Microsoft® Works 3.0 for Windows™

Microsoft® Works 3.0 for Windows™

JANET R. WILSON
Seattle University

PATRICIA SHEPARD
Skagit Valley College

Prentice Hall, Englewood Cliffs, New Jersey 07632

Library of Congress Cataloging-in-Publication Data
Wilson, Janet R. (Janet Ruth)
Microsoft Works 3.0 for Windows / Janet R. Wilson, Patricia Shepard.
p. cm.
Includes index.
ISBN 0-13-057192-X
1. Integrated software. 2. Microsoft Works for Windows.
I. Shepard, Patricia A. II. Title
QA76.76.I57W57 1995 94-23469
005.369--dc20 CIP

Acquisitions editor: Carolyn Henderson
Marketing manager: Nancy Evans
Director of production and manufacturing: Joanne Jay
Production editor: Cathleen Profitko
Production services manager: Lorraine Patsco
Electronic composition: John A. Nestor
Illustrations: Freddy Flake, John A. Nestor
Creative director: Linda Fiordilino
Cover design: Sheree Goodman
Cover Illustration: Marjory Dressler
Manufacturing buyer: Paul Smolenski

A Simon & Schuster Company
Englewood Cliffs, NJ 07632

ISBN 0-13-057192-X

Prentice-Hall International (UK) Limited, London
Prentice-Hall of Australia Pty. Limited, Sydney
Prentice-Hall of Canada Inc., Toronto
Prentice-Hall Hispanoamericana, S.A., Mexico
Prentice-Hall of India Private Limited, New Delhi
Prentice-Hall of Japan, Inc., Tokyo
Simon & Schuster Asia Ptd. Ltd., Singapore
Editora Prentice-Hall do Brasil, Ltda., Rio de Janeiro

Contents

Preface

Microcomputers have become commonplace in many schools, homes, offices, and other organizations. A vast array of software is available for use with these microcomputers, but the most common application programs are those for word processing, spreadsheet, and database functions. Works for Windows not only performs all three of these functions but also includes a communications tool. And Works for Windows is as easy to learn as it is powerful. The use of drop-down menus, two- or three-keystroke commands, and the small number of commands necessary to perform even complex operations combine to make Works for Windows remarkably easy to use.

This book provides you with step-by-step instructions in how to use Works for Windows for everything from basic procedures through its more sophisticated tools. As you work through the book, you will create, modify, and edit actual documents. In addition, tutorial documents and practice exercises are included at the end of every chapter so you can practice what you've learned on your own.

The practice documents include a wide variety of items. There are word processing documents, newsletters, and form documents (which are merged with database files). There are database files that require formulas and are used to compile reports. Queries, sorts, and searches are done on database files. Spreadsheets are created, and many types of formulas, searches, and sorts are performed on various spreadsheets.

Microsoft Works 3.0 for Windows is designed for use at a variety of levels. The user with no previous Works for Windows exposure can start at the beginning of the book and follow the step-by-step instructions through all of Works' features. An intermediate or advanced user could begin at any appropriate chapter and follow the guidelines for using the particular Works tool he or she is interested in.

BOOK ORGANIZATION

The book is divided into four parts. Each part covers a particular Works for Windows tool or background topic. Part I provides an introduction to computer concepts and to Windows. It also includes an overview of the Works for Windows features. Parts II through IV give in-depth instruction in using the three basic Works for Windows tools—the word processor, spreadsheet, database—and for integrating files. Appendix I covers some general instructions for using Works accessories, such as customizing the toolbar, using the WorksWizard, embedding and editing objects, and using templates. Appendix II provides guidelines for using the communications tool.

CHAPTER FEATURES

Objectives

A list of objectives is included at the beginning of each chapter. They summarize the features covered in the chapter and tell you exactly what you need to master by the chapter's close.

Preview

A preview is included at the beginning of each chapter. This overview of the features and commands covered in the chapter, their uses, and how they may be applied establishes a framework for all that follows.

Presentation/Practice

To keep things crystal clear, all instructions are given as numbered steps. These steps guide you through completing a word processing document, spreadsheet, or database file, as well as modifying and editing files and using other features available for each Works for Windows tool. Numerous screen captures are included to guide and to confirm your actions as you work through these steps.

Guided Tutorial

All of the features covered in a chapter are used to complete an extensive step-by-step practice document. This is an additional reinforcement of Works for Windows functions.

Review Questions

Review questions are included at the end of each chapter. They include questions on the commands discussed throughout the chapter and serve as a guideline for completing the practice documents. They also offer a reference as you complete the exercises and work on documents independently.

Hands-on Exercises

The hands-on documents are a key component of the book. They give the needed extra practice using commands covered in each chapter. Usually at least four exercises are included at the end of every chapter, and two examples of the final output are included in each chapter. These are best done independently using the book as a reference tool.

INSTRUCTOR'S MANUAL

An **Instructor's Manual with a Data Disk** is available to complement the *Microsoft Works 3.0 for Windows* text. The data disk includes the documents presented in the text and can be used in class to save inputting time. A test bank is also included in the Instructor's Manual, as well as answers to the Review Questions at the end of each of the chapters in the text.

ACKNOWLEDGMENTS

We would like to thank the many people who have been involved in making this book possible. Carolyn Henderson, Senior Editor, Application Software, at Prentice Hall was exceptionally helpful in coordinating all aspects that are required to produce a final manuscript and provided an atmosphere of cooperation and accessibility.

We would like to thank Cathleen Profitko, Production Editor, for her tireless involvement and supervision of the production of the book. Lorraine Patsco is greatly appreciated for her assistance with the art in the book and many other helpful suggestions. Both were always there when we needed them. We also thank copyeditor, Debbie Leighton and formatter, John Nestor. Their talents are truly appreciated.

Harriet Serenkin keystroke tested the manuscript; her comments and suggestions were invaluable. Many of her excellent ideas are incorporated in the final text.

We also greatly appreciated the work of the following reviewers.

Kenneth Avery, Spokane Falls Community College

Lo-An N. Tabar-Gaul, Mesa Community College

Lawrence J. Molloy, Oakland Community College

Arta Szathmary, Bucks County Community College

Finally, we want Patrick Randle and Dick Shepard to know how much we appreciated their encouragement and understanding when the task at hand seemed endless.

Microsoft® Works 3.0 for Windows™

CHAPTER 1

Introduction to the Microcomputer and to Windows

OBJECTIVES

Identify computer system components

Distinguish between hardware and software components

Become familiar with the standard keyboard

Learn about drive configurations and directories

Start Windows and identify Windows components

Use the mouse and the keyboard in Windows

PREVIEW

The combination of Works for Windows and your microcomputer provides you with a powerful tool to perform a variety of tasks either in a business environment, at school, or at home. You can use the word processing tool to produce letters, manuscripts, or other documents, the spreadsheet tool to present financial information, and the database tool to store information such as client names, addresses and phone numbers, records of sales, or personal or business inventories.

It is not necessary for you to be a computer hardware expert in order to use Works for Windows efficiently; however, it is helpful for you to understand some basic computer concepts and to be somewhat familiar with the Windows environment in order to make Works, or any other software program, easier to understand and use.

INTRODUCTION TO MICROCOMPUTER CONCEPTS

A discussion of microcomputer concepts generally falls into two categories-hardware and software. The computer hardware refers to the equipment that is used—the monitor, the CPU, the keyboard, printer, etc. Software refers to the programs used to run the equipment. Software includes operating system programs such as DOS and application programs such as Works.

Hardware

A microcomputer system is made up of a number of smaller pieces. Some of these pieces are mechanical—that is they have moving parts, such as the mechanism that pops your floppy disks out of the disk drive. The most central pieces, however, are electronic. That means they work by means of impulses running through silicon chips, which are connected with wires. The combination of electronic and mechanical pieces makes up what is referred to as **hardware**. Hardware is the tangible part of your computer-the part that you can touch. The hardware components that will be discussed here are the **central processing unit, memory, the monitor, keyboard, mouse, printer,** and storage devices.

Software

The hardware components are useless without the direction of computer programs. These programs, or computer codes, are called **software**. The software programs that run the computer system are called **operating systems**. One of the most common operating systems that runs the IBM computers or IBM compatible computers is PC- or MS-DOS. Other software programs are used to perform specific job-related tasks such as word processing, spreadsheets, or databases. These software programs are called application software.

Windows is a software program that is a graphic shell for the DOS environment, which means that you can use Windows to perform many DOS functions without actually having to enter DOS commands. DOS is covered later in this chapter, and a more detailed discussion of Windows is presented in Chapter 2.

The tasks performed by the various application software programs are saved as **files**. For example, a document produced by a word processing program is stored as a file; a spreadsheet is a file, just as is a database's list of addresses. These files are stored on a data disk—either on the internal hard disk or on floppy diskettes. Each file has a name that will help you remember what it contains and help you locate it among a group of files stored on the data disk.

HARDWARE COMPONENTS

All computer systems contain the same basic components. They are:

- Central processing unit
- Memory
- Monitor
- Keyboard
- Printer
- Storage devices
- Mouse (In a Windows environment, a mouse is generally included and used as a hardware component.)

Central Processing Unit

If you were to open up the cabinet of your computer and look inside, you would basically see hardware—silicon chips and wire. The central processing unit and the memory are contained on silicon chips. The **CPU** is often referred to as the *brain* of the computer system because the CPU literally controls the functions of the system and coordinates its activities—transmitting and receiving data through electrical impulses.

Memory

A microcomputer system has two kinds of memory: read-only memory (**ROM**) and random access memory (**RAM**). These memory components are also contained on silicon chips. ROM contains programs that are installed by the manufacturer. ROM generally can be read (i.e., the information can be used by the computer) but cannot be written to (i.e., data cannot be stored over it). These program instructions are necessary for many of the functions of the computer. RAM temporarily holds all program instructions and data used by the CPU. The operating system is loaded into RAM memory when the computer is first turned on. An application program such as Works for Windows is stored in RAM temporarily as are the data from files on which you are working.

The Monitor

The monitor resembles a TV screen. You can see your document on this screen as you type in Works for Windows. The monitor is a visual display of your interaction with the computer. It is therefore an **output device**. Instructions from the application program appear on the screen so that you can make decisions about what step to perform next. You can also check the results of revisions you have made to a document. You input from the keyboard and then see the results of the input on the screen. The display or output on monitor screens is usually either **monochrome** (one color) or **color** (multiple colors).

The Keyboard

The keyboard is an **input device**. It is used to put data into the computer. There are a variety of keyboard styles and sizes available with computer systems. All keyboards, however, have several major features in common. They all have the standard alphabetic and numeric character keys in the center of the keyboard. The keyboard is connected to the computer by a cable so that messages are sent directly to the computer's memory when keys are pressed. When you are typing a document or entering other data, the **cursor** appears on the screen at the point where your next character will be inserted. The cursor is usually a flashing square in some applications or a vertical line in Windows applications. It moves as you enter characters or numeric figures.

Most keyboards also contain a numeric keypad. The numeric keypad may be used as a calculator, and the numbers on the keypad frequently double as **cursor movement keys** often called **Arrow keys.** The switch between the numeric mode and the cursor movement keys usually is done using a key called the **Num Lock** key, located near the numeric keypad as shown in Figure 1-1. The figure shows an IBM-compatible keyboard. Although your keyboard design may vary somewhat, the function of the named keys will not.

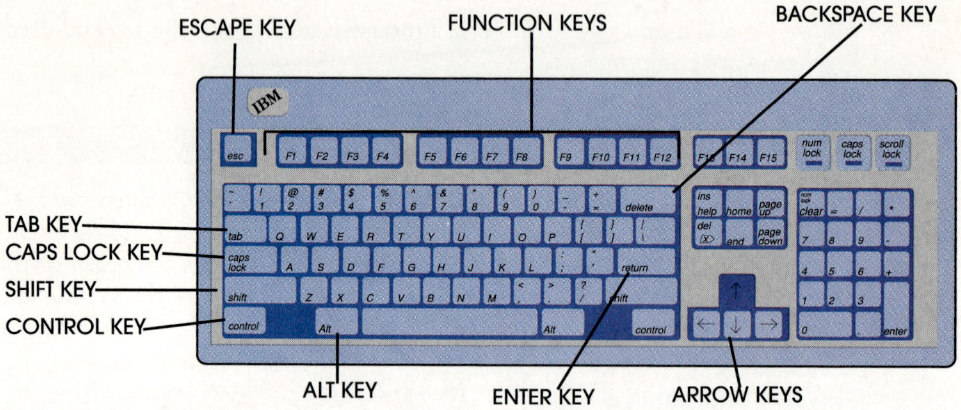

Figure 1-1
IBM-compatible keyboard

Function keys

Used for quick access to frequently used functions.

The Esc key

Returns to the document, or previous menu, or from a menu to the opening screen. Escapes from the current menu or dialog box.

The Tab key

Moves to the next tab, field, or cell, or when used with the Shift key moves back one field or cell (depending on whether you are using the word processor, database, or spreadsheet tool).

The Ctrl key

Used in combination with other keys to provide a secondary function to those keys.

The Shift key

Used to create uppercase lettering or to access a key's secondary function.

The Caps Lock key

Switches the keypad between upper- and lowercase letters.

The Alt key

Used in combination with other keys, such as the Ctrl key, to provide a secondary function. In Works, the Alt key is used to access the menu from the keyboard.

The Enter key

Used to select an option, or end an operation. In documents, it is used to terminate a paragraph, or insert a line in a report or script.

The Backspace key

Erases text to the left of the cursor. Also erases the current field (database) or cell (spreadsheet).

Alt/Backspace

Undoes an unwanted editing change or most recent insert in a word processor or clears the field or cell contents in the database or spreadsheet. This works as a toggle-deleting and reinserting most recent changes or insertions.

The Arrow keys

Used to move up, down, left, and right through a document. The left and right arrow keys will move one screen at a time in the spreadsheet and database tools when used in combination with other keys such as the Ctrl key.

Ctrl/Left and Right arrows

Allow you to move one selection left and right, such as one word in word processing or one cell in a spreadsheet or database.

Other keys

- **Print Screen key** copies all information on the screen to the Clipboard.
- **Scroll Lock key** toggles between allowing the screen image to move or the cursor to move through a document, except in the word processor.
- **Page Up** key redisplays the previous screen in a word processing document, spreadsheet, or database file.
- **Page Down** key redisplays the next screen in a word processing document, spreadsheet, or database file.
- **Delete** key deletes to the right of the cursor position.
- **End** key moves the cursor key to the end of a line in word processing or to the end of a record or end of a line in a database or spreadsheet.
- **Ctrl End** is used to move to the end of a file.
- **Home** key moves to the beginning of a line in word processing or to the beginning of a record or beginning of a line in a database or spreadsheet. **Ctrl Home** is used to move to the beginning of a file.
- **Insert** key toggles between Insert mode and Overtype mode in word processing in Works for Windows.

When using the keyboard to make menu selections in Works for Windows, the **Alt** key is used to make the menu bar active—the first option, File, will be highlighted. Then you can press the underlined letter of the option you want. For example, **Help** can be reached by pressing **Alt** to make the Works menu active, then pressing **h** to choose the Help option. This action displays the Help pull-down menu. You can then choose an option from the pull-down menu by pressing the underlined letter of the option you want or by clicking on the option.

Mouse

The mouse is also an input device that is often used in place of the keyboard, especially in a Windows environment. The mouse is used to quickly move the insertion point to a specific position in a file, to select text, to choose menu commands and options, and to open or close windows.

Printer

The printer is an **output device**. Your computer communicates with your printer through a cable connection, much like your keyboard communicates with the computer. There are many types of printers, ranging from daisy-wheel to dot matrix to ink jet to laser printer. Your instructor can tell you more about the printer you will be using and how to communicate with it.

The paper output from your printer is called **hard copy** because it is in a tangible form. The opposite of hard copy is **soft copy**. The image on your screen is a good example of soft copy. Soft copy is temporary, but it is also considered output.

Secondary Storage

Earlier in this chapter you learned about the internal memory in your computer called random access memory or RAM. RAM storage is temporary. When the power is turned off, everything contained in RAM is erased. For this reason, most data are stored semipermanently on a **secondary storage medium**. A secondary storage medium is commonly some kind of **magnetic disk** such as shown in Figure 1-2, or a rigid **hard disk.**

Secondary storage devices, such as a hard disk drive or diskette drive, are the hardware components that write data to, or read data from, either the hard disk or the diskette. These devices are slower than RAM because they contain mechanical parts. This is covered in more detail in the section on drive configurations later in this chapter.

Hard disk

Usually a hard disk is permanently mounted inside the computer; however, it can also be mounted in its own case. A single hard disk has a storage capacity of several million characters or bytes of information.

Diskettes

Diskettes are magnetic storage devices that can be inserted and removed from your computer. Depending upon your computer's diskette drive (or drives), these may be either 5 ¼ inch or 3 ½ inch diskettes as shown in Figure 1-2. Various application programs and operating systems are stored on diskettes when they are purchased. You can also store word processing, spreadsheet, and database files on diskettes.

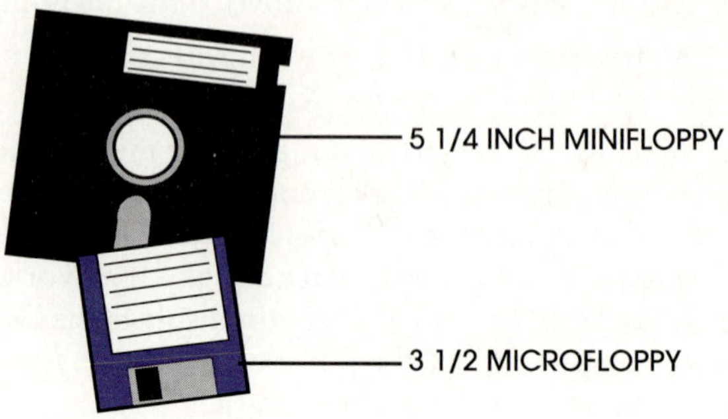

Figure 1-2
Two common types of diskettes

DRIVE CONFIGURATIONS

There are two kinds of disk drives: diskette drives and hard disk drives. Figure 1-3 shows two of the drive configurations that come with IBM PCs and IBM-compatible systems. Compatible systems are manufactured by companies other than IBM, but can use the same operating system and applications.

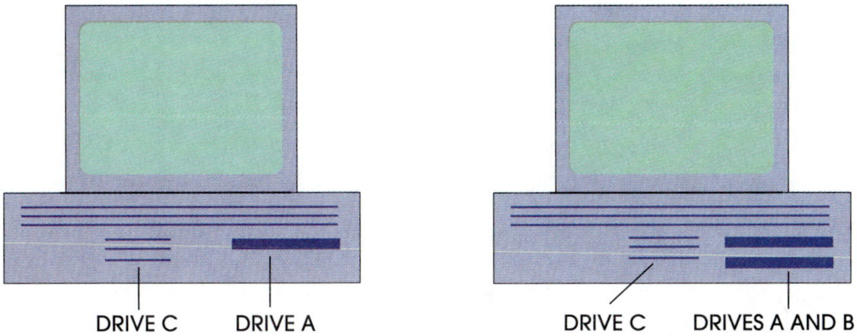

Figure 1-3
Disk drive configurations

The most common configurations are either the hard disk drive with two diskette drives or the hard disk system with one diskette drive. Your program and DOS and Windows files are stored permanently on the hard drive, and your files can be saved either on the hard drive or on a diskette in drive A or drive B.

> *NOTE:* One of the installation requirements for Windows is that it has to be installed on a hard drive. It cannot run on a dual-disk drive system because of the features and functionality of the Windows program.

DIRECTORIES

If you are using a hard drive, you will probably want to create directories where the program files and the various data files can be stored. Directories make it easier to locate and use your files. For example, when DOS, Windows, or Works are installed, the installation process automatically creates directories on the hard disk where each of these programs is stored. In addition to these directories, you can create your own directories or subdirectories to store data files.

To understand directories, compare the hard drive without directories to a filing cabinet without drawers. If there were no directories on the hard drive, all of the files could be there, but there would be no organization that makes it easy to locate specific files. Each directory can be thought of as a file drawer and within that directory (file drawer) are subdirectories (dividers) that provide organization for your files.

The Windows File Manager can show the directories and subdirectories on your hard drive as well as those on drives A and B. Figure 1-4 is an example of the File Manager in Windows displaying directories, subdirectories, and files that are stored on a hard drive.

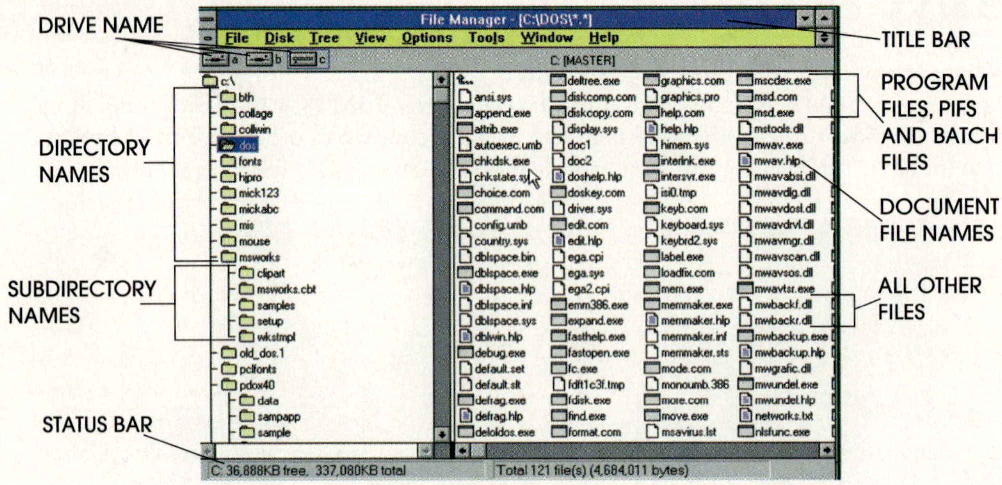

Figure 1-4
The File Manager in Windows showing directories, subdirectories, and files

In Figure 1-4, the column at the left lists some of the directories on drive C. (Notice that the button for drive C in the toolbar has a border around it. Also, the status bar at the bottom of the window shows that the current drive is C and the total bytes free.) Some of the directory names here are DOS, MSWORKS, PROCOMM, QUICKEN3, and WINDOWS. Some of these directories show subdirectories-for example, the MSWORKS directory shows CLIPART and MSWORKS.CBT as displayed in this illustration.

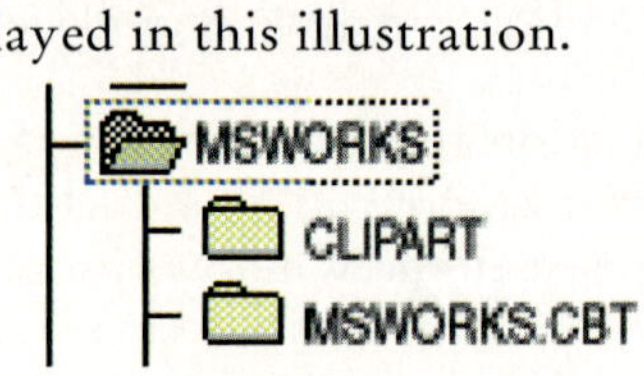

The four columns at the right list the various files that are located in the directory that is selected (highlighted) at the left. The DOS directory is selected in this example, and the files in the DOS directory are displayed at the right.

NOTE: If you are working in LAN or a network environment, your drive specifications and directories may be different than those shown here.

DOS

As mentioned earlier in this chapter, DOS, or a disk operating system, is required to run the computer. The operating system is a set of programs that tells a computer system how to control resources, execute programs, and manage data. Application programs such as Windows and Works could not run on the computer without the operating system to guide them.

When the DOS operating system is present, a symbol called the **prompt (>)** appears on the screen. Depending on the type of computer in use (hard drive or dual-disk drives), the symbol will vary. It is, however, always a letter of the alphabet, such as

A:\> (on a dual-disk system)

or

C:\> (on a hard disk system).

(The prompt may vary somewhat in appearance from the sample shown here.)

When you see one of these prompts, you are at the operating system and are ready to give system commands or to load an application program into memory (RAM).

DOS Files

DOS program files are stored on one or more diskettes and are usually purchased with the computer system. When DOS is installed on the hard drive, it is usually stored in its own directory, DOS. There are many programs stored on the DOS disks. They contain instructions for invoking certain commands, such as *Format, Copy, Diskcopy, DIR,* (Directory) and *CD* (Change Directory) that the user can access. Most of the functions that can be performed by using DOS commands (including those just listed) can be performed from Windows. You may, however, have to start Windows from the DOS prompt, C:\>, unless Windows appears automatically or is on a menu when you start up.

Some of the DOS programs are necessary for the operation of an application program such as Works for Windows. These programs are loaded automatically when the system is turned on and are stored in RAM prior to accessing the application program. Because the size of memory is limited, only the files needed for normal operation are loaded. These files are often referred to as **internal** or **resident** files. Other DOS files that are not needed for the everyday operation of the computer are not loaded into memory and are referred to as **external** or **transient** files. These files can be accessed by invoking a DOS comand such as ERASE, FORMAT, COPY, DIR, etc.

ABOUT WINDOWS

Windows is frequently referred to as a graphical interface to the DOS operating system. There are basically two main functions of Windows. One, it provides an environment where you can run several applications at once and move from one application to another without having to exit one program before loading another. This also allows you to cut, copy, and paste selected areas from a file in one program to a file in a different program. The second main function of Windows allows you to perform DOS operations from within the Windows environment.

The term *windows* is appropriate because each application that is running is shown in a box called a window. These windows can be overlapping, they can be arranged in tiles (not overlapping), or each window can be made full screen size. You can also change the size and move each window to further customize the screen.

> *NOTE:* This chapter is intended to give general information about Windows rather than to be used as a tutorial. You may not want to make the changes that are discussed here; however, it is helpful to run Windows when you read this chapter and work through some of the procedures enough to at least look at the menu options and experiment with the mouse actions. Check with your instructor about this.

STARTING WINDOWS

How you start Windows depends upon how the program is installed on your computer. Often Windows is made to start automatically when the system is turned on. It may also be included in a menu. If, however, you start Windows from the DOS prompt, use the following procedure. The command to load Windows is **win**. It can be entered from any prompt without changing to the Windows directory where the Windows files are located.

Start Windows

At whatever system prompt is displayed (For example C:\>):

1. Type: **win**
2. Press: **Enter.** The screen now shows the Windows screen. It may be similar to that shown in Figure 1-5.

IDENTIFYING WINDOWS COMPONENTS

Your Windows screen may resemble the one shown in Figure 1-5, or it may be considerably different depending upon the Windows programs that have been installed and the way the screen has been arranged.

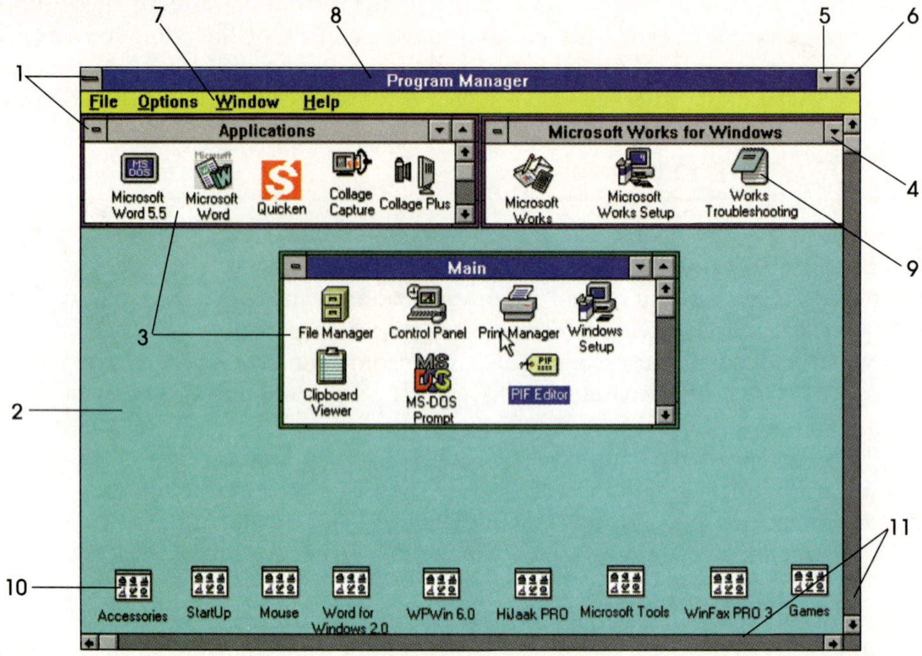

Figure 1-5
The Windows screen

The following components are shown in the Windows screen displayed here.

1	Control menu boxes	manage the active window
2	Desktop	is the background area upon which the windows are arranged
3	Group window	is a box showing the various application icons assigned to that group
4	Maximize button	expands the window to the full screen
5	Minimize button	reduces the window to an icon
6	Restore button	returns the window to its previous size
7	Menu bar	displays the options in the window
8	Title bar	contains the name of the application that is running
9	Program icon	represents an application that is not running but that can be started from Windows
10	Group icon	represents a specific group window. If you double-click on the group icon, it expands to show the group window containing various application icons

11	Scroll bars	are used with the mouse to move up and down or to the right or left in a window

USING THE MOUSE

The techniques of using a mouse are generally the same in any program. The mouse is used to move around in a window and to perform various selection functions. In some areas of a window the mouse is an arrow, in others it may be a vertical line, a double-headed arrow, or parallel lines with arrows on either side. It can be used to select an icon, make a window active, resize a window, move a window, and select options in a menu. In word processing programs it can be used to select blocks of text, or in spreadsheet and database to select contents of cells. The mouse is also used with the scroll bar to change the display on the screen, moving it either up and down or to the right or left.

The following terms are used when referring to the mouse.

Point	Move the mouse so that the arrow, vertical line, or whatever figure represents the mouse is in the position you want in the active window.
Click	Press the mouse button (usually the left button) to *select* (highlight) the position, option, or icon that you want.
Double-click	Tap the left mouse button twice when you have selected the icon. This executes the command to open it, or in some programs, it may perform a selection task.
Drag	Point to an area, hold down the left mouse button and move the mouse so that the selection is moved to a different area.

USING THE KEYBOARD

In most Windows environments, the mouse is easier to use than the keyboard; however, in some instances you may not want to move your hands from the keyboard to move the mouse around. For this reason the keyboard can be used for almost all actions that can be performed by the mouse. Both keyboard and mouse instructions will be given throughout this text. Use whichever is most efficient for you. In some instances the keyboard is better, in others the mouse is easier.

The following list of keystrokes and functions are the same in all windows.

Ctrl/Tab	Move the cursor from one group window or group icon to another. Hold down the Ctrl key and strike the Tab key to cycle through all windows or group icons.
Alt/Tab	Move from one active application to another. Hold down the Alt key and strike the Tab key to cycle through all active applications. When you see the icon or the box showing the name of the one you want, release the Alt key. The following is an example of the box showing an application that is currently running.

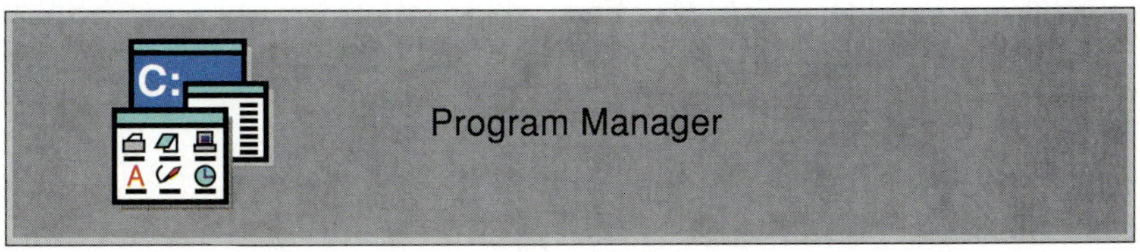

Arrow keys	Move from one icon to another in a group window, or move the cursor in an application file such as a word processing document.
Alt/Space or **Alt/- (minus)**	Display the pull-down Control menu.
Ctrl/Esc	Display the Task list.

The Control Menu

The Control menu is used to change the size or move the active window. It can also be used to close the current window or to switch to another application. Press **Alt/Space** or **Alt/-** (minus) to display the pull-down menu. Figure 1-6 shows an example of the Control menu in the active window that is displayed when **Alt/-** (minus) is pressed.

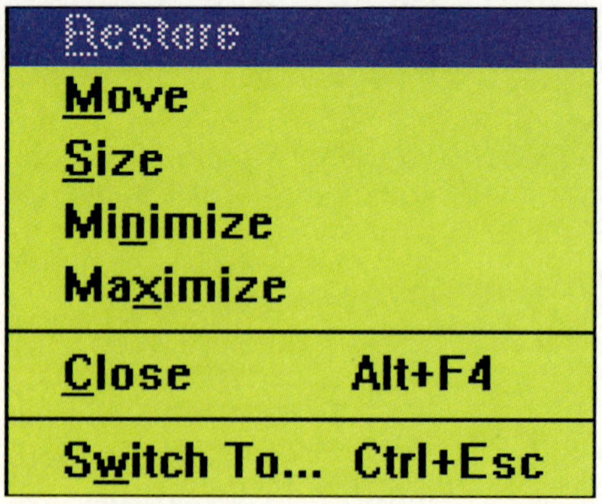

Figure 1-6
The Control Menu in the active window

The options in the Control menu perform the following functions:

Restore	Change the active window back to its previous size.
Move	Move the active window to a new position on the desktop.
Size	Change the size of the active window.
Minimize	Change the active window to an icon.
Maximize	Change the active window to full screen size.
Close	Close the active window.
Switch to	Switch to the next application that is running. (This option is not available in some windows.)
Next	Move to the next group icon or window. (This option is not available in some windows.)

Press **Esc** or click anywhere outside the menu box to leave the Control menu and remove it from the screen.

WORKING IN WINDOWS

In a Windows environment you can move, resize, maximize, minimize, or restore the active window to its previous size. You can also select an icon or a window, change the window to an icon or change an icon to a window, and switch from one window to another.

Select a Group Window

Selecting a group window or icon makes that window or icon active. The title bar in the window or the icon name will be highlighted. You can use either the keyboard or the mouse to perform this function. Figure 1-7 shows an example of a group window that is selected.

Mouse

1. Point to the window you want and click the left mouse button. The title bar will be highlighted. If you point to a group icon and click the left mouse button, the name is highlighted and a menu opens.

Keyboard

1. Press **Ctrl/Tab** until the window title bar you want is highlighted or the group icon name is highlighted.

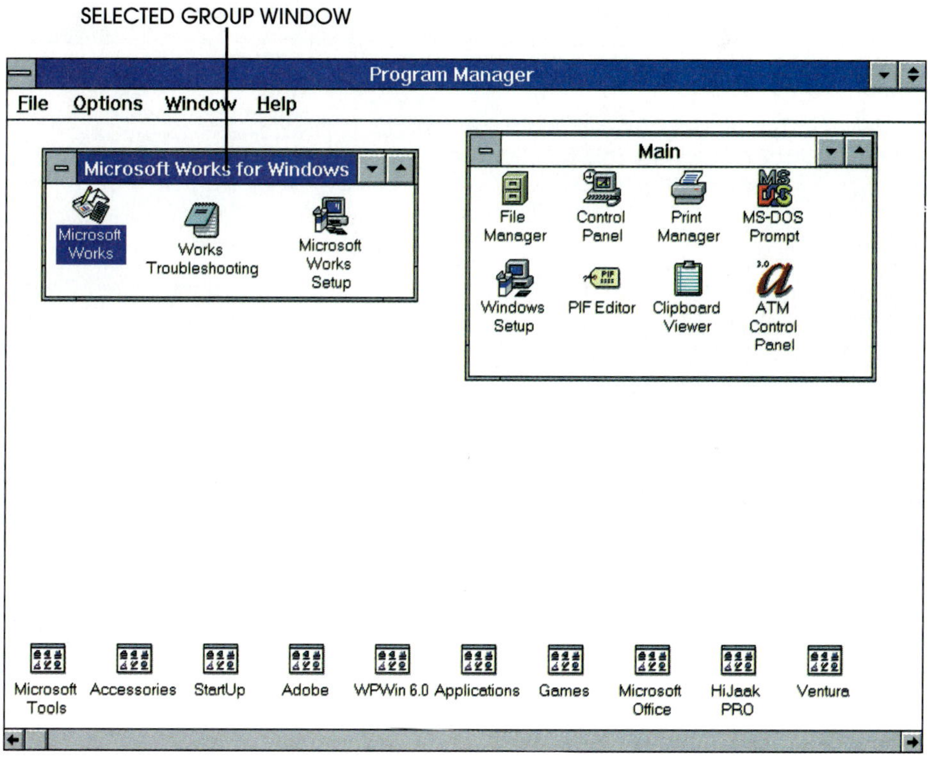

Figure 1-7
A selected window

Select a Program Icon

When a program icon is selected, it will be highlighted to indicate that it is now active. Figure 1-8 shows an example of a selected program icon.

Mouse

1. Point to the program icon and click the left mouse button. The icon name will be highlighted.

Keyboard

1. Press any **Arrow** key within the active window to move to the icon you want. Its name will be highlighted.

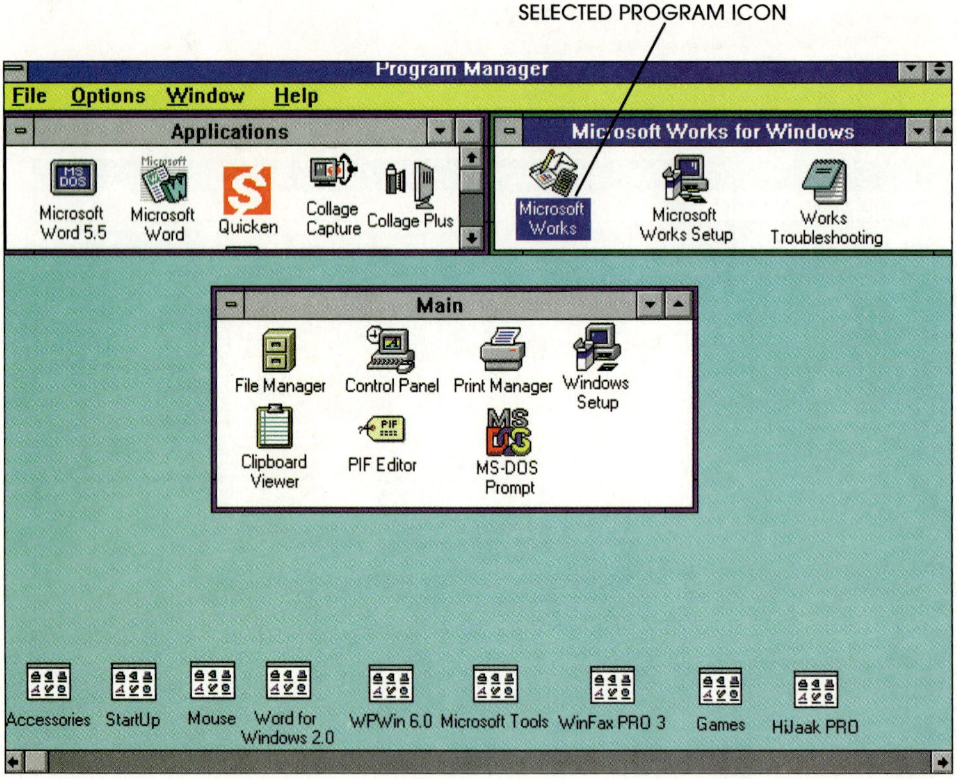

Figure 1-8
A selected program icon

NOTE: Loading (starting) a program will be covered in Chapter 2.

Change a Group Icon to a Window

The group icons are usually displayed near the bottom of the Windows screen. When a group icon is changed to a window, you are then able to see the applications in that group. Figure 1-9 shows a group icon that has been changed to a window.

Mouse

1. Point — to the group icon that you want.
2. Double-click — the left mouse button to change the icon to a window. The new window may overlap other windows.

Keyboard

1. Press **Ctrl/Tab** until the group icon you want is selected.
2. Press **Enter** to change the icon to a window. The new window may overlap other windows.

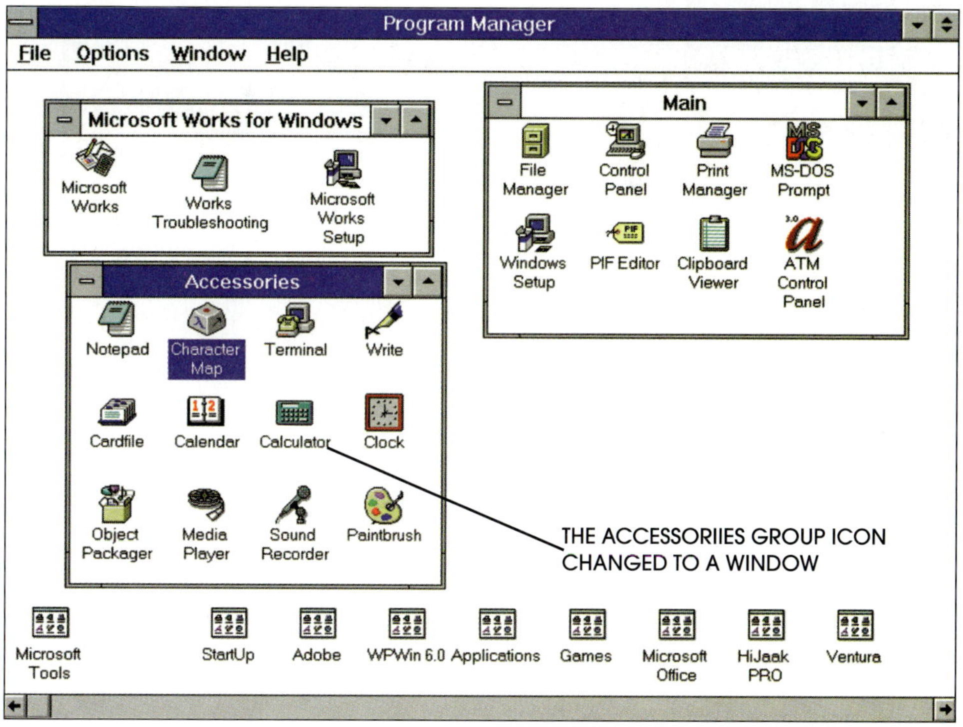

Figure 1-9
The Accessories group icon changed to a window

Change a Group Window to a Group Icon

If space is limited on your screen, you can change a group window back to a group icon so that it doesn't take up as much space on the desktop. Figure 1-10 shows the Accessories window reduced to a group icon.

Mouse

1. Click on the Minimize button (the down arrow) at the right end of the title bar in the active window as shown here.

Keyboard

1. Select the window to be changed to a group icon.
2. Press **Alt/-/n** to choose **Minimize.**

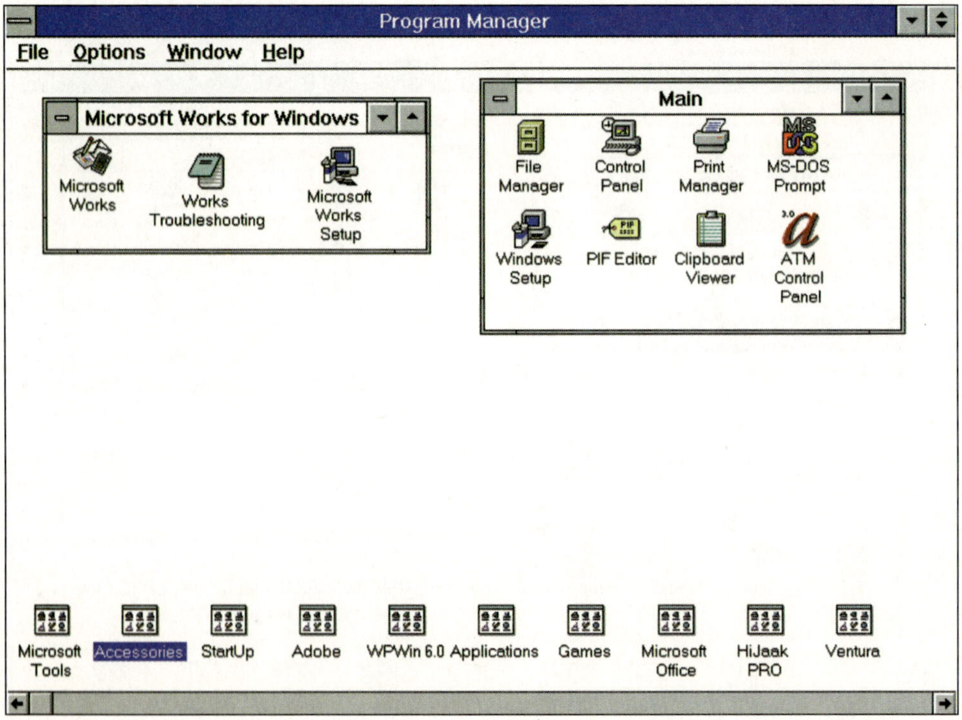

Figure 1-10
The Accessories window changed to a group icon

These are some of the basic functions that can be performed in the Windows Program Manager and they will get you started so you can use the Works for Windows program.

REVIEW QUESTIONS

1. Locate each of the following on your keyboard.
   a. Function keys
   b. Esc key
   c. Return or Enter key
   d. Backspace key
   e. Shift keys
   f. Delete key
   g. Numeric keypad
   h. Num Lock key
   i. Alt key
   j. Ctrl key
   k. Arrow keys
   l. Tab key
   m. Caps Lock key

Fill in the BEST answer for each item.

2. A computer system contains both ______________________ and ______________________ parts.
3. Written programs stored on the hardware or on a diskette are called ______________________.
4. Programs that do useful tasks for end users of computers are called (two words) ____________ ____________.
5. A software program called an ______________________ is required to run a computer.
6. The material you create with an application program is organized into ____________.
7. DOS programs necessary for everyday operation of a computer are stored in ____________ whenever the computer is being used.
8. Some DOS files that are not necessary for normal computer operation are referred to as ______________ because they remain in the DOS directory until needed.
9. DOS files may be described as either ______________________ or ______________________.
10. The ______________ command is entered at any system prompt to start Windows.
11. A ______________________ window displays a collection of program icons.
12. To reduce a group window to a group icon, click on the ____________ button at the right end of the ______________________ bar.
13. Press ______________________ to move from one window to another.
14. Press ______________________ to move from one active application to another.
15. Match each of the following definitions to the appropriate hardware component.
    a. Secondary storage
    b. RAM memory
    c. Keyboard
    d. Printer
    e. Microprocessor

f. Monitor

_____ An output device used to create hard copy

_____ Where documents can be saved permanently without concern about power failure

_____ An input device used to send messages to the computer

_____ The internal temporary storage section of a microcomputer

_____ The CPU (central processing unit)

_____ The screen where output is displayed on a microcomputer

Choose the BEST answer to the following items.

16. A diskette and a hard disk are examples of
    a. RAM.
    b. memory.
    c. secondary storage media.
    d. primary storage media.
17. The Shift, Ctrl, or Alt keys
    a. work only by themselves and perform no other function.
    b. work by pressing them in conjunction with the spacebar.
    c. work by pressing them in conjunction with another key.
    d. work by pressing two of them together.
18. The Delete key removes text
    a. to the left of the insertion point.
    b. to the right of the insertion point.
    c. from the insertion point to the end of the line.
    d. above or below the insertion point.
19. Works is an example of
    a. system software.
    b. programming languages.
    c. application software.
    d. programs stored permanently in ROM.
20. List two main functions of Windows.

CHAPTER 2

An Overview of Works for Windows

OBJECTIVES

Start Works

Identify the components of the Works for Windows Startup dialog box

Open and close a tool window

Make menu selections

Get help and use Cue Cards

Preview the word processor

Preview the spreadsheet

Preview the database

Exit Works for Windows

PREVIEW

This chapter will introduce you to Works for Windows. You will learn how to start the program on your PC, and review the tools included in the Works program. Also included in this chapter are instructions for opening the various tools, moving from one to the other, and arranging the opened windows.

STARTING WORKS

The following instructions assume that the program is installed on drive C and that you are ready to begin learning Works. Since you are in the Windows environment, the program is installed on drive C. You cannot run it from drive A or drive B.

Start Works

1. Open — the Microsoft Works for Windows group icon as shown here if it is not already opened. To do this, double-click on the group icon, or press **Ctrl/Tab** to select it and press **Enter.**

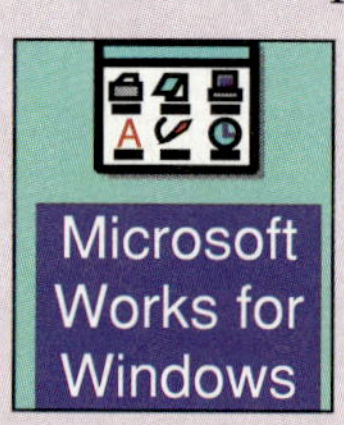

2. Open — the Microsoft Works icon as shown here. To do this, double-click on the icon, or press an arrow key to select the icon and press **Enter.**

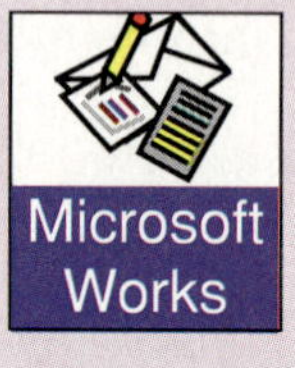

A Welcome to Microsoft Works window is displayed as shown in Figure 2-1.

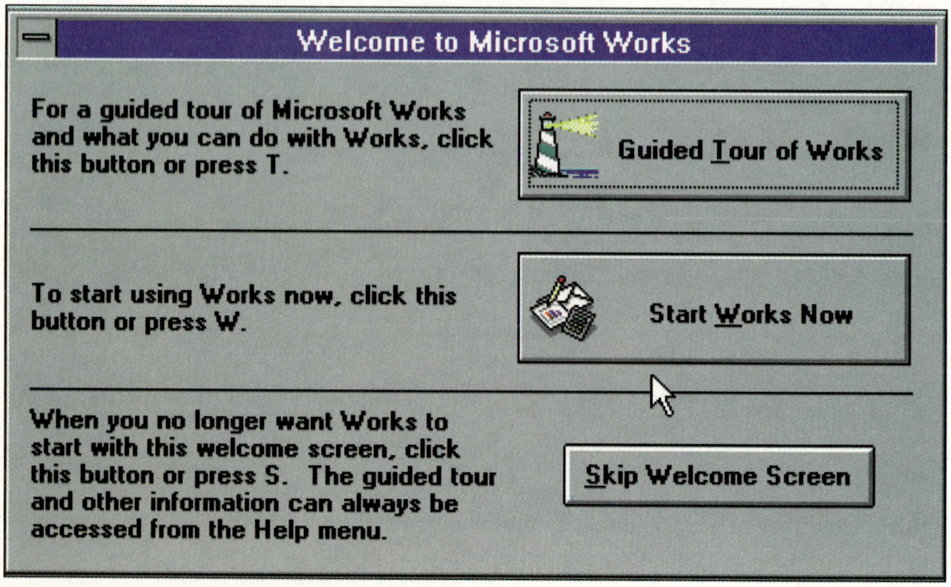

Figure 2-1
The Welcome to Microsoft Works dialog box

Start Works Now

1. Choose **Start Works Now** by clicking on the button or by pressing **W**. The Startup dialog box is displayed as shown in Figure 2-2.

NOTE: If you do not want the Welcome screen displayed each time you start Works, choose **Skip Welcome Screen.**

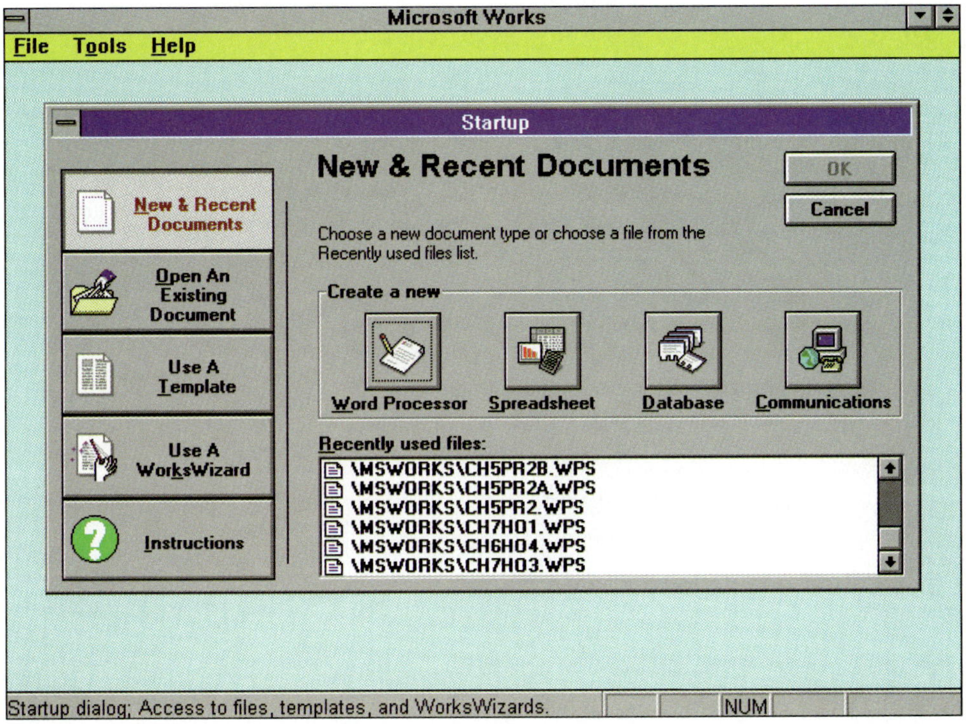

Figure 2-2
The Startup dialog box

NOTE: Your screen may shown a different list of files than that shown here.

IDENTIFYING THE COMPONENTS

The components of the Startup dialog box are used to open the word processor, spreadsheet, database, communications tool, document, templates, files, or WorksWizard tools. These are described in Table 2-1.

Word processor	 The word processor is used to create, edit, and format documents such as letters, manuscripts, memos, written reports, or any other type of text document. You can also include drawings, charts, and tables in documents created here.

Spreadsheet

The spreadsheet tool is used for financial recordkeeping tasks such as the option of preparing budgets, and creation of projections or other financial planning files. This information can be edited, and formulas for calculating values in the various cells can be entered. You can also use spreadsheet information to automatically create charts and insert them in word processing documents.

Database

The database tool is used to store information that is regularly kept in files, such as lists of names, addresses, and telephone numbers, records of sales, inventories, or student enrollment records. This tool allows you to sort information, query the files for specific records, and print reports based on the information in a file.

Communications

This tool allows you to connect with information services, send and receive text and files, and perform any other communications tasks. You need to have a modem in order to use this tool.

New and recent documents

This button is **on** by default when you start Works and displays the list of recently created documents.

Open an esixting document

Click on this button to display an Open dialog box which will show the complete list of Works files that can be opened.

Use a template

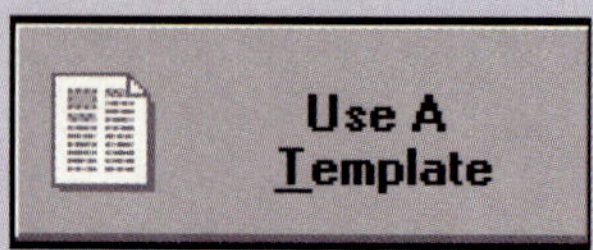

Click on the Template button to display a list of groups of templates. When you select a specific group, the categories that are available in that group are displayed and the templates available in each category are listed.

Use a WorksWizard

The WorksWizard button displays a list of features that can be used to automatically create items such as Address Book, Form Letter, or Letterhead. You will be guided through steps for using each of these tasks.

Instructions

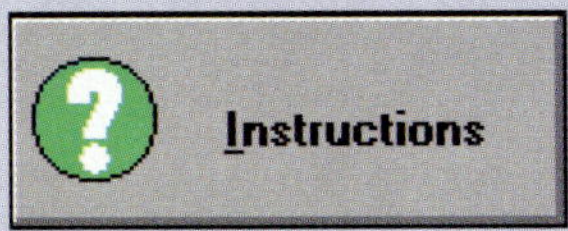

The Instructions button will display a description of each button in the current dialog box.

Recently used files

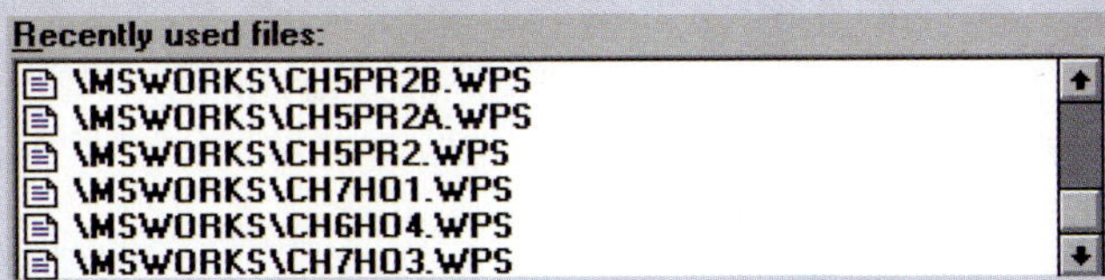

This list box shows the names of the most recently used files.

title bar

The Title Bar displays the name of the window. At the left end of the title bar is a control menu box which allows you to move or to close the window.

OK

The OK button is used to open a file that has been selected in the list of recently used files. You also can double click on a file to open it.

Cancel

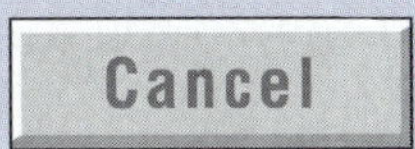

The Cancel button removes the Startup dialog box from the screen; however, you will still be in Works. The Startup dialog box can be redisplayed by choosing **File, Create New File** from the menu bar.

Table 2-1

The components of the Startup dialog box

OPENING WORKS WINDOWS

You can open a tool window from the Startup dialog box, or you can open it from the Works window. Both will be covered in this chapter to help you understand how to operate in the Works Windows environment.

Open the Word Processor

1. Choose **Word Processor** from the Startup dialog box by clicking on the button or by pressing **W**. The Works window is now displayed and it contains a Word document window. See an example in Figure 2-3. The components are identified, and their uses are described in Table 2-2.

NOTE: If this is the first time you have opened the word processor you may see the Cue Cards window at the right side of the screen.

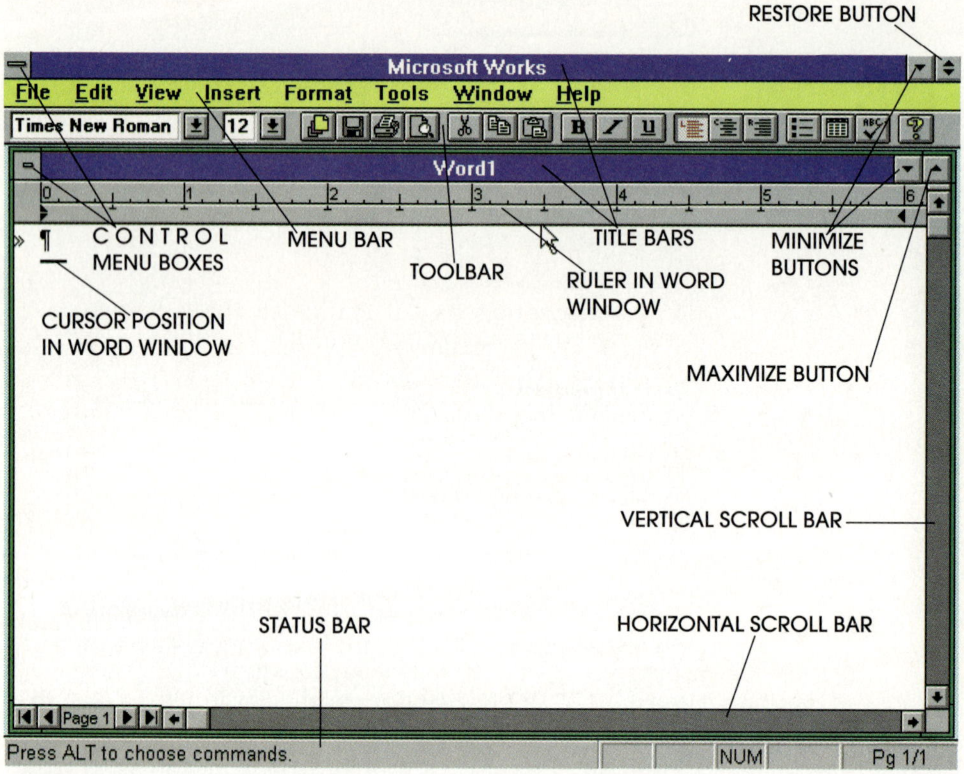

Figure 2-3
The Works window containing a Word document window

Table 2-2
Description of Works window components

Control menu box	Used to resize, move, or close a window. In the control menu box for Microsoft Works window, you can also switch to another application.
Menu bar	Contains the items from which you may choose to save files, perform formatting and editing tasks, work with Windows, and access the Help menu.
Toolbar	Displays buttons that can be selected to quickly perform various tasks. The buttons in this bar vary depending upon the Works tool window that is active.
Title bar	Displays the title for each window. When a file is saved, the title bar includes the file name.
Ruler	The Ruler is displayed only in the word processor window and is used to quickly set margins and tabs.
Minimize button	Reduces the active window to an icon when it is clicked.
Restore button	Returns the active window to its previous size when it is clicked.
Maximize button	Expands the active window to full screen size when it is clicked.
Vertical scroll bar	Used with the mouse to move up and down through the active window.
Horizontal scroll bar	Used with the mouse to move to the left or right through the active window. In the word processor window, this bar also contains buttons to move from one page to another. In the database window, this bar contains buttons to move from one record to another.
Status bar	Displays information about the file as well as how to use various procedures, depending upon the Works tool window that is active.

CHOOSING MENU OPTIONS

Each Works window contains the menu bar shown in the following illustration.

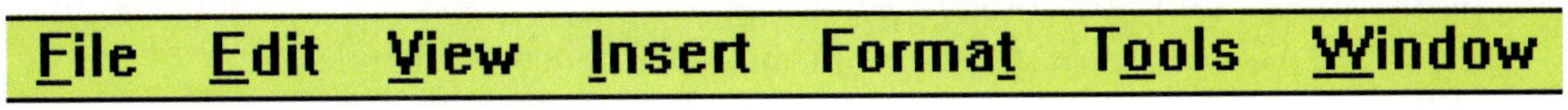

Choose an Option

1. **Click** on the menu item that you want.

   or

   Press **Alt** to access the menu bar and press the underlined letter shown in the menu item that you want. A drop-down menu of options will be displayed for each item chosen from the menu bar. See an example of the File menu shown in Figure 2-4.

2. **Choose** the option in the drop-down menu that you want by either clicking on the option or by pressing the underlined letter in the option that you want. (The drop-down menu can be closed by clicking anywhere outside the menu or by pressing the **Esc** key.)

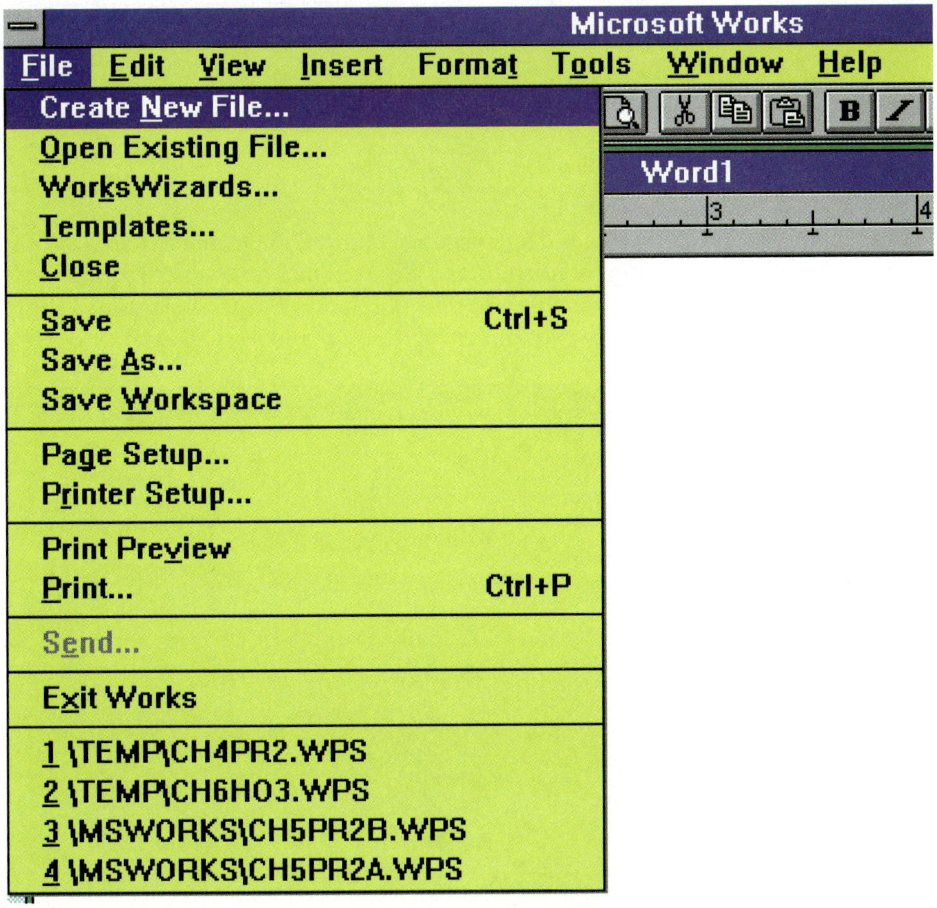

Figure 2-4
The drop-down menu for the File option

USING THE TOOLBAR

A toolbar is displayed for each Works window. The toolbars vary slightly depending upon the tool that you are using—word processor, spreadsheet, database, or communications. When you point to a button, its name will be displayed below the toolbar. The following is the toolbar displayed in the word processor window.

Choose a Toolbar Button

1. **Click** on the button that you want.
2. **Respond** to the screen depending upon the button that you choose. Some buttons, such as the Bold or Italic button do not require a response, but perform a task immediately.

NOTE: The toolbar for each tool will be covered in detail in the section pertaining to that tool.

USING LEARNING WORKS

Works provides a good deal of online help which can be accessed easily by using the toolbar that is displayed in the active Works window.

Choose Learning Works

1. **Click** on the Learning Works icon in the toolbar as shown here.

The Learning Works dialog box is displayed. See Figure 2-5. At the left are four buttons that can be used to help you learn to use Works. The box of instructions describes each of the choices available and tells you how each can help you. The Instructions button turns the display of instructions on and off in the box.

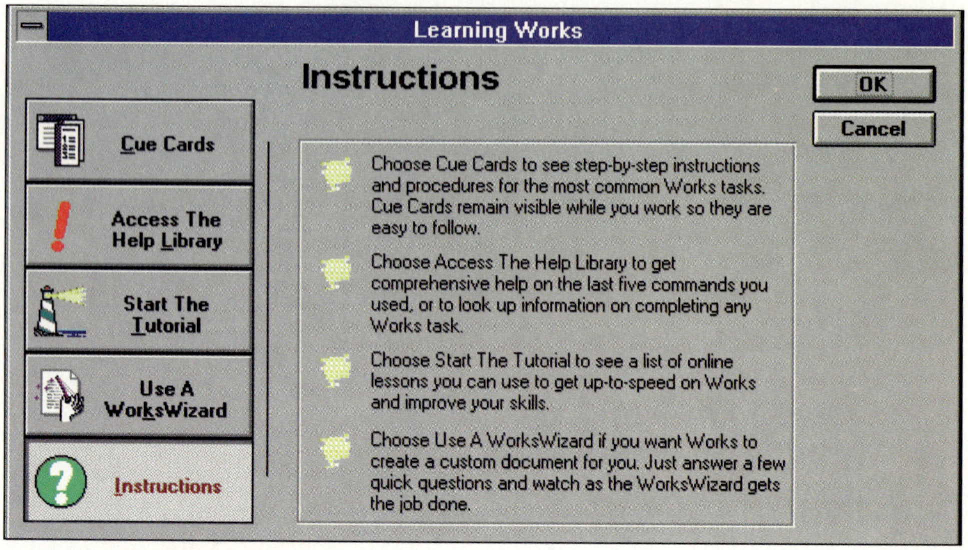

Figure 2-5
The Learning Works window

2. Click — on the button that you want and follow the screen instructions depending upon your choice of button. Experiment with these features as time permits.

When done:

3. Choose — **Cancel** or **Close** depending upon the feature you are using. To leave the Tutorial, choose **Exit Tutorial.** The Learning Works window will be closed and you will return to the active Works window.

CLOSING A TOOL WINDOW

You can close Works windows the same way you can close other windows.

Close a Works Window

1. Double-click — on the control menu box at the left end of the title bar of the active tool window.

   or

   Choose — **File, Close.** If you have an unsaved document, you will be prompted to save it or to close without saving.

USING HELP

The Help menu is available in all windows and in the Learning Works dialog box.

> *NOTE:* If the Startup dialog box is displayed, you will need to choose *Cancel* to remove it from the screen in order to go to the Help menu.

Use the Help Menu

1. Choose — **Help** from the menu bar. The drop-down menu that is displayed will depend upon the Works window that is active; however, all Help menus are similar. See an example in Figure 2-6.
2. Choose — the option that you want and respond to the screen menus and prompts to obtain the information you are looking for. The status bar describes the option that is selected. Experiment on your own with the Help menu as time permits.

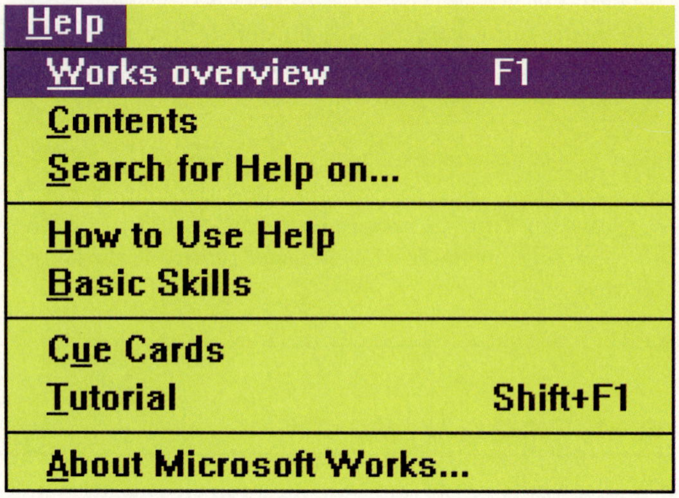

Figure 2-6
The Help menu in the Works window

USING CUE CARDS

The Cue Cards feature displays basic instructions at the right side of the window for using the tool (word processor, spreadsheet, or database) in which you are working and is on by default. If the Cue Cards window is not displayed, you can choose **Help** and turn on **Cue Cards**. (A check mark is displayed in front of Cue Cards when it is turned on.) Figure 2-7 shows an example of the first Cue Cards window that is displayed. If you leave Cue Cards turned on, the next time you open one of the tools, a Cue Card will be displayed relating to that particular tool.

> *NOTE:* A mouse is required to use Cue Cards. You can press **Shift/F3** to close the Cue Cards window if you do not have a mouse.

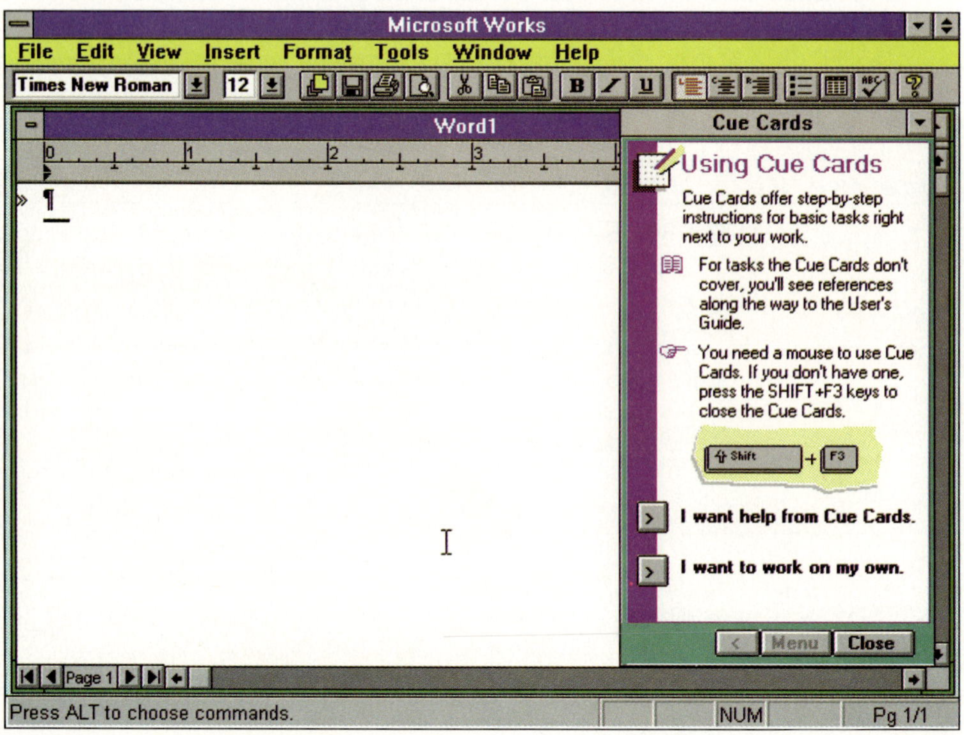

Figure 2-7
The Cue Cards window

Use the Word Processor Cue Cards

These steps assume you are at the Works window with nothing opened and that the Cue Cards are not turned on.

1. Choose **Help, Cue Cards** to turn on Cue Cards.
2. Choose **File, Create New File** to display the Startup dialog box.
3. Choose **Word Processor.** Your screen should be similar to Figure 2-7 if you have not previously had Cue Cards turned on.
4. Click on the arrow button  in front of **I**

   Want help from Cue Cards to display the Word Processor Cue Cards menu as shown in Figure 2-8.

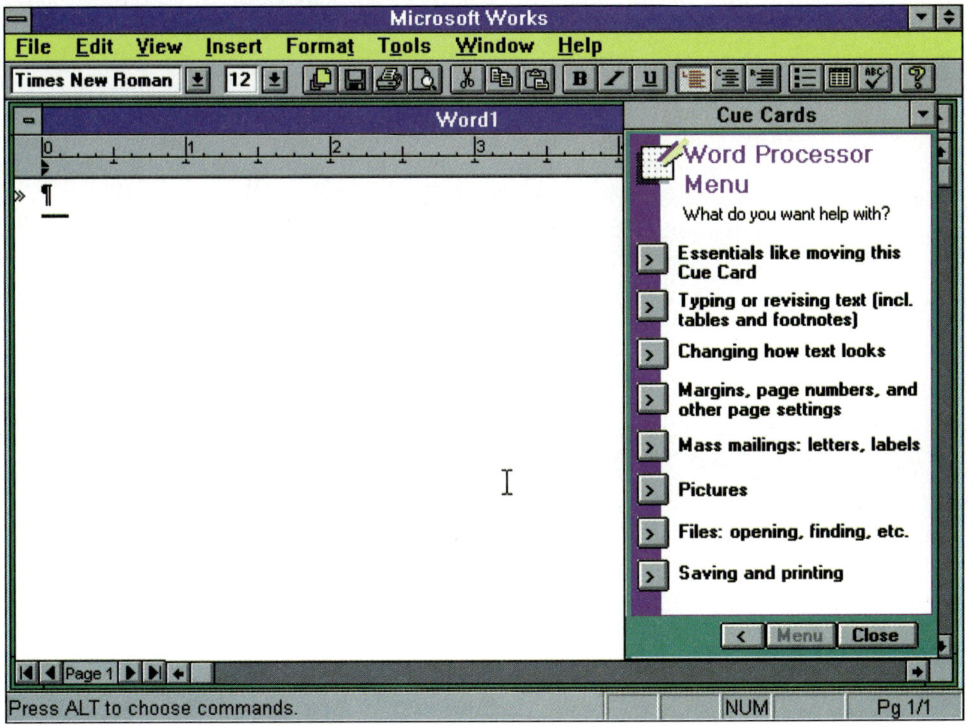

Figure 2-8
The Word Processor Cue Cards menu

5. Click on any of the arrows in front of an item about which you want instructions, then follow the screen instructions for completing that task.

When done you will see a message indicating you are done and asking to return to a menu. In Figure 2-9 the option **I'm done. Return to the main menu** is displayed.

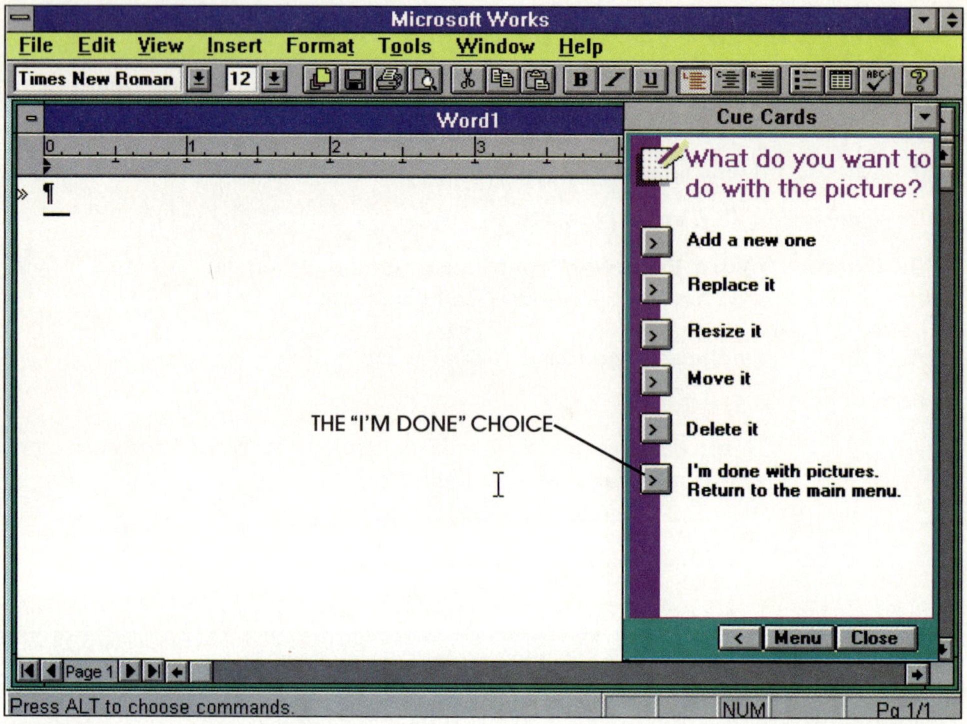

Figure 2-9
The options in a Cue Card

6. Choose whatever response is appropriate to return to the main menu. Your screen should once again resemble the screen shown in Figure 2-8.
7. Experiment with the various Cue Cards options as time permits.

Close the Cue Cards Window

If you do not want the Cue Cards window displayed you can turn it off.

1. Choose **Close** from the Cue Cards window. A second window will be displayed telling you how to turn Cue Cards on again.
2. Read the instructions in the Cue Cards window.
3. Choose either the **Close** button at the bottom of the window, or click on the arrow button in front of **Close Cue Cards**.

EXITING FROM WORKS

Exit the Works Window

1. Double -click on the control menu box at the left end of the Microsoft Works title bar.

or

Choose **File, Exit Works** from the menu bar. If there are any unsaved documents, you will be prompted to save each, or you can choose not to save.

GUIDED TUTORIAL

What You'll Do

- Start Works for Windows
- Open the word processor
- Open the spreadsheet
- Open the database
- Move from one window to another
- Arrange windows
- Size/Maximize/Minimize a window
- Move a window
- Review windows options
- Close a window
- Exit Works for Windows

How to Do It

1. Start Windows.
2. Start Works. Double-click on the Microsoft Works for Windows group icon or press **Ctrl/Tab** to select it and press **Enter.**

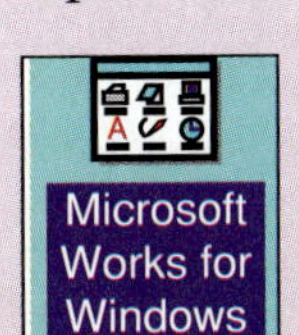

Then double-click on the Microsoft Works icon or use an arrow key to select it and press **Enter.**

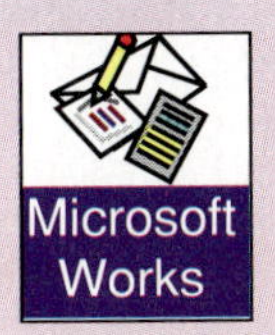

If the Welcome screen is displayed, choose **Start Works Now**—either click on the button or press **W**.

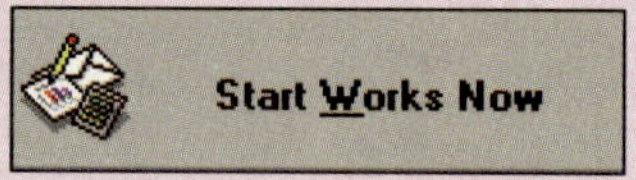

3. Open — the word processor by clicking on the **Word Processor** button, or by pressing **W**.

4. View — the options in the menu bar. An option is selected by clicking on it, or by pressing **Alt** and the underlined letter. When a pull-down menu is displayed, you can click on the choice you want or press the underlined letter to choose it.

5. Press — **Esc** twice or click anywhere outside an open drop-down menu to return to the document window.

6. Return — to the Startup dialog window by clicking on the Startup Dialog button in the toolbar.

7. Open — the spreadsheet window by clicking on the Spreadsheet button or pressing **S**.

8. View — the changes in the toolbar.

9. Return — to the Startup dialog window by clicking on the Startup Dialog button in the toolbar.

10. Open — a database window by clicking on the Database button or pressing **D**.

11. View — the changes in the toolbar.

12. Choose — **Window, Tile** to display the windows side by side. The active window is the one with the highlighted title bar. See Figure 2-10. The order of files shown on your screen may be different from that shown here.

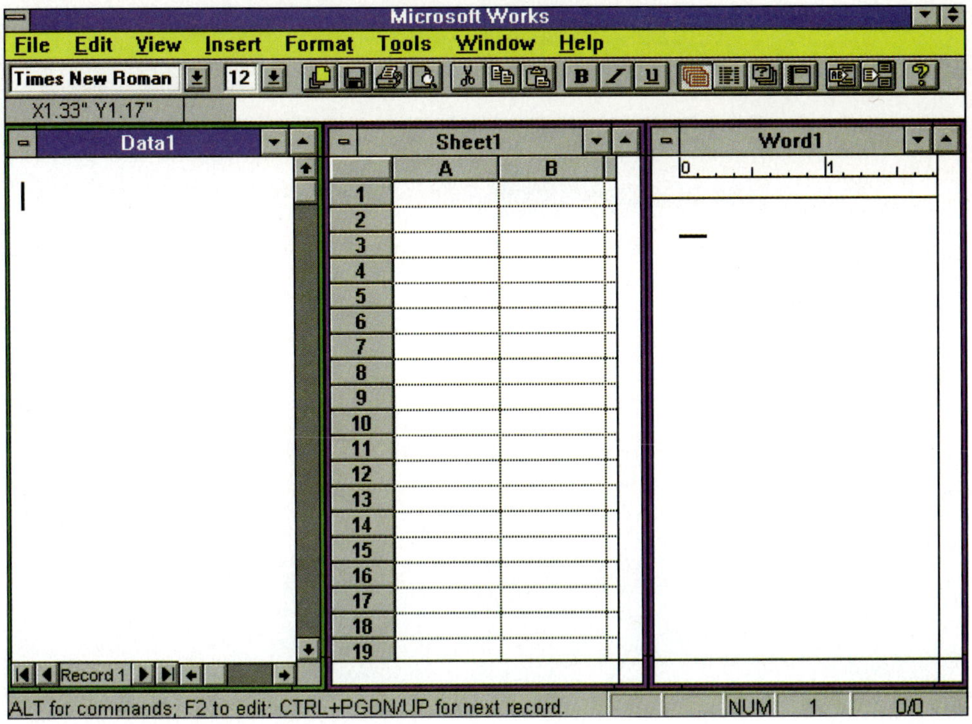

Figure 2-10
Side by side windows

13. Click — on the **Minimize** button  at the right end of the title bar in the active window to reduce it to an icon. The next window is now active and an icon is displayed in the lower left corner of the Works window.

14. Click — on the **Maximize** button  at the right end of the title bar in the new active window to make it full size.

15. Click — on the **Restore** button  at the right end of the menu bar in the active window to return it to its previous size.

16. Double-click — on the icon representing the first active window. (Your icon may represent a different tool.)

17. Choose — **Window, Cascade** to rearrange the windows. See Figure 2-11.

18. Drag — on the title bar of the top window to move it down to another position.

19. Click — on the title bar of the spreadsheet window to make it active.

20. Point — to the lower right corner of the active window. The pointer will become a double-headed arrow. See Figure 2-12.

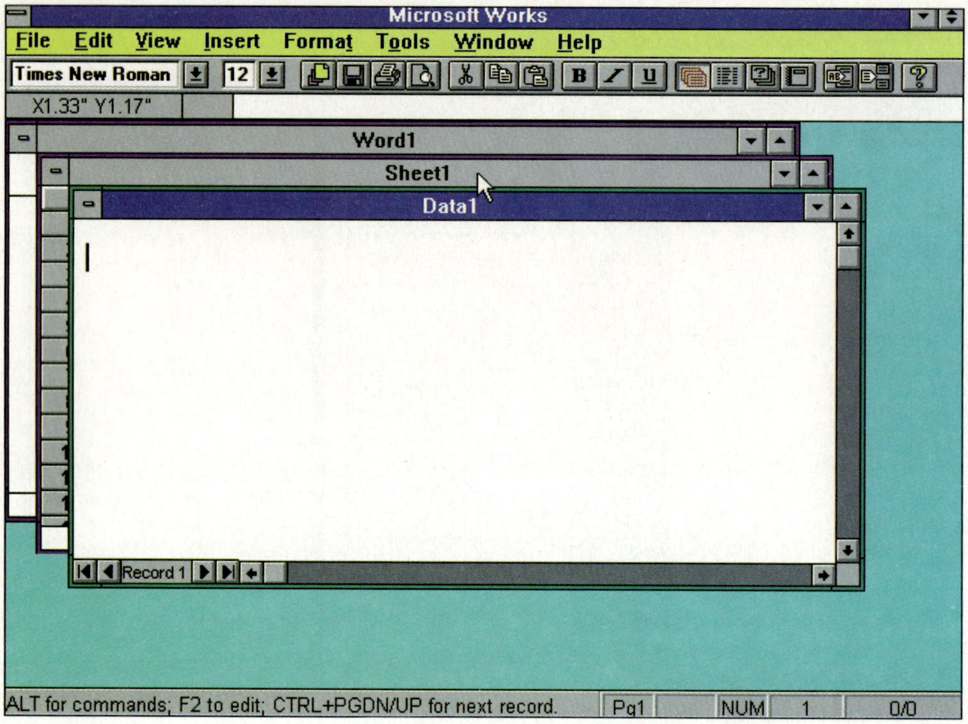

Figure 2-11
Cascading windows

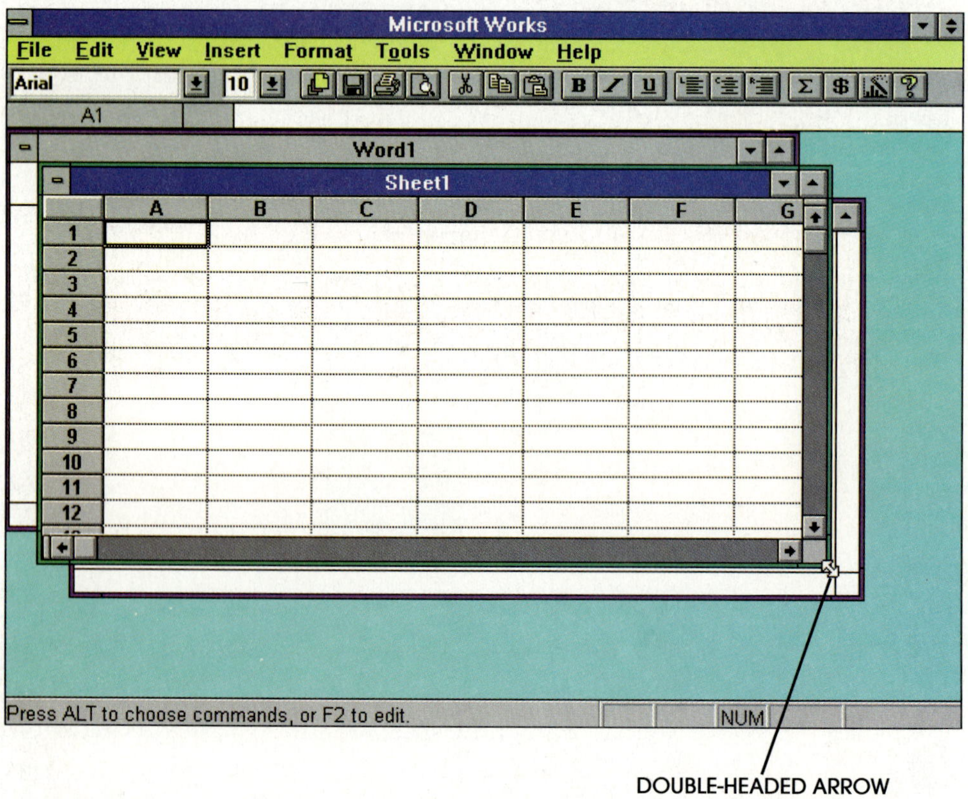

Figure 2-12
Active window changed from Figure 2-11

21. Drag — the corner up so that the window decreases in size.

22. Repeat — any of the steps above to experiment with making a window active and to resize it.

23. Close — the active window by double-clicking on the control menu box at the left end of the title bar.

or

Choose — **File, Close** from the menu.

24. Repeat — step 23 to close the remaining two windows and return to the Startup window.

25. Choose — **Cancel** to remove the Startup box from the Works window. This is necessary before you can exit from Works.

26. Exit — from Works by double-clicking on the control menu box at the left end of the Microsoft Works title bar.

or

Choose — **File, Exit Works.**

REVIEW QUESTIONS

1. List the steps to start Works for Windows on your system.
2. Identify each of the parts of the Works window that are marked in the following:

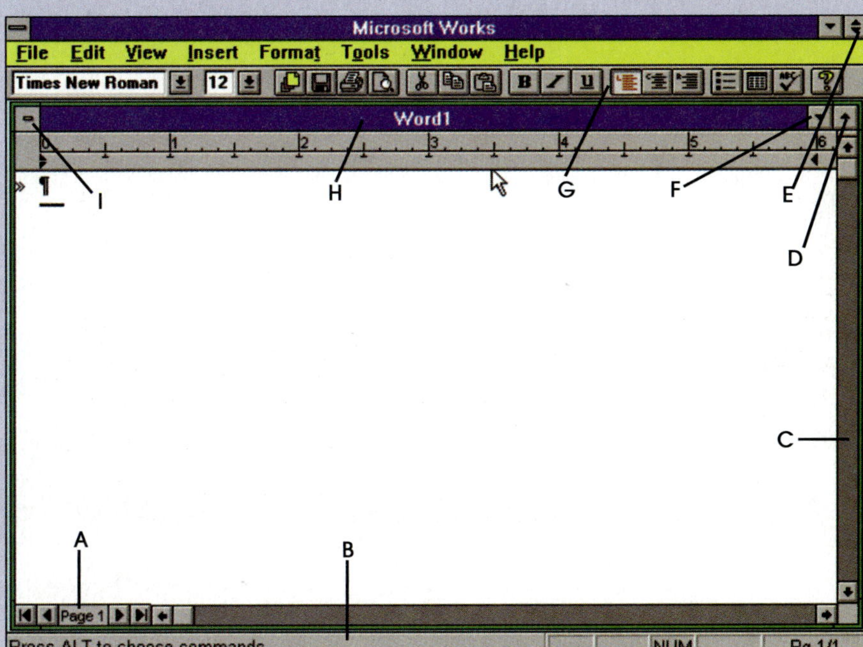

A ______________________________

B ______________________________

C ______________________________

D ______________________________

E ______________________________

F ______________________________

G ______________________________

H ______________________________

I ______________________________

3. Name each of the following buttons. Use the toolbar, if necessary, to see the exact name. The name of the tool is displayed when you point to it.

____

____

____

____

HANDS-ON EXERCISE

Exercise 1

1. Start Works.
2. Open the spreadsheet window.
3. Name each of the tools in the spreadsheet toolbar.

1 ______________________________

2 ______________________________

3 ______________________________

4 ______________________________

5 ______________________________

6 ______________________________

7 ______________________________

8 ______________________________

9 ______________________________

10 ______________________________

11 ______________________________

12 ______________________________

13 ______________________________

14 ______________________________

15 ______________________________

16 ______________________________

17 ______________________________

18 ______________________________

19 ______________________________

4. Make the spreadsheet full screen size.
5. Open the database window.
6. Arrange the windows as tiles.
7. Size and move the windows so that one is above the other rather than side by side. You can change the length or the width of the window by pointing to the side of the window to be sized—the pointer becomes a double arrow—and dragging the side to a different position. When done, your screen should be similar to the example shown below.

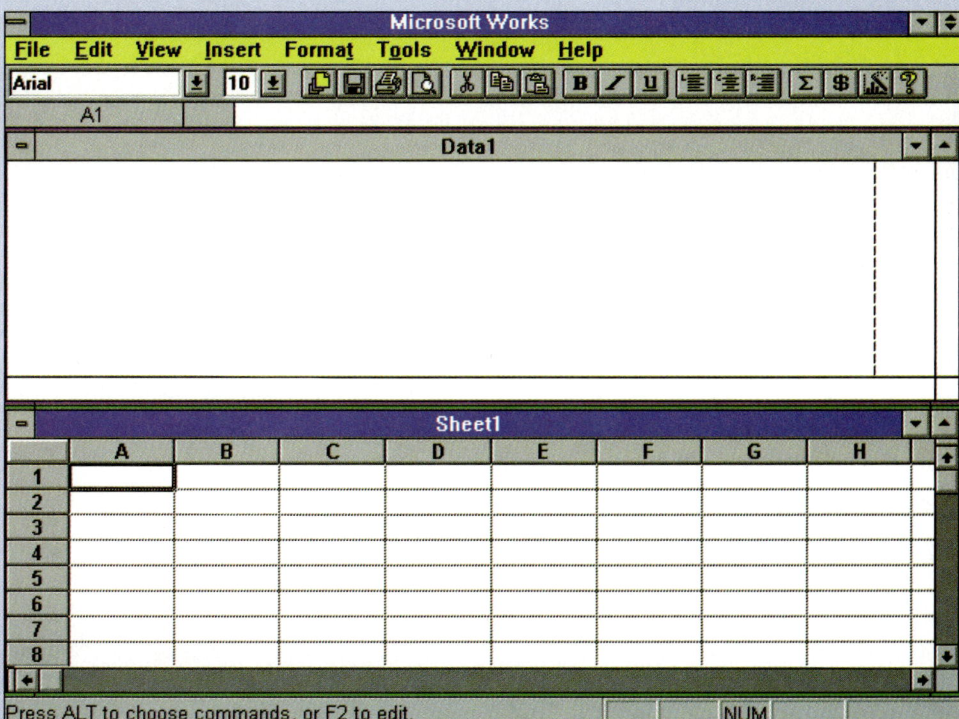

8. Exit from Works for Windows.

CHAPTER 3

Creating A Document

OBJECTIVES

Open a word processor window

Identify components of the word processor window and toolbar

Enter text

Move around in a document

Make corrections to text

Save the document

Close the document window

Retrieve a file

Preview and print the document

PREVIEW

In this chapter you will learn how to use the word processor tool in Works to create a document, make corrections, save the document, and print it. You will also learn how to preview the document before printing, as well as how to close a document and retrieve a document. Step-by-step instructions are given for these tasks, followed by a set of practice exercises where you can apply these functions on your own.

OPENING A NEW FILE

A new word processing file is displayed as soon as the Word Processor button is chosen in the Works Startup dialog box. The screen shows a blank document, where you can begin typing text for the document that you want to create.

Open the Word Processor

1. Start — Works by double-clicking on the Microsoft Works icon in the Microsoft Works for Windows group. (Refer to Chapter 2, if you need to review this procedure.) Then choose **Start Works Now** if the Welcome screen is displayed to go to the Startup dialog box.
2. Choose — **Word Processor** by clicking on the button 

or by pressing **W.** The Word1 window is displayed, as shown in Figure 3-1.

NOTE: A new file can also be opened from within the word processor window by choosing **File**, **Create New File**. If you do this, you are returned to the **Startup** dialog box where you can choose to open another word processing file, a spreadsheet file, or a database file.

THE WORD PROCESSOR WINDOW

The components of the word processor window are identified in Figure 3-1. Review these items. Refer to Table 3-2 to review explanations of each part if necessary. The word processor toolbar is discussed in this section.

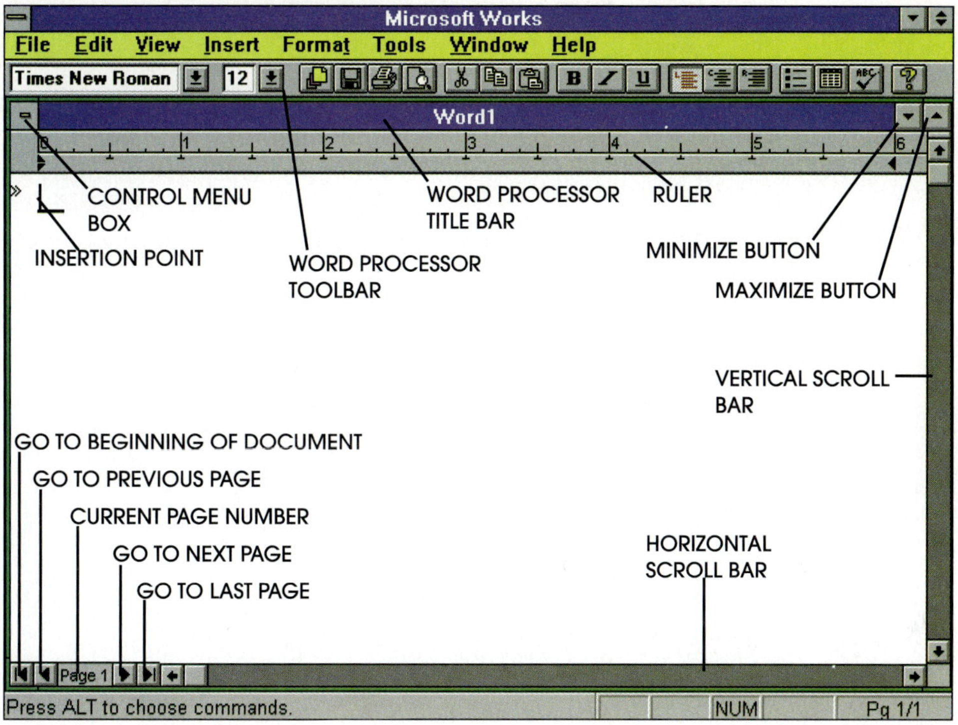

Figure 3-1
The Word Processor window

THE WORD PROCESSOR TOOLBAR

The following illustration is the toolbar in the word processor window. An explanation of each button is given in Table 3-1. When you point to a button, its name will be displayed below the toolbar.

Font name	 Lists available fonts. Click on the arrow at the right end of the button to see the list; then click on the name you want to apply to text at the insertion point.
Font size	 Lists available font sizes. Click on the arrow at the right end of the button to see the list; then click on the size that you want to apply to text at the insertion point.
Startup dialog	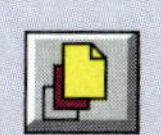 Returns to the Startup dialog box where you can open other Works tools.
Save	 Saves the document in the word processor window. You can name a new document, or save additional edits to a document that has already been named.

Print

Prints the document in the active window.

Print preview

Displays the document page where the insertion point is located as it will be printed.

Cut

Cuts selected text from the document and moves it to the Clipboard where it can then be inserted (pasted) again at a different position in the document.

Copy

Places a copy of the selected text in the Clipboard where it can then be inserted at a different position in the document.

Paste

Inserts the contents of the Clipboard in the document at the insertion point.

Bold

Turns bold formatting on or off (toggles on or off) for selected text.

Italic

Turns italic formatting on or off (toggles on or off) for selected text.

Underline

Turns underlining on or off (toggles on or off) for selected text.

Left align

Aligns paragraph text at the left margin.

Center align

Centers paragraph text.

Right align

Aligns paragraph text at the right margin.

Bullets

Formats paragraphs with bullets.

Insert table		Inserts a spreadsheet that can be used to create tables in the word processing document.
Spelling checker		Checks the spelling of the document in the active window.
Learning Works		Goes to the Learning Works dialog box. Refer to Chapter 2 for a review of these tools.

Table 3-1

The Word Processor toolbar

NOTE: If you inadvertently inserted text or formatting in the active document window as you were reviewing the toolbar buttons, close the document by choosing **File, Close.** You will be returned to the **Startup** dialog box. Choose the **Word Processor** button again to open a new document window.

ENTERING TEXT

Entering text is similar to typing on a sheet of paper; however, the word processor provides numerous tools, which will be covered in this chapter, for making this procedure easier than typing. After entering the text, you can save the document to disk. Works supplies a name for each document—Word1, Word2, Word3, etc., and these names can be used to save the document; however, you can give the document a different, more descriptive name, if you like.

Before entering text, look at the Ruler in the word processing document. In the following illustration the pointer is at the triangle representing the left paragraph indents. It is positioned at the left margin. This triangle is split (see next illustration) so that each part of it can be dragged to a different position. You will learn how to format with paragraph indents in Chapter 5, "Formatting Text."

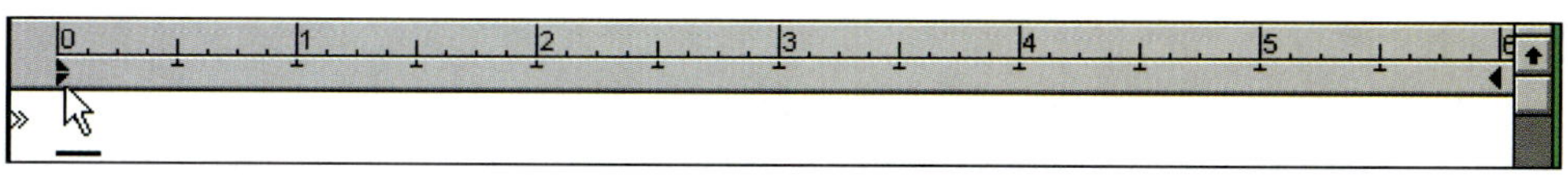

The illustration below shows the pointer at the triangle representing the right paragraph indent, and it is positioned at the right margin. The default margins are at 1.25, making a line that is 6" long. You will learn how to set margins in Chapter 7, "Page Design."

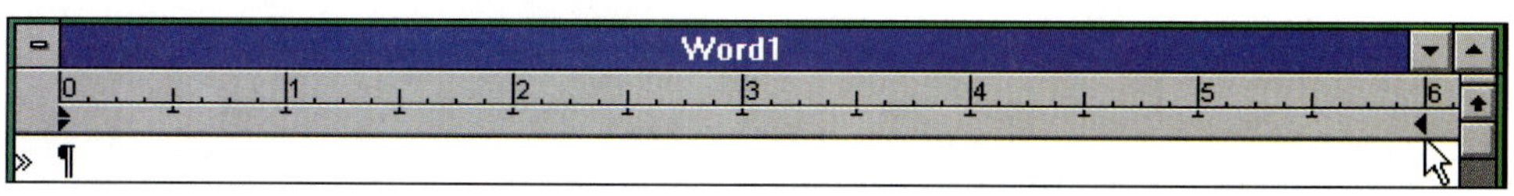

The following illustration shows the pointer at a mark that indicates a tab set. Default tabs are set every 1/2". You move from one tab to the next by pressing the **Tab** key. You will learn how to set new tab stops in Chapter 5, "Formatting Text."

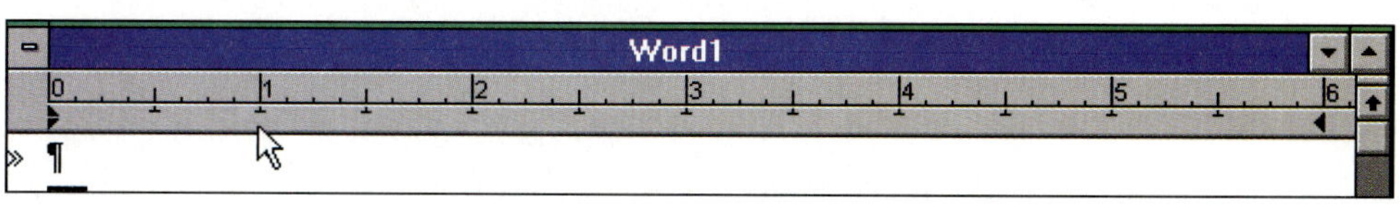

To enter text in a word processing document, just type the text as you would on a typewriter with one important exception—use **wordwrap**. Wordwrap means that you do not press **Enter** at the ends of lines-the computer will automatically end the lines for you. When text reaches the right margin, it will automatically move to the next line as you continue to type. You do need to press **Enter** at the end of each paragraph and also at the ends of short lines such as addresses, date lines, complimentary closes, and salutations. You also press **Enter** to insert blank lines.

It is important that you are aware of the position of the insertion point, which is the vertical blinking line. (Refer to Figure 3-1.) The insertion point indicates the position where you can insert text, graphics, tables, and other Works objects. The status bar in the word processor window indicates the page number where the insertion point is located, while the current page number and the total number of pages in the document display at the right end of the status bar in the Works window. See the example in the following illustration.

PAGE NUMBER IN WORD PROCESSING STATUS BAR   PAGE NUMBERS IN WORKS STATUS BAR

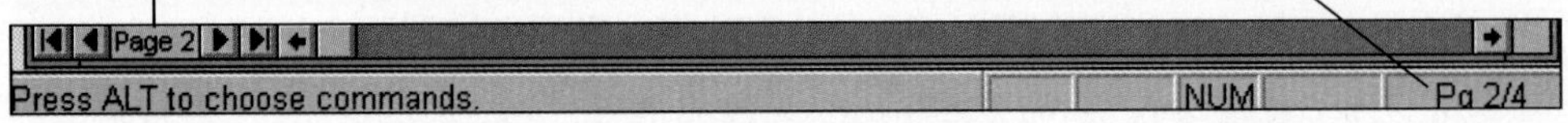

As you enter text, you can correct your typos by pressing the **Backspace** key to delete characters to the left of the insertion point, or you can press the **Delete** key to delete the characters to the right of the insertion point.

Enter Text

1. Type — the text shown in the box below. Remember to press **Enter** only at the ends of paragraphs, at the ends of short lines that do not extend to the right margin, and to insert blank lines. Also, press the **space-bar** twice at the end of each sentence. To enter text in all caps, press the **Caps Lock** key. Be sure to press it again to turn off Caps Lock. The word **and** in the list of boat sites is indented one tab stop—press the **Tab** key to indent.
2. Correct — any typos as you go, or just ignore them, if you like.

PROMOTIONAL OFFER

Next month Puget Sound Charters will offer two- and three-hour cruise tick-ets to all persons who visit one of our charter boats at any of their Puget Sound locations. Tickets will be available at reduced prices during the entire month, and will include brunch and dinner cruises.

The locations for visiting the boats are:

Kirkland on Lake Washington
Lake Union in downtown Seattle
Seward Park on Lake Washington
    and
Shilshole in Ballard

Drop in for a visit and learn about all of our cruising schedules.

MOVING AROUND IN THE DOCUMENT

Most Windows applications now use the term *insertion point* when referring to the cursor. In this section you will learn how to move the insertion point quickly to various positions in the document.

Use the Mouse to Move the Insertion Point

1. Click — on any position to immediately move the insertion point to that place.
2. Click — on the arrows in the scroll bars to move up or down or to the left or right. See example in Figure 3-2. Practice using both scroll bars to see the movement in the document.

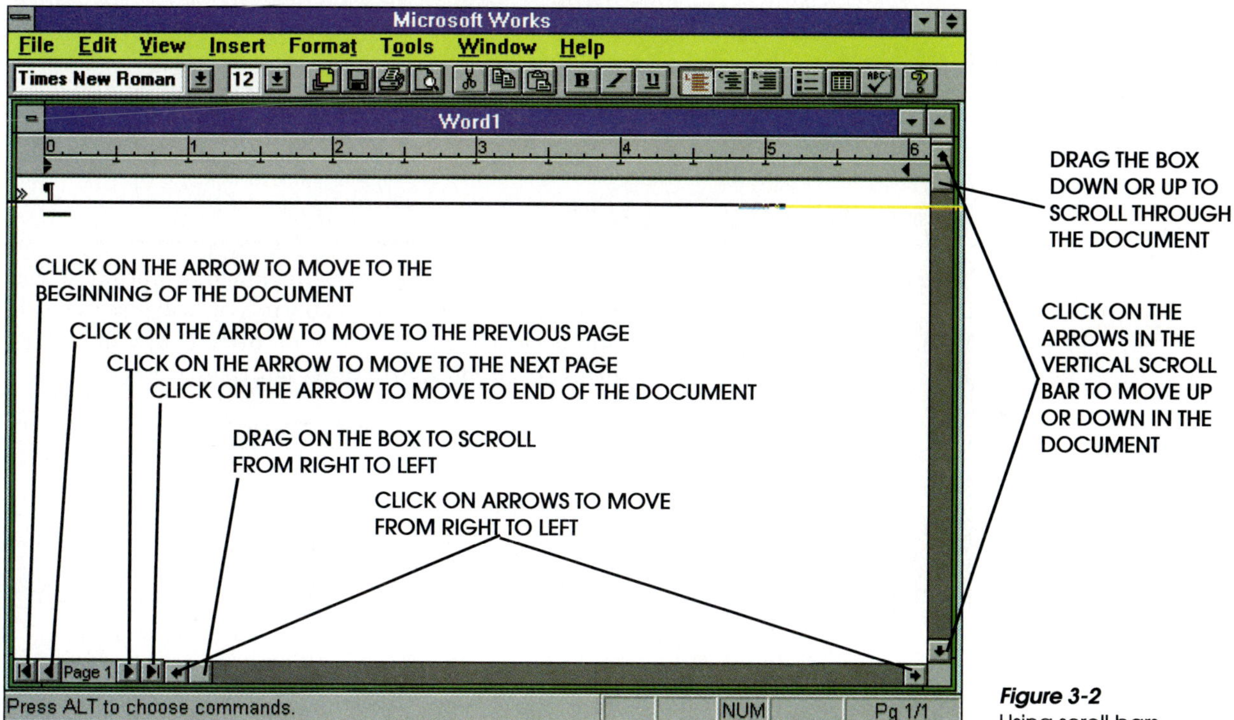

Figure 3-2
Using scroll bars

3. Click — on the arrows to the left and right of the page number in the word processor window status bar. See Figure 3-2 for an explanation of each of the arrows. You will not see a change in the page number because you only have one page; however, you will move from the top of the document to the bottom of the document.
4. Drag — on the boxes in the scroll bars to scroll through the document, either up or down or to the left or right. See Figure 3-2. Experiment with these actions.

Use the Keyboard to Move the Insertion Point

1.	Press	any of the arrow keys to move the insertion point up or down or to the left or right in the document.
2.	Press	**Ctrl/Home** to move to the top of the document.
3.	Press	**Ctrl/End** to move to the end of the document.
4.	Press	**Home** to move to the beginning of a line.
5.	Press	**End** to move to the end of a line.
6.	Press	**Page Up** to scroll up one screen length.
7.	Press	**Page Down** to scroll down one screen length.
8.	Press	**Ctrl/Right Arrow** to move right one word.
9.	Press	**Ctrl/Left Arrow** to move left one word.
10.	Press	**Ctrl/Page Down** to move to the bottom of the window.
11.	Press	**Ctrl/Page Up** to move to the top of the window.

SAVING DOCUMENTS

The process of saving a document copies it to a disk. If the document is not saved, the text on the screen is in RAM memory, and if your system aborts, you will lose the text. When it is saved on a disk, should the system shut down, your document will be preserved, unless in some very unfortunate circumstance the disk drives are damaged.

Save the Word Document

1. Click on the **Save** button in the toolbar 

   or

   Choose **File, Save As**. The Save As window will be displayed as shown in Figure 3-3.

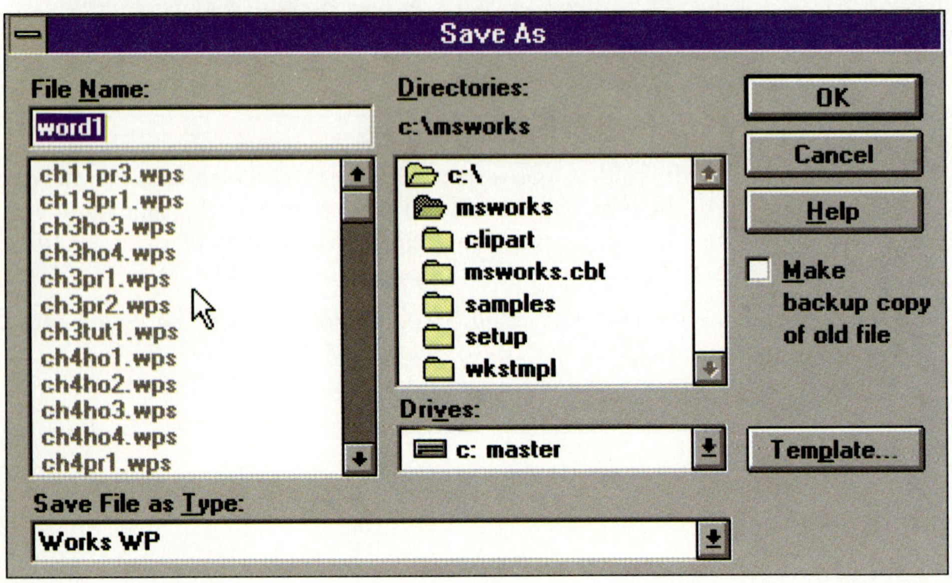

Figure 3-3
The Save As window

NOTE: If your system is set up to save to a diskette in drive A or B, then the Directories name in the Save As dialog box will be different than that shown here. It will display the default directories and drives as **a:** or **b:**.

A suggested name, **word1,** is displayed in the File Name text box. You may use this name or you may type a different name if you like. The file name is highlighted; therefore, if you begin typing a new name, the suggested name will be deleted immediately.

2. Type **CH3PR1** for the file name.

or

a:CH3PR1 or **b:CH3PR1** if you want to save to a diskette in drive A or B and the default directory is the same as that shown here, or if it is some directory other than A or B.

NOTE: The document name stands for Chapter 3, Practice Document 1.

3. Click on **OK** or press **Enter** to save.

When done, the new file name is now showing in the title bar in the word processor window as displayed here.

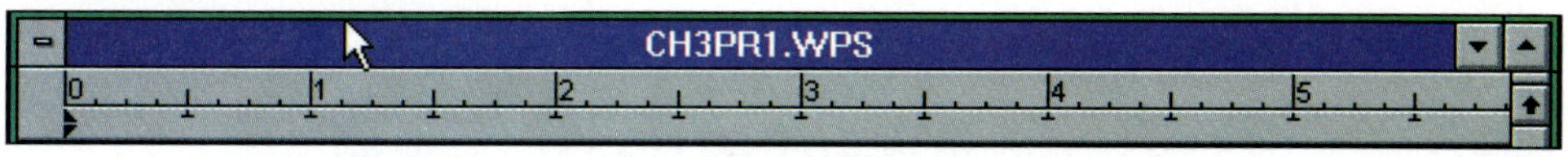

The extension **WPS** is automatically added. All word processing files will be assigned this extension unless you type a different three-character extension.

DISPLAYING CHARACTERS

It is helpful, particularly for beginners, to see all characters in a document when editing text. At this point you probably can see only the text; however, other characters representing paragraph marks and spaces can be shown so that you know exactly what has been entered in the document, making it easier to locate those characters if they need to be deleted.

Display All Characters

1. Choose **View, All Characters** from the Works menu bar. (If a check mark is already in front of All Characters, press **Esc** or click outside the menu to leave the drop-down menu without changing it.) Your document should now resemble that shown in Figure 3-4. Paragraph marks are displayed, which were inserted when you pressed **Enter**; dots between words show where the **spacebar** was pressed; and the right-pointing arrow was inserted when **Tab** was pressed.

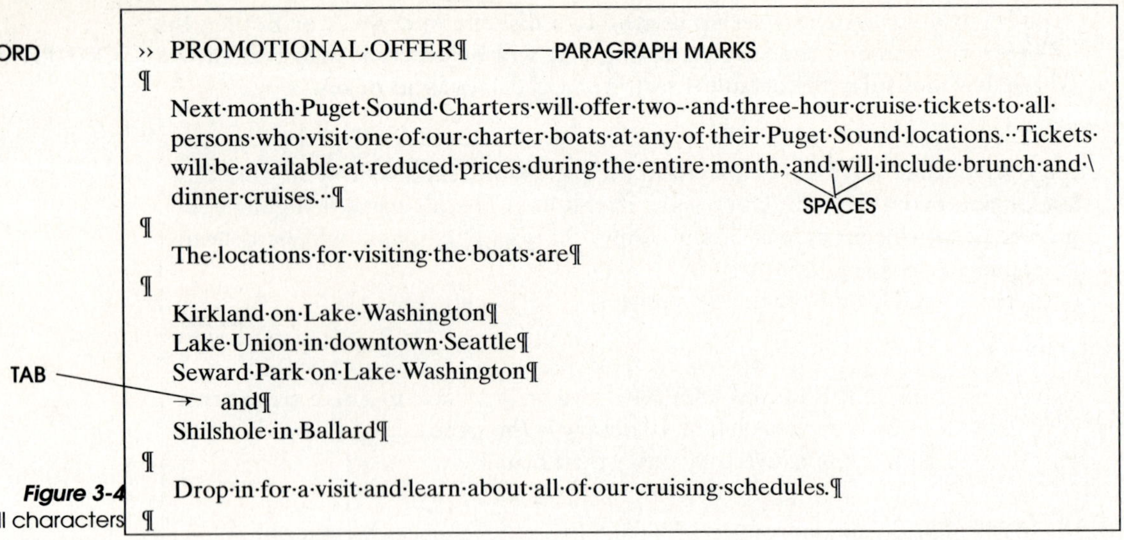

Figure 3-4
Showing all characters

NOTE: When you want to remove the characters from the screen, choose **View** from the Works menu bar. The choice **All Characters** has a check mark in front of it indicating that it is turned on. Choose **All Characters** to remove the check mark and turn off the display.

MAKING CORRECTIONS

You may have already used the **Backspace** and **Delete** keys. In this section you will learn how to make corrections and edits by inserting new text, typing over existing text, and combining and separating paragraphs. The edits that you will be making are shown in the following example.

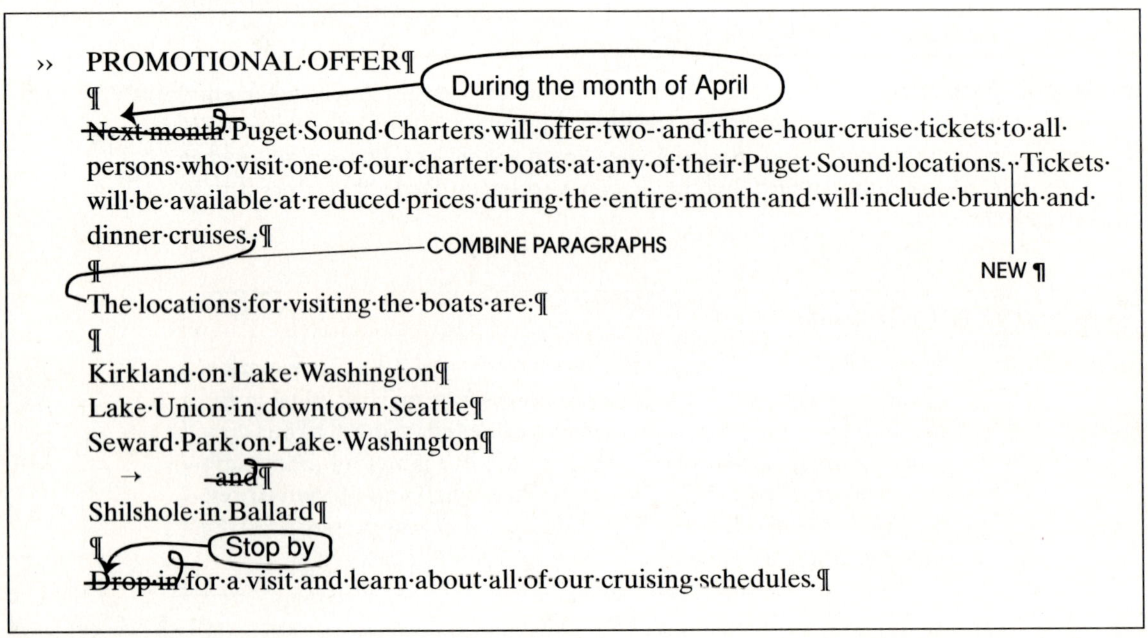

Delete and Insert Text

1. Move — the insertion point to the beginning of the first paragraph (see the following illustration) and press the **Delete** key enough times to delete **Next month.** The remaining text moves to the left to fill in the empty space.

Next·month·Puget·Sound·Charters·will·offer·two-·and·three-hour·cruise·tickets·to·all· persons·who·visit·one·of·our·charter·boats·at·any·of·their·Puget·Sound·locations.··Tickets· will·be·available·at·reduced·prices·during·the·entire·month·and·will·include·brunch·and· dinner·cruises.·¶

With the insertion point located in front of **Puget**

2. Type — **During the month of April** at the beginning of the paragraph. The remaining text moves to the right and down the page as you type.

3. Move — the insertion point directly following the word **and** in the list of locations as shown below and press **Backspace** to delete it.

Kirkland·on·Lake·Washington¶
Lake·Union·in·downtown·Seattle¶
Seward·Park,on·Lake·Washington¶
→ and¶
Shilshole·in·Ballard¶

PRESS BACKSPACE TO DELETE THE WORD "AND," THE TAB MARK, AND THE PARAGRAPH MARK

4. Press — **Backspace** again to delete the **Tab** and again to delete the paragraph mark following **Washington,** which removes the blank line between the last two locations.

Overtype Text

Overtype mode allows you to type over, or replace, existing text with new text. This is the opposite of Insert mode, which is also the default mode. Insert mode allows new text to be inserted within existing text, and the existing text that follows the newly inserted text moves automatically to the right and down the page. You toggle between Overtype and Insert mode by pressing the **Insert** key.

1. Move — the insertion point to the beginning of the last line of text shown in the illustration below.

2. Press — **Insert** key to change the typing mode to **Overtype.** The status bar should now show **OVR** to indicate the mode, as displayed here.

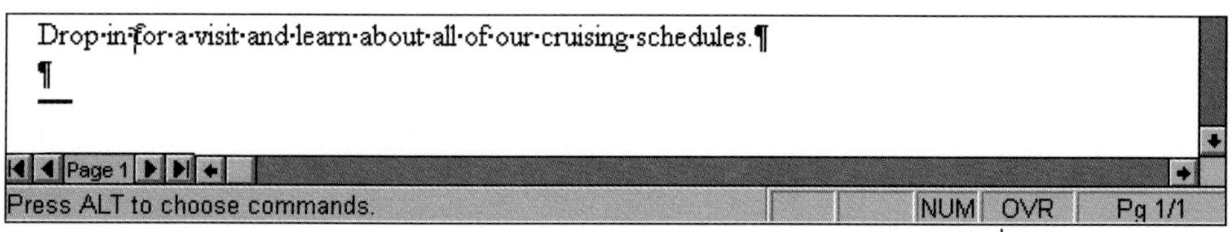

OVR SHOWING OVERTYPE MODE

3. Type — **Stop by** over the existing text **Drop in**. The old text is deleted and replaced with the new text.

4. Press — **Insert** key again to leave Overtype mode. The OVR is no longer displayed in the status bar.

NOTE: You do not necessarily use Overtype only when you are replacing the same number of characters. If extra characters remain, press **Backspace** or **Delete** to remove them. Be careful when using Overtype that you do not replace text that you do not want to delete.

Separate and Combine Paragraphs

1. Move — the insertion point to the beginning of the word **Tickets** in the first paragraph.

Next·month·Puget·Sound·Charters·will·offer·two-·and·three-hour·cruise·tickets·to·all·persons·who·visit·one·of·our·charter·boats·at·any·of·their·Puget·Sound·locations.··Tickets·will·be·available·at·reduced·prices·during·the·entire·month,·and·will·include·brunch·and·dinner·cruises.··¶
¶
The·locations·for·visiting·the·boats·are¶

PRESS ENTER TWICE
PRESS DELETE TO DELETE TWO PARAGRAPH RETURNS

2. Press — **Enter** key twice—once to end the first paragraph and a second time to insert a blank line.

3. Move — the insertion point to the end of the new second paragraph following the period after **cruises.**

4. Press — **Delete** key twice to combine that paragraph with the following line.

5. Press — **Spacebar** twice to insert two spaces between **cruises.** and **The.** Your document should now resemble the text shown in Figure 3-5.

›› PROMOTIONAL·OFFER¶
¶
During·the·month·of·April·Puget·Sound·Charters·will·offer·two-·and·three-hour·cruise·tickets·to·all·persons·who·visit·one·of·our·charter·boats·at·any·of·their·Puget·Sound·locations.··¶
¶
Tickets·will·be·available·at·reduced·prices·during·the·entire·month·and·will·include·brunch·and·dinner·cruises.··The·locations·for·visiting·the·boats·are:¶
¶
Kirkland·on·Lake·Washington¶
Lake·Union·in·downtown·Seattle¶
Seward·Park·on·Lake·Washington¶
Shilshole·in·Ballard¶
¶
Stop·by·for·a·visit·and·learn·about·all·of·our·cruising·schedules.¶

Figure 3-5
Edited document

SAVING EDITS

You have already named and saved the document; however, the corrections that have just been made are not saved to disk.

Save Edited Text

1. Click on the **Save** button 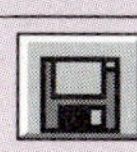, or choose **File, Save**, or press **Ctrl/S** to save the edits to disk. When you point to the **Save** button, a message, **Saves the active document,** will be displayed as shown in the following illustration. You will not see a dialog box; however, the status bar in the Works window will briefly display a message indicating that the file is being saved

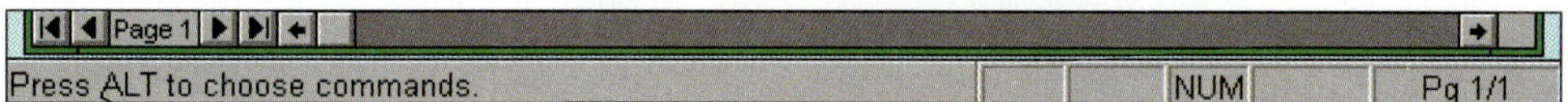

WORKS STATUS BAR INDICATING DOCUMENT WIL BE SAVED WHEN THE SAVE BUTTON IS USED.

CLOSING THE WINDOW

When done, you can close the active window and then retrieve the document at a later time.

Close the Word Processor Window

1. Double-click on the control menu box  at the left end of the **Word** title bar, or click on it once and choose **Close,** or press **Ctrl/F4.** If any changes have been made to the document since it was last saved, you will be prompted to save again before leaving the word processor window.

You will be returned to the Startup dialog box which now displays the new file name in the **Recently used files** list box.

If additional documents are open in the word processor window, you will not return to the Startup dialog box but will remain in the word processor window and the next remaining document will be active.

OPENING AN EXISTING FILE

You can open a file either from the Startup dialog box or from the word processor window. Both will be discussed here.

Open a File from the Startup Dialog Box

1. Choose **CH3PR1.WPS** from the **Recently used files** list box—click on the file name to select it, or press **Alt/R** and the **down arrow** to select the file name.

2. Choose **OK** or press **Enter**. The file is now displayed in the word processor screen.

Open a File from the Word Processor Window

1. Choose **File, Open Existing File.** The Open dialog box will be displayed as shown in Figure 3-6.

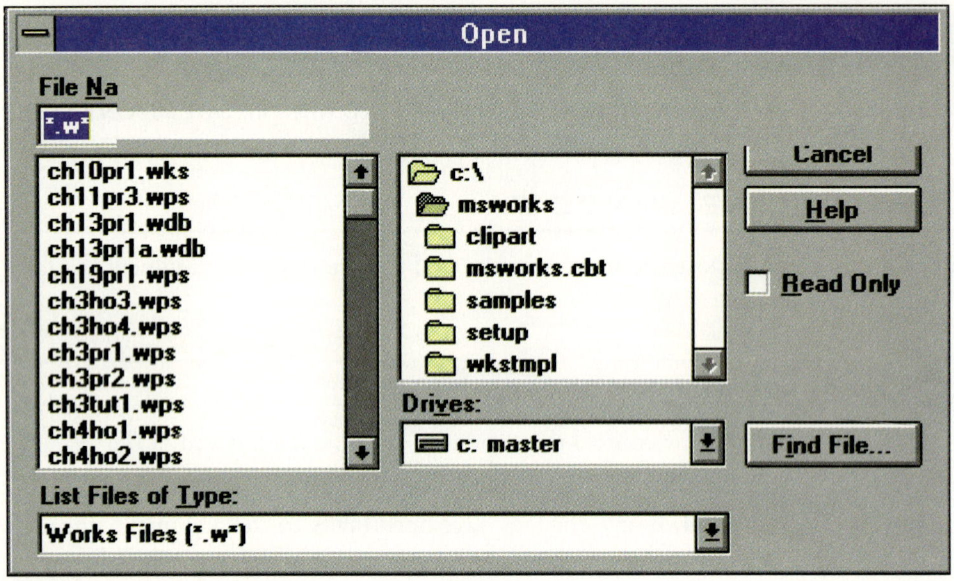

Figure 3-6
The Open dialog box

The File Name text box displays ***.w*** and the list box below shows the names of the files that are currently saved in the **msworks** directory. (Your dialog box will not show the files that are shown in Figure 3-6.)

2. Choose any other file that may be displayed there, if you like. You cannot retrieve the **CH3PR1.WPS** document because it is already open from the Startup dialog box.

3. Choose **OK** or press **Enter** to open another file, if one exists. If there are no other files, choose **Cancel.**

You can retrieve a file regardless of the Works tool window that is active. The **Open** dialog box displays all files—word processing, spreadsheet, and database files. These files are identified by the extension that is automatically assigned to them. Word processing files have the extension **.wps**; spreadsheet files have the extension **.wks**; and database files have the extension **.wdb.**

PREVIEWING THE DOCUMENT

It is often helpful to see how your document will look before printing. Print Preview will show margins, headers and footers (text printed at the top and the bottom of each page), and page breaks (page endings). You can also expand the size of the text in Print Preview to see how various font types and font sizes will look when they are printed.

Preview the Document

Be sure the **CH3PR1.WPS** document is in the active window.

1. Click on the **Print Preview** button , or choose **File, Print Preview** from the Works menu. The full document page is displayed as it will look when printed, and should be similar to the example below in Figure 3-7.

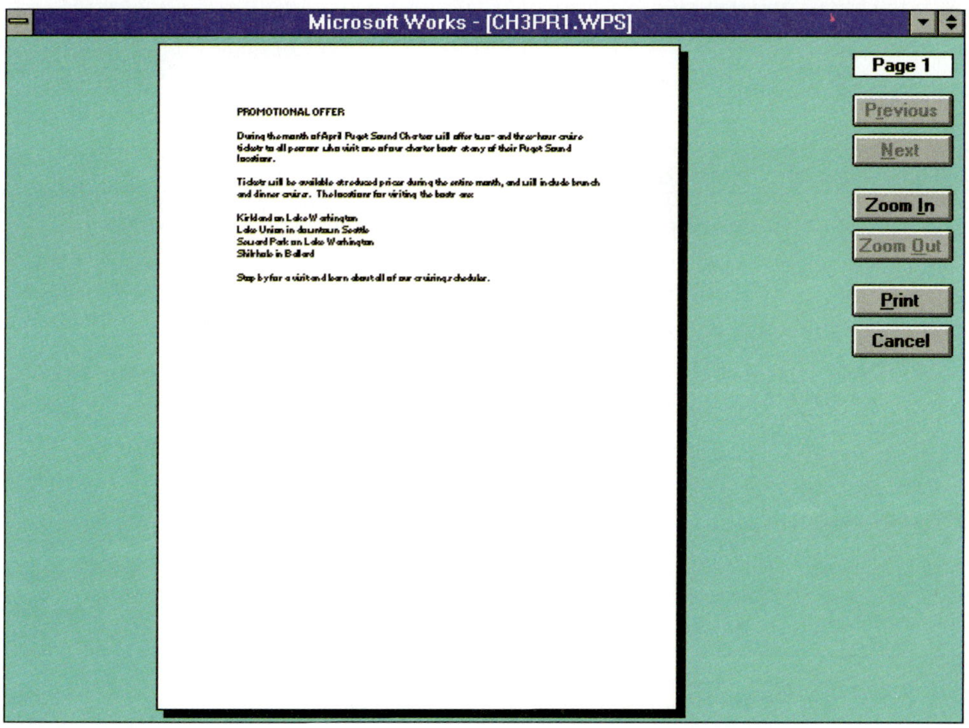

Figure 3-7
The current page in Print Preview

You can perform various functions from the Print Preview screen. The buttons at the right side of the screen are described in Table 3-2. Notice that only the **Zoom In, Print,** and **Cancel** buttons are available. The other options are not available because this document consists of only one page. **Zoom Out** will be available after **Zoom In** is chosen.

Page 1	Displays the number of the page that is currently being displayed.
Previous	Click on the Previous button to display the previous page. The Page Number button will reflect the change.
Next	Click on the Next button to display the next page. Again, the Page Number button will display the number of the page being viewed.
Zoom In	Expands the display to its maximum size.
Zoom Out	Reduces the display to its original size.
Print	Sends the entire file directly to the printer.
Cancel	Returns to the word processor window.

Table 3-2
The Print Preview buttons

Use Zoom In and Zoom Out

1. Choose **Zoom In** [Zoom In] to see an expanded view of the text.

   This allows you to see better how the characters used for the text will look, and the document will be easier to read.

2. Click on the up or down arrows in the scroll bars or press the arrow keys to see other text in the document.

3. Choose **Zoom Out** [Zoom Out] to return to viewing the full page.

You can also cycle through different zoom sizes.

4. Move the pointer to any position in the text. The pointer becomes a **Zoom** magnifying glass . See the example in Figure 3-8.

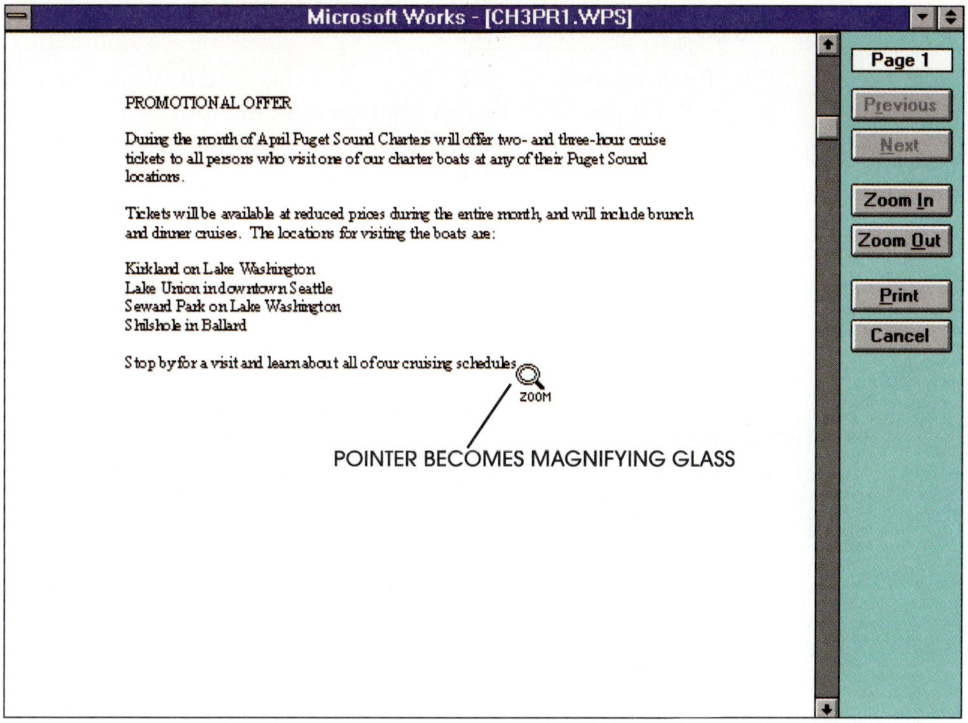

Figure 3-8
The Print Preview screen showing pointer as a magnifying glass

5. Click on the left mouse button to increase the size of the display.
6. Click again to further expand the display. You can move the insertion point around in the document, if you like.
7. Click again to return to the original text size.
8. Choose Cancel [Cancel] to return to the word processor window.

PRINTING A DOCUMENT

You can print from the Print Preview window; however, for now print the document from the Works word processor window.

Print the Document

1. Be sure the printer is on-line and the paper is adjusted correctly.
2. Click on the **Print** button, or; choose **File, Print,** or press **Ctrl/P** and press **Enter** to send the document directly to the printer. All pages of the document in the active window will be printed.

Print Two Copies of the Document

1. Choose **File, Print** or press **Ctrl/P.** The Print dialog box is displayed as shown in Figure 3-9. The Print button does not display the Print dialog box; therefore, it is not used when you want to change the default print options, which you will be doing here.

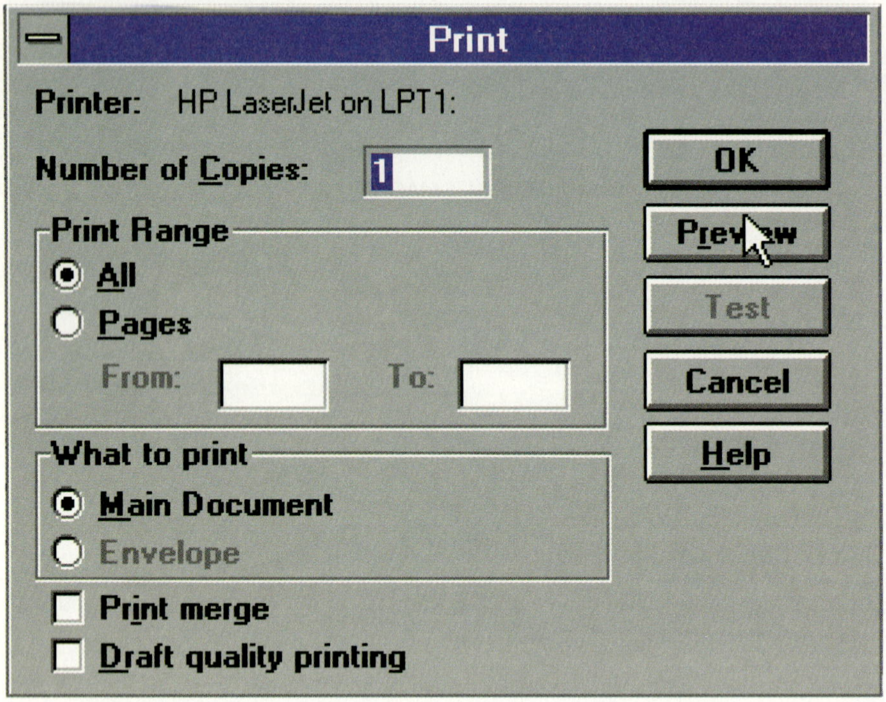

Figure 3-9
The Print dialog box

The number in the **Number of Copies** text box is highlighted.

2. Type **2** in the **Number of Copies** text box. The number **1** will be deleted and replaced with **2.**
3. Choose **OK** or press **Enter.**

Other options in the Print dialog box are described in Table 3-3.

All	**All** in the Print Range box is **on** by default, indicating that all pages of the active file will be printed.
Pages	Turn on **Pages** to print a selected range of pages. After turning this button on, enter page numbers in the **From** and **To** text boxes.
Main document	The document in the active window will be printed by default.
Envelope	Click on **Envelope** to print an accompanying envelope if one is available. Printing envelopes is covered in Chapter 6.
Print merge	Check the **Print merge** box when you are merging documents. This will be covered in Chapter 16.
Draft quality printing	Check the **Draft quality printing** box to print the document in draft quality (if that is available to you depending upon the type of printer being used). This can save time and is useful when you want to print a first draft of a document.

Exit the Works Window

1. Double-click on the control menu box  at the left end of the Works window title bar, or choose **File, Exit Works.** If any documents contain edits that have not been saved, you will be prompted to do that. If the **Save changes** prompt is displayed, choose **Yes** to save. Or you can choose **No** if you do not want to save the changes (or you can choose **Cancel** if you do not want to leave Works).

You will return to the Program Manager in Windows.

GUIDED TUTORIAL

What You'll Do

- Create a new document
- Practice editing
- Open an existing file
- Print a file

How to Do It

1. Load Works by double-clicking on the Microsoft Works icon in the Microsoft Works for Windows group.
2. Open the word processor in Works by clicking on the **Word Processor** button.

3. Type the text shown in the following example.

Today's date
¶
¶
¶
¶
Ms. Rebecca Barnes¶
1907 Seventh Avenue S. E.¶
Bellevue, WA 98005¶
¶
Dear Ms. Barnes:¶
¶
It has come to my attention that you are interested in exploring job opportunities with Data Enterprises.¶
¶
We are currently seeking applicants for a position as Junior Programmer in our EDS department. This position offers a competitive salary with flexible working hours. In addition to training, we offer successful employees a full range of opportunities for professional development.¶
¶
If you would like more information on this challenging position which is now open, please contact me.¶
¶
I shall look forward to hearing from you.¶
¶
Sincerely yours,¶
¶
¶
¶

3. Click — on the **Save** button  , or choose **File, Save As** to display the Save As dialog box similar to that shown here.
4. Type — **CH3TUT1** for Chapter 3, Tutorial practice 1 in the File Name text box.
5. Choose — **OK** or press **Enter** to save.

Turn on **All Characters:** (It may already be on. If so, skip step 6.)

6. Choose — **View, All Characters.**

Delete the text **interested in** the first paragraph:

7. Move — the insertion point in front of **interested in** and press **Delete** enough times to remove both words. Also delete extra spaces between words.

   or

   Move — the insertion point directly following **in** and press **Backspace** enough times to remove both words and delete extra spaces between words.

Use Overtype to change the text **employees** in the second paragraph to **personnel**:

8. Move — the insertion point in front of the **e** in **employees**.
9. Press — **Insert** key to change to Overtype. The status bar should now display OVR to indicate the change in typing mode.
10. Type — **personnel** over **employees**. Delete any extra spaces if they are displayed.
11. Press — **Insert** key to leave Overtype mode.

Combine the paragraph beginning **If you would like more . . .** and the following paragraph beginning **I shall look forward . . .**:

12. Move — the insertion point to the left of the paragraph mark following **me** in paragraph 3.
13. Press — **Delete** twice to combine these paragraphs, and press **spacebar** twice to insert spaces between the sentences.

Insert text between the paragraph beginning **We are currently. . .** and the next paragraph, **If you would like. . .**:

14. Move — the insertion point to the end of paragraph 2 after the words **professional development** and press **Enter** twice.
15. Type — the text shown in the following example. Press the **Tab** key to indent each item in the list.

Seminars are regularly offered in:

Employee Relations
Management Training
Job Satisfaction
Retirement Planning
and more

Save the document again:

16. Click — on the **Save** button , or choose **File, Save**, or press **Ctrl/S** to save the edits.

Open an existing file:

17. Choose — **File, Open Existing File** to display the Open dialog box.

18. Select — **CH3PR1.WPS**—the file created earlier in this chapter-or retrieve it from the instructor's data disk.

19. Choose — **OK** or press **Enter** to open the file. You now have two files in the word processor window.

20. Click — on the title bar for **CH3TUT1** to make it the active window.

21. Drag — on the title bar to move the document window down to a different position. You should now be able to see portions of both documents.

Print the active document:

Be sure the printer is on-line and the paper is adjusted correctly.

22. Click — on the **Print** button , or choose **File, Print** and **OK.**

23. Exit — from Works by double-clicking on the control menu box  at the left end of the Works title bar, or by choosing **File, Exit Works.** If the prompt to save is displayed, choose **Yes** if you want to save any changes or choose **No** if you do not want to save the changes.

REVIEW QUESTIONS

1. List the steps for creating and saving a new document.

2. Identify and describe the use of each of the following buttons in the word processor tool bar.

____

____

3. Match each of the following phrases to the keystrokes listed below.

___ Move the insertion point to the top of the document.

___ Move the insertion point to the beginning of the line.

___ Move the insertion point to the bottom of the window.

___ Move the insertion point to the end of the document.

___ Move the insertion point to the next word.

___ Move the insertion point to the end of the line.

___ Move the insertion point to the top of the window.

___ Move the insertion point to the previous word.

A. Ctrl/Right Arrow

B. Ctrl/Left Arrow

C. Ctrl/Home

D. Ctrl/End

E. Ctrl/Page Up

F. Ctrl/Page Down

G. Home

H. End

I. Page Up

J. Page Down

Fill in the best answer to complete the following statement.

4. Press the ____________________ key to change to Overtype mode.

5. If you are using the choices in the menu bar, name the commands for each of the following.

   Name and save the document ____________________

   Save a document that is already named ____________________

   Preview the document before printing ____________________

   Closing Works ____________________

   Open an existing file ____________________

6. Explain where will you see the following and how it is used.

ZOOM

7. Identify the following components of the word processor window.

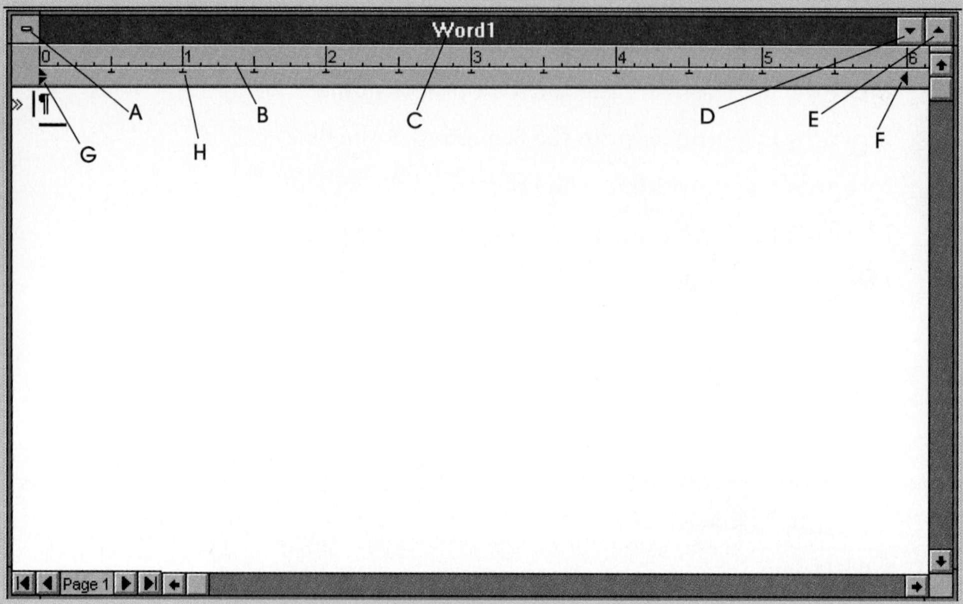

A ____

B ____

C ____

D ____

E ____

F ____

G ____

H ____

Hands-on Exercises

Exercise 1

1. Write a one-page résumé about yourself and your qualifications. Use the following format as a guideline. When listing skills, use a few words that focus on your experience such as:

   Four years of part-time work

   Excellent work record

   Training in accounting

Keep each skill on a single line. Leave space between each category.

NAME

ADDRESS

CITY, STATE ZIP

QUALIFICATIONS

Skill 1

Skill 2

Skill 3

EDUCATION

School 1

School 2

EXPERIENCE

Job or experience 1

Job or experience 2

HOBBIES AND SPECIAL INTERESTS

Activity 1

Activity 2

2. Save the document as **CH3HO1** for **Chapter 3, Hands-on Exercise 1**.
3. Correct any errors and save again.
4. Use **Print Preview** to see how the document will look when printed. Adjust the document on the page so that it is centered by inserting or deleting space at the top of the page. You may also need to delete some space between sections in order to get all information on one page.
5. Print one copy of the document. Proofread it carefully and correct any errors.
6. Save any edits.
7. Print a corrected copy.

Exercise 2

1. Use the word processor tool to complete a homework assignment or other project.

Exercise 3

1. Retrieve **CH3HO3** from your student data disk.
2. Display all characters using the **All Characters** command.
3. Change **Next Month** in the first paragraph to **In April**.
4. Add a blank line between each of the categories in the list by using the **Enter** key.
5. Preview the document.
6. Save the document and print a copy of it.

See an example of the final output at the end of this chapter.

Exercise 4

1. Retrieve **CH3HO4** from your student data disk.
2. Position the insertion point just prior to the number 1.
3. Press the **Backspace** key twice to merge the two paragraphs.
4. Delete the number 1, the period following it, and the tab. Also delete the space between **possible** and **During.**
5. Position the insertion point to the left of the **D** in **During.**
6. Press the **Enter** key twice.
7. Type the number **1.** and press **Tab.**
8. Save the document again as **CH3HO4.**
9. Preview the document.
10. Print a copy.
11. Close the documents and exit Works.

Exercise 3

OFFICE COSTUME PARTY

In April the office will have its annual costume party. Awards will be given in the following categories:

Most elaborate

Funniest

Most original

Worst

Plan now to attend this annual event. The Ebenezer prize will be awarded to those not attending and/or not appearing in costume.

Exercise 4

SUMMARY OF EVENTS

The following outstanding events were reported to us by Puget Sound Charters cruise members during the end-of-the-month business meeting. These should be noted by all employees so that we may concentrate on eliminating as many reoccurrences as possible.

1. During a cruise on the evening of March 25 one member of a particularly ambitious group of partiers fell off the stern end of the ship. She remained there until the boat docked since no one had missed her during the ongoing celebration. It is fortunate that in falling her clothing attached itself to the dinghy in such a way that she was dragged through the water and arrived safely upon docking.

2. Two members of the galley staff (names shall be withheld pending further investigation) were observed washing chicken legs off in the dishwasher before serving them to customers on the next cruise of the evening. This simply must stop!

3. One member slipped on a banana peel and bounced down the entire length of the spiral staircase, landing with a thump in the middle of the buffet line (narrowly missing the buffet table). It is perhaps fortunate that he remembered nothing of the incident and commented excessively about the wonderful trip he had. Please keep an eye out for dangerous objects in the future.

4. Thanks to the astute eye of the captain, the ship narrowly missed ramming a cargo freighter during a late-night cruise. A bolt of lightning struck at just the right moment to arouse the attention of the captain as he was heading toward its bow. We are grateful for the quick reaction of the captain, and will give an appreciation party in his honor in the near future.

CHAPTER 4

Revising Text

OBJECTIVES

Select blocks of text

Delete text

Undo edits

Move text

Copy text

Search and replace text

Use the spelling checker

PREVIEW

In Chapter 4 you will learn how to perform various editing tasks. You have already edited text by pressing **Backspace** and **Delete**, combined and separated paragraphs, and shown all characters on the screen. In this chapter, you will learn how to select text, which will enable you to move, copy, and delete large blocks of characters. In addition, the Find and Replace commands will be covered, as well as the spelling checker.

CREATING AND SAVING A NEW DOCUMENT

You will be creating a new document here that will then be edited, both in this chapter and in Chapter 5.

Create a Document

1. Open — Works for Windows and click on the word processor button in the Startup dialog box 

. A new *Word* document screen is displayed.
2. Type — the text shown in the box below or retrieve **CH4PR1A** from the Instructor data disk. *(The list that is referred to in the text is not entered at this time. It will be added in Chapter 5.)*

¶
PUGET SOUND CHARTERS¶
AGENDA FOR MARKETING MEETING¶
NOVEMBER 20, 1994¶
¶
¶
This agenda contains a list of items to be discussed at the next marketing meeting. Please read through each item carefully prior to the meeting. If you have any additional comments, suggestions, or questions, be prepared to discuss them at the meeting.¶
¶
The meeting will be held promptly at 2 p.m. in the conference room.¶
¶
Please bring progress reports with you.¶
¶

Name and Save the Document

Save the document as **CH4PR1** if you typed it rather than retrieved the document from the Instructor data disk.

1. Click — on the Save button , or choose **File, Save As**, to display the Save As dialog box shown in Figure 4-1.

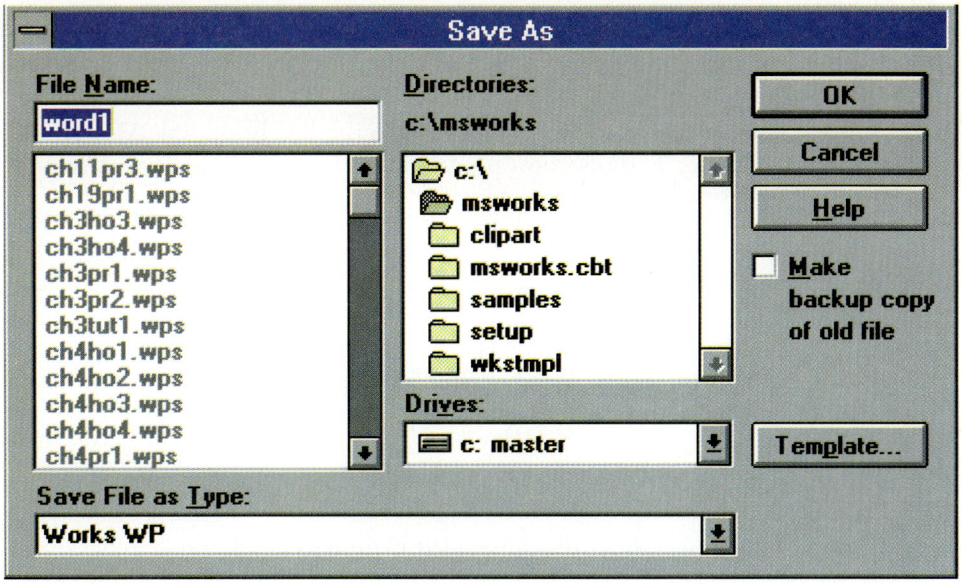

Figure 4-1
The Save As dialog box

2.	Type	**CH4PR1** in the File Name text box.
3.	Choose	**OK** or press **Enter** to save. The title bar now shows the document name as displayed here.

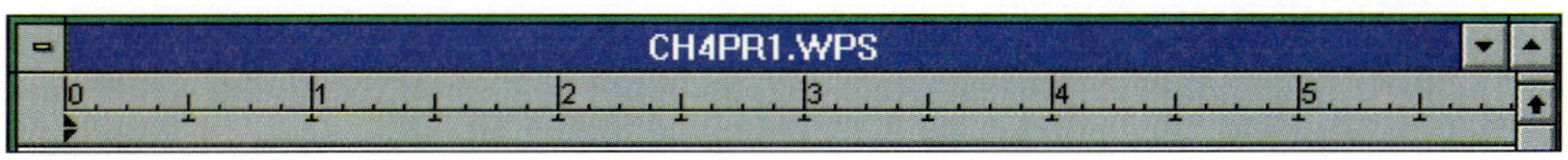

SELECTING TEXT

Selecting text can make your word processing work much easier. You can select large blocks of text and delete, move, or copy them; or, as you will learn in Chapter 5, you can add formatting to blocks of text. In this section, you will learn how to use various mouse actions or keystrokes to select specified text.

Use the Mouse to Select Text

Table 4-1 on page 74 summarizes the mouse actions and keystrokes that are used to select text.

To select a word

1. Point — to the word **PUGET** in the first line and double-click the left mouse button. See the following example.

›› PUGET SOUND CHARTERS
AGENDA FOR MARKETING MEETING
NOVEMBER 20, 1994

2. Click — anywhere in the window to deselect it.

To select a line

3. Point — to the left window margin next to the line beginning **AGENDA FOR...** The insertion point becomes an arrow as shown in the illustration following step 4

4. Click — the left mouse button once to select the entire line as shown here.

›› PUGET SOUND CHARTERS
AGENDA FOR MARKETING MEETING
NOVEMBER 20, 1994

5. Click — anywhere other than in the left margin to deselect it.

To select a paragraph

6. Point — to any position in the left window margin next to the first paragraph.

7. Click — the left mouse button twice to select the paragraphs as shown here.

→ This·agenda·contains·a·list·of·items·to·be·discussed·at·the·next·marketing·meeting.··
Please·read·through·each·item·carefully·prior·to·the·meeting.··If·you·have·any·additional·
comments,·suggestions,·or·questions,·be·prepared·to·discuss·them·at·the·meeting.¶
¶

8. Click — anywhere other than in the left margin to deselect it.

To select a block of text

9. Point — to the Tab mark at the beginning of the second paragraph.

10. Hold — down the left mouse button and drag to the end of the third paragraph to select both paragraphs as shown here.

→ The meeting will be held promptly at 2 p.m. in the conference room.

→ Please bring progress reports with y

11. Click — anywhere other than on the selected text to deselect it.

To select the entire document

12. Point — to the left margin—anywhere in the document.

13. Press — **Ctrl** and click the left mouse button.

14. Click — anywhere to deselect.

Use the Keyboard to Select Text

To select a word

1. Move the insertion point to any position in the word **PUGET**.
2. Press **F8** twice to select the word. Extend is turned on and EXT is displayed in the status bar as shown here.

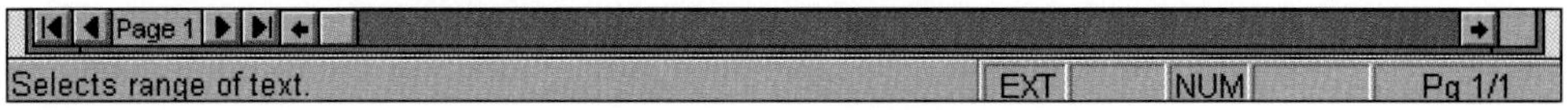

3. Press **Esc** to turn off Extend (EXT is no longer showing in the status bar), and move the insertion point away from the word to deselect it.

To select a line

4. Move the insertion point to the beginning of the second line-**AGENDA . . .**
5. Press **Shift/End** to select the entire line.

NOTE: This method selects the line from the insertion point to the end of the line; therefore, you can select all or part of a line.

6. Move the insertion point away from the line to deselect it.

To select a sentence

7. Move the insertion point to any position in the first sentence in the first paragraph.
8. Press **F8** three times to select the sentence. Extend is turned on again by doing this. EXT is displayed in the status bar.
9. Press **Esc** to turn off Extend, and move the insertion point away from the sentence to deselect it.

To select a paragraph

10. Move the insertion point to any position in the first paragraph. (It may already be there.)
11. Press **F8** four times to select the paragraph. Extend is turned on and EXT is displayed in the status bar.
12. Press **Esc** to turn off Extend, and move the insertion point away from the paragraph to deselect it.

To select the entire document

13. Press **F8** five times. Extend is turned on and EXT is displayed in the status bar.
14. Press **Esc** to turn off Extend, and press any of the arrow keys to deselect the document.

To select a block of text

15.	Move	the insertion point to the beginning of the second paragraph in front of the Tab mark.
16.	Press	**F8**. EXT is now displayed in the status bar.
17.	Press	the **Down Arrow** and the **Right Arrow** if necessary to extend the selection to the end of the third paragraph.
18.	Press	**Esc** to turn off Extend, and press any arrow key to deselect the text.

NOTE: You can also select a block of text by holding down the Shift key and pressing any of the arrow keys to extend the selection. Experiment with this as time permits.

The following Table 4-1 summarizes the mouse actions and keystrokes used to select text.

Table 4-1
Keyboard and mouse actions for selecting text

Selection	Keyboard	Mouse
Word	Press F8 twice.	Double-click on the word.
Line	Press Shift/End.	Click in the margin to the left of the line.
Sentence	Press F8 three times.	Point to the beginning of the sentence, hold down the left mouse button and drag to the end of the sentence.
Paragraph	Press F8 four times.	Double-click in the margin to the left of the paragraph.
Entire document	Press F8 five times.	Point to the left margin, hold down Ctrl, and click the left mouse button.
Any amount of text	Move the insertion point to the place where you want to select the text, press F8, and move the insertion point to the end of the text.	Point to the beginning of the text, hold down the left mouse button and drag to the end of the text.

DELETING TEXT

In this section text will be deleted, and in the following section it will be restored using the Undo command.

Delete a Block of Text

The first paragraph of the document **CH4PR1** will be deleted.

1.	Double-click	in the left margin beside the first paragraph, or move the insertion point to the paragraph and press **F8** four times to select the paragraph. See the following illustration.

> This agenda contains a list of items to be discussed at the next marketing meeting. Please read through each item carefully prior to the meeting. If you have any additional comments, suggestions, or questions, be prepared to discuss them at the meeting.

2. Press **Delete** to remove the block of text from the window.

   NOTE: Do not enter any new text. If you do, you will not be able to restore the deleted text.

UNDOING AN EDIT

Text that has been deleted can be restored if the Undo command is used as soon as the deletion has taken place. You can also use Undo to remove text that has inadvertently been entered. Both actions will be covered here.

Undo a Deletion

1. Choose **Edit, Undo Editing** or press **Ctrl/Z.** The deleted text is reinserted in the document at the insertion point.

Undo Typing

1. Type your name at the insertion point, regardless of where it is.
2. Choose **Edit, Undo Editing** or press **Ctrl/Z.** The inserted text is removed from the screen.

Redo Editing

Redo editing reverses the last Undo command. Here you will restore your name at the insertion point.

1. Choose **Edit, Redo Editing** or press **Ctrl/Z.** The latest text that was removed, is restored. In the Edit menu the **Undo Editing** option was changed to **Redo Editing**

To remove the restored text again

2. Choose **Edit, Undo Editing** or press **Ctrl/Z.**

MOVING A BLOCK

You can move blocks of text, graphics, tables, or any other objects in a word processing document. Here, text will be moved.

Move a Block of Text

The second paragraph will be moved to the end of the document.

1. **Select** the second paragraph—either double-click in the left margin by the paragraph, or move the insertion point to the paragraph and press **F8** four times.

   NOTE: Actually, in this case you only need to click the left mouse button once because the paragraph is only one line.

2. **Click** on the Cut button in the toolbar 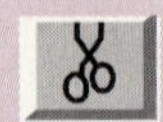, or choose **Edit, Cut**, or press **Ctrl/X.** The block of text is deleted and moved to the Clipboard. Your document should now resemble the following example.

```
Comments,·suggestions,·or·questions,·be·prepared·to·discuss·them·at·the·meeting¶
¶
¶
→       Please·bring·progress·reports·with·you.¶
¶
```

3. **Press** **Delete** to remove the extra paragraph mark between the first and the new second paragraph. See the following illustration

```
→       This·agenda·contains·a·list·of·items·to·be·discussed·at·the·next·marketing·meeting.··¶
Please·read·through·each·item·carefully·prior·to·the·meeting.··If·you·have·any·additional·
coments,·suggestions,·or·questions,·be·prepared·to·discuss·them·at·the·meeting.¶
¶
→       Please·bring·progress·reports·with·you.¶
¶
```

4. **Move** the insertion point to the end of the document—press **Ctrl/End** or click at the end of the document with the left mouse button. If necessary, press **Enter** to insert extra paragraph marks following the last sentence as shown here.

```
→       Please·bring·progress·reports·with·you¶
¶
¶
```

5. **Click** on the Paste button in the toolbar , or choose **Edit, Paste,** or press **Ctrl/V**. The block of text is inserted at the new position as shown here.

comments,·suggestions,·or·questions,·be·prepared·to·discuss·them·at·the·meeting¶
¶
→ Please·bring·progress·reports·with·you.¶
¶
→ The·meeting·will·be·held·promptly·at·2·p.m.·in·the·conference·room.¶
¶

NOTE: You can also drag selected text to a new position. When you point to the selected text, the mouse pointer displays the word **Drag** DRAG. Hold down the left mouse button and drag the selected text to a new position. This is covered in the Guided Tutorial for this chapter. You can undo a drag and return the text to its original position.

COPYING A BLOCK

You can copy a block of text, graphics, tables, etc., in much the same way you moved the block. Here, text, including the word **Suggestion:**, will be entered and then **Suggestion:** will be copied to two additional positions.

Copy a Block of Text

1. Move the insertion point directly following the period following **conference room** as shown here.

→ Please·bring·progress·reports·with·you.¶
¶
→ The·meeting·will·be·held·promptly·at·2·p.m.·in·the·conference·room.|¶
¶

2. Press **Spacebar** twice and type the text in the box below. Press **Enter** twice at the end of the paragraph, and press **Enter** twice following the word **Suggestion.**

Bring your suggestions to the meeting. Jot them down in the area provided at the bottom of this agenda.¶
¶
¶
Suggestion:¶
¶
¶
¶

Now you will copy the word **Suggestion:** two times.

3. Select — the word **Suggestion:** and the following *two* paragraph marks below the word. To do this, move the insertion point to the beginning of the word, click the left mouse button and drag to the second paragraph mark, or press **F8** and press the **down arrow** three times to select the word and the second paragraph mark. See the following illustration.

Suggestion:¶
¶
¶
¶

4. Click — on the Copy button in the toolbar , or choose **Edit, Copy**, or press **Ctrl/C**. The block is copied to the Clipboard.

5. Move — the insertion point to the last paragraph mark.

6. Click — on the Paste button in the toolbar , or choose **Edit, Paste**, or press **Ctrl/V.** Your document should now resemble the following.

Suggestion:¶
¶
¶
¶
Suggestion¶
¶
¶
¶

7. Repeat — steps 5 and 6 to insert another copy of the word at the end of the document. See the following example.

suggestions·to·the·meeting.··Jot·them·down·in·the·area·provided·at·the·bottom·of·this·agenda¶
¶
Suggestion:¶
¶
¶
Suggestion:¶
¶
¶
Suggestion:¶
¶
¶
¶

SEARCHING FOR TEXT

The Find command in the Edit menu is used to locate specific text. You can specify whether you want to match a whole word or not. If you do not turn on **Match Whole Word Only**, then the word will be located even if it is part of another word. For example, if you are searching for **or** and do not specify **Match Whole Word Only**, words such as *information, forward,* and *history* will be located as well as **or**. Turn on **Match Case** if you want to locate **Brown** (not *brown*). When **Match Case** is turned on, **Brown** will be found only when the **B** is uppercase.

Find Text

Locate the text **Please bring** and insert text **this month's** following it in the second paragraph.

1. Move the insertion point to the beginning of the document—press **Ctrl/Home to do this.**
2. Choose **Edit, Find** to display the Find dialog box.
3. Type **Please bring** in the **Find What** text box as shown in Figure 4-2.

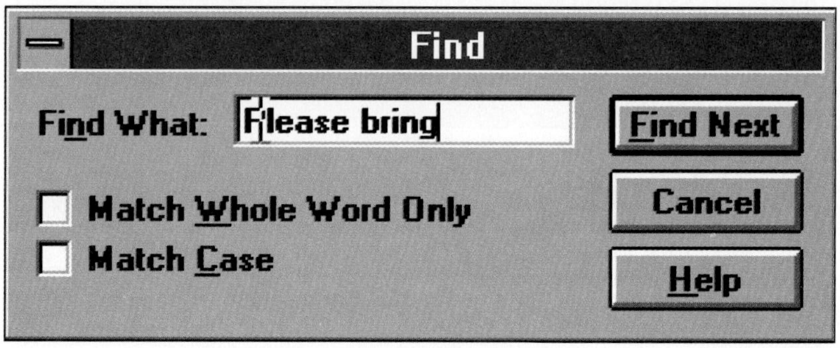

Figure 4-2
The Find dialog box

4. Press **Enter** or choose **Find Next** to go to the text. Your screen should resemble Figure 4-3.

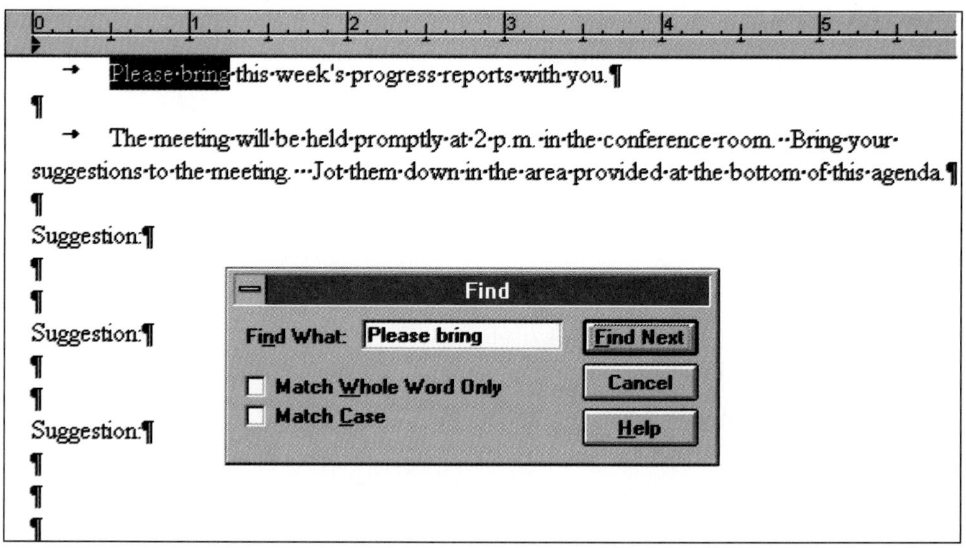

Figure 4-3
Locating specific text

5. Press **Esc** or choose **Cancel** to remove the Find dialog box from the screen.
6. Press the **Right Arrow** once and press the **Spacebar** once.
7. Type **this month's.**

REPLACING TEXT

The Replace command in the Edit menu is used to locate specific text and replace with other text. As with the Find command, you can specify whether you want to **Match Whole Word Only** or **Match Case**. You also can choose to **Replace All** which would replace all occurrences of the located text with the text that you entered in the **Replace With** text box.

Replace Text

Here you will replace the word **month's** with the word **week's**—part of the text that was just inserted using the Find command.

1. Move the insertion point to the top of the document.
2. Choose **Edit, Replace** to display the Replace dialog box as shown in Figure 4-4.

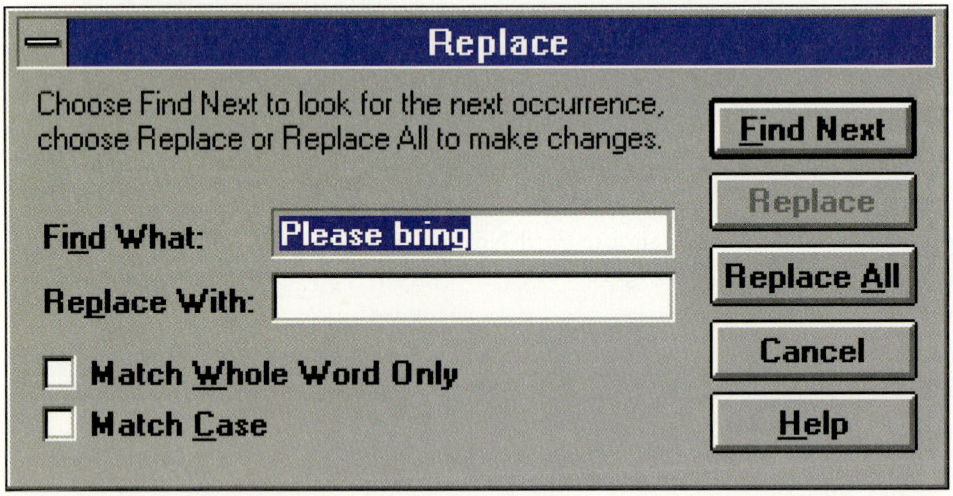

Figure 4-4
The Replace dialog box

The previously located text is displayed in the Find What text box, but as soon as you start typing it will be removed.

3. Type **month's** in the **Find What** text box.
4. Choose **Replace With**—either click in the text box; press **Alt/P**; or press the **Tab** key to move to it.
5. Type **week's** in the **Replace With** text box. Your dialog should resemble Figure 4-5.

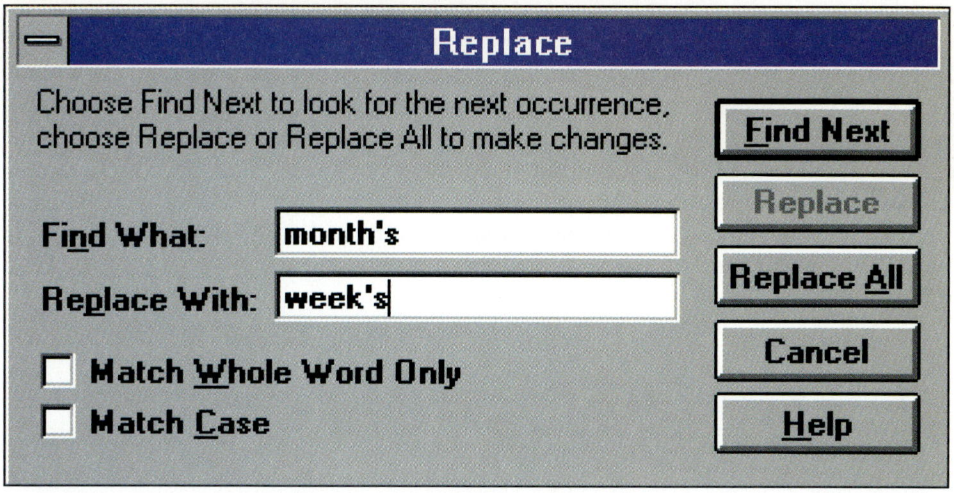

Figure 4-5
The Replace dialog box containing text to find and replace

6. Press **Enter** or choose **Find Next.** Your screen should now resemble Figure 4-6.

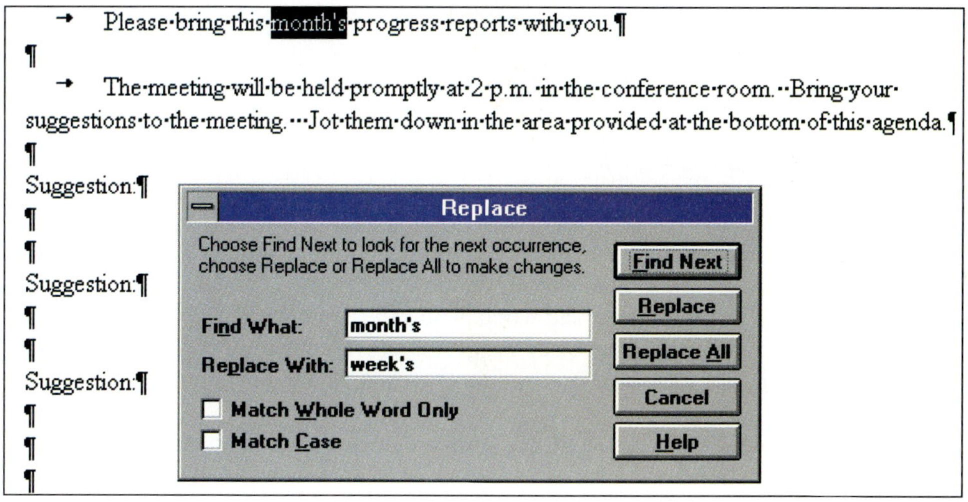

Figure 4-6
The Replace dialog box and the selected text to be replaced

7. Choose **Replace**. The word **month's** should now be replaced with **week's.**
8. Choose **Close** to remove the Replace dialog box from the screen.

If additional occurrences of **month's** were in this document, you could choose **Replace All**, if you like, and all occurrences would be replaced automatically. If you did not want to replace all occurrences, then repeat steps 4 and 5 above for each replacement.

SAVING THE DOCUMENT

Save the Edits

1. Click on the Save button 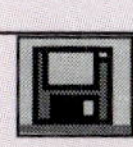 , or choose **File, Save,** or press **Ctrl/S** to save **CH4PR1** with the changes. Do not close the file.

SEARCHING FOR SPECIAL CHARACTERS

The Find and Replace functions can locate and replace special characters as well as text. Using special characters is discussed in Chapter 6, "Built-in Word Processing Assistance." Table 4-2 lists the special characters that can be located and the keystrokes that are entered in the Find and Replace dialog boxes to locate them. Special characters that can be located include paragraph marks, tab marks, page breaks as well as white space. White space is any combination of spaces, tab marks, and nonbreaking spaces (those that will not break at the end of a line).

Table 4-2

Special characters used in the Find or Replace dialog boxes

Type this	To search for or replace this
^t	Tab mark
^p	Paragraph mark
^n	End-Of-Line mark
^d	Page break
^s	Nonbreaking space
^^	Caret
^?	Question mark
^num	Extended ANSI character. These are other characters that are inserted in text by typing numbers that represent the characters.
^w	White space
?	Any character

USING THE SPELLING TOOL

Works contains a built-in dictionary that is used to check for spelling errors, words with incorrect capitalization, words that are incorrectly hyphenated, and words that are repeated, such as **an an**. When Works has located an incorrect word (a word that is not in its dictionary), it highlights the word. You can then change the word by typing it correctly, or you can look at a list of suggested correct spellings. You can also add words to the dictionary that you use frequently, such as proper names of cities, persons, or company names.

Refer to Table 4-3 for a list of the options in the Spelling dialog box and the description of each choice.

Check for Spelling Errors

1. Open — the existing file, **CH4PR2**, from the Student data disk to use for the spell check. This document is shown in the box below.

   NOTE: Leave the current document, **CH4PR1**, open. The new document will be stacked on top of the previous document.

HISTORY OF PUGET SOUND CHARTERS

Puget Sound Charters was founded in early 1980. The compeny opened its doors to the public in February with a pormotional campagne offering free dinner cruises and an open house held on the the second Saturday of the month.

The first shop was located in teh old part of town, on First and Madeson. The showroom was capible of holding approxamately 15 boats and was convenently located for heavy foot traffic. Tourists, business personnel, and shoppers were regular customers in teh store.

With the advent of addisional construction and highrises, however, the location became less accessable. A decision was made in early 1989 to move to the north of town. The new location has proven to have even better access. Patking is available and the population base north of town provides a heavy flow of customers.

2. Move the insertion point to the beginning of the document if necessary.

3. Click on the Spelling Checker button ABC or choose **Tools, Spelling.** The Spelling dialog box is displayed as shown in Figure 4-7.

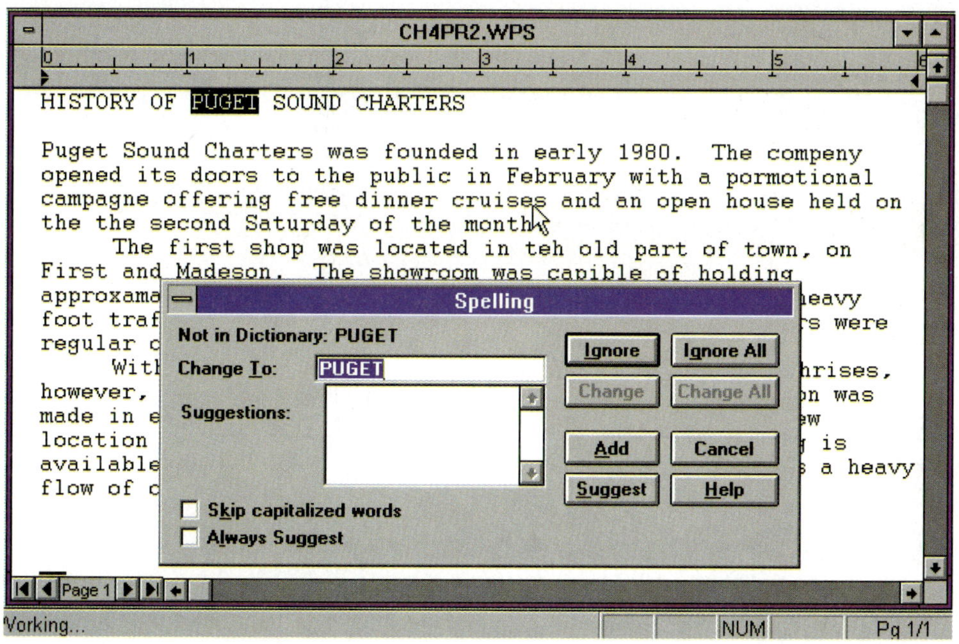

Figure 4-7
The Spelling dialog box

The Spelling dialog box offers the choices listed and described in Table 4-3.

This option	will do this
Change To:	Displays the word that will replace the highlighted word in text if **Enter** is pressed or if you choose **Change.** You can enter a new word here either by by choosing **Suggest** and selecting a new word from the list in the **Suggestions** box, or by typing in the correct spelling.

Button	Description
Suggestions:	Displays a list of suggested spellings if **Suggest** is chosen.
Skip capitalized words	Skips over all words in uppercase.
Always Suggest	Displays a list of correct spellings in the **Suggestions** text box corresponding to the highlighted word when this option is turned on. You do not have to choose **Suggest** to display the list.
Ignore	Skips over the highlighted word without changing the spelling.
Ignore All	Skips over the highlighted word and all subsequent words that are the same as the word that is highlighted.
Change	Replaces the highlighted word with the word that is displayed in the **Change To** text box.
Change All	Replaces all words that are the same as the highlighted word in the document with the word that is displayed in the **Change To** text box.
Add	Adds the highlighted word in the document to the dictionary where it will be available in other spell checks.
Cancel	Ends the spell check and returns to the document screen.
Suggest	Displays a list of correctly spelled words contained in the Works dictionary that may be used to replace the highlighted word in the document.
Help	Displays the Help screen that contains information about the spelling command.

Table 4-3

The choices in the Spelling dialog box

The first word that is not in the Works dictionary is highlighted—**PUGET—**and is displayed in the **Change To** text box in the Spelling dialog box.

Add Word to the Dictionary

Because the word **PUGET** is not a common word, it is not in the dictionary; however, because this is a company name it would be best to add it to the dictionary so that the spell check does not stop at this word when it is used in other documents.

1. Choose Add **Add** from the Spelling dialog box. The spelling checker goes to the next word which is **Puget** (not in uppercase).
2. Choose Add **Add** again to add **Puget** with an initial cap to the dictionary.

Suggest a Correct Spelling

The next word that is highlighted is **compeny**. A correct spelling can be displayed in the **Suggestions** box.

1. Choose **Suggest** [Suggest]. The **Suggestion** box now shows the correct spelling of **company**. It is the only suggestion displayed here. Notice that the spelling in the **Change To** box has been changed to correspond to the word that is highlighted in the **Suggestion** box.

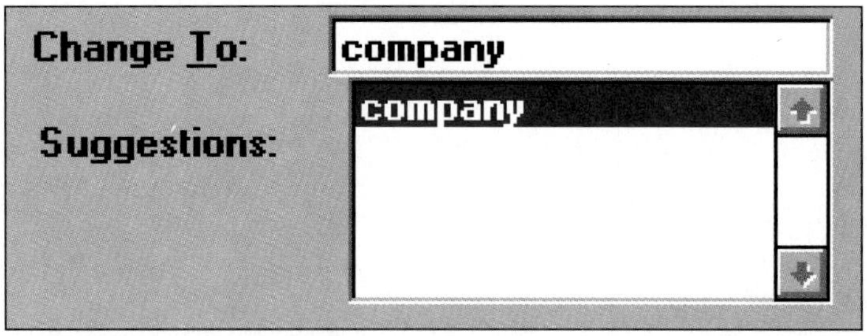

2. Choose **Change** [Change] . The correct spelling of **company** replaces the incorrect spelling and the next incorrect word, **pormotional**, is displayed.
3. Choose **Suggest** [Suggest] to display the correct spelling.
4. Choose **Change** [Change] to insert the correct spelling. The incorrect word **campagne** is now displayed.
5. Choose **Suggest** [Suggest] Two words are now displayed. Be sure the correct word (**campaign**) is highlighted.
6. Choose **Change** [Change] .

Delete an Extra Word

The next word that is highlighted is a second **the**, which is a frequent typing error. The dialog box indicates **Repeated Word** above the **Change To:** text box.

1. Choose **Change** [Change] to remove the extra word.

Use Change All

The next highlighted word is **teh**, which is also a frequent typo. In this case, if you choose **Change All**, all subsequent errors where **the** is misspelled in this way will be changed automatically without the spelling checker stopping at each word.

1. Choose **Suggest** [Suggest] . to display the correct spelling of **the**.
2. Choose **Change All** [Change All] to change all remaining occurrences of **teh** to **the.**

3. Continue making suggestions and changing the following words:

   Madeson

   capible

   approxamately

   convenently

   addisional

   highrises (The spell checker knows to insert a hyphen.)

   accessible

4. See the next section for typing the correct word at **patking.**

Type the Correct Word

In some instances, the correct spelling will not be displayed in the **Suggestions** box. Here, the word **patking** should be **parking**; however, the correct spelling will not be displayed. You will have to type the correct spelling in the **Change To** box.

1. Choose **Suggest** [Suggest]. The **Suggestions** box now shows only **Patching** as displayed in Figure 4-8.

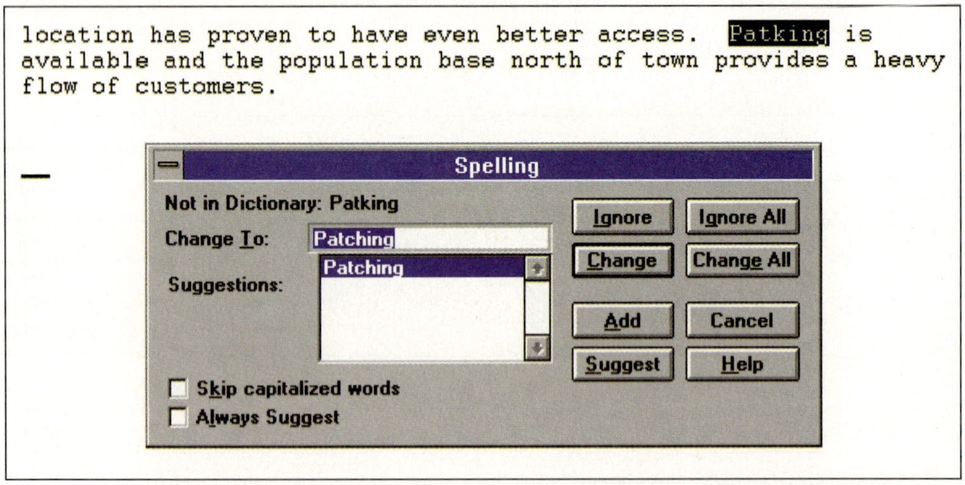

Figure 4-8
The Spelling dialog box showing a word that is to be retyped

2. Type **Parking** in the **Change To** box.
3. Choose **Change** [Change] to insert the correct spelling. The prompt indicating that the spell check is complete is displayed as shown in Figure 4-9.

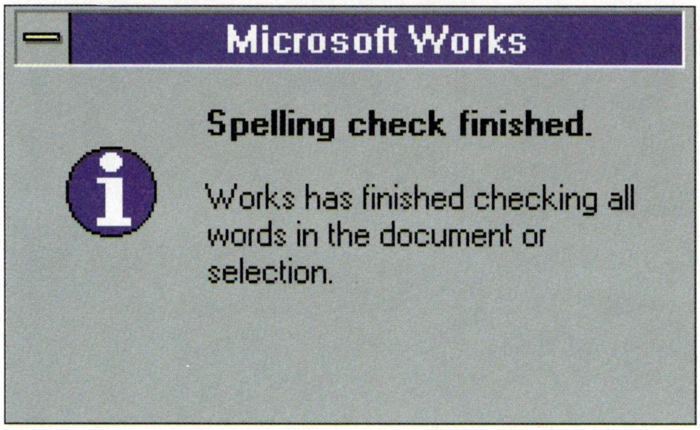

Figure 4-9
The Spelling check finished box

4. Choose **OK** or press **Enter** to end the spell check.

NOTE: If your insertion point was not at the beginning of the document when you started the spell check, the prompt indicating you are at the end of the document is displayed as shown in Figure 4-10. You can either choose **Cancel** to end the spell check, or you can choose **OK** which will return the spelling checker to the beginning of the document when it will continue checking from that point.

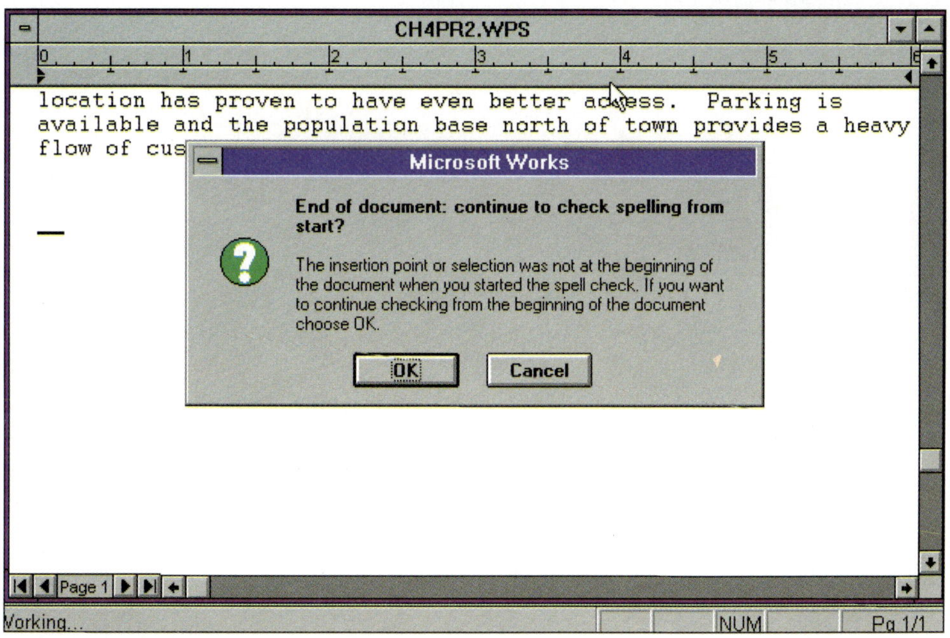

Figure 4-10
The prompt for continuing or canceling the spell check

NOTE: At the beginning of this spell check, you were instructed to move the insertion point to the beginning of the document. Actually the insertion point could be at any position in the document. When the spelling checker gets to the end of the document, the prompt shown in Figure 4-10 will be displayed, and you can continue on with the spell check from the beginning of the document.

5. Save — the edited document. Click on the Save button , or choose **File, Save**, or press **Ctrl/S**.

6. Close — both documents. Save any changes, if prompted to do so, and return to the Startup dialog box.

GUIDED TUTORIAL

What You'll Do

- Select text
- Delete and undo text
- Move text
- Use Find and Replace to edit text
- Use the Undo command to reverse edits
- Run a spell check

How To Do It

1. Open — the **Word Processor**.

2. Type — the text shown in the box below—press **Enter** twice after the last paragraph—or retrieve **CH4TUTA** from the Instructor data disk.

PUGET SOUND CHARTERS

To: All Staff

From: Management

Subject: Upcoming Cruise Events

The following evening cruises are scheduled for this weekend. Please review them carefully. If there is any question about your responsibility with a cruise, please call the office.

HAWAIIAN LUAU DINNER CRUISE

This cruise will include a lei greeting at the top of the gangway. Dark green will be the color theme. Pineapples will be on each of the tables. The staff should wear Aloha shirts, shorts, tennis shoes, and leis (available from management). Taped Hawaiian music will play in the background. Pictures will be taken on the pier. The cruise will depart at exactly 7 p.m. and conclude at 10:30 p.m.

WASHINGTON STATE ASSOCIATION FOR EDUCATION DEVELOPMENT

Nothing special on this cruise. It will be the standard evening cruise from 7 to 10 p.m. It will include the beef and turkey breast buffet, Northwest salmon, and assorted salads, rice, and potatoes. Music will include the Puget Sound Charters theme song and the Broadway Hits show by the staff. The cruise will include dancing from 8:30 to 10:00 p.m.

3. Save the document as **CH4TUT1.**

To select the first paragraph and delete it

4. Move the insertion point to the first paragraph and press **F8** four times, or double-click in the left margin beside the first paragraph. See the following example.

¶
The·following·evening·cruises·are·scheduled·for·this·weekend.··
Please·review·them·carefully.··If·there·is·any·question·about·
your·responsibility·with·a·cruise,·please·call·the·office¶
¶
HAWAIIAN·LUAU·DINNER·CRUISE¶

5. Press **Delete** to remove the paragraph.

To restore the text using Undo

6. Choose **Edit, Undo** or press **Ctrl/Z** to reverse the deletion.

To drag the last sentence in the first paragraph to the end of the document

Here you will use the mouse to drag the selected text to a new position.

7. Select the sentence beginning with **If there is any question....** To do this, move the insertion point in front of **If**, hold down the left mouse button, and drag to the end of the sentence. See the following example.

NOTE: Do not use F8 if you are going to use the mouse button to drag. Because F8 turns on Extend, when you begin to drag you will either reduce the amount of selected text or add to it, rather than dragging the selection to a new position.

The·following·evening·cruises·are·scheduled·for·this·weekend.··
Please·review·them·carefully.··If·there·is·any·question·about·
your·responsibility·with·a·cruise,·please·call·the·office¶
¶
HAWAIIAN·LUAU·DINNER·CRUISE¶

8. Point to the selection with the pointer showing **Drag**. See the illustration above.

9. Hold down the left mouse button and begin to drag the selected text. The pointer now shows the word **Move** as displayed here.

10. Drag down to the end of the document until the insertion point is two lines below the last paragraph as shown here. When you are dragging, hold the pointer on the horizontal scroll bar which will then show a circle with a diagonal line through it. ⃠ This will scroll down through the document.

When the insertion point is positioned where you want to insert the text:

11. Release the left mouse button. The text will be moved to the insertion point as shown here.

staff.··The·cruise·will·include·dancing·from·8:30·to·10:00·p.m¶
¶
If·there·is·any·question·about·your·responsibility·with·a·cruise,·please·call·the·office.¶

To replace the word pier with the words upper deck

12. Move — the insertion point to the beginning of the document—press **Ctrl/Home.**
13. Choose — **Edit, Replace** to display the Replace dialog box as shown here.

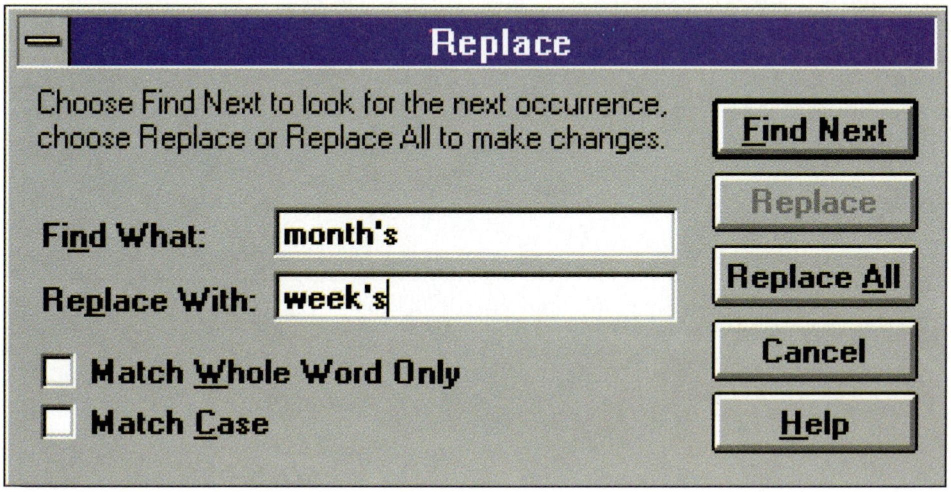

14. Type — **pier** in the **Find What** text box.
15. Choose — **Replace With.**
16. Type — **upper deck** in the **Replace With** text box.
17. Press — **Enter** or choose **Find Next. Pier** will be highlighted in the document.
18. Choose — **Replace.**
19. Choose — **Close** to remove the dialog box from the screen.
20. Save — the edits to the **CH4TUT1.**

To run a spell check

21. Click — on the Spelling Checker button , or choose **Tools, Spelling**.

22. Respond — to the Spelling dialog box to correct any errors.

23. Save — any changes to the document.

24. Close — Works by double-clicking on the Control menu box at the left end of the Works title bar 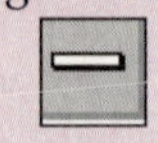.

25. Respond — to any prompts that may be displayed to save documents.

REVIEW QUESTIONS

1. Name each of the following buttons in the word processor toolbar and describe its editing function.

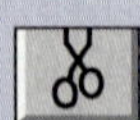

____

____

____

____

____

____

____

____

____

2. The ____________________ option in the ________________ menu is used to reverse the last edit.

3. Match each of the following with the action. (You may use answers more than one time.)

   ____ F8

   ____ Click once in the left margin

   ____ Shift Right Arrow

____ F8 twice

____ Double click in the left margin

____ Hold down Ctrl and click the left mouse button in the left margin

____ F8 three times

____ Esc

____ F8 four times

A. Select a word

B. Select a paragraph

C. Select a sentence

D. Select entire document

E. Select continuous characters to the right

F. Turn on Extend

G. Turn off Extend

H. Select a line

4. Name and briefly describe what each of the following buttons in the Spelling dialog box will do.

Ignore

____

____

____

Change

____

____

____

Add

____

____

____

Suggest

Ignore All

Change All

Hands-on Exercises

Exercise 1

1. Type the document shown in the box below. Press **Tab** following each number in the numbered paragraphs. This document will be used again in Chapter 5 where different formatting will be applied.

CONTRACT

This contract will confirm the agreement between Puget Sound Charters and Lake Union Food Services, covering the handling of all catering duties on cruises during the next year. Lake Union Food Services will provide brunch and dinner meals according to the following terms and conditions agreed upon by both parties.

The terms and conditions are set forth as follows:

1. Puget Sound Charters hereby commissions Lake Union Food Services to prepare brunch and dinner meals for all scheduled cruises during the next calendar year.

2. All conditions to this contract shall be agreed upon by both parties. Puget Sound Charters will maintain the right to cancel this contract if Lake Union Food Services fails to provide services set in this contract.

3. Catering shall include a full brunch buffet each Saturday and Sunday unless otherwise specified. It shall further include dinner meals Tuesday through Friday unless otherwise specified by Puget Sound Charters.

4. In consideration of the services to be provided by Lake Union Food Services, Puget Sound Charters will pay them at a rate of $25 per meal.

This agreement shall be in effect as of January 1, 1995, and will continue through December 31, 1995, or until the contract is terminated by one of the parties.

2. Save the document as **CH4HO1.**
3. Run a spell check on the document and save any changes.
4. Print a draft copy of the document.
5. Proof the copy, make any changes, and save the edits.
6. Print a final copy of the document.
7. Close the file.

Exercise 2

1. Open the document **CH4HO1** created in Hands-on Exercise 1, or retrieve it from the Instructor data disk.
2. Move the numbered paragraph 1 so that it is the third numbered paragraph. Renumber the paragraphs so that they are again in sequence and adjust the spacing.
3. Copy numbered paragraph 4 below its present position, making a new numbered paragraph 5. In that paragraph, however, replace the words **$25 per meal** with **$30 per hour for services.**
4. Replace the words **Food Services** with **Caterers** throughout the document.

5. Save the document as **CH4HO2.**
6. Print the document.
7. Exit Works.

Exercise 3

1. Retrieve **CH3HO3** from your data disk.
2. Highlight the last paragraph in the document.
3. Move the highlighted paragraph so that it appears after the first sentence in the first paragraph.
4. Add or delete any extra spaces in the new paragraph.
5. Replace the word **annual** with **semi-annual** wherever it occurs.
6. Save the document with a different name, **CH4HO3**. To do this, choose **File, Save, As,** type **CH4HO3** in the **File Name** text box, and press **Enter**.
7. Preview and print a copy of the document.

Exercise 4

1. Retrieve **CH3HO4** from your data disk.
2. Search for the word **further** in paragraph number 2 and delete it.
3. Search for and replace the word **Captain** with a lowercase **captain**.
4. Move paragraph number 4 between paragraphs numbered 1 and 2.
5. Renumber the paragraphs. Also adjust the spacing if necessary.
6. Save this document as **CH4HO4**. Use the same procedure given in step 6 in Exercise 3.
7. Preview and print a copy of the document.

Exercise 2: CH4HO2

CONTRACT

This contract will confirm the agreement between Puget Sound Charters and Lake Union Caterers, covering the handling of all catering duties on cruises during the next year. Lake Union Caterers will provide brunch and dinner meals according to the following terms and conditions agreed upon by both parties.

The terms and conditions are set forth as follows:

1. All conditions to this contract shall be agreed upon by both parties. Puget Sound Charters will maintain the right to cancel this contract if Lake Union Caterers fails to provide services set in this contract.

2. Catering shall include a full brunch buffet each Saturday and Sunday unless otherwise specified. It shall further include dinner meals Tuesday through Friday unless otherwise specified by Puget Sound Charters.

3. Puget Sound Charters hereby commissions Lake Union Caterers to prepare brunch and dinner meals for all scheduled cruises during the next calendar year.

4. In consideration of the services to be provided by Lake Union Caterers, Puget Sound Charters will pay them at a rate of $25 per meal.

5. In consideration of the services to be provided by Lake Union Caterers, Puget Sound Charters will pay them at a rate of $30 per hour for services.

This agreement shall be in effect as of January 1, 1995, and will continue through December 31, 1995, or until the contract is terminated by one of the parties.

OFFICE COSTUME PARTY

In April the office will have its semi-annual costume party. Plan now to attend this semi-annual event. The Ebenezer prize will be awarded to those not attending and/or not appearing in costume. Awards will be given in the following categories:

Most elaborate

Funniest

Most original

Worst

CHAPTER 5

Formatting Text

OBJECTIVES

Format text in bold, underline, italic, and superscript

Change font type and size

Center lines

Align text at right margin

Indent paragraphs

Change the line spacing

Create bulleted lists

Copy formatting

Set tabs

PREVIEW

One of the advantages of using a word processor is that formatting can be added to text easily. Now that a variety of fonts and sizes is available, you can produce documents that look as though they were professionally typeset. You can also easily change the way text is aligned at the margins, quickly change the spacing in the entire document, add bulleted lists, and format text in tabular columns.

FORMATTING CHARACTERS

Character formatting includes adding bold, underlining, and italic to text, as well as changing the font type and size. Also, text can be formatted in superscript or subscript.

There are two ways to apply character formats to text. One is to give a command prior to typing text, and the second is to apply the formatting after the text is typed. Both will be covered here.

For most Windows users, the easiest way to apply formatting is to use the formatting buttons on the toolbar, and those are used in the following instructions. However, the **Format, Font and Style** menu is also used, as well as shortcut keys. A table of shortcut keys for both character and paragraph formatting is included at the end of this chapter.

Apply Bold to Text

In this section, bold formatting will be added to text that has already been typed. You will use the documents created in Chapters 3 and 4.

1. Open — the word processor if it is not already opened.
2. Retrieve — **CH3PR1** that you created in Chapter 3 or retrieve it from the Instructor's data disk. This is the document titled **PROMOTIONAL OFFER**. Your document should resemble the text shown here.

›› PROMOTIONAL OFFER

During the month of April Puget Sound Charters will offer two- and three-hour cruise tickets to all persons who visit one of our charter boats at any of their Puget Sound locations.

Tickets will be available at reduced prices during the entire month, and will include brunch and dinner cruises. The locations for visiting the boats are:

Kirkland on Lake Washington
Lake Union in downtown Seattle
Seward Park on Lake Washington
Shilshole in Ballard

Stop by for a visit and learn about all of our cruising schedules.

To format the title in bold

3. Select the title **PROMOTIONAL OFFER**, as shown below. Either click in the left margin or press **F8** three times to select the line.

NOTE: If you use the mouse, the paragraph mark at the end of the line will be selected. If you use the **F8** key only the words will be selected. This is not critical here; however, if you use the mouse to select a line including the paragraph mark, the formatting in that line will be repeated if **Enter** is pressed.

›› PROMOTIONAL OFFER

During the month of April Puget Sound

4. Click on the Bold button in the toolbar **B** .

NOTE: The button in the toolbar is depressed to show that it is on.

5. Click anywhere in the document to remove the highlighting, or if you used the **F8** key to select the text, press **Esc** to turn off Extend and then press any arrow key.

Underline Text As It Is Typed

To add underlined text <u>See Seattle by boat</u>

1. Move the insertion point to the beginning of the first paragraph and press **Enter** twice. Then press the **Up Arrow** twice to move above the first line of the paragraph. The text **See Seattle by boat** will be inserted here.

To underline new text

2. Click on the Underline button **u** .
3. Type **See Seattle by boat**. The text will appear underlined as shown here.

›› PROMOTIONAL OFFER

<u>See Seattle by boat</u>

During the month of April Puget Sound Charters will offer two- and three-hour cruise

At the end of the line

4. Click on the Underline button to turn off underlining. The button is no longer depressed.

Format Text in Italic

The text **Puget Sound Charters** will be formatted in italic in this section.

1. Select **Puget Sound Charters** in the first paragraph as shown here. Either point to the beginning of the text with the left mouse button and drag to the end of the word **Charters**, or move the insertion point to the beginning of the text, hold down the **Shift** and **Ctrl** keys and press the **Right Arrow** key three times to select the three words.

NOTE: If you select with the mouse, the space following **Charters** is selected. If you use the arrow keys, it is not. Either way is okay here.

See Seattle by boat

During the month of April Puget Sound Charters will offer two- and three-hour cruise tickets to all persons who visit one of our charter boats at any of their Puget Sound locations.

2. Click on the Italic button.
3. Press any arrow key or click anywhere in the document to remove the highlighting.

Format Text in Superscript

A **(tm)** mark will be inserted following **Puget Sound Charters** indicating that the name is a registered trademark. The Format, Font and Style menu is used for formatting in superscript. The formatting will be applied before text is typed and then turned off after the text is entered.

1. Move the insertion point directly following the word **Charters** in the first paragraph.
2. Choose **Format, Font and Style**. The Font and Style dialog box will be displayed as shown in Figure 5-1.

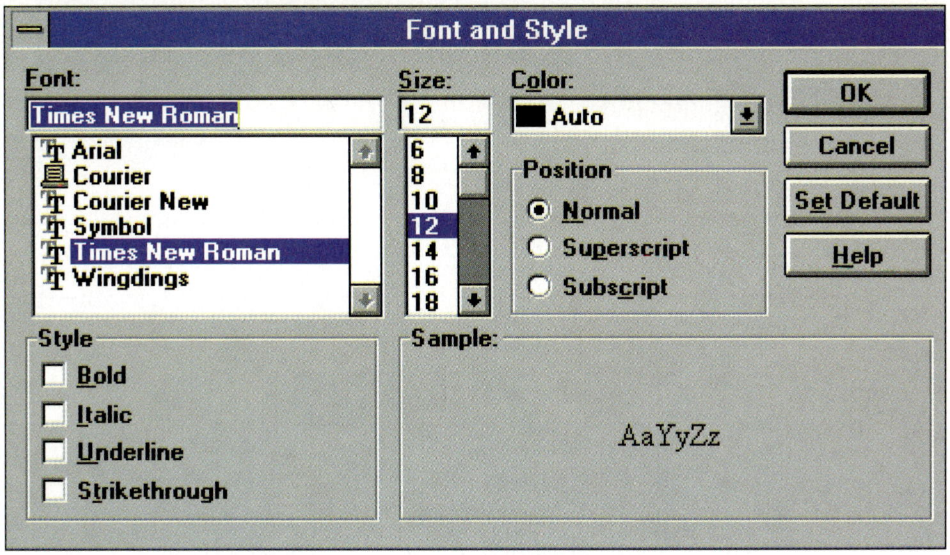

Figure 5-1
The Font and Style dialog box

This dialog box shows the available fonts and sizes as well as colors, if they are available.

NOTE: You can also turn on Bold, Italic, Underline, and Strikethrough from here, if you like. (Strikethrough is used to print horizontal lines across existing text. This is used primarily when you are editing a first draft and want to mark text that may be deleted later.)

3. Choose **Superscript** to turn it on. A dot appears in the radio button.
4. Choose **OK** or press **Enter** to return to the document.
5. Type **(tm)**.
6. Press **Ctrl/Spacebar** to end the superscript formatting.

NOTE: **Ctrl/Spacebar** can be used to turn off any character formatting.

Format Text with a Different Font Type and Size

The fonts and sizes that are available depend upon the printer that is being used; therefore, your dialog box may not show the same fonts that are displayed in Figure 5-1. When you format text with a different fonts, you can either choose a font type and size from the buttons in the toolbar, or you can choose **Format, Font and Style** and select fonts from the Font and Style dialog box.

Here, you will format **(tm)** that you just formatted as a superscript with a different font and size.

1. Select **(tm)** as shown here. To do this, either drag through the four characters, or move the insertion point in front of the left parenthesis, hold down the **Shift** key and press the **Right Arrow** four times.

In the toolbar

2. Click on the **Down Arrow** at the right end of the Font Name button to display the list of font names as shown below.

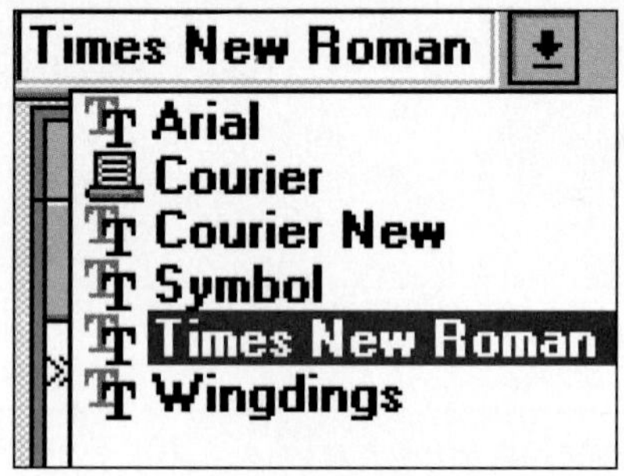

3. Select a font name other than the one that is highlighted. To do this, scroll up and down through the list to see the fonts that are available. If possible, choose a sans serif font such as Helvetica or Arial. When you see the one you want, click on it to select it. The list will be removed from the screen, and the selected text will be formatted with the new font name.

NOTE: Fonts usually are either sans serif or serif. Sans serif fonts do not have the extra angles at the ends of lines that make up the characters. Serif fonts do have the extra angles. Times Roman and Times New Roman are examples of serif-type fonts.

To format the selection with a different font size

4. Leave the text selected as shown in step 1.

5. Click on the **Down Arrow** at the right end of the Font Size button to display the list of font sizes as shown here

6. **Select** the font size that you want. To do this, scroll up and down through the list of sizes. Choose a small font size—probably 8 or 10 points—for the characters. Click on the size you want. The list will now be removed from the screen and the selected text will be formatted.

NOTE: Formatting with a different font name and size is the same as formatting with any other attribute. You can apply the formatting after you type the text, or you can enter the formatting before typing and end formatting by pressing **Ctrl/Spacebar**. You can also use the Font and Style dialog box to end formatting.

7. **Save** the document with a new name, **CH5PR1**.

FORMATTING PARAGRAPHS

In this section, paragraphs will be formatted with centered and right alignments as well as with indents. In addition, spacing will be changed in selected paragraphs.

The basic formatting concepts applied to character formatting are also used in paragraph formatting. You can either turn on the formatting you want, type text, and end formatting, or you can type the text first, then select the text and apply formatting. Also, toolbar buttons are available for the most common paragraph formatting and will be used here; however, the **Format, Paragraph** menu is also used for formatting. Shortcut keys for paragraph formatting are included in a table at the end of the chapter.

Center Text

1. **Retrieve** **CH4PR1** created in Chapter 4 or retrieve from the Instructor data disk. This is the document about the agenda for marketing. It should resemble the document shown below.

PUGET SOUND CHARTERS
AGENDA FOR MARKETING MEETING
NOVEMBER 20, 1994

This agenda contains a list of items to be discussed at the next marketing meeting. Please read through each item carefully prior to the meeting. If you have any additional comments, suggestions, or questions, be prepared to discuss them at the meeting.

Please bring this week's progress reports with you.

The meeting will be held proptly at 2 p.m. in the conference room. Bring your suggestions to the meeting. Jot them down in the area provided at the bottom of this agenda.

Suggestion

To center the first two lines

2. Select — both lines as shown in the illustration below. Either drag from the beginning of the first line through the end of the second line, or move the insertion point to the beginning of the first line, press **F8** and press the **Down Arrow** and the **End** key to select the lines.

NOTE: If you are going to apply formatting to more than one paragraph, then all paragraphs to be formatted must be selected. If formatting is to be added to only one paragraph, just move the insertion point to any position in the paragraph and apply the formatting. Formatting is stored in the paragraph mark at the end of the paragraph.

```
›› PUGET SOUND CHARTERS
   AGENDA FOR MARKETING MEETING
   NOVEMBER 20, 1994
```

3. Click — on the Center Align button 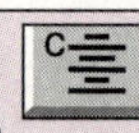. Your text should now resemble the following illustration.

```
››                 PUGET SOUND CHARTERS
              AGENDA FOR MARKETING MEETING
   NOVEMBER 20, 1994
```

4. Move — the insertion point away from the selection to remove the highlighting.

NOTE: You can also choose **Format**, **Paragraph** to go to the Paragraph dialog box and choose **Indents and Alignment** and **Center**. Then choose **OK** or press **Enter** to return to the document. **Ctrl/E** is the shortcut key for centering.

Align Text at the Right Margin

In this section, the date line will be aligned at the right margin.

1. Move — the insertion point to any position in the date **November 20, 1994**. You do not need to select the paragraph because formatting is going to be applied to only one paragraph.
2. Click — on the Right Align button 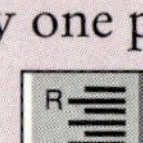. The text should now look like the following example.

›› PUGET·SOUND·CHARTERS¶
AGENDA·FOR·MARKETING·MEETING¶
NOVEMBER·20,·1994¶

NOTE: Left alignment (which is the default paragraph alignment) and Justified are two additional alignments that can be used in paragraph formatting. Justified aligns text at both the left and right margins. To do this, Works adds extra spaces automatically between words. You can either press **Ctrl/J** or choose **Format, Paragraph, Indents and Alignment, Justified** to apply Justified alignment. Left alignment is applied by clicking on the Left Align button in the toolbar.

Indent a Paragraph

Here, you will begin paragraph formatting with a first line indent before typing the text. The text shown below will be inserted following the first paragraph.

The following items are carried over from the two previous marketing meetings. No firm decisions have been made about which approach would be most suitable for the upcoming sales campaign; however, after the success of recent months, an approach similar to last quarter's might prove successful again.

1. Move — the insertion point to the end of the first paragraph and press **Enter** twice.
2. Choose — **Format, Paragraph** to display the Paragraph dialog box as shown in Figure 5-2.

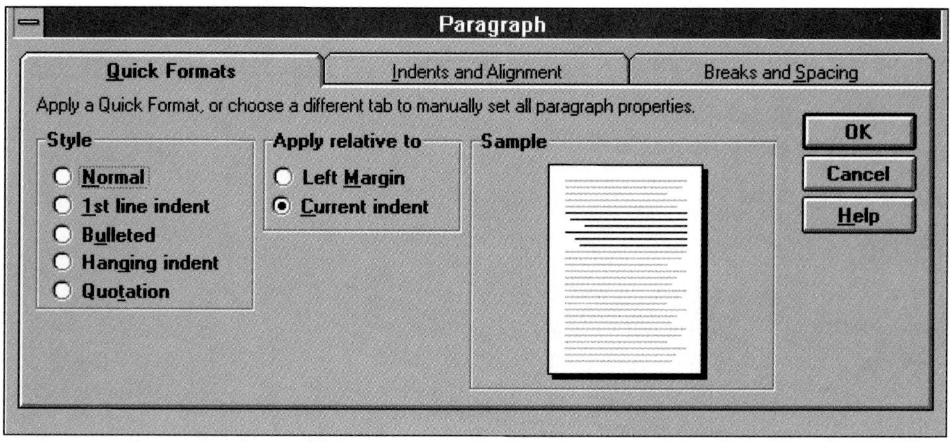

Figure 5-2
The Paragraph dialog box

The dialog box shows three "file cards" or **tabs** which is the term Works uses to identify each section. The titles refer to the types of options available on each "tab." The Quick Formats tab is probably showing.

3.	Choose	**Quick Formats** if it is not showing.
4.	Choose	**1st line indent**. The Sample box at the right displays an example of the formatting. Your screen should resemble Figure 5-2.
5.	Choose	**OK** or press **Enter** to return to the document. Your paragraph is now indented one tab stop. The advantage of using this option is that each time **Enter** is pressed to go to the next paragraph, the formatting will be repeated automatically.
6.	Type	the text in the box below. The first line of text will automatically be indented one tab stop.

The following items are carried over from the two previous marketing meetings. No firm decisions have been made about which approach would be most suitable for the upcoming sales campaign; however, after the success of recent months, an approach similar to last quarter's might prove successful again.

7.	Press	**Enter** once at the end of the paragraph.
8.	Press	**Ctrl/Q** or choose **Format, Paragraph, Normal** and press **Enter** to return to normal paragraph formatting.

NOTE: Other Quick Formats options are described in Table 5-1.

Normal — Aligns text at the document's margins.

1st line indent — Indents the first line of each paragraph.

Bulleted	Inserts a bullet at the beginning of each paragraph and aligns all lines of text at the first tab stop. 
Hanging indent	Aligns the first line at the left margin and the remaining lines at the first tab stops. 
Quotation	Indents all lines of the paragraph one tab stop from both margins. 
Apply relative to Left Margin	Indents the paragraph from the left margin.
Apply relative to Current indent	Indents the paragraph in relation to indents in the paragraph that is highlighted.

Table 5-1

The choices in the Quick Formats tab in the Paragraph dialog box

NOTE: You can also set indents manually at specified measurements. To do this, choose **Format**, **Paragraph**, **Indents** and **Alignment** and enter measurements in the boxes for **Left**, **Right**, or **First Line**. To return to normal paragraph formatting after you have entered custom measurements for indents, you should return again to the **Indents and Alignment** tab and set 0 as the measurement for the indents you have set.

Format with a Hanging Indent

Hanging indents are used frequently for numbered lists. The following text will be inserted below the new paragraph.

1. Open house and drawing for a discount on any weekday brunch cruise.¶

¶

2. Free dinner tickets and a 10 percent discount on purchases of additional tickets prior to March 1.¶

¶

3. Free dinner or brunch tickets to the first 100 persons visiting one of our boats during the next two weeks.¶

¶

¶

1. Press **Enter** a second time to insert a blank line below the new paragraph.
2. Choose **Format, Paragraph, Quick Formats** if the Quick Formats tab is not the active one. See example in Figure 5-3.

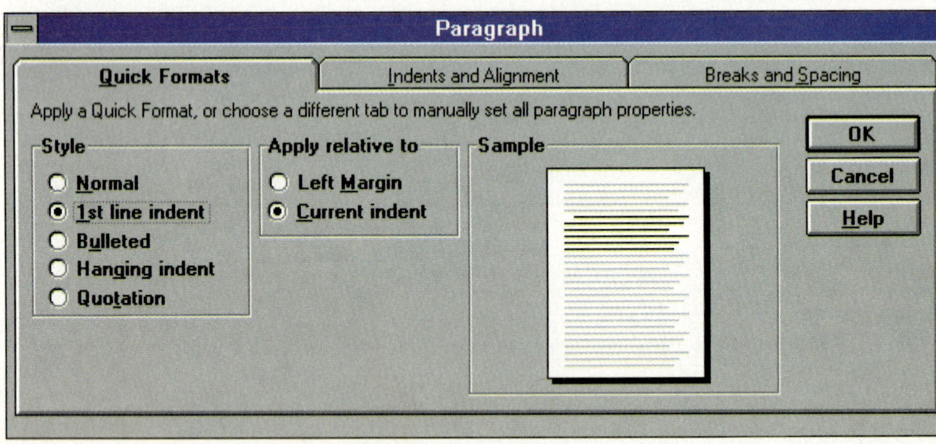

Figure 5-3
The Quick Formats tab in the Paragraph dialog box

3. Choose **Hanging indent**. The Sample box should resemble the following illustration.

4. Choose **OK** or press **Enter** to return to the document. In the Ruler, the left indent marker that is split now shows the lower triangle moved to the first tab stop as displayed here.

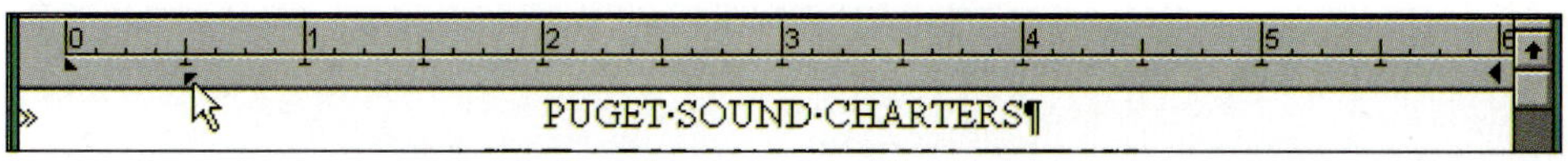

5. Type the number **1.** (period) and press **Tab** to go to the first tab stop. Type the sentence in the box below. The text in the second line automatically wraps to the first tab stop because the paragraph is formatted with a hanging indent.

NOTE: If you are using a small-sized font, the sentence may not wrap to the second line. When you type the next numbered item, the sentence will be long enough to wrap to the next line.

1. Open house and drawing for a discount on any weekday brunch cruise.¶

¶

¶

6. Press **Enter** twice to insert a blank line as shown above. In the Ruler, the lower half of the left indent marker should still be at the first tab stop.

7. Type the numbered items in the box below. Press **Tab** once after the period following each number, and press **Enter** twice after each paragraph.

2. Free dinner tickets and a 10 percent discount on purchases of additional tickets prior to March 1.¶

¶

3. Free dinner or brunch tickets to the first 100 persons visiting one of our boats during the next two weeks.¶

¶

¶

NOTE: If you are using a mouse, you can format a paragraph with a hanging indent by holding down the **Shift** key and dragging the lower half of the left indent marker to the first tab stop or to any other tab stop.

Double-space Text

In this section, the first, second, and last paragraphs will be double-spaced.

1. Move the insertion point to the beginning of the first paragraph and select paragraphs one and two, as shown below—drag through the paragraphs, or press **F8** and press the **Down Arrow** to select all text.

> This agenda contains a list of items to be discussed at the next marketing meeting. Please read through each item carefully prior to the meeting. If you have any additional comments, suggestions, or questions, be prepared to discuss them at the meeting.
>
> The following items are carried over from the two previous marketing meetings. No firm decisions have been made about which approach would be most suitable for the upcoming sales campaign; however, after the success of recent months, an approach similar to last quarter's might prove successful again.

2. Press **Ctrl/2** or choose **Format, Paragraph, Breaks and Spacing** to display the Breaks and Spacing tab as shown in Figure 5-4.

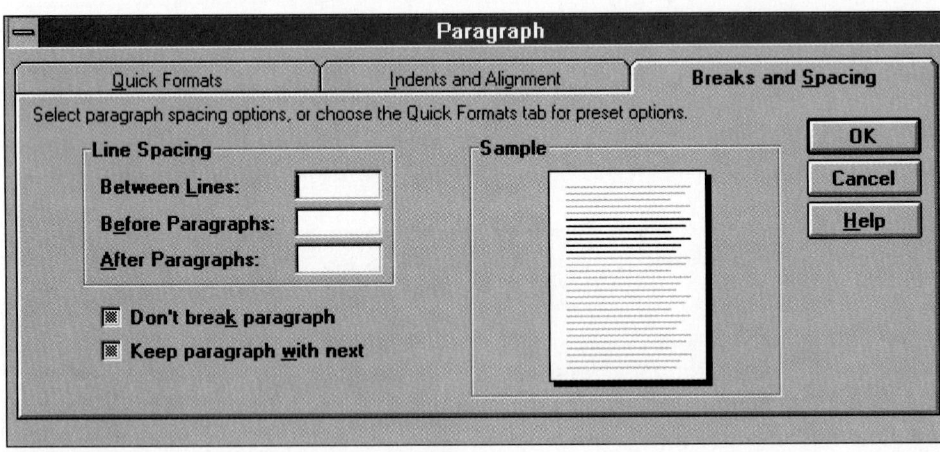

Figure 5-4
The Breaks and Spacing tab in the Paragraph dialog box

If you displayed the Paragraph dialog box

3. Type **2** for double-spacing in the **Between Lines** text box as shown below.

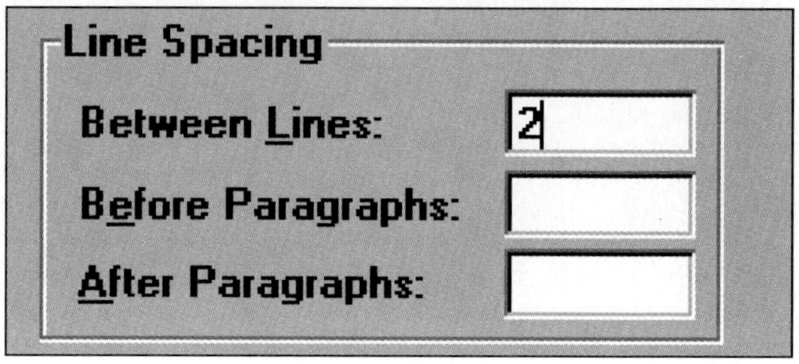

4. **Choose** **OK** or press **Enter** to return to the document. The text is now double-spaced, as shown here.

> This agenda contains a list of items to be discussed at the next marketing meeting. Please read through each item carefully prior to the meeting. If you have any additional comments, suggestions, or questions, be prepared to discuss them at the meeting.
>
> The following items are carried over from the two previous marketing meetings. No firm decisions have been made about which approach would be most suitable for the upcoming sales campaign; however, after the success of recent months, an approach similar to last quarter's might prove successful again.

5. **Move** the insertion point away from the text to remove the highlighting.
6. **Move** the insertion point to the space between the two paragraphs and press **Delete** to remove the extra line.
7. **Move** the insertion point to any position in the last paragraph.
8. **Press** **Ctrl/2** or choose **Format, Paragraph**. Be sure the **Breaks and Spacing** tab is active. Type **2** in the text box and choose **OK** or press **Enter** to return to the document. See the example in the following illustration. See Table 5-2 for a description of other choices in the Breaks and Spacing tab.

> The meeting will be held promptly at 2 p.m. in the conference room. Bring your suggestions to the meeting. Jot them down in the area provided at the bottom of this agenda.

NOTE: If you want to enter a different measurement for line spacing, enter the amount (instead of **2**) in the **Between Lines** text box.

Between Lines	Sets the amount of space between lines in the paragraph. Type the measurement. If you want it to be measured by the height of the current font, type **auto**.
Before Paragraphs	Enter the number of blank lines you want inserted above the paragraph.
After Paragraphs	Enter the number of blank lines you want to be inserted below the paragraph.
Don't break paragraph	Prevents a page break within the selected paragraph.
Keep paragraph with next	Prevents a page break between the selected paragraph and the following paragraph.

Table 5-2
Options in the Breaks and Spacing tab in the Paragraph dialog box

NOTE: Refer to Table 5-3 at the end of the chapter for a list of shortcut keys for paragraph and character formatting.

FORMATTING WITH BULLETED LISTS

Formatting with bulleted lists is a type of paragraph formatting. You have already seen this option in the Paragraph dialog box in the Quick Formats tab section. However, it is much quicker to use the Bullets button in the toolbar to apply this formatting.

Use the Bullets Button

The following text will be inserted below item number 3.

- Discount on all brunch and dinner tickets during the next quarter. Discount amount to be determined.
- Discount on dinner cruises for persons purchasing more than five tickets during the quarter.

1. Move the insertion point two lines below numbered item 3 as shown in the following illustration.

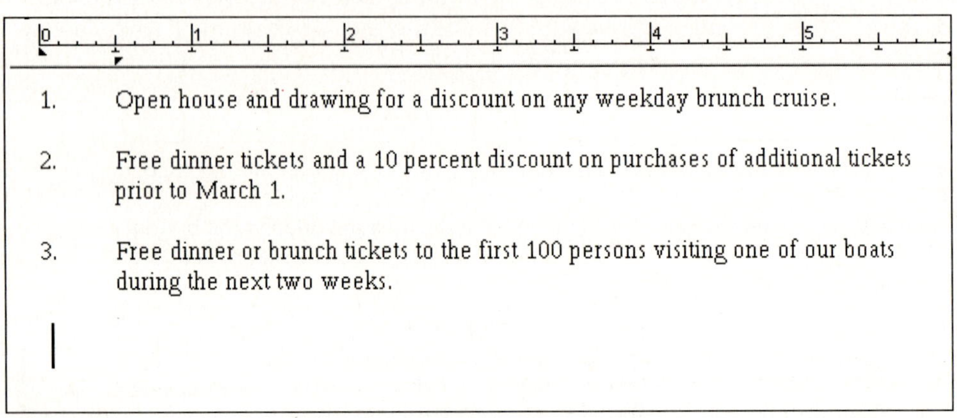

2. Press **Ctrl/Q** to return to normal paragraph formatting. Confirm the change in the Ruler. Both triangles at the left end of the Ruler should be at the same position as shown in the illustration above.

NOTE: If you don't do this, the bullet will be placed at the first tab stop, because the previous paragraph was formatted with a hanging indent.

3. Click on the Bullets button  . A bullet is displayed at the left margin and the insertion point is at the first tab stop.

NOTE: The indents for bulleted lists are different from indents for numbered lists.

4. Type the text in the box below.

- Discount on all brunch and dinner tickets during the next quarter. Discount amount to be determined.

5. Press **Enter** once at the end of the paragraph. The bullet is repeated.

6. Type the following text.

- Discount on dinner cruises for persons purchasing more than five tickets during the quarter.

Your text should now resemble the following example.

1. Open house and drawing for a discount on any weekday brunch cruise.
2. Free dinner tickets and a 10 percent discount on purchases of additional tickets prior to March 1.
3. Free dinner or brunch tickets to the first 100 persons visiting one of our boats during the next two weeks.

- Discount on all brunch and dinner tickets during the next quarter. Discount amount to be determined.
- Discount on dinner cruises for persons purchasing more than five tickets during the quarter.

7. Delete any extra spaces between paragraphs if necessary. There should be one blank line between each paragraph.

NOTE: If you want to insert a blank line between the bulleted items, press **Ctrl/Q** to return to normal formatting after pressing **Enter** following the first paragraph. Then press **Enter** again to insert a blank line and click on the Bullets button to format the next paragraph with a bullet.

Copy Paragraph Formatting

You can copy character or paragraph formatting without copying text. In this section, you will copy the formatting of the last bulleted item to the paragraph directly below it.

1. **Select** the last bulleted item as shown in the following illustration. Either double-click in the left margin by the paragraph, or press **F8** four times in the paragraph.

- Discount on all brunch and dinner tickets during the next quarter. Discount amount to be determined.
- Discount on dinner cruises for persons purchasing more than five tickets during the quarter.

Please bring this week's progress reports with you.

2. **Click** on the Copy button, or choose **Edit, Copy,** or press **Ctrl/C.**
3. **Move** the insertion point to the following line **Please bring this week's progress report with you.**
4. **Choose** **Edit, Paste Special.** The Paste Special dialog box is shown here.

5. **Choose** **Paragraph Format** if it is not already turned on.
6. **Choose** **OK** or press **Enter.** The line is formatted with a bullet. Use the following steps to remove extra indents if needed.
7. **Press** **Home** to go to the beginning of the line following the bullet.
8. **Press** **Delete** to remove the tab.

NOTE: You can copy either paragraph or character formatting using the procedure just presented.

9. **Save** the document as **CH5PR2A.**

SETTING TABS

Setting tabs is a type of paragraph formatting. The tab settings are carried from paragraph to paragraph the way other paragraph formatting is repeated. The following information will be inserted.

Salesperson	Closing	Total
Gail Saunders	9-28-94	10,975.00
John Stevenson	9-30-94	8,525.00
Beverly Simms	9-27-94	13,550.00
Jerry Randall	9-30-94	11,180.00

Tabular text showing the names of salespersons and the total amount of sales for each will be entered directly following the bulleted lists.

Set Tabs for Three Columns

To set a left tab, which aligns the left side of the text

1. Move the insertion point to the left margin at the beginning of the paragraph **The meeting will be held....** Be sure the insertion point is to the left of the tab. Choose **View, All Characters** if it is not already on to see the tab mark.
2. Press **Enter** twice to insert blank lines.
3. Press the **up arrow** twice to move two lines above the **The meeting** paragraph.
4. Press **Ctrl/1** (the number one) to return to single spacing.
5. Choose **Format, Tabs** to display the Tabs dialog box as shown in Figure 5-5

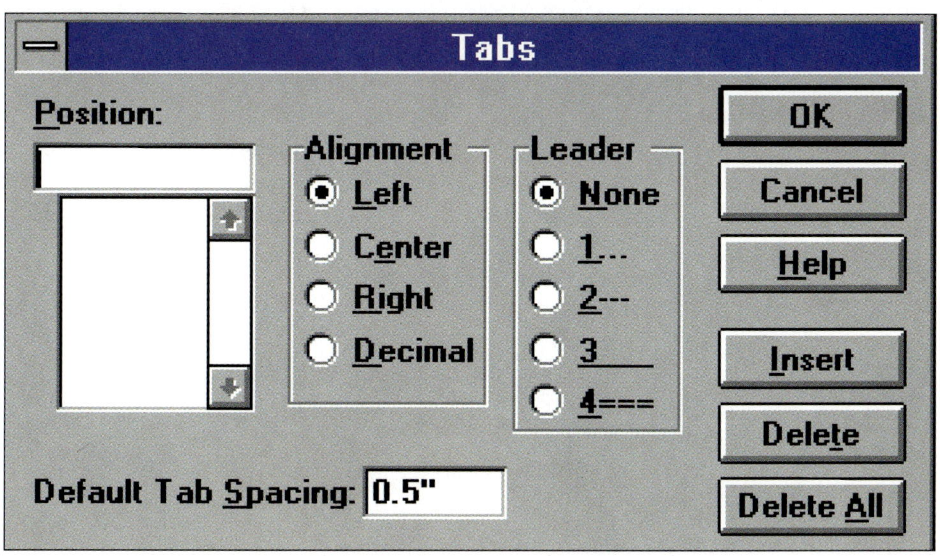

Figure 5-5
The Tabs dialog box

6. Type .5 in the Position text box as shown here 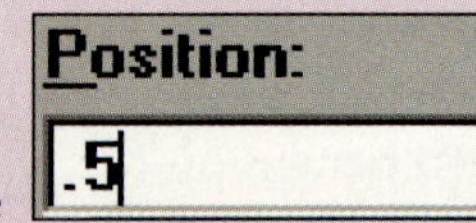

. The default alignment is **Left** which will be used for this tab set.

7. Choose **Insert** 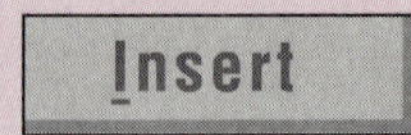

to add the tab position to the Position list box as shown here.

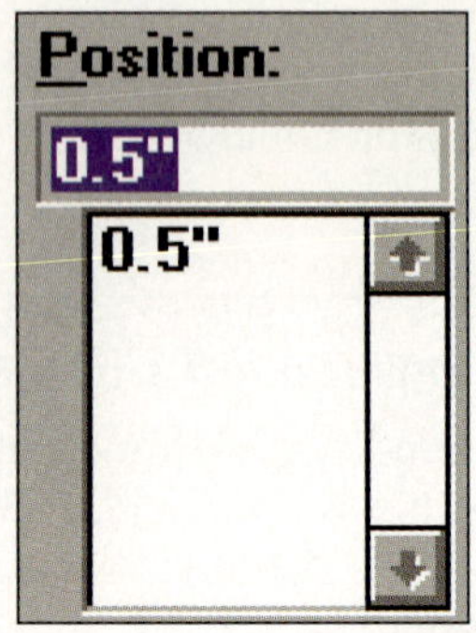

To set a right tab which aligns the right side of the text

8. Type **3** in the Position text box 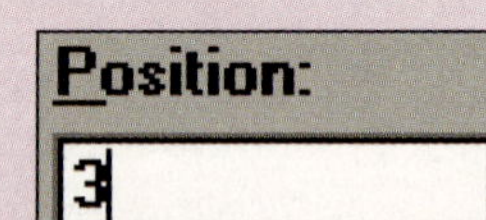

.

9. Choose **Right** 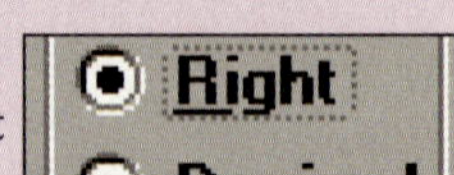

to choose the alignment you want.

10. Choose **Insert** 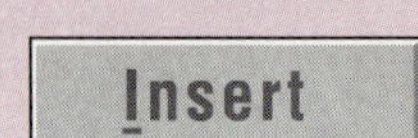

. The new tab stop is now displayed in the Position list box as shown in the following illustration.

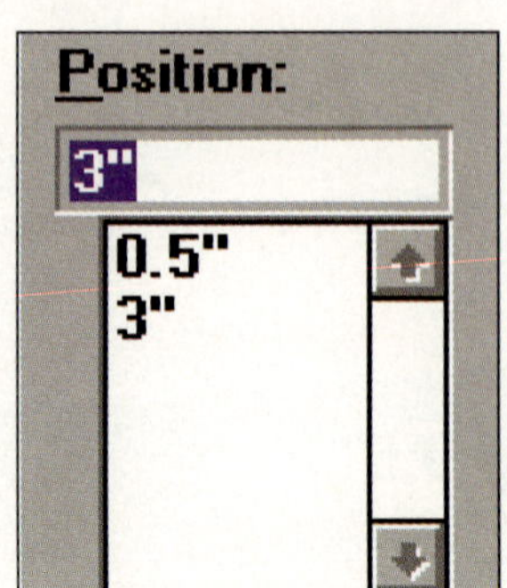

To set a decimal tab with dot leaders

A decimal tab aligns the decimals in the text and formats the tab with a dot leader which connects this column and the previous column with dots.

11. Type **4.5** in the Position text box.

12. Choose **Decimal** 

.

13. Choose **1. . .** in the **Leader** box 

to set a dot leader.

14. Choose **Insert** 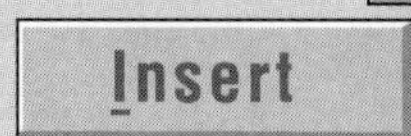

to set the tab and display the measurement in the **Position** list box, as shown here.

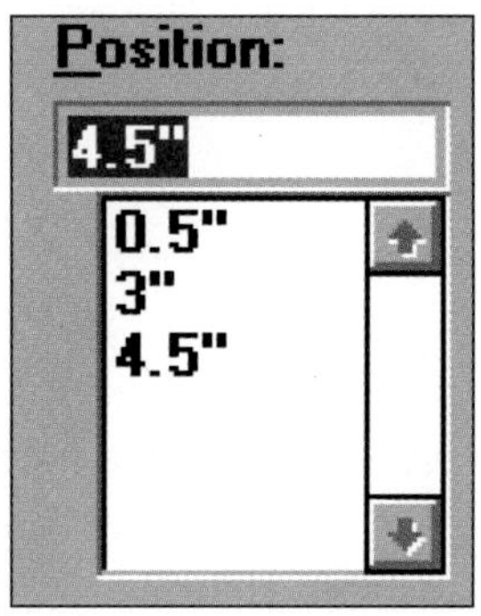

15. Choose **Close** to return to the document. Your Ruler should now resemble the following example. The default tabs are removed and replaced with the three tabs that were just set.

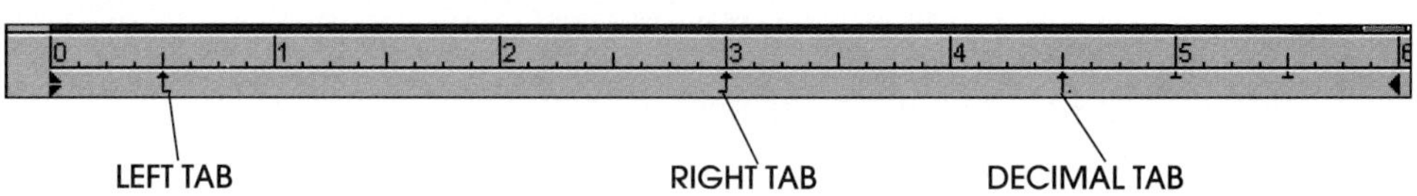

Type Text in Tabular Columns

The information shown in the box below will be entered in tabular columns. Do not type the headings for each column now. They will be entered later.

Salesperson	Closing	Total
Gail Saunders	9-28-94	10,975.00
John Stevenson	9-30-94	8,525.00
Beverly Simms	9-27-94	13,550.00
Jerry Randall	9-30-94	11,180.00

1. Press **Tab** to move to the tab stop at .5.
2. Type **Gail Saunders** and press **Tab** to move to the tab stop at 3.
3. Type **9-28-94** and press **Tab**. The insertion point will move to the decimal tab and dot leaders will be displayed.
4. Type **10,975.00.** As you type, the numbers to the left of the decimal will be entered from right to left. After typing the decimal (.), the remaining numbers will be entered from left to right.
5. Press **Enter** to go to the next line. The formatting for the tabs is repeated in the next paragraph. Confirm this in the Ruler.
6. Type the three remaining lines of the text, as shown here.

John Stevenson	9-30-94	8,525.00
Beverly Simms	9-27-94	13,550.00
Jerry Randall	9-30-94	11,180.00

Set Tabs for Headings

To enter headings that are centered over each column

New tab sets will be set with centered alignment at 1, 2.75, and 4.4 in a paragraph above the first row. Center tab alignment centers the text at the tab position.

1. Move the insertion point to the left margin in the first row.
2. Press **Enter** once and the **Up Arrow** to move up to the new blank line. Look at the Ruler to confirm that the tabs are still the same as those in the columns.
3. Choose **Format, Tabs** to display the Tabs dialog box.
4. Choose **Delete All** [Delete All]. The previous tab set positions are removed from the Position list box.
5. Type **1** in the Position text box.
6. Choose **Center.**
7. Choose **Insert.** The Tabs dialog box should now resemble Figure 5-6.

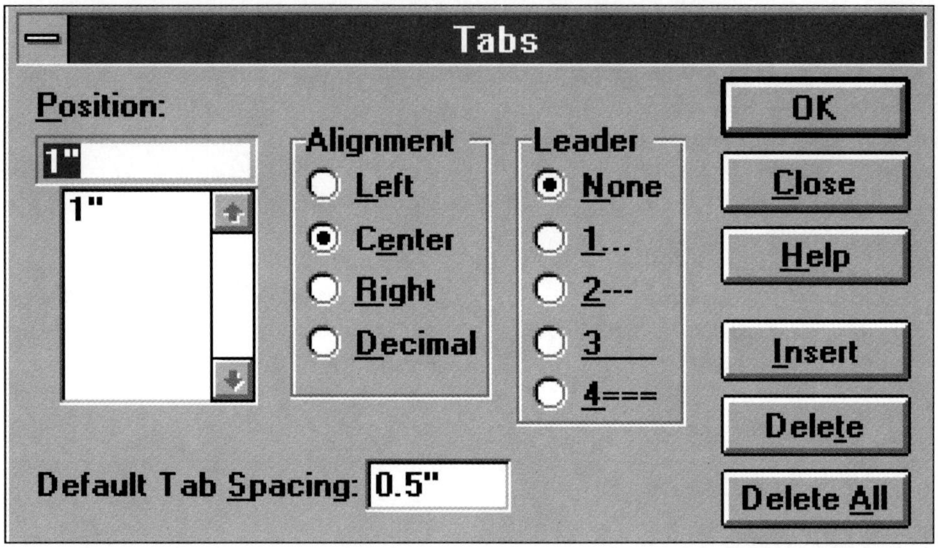

Figure 5-6
The Tabs dialog box

8. Repeat — steps 5 and 7 above to set center tabs at 2.75 and 4.4. **Center** will remain turned on until you choose another alignment, so you can skip step 6.
9. Choose — **Close**. The Ruler should now resemble the following example.

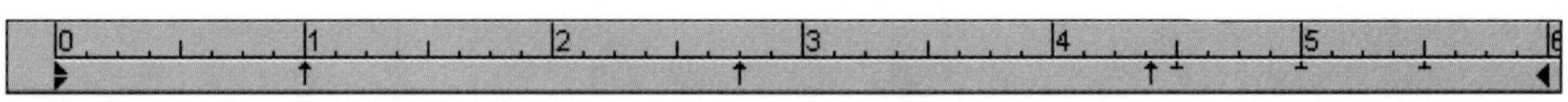

10. Press — **Tab** to move to the first tab stop.
11. Click — on the Bold button **B**.
12. Type — **Salesperson.**
13. Press — **Tab** to go to the next tab stop and type **Closing**.
14. Press — **Tab** again to go to the last tab stop and type **Total**.
15. Click — on the Bold button **B** to end bold.
16. Press — **Enter** to insert a blank line between the heading line and the remainder of the text.
17. Move — the insertion point to the line above the heading and type the following paragraph. When done, press **Enter** to insert a blank line between the paragraph and the table headings.
18. Save — the document as **CH5PR2B** (you should now have two files, **CH5PR2A** and **CH5PR2B**)
19. Close — all the opened files.

The table below shows the top four salespersons during the past quarter ending September 30. The total sales figure depicts the total dollar amount of bookings during the period. This is an outstanding effort. Other members of the team are to be commended as well.

OTHER FORMATTING

Other options in the Format menu include Borders and Columns. Borders can be added to text—just select all paragraphs to have a border and choose **Format, Borders**. In the Border dialog box, select **Outline** to add a border around all paragraphs, or select only a specific side(s). Then select the type of border and choose OK.

Formatting text in newspaper type columns is discussed in Chapter 7, "Page Design."

Text can also be entered (formatted) in a table by inserting a spreadsheet/table in a word processing document. The table is inserted by clicking on the Insert Table button or choosing **Insert, Spreadsheet/Table**. This is covered in Chapter 11, "Increased Spreadsheet Power."

SHORTCUT KEYS FOR FORMATTING

Table 5-3 below lists the shortcut keys that can be used to apply both character and paragraph formatting.

Table 5-3

List of shortcut keys for formatting

Shortcut key	Formatting
Ctrl/B	Bold
Ctrl/I	Italic
Ctrl/U	Underlining
Ctrl/Equal sign	Subscript
Ctrl/Shift/Equal sign	Superscript
Ctrl/spacebar	Restore normal (default) font with no formatting
Shift/F7	Repeat formatting that has just been applied to text to a different block of selected text
Ctrl/1	Single-spaced paragraph
Ctrl/2	Double-spaced paragraph
Ctrl/5	1.5 line spacing in paragraphs
Ctrl/H	Hanging indent
Ctrl/G	Undo a hanging indent
Ctrl/N	Indent all lines at the left
Ctrl/M	Move left indent back one tab stop
Ctrl/E	Center lines in a paragraph
Ctrl/J	Justify lines in a paragraph
Ctrl/L	Left align paragraph lines
Ctrl/R	Right align paragraph lines
Ctrl/Q	Restore normal paragraph formatting: left align, single-spacing, restore default tabs every 1/2 inch

GUIDED TUTORIAL

What You'll Do

- Add bulleted lists
- Change font type and style
- Copy format changes
- Change paragraph indents
- Set and change tab positions

How To Do It

The document you will be creating is shown in the box below.

PUGET SOUND CHARTERS
NEEDS ANALYSIS

Report Presented to Management
for Computer Equipment Purchases

Introduction

This is a needs analysis requested by the management of Puget Sound Charters. The management team is interested in researching the possibility of purchasing computer equipment for the office to increase productivity.

Justification: The microcomputer has more than proved itself to be a valuable office tool during the past two decades since its inception. In numbers alone, it has shown that people are demanding and using their computers. In 1980, $1 billion worth of microcomputers had been sold; in 1990 that figure reached beyond $50 billion. Microcomputers have consistently increased in speed and efficiency. The storage capacity, processing speed, and power of the microcomputer are the most competitive marketing tactics in use by vendors. Another keen focus of the microcomputer community has been in the development of software programs. Where micros initially were capable of running only a single, and somewhat limited, program at a time, they now run very complex and sophisticated programs that do more for the user and perform faster.

The user interface is also important. Users want operating systems and software that are easy to use and take a minimum amount of time to learn. This has been provided by both the Macintosh system and the IBM personal computers and compatibles.

Programs: Word processing was perhaps the most popular use of microcomputers in the early years of software development; however, other software programs were also heavily used. Among the most popular programs were those for file management and spreadsheet applications. Today, many programs are available. Nearly any need for a particular application can be met. Among some of the popular ones in use today are very sophisticated word processing programs capable of outputting graphic images, using tables, performing calculations, and merging documents, to name a few. Database management programs are not only more sophisticated, but easier to use and capable of handling complex queries on multiple tables. Spreadsheet programs offer worksheets that hold thousands of cells and perform quick calculation. Many programs, such as Microsoft Works, combined these tools into a single application, thus making it easy to move quickly from one application to another and to integrate applications.

Integrated programs may include:

Word Processing ....A document tool
Spreadsheet ....A numbers tool
Database ....A facts collection tool
Communications............A sending/receiving tool
Draw ....A graphics tool

1. Open — a new document file—Choose **File, Create New File**, or click on the Startup dialog button to return to the Startup dialog box.
2. Choose — **Word Processor** to display a new blank document window. Or retrieve the document **CH5TUT1A** from the Instructor's data disk.

To type the centered title in bold

3. Click — on the Center Align button 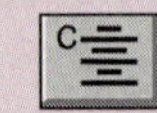.
4. Click — on the Bold button 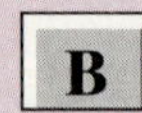, and press **Caps Lock**.
5. Type — the first two lines and click on the Bold button to turn off bold. Also, press **Caps Lock** to return to lowercase and press **Enter**.
6. Type — the last two lines of the title. Your screen should now resemble the following.

››

PUGET·SOUND·CHARTERS¶
NEEDS·ANALYSIS¶
Report·Presented·to·Management¶
for·Computer·Equipment·Purchases¶
¶

7. Press — **Enter** twice to insert blank lines and click on the Left Align button  to return to normal formatting.

At **Introduction**

8. Click — on the Bold button  and on the Underline button 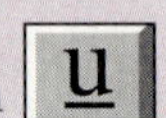.
9. Type — **Introduction** and press **Ctrl/Spacebar** to end the character formatting, and press **Enter** twice.
10. Type — the remaining text shown in the box at the beginning of the tutorial. Format **Justification:** and **Programs:** in bold. Type only the text through the paragraph following **Programs:**. Instructions for typing **Integrated programs...** and the following list are given below.

Following the **Programs:** paragraph

11. Press — **Enter** twice.
12. Press — **Tab,** type **Integrated programs may include:** and press **Enter** twice.

To set tabs at .5 and at 5.5

13. Choose — **Format, Tabs** to go to the Tab dialog box.

14.	Type	**.5** in the Position text box. Be sure the alignment is set at **Left** and choose **Insert** 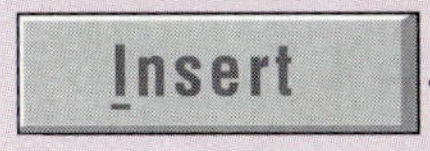 .
15.	Type	**5.5** in the Position text box, choose **Right**, choose leader **1. . .**, and then choose **Insert** 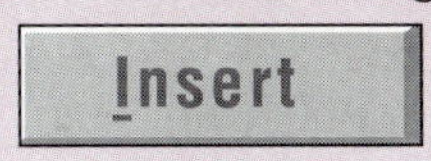 . The Tab dialog box should now resemble the following.

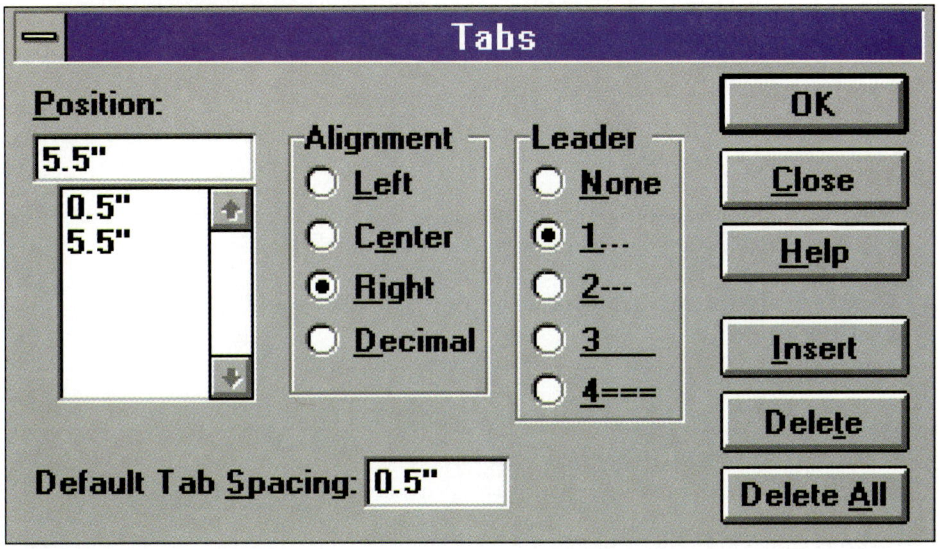

16.	Choose	**Close** to return to the document. Your Ruler should now resemble the following illustration.

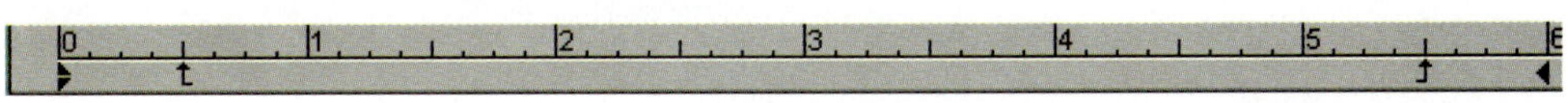

17.	Press	**Tab** and type **Word Processing.**
18.	Press	**Tab** and type **A document tool.** Press **Enter** to go to the next line.
19.	Repeat	pressing **Tab** and typing the remaining lines as shown here.

Spreadsheet . . . . .A numbers tool
Database . . . . .A facts collection tool
Communications . . . . .A sending/receiving tool
Draw . . . . .A graphics tool

To add bullets

Here, text in the **Programs** section will be reformatted with bullets as shown in the following illustration.

<u>**Programs:**</u> Word processing was perhaps the most popular use of microcomputers in the early years of software development; however, other software programs were also heavily used. Among the most popular programs were those for file management and spreadsheet applications. Today, many programs are available. Nearly any need for a particular application can be met. Among some of the popular ones in use today are:

- Very sophisticated word processing programs capable of outputting graphic images, using tables, performing calculations, and merging documents, to name a few.
- Database management programs are not only more sophisticated, but easier to use and capable of handling complex queries on multiple tables.
- Spreadsheet programs offer worksheets that hold thousands of cells and perform quick calculations.

20. Move the insertion point following the word **are** in the sentence beginning **Among some of the popular ones in use today are.**

21. Type a colon **(:)** and press **Enter** twice.

22. Click on the Bullets button 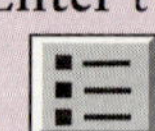, or choose **Format, Paragraph, Quick Formats, Bulleted** (see the following illustration) and choose **OK** or press **Enter.**

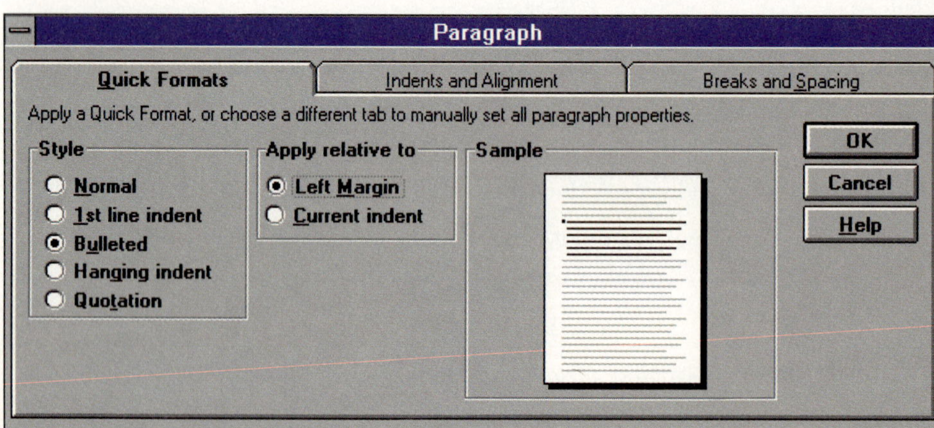

Your text should now resemble the following example.

application can be met. Among some of the popular ones in use today are:

- Very sophisticated word processing programs capable of outputting graphic images, using tables, performing calculations, and merging documents, to name a few. Database management programs are not only more sophisticated, but easier to use and capable of handling complex queries on multiple tables. Spreadsheet programs offer worksheets that hold thousands of cells and perform quick calculations.

23. Press — **Delete** twice to remove the blank space at the beginning of the line and to delete **v** in **very.**

24. Type — **V** to insert a capital letter in **Very.**

To format the next bulleted item

25. Move — the insertion point directly following the period after **few.** in **to name a few.**

26. Press — **Enter** twice. Two bullets are inserted.

27. Press — the **Up Arrow** to go to the bullet at the beginning of the blank line as shown here.

- Very sophisticated word processing programs capable of outputting graphic images, using tables, performing calculations, and merging documents, to name a few.
-
- Database management programs are not only more sophisticated, but easier to use and capable of handling complex queries on multiple tables.

28. Press — **Ctrl/Q** to restore normal paragraph formatting. The bullet will be removed.

29. Press — the **Down Arrow** once to return to the extra space before **Database** and press **Delete** to remove any extra spaces.

30. Move — the insertion point in front of the sentence **Spreadsheet programs offer . . .** and repeat steps 26 through 29 to make that sentence a bulleted paragraph.

31. Move — the insertion point in front of the **M** in **Many programs, such as Microsoft Works . . .**

32. Press — **Enter** twice and remove the bullets from this paragraph and the blank line above it by pressing **Ctrl/Q** in each paragraph. Delete any extra spaces to the left of **Many**. Your document should now look like the following example.

application can be met. Among some of the popular ones in use today are:

- Very sophisticated word processing programs capable of outputting graphic images, using tables, performing calculations, and merging documents, to name a few.
- Database management programs are not only more sophisticated, but easier to use and capable of handling complex queries on multiple tables.
- Spreadsheet programs offer worksheets that hold thousands of cells and perform quick calculations.

Many programs, such as Microsoft Works, combined these tools into a single application.

To copy character formatting

Format the word **Introduction** with a sans serif font type such as Helvetica or Arial, and copy that formatting plus the underlining to **Justification:** and to **Programs:**.

33. Select the word **Introduction** by double-clicking on it or by pressing **F8** twice.

34. Click on the Font Name button and choose a sans serif font as shown here.

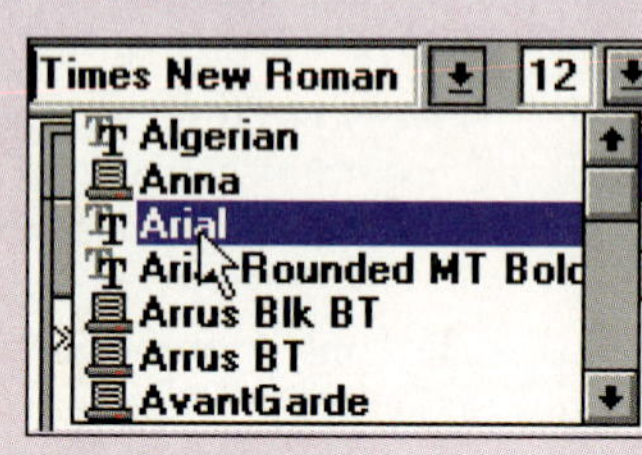

35. Click on the Font Size button and choose 12 point if it is not already chosen.

To copy the formatting

36. Select the word **Introduction** if it is not already selected, and click on the Copy button .

37. Select the word **Justification**. Do not include the colon.

38. Choose **Edit, Paste Special** to display the Paste Special dialog box and choose **Character Style** as shown in the following illustration.

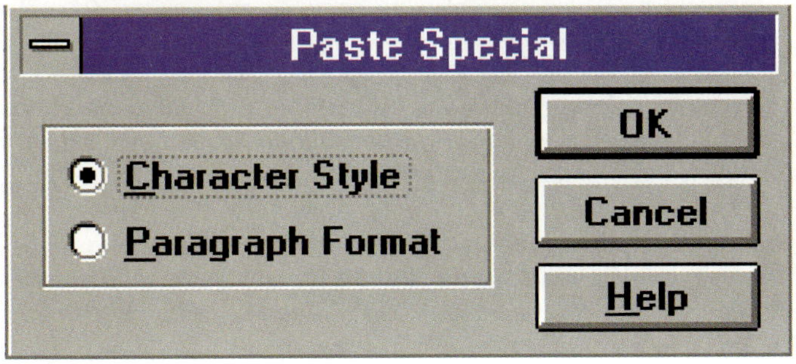

39. Choose **OK** or press **Enter** to apply the character formatting to the selection.

40. Select **Programs:** Do not include the colon.

41. Choose **Edit, Paste Special, Character Style** and choose **OK** or press **Enter** to copy the character formatting to **Programs**.

To change paragraph indent

Here you will indent paragraphs using shortcut keys. See Table 5-3 at the end of the chapter for a list of shortcut keys that can be used to apply common types of paragraph formatting.

42. Move the insertion point to the first **Justification** paragraph.

43. Press **Ctrl/H** to format it with a hanging indent as shown here.

Justification: The microcomputer has more than proved itself to be a valuable office tool during the past two decades since its inception. In numbers alone, it has shown that people are demanding and using their computers. In 1980, $1 billion worth of microcomputers had been sold; in 1990 that figure reached beyond $50 billion. Microcomputers have consistenly increased in speed and efficiency. The storage capacity, processing speed, and power of the microcomputer are the most competitive marketing tactics in use by vendors. Another keen focus of the microcomputer community has been in the development of software programs. Where micros initially were capable of running only a single, and somewhat limited, program at a time, they now run very complex and sophisticated programs that do more for the user and perform faster.

The user interface is also important. Users want operating systems and software that are easy to use and take a minimum amount of time to learn. This has been provided by both the Macintosh system and the IBM personal computers and compatibles.

To indent the next paragraph

44. Move the insertion point to any position in the paragraph beginning, **The user interface . . .**

45. Press **Ctrl/N** to indent the entire paragraph one tab stop. The indented first line remains indented as shown here.

capacity, processing speed, and power of the microcomputer are the most competitive marketing tactics in use by vendors. Another keen focus of the microcomputer community has been in the development of software programs. Where micros initially were capable of running only a single, and somewhat limited, program at a time, they now run very complex and sophisticated programs that do more for the user and perform faster.

The user interface is also important. Users want operating systems and software that are easy to use and take a minimum amount of time to learn. This has been provided by both the Macintosh system and the IBM personal computers and compatibles.

To format the **Programs:** paragraph with a hanging indent

46. Move the insertion point to any position in the Programs paragraph.

47. Press **Ctrl/H.**

To format the bulleted paragraphs with indents

48. Move the insertion point to any position in the first bulleted paragraph.

49. Press **Ctrl/N.**

50. Repeat steps 48 snd 49 for the two remaining bulleted paragraphs. These last paragraphs should look like the following example.

Programs: Word processing was perhaps the most popular use of microcomputers in the early years of software development; however, other software programs were also heavily used. Among the most popular programs were those for file management and spreadsheet applications. Today, many programs are available. Nearly any need for a particular application can be met. Among some of the popular ones in use today are:

- Very sophisticated word processing programs capable of outputting graphic images, using tables, performing calculations, and merging documents, to name a few.
- Database management programs are not only more sophisticated, but easier to use and capable of handling complex queries on multiple tables.
- Spreadsheet programs offer worksheets that hold thousands of cells and perform quick calculations.

To use the mouse to change the tab settings in the tabular columns

51. Select all lines in the tabular columns as shown here.

Integrated programs may include:

Word Processing ....A document tool
Spreadsheet ....A numbers tool
Database ....A facts collection tool
Communications ....A sending/receiving tool
Draw ....A graphics tool

52. Point — to the Left tab stop at .5 as shown here

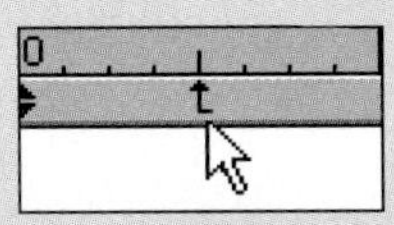

53. Hold — down the left mouse button and drag the tab set arrow to **1** in the Ruler. Release the mouse button. The selected text in the first column moves automatically to align with number 1 in the Ruler.

With the text still selected

54. Point — to the Right tab stop at 5.5 as shown here

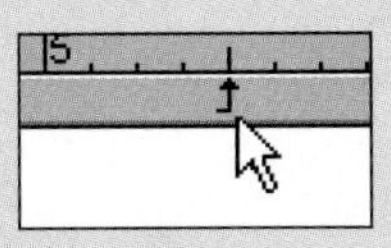

55. Hold — down the left mouse button and drag the tab set arrow to the left to **5**. Release the mouse button. The selected text in the second column moves automatically to the left. Your text should now resemble the following example.

Integrated programs may include:

Word Processing . . . . .A document tool
Spreadsheet . . . . .A numbers tool
Database . . . . .A facts collection tool
Communications . . . . .A sending/receiving tool
Draw . . . . .A graphics tool

56. Save — the document as **CH5TUT1B.**

57. Print — the document and close the window.

REVIEW QUESTIONS

1. Name the keystrokes that can be used for each of the following actions.

________	Indent all lines of a paragraph one tab stop.
________	Format a paragraph with a hanging indent.
________	Center all lines of a paragraph.
________	Move indented lines of a paragraph back one tab stop to the left.
________	Restore normal paragraph formatting.
________	Remove a hanging indent.
________	Align all lines of the paragraph at the right margin.
________	Justify all lines of the paragraph.
________	Double-space all lines in a paragraph.

2. The following dialog box can be displayed by choosing ________, ________.

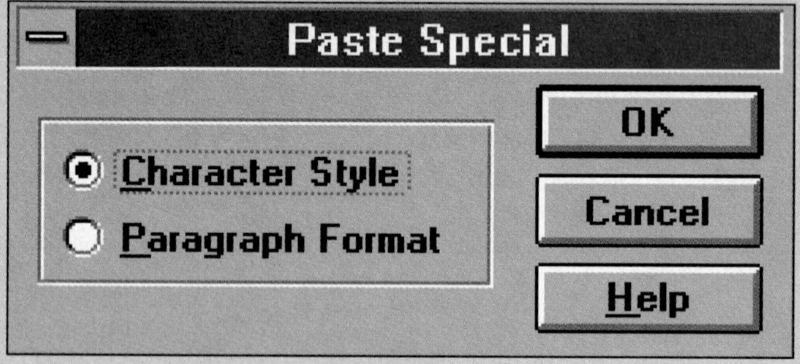

3. The following dialog box can be displayed by choosing ________, ________.

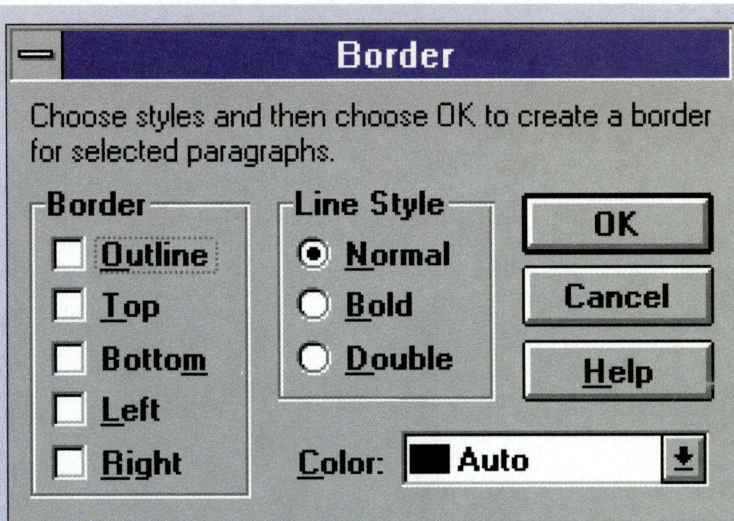

4. The following dialog box can be displayed by choosing ______________________, ____________________________.

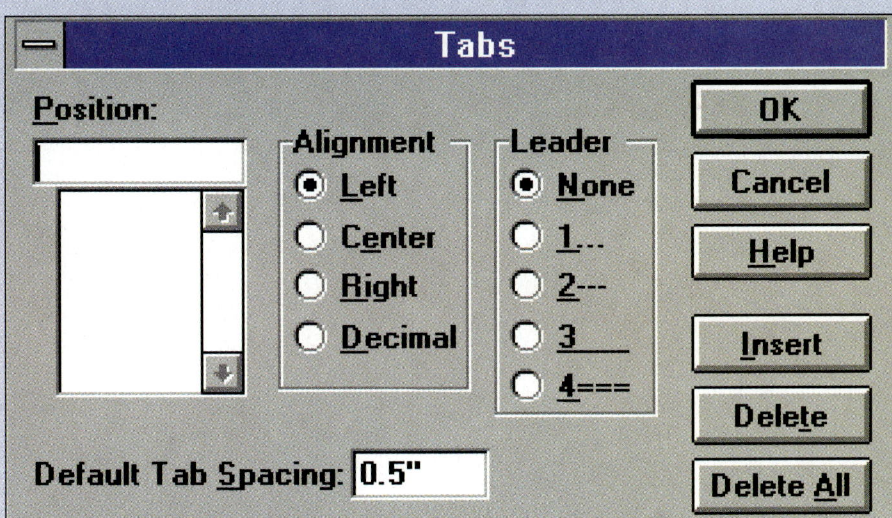

5. Name and describe what each of the following buttons can do.

____

____

____

Hands-on Exercises

Exercise 1

1. Retrieve the document **CH5TUT1B** that you created in the Guided Tutorial section here in Chapter 5, or retrieve it from the Instructor's data disk.
2. Add the following text at the bottom of the document. Leave a single blank line below the table before adding this text. Format the paragraphs as follows:
   - First paragraph-use a hanging indent.
   - Bulleted list-indent one tab stop (press **Ctrl/N** once.)
   - Paragraph following bulleted list-indent all lines one tab stop.
   - Last paragraph-use a hanging indent.

Need: The point at which a company needs to make a decision about the purchase of a microcomputer or other computer equipment can vary. Some of the major factors include:

- Increased volume of paperwork
- Need for additional office personnel
- Difficulty in locating information quickly
- Excessive time spent in organization
- Lack of proper backup of company-related documents

When the efficiency of an office seems to be less than at its peak, it is probably time for an analysis of the situation, as in the case of Puget Sound Charters.

Results: This team has spent the past month monitoring the activities performed on a daily basis at Puget Sound Charters and, as a result, arrived at the following account of time and money spent on individual activities.

3. Run a spell check on the document and proof the content.
4. Double-space the document except the top heading, the itemized lists, and the table. Press **Enter** twice at the end of each paragraph to insert two blank lines between each paragraph.
5. Save the document as **CH5HO1**.
6. Print the document.

Exercise 2

1. Open the document **CH5HO1** if necessary.
2. Move the **Need:** paragraph, including the itemized list and its following paragraph, to just above the **Justification:** paragraph.
3. Add the following table at the bottom of the document. If necessary, press **Enter** twice following the last paragraph to insert two blank lines before typing the table. Use your own judgment in setting the tab positions (you can drag the tab stops to different positions after typing the text, if you think they need to be changed). However, set tab types as follows:

   Left tab stop for the first column
   Right tab stop for the second column
   Decimal tab stop for the third column
   Reset the tab stops for the headings, using center tab stops for all three.

Activity	Average Time	Average Overall Cost
Typing	4.5 hours	45.00
Editing and revisions	3.0 hours	30.00
Photocopying	1.5 hours	35.00
Mailing activities	1.0 hours	20.00
Printing services	NA	15.00
Accounting	6.0 hours	120.00
Advertising	4.0 hours	100.00

4. After the last line of the tabular columns, press **Enter** twice and restore the default tabs.
5. Add the following paragraphs beginning on the second blank line below the table. Format as shown.

Summary: It is the recommendation of this team that time could be saved in all the activities observed during the past month. Time spent making revisions of documents could be lessened through the use of a word processing program. Many observations of documents being completely retyped were made.

Photocopies are being made of all documents. This is the only method of making multiple copies to send to clients, company personnel, and others. While a photocopy is a good copy, it is not as good as an original, and it costs more. It is far less expensive to print multiple copies using a good letter-quality printer or laser printer than to photocopy pages.

Mailing activities include typing original mailing labels. Again, a database file and a word processing program would eliminate the need to retype frequently used mailing labels. The labels can also be used to merge with form letters and a file in a database program to gather information about clients' needs.

The same observations are true for the printing and accounting expenses and some of the advertising expenses. Many of the printing services could be eliminated with either a sophisticated word processing program or a desktop publishing program.

Recommendations: It is the recommendation of this team that the following equipment be purchased to increase productivity and decrease costs.
A personal computer using the DOS operating system.
A word processing program.
An accounting or spreadsheet program.
A database program
OR
An integrated software program, such as Microsoft Works, that includes word processing, graphics, spreadsheet, database, and communications capabilities.
A letter-quality or laser printer.

Information on cost will be provided early next month

6. Double-space this part of the document with the exception of the itemized list in the **Recommendations:** paragraph.
7. Create hanging indents of the **Summary:** and **Recommendations:** paragraphs to correspond to the previous paragraphs created in Exercise 1 and indent the other paragraphs in the **Summary:** section.

8. Format the list with bullets and indent each item (**Ctrl/N**) one tab stop.
9. Align the last paragraph at the left margin with no indents.
10. Copy the character formatting from **Justification** to all of the new headings: **Need:**, **Results:**, **Summary:**, and **Recommendations:**.
11. Run a spell check on the document.
12. Use Print Preview to see how the text is divided into pages. Make any adjustments by inserting blank lines or deleting unwanted extra spaces between paragraphs.
13. Save the document as **CH5HO2**.
14. Print the document.

Exercise 3

1. Retrieve **CH4HO3** from your data disk.
2. Select and bold the main heading.
3. Select the main heading, and change the font and point size to any other font in a larger size.
4. Center the main heading.
5. Preview the document to note the changes.
6. Center the four categories following the first paragraph.
7. Indent the first paragraph using the Tab key.
8. Preview the document.
9. Save the document as **CH5HO3** and print a copy.

Exercise 4

1. Retrieve **CH4HO4** from your data disk.
2. Center and bold the main heading.
3. Justify the left and right margins of the entire document. To do this, select the entire document, and choose **Format, Paragraph, Indents and Alignment, Justified.**
4. Select and create hanging indents for paragraphs 1 through 4.
5. Double space the first paragraph in the document (not the itemized, numbered paragraphs).
6. Preview and print a copy of the document with the numbered paragraphs.
7. Change the numbered paragraphs to bulleted paragraphs. To do this, select the paragraphs and click on the Bullet button. Be sure to delete each paragraph number, and the period and the tab mark following each number.
8. Add the text in the following box to the bottom of the document. Set appropriate tabs for each column. Use center tabs for the column headings and left align tabs for column data below the headings.

Total damages reported due to employee mishaps.

Employee	Division	Mishap
Kyler Graham	Food Service	Tripped on customer's foot; soiled carpet
Linette Alvarado	Food Service	Spilled coffee in customer's lap
Chad Palafox	Galley	Started fire on galley range
Edward Mahoney	Deck Hand	Dropped line in water causing engine to tangle

9. Preview the document and make any necessary adjustments.
10. Run a spell check
11. Save the document as **CH5HO4** and print a copy.

Examples Of Exercises

Exercise 2: CH5HO2

PUGET SOUND CHARTERS
NEEDS ANALYSIS
Report Presented to Management
for Computer Equipment Purchases

Introduction

This is a needs analysis requested by the management of Puget Sound Charters. The management team is interested in researching the possibility of purchasing computer equipment for the office to increase productivity.

Need: The point at which a company needs to make a decision about the purchase of a microcomputer or other computer equipment can vary. Some of the major factors include:

- Increased volume of paperwork
- Need for additional office personnel
- Difficulty in locating information quickly
- Excessive time spent in organization
- Lack of proper backup of company-related documents

When the efficiency of an office seems to be less than at its peak, it is probably time for an analysis of the situation, as in the case of Puget Sound Charters.

Justification: The microcomputer has more than proved itself to be a valuable office tool during the past two decades since its inception. In numbers alone, it has shown that people are demanding and using their computers. In 1980, $1 billion worth of microcomputers had been sold; in 1990 that figure reached beyond $50 billion. Microcomputers have consistently increased in speed and efficiency. The storage capacity, processing speed, and power of the microcomputer are the most competitive marketing tactics in use by vendors. Another keen focus of the microcomputer community has been in the development of software programs. Where micros initially were capable of running only a single, and somewhat limited, program at a time, they now run very complex and sophisticated programs that do more for the user and perform faster.

The user interface is also important. Users want operating systems and software that are easy to use and take a minimum amount of time to learn. This has been provided by both the Macintosh system and the IBM personal computers and compatibles.

Programs: Word processing was perhaps the most popular use of microcomputers in the early years of software development; however, other software programs were also heavily used. Among the most popular programs were those for file management and spreadsheet applications. Today, many programs are available. Nearly any need for a particular application can be met. Among some of the popular ones in use today are:

- Very sophisticated word processing programs capable of outputting graphic images, using tables, performing calculations, and merging documents, to name a few.
- Database management programs are not only more sophisticated, but easier to use and capable of handling complex queries on multiple tables.
- Spreadsheet programs offer worksheets that hold thousands of cells and perform quick calculations.

Many programs, such as Microsoft Works, combined these tools into a single application, thus making it easy to move quickly from one application to another and to integrate applications.

Integrated programs may include:

Word Processing .... A document tool

Spreadsheet .... A numbers tool

Database .... A facts collection tool

Communications....... A sending/receiving tool

Draw........................ A graphics tool

Results: This team has spent the past month monitoring the activities performed on a daily basis at Puget Sound Charters and as a result arrived at the following account of time and money spent on individual activities

Activity	Average Time	Average Overall Cost
Typing	4.5 hours	45.00
Editing and revisions	3.0 hours	30.00
Photocopying	1.5 hours	35.00
Mailing activities	1.0 hours	20.00
Printing services	NA	15.00
Accounting	6.0 hours	120.00
Advertising	4.0 hours	100.00

Summary: It is the recommendation of this team that time could be saved in all the activities observed during the past month. Time spent making revisions of documents could be lessened through the use of a word-processing program. Many observations of documents being completely retyped were made.

Photocopies are being made of all documents. This is the only method of making multiple copies to send to clients, company personnel, and others. While a photocopy is a good copy, it is not as good as an original, and it costs more. It is far less expensive to print multiple copies using a good letter-quality printer or laser printer than to photocopy pages.

Mailing activities include typing original mailing labels. Again, a database file and a word processing program would eliminate the need to retype frequently used mailing labels. The labels can also be used to merge with form letters and a file in a database program to gather information about clients' needs.

The same observations are true for the printing and accounting expenses and some of the advertising expenses. Many of the printing services could be eliminated with either a sophisticated word processing program or a desktop publishing program.

Recommendations: It is the recommendation of this team that the following equipment be purchased to increase productivity and decrease costs.

- A personal computer using the DOS operating system.
- A word processing program.
- An accounting or spreadsheet program.
- A database program
  OR
- An integrated software program, such as Microsoft Works, that includes word processing, graphics, spreadsheet, database, and communications capabilities.
- A letter-quality or laser printer.

Information on cost will be provided early next month.

Exercise 3: CH5HO3

OFFICE COSTUME PARTY

Next month the office will have its semi-annual costume party. Plan now to attend this semi-annual event. The Ebenezer prize will be awarded to those not attending and/or not appearing in costume. Awards will be given in the following categories:

Most elaborate

Funniest

Most original

Worst

CHAPTER 6

Built-In Word Processing Assistance

OBJECTIVES

Change document window views

Place and use bookmarks

Use the thesaurus

Insert special characters

Create an envelope

PREVIEW

In this chapter, special features that are available in Works for Windows will be used to speed up and enhance document production. You will change the window so that the document can be viewed and edited in various ways. Bookmarks will be created that mark locations in the document and will then be used to go quickly to that location. In addition, you will learn how to use the Thesaurus and how to create envelopes. (You will not print envelopes here, because the process varies depending upon your particular printer and you may not be able to insert envelopes.)

CHANGING VIEWS

The options available in the View menu are used to change the way text is displayed in the window and to allow editing. When you start the word processor, the default view is *Normal,* which means that text is displayed as it is formatted and shows any pictures or other objects. *Page Layout* view displays not only the formatting and pictures but also shows headers, footers, and footnotes. Working in this view is slower than in Normal view. You can change to *Draft* view which is the fastest view, but it does not display different font types and sizes, nor does it show headers and footers, other formatting, or pictures. You can also use *Zoom* to increase or decrease the size of the text that is displayed.

NOTE: **File, Print Preview** also displays text, but it does not allow editing.

Use Page Layout

The default view is Normal. Here you will change to Page Layout so that you can see the margins and line endings as they will be printed.

1. Retrieve **CH5PR2B** or retrieve it from the Instructor data disk.
2. Choose **View, Page Layout.** Your screen should resemble Figure 6-1.

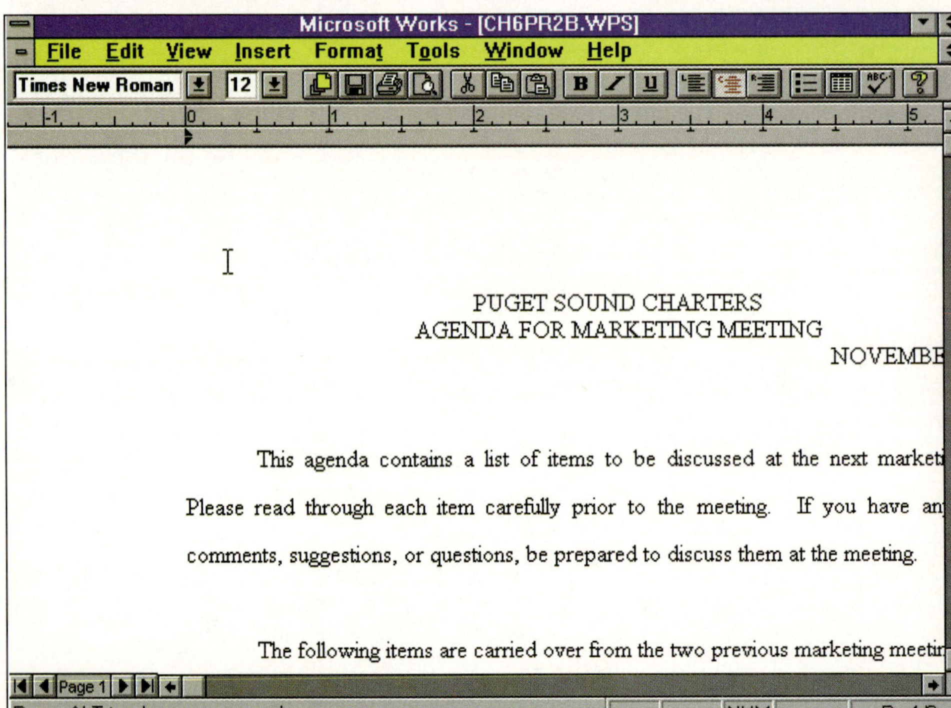

Figure 6-1
Document in Page Layout view

Notice the change in the Ruler. Also, the margins are displayed on the screen as the document will be printed.

3. Click — on the up arrow in the vertical scroll bar. As you do this the top edge of the paper will be displayed as shown here.

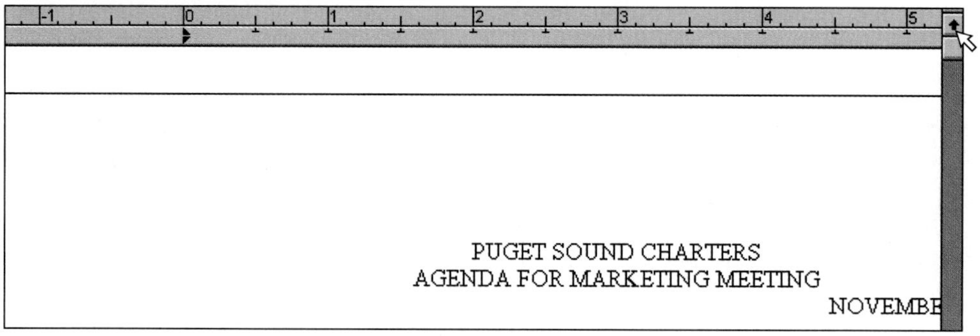

4. Click — on the left arrow in the horizontal scroll bar to display the left edge of the paper as shown in the following illustration.

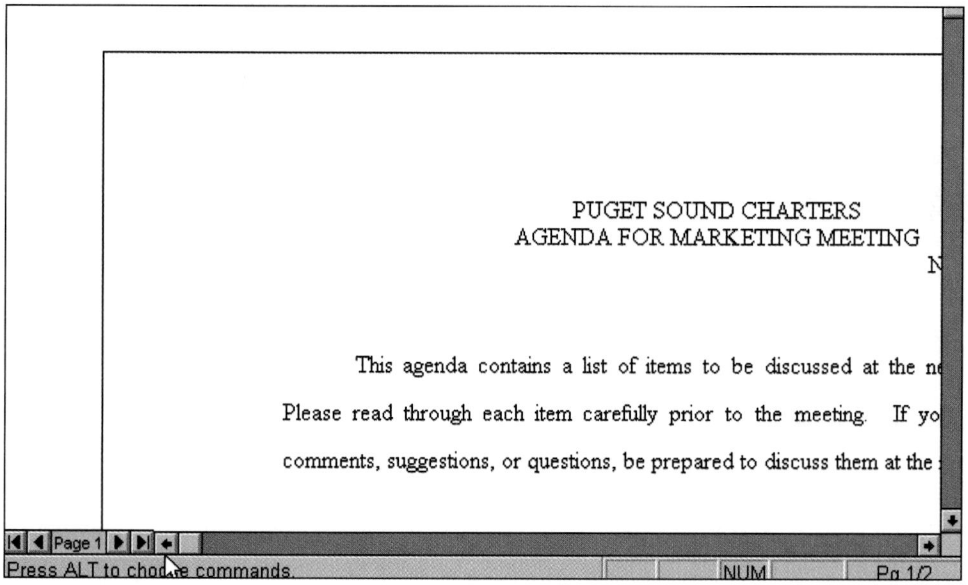

5. Scroll — through the document by clicking on the arrows in the vertical and horizontal scroll bars to see other portions of the document.

Use Draft View

Draft view will show the text in one font type and size and will not show any formatting.

1. Choose **View, Draft View**. Your screen should now resemble the example shown in Figure 6-2.
2. Scroll through the document to see the entire text. The insertion point moves very quickly from one point to another whether you use the mouse or the arrow keys.

NOTE: If your text does not look exactly as shown in Figure 6-2, you may have **Wrap for Window** turned off. To turn it on, choose **View, Wrap for Window**. Be sure a check mark is in front of the option. Wrap for Window shows the entire line on the screen, but this is not necessarily the line endings as it will be printed. Page Layout view shows the exact line endings.

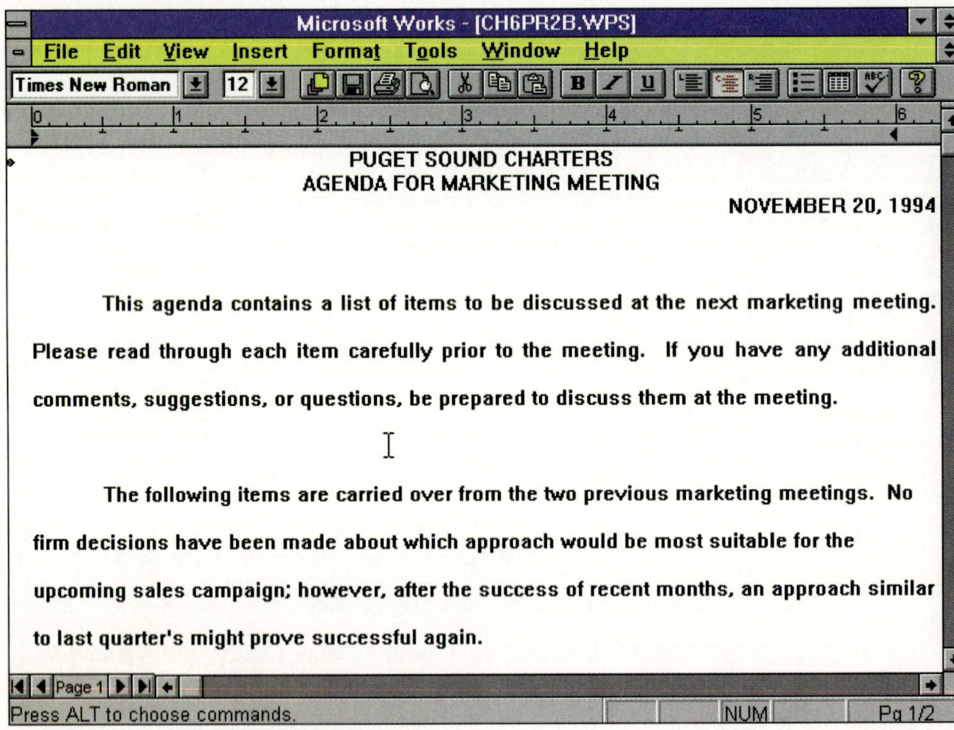

Figure 6-2
The document in Draft view

Use Zoom

The Zoom option in the View menu allows you to increase the size of the display so that you can see the way text formatted in various font types and sizes will be printed. Or you can decrease the display so that you can see more text on the screen at one time.

1. Choose **View, Normal** to return to Normal view to see the different font types and sizes that have been used.
2. Choose **View, Zoom** to display the Zoom dialog box as shown in Figure 6-3.

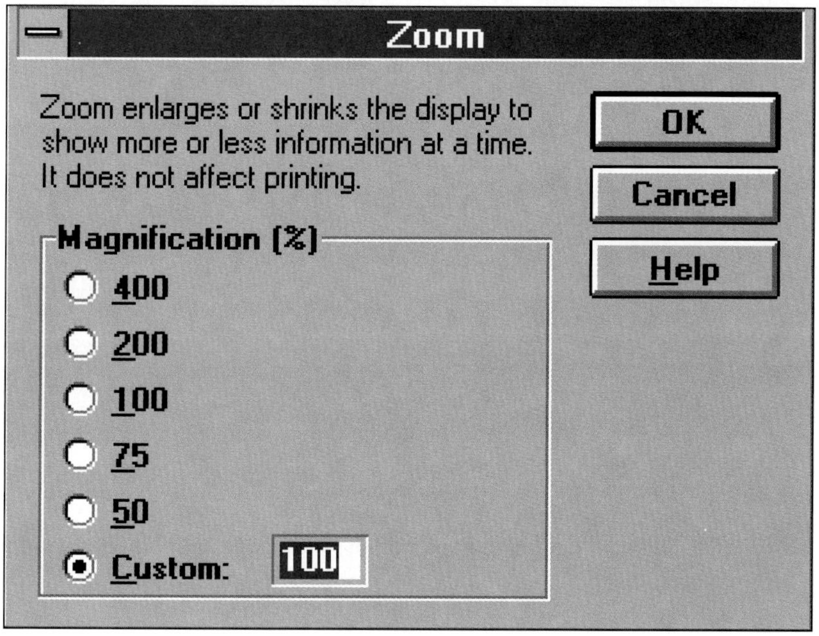

Figure 6-3
The Zoom dialog box

3. Choose 400 to display the largest percentage increase. The default Normal view is 100% magnification.
4. Choose **OK** or press **Enter** to return to the document window which now shows the text as displayed in Figure 6-4. The line endings have changed so that text can be displayed on the screen. You can easily see exactly how the formatting for the font type and size will be printed.

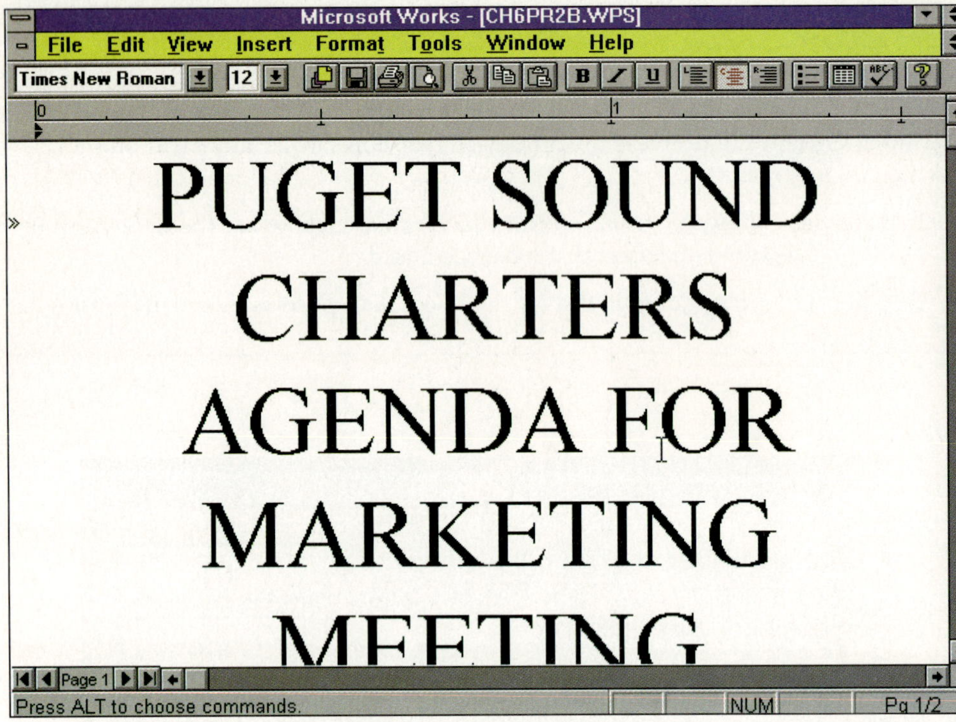

Figure 6-4
The document in Zoom 400% view

5. Scroll through the document to see other portions of text as it is displayed in Zoom view.
6. Choose **V̲iew, Z̲oom** again to display the Zoom dialog box.
7. Choose 0 to decrease the size of the display.
8. Choose **OK** or press **Enter** to return to the document. Your screen should resemble Figure 6-5. You can see more text; however, the font type and size are not as easily seen.

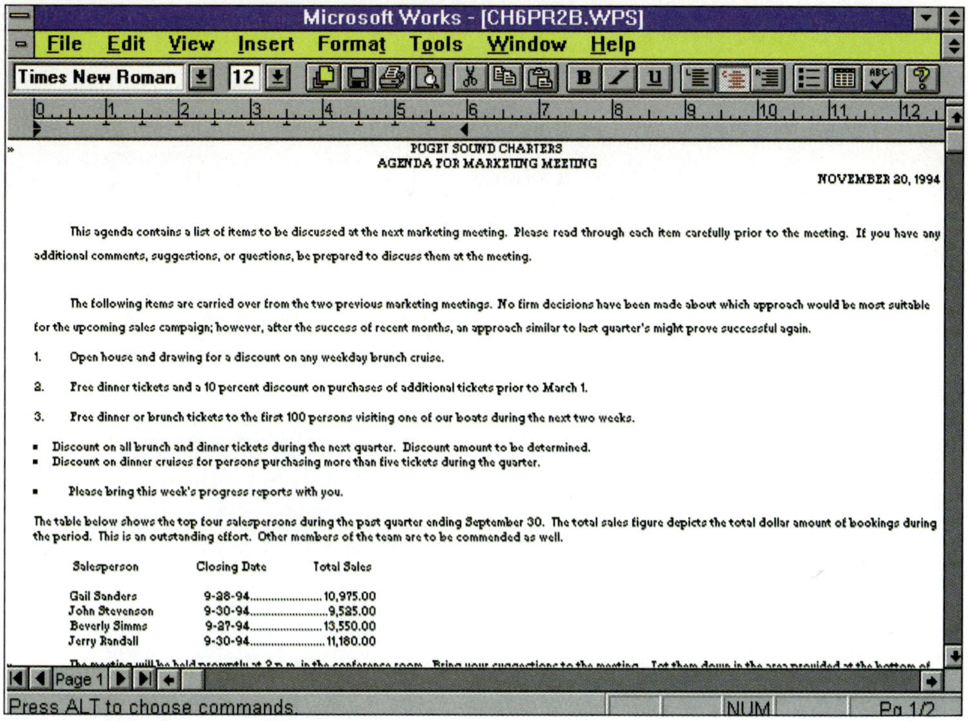

Figure 6-5
The document in Zoom 50% view

To return to normal view

9. Choose **View, Zoom.**

NOTE: You can customize the settings, if you like, by choosing **Custom** and entering a percentage other than the choices that are available in the Magnification box in the Zoom dialog box

10. Choose 100 to return to the percent of magnification for Normal view.
11. Choose **OK** or press **Enter** to return to the document.

PLACING BOOKMARKS

Bookmarks are hidden markers that you place at specific positions in the document that enable to you go directly to these marks when you want to locate certain text. These are particularly useful in long documents. In this section, a bookmark will be placed at the table in the **CH5PR2B** document so that you can go quickly to that area of text.

Insert Bookmarks

1. Open the document **CH5PR2B** if it is not already opened.
2. Move the insertion point to **Salesperson** in the header line of the table.
3. Choose **Insert, Bookmark Name** to display the Bookmark Name dialog box as shown in Figure 6-6.

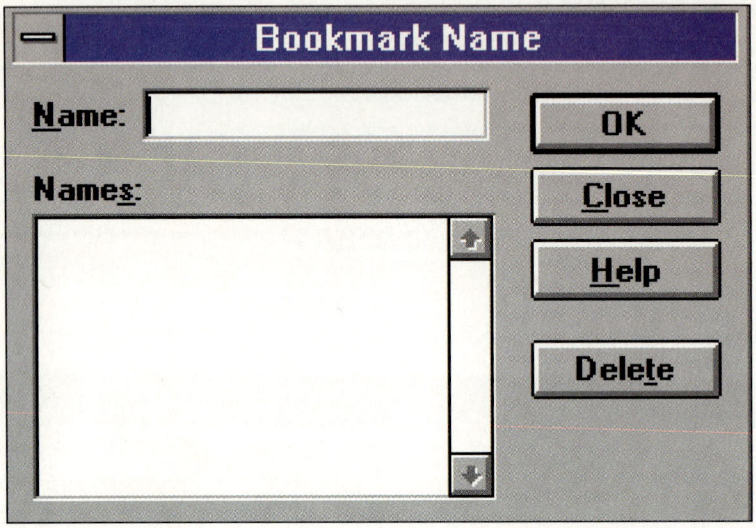

Figure 6-6
The Bookmark Name dialog box

4. Type **Sales table** in the **Name** box as shown in the following illustration.

5. Choose **OK** or press **Enter** to return to the document.

NOTE: You can enter as many characters as you like for the name; however, only 15 characters are displayed.

Use A Bookmark

The advantage of placing a bookmark is that you can go quickly to that location.

To go to the bookmark **Sales table.**

1. Move the insertion point to the end of the document. (It can actually be at any position.)
2. Choose **Edit, Go To** or press **F5** to display the Go To dialog box as shown in Figure 6-7. The bookmark name is now displayed here. It is also in the **Bookmark Name** dialog box.

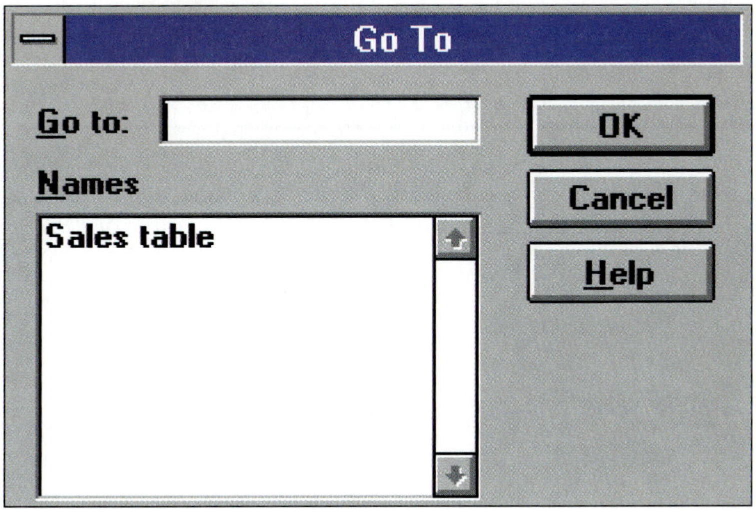

Figure 6-7
The Go To dialog box

3. Click on **Sales table** or press **Tab** and the **Down Arrow** to select it. **Sales table** is now displayed in the **Go to** text box as shown in Figure 6-8.

Figure 6-8
The Go To dialog box showing the bookmark selection

4. Choose **OK** or press **Enter** to go immediately to **Salesperson** at the beginning of the table.

   NOTE: You can delete a bookmark by choosing **Insert, Bookmark Name,** selecting the bookmark you want to remove, and choosing **Delete.** The bookmark name is removed from the Names list box. Choose **OK** or press **Enter** to return to the document.

5. Save the document as **CH6PR1** and print one copy. The bookmark is saved in the file.

USING THE THESAURUS

The Thesaurus is a valuable aid in composing text. It contains synonyms—words with the same meaning as a word you are using. When you use it, a dialog box will be displayed that lists alternate words that can be used to replace the word in the text.

Use The Thesaurus

1. Open the file **CH4PR2** that you used in the spell check in Chapter 4, or retrieve it from the Student data disk.
2. Move the insertion point to any position in the word **location** in the third paragraph.
3. Choose **Tools, Thesaurus** to display the Thesaurus dialog box as shown in Figure 6-9.

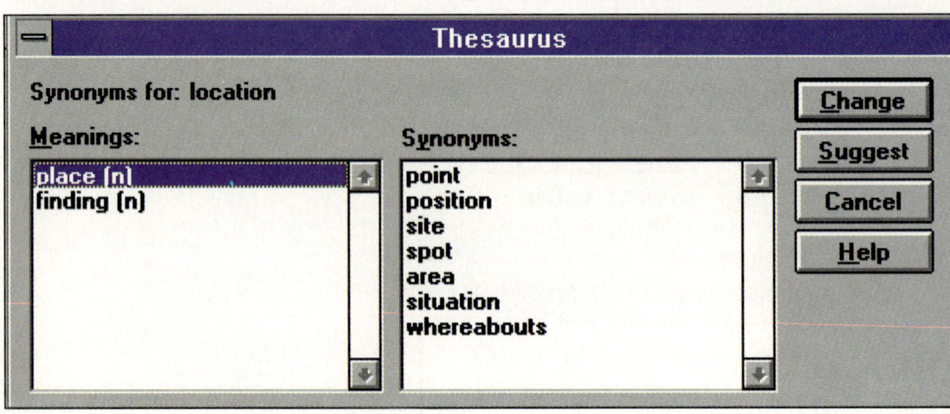

Figure 6-9
The Thesaurus dialog box

The **Meanings** box at the left of the screen shows the meanings and corresponding part of speech for the selected word. The **Synonyms** box on the right shows a list of possible alternate words for the selected word in the **Meanings** box. When you select another word in the **Meanings** box, the list of synonyms changes.

4. Choose **site** as the new word-either click on it or press **Tab** and the **Down Arrow** enough times to select it.
5. Choose **Change** to return to the document and replace the word **location** with the word **site**.

NOTE: You can see other words that are synonyms for the selected word by choosing **Suggest**. When you find a word that you want, then select it and choose **Change** to replace the word in the document with the new word. Experiment with this as time permits.

6. Save the document as **CH6PR2**.

INSERTING SPECIAL CHARACTERS

This feature allows you to insert characters that will automatically perform a variety of functions, such as printing the current date or time, printing the page number or filename, or inserting types of hyphens or line endings. The current date option will be used here; however, Table 6-1 lists all available special characters options and describes each.

Print The Date

When you insert an instruction to print the date, the current date will be printed regardless of when the document was created. The advantage here is that you can use the document repeatedly and each time it is printed, the date will change to reflect the date when it is printed. If you choose to insert **Current date** or **Current time**, the current date and current time will be inserted in the document; however, this information will not be updated if the document is printed on a different date.

1. Open the document **CH3TUT1** that you created in the guided tutorial in Chapter 3 or retrieve it from the Instructor data disk.

2. Delete the line containing the date and leave the insertion point on that line.
3. Choose **Insert, Special Character** to display the **Special Character** dialog box as shown in Figure 6-10.

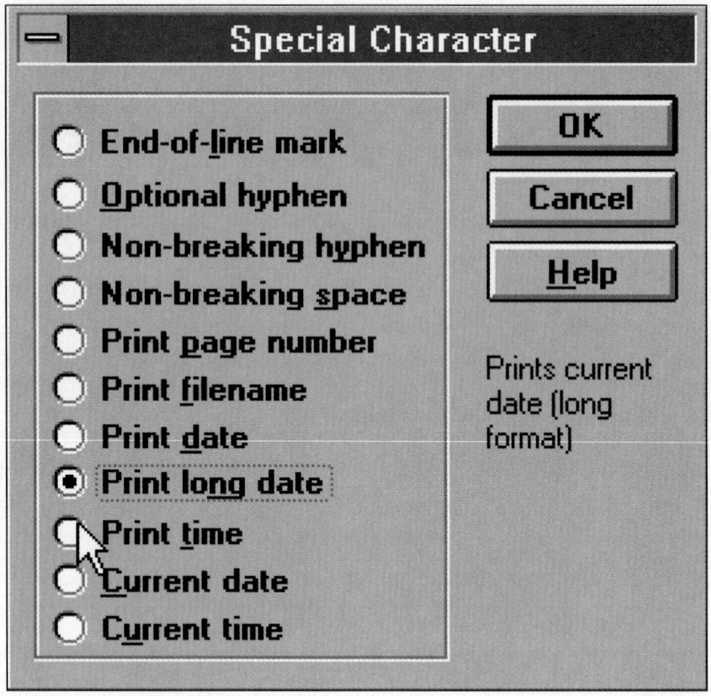

Figure 6-10
The Special Character dialog box

4. Choose **Print lo<u>n</u>g date.** (See the pointer in Figure 6-10.) The long date option prints the date as **November 15, 1994,** for example. The **Print date** and the **Current date** options print the date as **11/15/94.** Be sure a dot is showing in the radio button as shown in Figure 6-10.

5. Choose **OK** or press **Enter** to return to the document. The code ***longdate*** is displayed as shown in the following illustration.

longdate

Ms. Rebecca Barnes
1907 Seventh Avenue S.E.
Bellvue, WA 98005

To see the date that will be printed, use Print Preview.

6. Choose **File, Print Preview.** The date in the long format is shown at the place where the ***longdate*** field is inserted. To view the text, click with the left mouse button to zoom (increase) the size of the display as displayed in the following illustration.

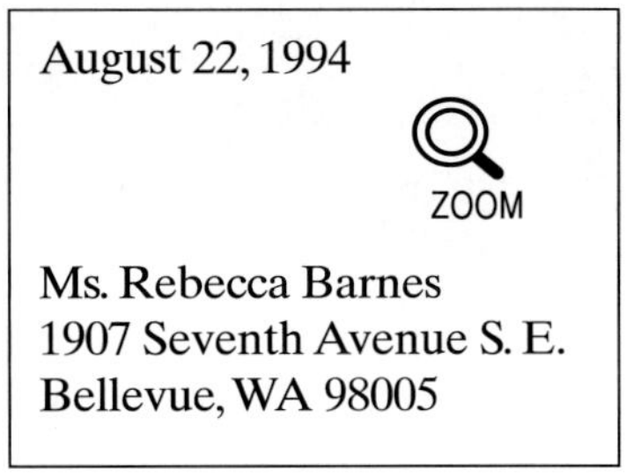

7. Choose **Cancel** when done viewing to return to the document.
8. Save the document as **CH6PR3A.**

Other Special Characters

Table 6-1 lists the other options in the Special Character dialog box. The procedure for inserting any of these characters is the same as inserting the current date.

Character		Description
End-of-line mark	↵	Inserts a mark that begins a new line with-out starting a new paragraph. This is used to keep several lines or a table together formatted as one paragraph.
Optional hyphen	-	Inserts a hyphen in a word at the place where you would want the word to be divided if it appeared at the end of a line. The hyphen shows only when the word is hyphenated; otherwise it is hidden. It will be displayed, however, if you turn on View, All Characters.
Nonbreaking hyphen	-	Inserts a hyphen in compound words such as mother-in-law. This hyphen keeps all of the words together on one line. They will not break at the end of a line.
Nonbreaking space		Inserts a space between words that you want to keep together on one line, such as titles, addresses, or dates. A nonbreaking space will prevent these words from breaking at the end of a line.
Print page number ***page***		Inserts a placeholder that will print the current page number.
Print filename ***filename***		Inserts a placeholder that will print the name of the current file with the document.
Print date ***date***		Inserts a placeholder that will print the current date whenever the document is printed. The format is 10/10/94, for example.
Print long date ***longdate***		Inserts a placeholder that will print the current date whenever the document is printed. The long format is October 10, 1994, for example.
Print time ***time***		Inserts a placeholder that will print the current time whenever the document is printed. The format for the time is 11:45 AM.
Current date		Inserts the current date in the document. The format is 10/10/94. The date is not updated if the document is printed on a different day.
Current time		Inserts the current time in the document. The format is 11:45 AM. The time is not updated if the document is printed at a different time.

Table 6-1

The Special Characters options

USING ENVELOPES

You can address and print an envelope for the current document. The envelope is created at the beginning of the document. If you do not have an envelope feeder for your printer, you can insert the envelope manually to print it. In this section, only instructions for creating an envelope will be covered. You will not print an envelope because printers vary: and, in your specific situation, you may not be able to insert envelopes.

Create An Envelope

1. Open the document **CH6PR3A** if it is not already opened.

   NOTE: If the document is open but is not in the active window, choose **Window** and select **CH6PR3A** to make it active.

2. Choose **Tools, Envelopes and Labels** to display the **Envelopes and Labels** dialog box as shown in Figure 6-11.

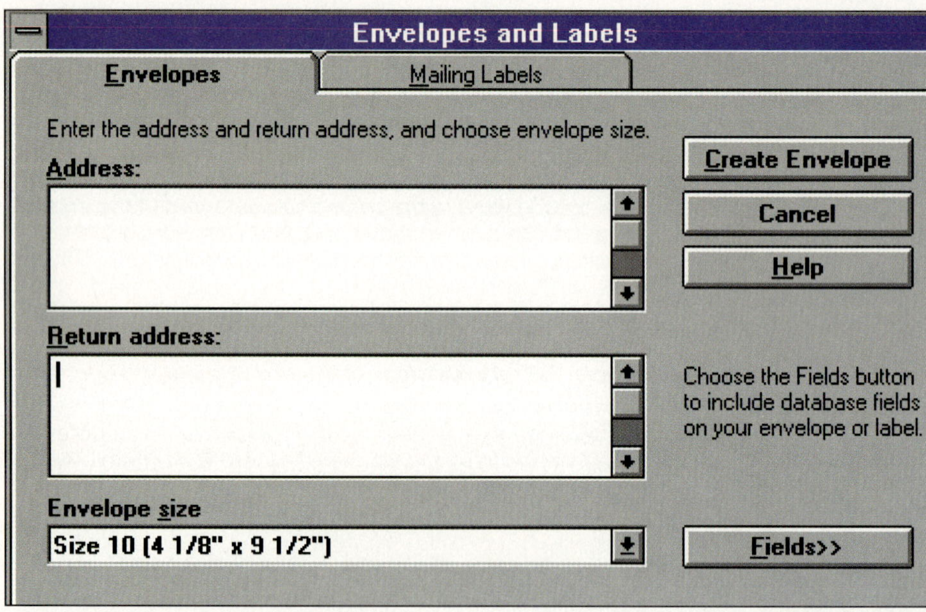

Figure 6-11
The Envelopes and Labels dialog box

The default envelope size is 10 (4 ⅛" x 9 ½"), which is the standard business envelope size. A variety of envelope sizes are available if you click on the down arrow at the right end of the **Envelope size** list box as shown in the following illustration. For now, use the Size 10 envelope.

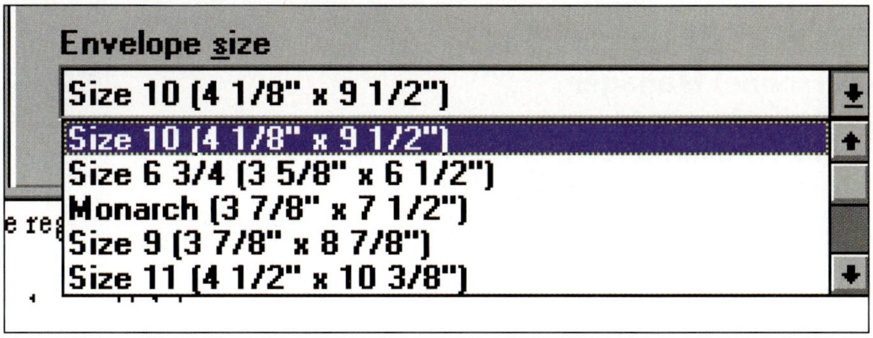

3. Choose **Address** to return to the **Address** text box if you looked at the envelope sizes. You can either click on the **Address** text box or press **Alt/A** to do this.

4. Type the address in the **Address** text box as shown here. Press **Enter** at the end of each line in the address.

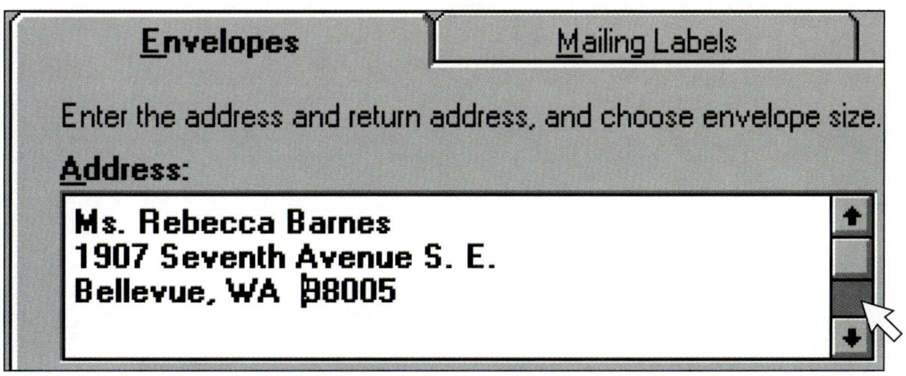

5. Choose **Return address** to move to the **Return Address** text box. You can click on the **Return Address** text box or press **Alt/R** to do this.

NOTE: If a different address is displayed here, it means the dialog box was used previously. Select the entire address and press **Delete** to remove it.

6. Type the following for the return address: Press **Enter** at the end of each line.

   George Bellfield
   Personnel Manager
   Data Enterprises
   1111 Redmond Ave.
   Redmond, WA 98555

7. Scroll up and down through the text box to proofread all lines. The text box only displays four lines, but additional lines can be seen by moving up and down in the box. See the following illustration.

8. Choose **Create Envelope** to return to the document. An envelope is now displayed at the beginning of the document as shown in Figure 6-12.

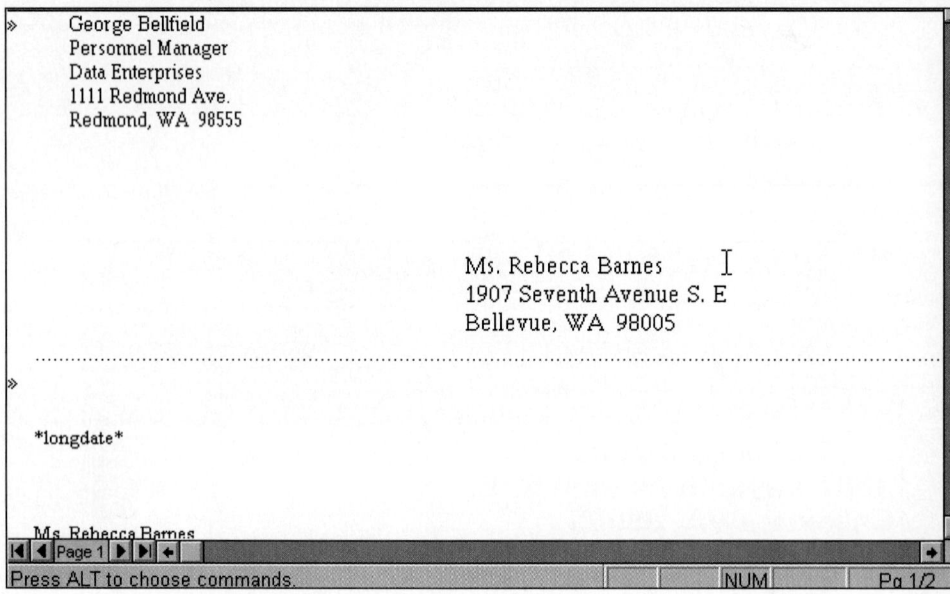

Figure 6-12
The envelope for the current document

Print The Envelope

The following instructions show you how to print, but you will not actually print the envelope here. The instructions tell you when to choose **Cancel** to avoid printing.

1. Insert an envelope in the paper tray or bin, or in the manual feeder if that is necessary.

If you have an envelope feeder

2. Choose **Tools, Options** to display the Options dialog box as shown in Figure 6-13.

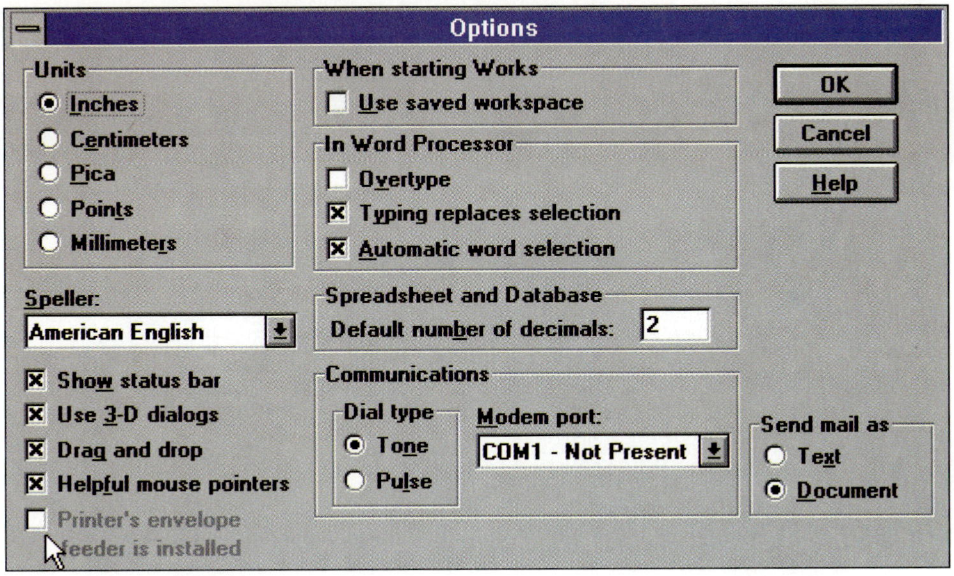

Figure 6-13
The Options dialog box

3. Choose **Printer's envelope feeder is installed** to display a check mark in the box. (If you do not have an envelope feeder this option will be dim and you cannot check it.) If an envelope feeder is installed and a checkmark is displayed in the box shown in Fgiure 6-14, the feeder will be used automatically when the envelope is printed. If you do not have an envelope feeder, or if this box is not checked, you will be prompted to insert the envelope manually.

4. Choose **OK** or press **Enter** to return to the document.

To print

5. Choose **File, Print** or press **Ctrl/P** to go to the Print dialog box as shown here in Figure 6-14.

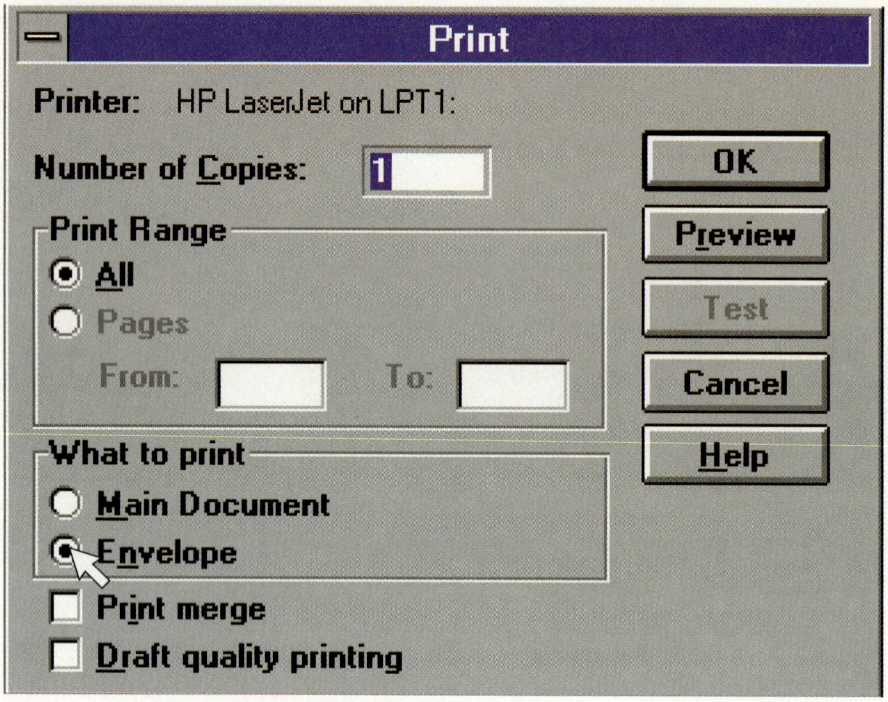

Figure 6-14
The Print dialog box

6. Choose **Envelope** to turn it on if it is not already turned on. If your insertion point is in the envelope section of the active document when you go to the Print dialog box, then **Envelope** is automatically chosen.

7. Choose **Preview** to see how the envelope will look when printed as shown in the following illustration. You can return to the document and make adjustments if you like.

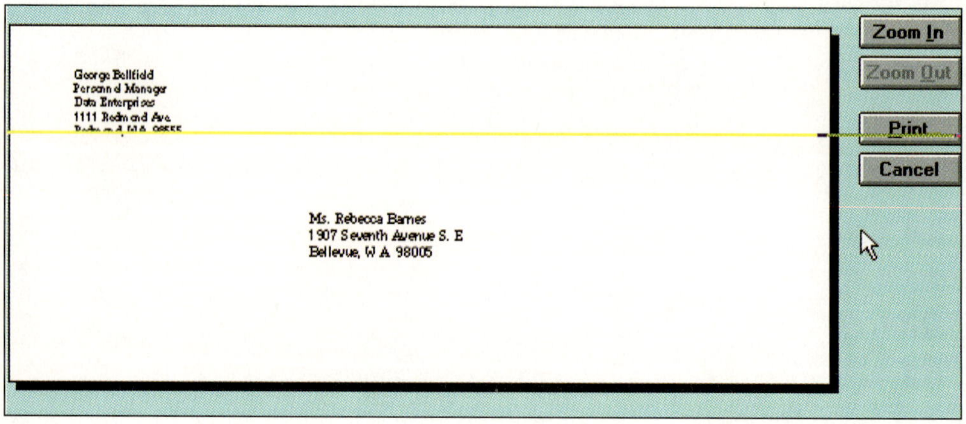

8. Choose **Print** to return to the Print dialog box.
9. Choose **Cancel** at this point. Do not print the envelope.
10. Save the document as **CH6PR3B**. This saves the envelope with the letter.

Print The Document

1. Choose **File, Print** or press **Ctrl/P**.
2. Choose **Main Document.**

NOTE: If your insertion point is moved to the letter rather than the envelope, **Main Document** is turned on automatically.

3. Choose **OK** or press **Enter** to print.
4. Close all opened documents. Save any changes, if prompted to do so.

GUIDED TUTORIAL

What You'll Do

- Create a memo.
- Insert a special character that will show the current date.
- Use Replace.
- Use the spell checker.
- Use the Thesaurus to edit text.
- Create an envelope. (Do not print the envelope).

How To Do It

The document you will be creating is shown in the box below.

TO: Roberta Melbourne
FROM: (type your name)
DATE: (insert current date)
SUBJECT: Word processing slides

Here are the word processing slides you requested. A check for $25, to cover processing and duplication, may be sent directly to me. Note that I have added a few slides to the series since the program at the recent Arizona Computer Education meeting. They are:

New software products
New computer monitors
Upgrades in laser printers
Advances in software products

I do not have a script for the slides. If you have questions about any of them, please drop me a line or give me a call. Note that I have numbered the slides. If you have a question, you can refer to them by number.

1. Open — a new blank word processing window or retrieve **CH6TUT1A** from the Instructor data disk.
2. Type — the first two lines in the memo. Press **Tab** twice between **TO:** and **Roberta Melbourne**. Also, depending upon the size of font you are using, you may have to press **Tab** twice following **FROM:** to align your name under **Roberta Melbourne**.

To insert the current date

3. Type — **DATE:** and press the **Tab** enough times to align the text under **Roberta Melbourne**.
4. Choose — **Insert, Special Character** and turn on **Current date** as shown in the following illustration.

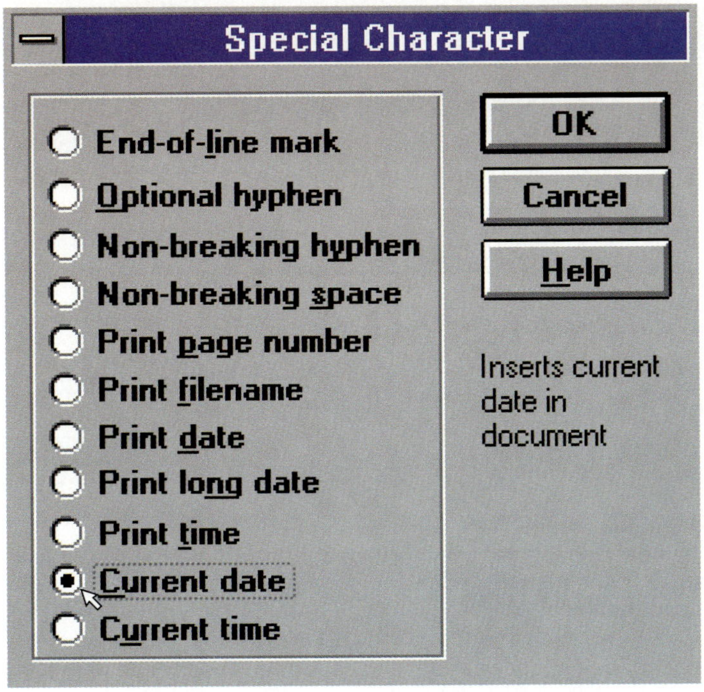

5. Choose **OK** or press **Enter** to insert the current date.

6. Type the remainder of the document as shown in the box on page 175 .

NOTE: If you are using a proportionally spaced font such as Times New Roman and if you are in Normal view, the alignment of text following the guide words may not be displayed as it will be printed. Choose **View, Page Layout** to see how the text will look when printed. If necessary, make any adjustments by deleting or adding tabs.

To add a heading MEMORANDUM centered at the top of the page

7. Press **Ctrl/Home** to go to the top of the document.

8. Press **Enter** three times to insert blank lines, and then move the insertion point to the top line.

9. Click on the Center button .

10. Click on the Bold button **B** .

11. Type **MEMORANDUM**. Press **Caps Lock** to type this in uppercase.

To use Replace to change "slides" to "films"

12. Move the insertion point to the beginning of the document.

13. Choose **Edit, Replace** to display the Replace dialog box.

14. Type **slides** in the **Find What** text box.

15. Choose **Replace With** and type **films** in the **Replace With** text box as shown in the following illustration.

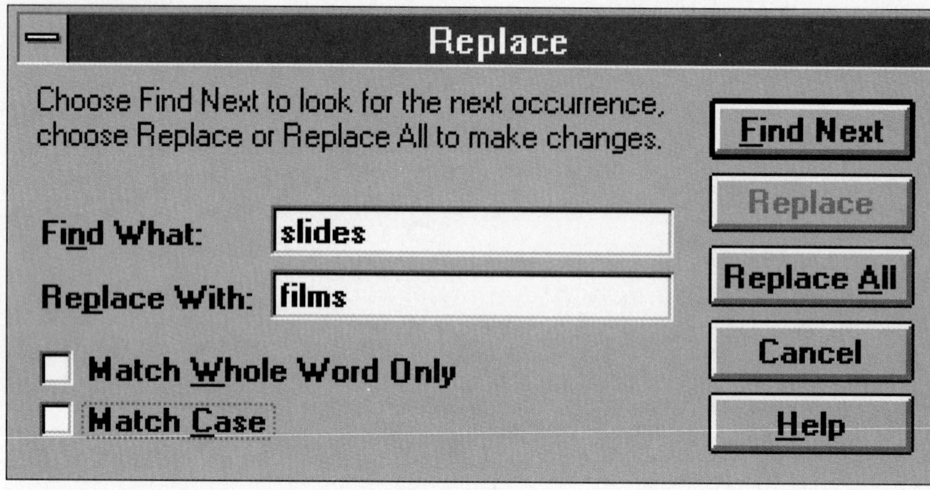

16. Choose **Find Next** to go to the first occurrence of **slides.**

17. Choose **Replace All** to replace all occurrences of **slides** with the word **films.**

18. Choose **Close to remove the Replace dialog box and return to the document.**

To use the thesaurus to look for a new word in place of duplication

19. Move the insertion point to **duplication** in the first paragraph.

20. Choose **Tools, Thesaurus** to display the Thesaurus dialog box as shown in the following illustration.

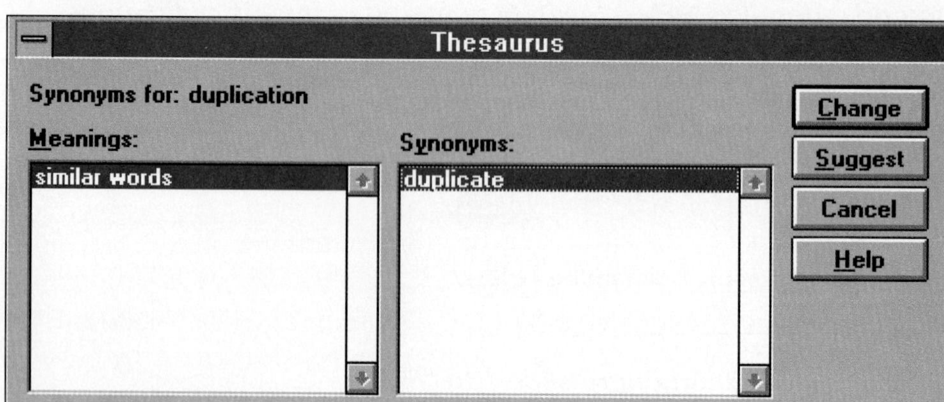

At this point, no new words are shown in the **Meanings:** box. The word **duplicate** is in the **Synonyms:** list boxes.

21. Choose **Suggest** 

. A list of new words is now displayed in both list boxes as shown in the following example.

NOTE: The word **duplicate** has now replaced the word **duplication** following **Synonyms for:** because that was the word display originally in the **Synonyms:** list box.

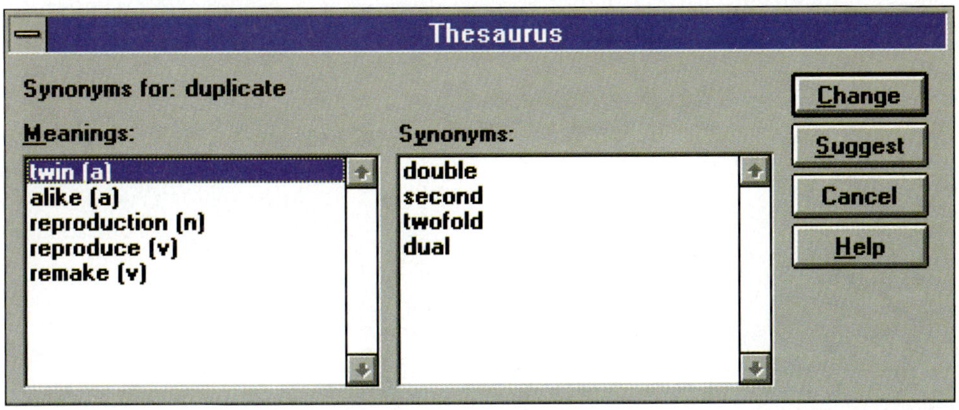

22. Choose **reproduction** to highlight it as shown here. A new list of synonyms is displayed.

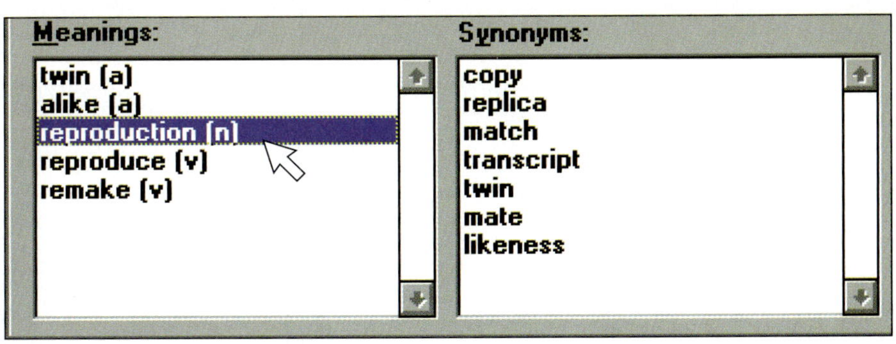

23. Choose **Change** 

to replace **duplication** with **reproduction** in the document.

To add bullets to the list

24. Move the insertion point to the beginning of the line **New Software products.**

25. Select all four lines in the list by dragging from the first line to the last line.

26. Click on the Bullets button.

27. Click anywhere away from the selected text to remove the highlighting.

To run a spell check

28. Click on the Spelling Checker button or choose **Tools, Spelling** to display the Spelling dialog box as shown in the following illustration. The text that is displayed depends upon the position of the insertion point when you started the spell check.

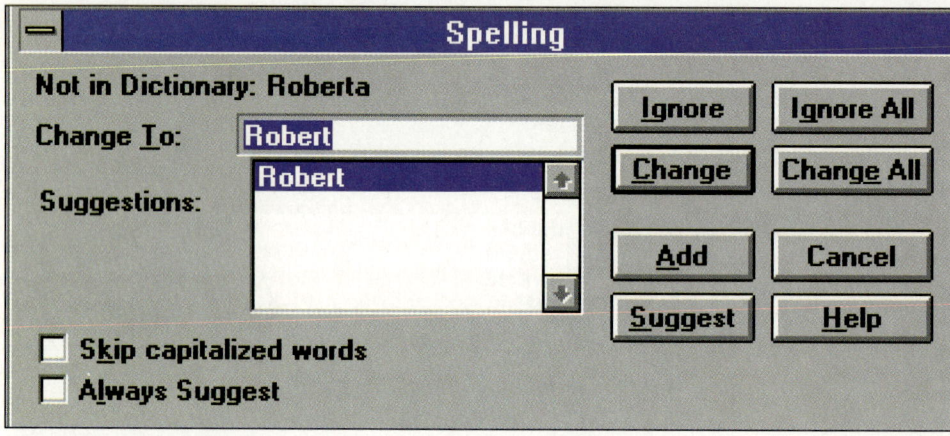

29. Respond to the choices in the Spelling dialog box depending upon the errors or the words not in the dictionary that are in your document.

To create an envelope

30. Choose **Tools, Envelopes and Labels** to display the Envelopes and Labels dialog box as shown in the following example.

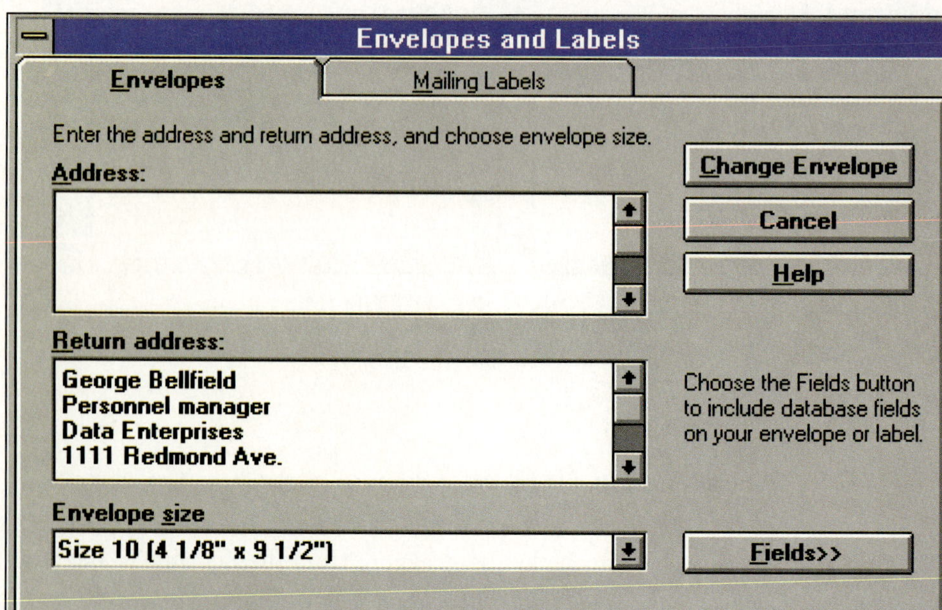

The previous address is displayed in the **Return address** text box.

31. Type the following address for Roberta Melbourne in the **Address** text box.

Ms. Roberta Melbourne
Training Supervisor
CompuTech, Inc.
1000 Denali St.
Anchorage, AK 99503

32. Choose **Return address**-either click on the box or press **Alt/R** to do this. All lines in the text box will be selected automatically. Press **Delete** to remove the previous return address.

NOTE: If this were the return address that you usually used, it is convenient to have it always displayed here and not have to retype it each time you address an envelope.

33. Type your address in the **Return address** text box.

34. Choose **Create Envelope** when done. (Do not print the envelope.)

To print the document

35. Choose **File, Print** and turn on **Main Document** as shown in the following example.

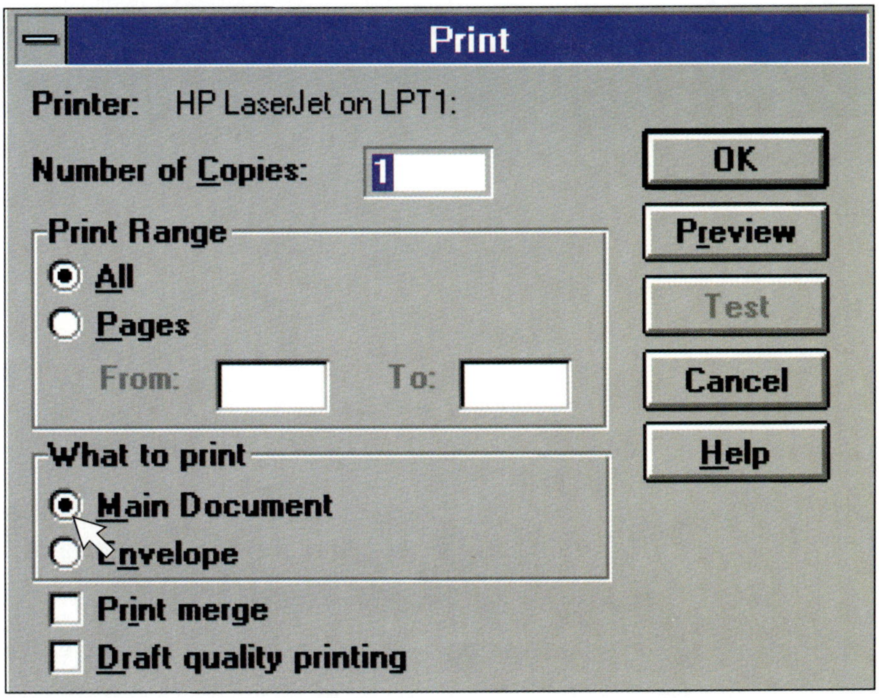

36.	Choose	**OK** or press **Enter** to print.
37.	Save	the document as **CH6TUT1B.**
38.	Close	the document.

REVIEW QUESTIONS

1. Identify the type of view chosen for each of the following examples.

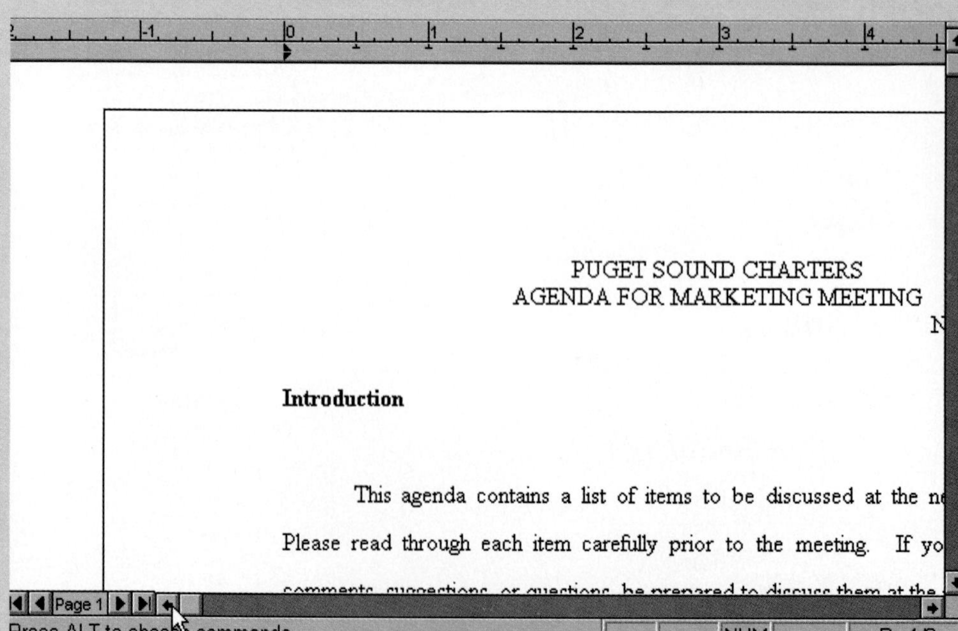

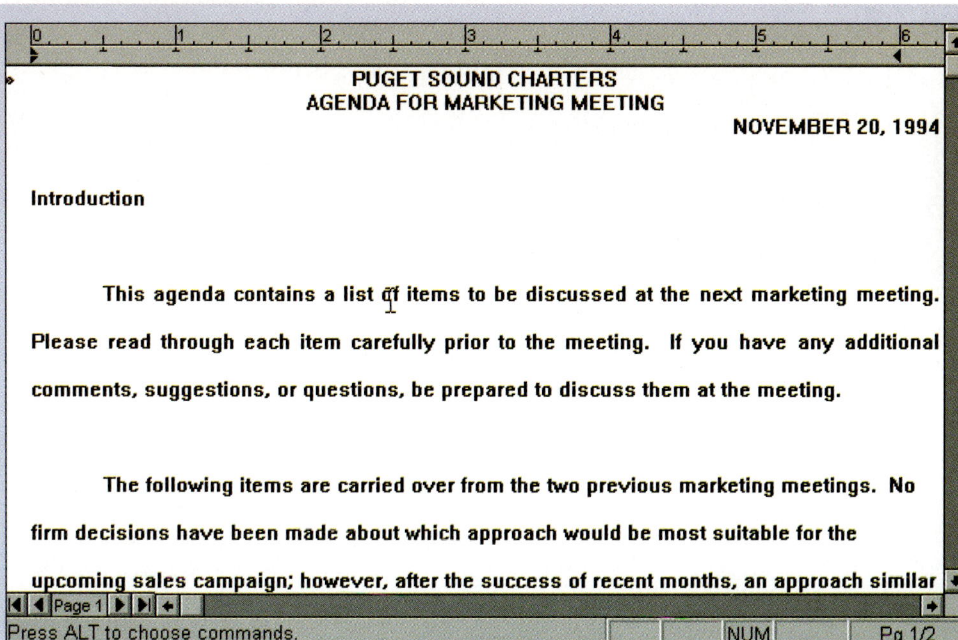

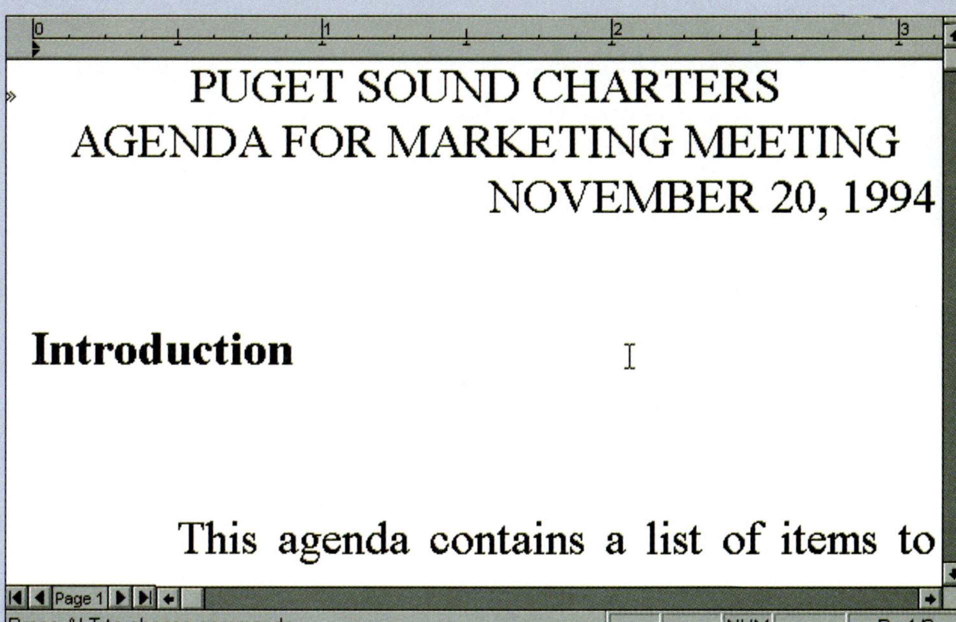

2. A bookmark is placed in a document by choosing ______________________, __________________________ from the menu bar.

3. You can go to a bookmark by choosing ____________________________, __________________________ from the menu bar.

4. Delete a bookmark by choosing ______________________________, ______________________________ from the menu bar.

5. Choose ______________________ ______________________ to create an envelope.

6. Identify each of the following features in the Thesaurus dialog box and describe its function.

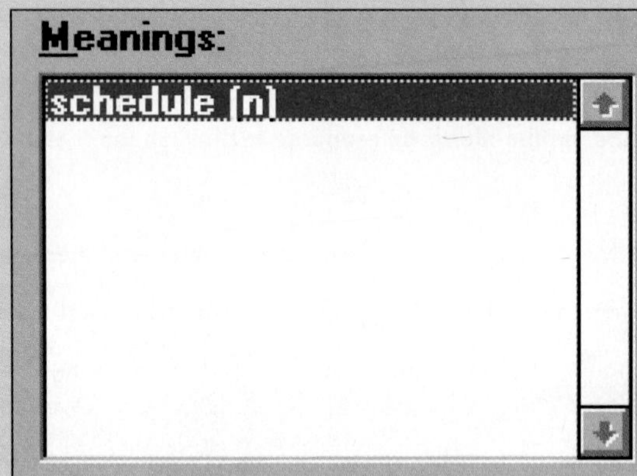

____

____

____

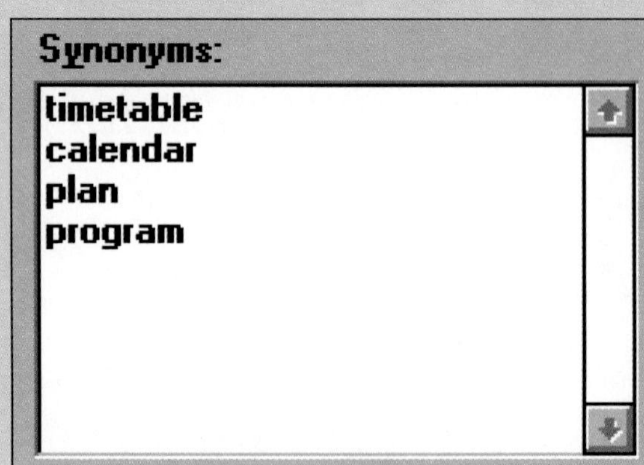

____

____

____

____

____

____

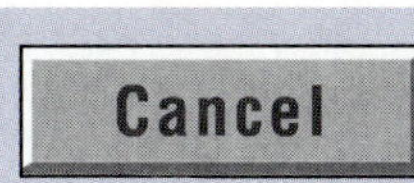

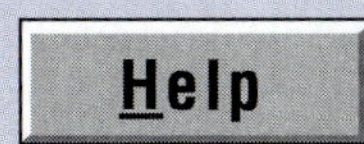

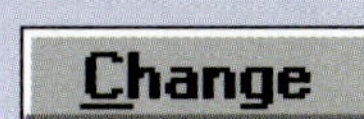

7. Match each of the following descriptions with the correct special character.

________ Prints the time automatically when the document is printed.

________ Displays the filename of the active document in the text.

________ Keeps two hyphenated words together on one line.

________ Displays the current page number in the text.

________ Prints the date automatically when the document is printed and uses the format April 15, 1994, for example.

________ Ends a line without ending the paragraph.

________ Inserts the time in the document, but does not update it.

A. Current time
B. Current date
C. Print time
D. Print long date
E. Print date
F. Print filename
G. Print page number
H. Nonbreaking space
I. Nonbreaking hyphen
J. Optional hyphen
K. End-of-line mark

Hands-on Exercises

Exercise 1

1. Open the document **CH4HO2** as shown below, or retrieve the following document from the Instructor data disk.

> CONTRACT
>
> This contract will confirm the agreement between Puget Sound Charters and Lake Union Caterers covering the handling of all catering duties on cruises during the next year. Lake Union Caterers will provide brunch and dinner meals according to the following terms and conditions agreed upon by both parties.
>
> The terms and conditions are set forth as follows:
>
> 1. All conditions to this contract shall be agreed upon by both parties. Puget Sound Charters will maintain the right to cancel this contract if Lake Union Caterers fails to provide services set in this contract.
>
> 2. Catering shall include a full brunch buffet each Saturday and Sunday unless otherwise specified. It shall further include dinner meals Tuesday through Friday unless otherwise specified by Puget Sound Charters.
>
> 3. Puget Sound Charters hereby commissions Lake Union Caterers to prepare brunch and dinner meals for all scheduled cruises during the next calendar year.
>
> 4. In consideration of the services to be provided by Lake Union Caterers, Puget Sound Charters will pay them at a rate of $25 per meal.
>
> 5. In consideration of the services to be provided by Lake Union Caterers, Puget Sound Charters will pay them at a rate of $30 per hour for services.
>
> This agreement shall be in effect as of January 1, 1995, and will continue through December 31, 1995, or until the contract is terminated by one of the parties.

2. Center and underline the main heading **CONTRACT**.
3. Format the company names in the first paragraph in bold.
4. Format each of the numbered items with a hanging indent.
5. Format the last paragraph with a bullet.
6. Double-space the first paragraph in the contract.
7. Use a special character marker to insert the current date at the top of the document-centered two lines above the main heading.
8. Use the Thesaurus to find better words for the following:
   duties in the first paragraph
   specified in the first sentence in numbered paragraph 2

   NOTE: The synonyms that are displayed may not necessarily be the correct form of the word. For example, if you choose **identify** to replace **specified**, you will need to change it to **identified**.

9. Save the document as **CH6HO1**.
10. Preview the document and print it.

Exercise 2

1. Open a new, blank word processing window and type the letter shown in the following box.

(Insert Current date special character)

Teresa Chow, Owner
Lake Union Caterers
22525 Center Blvd.
Seattle, WA 98111

Dear Teresa:

During the last quarter, sales increased dramatically at Puget Sound Charters. We believe that this is due in part to increased emphasis on new marketing strategies. It is, however, important to bring to your attention that this could not have happened without the excellent service and attention your company has given to us.

As you know, prior to signing Lake Union Caterers on as our primary caterer late last year, we had been experiencing some difficulty finding responsible, competitive, and friendly catering services. We had experimented with several catering companies prior to our first experience with yours. That first experience was a memorable one and led to many others, and finally, to a full-time permanent contract.

A successful charter business cannot be that without the effort of many persons from many different directions. Timeliness is one of the most critical factors, and you have always been there on time and ready to go.

Thank you for your efforts and your part in making Puget Sound Charters so successful. We look forward to many more years of business with your company.

Sincerely,

P. J. MacRannall
President

2. Run a spell check on the document.
3. Use Find to locate all occurrences of the company name, **Puget Sound Charters**, and format it in italic.
4. Create an envelope for the letter to Ms. Chow. The return address is:

   P. J. MacRannall, President
   Puget Sound Charters
   West Lake Union Way
   Seattle, WA 98108

5. Save as **CH6H02**.
6. Print only the letter. Do not print the envelope.

Exercise 3

1. Retrieve **CH6HO3** from your data disk.
2. Choose a different font and point size for the main heading and date. Use Print Preview to view the change in the heading style.
3. Underscore each of the side headings: **Introduction, Outstanding Events, Past Successes, Building Future Successes,** and **Conclusion.**
4. Create a bookmark for each of the side headings.
5. Use the bookmark to locate the heading, **Outstanding Events**. Change **paragraphs a** and **b** to hanging indent paragraphs.
6. Double-space all text with the exception of paragraphs **a** and **b** in the Outstanding Events section.
7. Add the date two lines below the last paragraph in the document. Insert the Current date using the Special Character commands.
8. Preview the document. Zoom in on the text on page two. Return to the reduced mode when finished.
9. Save again as **CH6HO3** and print a copy.

Exercise 4

1. Retrieve **CH6HO3** from your data disk.
2. Use the Thesaurus to locate and find a new word for the word **focused** in the first paragraph.
3. Change paragraphs **a** and **b** in the Outstanding Events section to bulleted paragraphs. Delete the letters **a** and **b**.
4. Change the format for all paragraphs, including the bulleted paragraphs, to justified.
5. Preview the document.
6. Save the document under the new name **CH6HO4**. Print a copy.

Exercise 2: CH6HO2

Envelope

P. J. MacRannall, President
Puget Sound Charters
West Lake Union Way
Seattle, WA 98108

Ms. Teresa Chow, Owner
Lake Union Caterers
22525 Center Blvd.
Seattle, WA 98111

Letter (Your letter should show 4 blank lines between the date and address and between the complimentary close and signature name.)

11/17/93

Teresa Chow, Owner
Lake Union Caterers
22525 Center Blvd.
Seattle, WA 98111

Dear Teresa:

During the last quarter, sales increased dramatically at Puget Sound Charters. We believe that this is due in part to increased emphasis on new marketing strategies. It is, however, important to bring to your attention that this could not have happened without the excellent service and attention your company has given to us.

As you know, prior to signing Lake Union Caterers on as our primary caterer late last year, we had been experiencing some difficulty finding responsible, competitive, and friendly catering services. We had experimented with several catering companies prior to our first experience with yours. The first experience was a memorable one and led to many others, and finally, to a full-time permanent contract.

A successful charter business cannot be that without the effort of many persons from many different directions. Timeliness is one of the most critical factors, and you have always been there on time and ready to go.

Thank you for your efforts and your part in making Puget Sound Charters so successful. We look forward to many more years of business with your company.

Sincerely,

P. J. MacRannall
President

Exercise 4: CH6HO4

BUSINESS MEETING REPORT

May 5

Introduction

The fifth business meeting for the year was held on May 5. The primary agenda for the meetings was to discuss both past successes and past failures, although we in the company look at failures as potential successes; therefore, all agenda items were viewed in a positive light. In addition, discussion also concentrated on possible promotional issues for the busy, upcoming summer schedule. The following is a summary of key issues the company faces. Open discussion is encouraged among all employees, and feedback is desired by administrative personnel.

Outstanding Events

Several outstanding events were reported during the month of March. They included incidents involving passengers overboard, banana peels, near vessel collisions, and scrubbed chickens. Needless to say the administration and particularly the visiting vice president of the company found this news somewhat disturbing. All present agreed on the following steps (in order of priority) to assist in avoiding future incidents.

- All employees should read the manual on ship safety and focus in particular on steps to take when passengers fall into the sea.
- All employees should report any unseemly incidents immediately. They should focus in particular on dangerous objects that might cause accidents, such as the banana peel. If one approaches a potentially hazardous situation, the immediate action should be to make an announcement over the speaker system. Be sure to scream loudly into the speaker so that the message is heard by all on board. For example, "Watch out! Watch! Hand rail missing on stern deck."

Inform the administration or the captain of any and all other outstanding events as they may occur.

Past Successes

The most recent outstanding success story on board occurred last week when the governor visited the ship for dinner. The dinner and reception following could not have gone more smoothly. The main course included chicken legs in a banana cream sauce. Champagne was served (although it was accidentally placed near the galley ovens and so was served warm). Following the governor's speech, pictures with the captain and staff were scheduled. Somehow the captain's hat and jacket appeared on the galley chief just as the camera clicked. In the photo the galley chief's face was obscured from the oversized hat. The captain could not be found; however, no one, including the governor, seemed to notice and all had a very good time. We are delighted with the governor's timing. It seems she came down with severe chills and sweats the following morning-a reminder that we should all get our flu shots.

Building Future Success

As mentioned in the introduction, we do not focus on failures, but rather look at them as potentials for building success. Following the avoided collision (due to a lightning storm and the quick reactions of the captain) we have put the sales staff to work on increasing the number of cruises during the winter storm months. It is clear that lightning storms aid in a safer journey for our crew and passengers and so the number of trips should be increased on dark and stormy nights. We will also monitor the effects of other natural aids such as high winds, turbulent seas, and so on.

Conclusion

Your comments are welcome as always. We are collecting reports for the next outstanding events bulletin, and will keep you informed of important issues directly affecting you. More information is due out this week on the merit raises of .025 percent due to the top two employees of the year. Keep up the good work!

CHAPTER 7

Page Design

OBJECTIVES

- Change margins
- Insert page break
- Use paginate now
- Create headers and footers
- Create footnotes
- Print specific pages
- Format in columns
- Use landscape orientation

PREVIEW

This chapter focuses on the options available for customizing pages of text. These include adjusting margins, adding headers and footers, inserting page numbers, and entering manual page breaks. Also included in this chapter will be instructions for using landscape orientation and formatting text in newspaper style columns.

CHANGING MARGINS

One of the most frequently used procedures in page design is that of changing the margin settings so that text fits better on the page. You can change all margins or change only one. For example, if you want to bind the pages at the left, you can set a wider left margin. Or you can change the margin allowances for the headers and footers. The **Page Setup** command is located in the **File** menu.

Adjust the Margins

In this section, change the top and left margins in the agenda for marketing meeting document, **CH6PR1,** that you edited in Chapter 6.

1. Start   Works if it is not already running.
2. Open   the document **CH6PR1** or retrieve it from the Instructor data disk. Your screen should resemble Figure 7-1.

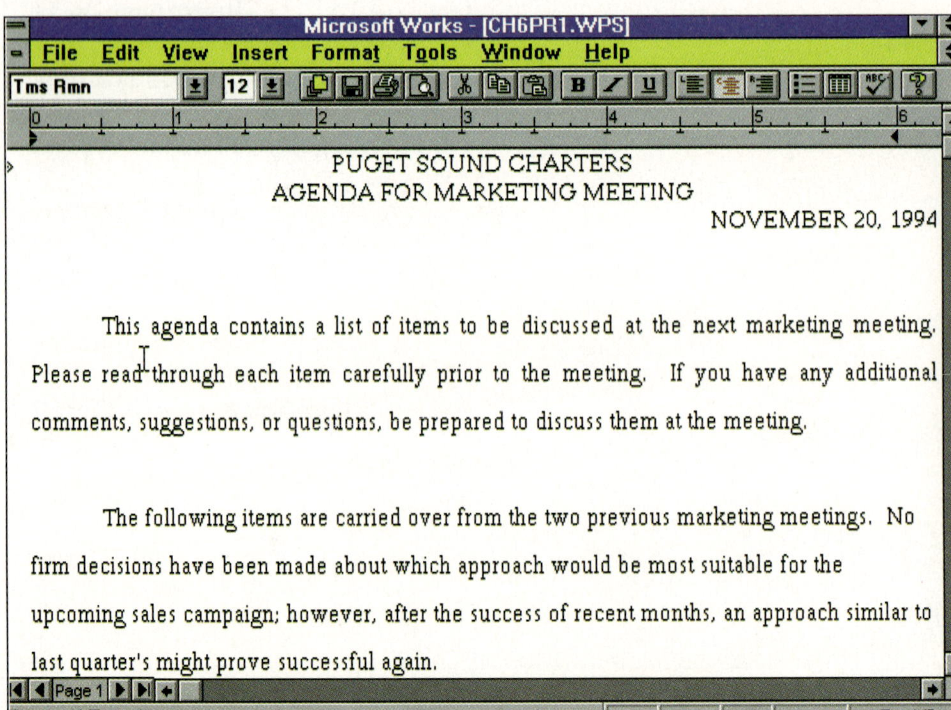

Figure 7-1
The Agenda for Marketing Meeting document

3. Choose **File, Page Setup** to display the Page Setup dialog box as shown in Figure 7-2. This dialog box is similar to the **Format, Paragraph** dialog box in that it contains three "file cards" (or tabs as Works calls them) that contain the options that affect page formatting.

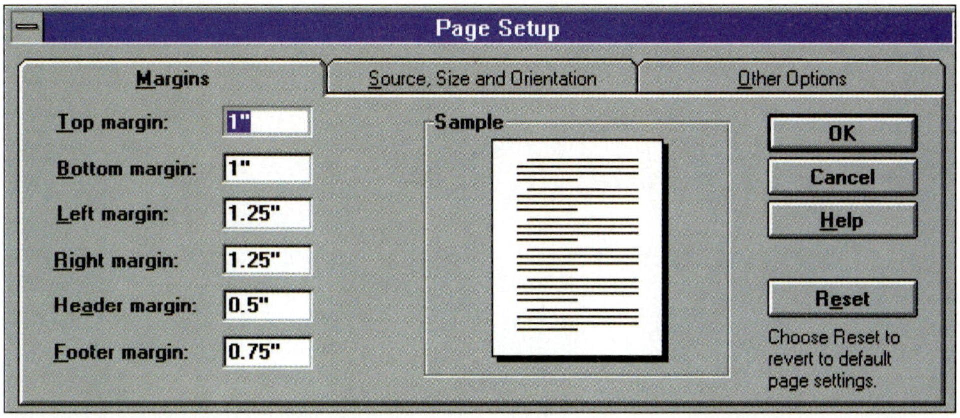

Figure 7-2
The Page Setup dialog box

The **Margins** tab is active and is used to change margin settings.

To change the top margin to 2"

4. Choose **Top margin**. It is probably already highlighted.
5. Type 2 in the text box as shown here. 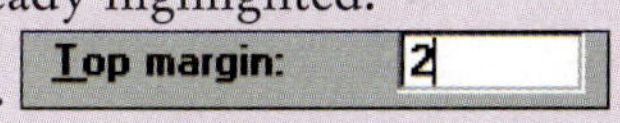

. As soon as you start typing, the previous default number is deleted.

To change the left margin to 1.5"

6. Choose **Left margin**. The default measurement is highlighted. Also notice that the Sample box at the right now reflects the new top margin setting as shown in the following example.

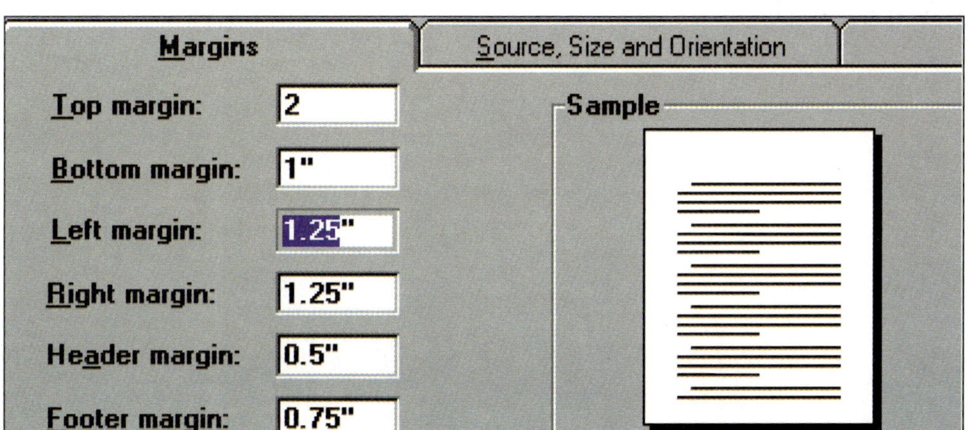

7.	Type	**1.5** for the new left margin setting.
8.	Select	any other margin text box to change the display to reflect the new left margin setting as shown here.

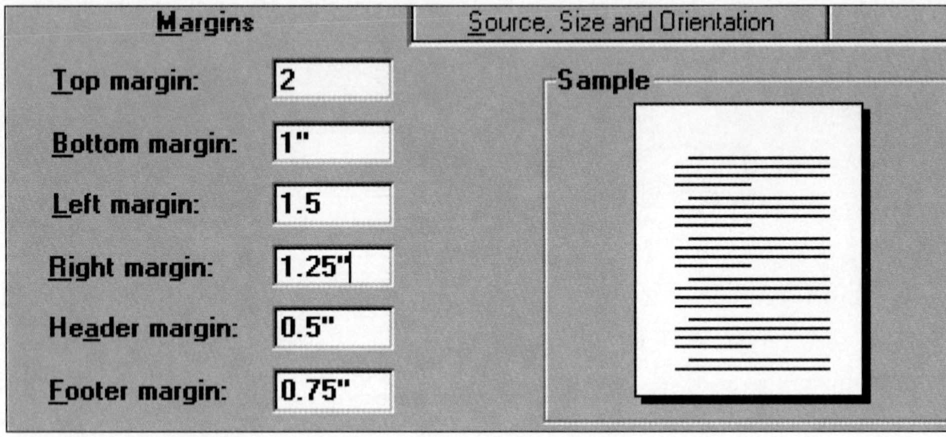

9.	Choose	**OK** or press **Enter** to return to the document. You do not see a change if you are in Normal view; however, the Ruler now shows a line that is 5.75" long rather than the previous 6" as shown here.

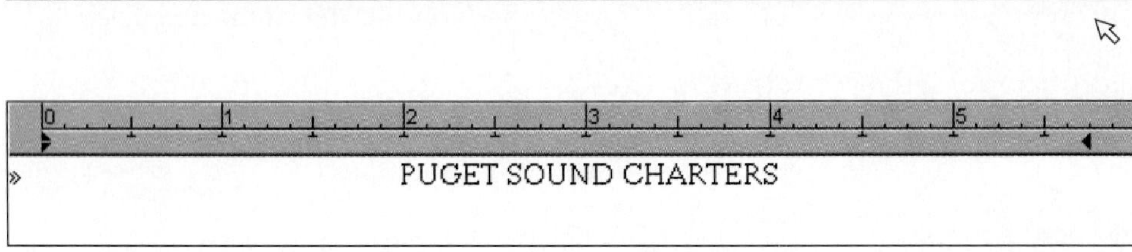

10.	Choose	**File, Print Preview** to see how the document will look with the new margin settings. The Print Preview screen should resemble the following example.

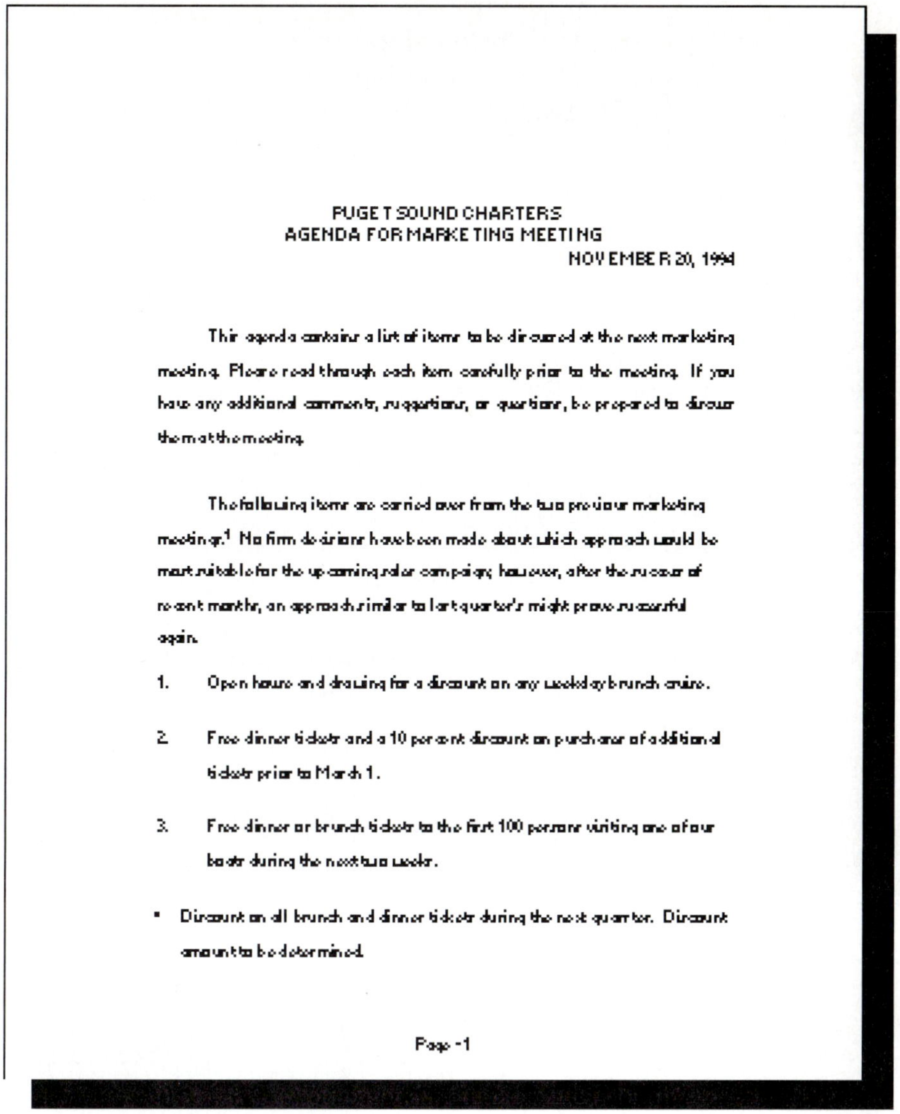

PUGET SOUND CHARTERS
AGENDA FOR MARKETING MEETING
NOVEMBER 20, 1994

This agenda contains a list of items to be discussed at the next marketing meeting. Please read through each item carefully prior to the meeting. If you have any additional comments, suggestions, or questions, be prepared to discuss them at the meeting.

The following items are carried over from the two previous marketing meetings.[1] No firm decisions have been made about which approach would be most suitable for the upcoming sales campaign; however, after the success of recent months, an approach similar to last quarter's might prove successful again.

1. Open house and drawing for a discount on any weekday brunch cruise.

2. Free dinner tickets and a 10 percent discount on purchase of additional tickets prior to March 1.

3. Free dinner or brunch tickets to the first 100 persons visiting one of our boats during the next two weeks.

- Discount on all brunch and dinner tickets during the next quarter. Discount amount to be determined.

Page -1

To leave Print Preview

11. Choose **Cancel**  to leave the Print Preview screen.

INSERTING A PAGE BREAK

Page breaks tell the printer where a page is going to stop and where another page will begin. When looking at **Print Preview** in the preceding exercise, the document on which you were working was automatically divided into two pages. Works inserts a page break when you have filled up all of the default text lines on a page. The page break is identified by a double greater than symbol as shown in the following example.

1. Scroll through the document until you locate this mark. Choose **View, All Characters** to help locate marks, if you like.

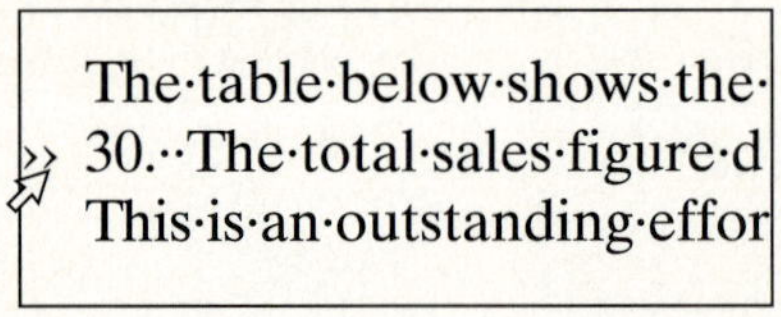

This symbol may not appear at this position in your document if you are using a font type and size that is different than used in this example.

Add Double-spacing

Before you insert page breaks in this document, adjust the spacing so that the text expands to three pages by doing the following:

1. Move the insertion point to every paragraph that is not currently double-spaced and press **Ctrl/2** to format them with double-spacing. This includes the numbered and bulleted lists but not the table.
2. Press **Enter** following each bulleted list item to insert a blank paragraph, and press **Ctrl/Q** to remove the extra bullet.
3. Move the insertion point to the second suggestion and press **Enter** two or three times to insert extra lines. Repeat this step for the last suggestion. Look at the status bar to determine if three pages have been created. If not, insert additional spaces between the suggestions until there are three pages in the document.
4. Choose **File, Print Preview** and then choose **Next** to go from page to page to see how the text looks on each page. Be sure that there is at least one suggestion on page three as shown in the following example.

The third page may contain only one suggestion and the bulleted list is probably displayed on both page one and page two. This is not the best layout for the document. You could add or delete lines between paragraphs to adjust the pages, but it probably makes more sense to manually insert page breaks at locations different from those assigned automatically by Works.

Insert Page Breaks

1. Move the insertion point to the first bulleted item that begins **Discount on all brunch...**as shown here. Notice that in this example the automatic page break is below the second bulleted item. Look for this symbol in your document to determine where the automatic page break is located.

• Discount·on·all·brunch·and·dinner·tickets·during·the·next·qua
to·be·determined.¶
¶
• Discount·on·dinner·cruises·for·persons·purchasing·more·than·
quarter.¶
››¶

PAGE BREAK

2. Choose **Insert, Page Break** or press **Ctrl/Enter**. A dotted line is now displayed above the first bulleted item, indicating the manual page break. The double greater than symbol is also above the first bulleted item, as shown here. Also, notice the status bar now shows page 2.

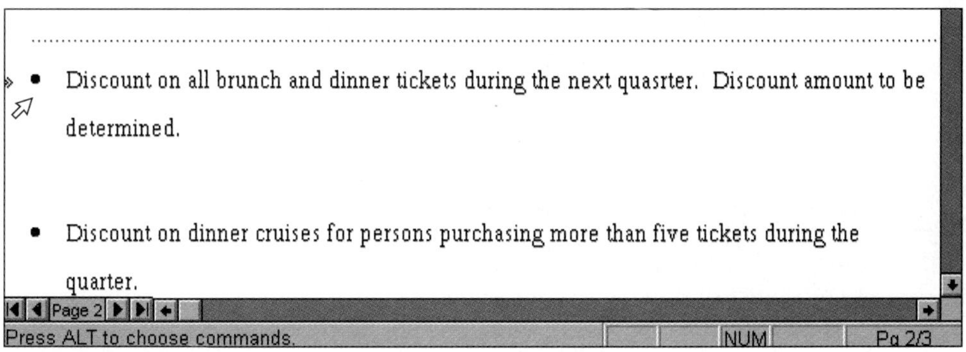

To insert a page break for page three

3. Move the insertion point to the left margin at **The meeting** as shown here.

The meeting will be held promptly at 2 p.m. in the conference room. Bring your suggestions to the meeting. Jot them down in the area provided at the bottom of this agenda.

4. Choose **Insert, Page Break** or press **Ctrl/Enter** to insert a manual page break as shown in the following example. Notice the double greater than symbol to the left of **The meeting** as well as the dotted line above, indicating the manual page break.

›› The meeting will be held promptly at 2 p.m. in the conference room. Bring your suggestions to the meeting. Jot them down in the area provided at the bottom of this agenda.

If you paused, your status bar should now show page 3 and Pg 3/3 as displayed here; otherwise use **Paginate Now** as described next.

Paginate Now

When page endings have been changed, the status bar changes to reflect the new pages when you pause. If you want the status bar to show changes immediately, use **Paginate Now**.

1. Choose **Tools, Paginate Now** or press **F9.** The status bar shows the new pages immediately.
2. Choose **File, Print Preview** and view each of the pages.
3. Choose **Cancel** when done to return to the document.

CREATING HEADERS AND FOOTERS

Headers are blocks of text that appear at the top of every page, and footers appear at the bottom of every page. These options are commonly used to include elements such as chapter headings, text titles, and page numbers. Headers and footers can be formatted just like any other text. Bold print, underlining, and right alignment are some of the formats that can be applied just as in a document.

Works includes some preset tab positions that are commonly used such as a centered tab and right aligned tab position. Page numbers are often centered and information is often right aligned within a header or footer.

Works provides two ways of creating headers and footers. You can choose **View, Headers and Footers** and enter only <u>one</u> line of text for each in the **Headers and Footers** dialog box, or you can turn on **Use header and footer paragraphs** in the **Headers and Footers** dialog box and return to the document where more than one line of text can be entered in the header or footer. This text is marked at the top of the document to indicate it is header and footer text. Both will be discussed here.

Create Single-line Headers and Footers

Text and formatting codes can be inserted in the single-line headers and footers. Here, the filename and the date will be entered in a header and aligned at the right margin,.and a footer will be created that prints the page number and centers it at the bottom of each page. Table 7-1 shows a list of the codes and their descriptions that can be entered in headers and footers to produce specific information.

Type this	To show this when printed
&l	Aligns following characters at the left margin.
&r	Aligns following characters at the right margin.
&c	Centers the following characters.
&p	Prints the page number.
&f	Prints the filename.
&d	Prints the date and automatically updates it whenever the document is printed.
&n	Prints the date in long format and automatically updates it whenever the document is printed.
&t	Prints the time and automatically updates it whenever the document is printed.
&&	Prints a single ampersand (&).

Table 7-1
Commands used for single-line headers and footers

To create a header that prints the filename and the date

1. Choose **View, Headers and Footers** to display the Headers and Footers dialog box as shown here in Figure 7-3. Your insertion point can be at any position in the document.

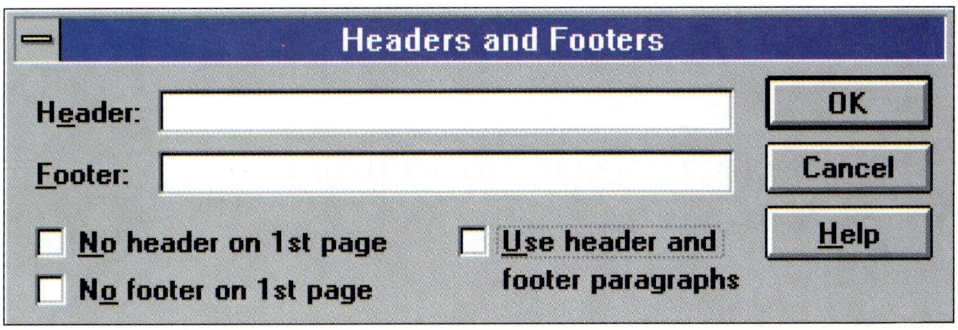

Figure 7-3
The Headers and Footers Dialog box

In the Header box

2. Type **&r&f, &d**. The characters **&r** will align the text at the right margin, **&f** will print the filename followed by a comma, and **&d** will print the current date. See an example as shown in Figure 7-4.

To insert a footer containing a centered page number

3. Choose **Footer** to move the insertion point to the Footer text box. You can either click on the **Footer** text box, or press **Alt/F**.
4. Type **&cPage &p**. The characters **&c** will center the word **Page** followed by a space, and **&p** prints the current page number. See the example in Figure 7-4.
5. Choose **No footer on 1st page.** See Figure 7-4.

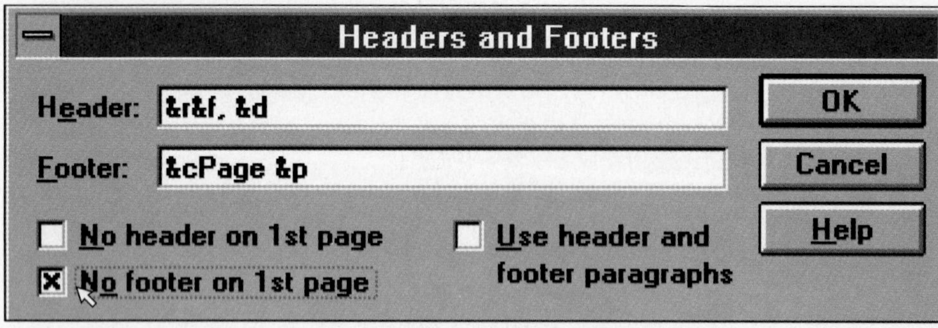

Figure 7-4
Text for headers and footers

6. Choose **OK** or press **Enter** to return to the document. If you are in Normal view, the headers and footers are not showing.

To see the headers and footers

7. Choose **File, Print Preview**. On the first page, only the header is displayed as shown in the following illustration, because **No Footer on 1st page** is turned on in the **Headers and Footers** dialog box.

CH6PR1.WPS, 8/21/94

PUGET·SOUND·CHARTERS¶
AGENDA·FOR·MARKETING·MEETING¶
NOVEMBER·29,·1994

8. Choose **Next** 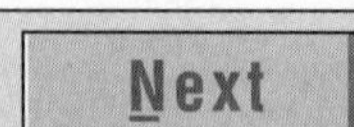 to see page two. The page number should now be showing at the bottom of the page as displayed in the following example.

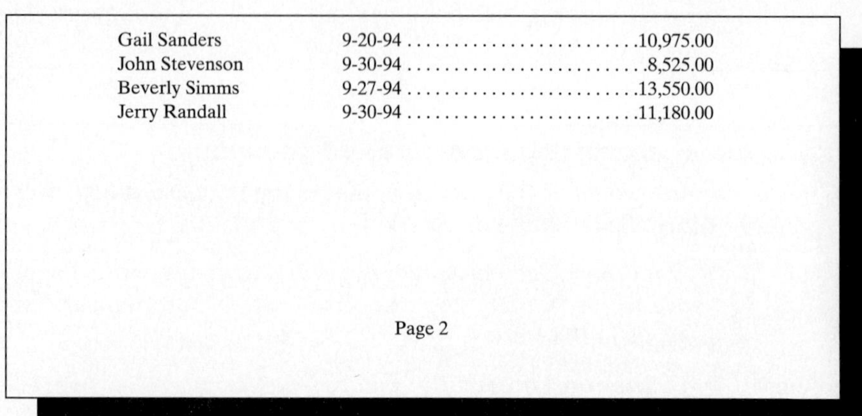
Gail Sanders	9-20-94	10,975.00
John Stevenson	9-30-94	8,525.00
Beverly Simms	9-27-94	13,550.00
Jerry Randall	9-30-94	11,180.00

Page 2

9. Choose **Cancel** to return to the document.

Remove Headers and Footers

The single-line header and footer will be removed and replaced with paragraph headers and footers.

1. Choose **View, Headers and Footers**. The dialog box is displayed and the header text is highlighted.
2. Press **Delete** to remove it.
3. Choose **Footer** to highlight the footer text and press **Delete**. Your dialog box should now look like that shown in Figure 7-5. (Leave it open to create paragraph headers and footers in the next section.)

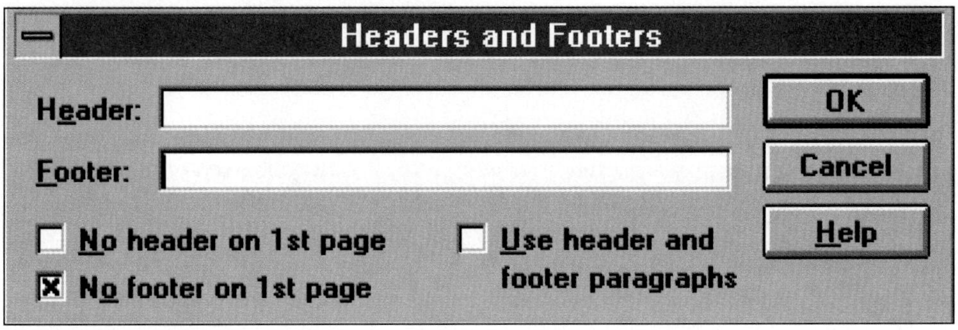

Figure 7-5
The Headers and Footers dialog box with header and footer text deleted

Create Paragraph Headers and Footers

A paragraph header containing two lines of text and a paragraph footer will be created. Also, turn on **No header on 1st page**, turn off **No footer on 1st page** so that a page number will be printed on the first page but no header, and, finally, turn on **Use header and footer paragraphs**.

1. Choose **No header on 1st page** to display an X in the check box. See an example in Figure 7-6.
2. Choose **No footer on 1st page** to turn off and remove the X in the check box. See Figure 7-6.
3. Choose **Use header and footer paragraphs** to turn it on and display an X in the check box. See Figure 7-6.

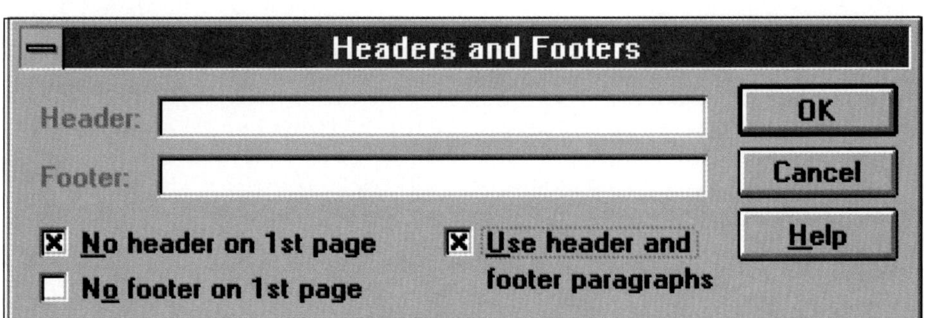

Figure 7-6
The Headers and Footers dialog box showing new choices

4. Choose **OK** or press **Enter** to return to the document. If your insertion point is not at the top of the document, you will not see the header and footer paragraph marks.

5. Move the insertion point to the beginning of the document (press **Ctrl/Home**). Your document should now resemble the following example.

The footer mark shows the word **Page** centered followed by a special character that will print the page number. This is the default footer and will be used here; however, you can add more text to the footer paragraph if you like. For now, two lines of text will be entered for the header paragraph.

The formatting in the paragraph header will be applied the same way you apply formatting to regular document text. The following text will be used for the header.

AGENDA	Puget Sound Charters, *date*
	Marketing Department

6. Move the insertion point so that it is directly to the right of the header mark (H) in the first line as shown in the following example.

7. Type **AGENDA** at the left margin.

8. Press **Tab** twice. The first tab stop is at the Center tab and the second is at the Right align tab at the right margin. These are default tab sets for the header paragraph.

9. Type **Puget Sound Charters,** (be sure to type a comma after **Charters**) and space once.

To insert a special character that prints a date and automatically updates it

10. Choose **Insert, Special Character** and choose **Print date**. See the example below.

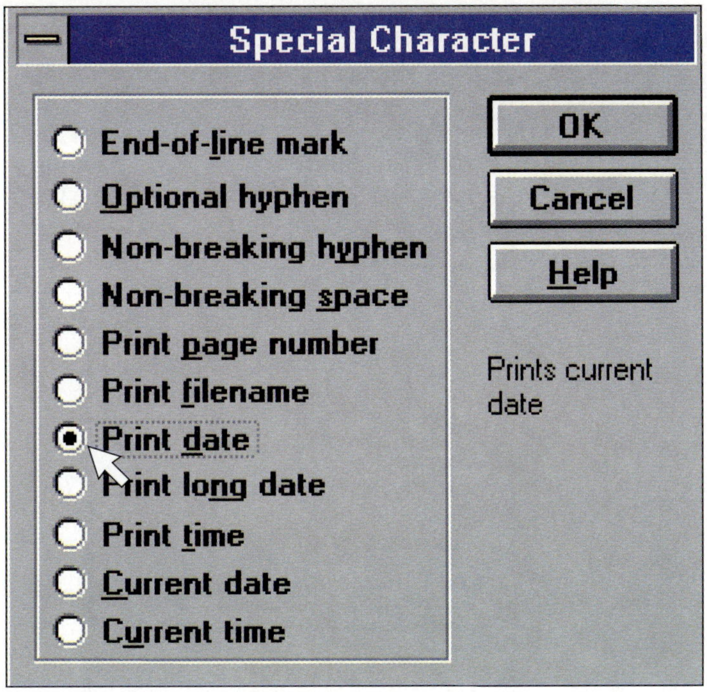

11.	Choose	**OK** or press **Enter** to return to the header paragraph. A date code is now displayed as shown in the following example.

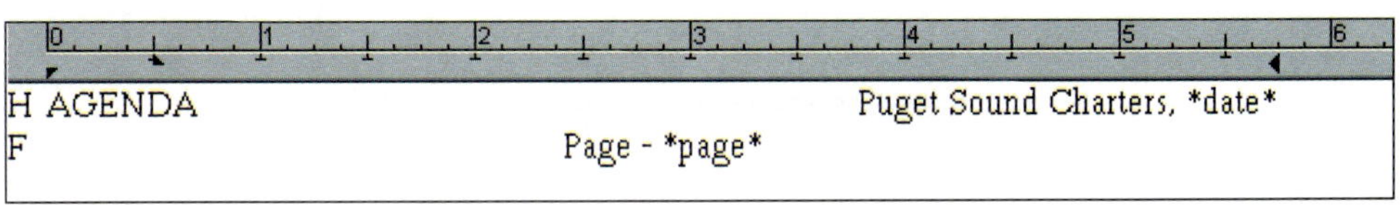

12.	Press	**Enter** to insert another header line.
13.	Press	**Tab** twice to go to the Right align tab stop at the right margin.
14.	Type	**Marketing Department**. Your screen should now resemble the following example.

The header and footer are now created. No text will be added to the footer.

To see the header and footer as they will be printed

15. Choose **File, Print Preview** and choose **Next** to go from one page to the next to see how your document will look. The second page should resemble the following example with both the header and the footer text displayed.

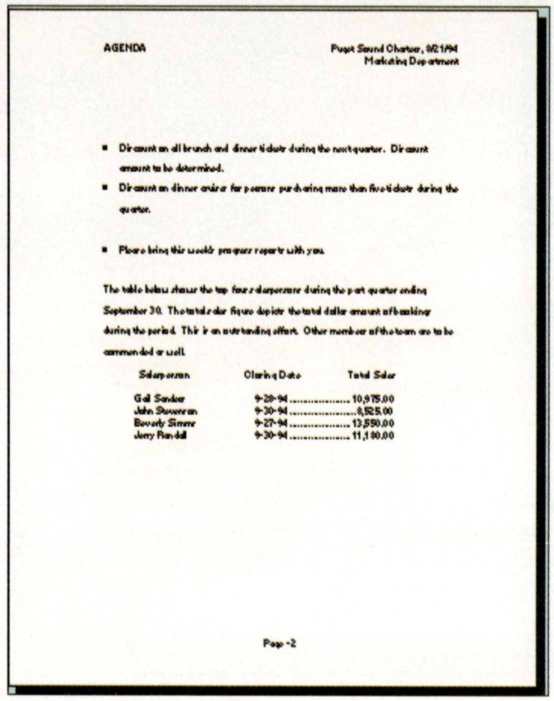

AGENDA

Puget Sound Charter, 8/21/94
Marketing Department

- Discount on all brunch and dinner tickets during the next quarter. Discount amount to be determined.
- Discount on dinner cruises for persons purchasing more than five tickets during the quarter.

- Please bring this weeks progress reports with you.

The table below shows the top four salespersons during the past quarter ending September 30. The total sales figure depicts the total dollar amount of bookings during the period. This is an outstanding effort. Other members of the team are to be commended as well.

Salesperson	Closing Date	Total Sales
Gail Sanders	9-28-94	10,975.00
John Stevenson	9-30-94	8,525.00
Beverly Simms	9-27-94	13,550.00
Jerry Randall	9-30-94	11,180.00

Page -2

16. Choose **Cancel** to return to the document.

CREATING FOOTNOTES

Footnotes are often used to cite references in a document. When a footnote is created, Works inserts a reference number that is superscripted, such as the number 1. You can insert other characters such as an asterisk to make the reference if you prefer. The Footnote dialog box contains a new WorksWizard feature that will automatically format your reference if you like. In this section a footnote referring to previous meetings will be inserted, as well as a footnote using the WorksWizard that refers to a newspaper article.

Create a Footnote Without Using Workswizard

Create a footnote using an asterisk as a character mark. The text of the footnote is shown in the following box.

See minutes for September 18 and October 15 meetings.

1. Move the insertion point to the space following the word **meetings** at the end of the first sentence in the second paragraph as shown in the following example.

INSERTION POINT

The following items are carried over from the two previous marketing meetings. No firm decisions have been made about which approach would be most suitable for the upcoming sales campaign; however, after the success of recent months, an approach similar to

2. Choose **Insert, Footnote** to display the Footnote dialog box as shown in Figure 7-7. **Numbered** is turned on which would automatically insert the next consecutive footnote number. In this case it would be **1** since this is the first footnote; however, here an asterisk will be used instead of a number.

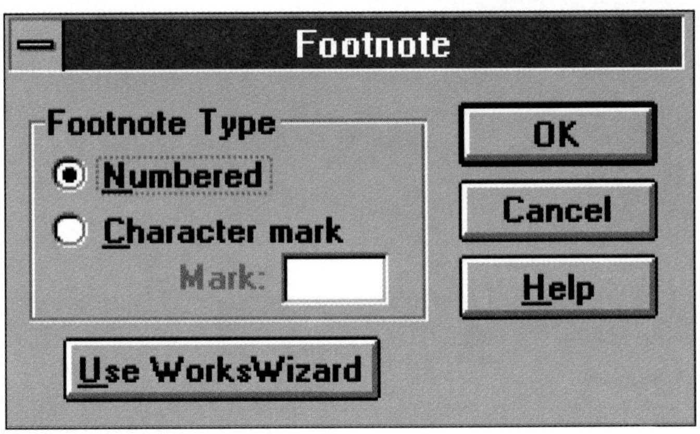

Figure 7-7
The Footnote dialog box

3. Choose **Character mark**. The **Mark** text box is no longer dimmed.
4. Choose **Mark** to move the insertion point to the text box.
5. Type * (an asterisk) in the text box as shown here.

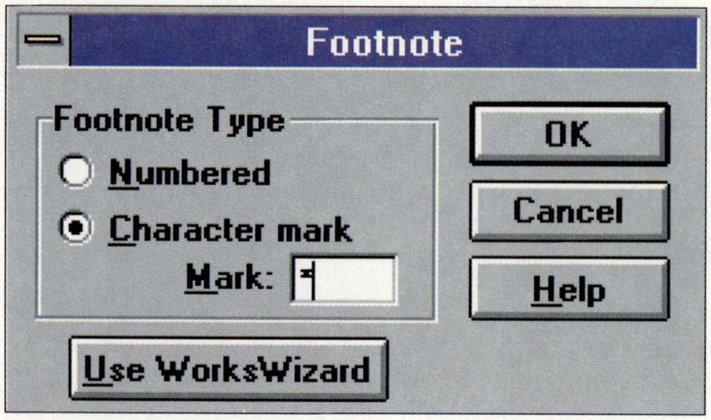

6. Choose **OK** or press **Enter** to return to the document. An asterisk is now showing in the text, and a footnote pane is opened at the bottom of the window. See the example in Figure 7-8.

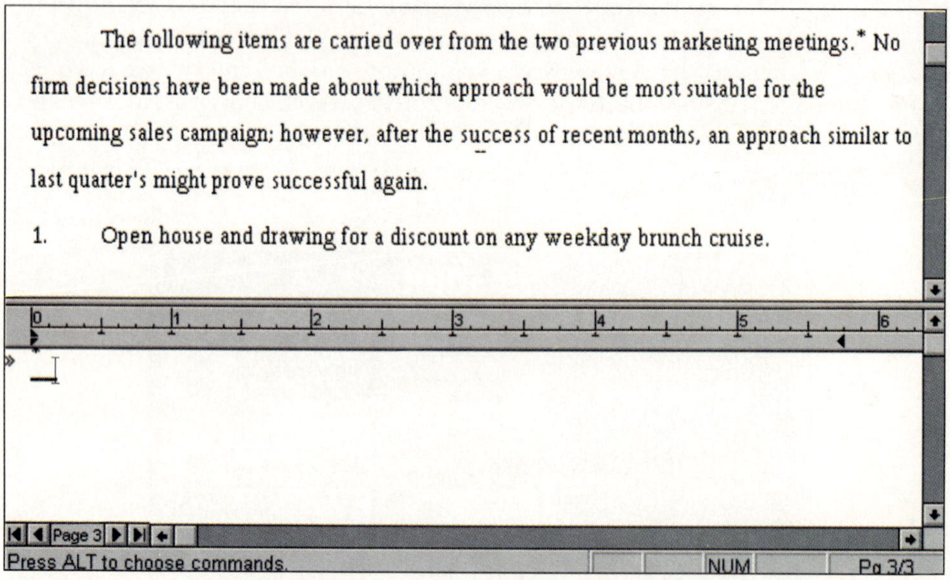

Figure 7-8
The Footnote pane

The insertion point is located in the footnote pane, and this is where you type the footnote text.

7. Type **See minutes for September 18 and October 15 meetings.** See the following example.

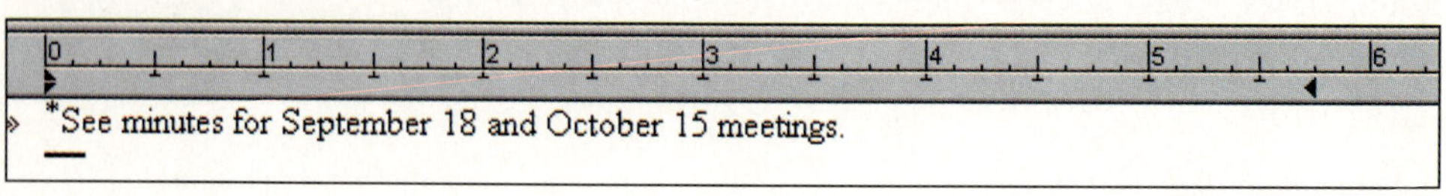

Move from Footnote Pane to Document and Reverse

1. Click anywhere in the document text or press **F6.**
2. Repeat step 1 to move back to the footnote pane.

Close a Footnote Pane

You can close the footnote pane without losing the footnote text. The footnote text will be placed by default at the bottom of the page on which the reference mark or number has been entered, and it will be separated from other text by a line above the footnote. You can either use the mouse or the **View** menu to close the pane.

To use the mouse

1. Double-click on the split bar at the top of the pane as shown in the following example. The pointer becomes a double-headed arrow and shows **adjust** as displayed as follows.

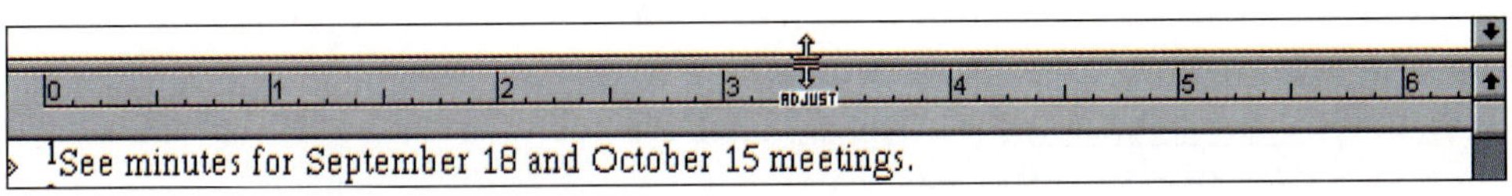

NOTE: You also can change (adjust) the size of the pane by dragging up or down on the split bar.

To use the menu to open or close the pane

2. Choose **View, Footnotes.**

To see how the footnote will look when printed

3. Choose **File, Print Preview.** Your page should resemble that shown in Figure 7-9.

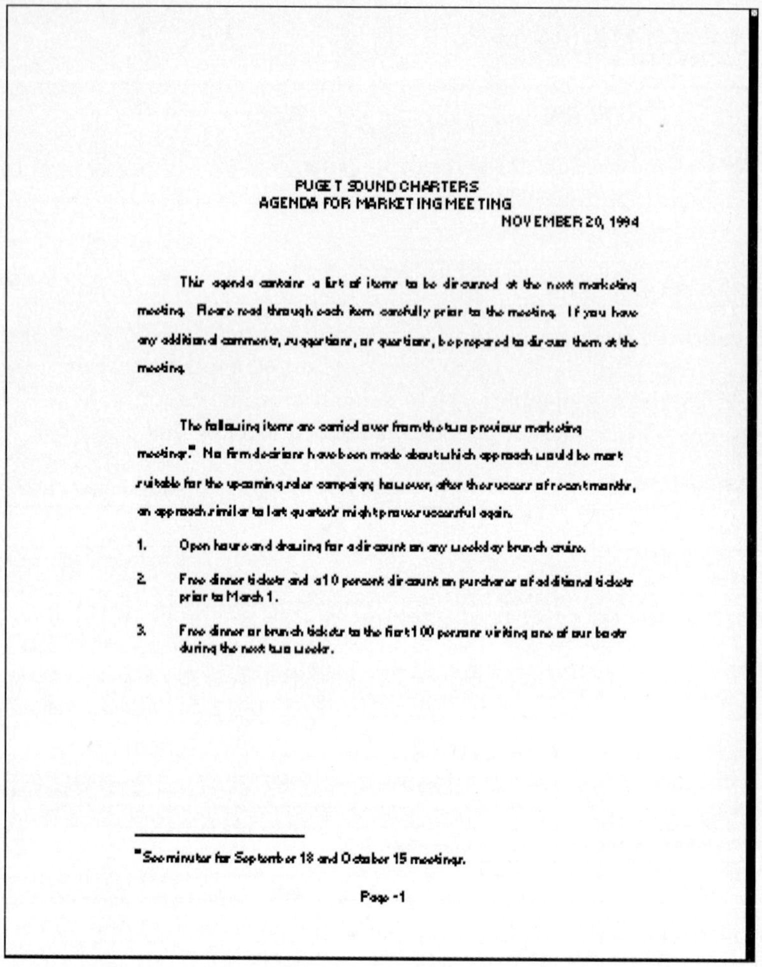
PUGET SOUND CHARTERS
AGENDA FOR MARKETING MEETING
NOVEMBER 20, 1994

This agenda contains a list of items to be discussed at the next marketing meeting. Please read through each item carefully prior to the meeting. If you have any additional comments, suggestions, or questions, be prepared to discuss them at the meeting.

The following items are carried over from the two previous marketing meetings.* No firm decisions have been made about which approach would be most suitable for the upcoming sales campaign; however, after the success of recent months, an approach similar to last quarter's might prove successful again.

1. Open house and drawing for a discount on any weekday brunch cruise.
2. Free dinner tickets and a 10 percent discount on purchases of additional tickets prior to March 1.
3. Free dinner or brunch tickets to the first 100 persons visiting one of our boats during the next two weeks.

*See minutes for September 18 and October 15 meetings.

Page -1

Figure 7-9
The footnote showing in Print Preview

4. Choose **Cancel** to return to the document window.

Use Workswizard To Format a Footnote

A footnote reference to a newspaper article will be entered here, and the format for it will be applied automatically using the footnote WorksWizard. Before doing that, an additional sentence (shown in the box below) will be inserted in the paragraph directly above the sales table.

Our excellent staff was recently featured in an article in a local marine journal.

1. Move the insertion point to the end of the paragraph **. . . commended as well.** just above the table showing the sales report. See the following example.

The total sales figure depicts the total dollar amount of bookings during the period. This is an outstanding effort. Other members of the team are to be commended as well.

Salesperson	**Closing Date**	**Total Sales**
Gail Sanders	9-28-94	10,975.00

2. Type **Our excellent staff was recently featured in an article in a local marine journal.**

To create the footnote

3. Choose **Insert, Footnote** to go to the Footnote dialog box.
4. Choose **Use WorksWizard**. The Footnote WorksWizard window is displayed as shown in Figure 7-10.

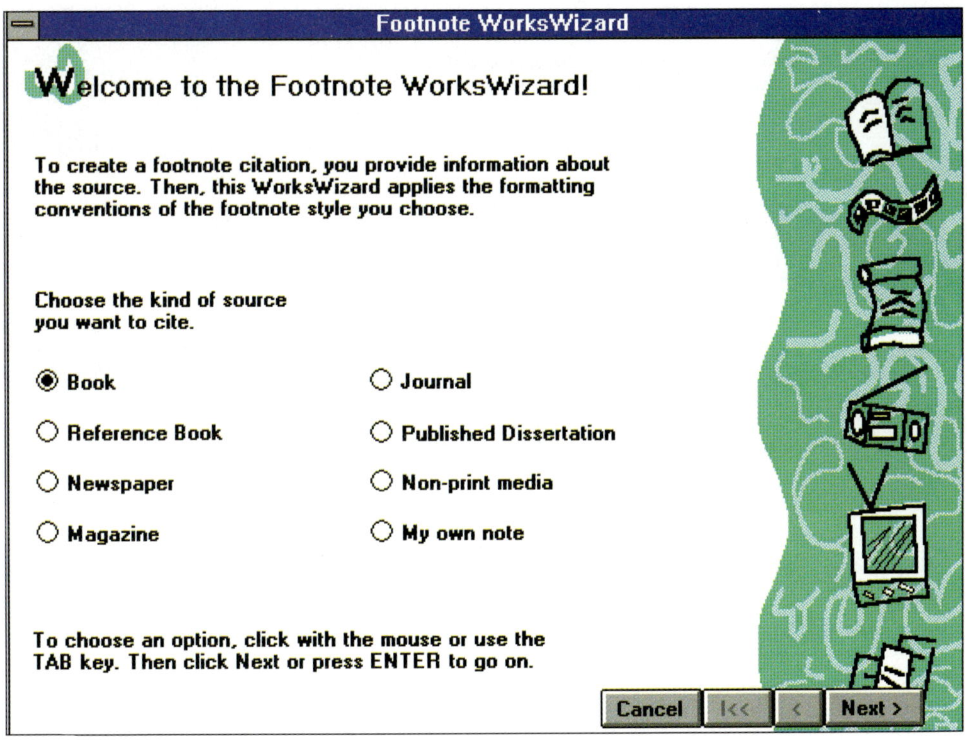

Figure 7-10
The Footnote WorksWizard window

Read the information in the WorksWizard window. As you can see, this feature is used to automatically format your footnote correctly to match the footnote style you want.

5. Choose **Newspaper** to turn it on as shown in the following example.

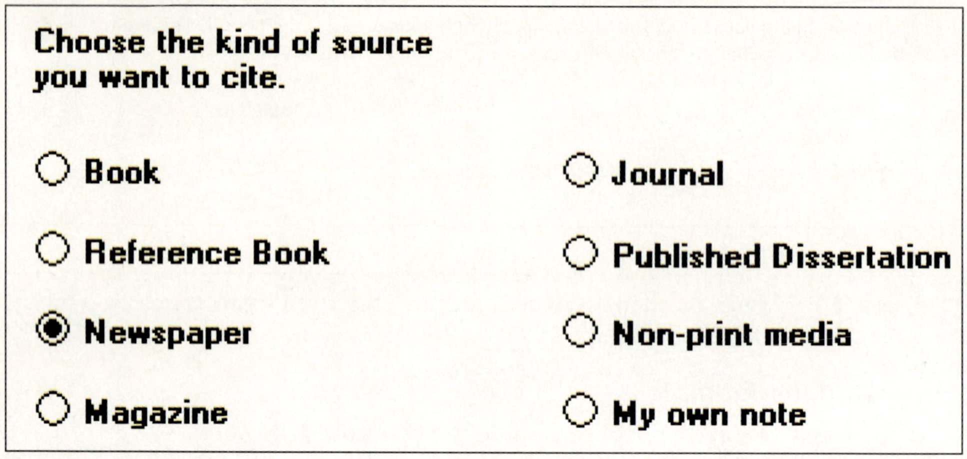

6. Choose **Next >** as shown in the following example.

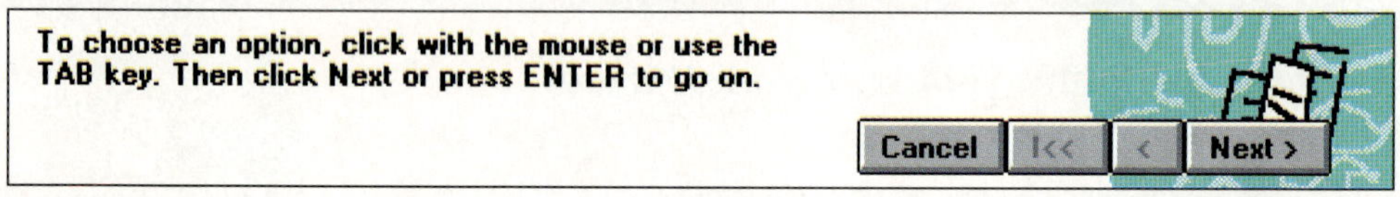

The Footnote WorksWizard window for the Newspaper option is displayed. See Figure 7-11.

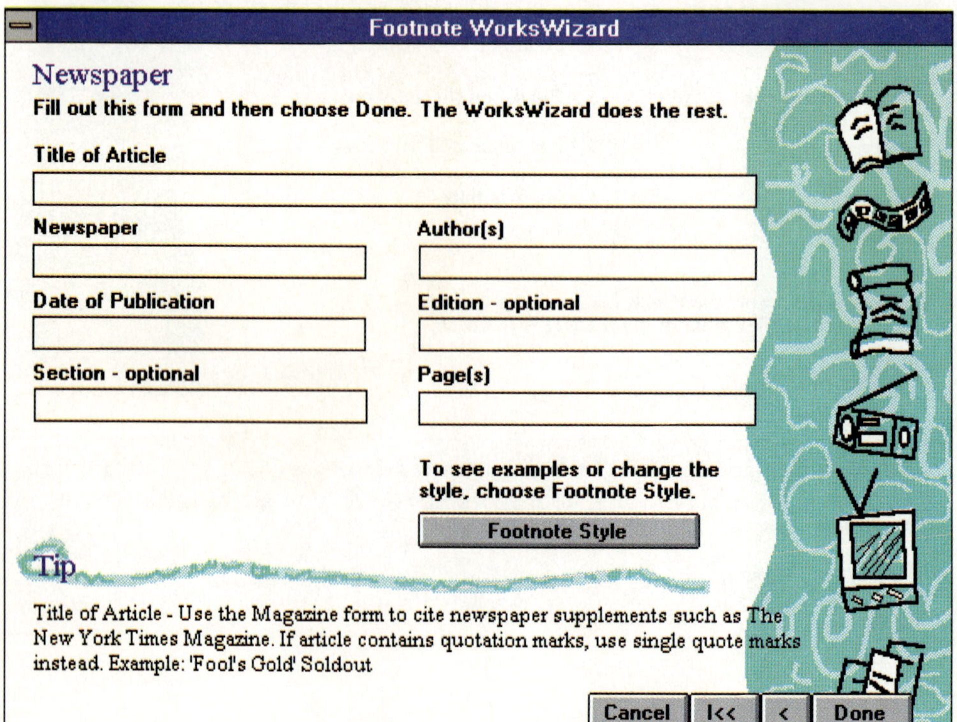

Figure 7-11
The Footnote WorksWizard window for newspaper formatting

You can now insert information in the various boxes.

In the **Title of Article** box

7. Type **Super Sales Staff for Charter Service.**
8. Press **Tab** to go to the **Newspaper** box.

In the **Newspaper** box

9. Type **Puget Sound Marine Journal** and press **Tab** to go to the next box.

In the **Author(s)** box

10. Type **W. E. Erickson.** and press **Tab.**

In the **Date of Publication** box

11. Type **July 20, 1994,** and press **Tab** twice. Skip the **Edition** box and go to the **Section** box.

In the **Section** box

12. Type **Business** and press **Tab.**

In the **Page(s)** box

13. Type **B1.**

To see the newspaper style

14. Choose **Footnote Style.** The window now shows the format choices in which your information can be printed as displayed in Figure 7-12.
15. Choose **Chicago Manual of Style** for the footnote style. See Figure 7-12.

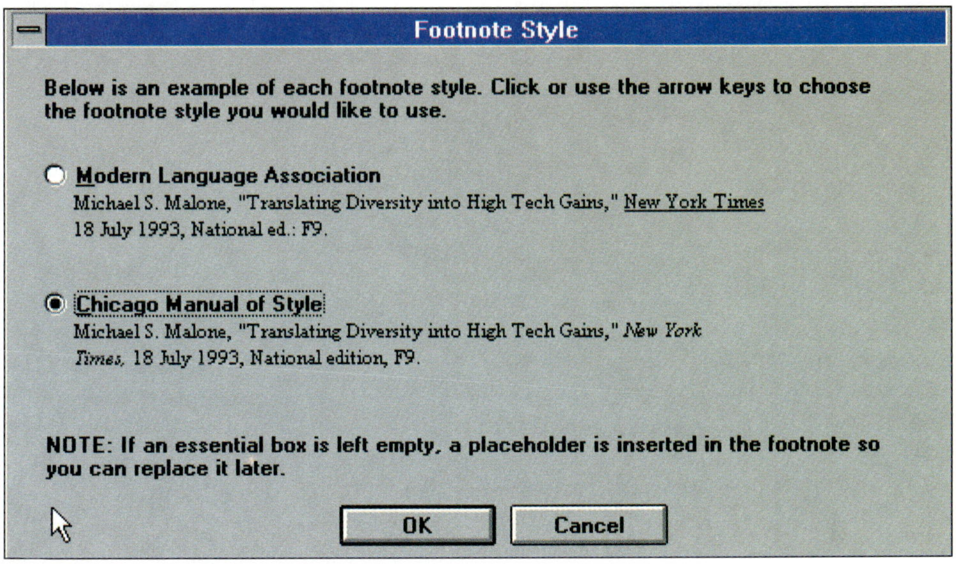

Figure 7-12
The Footnote Style window

16. Choose **OK** or press **Enter** to return to the Footnote WorksWizard window.

17. Choose **Done** 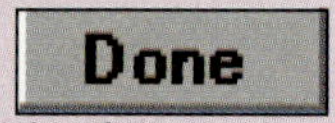

to return to the footnote pane in the document. The footnote is entered automatically in the chosen format, and should now look like the following example.

NOTE: A footnote number has been used here, and the number is **2** even though the first footnote was marked with an asterisk. In the next section, you will learn how to change the asterisk to a number.

Change a Footnote Mark

Change the asterisk to a number

1. Select the asterisk in the document window as shown here.

2. Choose **Insert, Footnote** to display the Footnote dialog box.
3. Choose **Numbered** as shown here.

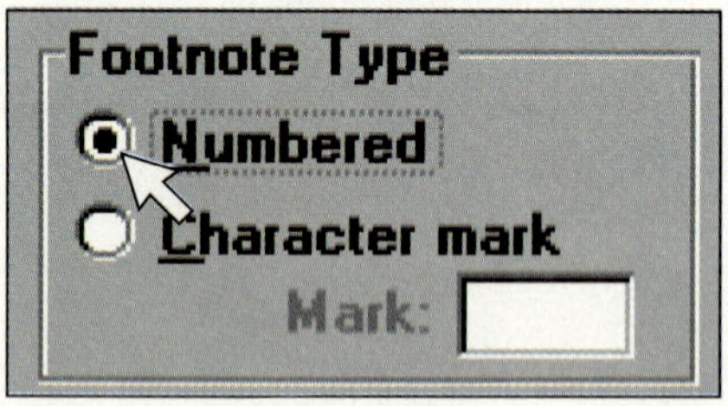

4. Choose **OK** or press **Enter** to return to the document. The asterisk is now a number 1. The number is entered automatically and reflects its appropriate order in the document.

If the footnote pane is not displayed

5. Choose **View, Footnotes**. The footnote pane now shows the first footnote with a number in place of the asterisk as shown in the following example.

The following items are carried over from the two previous marketing meetings.[1] No firm decisions have been made about which approach would be most suitable for the upcoming sales campaign; however, after the success of recent months, an approach similar to last quarter's might prove successful again.

1. Open house and drawing for a discount on any weekday brunch cruise.

[1]See minutes for September 18 and October 15 meetings.
[2] W. E. Erickson, "Super Sales Staff for Charter Service," *Puget Sound Marine Journal,* July 20, 1994, sec. Business, B1.

If you want to see how the footnotes will look

6. Choose **File, Print Preview** and choose **Next** to see how each page will look.
7. Choose **Cancel** to return to the document
8. Save the document as **CH7PR1**.

PRINTING SPECIFIC PAGES

It is possible to print only specified pages of a document if you wish, or you can print several copies of a single page, several pages, or the entire document.

Print Two Copies of a Single Page

Print two copies of the first page of the Agenda document.

Be sure the printer is on and that paper is adjusted properly.

1. Choose **File, Print** or press **Ctrl/P** to display the Print dialog box.
2. Type 2 in the **Number of Copies** text box. See Figure 7-13.
3. Choose **Pages** to turn it on. The insertion point is now flashing in the **From** box.
4. Type 1 in the **From** box.
5. Choose **To** to move the insertion point to the **To** box.
6. Type 1 in the **To** box. The Print dialog box should now look like that displayed in Figure 7-13.

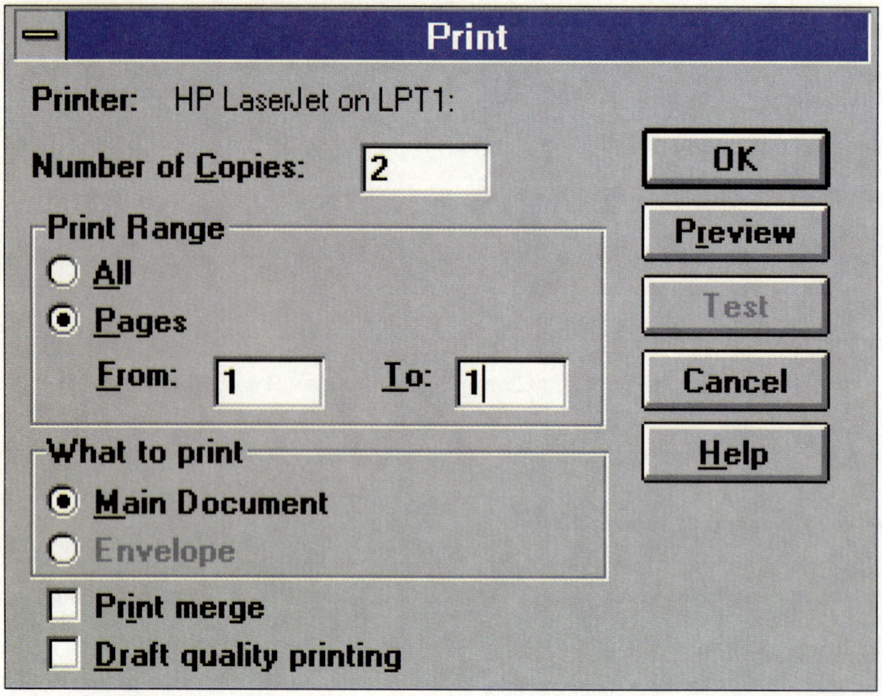

Figure 7-13
The Print dialog box

7. Choose **OK** or press **Enter** to print two copies of the first page.

   NOTE: If you want to print several consecutive pages, use these same steps but enter the number of the first page to print in the **From** text box and the number of the last page to print in the **To** box.

Print Footnotes at End of Document

In the previous exercise, footnotes were printed at the bottom of each page. You can; however, change this and print all footnotes at the end of the document.

1. Choose **File, Page Setup** to display the Page Setup dialog box.
2. Choose **Other Options** tab.
3. Choose **Print footnotes at end of document** to turn it on. Your screen should now resemble Figure 7-14.

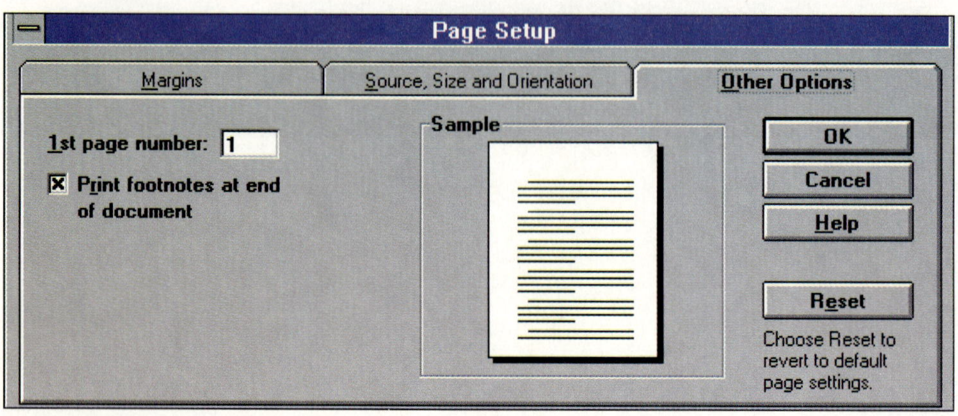

Figure 7-14
The Other Options tab in the Page Setup dialog box

4. Choose **OK** or press **Enter** to return to the document.
5. Choose **File, Print Preview** and choose **Next** enough times to go to the last page. You should now see the footnotes on that page as shown here.

AGENDA

Puget Sound Charter, 8/21/94
Marketing Department

The meeting will be held promptly at 2 p.m. in the conference room. Bring your suggestions to the meeting. Jot them down in the area provided at the bottom of this agenda.

Suggestion:

Suggestion:

Suggestion:

[1]*See* minutes for September 18 and October 15 meeting.
[2]W.E.Erickson, "Super Sales Staff for Charter Services," *Puget Sound Maine Journal* of July 20, 1994, sec Business, B1.

Page-3

6. Choose **Print** from the **Print Preview** window to print the entire document, and change the command to print 2 copies to 1 copy.
7. Save the document again as **CH7PR1** to save the command to print footnotes at the end of the document.

FORMATTING IN COLUMNS

Assume you want to use the text in the History of Puget Sound Charters document in a brochure to be distributed to customers. The presentation of the information could be enhanced if it were formatted in three columns. In this section, the document, **CH6PR2** will be retrieved and formatted in columns, and then additional text will be typed so that you can see how it is formatted automatically in columns.

Format in Columns

1. Open the document **CH6PR2** or retrieve it from the Instructor data disk.

To format in columns

2. Choose **Format, Columns** to display the Columns dialog box.
3. Type **3** in the **Number of columns** text box.
4. Press **Tab** to go to the **Space between** text box.

No change will be made here; however, a new measurement could be typed. When the insertion point is moved to another text box, the Sample box displays showing how the text will look with three columns. **Line Between** is turned on by default. That will not be changed. Your screen should now resemble Figure 7-15.

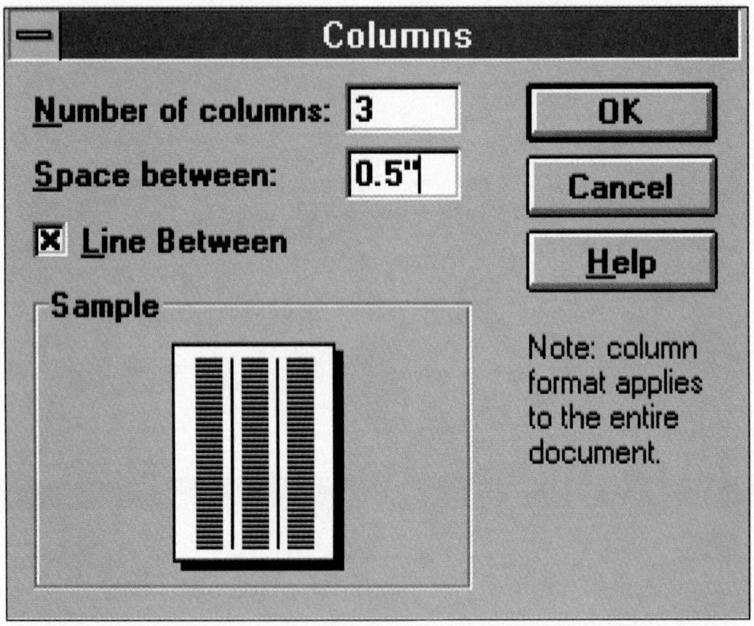

Figure 7-15
The Columns dialog box

5. Choose **OK** or press **Enter**. You are probably working in Normal view. If you are, you will be prompted to change to Page Layout view as shown here.

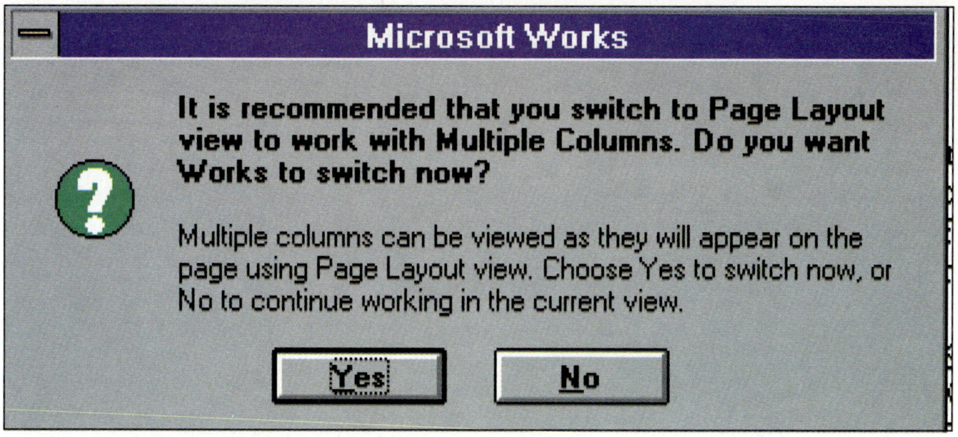

6. Choose **Yes** to return to the document.

NOTE: The amount of text in the first column depends upon the font type and size you are using. Your document may or may not show additional text in the second column. The font used here is Courier 12 pt.

Your screen may now resemble the following example. Notice the indent markers have changed in the Ruler to reflect the column formatting. They now show the width of the column.

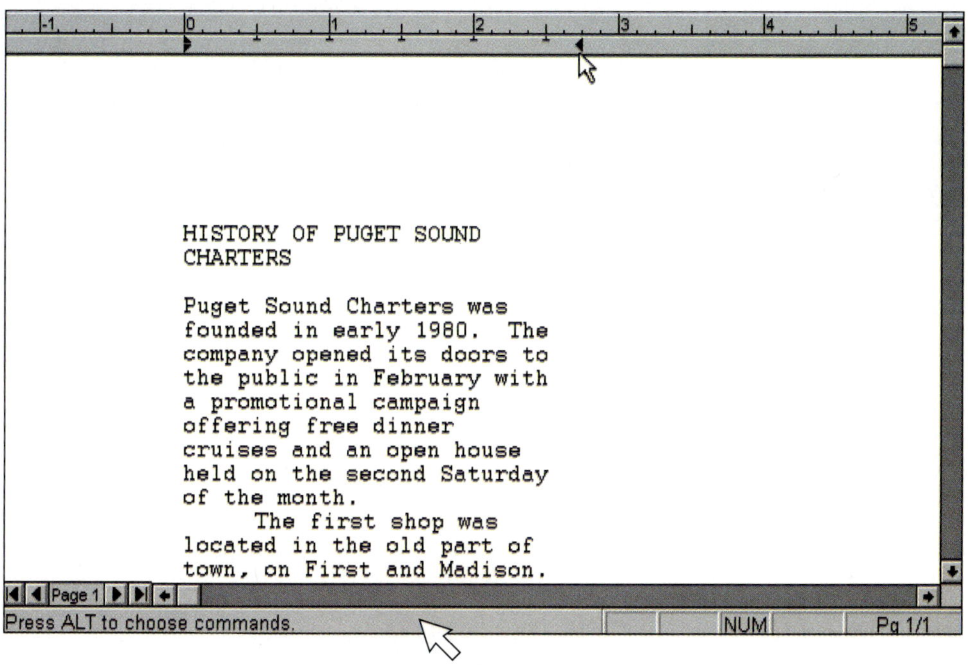

The following text will be added to the document

7. Move the insertion point to the end of the document (press **Ctrl/End**) directly following the last words **. . . heavy flow of customers**. If there are extra paragraph marks showing at the end, delete them.

8. Type the following text. It is formatted automatically in the second column. If you are using a large font size, it will "snake" to the third column when the second column is filled.

This location is situated on the east side of Lake Union and has space for two additional boats.

In 1990 a location in Kirkland on Lake Washington was obtained, and Puget Sound Charters was able to increase its fleet with three more boats. This site proved to be very popular with both local residents and visitors.

Another site on Lake Washington at Seward Park was obtained in 1991 and became very busy, providing cruises for several of the large industries located at the south end of Lake Washington.

By 1993 space for two large cruisers was acquired at Shilshole which allowed us to easily provide sightseeing tours of Puget Sound as well as tours of Lake Union and Lake Washington. Newcomers to the area were particularly interested in these cruises, and organizations meeting in Seattle frequently reserved one of these cruisers for an evening's entertainment.

To double-space the text

9. Select the entire document by holding down the **Ctrl** key and clicking in the left margin or by pressing **F8** five times.

10. Press **Ctrl/2** to apply double-spacing to expand the text to the third column. Depending upon the type and size of font you are using, your text may be moved on to the first column on page 2.

11. Choose **File, Print Preview** to see how it looks.

12. Choose **Cancel** to return to the document.

Add a Banner Headline

You can add a headline that extends across all columns by creating it as a header. Here you will delete the title and use it in a header paragraph to create a banner headline.

1. Delete — the title **HISTORY OF PUGET SOUND CHARTERS** at the top of column one.
2. Delete — any extra space at the top of the document.
3. Choose — **View, Normal** so that you will be able to see the paragraph header mark. Page Layout view does not show the header and footer marks.
4. Choose — **View, Headers and Footers** to go to the dialog box.
5. Choose — **Use header and footer paragraphs.**
6. Choose — **OK** or press **Enter** to display the paragraph header and footer marks as shown in the following example.

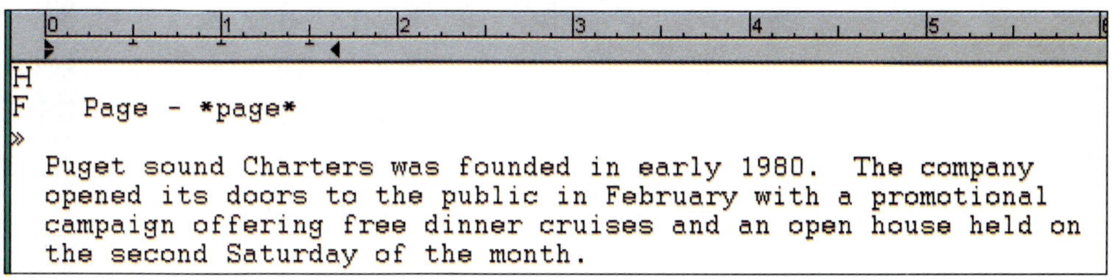

To remove the footer text

7. Select — the text **Page -** and the special character ***page*** as shown in the following example.

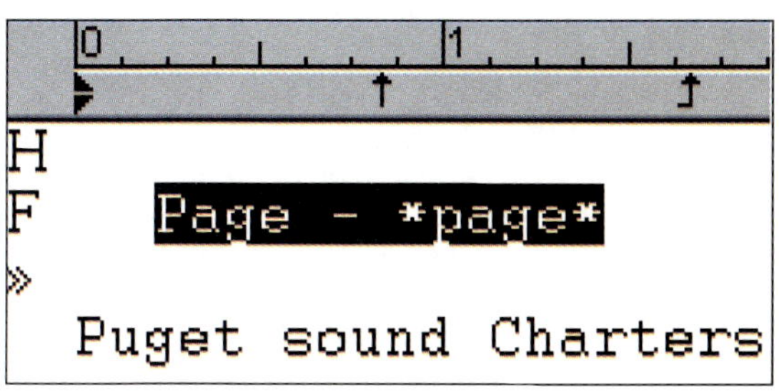

8. Press — **Delete** so that there will not be a footer in this document.

To change the tab positions in the header

9. Move — the insertion point to the header mark (H).
10. Drag — the **Right** tab mark to the far right side of the Ruler. It will not be used here.
11. Drag — the **Center** tab mark to **3,** which is the center of the entire page. See the following example.

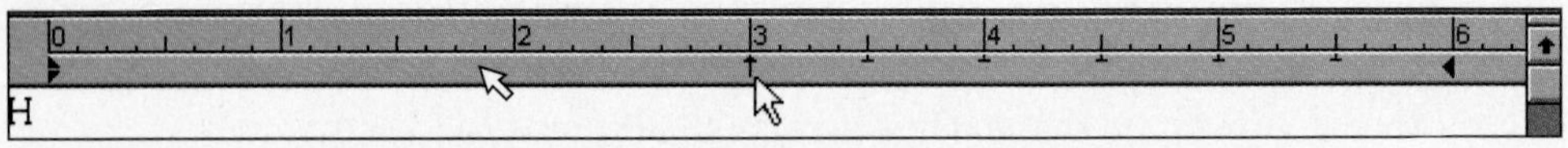

12. Press **Tab** to go to the Center tab.

To enter the text

13. Type **HISTORY OF PUGET SOUND CHARTERS** and press **Enter** to insert a blank line.

To go to Print Preview to see how the page looks

14. Choose **File, Print Preview**. Your screen should resemble the following example. Choose **Next** to see page 2.

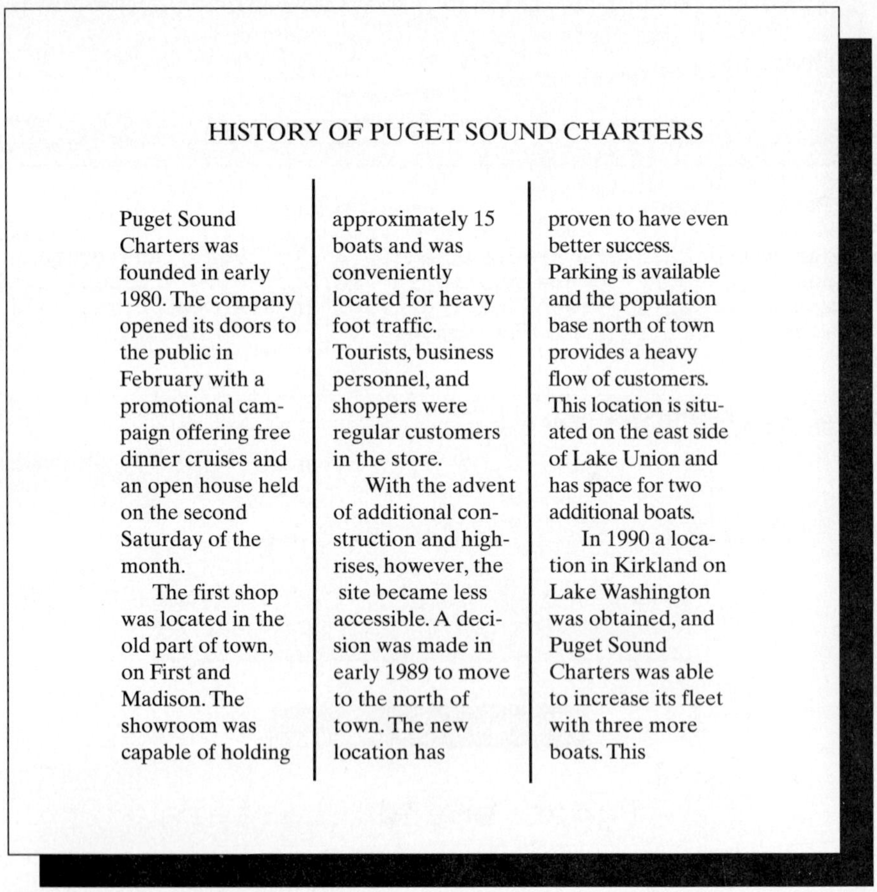

HISTORY OF PUGET SOUND CHARTERS

Puget Sound Charters was founded in early 1980. The company opened its doors to the public in February with a promotional campaign offering free dinner cruises and an open house held on the second Saturday of the month.

The first shop was located in the old part of town, on First and Madison. The showroom was capable of holding approximately 15 boats and was conveniently located for heavy foot traffic. Tourists, business personnel, and shoppers were regular customers in the store.

With the advent of additional construction and high-rises, however, the site became less accessible. A decision was made in early 1989 to move to the north of town. The new location has proven to have even better success. Parking is available and the population base north of town provides a heavy flow of customers. This location is situated on the east side of Lake Union and has space for two additional boats.

In 1990 a location in Kirkland on Lake Washington was obtained, and Puget Sound Charters was able to increase its fleet with three more boats. This

15. Choose **Cancel** when done.

16. Save the document as **CH7PR2**.

17. Print the document by clicking on the Print button  or by choosing **File, Print**.

USING LANDSCAPE ORIENTATION

Landscape orientation prints a document on paper that is wider than it is long. The default orientation is portrait, which is the way you have normally been printing documents. Landscape orientation is frequently used for column typing or for large spreadsheets. In this section the document on the History of Puget Sound Charters is formatted in landscape orientation.

Landscape orientation and column formatting apply to the entire document.

Use Landscape Orientation

1. Open the document **CH7PR2** if it is not already active, or retrieve it from the Instructor data disk.

To change to landscape orientation

2. Choose **File, Page Setup** to go to the Page Setup dialog box.
3. Choose **Source, Size and Orientation** tab.
4. Choose **Landscape**. Your screen shows the Page Setup dialog box with Landscape turned on as displayed in Figure 7-16. Notice the Sample box now shows the page in landscape orientation.

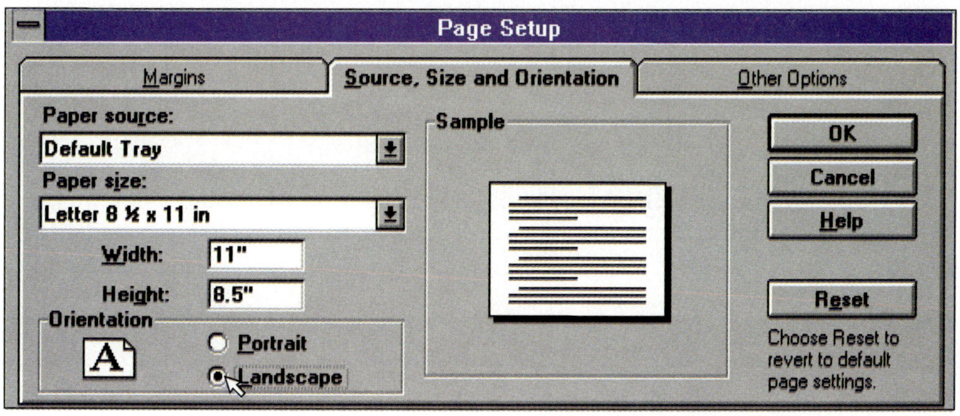

Figure 7-16
The Page Setup dialog box showing the Source, Size and Orientation tab and Landscape turned on

5. Choose **OK** or press **Enter** to return to the document.
6. Choose **File, Print Preview** to see how the document will look when printed. Your screen should resemble the following example.

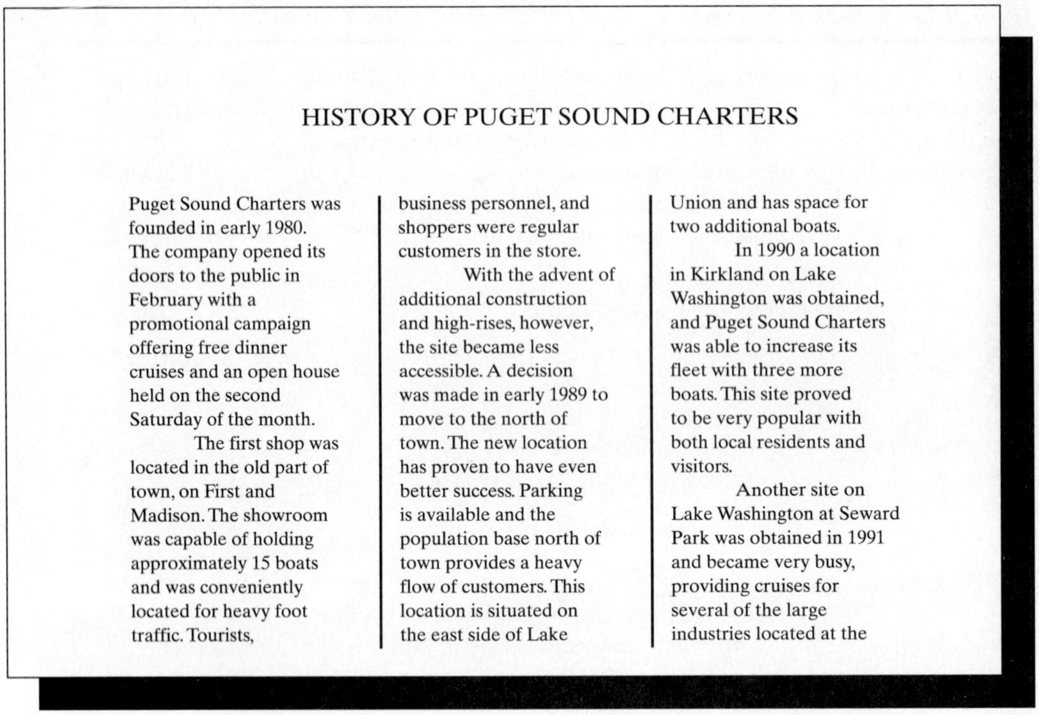

HISTORY OF PUGET SOUND CHARTERS

Puget Sound Charters was founded in early 1980. The company opened its doors to the public in February with a promotional campaign offering free dinner cruises and an open house held on the second Saturday of the month.

The first shop was located in the old part of town, on First and Madison. The showroom was capable of holding approximately 15 boats and was conveniently located for heavy foot traffic. Tourists, business personnel, and shoppers were regular customers in the store.

With the advent of additional construction and high-rises, however, the site became less accessible. A decision was made in early 1989 to move to the north of town. The new location has proven to have even better success. Parking is available and the population base north of town provides a heavy flow of customers. This location is situated on the east side of Lake Union and has space for two additional boats.

In 1990 a location in Kirkland on Lake Washington was obtained, and Puget Sound Charters was able to increase its fleet with three more boats. This site proved to be very popular with both local residents and visitors.

Another site on Lake Washington at Seward Park was obtained in 1991 and became very busy, providing cruises for several of the large industries located at the

The title now needs to be changed since the center is no longer at **3.**

7. Choose **Cancel** to return to the document.

8. Move the insertion point to the header paragraph at the top of the document.

9. Drag the **Center** tab mark to **4.25** as shown in the following example. The title moves automatically when the tab mark is changed.

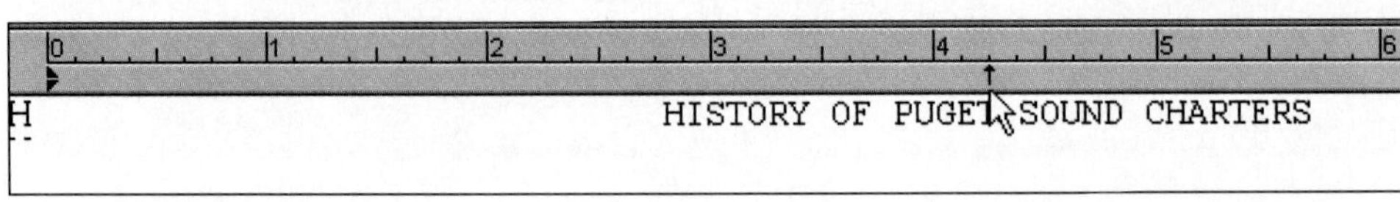

10. Save the document as **CH7PR3.**

11. Print the document and close all opened documents.

NOTE: If you have difficulty printing in landscape, you may have to choose **File, Printer Setup**. Make sure you have selected the correct printer as displayed in the Printer Setup dialog box, and then choose **Setup** to go to the dialog box for the selected printer. In that box, choose **Landscape** and choose **OK** enough times to return to the document. Then you can click on the print button or choose **File, Print**.

NOTE: When you open another new document window, the orientation for the new document is automatically returned to the default portrait orientation.

What You'll Do

- Change to landscape orientation.
- Format in columns.
- Create headers and footers.
- Create footnotes.
- Adjust tab sets in tabular columns.

How To Do It

1. Open the document **CH5HO2**, (the Needs Analysis document), or retrieve it from the Instructor data disk.

To change to landscape

2. Choose **File, Page Setup** to go to the **Page Setup** dialog box. Choose the **Source, Size and Orientation** tab if necessary.
3. Choose **Landscape** to turn it on and choose **OK** or press **Enter** to return to the document.

To format in columns

4. Choose **Format, Columns** to go to the **Columns** dialog box.
5. Type **2** in the **Number of columns** text box.
6. Choose **Line Between** to turn it off. The **Columns** dialog box should look like the following example.

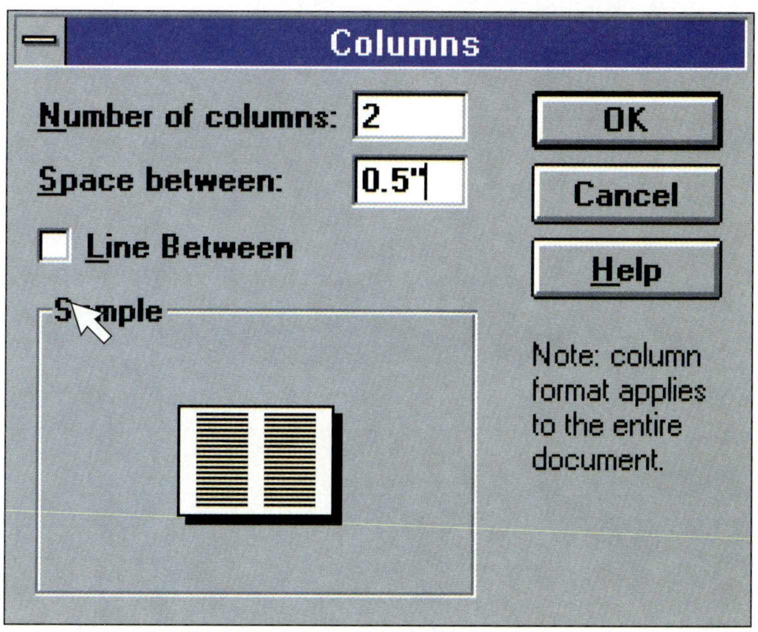

7. Choose **OK** or press **Enter**. The prompt asking if you want to change to Page Layout will be displayed if you are working in Normal view.

8. Choose **Yes** to return to the document.

9. Delete the titles **PUGET SOUND CHARTERS** and **NEEDS ANALYSIS.** Also delete any extra space, if there is any, so that the two subtitle lines are at the top of the document.

To center the subtitles in the first column

10. Select both subtitles and the following paragraph mark as shown here. Your screen should be similar to the following example. Notice the position of the margin markers in the Ruler.

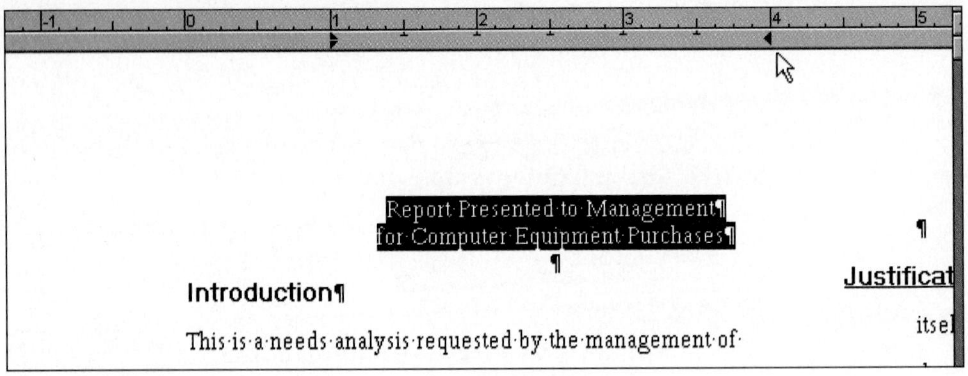

11. Press **Ctrl/Q** to return to normal formatting.

12. Press **Ctrl/E** to center the selected text in the first column. :See the following illustration. Notice the change in the margin markers. They are at 0 and 4 for both the heading and the text.

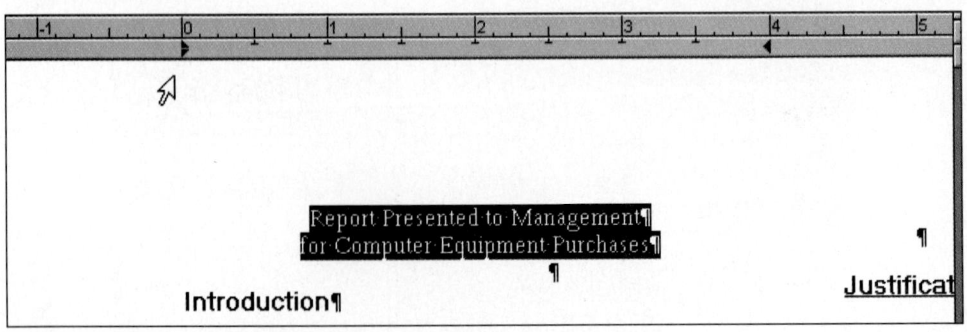

To create a header

The header will consist of the following text. PUGET SOUND CHARTERS will be aligned at the top left of the first column and NEEDS ANALYSIS will be aligned at the top right of the second column as shown in the following box.

PUGET SOUND CHARTERS NEEDS ANALYSIS

13. Choose **View, Headers and Footers** to go to the **Headers and Footers** dialog box.

14. Choose **Use header and footer paragraphs** to turn it on and choose **OK** or press **Enter** to return to the document.

15. Choose **View, Normal** and press the **Up Arrow** if necessary to go to the top of the document. The paragraph header and footer marks should be showing there as displayed in the following example.

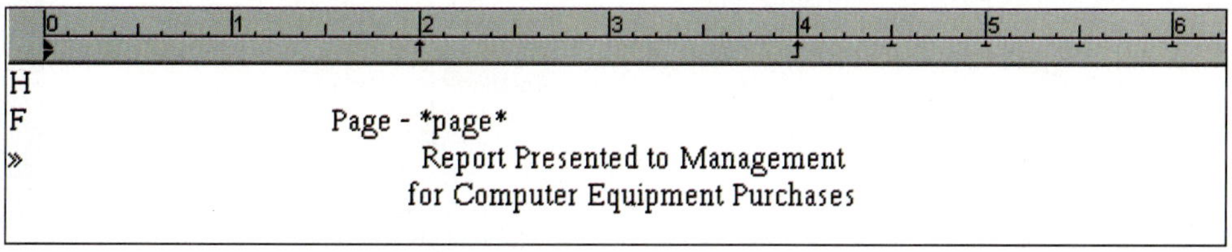

16. Type **PUGET SOUND CHARTERS** at the left margin in the paragraph header.

17. Drag the **Right** tab marker to the right edge of the Ruler and then click on the arrow at the right end of the horizontal scroll bar until **8.5** is displayed. Then continue dragging the **Right** tab marker to **8.5.** The screen jumps back to the left.

18. Press **Tab** once. Your screen will probably show the insertion point at **2.5** because you are in Normal view which does not show the text exactly as it will be printed.

NOTE: If you are using a smaller font type and size, you may have to drag the center tab to the left so that it does not affect the alignment when you pressed the **Tab** key in step 18.

19. Type **NEEDS ANALYSIS** at the insertion point. Your screen should resemble the following example. **View, All Characters** is turned on here so that you can see where the **Tab** key was pressed.

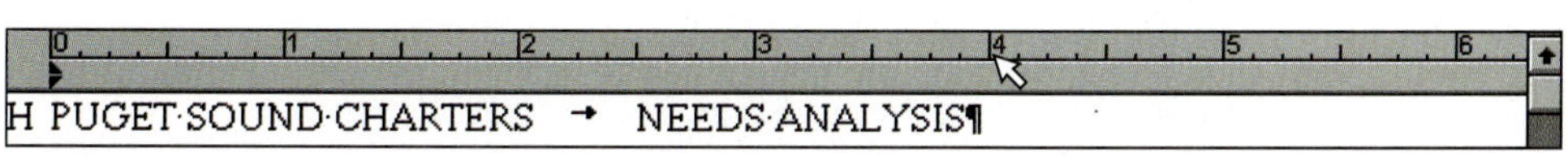

20. Choose **File, Print Preview** to confirm that the alignment is correct. Your screen should resemble the following example.

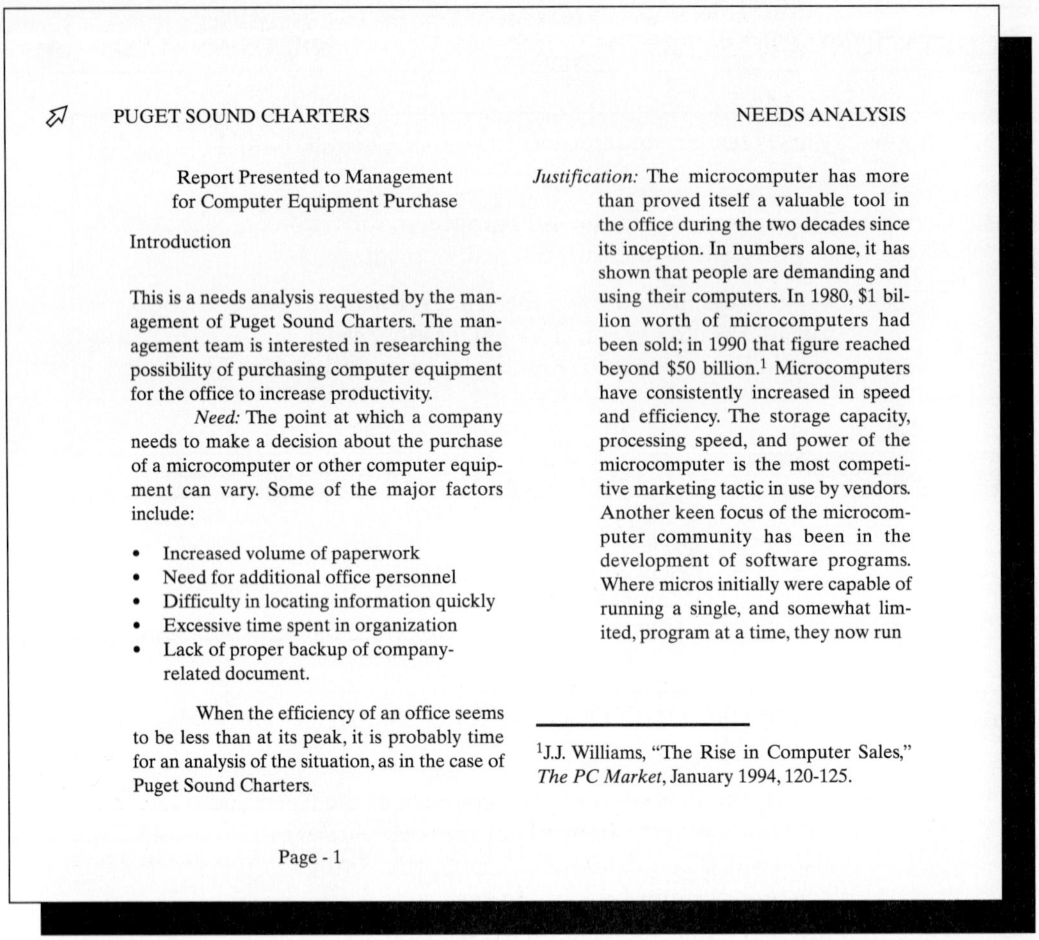

PUGET SOUND CHARTERS NEEDS ANALYSIS

Report Presented to Management
for Computer Equipment Purchase

Introduction

This is a needs analysis requested by the management of Puget Sound Charters. The management team is interested in researching the possibility of purchasing computer equipment for the office to increase productivity.

Need: The point at which a company needs to make a decision about the purchase of a microcomputer or other computer equipment can vary. Some of the major factors include:

- Increased volume of paperwork
- Need for additional office personnel
- Difficulty in locating information quickly
- Excessive time spent in organization
- Lack of proper backup of company-related document.

When the efficiency of an office seems to be less than at its peak, it is probably time for an analysis of the situation, as in the case of Puget Sound Charters.

Justification: The microcomputer has more than proved itself a valuable tool in the office during the two decades since its inception. In numbers alone, it has shown that people are demanding and using their computers. In 1980, $1 billion worth of microcomputers had been sold; in 1990 that figure reached beyond $50 billion.[1] Microcomputers have consistently increased in speed and efficiency. The storage capacity, processing speed, and power of the microcomputer is the most competitive marketing tactic in use by vendors. Another keen focus of the microcomputer community has been in the development of software programs. Where micros initially were capable of running a single, and somewhat limited, program at a time, they now run

[1]J.J. Williams, "The Rise in Computer Sales," *The PC Market*, January 1994, 120-125.

Page - 1

21. Choose **Next** in the Print Preview screen to see the following pages and to confirm the placement of the header.

22. Choose **Cancel** to return to the document.

To create a footer

Notice in the previous illustration that the footer is only under the first column. This will be changed-the page number will be deleted and the filename of the document will be displayed at the left margin and the date at the right margin. See the illustration following step 32.

23. Delete the text **Page -** and the code ***page***. in the footer paragraph.

24. Drag the **Right** tab marker to **8.5** as you did for the header.

25. Drag the **Center** tab marker to **4.25** as you did for the header.

26. Move the insertion point to the left margin in the footer paragraph if it is not already there.

27. Choose **Insert, Special Character** to display the dialog box as shown here

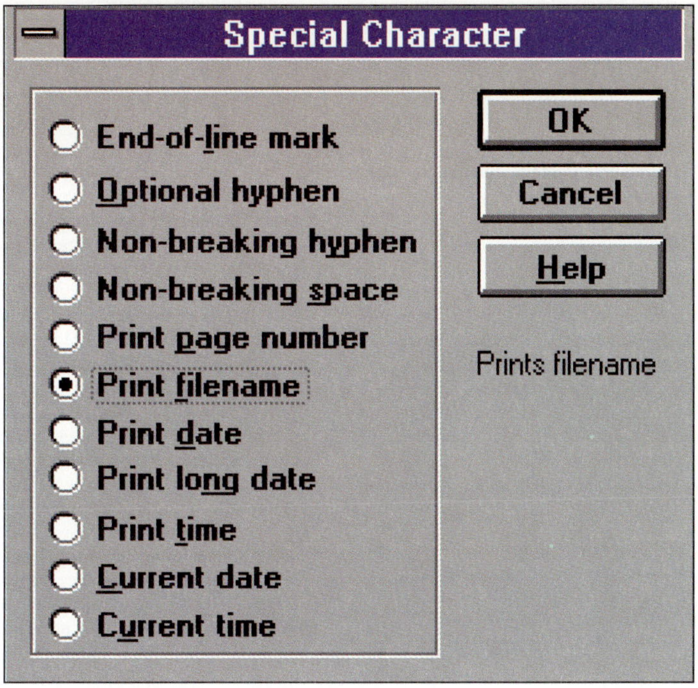

28. Choose **Print filename** and choose **OK** or press **Enter** to insert the code in the footer.

29. Press **Tab** twice. Again the insertion will be at **4.5** not at the right margin, but that is okay.

30. Choose **Insert, Special Character.**

31. Choose **Print date** and choose **OK** or press **Enter** to insert the date code in the footer. Your footer should now look like the following example.

32. Choose **File, Print Preview** to confirm the correct placement of the footer text. Your screen should resemble the following illustration.

PUGET SOUND CHARTERS — NEEDS ANALYSIS

Report Presented to Management
for Computer Equipment Purchase

Introduction

This is a needs analysis requested by the management of Puget Sound Charters. The management team is interested in researching the possibility of purchasing computer equipment for the office to increase productivity.

Need: The point at which a company needs to make a decision about the purchase of a microcomputer or other computer equipment can vary. Some of the major factors include:

- Increased volume of paperwork
- Need for additional office personnel
- Difficulty in locating information quickly
- Excessive time spent in organization
- Lack of proper backup of company-related document.

When the efficiency of an office seems to be less than at its peak, it is probably time for an analysis of the situation, as in the case of Puget Sound Charters.

Justification: The microcomputer has more than proved itself a valuable tool in the office during the two decades since its inception. In numbers alone, it has shown that people are demanding and using their computers. In 1980, $1 billion worth of microcomputers had been sold; in 1990 that figure reached beyond $50 billion.[1] Microcomputers have consistently increased in speed and efficiency. The storage capacity, processing speed, and power of the microcomputer is the most competitive marketing tactic in use by vendors. Another keen focus of the microcomputer community has been in the development of software programs. Where micros initially were capable of running a single, and somewhat limited, program at a time, they now run

[1]J.J. Williams, "The Rise in Computer Sales," *The PC Market*, January 1994, 120-125.

CH7TUT1.WPS — 8/22/94

33. Choose **Cancel** to return to the document.

To add footnotes

When the footnotes are inserted, they will be printed at the bottom of the appropriate column.

34. Move the insertion point following the period after the text **$50 billion.** at the end of the third sentence in the **Justification** paragraph.

HINT: You may want to stay in Normal view for this, because it is easier to move around in the document than in Page Layout..

35. Choose **Insert, Footnote** and choose **Use WorksWizard.** The footnote text is a reference to a magazine article, therefore, using the WorksWizard makes entering the footnote much easier.

36. Choose **Magazine** and choose **Next >** to go to the **Magazine Footnote WorksWizard** screen.

37. Fill in the boxes as follows:

In **Title of Article** type **The Rise in Computer Sales**

In **Name of Magazine** type **The PC Market**

In **Author(s)**	type **J. J. Williams**
In **Date of Publication**	type **January 1994**
In **Page(s)**	type **120-125**

The Magazine Footnote WorksWizard window should look like the following example.

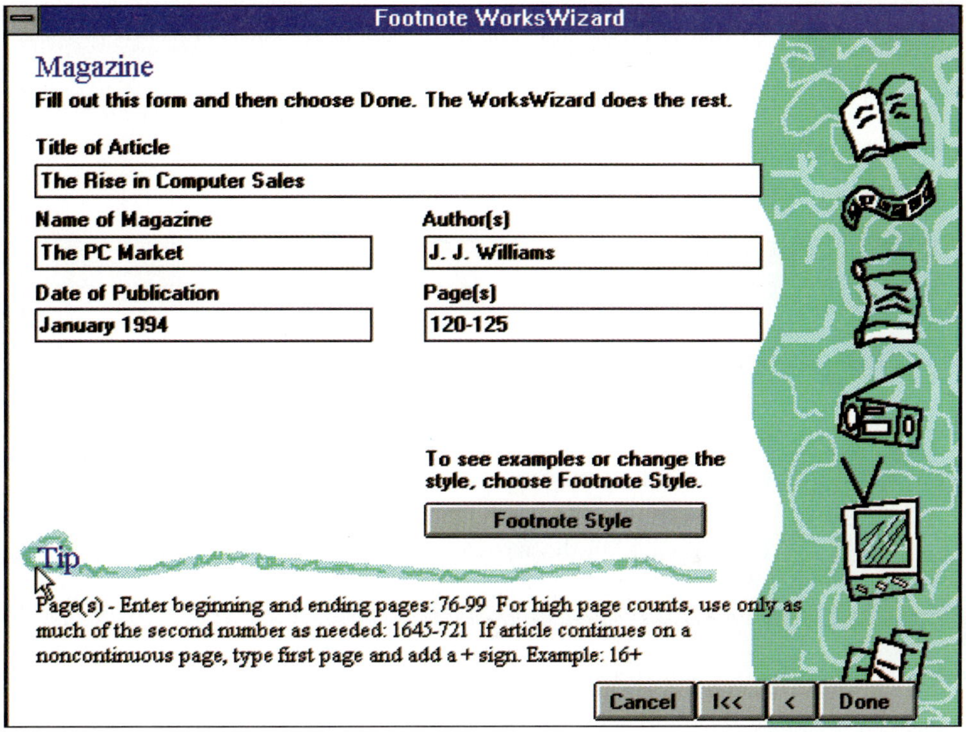

38. Choose **Footnote Style**. Then choose **Chicago Manual of Style** if it is not turned on.

39. Choose **OK** and then choose **Done**. Your footnote pane should resemble the following.

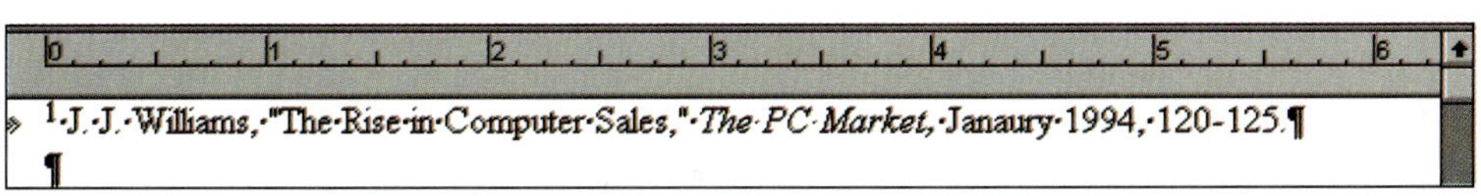

The second footnote information is shown in the box below.

"A New Market", by S. Johansson, published in Technology Today**, March 1992, p. 270.**

40. Move the insertion point to the end of the first **Justification** paragraph following the word **faster**.

41. Choose **Insert, Footnote, Use WorksWizard**.

42. Choose **Magazine** and **Next >**.

43. Type the information in the box shown above step 41 in the appropriate text boxes in the **Magazine Footnote WorksWizard** window. The **Chicago Manual of Style** is still turned on.

44. Choose **Done**. Your footnote pane should now resemble the following example.

45. Close the footnote pane by double-clicking on the split bar at the top of the pane.

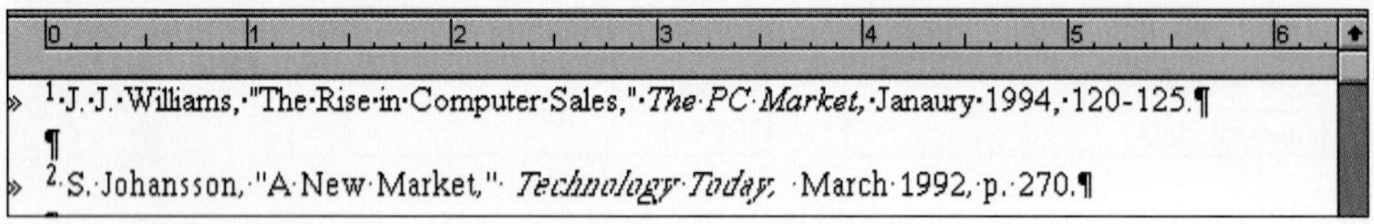

To adjust tabs in tabular columns

46. Select all lines in the table as shown in the following example. You may have to click on the arrows in the horizontal scroll bar to display the entire table. The Ruler now shows the tab stops for this table.

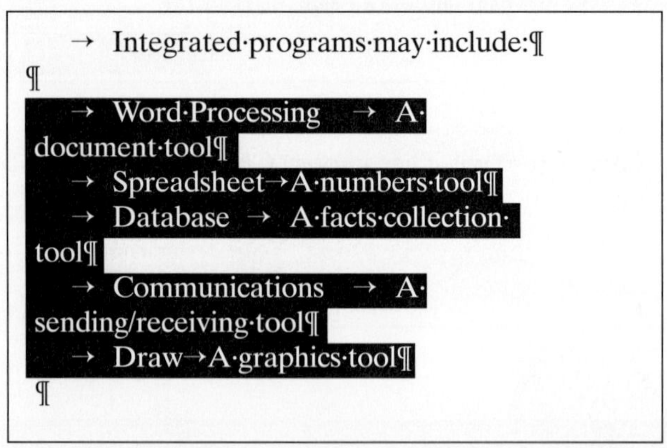

47. Drag the **Left** tab marker 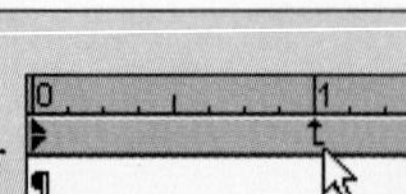 (which is at **1**) to the left to **.25**.

48. Drag the **Right** tab marker 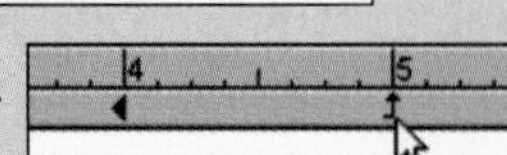 (which is probably at **5**) to the left to **3.75**. Your Ruler and table should now look like the following.

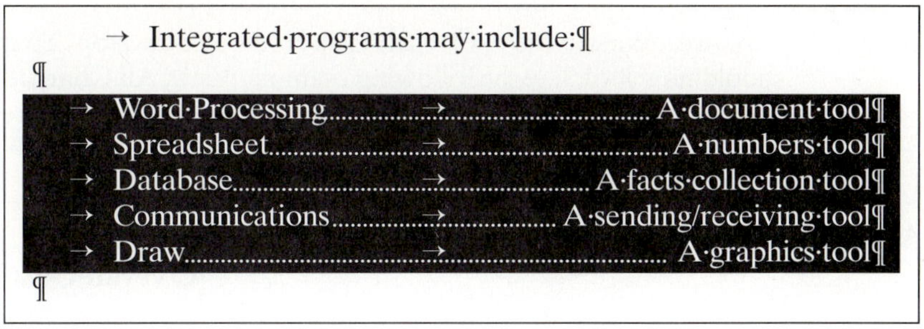
→ Integrated·programs·may·include:¶
¶
→ Word·Processing........→........A·document·tool¶
→ Spreadsheet........→........A·numbers·tool¶
→ Database........→........A·facts·collection·tool¶
→ Communications........→........A·sending/receiving·tool¶
→ Draw........→........A·graphics·tool¶
¶

To repeat this procedure for the tabular columns in the Results section

49. Select — all lines in the tabular columns. D not include the headings; they are adjusted separately.

50. Drag — the **Left** tab marker to **.1**.

51. Drag — the **Right** tab marker to **2.6**.

52. Drag — the **Decimal** tab marker to **3.5**. Your text and Ruler should now resemble the following example.

NOTE: If these measurements do not look like they are going to place the columns at good positions, drag them to different positions. As noted previously, if you are using a font that is a different size, your text may be aligned differently than that shown here.

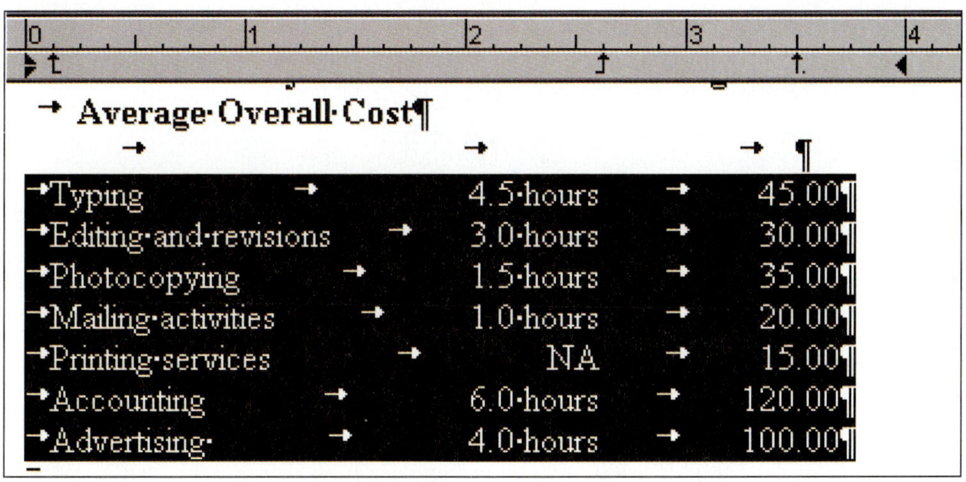

→ **Average·Overall·Cost¶**
→ → → ¶
→Typing → 4.5·hours → 45.00¶
→Editing·and·revisions → 3.0·hours → 30.00¶
→Photocopying → 1.5·hours → 35.00¶
→Mailing·activities → 1.0·hours → 20.00¶
→Printing·services → NA → 15.00¶
→Accounting → 6.0·hours → 120.00¶
→Advertising· → 4.0·hours → 100.00¶

To adjust the headings

53. Select — all text for the three headings. They are probably on two lines.

54. Drag — the three **Center** tabs to the following positions: **.5**, **2.25**, and **3.5**. The last heading needs further adjustment.

55. Move — the insertion point in front of **Overall** and press **Enter** to move it to the next line.

56. Press — **Tab** three times to move **Overall Cost** to the last tab stop. Your text should now look like the following example. **View, All Characters** is turned on here so that you can see where **Tab** and **Enter** were pressed.

→ **Activity** →	**Average·Time** →	**Average¶**
→ →	→	**·Overall·Cost¶**
→	→	¶
→Typing	→ 4.5·hours →	45.00¶
→Editing·and·revisions	→ 3.0·hours →	30.00¶
→Photocopying	→ 1.5·hours →	35.00¶
→Mailing·activities	→ 1.0·hours →	20.00¶
→Printing·services	→ NA →	15.00¶
→Accounting	→ 6.0·hours →	120.00¶
→Advertising·	→ 4.0·hours →	100.00¶

57. Go — to **Print Preview** to see how the document looks, Choose **Cancel** to return to the document, and make any adjustments that seem more appropriate for your text.

58. Save — the document as **CH7TUT1**.

59. Print — one copy of the document, and then close the document window.

REVIEW QUESTIONS

1. The ____________________ command from the ______________ menu is used to change margins in a document.
2. What are the standard settings for margins in a document?

____

____

____

3. A header is printed in the ________________ margin.
4. A footer is printed in the ________________ margin.
5. Identify each of the following marks and explain how they are entered in a document.

¶
Suggestion:¶
¶

____

____

____

____

____

____

6. Name the two types of references that can be used for footnotes.

____

____

7. Identify the following window and briefly describe what it does.

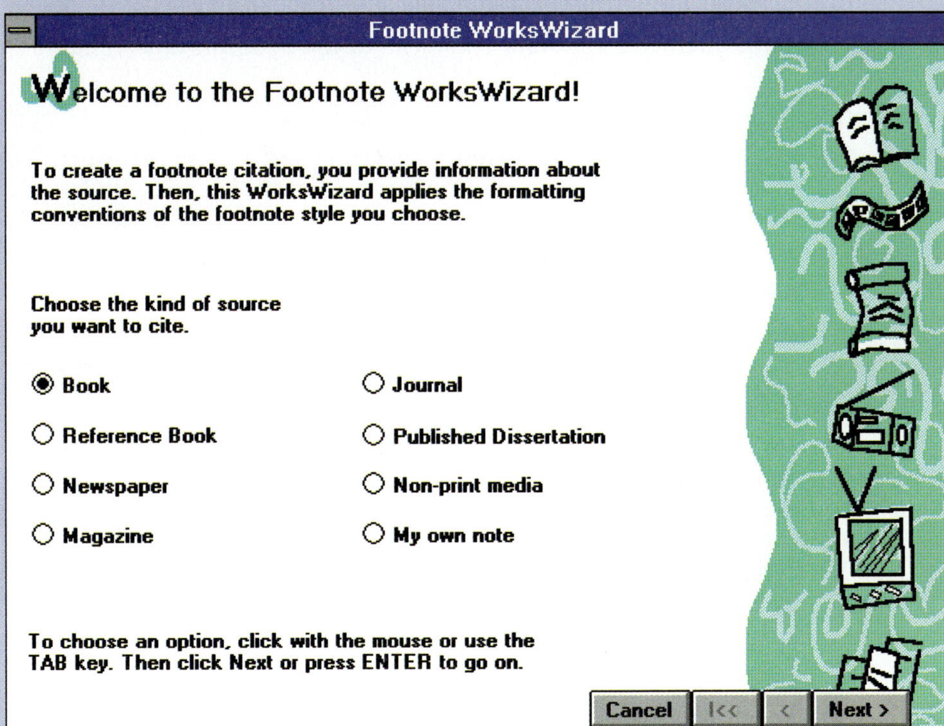

____

____

____

8. In order to use the window shown in question 7, choose the ______________ command from the ______________ menu and then choose ______________.

9. List two ways to close the footnote pane.

10. To format text in columns, choose the ______________ command from the ______________ menu.

11. To display text in the document window in columns, choose the ______________________ command from the ____________________ menu.
12. To display the entire page on the screen formatted in columns, choose the ______________________ command from the ____________________ menu.

Hands-on Exercises

Exercise 1

1. Open the document, **CH7TUT1** or retrieve it from the Instructor data disk.
2. Change the formatting from two columns to one column.
3. Change the orientation from landscape to portrait.
4. Change the margins to a left margin of **2** and a right margin of **1**. The left margin of this document can then be bound in a cover.
5. Adjust the tab sets in the two tabular column tables to fit the full-sized page.
6. Create a third numbered footnote at the end of the **Programs:** paragraph following

   . . . in use today are:. The footnote text is shown below. You do not necessarily need to use the WorksWizard for this; however, if you do, use the **Journal** or **My own note** option. If you chose the Journal style, placeholders for volume/issue and pages will be inserted in the footnote. Delete these manually from the footnote after it is displayed on your screen.

Zeigler, B., "Productivity Research Results," Puget Sound Charters, 1991.

7. Modify the header so that it does not appear on the first page. Change the text so that both titles are aligned at the right margin and are on two lines. To do this, drag the **center** tab away from the Ruler. Then locate the **right** tab that you dragged previously to 8.5, and drag it back to the new right margin at 5. Then press **Tab** in front of PUGET SOUND CHARTERS to align it at the right margin. If necessary, move the insertion point directly following CHARTERS, and press **Enter** to move NEEDS ANALYSIS to the next line. If NEEDS ANALYSIS does not align at the right margin you may have an extra tab mark in front of it that will need to be deleted.
8. Modify the footer. Delete all of the previous footer text, drag the Center tab to **2.75**, and center the following text and code, **Page - *page***.
9. Use **Print Preview** to see how the pages look. Make any adjustments that you think would enhance the appearance of the document.
10. Save the document as **CH7HO1** and print a copy of it.
11. Close the document.

Exercise 2

1. Open a new word processing window. The text shown in the box below will be used to create a new document.

TOTAL SALES
FIRST AND SECOND QUARTER
PUGET SOUND CHARTERS

Boat Name	Location	Last Year's Sales	This Year's Sales
Delano	Kirkland	36,890.00	42,520.00
The Spirit	Lake Union	35,550.00	41,236.00
Sea Wolf	Seward Park	38,950.00	45,780.00
Irish Sea	Shilshole	40,150.00	58,695.00

Needless to say, we are delighted with the increase in our business and our increased popularity in the Puget Sound area as one of the outstanding charter boat companies. We believe that we offer excellent service, fine dining, an outstanding staff, and scenic cruises.

P. J. MacRannall
President

2. Change to landscape orientation.
3. Choose a sans serif font type and a size that is at least 12 or 14 point for the titles, and choose a serif font type and a size that is at least 12 point for the table and remaining text.
4. Center the titles and type them in bold.
5. Set left tabs for the first two columns at positions that seem appropriate for you.
6. Set decimal tabs for the last two columns at positions that seem appropriate for you.
7. You may want to change to Page Layout view when typing the text in the columns in order to see exactly where they will be placed.
8. After entering the text in the columns, type the headings in bold and center over each column. Use Print Preview to see how the columns look. Drag the tab sets to different positions if adjustments are necessary.
9. Add the following footnote at the end of the title **Last Year's Sales.**

   From Financial Report for Fiscal Year 1993.

10. Run a spell check and then save the document as **CH7HO2.**
11. Print a copy of the document and close the document window.

Exercise 3

1. Retrieve **CH6HO4** from your data disk.
2. Set both the left and right margins at **1.5** using **File, Page Setup.**

3. Create the header shown below. Include your name and the name of the report.

BUSINESS MEETING REPORT	Your name
May 5, 1994	

4. Format the text in 2 columns with a line between the columns.
5. Delete the original title, BUSINESS MEETING REPORT, MAY 5 that appears at the top of the first column. (The header will serve as the title, in this case.)
6. Insert page numbers at the bottom of each page except the first.
7. Change to single spacing for the entire document.
8. Change the justified alignment to left alignment for the entire document.
9. Preview the document. Be sure that page breaks are appropriate. If a heading is at the bottom of a column by itself, move it so that it is above its accompanying text in the following column.
10. Save the document as **CH7HO3**.
11. Print a copy of the entire document.

Exercise 4

1. Retrieve **CH7HO3** from your data disk if necessary.
2. Add footnotes to the document as follows:

After paragraph 1 in the Introduction	[1]The Admininstration, Business Meeting Report, Vol. 1, No.1, May 5.
After the second bulleted paragraph in the Outstanding Events section	[2]The Captain, Puget Sound Charters Guidelines, 1995.
At the end of the Past Successes paragraph	[3]The Galley Crew and Staff, Outstanding Events Report, March 1995.

3. Change the left and right margins back to **1.25**.
4. Change the report layout to landscape mode and to three columns with line between.
5. Change paragraph text, except for the bulleted paragraphs, to double spacing. Adjust page breaks. Delete extra paragraph marks between headings and paragraphs to reduce the increased space that has been inserted as the result of change to double spacing. Change to Normal view to make it easier to locate these paragraph marks.
6. Adjust the header and footer text to fit the page. Items at the right should be aligned at the right margin. (Hint: In the Ruler, drag the tab stops to appropriate positions.)
7. Save the revised document as **CH7HO4** and print a copy of it.
8. Close all documents.

Exercise 1: CH7HO1

Report Presented to Management
for Computer Equipment Purchases

Introduction

This is a needs analysis requested by the management of Puget Sound Charters. The management team is interested in researching the possibility of purchasing computer equipment for the office to increase productivity.

Need: The point at which a company needs to make a decision about the purchase of a microcomputer or other computer equipment can vary. Some of the major factors include:

- Increased volume of paperwork
- Need for additional office personnel
- Difficulty in locating information quickly
- Excessive time spent in organization
- Lack of proper backup of company-related document.

When the efficiency of an office seems to be less than at its peak, it is probably time for an analysis of the situation, as in the case of Puget Sound Charters.

Justification: The microcomputer has more than proved itself a valuable tool in the office during the past two decades since its inception. In numbers alone, it has shown that people are demanding and using their computers. In 1980, $1 billion worth of microcomputers had been sold; in 1990 that figure reached beyond $50 billion.[1] Microcomputers have consistently increased in speed and efficiency. The storage capacity, processing speed, and power of the microcomputer is the most competitive marketing tactic in use by vendors. Another keen focus of the microcomputer community has been in the development of software programs. Where micros initially were capable of running a single, and somewhat limited, program at a time, they now run very complex and sophisticated programs that do more for the user and perform faster.[2]

The user interface is also important. Users want operating systems and software that are easy to use and take a minimum of time to learn. This has been provided by both the Macintosh system and the IBM personal computers and compatibles.

Programs: Word processing was perhaps the most popular use of microcomputers in the early years of software development; however, other software programs were also heavily used. Among the most popular programs were those for file

---

[1]J. J. Williams, "The Rise in Computer Sales," *The PC Market, **January 1990, 120-125.***

[2]S. Johnsson, "A New Market," *Technology Today, March 1992, p. 270.*

Page - 1

management and spreadsheet applications. Today, many programs are available. Nearly any need for a particular application can be met. Among some of the popular ones in use today are:[3]

- Very sophisticated word processing programs capable of outputting graphic images, using tables, performing calculations, and merging documents, to name a few.
- Database management programs are not only more sophisticated, but easier to use and capable of handling complex queries on multiple tables.
- Spreadsheet programs offer worksheets that hold thousand of cells and perform quick calculations.

  Integrated programs may include:

  Word Processing..................................A document tool
  Spreadsheet...A numbers tool
  Datebase.......................................A facts collection tool
  Communications ....A sending/receiving tool
  Draw...A graphics tool

Results: This team has spent the past month monitoring the activities performed on a daily basis at Puget Sound Charters and as a result arrived at the following as an account of the time and money spent on individual activities

Activity	Average Time	Average Overall Cost
Typing	4.5 hours	45.00
Editing and revisions	3.0 hours	30.00
Photocopying	1.5 hours	35.00
Mailing activities	1.0 hours	20.00
Printing services	NA	15.00
Accounting	6.0 hours	120.00
Advertising	4.0 hours	100.00

Summary: It is the recommendation of this team that time could be saved in all the activities observed during the past month. Time spent making revisions of documents could be lessened through the use of a word processing program. Many observations of completely retyping documents were made.

Photocopies are made of all documents. This is the only method of making multiple copies to send to clients, company personnel, and others. While a photocopy is a good copy, it is not as good as an original and it costs more. It is far less expensive to print multiple copies using a good letter-quality printer or laser printer than to photocopy pages.

---

[3]B. Zeigler, "Productivity Research Results," *Puget Sound Charters*, Vol./Issue (1991)

PUGET SOUND CHARTERS
NEEDS ANALYSIS

Mailing activities included typing original mailing labels. Again, a database file and a word processing program would eliminate the need to retype frequently used mailing labels. The labels can also be used to merge with form letters and a file in a database program to gather information about clients needs.

The same observations are true for the printing and accounting expenses and with some of the advertising expenses. Many of the printing services could be eliminated with either a sophisticated work processing program or a desktop publishing program.

Recommendations: It is the recommendation of this team that the following equipment be purchased to increase productivity and decrease costs.

- A personal computer using the DOS operating system.
- A word processing program.
- An accounting or spreadsheet program.
- A database program.

OR

- An integrated software program such as Miscrosoft Works which includes word processing, graphics, spreadsheet, database, and communications capabilities
- A letter-quality or laser printer.

Information on cost will be provided early next month.

Page - 3

Exercise 3: CH7HO3

BUSINESS MEETING REPORT Your name

May 5, 1994

Introduction

The fifth business meeting for the year was held on May 5. The primary agenda for the meetings was to discuss both past successes and past failure, although we in the company look at failures as potential successes; therefore, all agenda items were viewed in a positive light. In addition, discussion also concentrated on possible promotional issues for the busy, upcoming summer schedule. The following is a summary of key issues the company faces. Open discussion is encouraged among all employees, and feedback is

- All employees should read the manual on ship safety and focus in particular on steps to take when passengers fall into the sea.
- All employees should report any unseemly incidents immediately. They should focus in particular on dangerous objects that might cause accidents, such as the banana peel. If one approaches a potentially hazardous situation, the immediate action should be to make an announcement over the speaker system. Be sure to scream loudly into the speaker so that the

desired by administrative personnel.

Outstanding Events

Several outstanding events were reported during the month of March. They included incidents involving passengers overboard, banana peels, near vessel collisions, and scrubbed chickens. Needless to say the administration and particularly the visiting vice president of the company found this news somewhat disturbing. All present agreed on the following steps (in order of priority) to assist in avoiding future incidents.

message is heard by all on board. For example, "Watch out! Watch! Hand rail missing on stern deck."

Inform the administration or the captain of any and all other outstanding events as they may occur.

Past Successes

The most recent outstanding success story on board occurred last week when the governor visited the ship for dinner. The dinner and reception following could not have gone more

Page - 1

BUSINESS MEETING REPORT Your name

May 5, 1994

smoothly. The main course included chicken legs with banana cream sauce. Champagne was served

(although it was accidentally placed near the galley ovens and so was served warm). Following the governor's speech, pictures with the captain and staff were scheduled. Somehow the captain's hat and jacket appeared on the galley chief just as the camera clicked. In the photo the galley chief's face was obscured from the oversized hat. The captain could not be found; however, no one, including the governor, seemed to notice and all had a very good time. We are delighted with the governor's timing. It seems she came down with severe chills and sweats the following morning-a reminder that we should all get our flu shots.

Building Future Success

As mentioned in the introduction, we do not focus on failures, but rather look at them as potentials for building success. Following the avoided collision (due to a lightning storm and the quick reactions of the captain) we have put the sales staff to work on increasing the number of cruises during the winter storm months. It is clear that lightning storms aid in a safer journey for our crew and passengers and so the number of trips should be increased on dark and stormy nights. We will also monitor the effects of other natural aids such as high winds, turbulent seas, and so on on.

Conclusion

Your comments are welcome as always. We are collecting reports for the next outstanding events bulletin, and will keep you informed of important issues directly affecting you. More information is due out this week on the merit raises of .025 percent due to the top two employees of the year. Keep up the good work!

5/2/94

Page - 2

CHAPTER 8

Creating A Spreadsheet

OBJECTIVES

- Create a spreadsheet
- Move through a spreadsheet
- Enter text and values
- Change column width
- Edit cells
- Save a spreadsheet
- Close and retrieve a file
- Use a formula to compute values

PREVIEW

A spreadsheet is much like an accountant's worksheet. In fact, the area in which you work in a spreadsheet program is often called a worksheet. It can be used for financial planning and for creating income statements and budget projections, and other financial record keeping documents. Spreadsheets can also allow for the extensive use of computations through formulas. Formulas can be entered for minor calculations, such as adding two values together, or for more complex calculations. Formulas can also be used to perform searches using IF-THEN-ELSE structures.

CREATING A SPREADSHEET

Beginning a new spreadsheet is similar to starting other documents in Works.

Create a Spreadsheet

1. Choose **File, Create New File** to display the Startup window if it is not already displayed.
2. Choose **Spreadsheet.**

The spreadsheet window shown in Figure 8-1 appears.

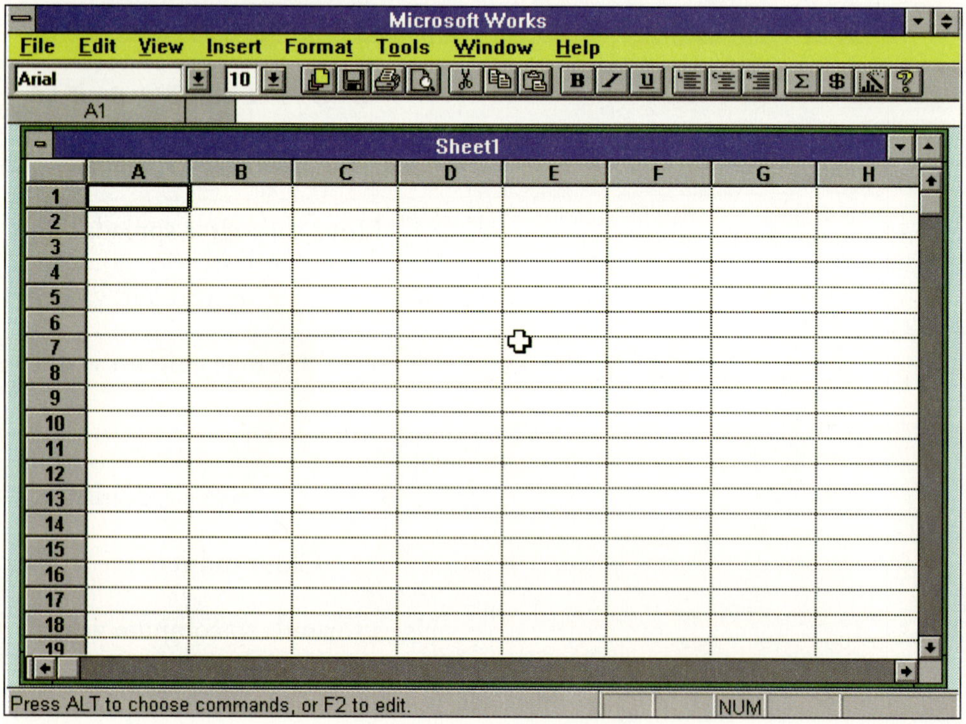

Figure 8-1
New spreadsheet document

The parts of the screen are identified in Table 8-1.

Menus

The menus are very similar to those used in word processing.

Toolbar

Shows tools used for quick access to commands and functions.

Title bar

Shows the current title of the spreadsheet. When the file is named and saved, the filename is displayed here.

Columns

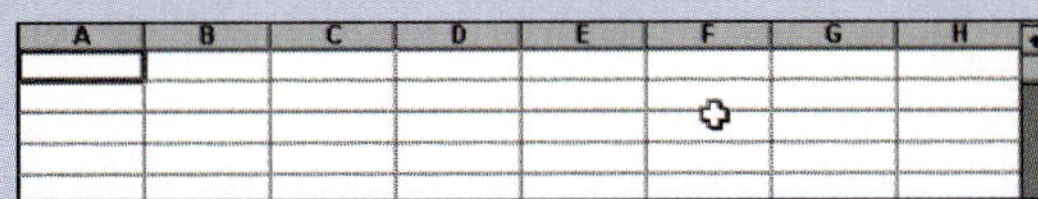

Columns are set at 10 spaces unless the width is changed. The column labels appear across the top of all spreadsheets. They are identified as A, B, C, and so on.

Rows

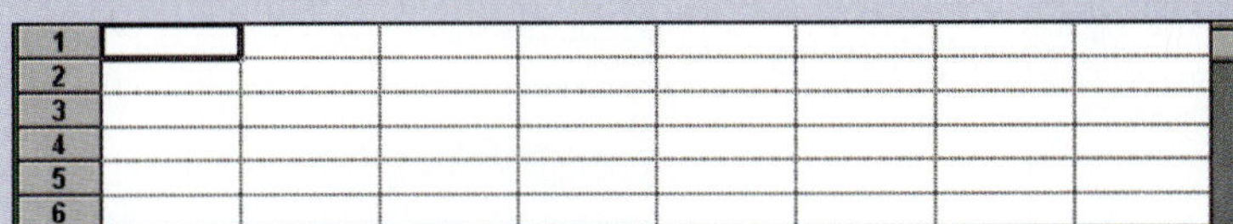

Rows are numbered down the left side of the spreadsheet: 1, 2, 3, and so on.

Active cell

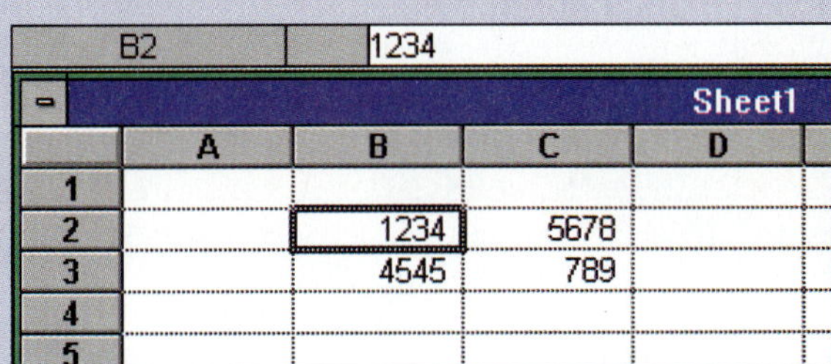

The active or current cell is the one that is highlighted. This is like the insertion position except that it fills up the entire width of the cell. A cell is the intersection of a row and a column. The active cell address appears in the upper left corner above the title bar.

Split box

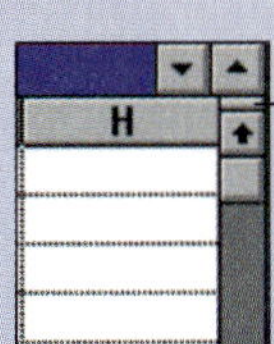

SPLIT BOX

Splits the current window horizontally into two sections by dragging the mouse button on it.

Formula bar

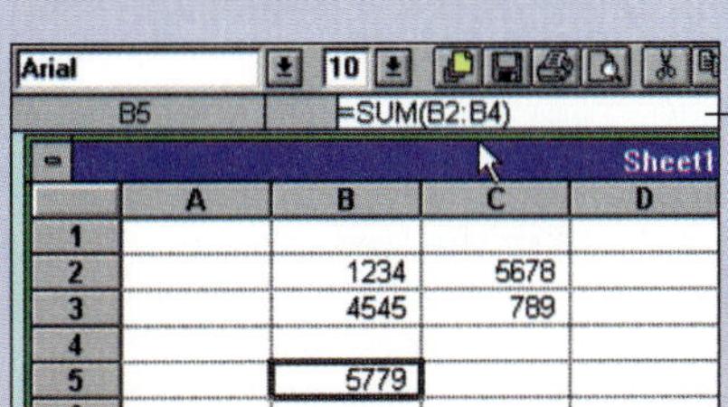

FORMULA BAR

The formula bar shows the contents of the active cell. It also shows

	values or labels as you are entering them into a cell. The values in the formula bar can be edited by pressing the **F2** key or clicking on the value in the bar with the left mouse button. It also shows the formula used, such as in the above example. The active cell, however, will display the answer.
Scroll Bar	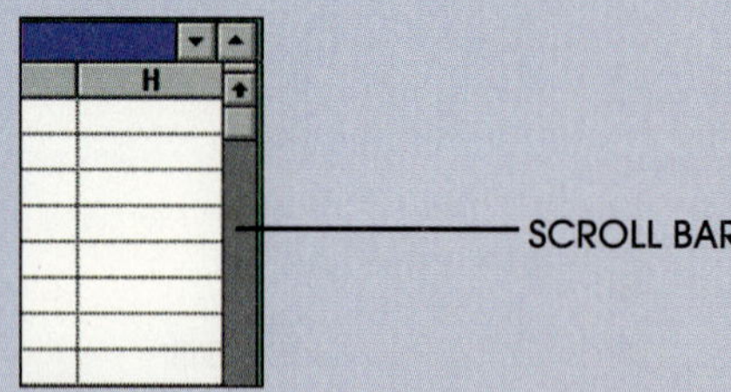 The scroll bars are used the same as in word processing or other Works windows. Using the mouse, you can drag the box in the bar to a different position. Scroll bars are located at the right (as shown above) and at the bottom of the screen.
Control menu boxes	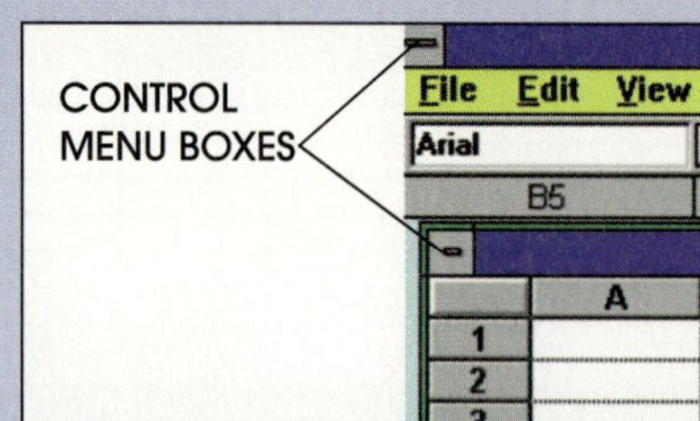 The Control menu boxes adjust the size of either the Works window or the active spreadsheet window. You can also double click on the box to either close the active spreadsheet or to exit from Works.
Status and message lines	 Indicates extend (EXT), which is turned on and off by pressing **F8**, Caps Lock (CAPS), or Num Lock (NUM). 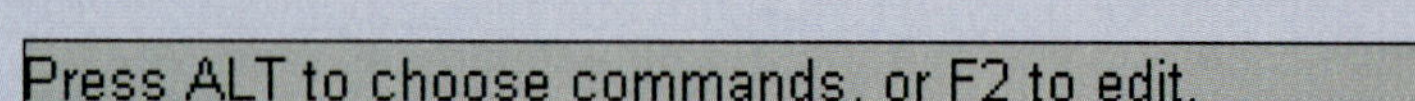 Shows actions to be taken next or keys that can be pressed during the current action.

Table 8-1
Parts of the screen

MOVING THROUGH A SPREADSHEET

When a cell is selected, it is referred to as being highlighted. Sometimes a range of cells is highlighted, much like a block of text in word processing, so that special formats can be applied to it or so that it can be printed. For now, you will practice moving the highlighting to various positions in the worksheet by using the keyboard, pressing the left mouse button, or choosing menu commands.

Use the Keyboard or Mouse for Scrolling

Table 8-2 shows ways of moving around in the spreadsheet.

Press the following keys	Or the left mouse button	To move to this position
Left or Right Arrow	Click in the cell	Left or right
Down or Up Arrow	Click in the cell	Up or down
Home	Click in the cell	To the first cell in the row
End	Click in the cell	To the last non-empty cell in the row
Page Down	Click once in the lower right of the vertical scroll (bar above the arrow)	To move down one screen
Page Up	Click once in the upper right of the vertical scroll (bar below the arrow)	To move up one screen
Ctrl/Page Down	Click once in the right corner of the bottom scroll bar (left of the arrow)	To move right one screen
Ctrl/Page Up	Click once in the left corner of the bottom scroll bar (right of the arrow)	To move left one screen
Ctrl/Home	Drag the scroll bar(s) and click in the cell	To move to the upper left cell of the spreadsheet, usually cell A1
Ctrl/End	Drag the scroll bar(s) and click in the cell	To move to the lower right corner of the spreadsheet; the last cell in a column and row in the spreadsheet
F5 (the Go To key) or choose **Edit, Go To**		To move to a specific cell
Ctrl/Arrow Keys		To move the cursor to the outermost cell as follows:
Ctrl/Right Arrow		to column IV (last column)
Ctrl/Left Arrow		to column A
Ctrl/Down Arrow		to row 16,384 (last row)
Ctrl/Up Arrow		to row 1

Table 8-2

Selection of movements in a spreadsheet

1. Practice moving through the empty spreadsheet on the screen. The **End** commands used at this time will only move to the first column.

LOOK AT THE SPREADSHEET SIZE

The area of the spreadsheet now visible is only a small portion of the entire worksheet area. Column letters repeat themselves and rows extend into the thousands. The last column and row is number IV16,384. That is column IV and row 16,384; therefore, what you now see on your screen is only a small representation of the entire spreadsheet. Figure 8-2 graphically represents the size of the screen in relation to the entire worksheet. The small box in the upper left corner is the visible worksheet on the screen, and the remaining area is all of the spreadsheet space available.

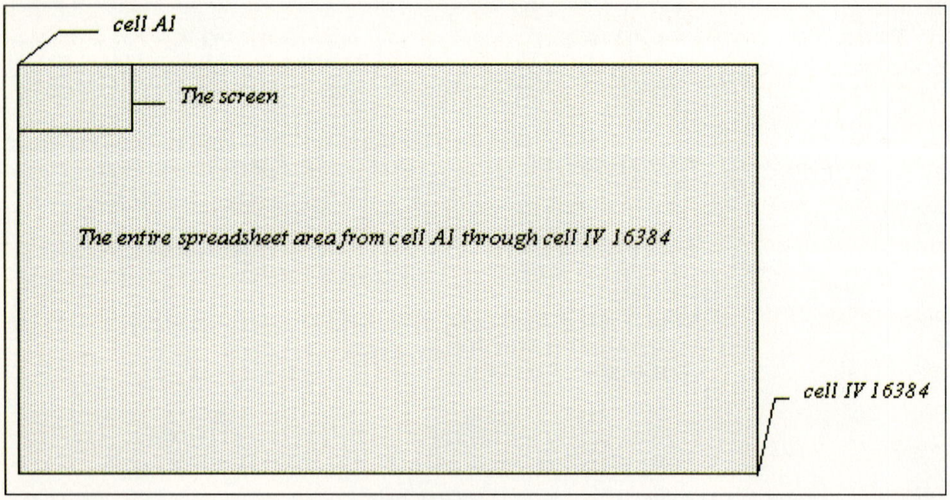

Figure 8-2
The Works Spreadsheet Screen

1. **Position** the highlight in cell **A1** by pressing **Ctrl/Home** or by dragging the scroll bars with the left mouse button.

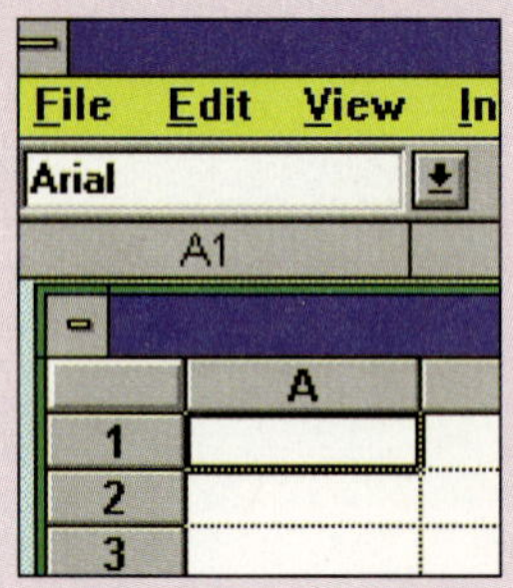

cell A1

2. **Move** the highlight across the spreadsheet to cell **AA1** by pressing the **Right Arrow** key or by clicking on the right arrow in the horizontal scroll bar as shown here.

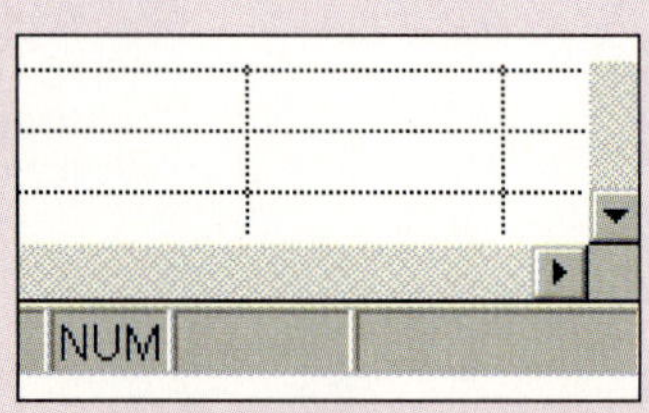

NOTE: Watch the upper left corner just above the column labels as the cell position indicator changes from A1 to AA1. Whichever cell address is showing in the upper left corner is referred to as the current cell.

As the cell location moves right, the column letters change. They increase from A through Z and then begin repeating themselves. The first repeat begins by inserting an A in front of each column, such as AA, AB, AC, and so on. If you continue moving to the right, the letters (columns) will adjust again to BA, BB, BC, and so on, until the final columns increase through the I's and become IA, IB, IC through IV as shown in Figure 8-2. The rows in the spreadsheet increase as well, through approximately 16,384.

ENTERING TEXT AND VALUES

Text and *values* are entered into the cells in a worksheet. A *value* is a number, such as 175.42 or 10. *Text* is any label, such as First Quarter or Balance Sheet. When text is entered into a cell in which there is no text or value in the cell to the right, it will overlap automatically into the next cell or cells. This is the procedure normally used to enter a long heading at the top of a spreadsheet. Other cells in the spreadsheet that contain text, or where values or text appear in the cells to the right, usually have the width of the column adjusted so that the contents of the cell fit within the cell boundaries. Here, you will enter a heading at the top, and then enter text and values in the spreadsheet body. As the spreadsheet is modified, it will be necessary to adjust the width of the columns and edit text and values.

Enter Text in Cells

1. Position the highlight in cell **A1** by pressing **Ctrl/Home** or by using the scroll bar and mouse.
2. Move to cell **C1** by pressing the **Right Arrow** key or by clicking once in the cell with the left mouse button.

NOTE: The cell address C1 appears in the upper left corner of the window.

3. Type **PUGET SOUND CHARTERS.**

NOTE: As you are typing, watch the formula bar (box) located above the spreadsheet title bar. The text you are typing appears in the formula bar as shown in Figure 8-3. You can view the contents you are typing either in the formula bar or in the cell. This is helpful for checking for accuracy. Use the **Backspace** key or the **Delete** key to make corrections if necessary.

When the title appears correct,

4. Press **Enter.** When **Enter** is pressed, the title appears in cells C1, D1, and E1.

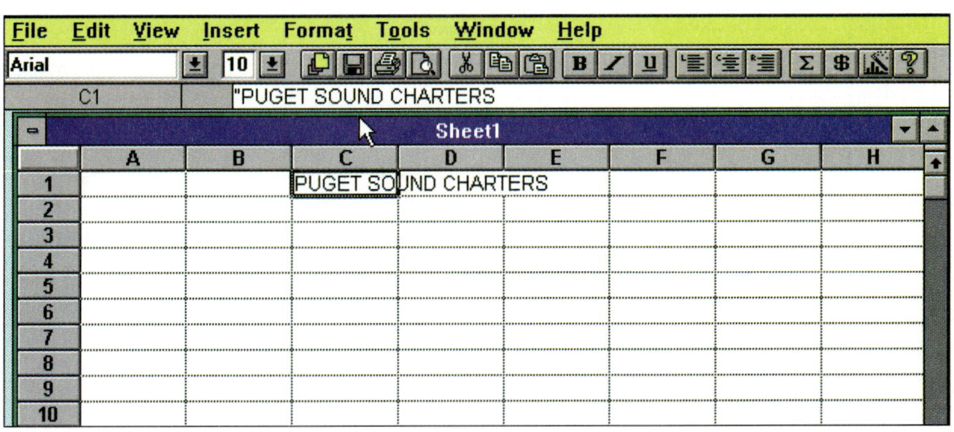

Figure 8-3
The formula bar

Because you entered this heading in cell C1, you will always need to be in that cell to make changes to its contents. The entire heading is contained in cell C1, even though it overlaps into another cell. Look in the formula bar where the title appears. This shows the title as it is entered into the cell.

5. Press the **Right Arrow** key once or click the left mouse button in cell **D1**.

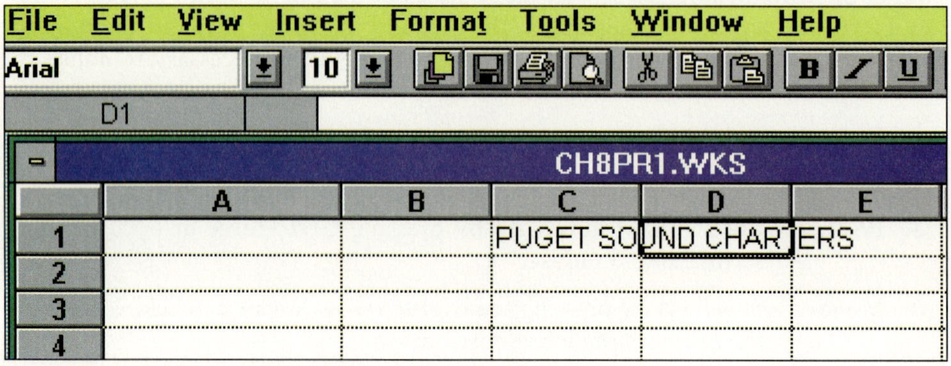

Notice that this cell does not show any contents in the formula bar. The cell is recognized as empty. If you entered a value or other text into it, it would replace the text overlapping into the cell, in this case the *UND CHARTERS*; however, it would not affect the contents of the cell.

6. Position the highlight in cell **C1** again. The text appears as shown in Figure 8-4.

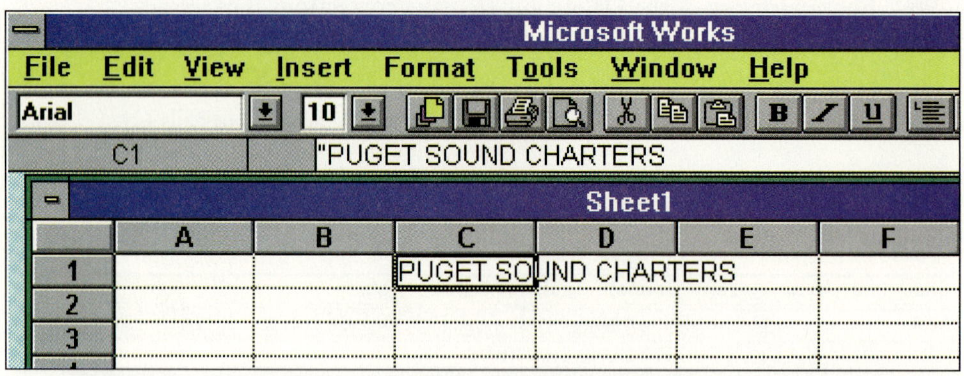

Figure 8-4
Text in the formula bar

The double quotation mark showing in the formula bar identifies the heading as text and not as values that could be used in calculations. It is inserted in front of text automatically. If labels such as column headings begin with values such as 1992, a double quote mark must be typed prior to typing the heading.

7. Position the highlight in cell **B3**. Watch the upper left corner of the formula bar as the cell address changes.

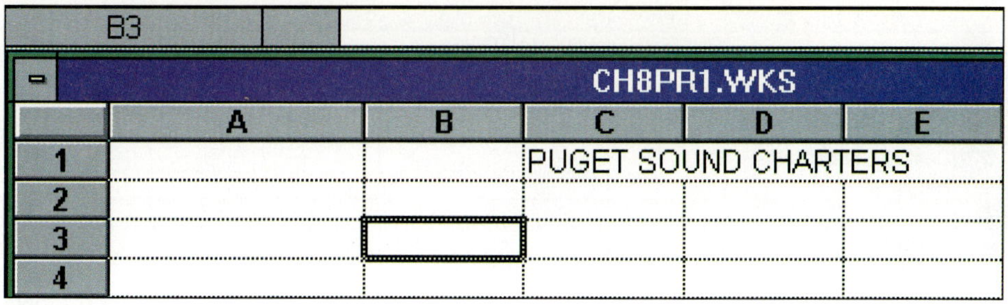

8. Type	**"1991** (including the double quote).
9. Press	**Enter** or click the left mouse button once in the cell.

The column heading, 1991, is entered into the cell as text because of the double quote mark prior to the numbers. Notice that this text is also aligned on the left side of the cell. If it had been entered as a value, it would align on the right side of the cell. Pressing **Enter** or clicking the left mouse button once in the same cell inserts the text into the cell and leaves it highlighted. Pressing an arrow key moves the highlight to an adjacent cell and inserts the text in the current cell as shown in Figure 8-5.

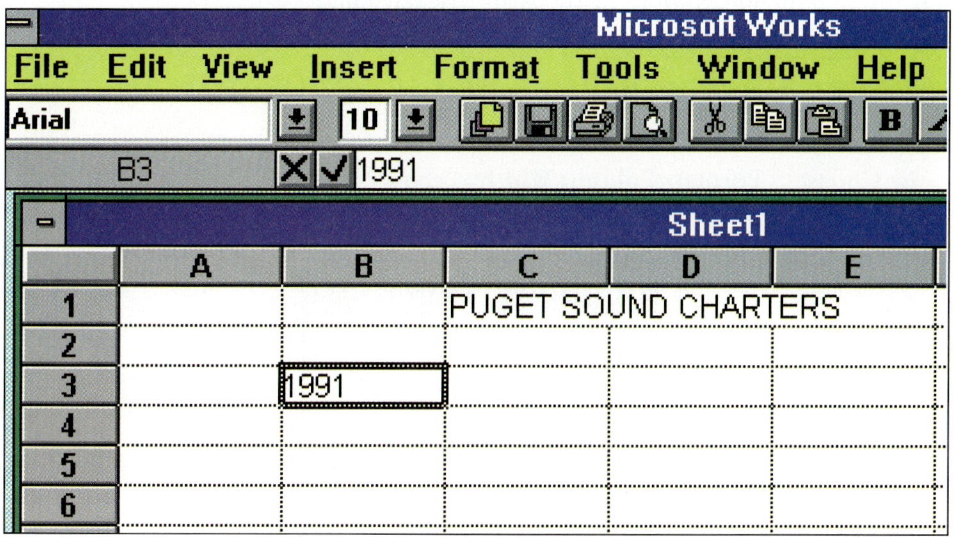

Figure 8-5
Ways to insert text

10. Position	the highlight in cell **C3**.
11. Type	**"1992**. (Do not type the period.)
12. Press	the **Right Arrow** key once or click the left mouse button in the cell to the right (D3).

Use any of the methods in the paragraph above Figure 8-5 to enter the following column headings.

13. Type	**"1993** as text (with the double quote, ") in cell D3.
14. Type	**"1994** in cell E3 as text.
15. Position	the highlight in cell **A4** and type the following text down the column in A5, A6, and so on, as shown (do not worry if they overlap into other cells).

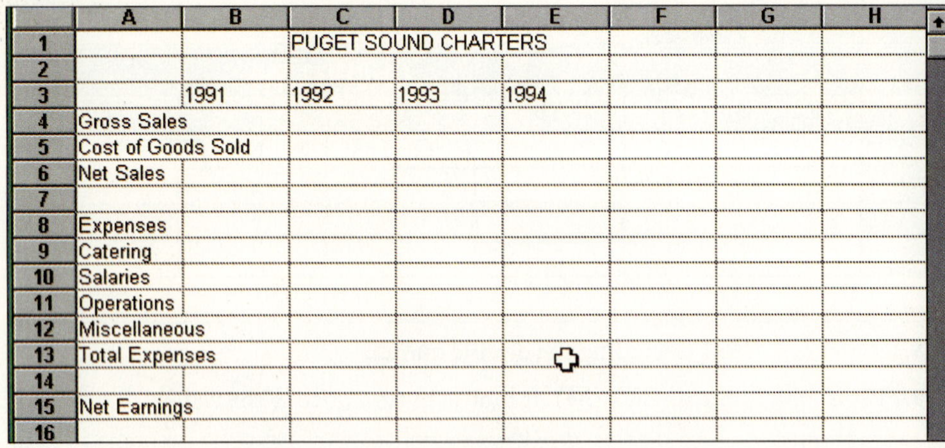

CHANGING COLUMN WIDTH

The text entered into column A in this spreadsheet overlaps into column B. Cost of Goods Sold, for example, extends under the column heading, 1991. To adjust the width use the **Column Width** command in the **Format** menu or use the mouse to drag the column border. Both methods are discussed here.

Change Column Width Using the Format Menu

1. Position the highlight anywhere in column A.
2. Choose **Format, Column Width** as shown here.

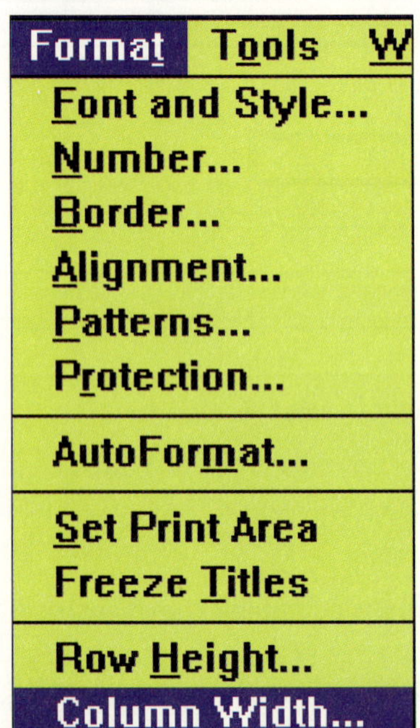

The Column Width dialog box is displayed as shown below. The default width of 10 characters is showing.

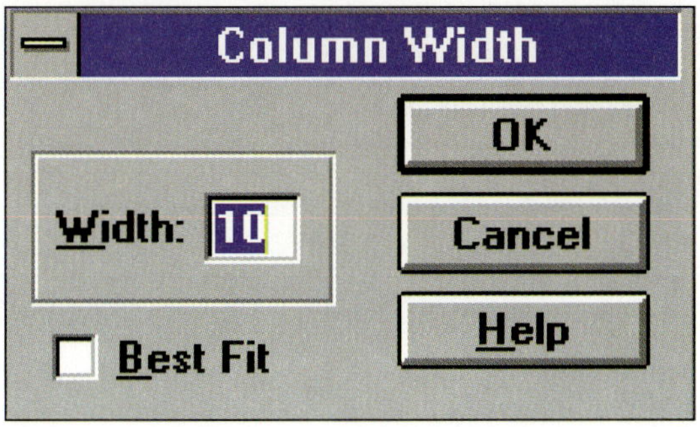

Since Cost of Goods Sold is the widest block of text, the column width should be slightly wider than this label, which is 18 characters wide. Make the column width 20.

3. Type 20 in the Width text box.

NOTE: As soon as 20 is typed, the 10 will be removed automatically.

4. Choose **OK** or press **Enter**.

NOTE: If you have any questions about how to make dialog box or menu selections, read through Chapter 2. It explains the procedure in more detail. This part on the Spreadsheet tool assumes that you have completed the Word Processing part and are experienced with making menu and dialog box selections.

The column width is adjusted and the labels no longer overlap into column B as shown in the following illustration.

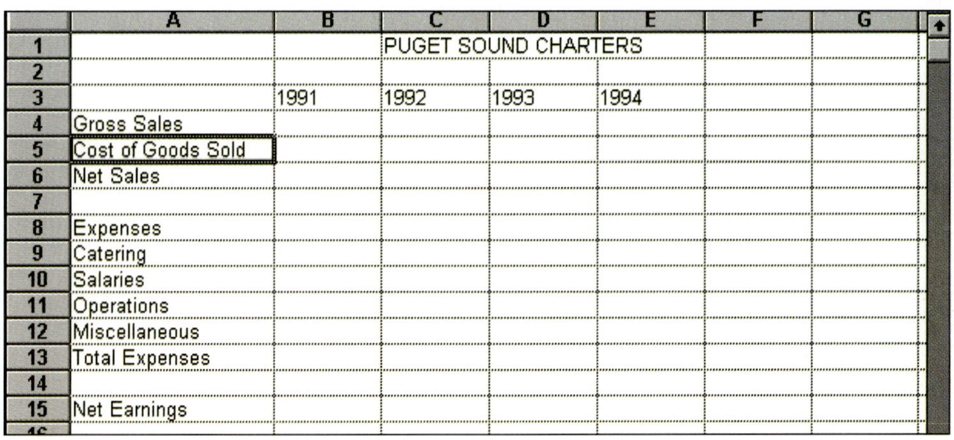

Change the Width Using the Mouse

Column width may also be changed by dragging the right border of a column label to a new position. You can also select the entire column and drag the right border of the column to a different position.

1. Position the pointer on the right border of column A. The pointer becomes a double arrow and the word *adjust* is displayed below it as shown here.

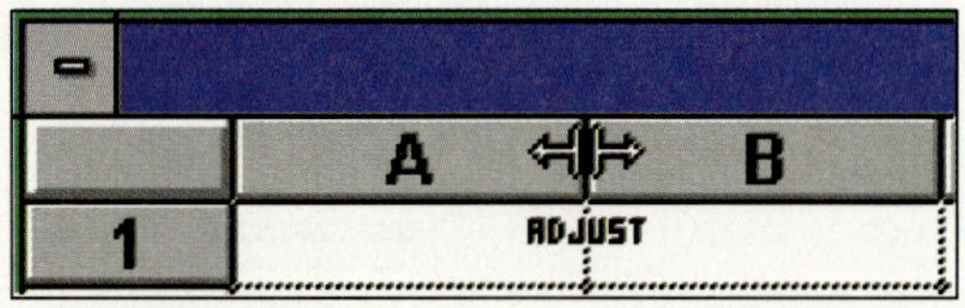

2. Hold — the left mouse button down and practice dragging the border to the left and right.
3. Release — the left mouse button when the border is positioned just to the right of the widest text in column A.

Use this method whenever you want to adjust the column width quickly.

Enter Values in Cells

Values are typed directly in a cell without inserting special characters (such as double quotes) prior to the numbers.

1. Position — the highlight in cell **B4**.
2. Type — **110950**.
3. Press — the **Right Arrow** key once or click the left mouse button in cell **C4**.
4. Type — **116300** in cell C4.
5. Continue — entering all the values as shown in the following example.

	A	B	C	D	E	F	G
1			PUGET SOUND CHARTERS				
2							
3		1991	1992	1993	1994		
4	Gross Sales	110950	116300	151540	188231		
5	Cost of Good Sold	8540	9430	10500	18900		
6	Net Sales						
7							
8	Expenses						
9	Catering	8800	9250	12325	15800		
10	Salaries	15000	22500	60600	60800		
11	Operations	5500	3000	5500	7530		
12	Miscellaneous	4000	6500	8000	2500		
13	Total Expenses						
14							
15	Net Earnings						
16							

EDITING CELLS

Cells can be edited in a number of ways using any of the methods listed in Table 8-3.

Function	Procedure
Type new contents	Type over the old cell contents. When an **Arrow** key or the **Enter** key is pressed, the new contents will replace the old.

Replace with a blank space	Enter a blank space into the cell by pressing the **Spacebar** once and then pressing **Enter**.
Use **F2**	Press the **F2** key to go to the formula bar where text can be edited. Changes may also be viewed in the cell as edits are made. You can use the **Backspace, Delete,** and any of the arrow keys to edit in the formula Bar. When the **Enter** key is pressed, the edit is completed.
Clear the cell	Choose the **Clear** command from the **Edit** menu.

Table 8-3
Editing in a spreadsheet

Replace Cell Contents

1. Highlight cell **A4**.

NOTE: From now on the instructions will use "Highlight" when referring to selecting a particular cell on the spreadsheet.

2. Type **GROSS SALES** in all CAPS.
3. Press **Enter.**

The word in capital letters replaced the old cell contents as shown in Figure 8-6.

	A	B	C	D	E
1			PUGET SOUND CHARTERS		
2					
3		1991	1992	1993	1994
4	GROSS SALES	110950	116300	151540	188231
5	Cost of Good Sold	8540	9430	10500	18900

Figure 8-6
Replacing Cell Contents

4. Highlight cell **A6.**
5. Type **NET SALES** in all CAPS and press **Enter.**

Edit with F2 Key

1. Highlight cell **A8.**
2. Press **F2.**

The cursor moves to the formula bar.

3. Press the **Backspace** key to remove all lowercase letters.
4. Type **XPENSES** (the E is already in place).
5. Press **Enter.**

NOTE: You can edit the contents of cells at any time by using the F2 key to go to the formula bar where you can use the arrow keys, **Backspace, Delete,** and type new text to make your edits. The advantage of this option is that you do not have to retype the entire contents.

CLEARING AND DELETING CELL CONTENTS

Cell contents can be removed using the **Clear** command in the **Edit** menu. This command erases the contents of one or more highlighted cells.

Clear and Delete Cell Contents

1. Highlight cell **A13**.
2. Choose **Edit, Clear** from the **Edit** menu shown here.

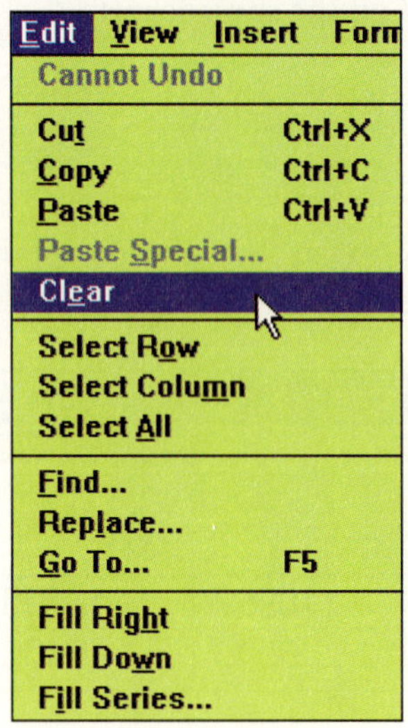

The cell contents are erased.

3. Type **TOTAL EXPENSES** in all CAPS.
4. Press **Enter**.

   NOTE: For future reference, it is not necessary to clear a cell with Edit/Clear before entering new data.

5. Capitalize: **NET EARNINGS** in cell A15 using one of the editing methods.

SAVING A SPREADSHEET

Saving a spreadsheet is the same as saving a word processing document. Use the **Save As** command for the first save or for saving the spreadsheet under a second name. Use the **Save** command for each save thereafter.

Save the Spreadsheet

1. Choose **File, Save As** (for this first save).

A dialog box similar to the one shown in Figure 8-7 appears.

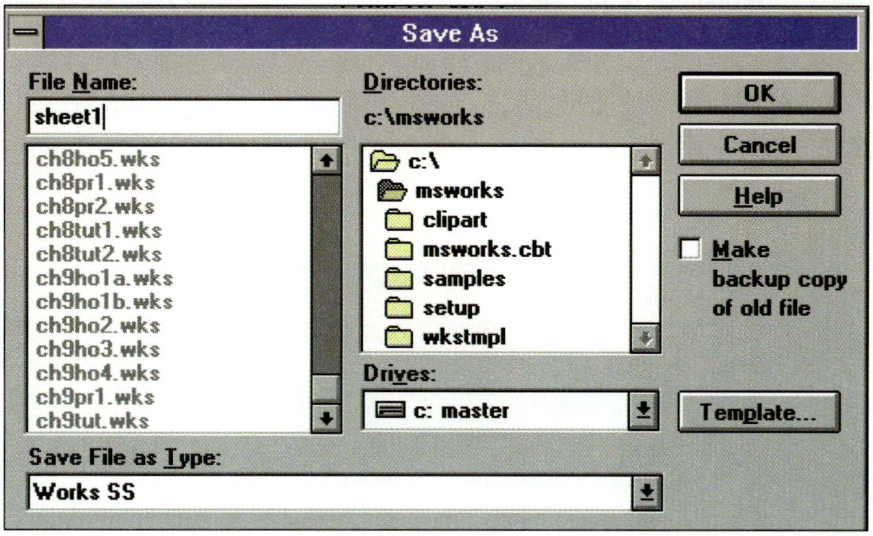

Figure 8-7
The Save As dialog box

The content of your dialog box may appear somewhat different from the one shown, but the following features are the same. The box to the left contains the current File Name. The list box to the right contains a list of Directories. All Works files may be saved in different formats. To see a list of the formats, click on the down arrow to the right of the Save File as Type box. If you want to change disk drives, for example change to Drive B or A where a floppy disk is located, then click on the down arrow to the right of the Drives list box and select the correct drive location.

2. Change the directory in the **Directories** list box if necessary.

   OR

   Change the drive in the **Drives** list box if you are saving to a floppy disk in Drive A or B.

3. Choose **File Name** to return to the File Name text box if you changed the drive or directory. This will select the name that is shown there. If you did not change the drive or directory, the file name showing here will already be selected. When you begin typing a new name, the previous name will be automatically deleted.

4. Type **CH8PR1** in the **File Name** box.

5. Choose **OK** or press **Enter**.

The name of the document now appears in the title bar at the top of the spreadsheet as **CH8PR1.WKS**. The WKS is the default extension for a worksheet. As in word processing, you could type your own three-character extension to replace the WKS.

For the most part, this is a good extension because it is a unique identifier of spreadsheet documents.

CLOSING A SPREADSHEET

You can close the worksheet by choosing **File, Close** or by double-clicking on the control menu box at the left end of the spreadsheet title bar with the left mouse button.

Close the Spreadsheet

1. Choose **File, Close** or double-click on the control menu box at the left end of the spreadsheet title bar as shown here.

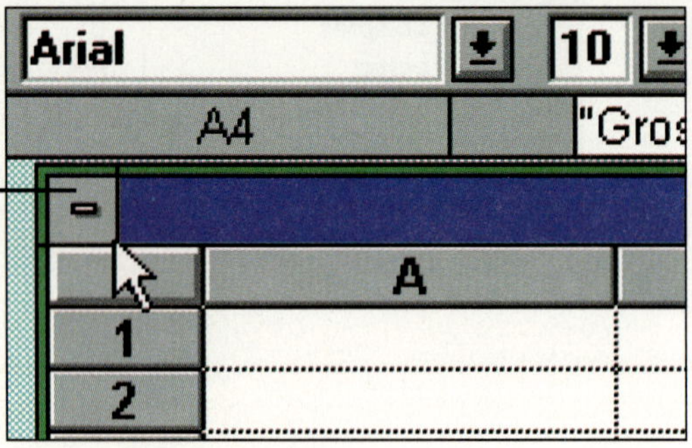

NOTE: You can also close a file when you exit Works by choosing the **File, Exit Works**, or by double-clicking on the control menu box at the left end of the Works window title bar as shown in the following example. If documents have not been saved, Works will prompt you with a message to save.

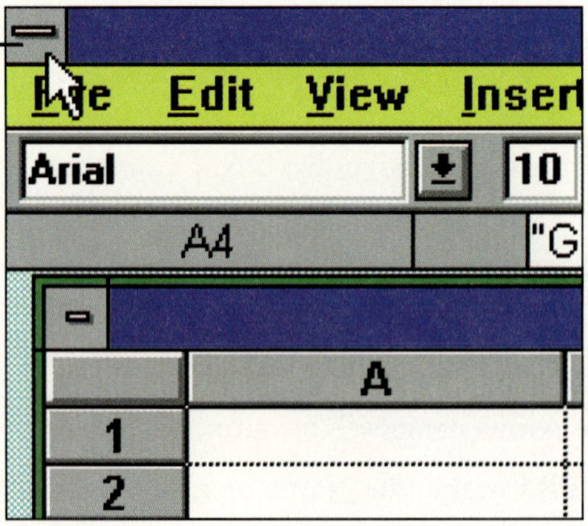

RETRIEVING A FILE

Retrieving a spreadsheet is done in the same way as retrieving a word processing file. In fact, as you proceed through this chapter and continue through the book, most of the commands are performed in the same way from one application to another.

Retrieve a File

1. Choose **File, Open Existing File** or **Open** An Existing Document from the Startup dialog box.

2. Change the directory in the **Directories** list box or the Drive in the **Drives** list box if necessary to that of your data disk. The options should look similar to those shown in Figure 8-8.

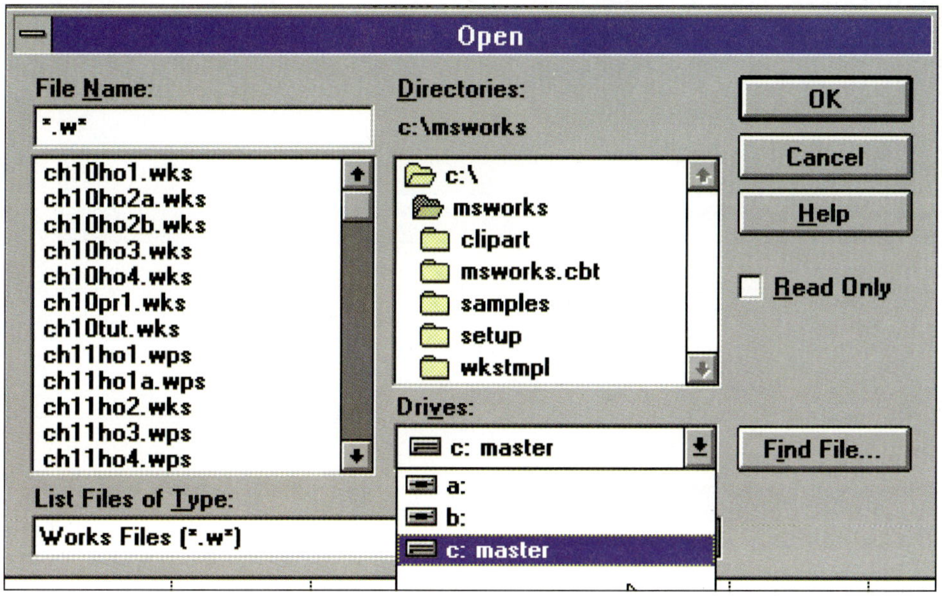

Figure 8-8
The Open dialog box

Figure 8-8 shows the Open dialog box. This box contains all of the options for opening an existing document. You can choose the drive containing your data disk from the Drives list box (click on the arrow to the right of the box). You can also choose the appropriate directory from the Directories box as shown in the figure. When you select a new drive or directory, the filenames will change in the File Name box to display the files stored in the selected directory.

3. Scroll through the list in the **File Name** list box using the arrow keys or the mouse.

NOTE: As you are scrolling, file extensions appear in this list box. They are for each of the applications in Works—.WPS for word processing, .WKS for spreadsheets, and .WDB for database. Look at the spreadsheet files for all retrievals in this part. If you want, you may also choose *.wks from the List Files of Type box as shown in Figure 8-9. This option will display only spreadsheet files with extensions of .wks.

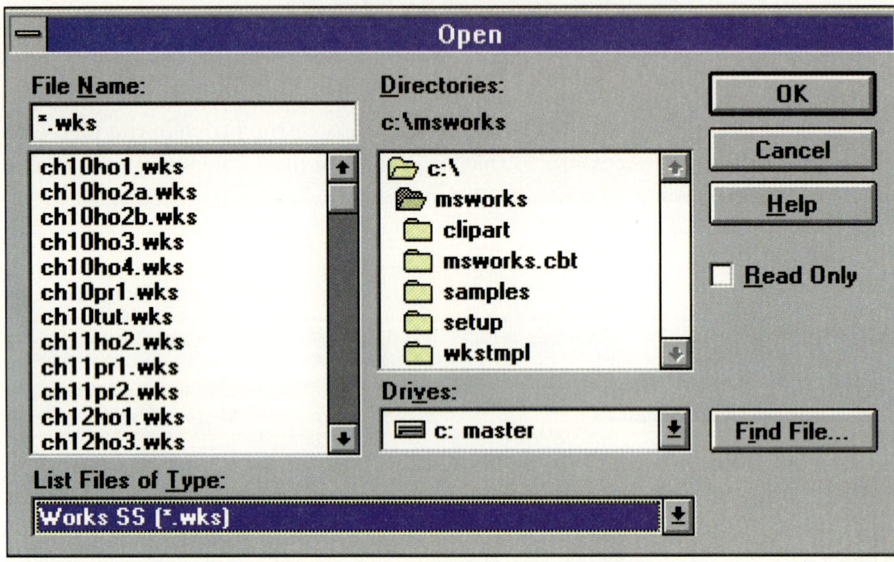

Figure 8-9
The Open dialog box showing the List Files of Type list

4. Choose **CH8PR1.WKS** from the **File Name** list box by selecting the name and choosing **OK** or by clicking the left mouse button twice on the name. The spreadsheet appears on the screen as follows.

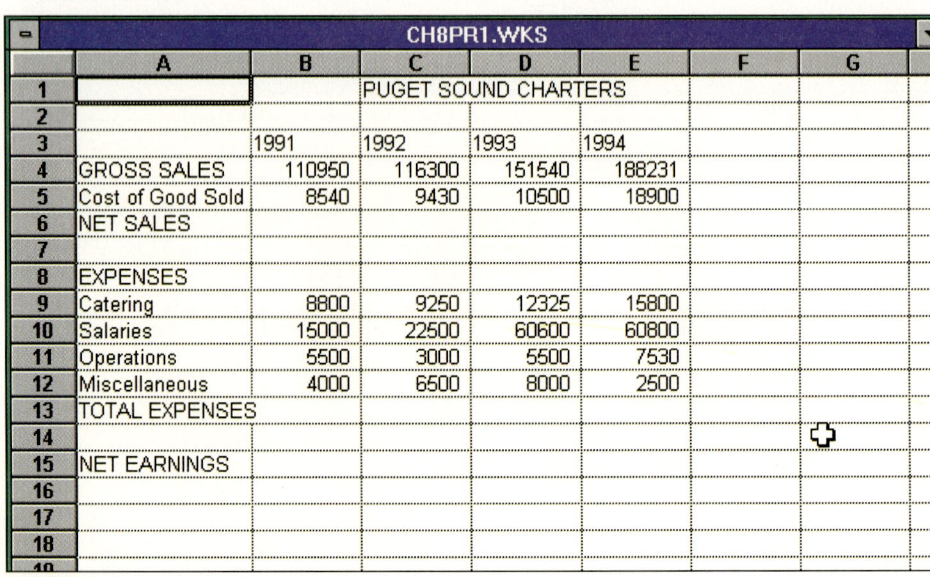

USING FORMULAS

Formula are used to calculate new values based on values that have been entered in a spreadsheet. The primary advantage of using formulas is that values are computed quickly and accuracy is assured as long as the formula is correct. A second advantage is that the values calculated by the formula are recalculated automatically any time values used as part of the equation are changed. Formulas can include any of the figures and text as well as functions, operands, and operators as shown in Table 8-4.

Operators:	
Addition	+
Subtraction	-
Multiplication	*
Division	/
Operands:	
Constant values: any number, such as:	10,20,-25,56.25, and so on
Cell and range references, such as	A1, B3, D25, B5:B25, and so on
Range names, such as	Net Earnings and Total Expenses
Functions:	
Functions that come with Works, such as	SUM (Addition), IF (IF-THEN-ELSE), and SQRT (Square Root). (See the *User's Guide* for a complete list of functions.)

Table 8-4

Text and figures used in formulas

Subtract One Value from Another

All formulas begin with an equal sign (=). The cell into which the answer to the formula should appear is first highlighted; then the formula is typed and entered into the cell. When it is entered into the cell, the answer to the formula will appear in the cell and the formula will appear in the formula bar.

1. Highlight cell **B6**.
2. Type **=b4-b5** (in upper or lowercase) as shown in the following illustration.

This formula will subtract the value found in cell B5 from that in B4. You can use either uppercase or lowercase when typing the location of the cell. The cell in a formula is often referred to as the *address*. B4 and B5 are the cell addresses in the formula above.

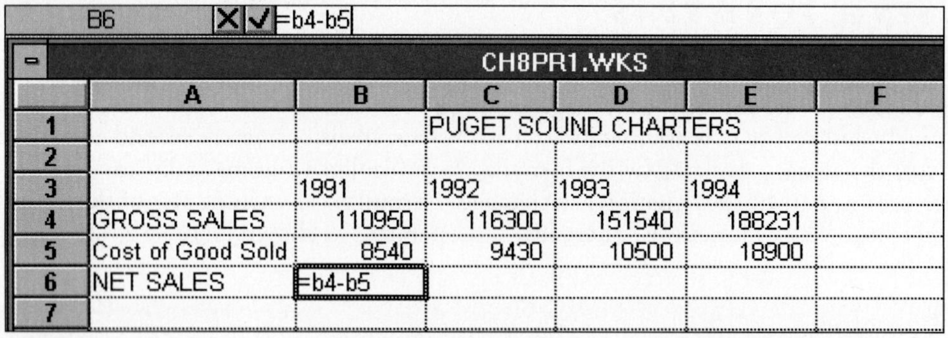

> ### *Canceling or Entering Data*
>
> When entering data or a formula into a cell, the formula bar displays an X and a check mark as shown below.

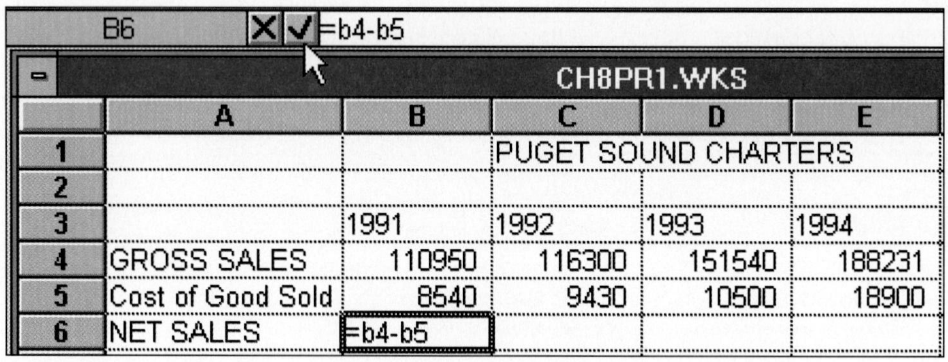

The X may be used to cancel entries in the formula bar. The check mark is referred to as the **Enter** tool and may be used, just like pressing the Enter key, to insert data into a cell. Use any of the methods discussed in this and other spreadsheet chapters.

3. Press **Enter** or click the left mouse button once at any place in the window.

The Net Sales amount, 102410, appears in cell B6.

In the following exercise, you will sum the values in cells B9, B10, B11, and B12.

Sum A Range Of Values

A series of values can be summed by typing each of the cells in a string, such as the values found in cells B9 through B12. These values could be added together using cell addresses such as =B9+B10+B11+B12. This could, however, become long and tedious when summing many cells. For this reason, Works uses ranges to identify a group of cells from one point to another. The group of cells used in the formula above could be abbreviated to read B9:B12, which is much more compact. When a range is used, the SUM function is also used. SUM is one of Works' built-in functions used to identify the type of calculation being done. Examples of a few of Works' functions are given in Table 8-1. For a more complete list see the *User's Guide* for Microsoft Works. SUM is used when performing addition, subtraction, multiplication, division, and other mathematical functions on a group or range of cells.

1. Highlight cell **B13**.
2. Type **=SUM(B9:B12)** (in uppercase or lowercase).

   NOTE: The equal sign (=) is required in a formula. If it is not entered, the formula will be entered as text in the cell and will not perform a calculation. The parentheses () is used to indicate a range, and the colon (:) is used to specify that all cells between two cell addresses are included in the calculation.

3. Press **Enter** or click the left mouse button in the cell. The total of all values in B9, B10, B11, and B12, 33300, is inserted into B13.

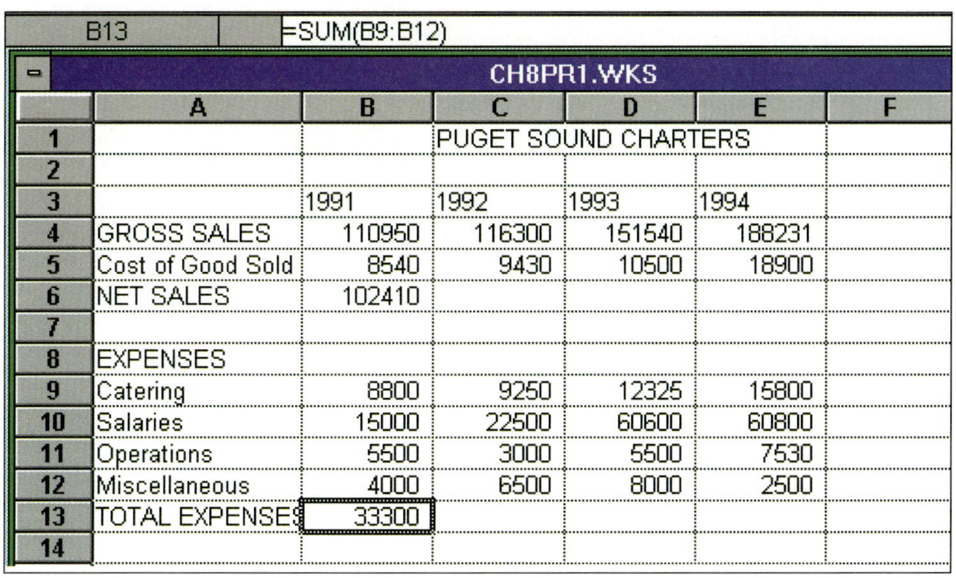
B13 =SUM(B9:B12)

CH8PR1.WKS

	A	B	C	D	E	F
1			PUGET SOUND CHARTERS			
2						
3		1991	1992	1993	1994	
4	GROSS SALES	110950	116300	151540	188231	
5	Cost of Good Sold	8540	9430	10500	18900	
6	NET SALES	102410				
7						
8	EXPENSES					
9	Catering	8800	9250	12325	15800	
10	Salaries	15000	22500	60600	60800	
11	Operations	5500	3000	5500	7530	
12	Miscellaneous	4000	6500	8000	2500	
13	TOTAL EXPENSES	33300				
14						

Use the Toolbar to Calculate a Sum

You may also use the toolbar to sum a range of values. The Autosum button, Σ, is used to automatically sum a range of values.

1. Highlight cell **B13** (over the existing total).
2. Choose **Edit, Clear**.
3. Click **once** on the Autosum button Σ. The format, =SUM(B9:B12), appears in cell B13 and also in the formula bar.. It will sum the range of values just above the highlighted cell.

   NOTE: When the summation tool is used, Works looks to the cells adjacent to those of the highlight. In this case, the cells filled with values were those just above the highlighted cell. If values are located to the left of the highlighted cell (in a row) and no values are above the cell, the Works summation tool will sum that range. You may also move to the formula bar and edit the range in the function.

4. Press **Enter** to insert the total.

SELECTING CELLS FOR FORMULAS

The Arrow keys or the mouse pointer can be used to highlight cells to be used in formulas. Selection of cells is used in place of typing the cell address from the keyboard. Either option may be used. Sometimes it is convenient to use the Arrow keys or the mouse pointer when spreadsheets are extremely large and the cells are not visible on the screen. After making the following selections, use whichever method is easiest for you when entering cell addresses into formulas.

Select Cells for the Formula

1. Highlight cell **B15**.
2. Type =
3. Press the **Up Arrow** key until cell B6 is highlighted, or click the left mouse button in cell B6.

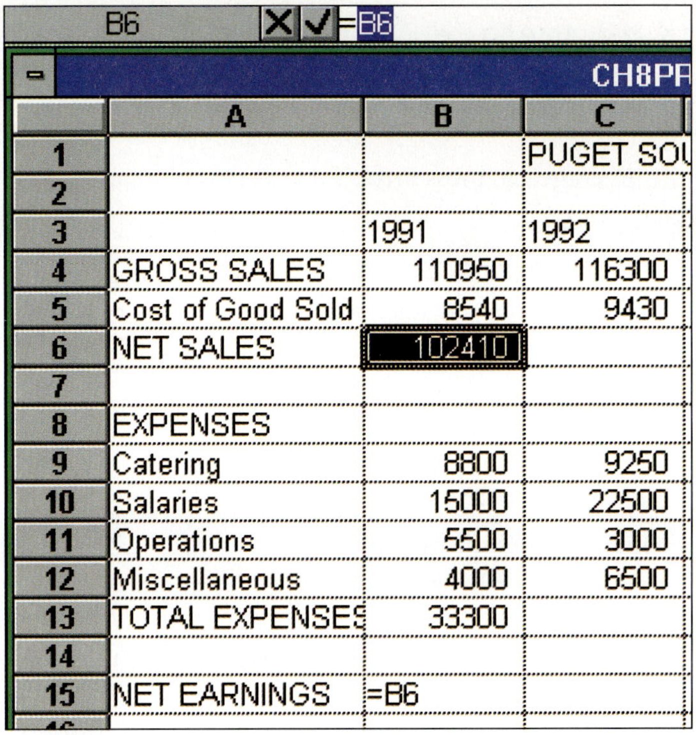

4. Type - to subtract the next value (the highlight returns to the formula cell, B15).
5. Press the **Up Arrow** key until cell B13 is highlighted, or click the left mouse button in cell B13. The formula is complete. Cell B13 should be highlighted.
6. Press **Enter.** A net earnings of 69110 is entered into cell B15.

COMPUTING AVERAGES

Averages are computed using AVG, the built-in function for average. This function is written in the same way as a SUM function and uses a range of values to compute the answer. To enter the average of cells B9, C9, D9, and E9 in cell F9, you would do the following.

Compute an Average

To enter the text, **Average,** in column F

1. Highlight cell **F3**.
2. Type **Average** and press **Enter** to name the column.
3. Highlight cell **F9**.
4. Type **=AVG(B9:E9).** This function will compute the average of all catering expenses over the four-year period.
5. Press **Enter** or click the left mouse button once in cell F9. The average, 11543.75, appears in the cell.

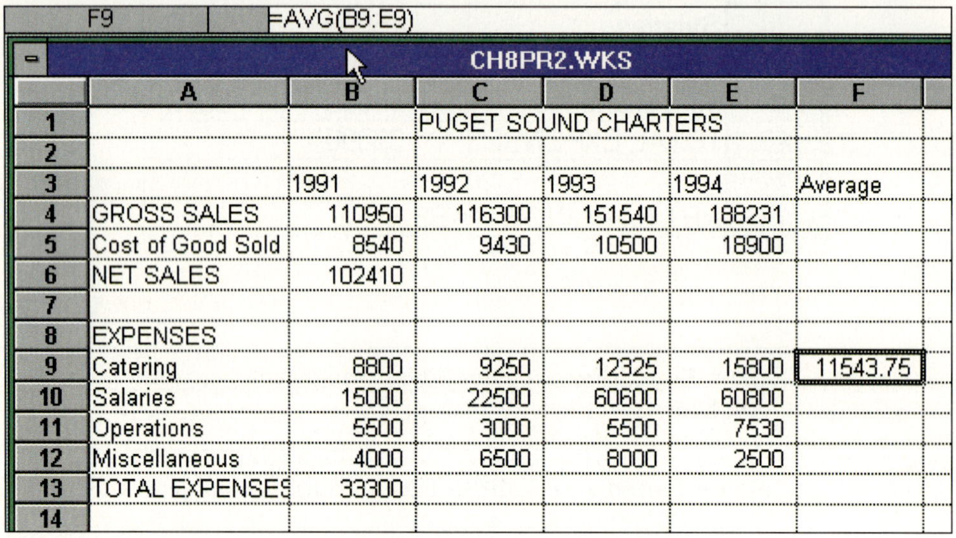

F9 =AVG(B9:E9)

CH8PR2.WKS

	A	B	C	D	E	F
1			PUGET SOUND CHARTERS			
2						
3		1991	1992	1993	1994	Average
4	GROSS SALES	110950	116300	151540	188231	
5	Cost of Good Sold	8540	9430	10500	18900	
6	NET SALES	102410				
7						
8	EXPENSES					
9	Catering	8800	9250	12325	15800	11543.75
10	Salaries	15000	22500	60600	60800	
11	Operations	5500	3000	5500	7530	
12	Miscellaneous	4000	6500	8000	2500	
13	TOTAL EXPENSES	33300				
14						

LOCATING UNKNOWN FUNCTIONS

If you are not sure of the correct format for a function, you can **Insert, Function** to display the Insert Function dialog box as shown in Figure 8-10.

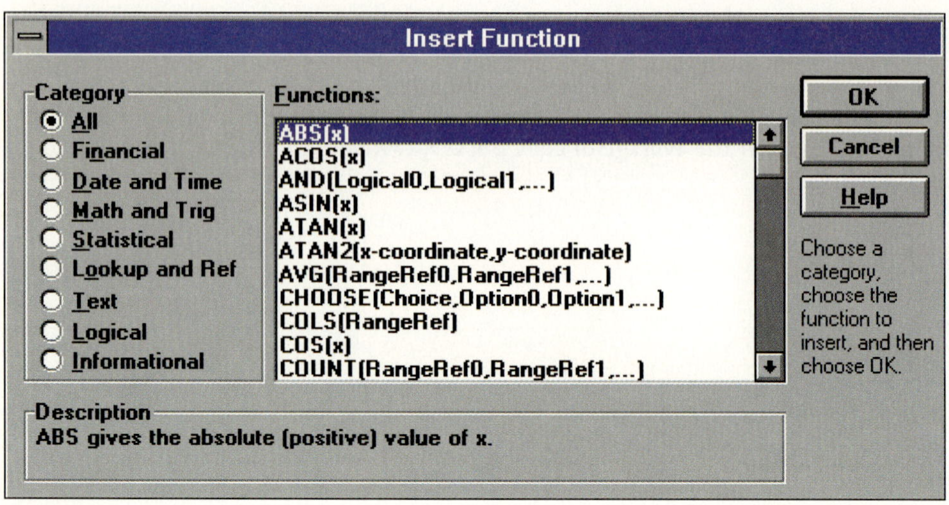

Figure 8-10
The Insert Function dialog box

10. Write the correct syntax (format) that will display a value greater than 3000.

True or False:

11. ______ Cell A1 is always considered the **active** cell.
12. ______ Ctrl/Home will position the highlight in cell A1.
13. ______ The Spacebar may be used to erase cell contents quickly.
14. ______ The entire column must be highlighted when changing column width.

Hands-on Exercises

Exercise 1

1. Type the following spreadsheet. As you are entering labels in column A, adjust the column width as necessary.

	A	B	C	D	E	F
1		MISCELLANEOUS EXPENDITURES WORKSHEET				
2						
3		January	February	March	Total	
4	Passenger Overboard Fees	100	200	100		
5	Stress Management	1600	1000	2500		
6	Food Replacement	1200	1600	1400		
7	Safety Training	2000	3000	1500		
8	Vessel Collision Lessons	800	350	700		
9						
10	Total					
11	Average					
12	Maximum					
13						
14						
15						

2. Change the text in cells A10 to A12 to all CAPS.
3. Change the value in cell B4 to 200; in C4 to 500; and in D4 to 300.
4. Change the width of columns B through E to 12.
5. Save the spreadsheet as **CH8HO1**.
6. Preview and print a copy of the spreadsheet.
7. Close the file.

Exercise 2

1. Type the following spreadsheet. To indent the items in cells A8 through A12, in the formular bar press the **spacebar** several times before typing the text.

	A	B	C	D	E	F
1		Staff Training Courses				
2		Enrollment Figures				
3						
4	Course title		Date of Course			
5		January 15	February 10	March 08		
6	Galley Safety Tips	5	4	6		
7	Crash Courses					
8	Captaining	82	80	75		
9	Deck Hand	2	3	4		
10	Life Saving	82	85	87		
11	First Aid	4	6	3		
12	Jumping Overboard	80	79	88		
13	Personal Safety First	2	3	1		
14	Emergency Evacuation	67	89	76		
15	Avoiding Sharks	6	7	8		
16	Narrow Misses	17	24	19		
17	Riding the Storm	77	71	76		
18	Minding Holes	4	9	6		
19						
20	Total					

2. Change the two lines of the main heading to all CAPS.
3. Adjust the column width in A to 25.
4. Adjust the column width in columns B through D to 12.
5. Change Course Title in A4 to all caps followed by a colon (:).
6. Save the spreadsheet as **CH8HO2**.
7. Print a copy of the spreadsheet.
8. Close the file.

Exercise 3

1. Retrieve **CH8HO1** from your data disk.
2. Compute the total of all Passenger Overboard Fees (January through March).
3. Compute the total of all fees for the month of January.
4. Compute the average of all fees for the month of January.
5. Compute the maximum value of all fees for the month of January. To do this, choose **Insert, Function**, scroll down through the **Functions:** list box, select **MAX**, press **Enter**. The MAX function and the range reference will be displayed in the formular bar. Edit the range reference to show **(B4:B8)**. MAX is the function that will display the maximum value in this range. You can also type in the formula bar, **=MAX(B4:B8)** and press **Enter**.
6. Save this spreadsheet as **CH8HO3**.
7. Print a copy and close the file.

Exercise 4

1. Retrieve **CH8HO2** from your data disk.
2. Compute the monthly total enrollment for January in B20. Hint: In the formula bar, change the range from B8:B19 to B6:B19.

3. Add a new Total heading in E5 to the right of March.
4. Compute the total enrollment figures for Galley Safety Tips for all 3 months in cell E6.
5. Add a new label, Average, in A21 and compute the average for all values in January in B21.
6. Add a new label, Minimum, in A22 and compute the minimum enrollment of all values in January in B22.
7. Add a new label, Maximum, in A23 and compute the maximum enrollment of all values in January in B23.
8. Save the spreadsheet as **CH8HO4**.
9. Print a copy and close the file.

Exercise 5

1. Create the following partial spreadsheet.

	A	B	C	D	E	F	G	H
1			PUGET SOUND CHARTERS					
2								
3		Current	Next	Five-year	Ten-year	Percentage		
4		Year	Year	Projection	Projection	of increase		
5								
6	Delano	37890						
7	The Spirit	35550						
8	Sea Wolf	38950						
9	Irish Sea	41250						
10								

2. Save the spreadsheet as **CH8HO5**.
3. In C6 Compute the **Next Year** projected sales for Delano by multiplying the **Current Year** sales by **1.10** percent (110%, an increase of 10 percent over this year).
4. In D6 Compute **Delano's Five-year Projection** amount by multiplying **Next Year's** projected sales by **1.10** percent.
5. In E6 Compute Delano's **Ten-year Projection** by multiplying the **Five-year Projection** by **1.30** percent.
6. In F6 Compute the **Percentage of Increase** value for **Delano** by dividing the **Ten-year Projection** amount into the **Current Year** amount. The completed worksheet should appear similar to the one below. Do not worry if your decimal places vary from those shown.

	A	B	C	D	E	F	G	H
1			PUGET SOUND CHARTERS					
2								
3		Current	Next	Five-year	Ten-year	Percentage		
4		Year	Year	Projection	Projection	of Increase		
5								
6	Delano	37890	41679	45846.9	59600.97	0.6357279		
7	The Spirit	35550						
8	Sea Wolf	38950						
9	Irish Sea	41250						
10								

7. Proof for typographical errors and save the spreadsheet again as **CH8HO5.**
8. Print a copy of the spreadsheet and close the file.

Examples of Exercises

Exercise 1: CH8HO1

	A	B	C	D	E	F
1		MISCELLANEOUS EXPENDITURES WORKSHEET				
2						
3		January	February	March	Total	
4	Passenger Overboard Fees	200	500	300		
5	Stress Management	1600	1000	2500		
6	Food Replacement	1200	1600	1400		
7	Safety Training	2000	3000	1500		
8	Vessel Collision Lessons	800	350	700		
9						
10	TOTAL					
11	AVERAGE					
12	MAXIMUM					
13						
14						

Exercise 4: CH8HO4

	A	B	C	D	E	F
1			STAFF TRAINING COURSES			
2			ENROLLMENT FIGURES			
3						
4	COURSE TITLE:		Date of Course			
5		January 15	February 10	March 08	Total	
6	Galley Safety Tips	5	4	6	15	
7	Crash Courses					
8	Captaining	82	80	75		
9	Deck Hand	2	3	4		
10	Life Saving	82	85	87		
11	First Aid	4	6	3		
12	Jumping Overboard	80	79	88		
13	Personal Safety First	2	3	1		
14	Emergency Evacuation	67	89	76		
15	Avoiding Sharks	6	7	8		
16	Narrow Misses	17	24	19		
17	Riding the Storm	77	71	76		
18	Mending Holes	4	9	6		
19						
20	Total	428				
21	Average	35.6666667				
22	Minimum	2				
23	Maximum	82				

CHAPTER 9

Editing A Spreadsheet

OBJECTIVES

Understand relative and absolute cell references

Copy to adjacent and nonadjacent cells

Insert and delete rows and columns

Move a range of cells

Select cells

Remove a range of cells

PREVIEW

Modifications can be made to a spreadsheet, such as inserting or deleting rows and columns. Entire blocks of text or values can also be moved from one section of the worksheet to another, and formulas can be copied from one cell to a single cell or to a range of cells. Chapter 8 covered using the F2 key for editing, using the **Clear** command in the **Edit** menu, as well as replacing the contents of a cell by typing a new entry. Other editing commands including copying and moving cell contents, clearing ranges of cells, and inserting and deleting rows and columns will be covered in this chapter.

COPYING RELATIVE CELL ADDRESSES

You can copy the cell contents from one cell to another single cell or to a range of cells. If the cell contains a formula, the formula is copied. Any cell addresses in the formula are automatically adjusted to apply to the row and column to which they are copied. For example, copying a formula in cell B6 containing the cell addresses B2:B4 to columns C through D in row 6 would change the addresses to C2:C4 and D2:D4. The address is copied two columns to the right, and the cell addresses are changed automatically. In this case, the columns change. The address in a formula changes *relative* to the new location. If formulas are copied to another row, the same occurs; that is, copying from row 6 to row 7 would result in the formula showing B3:B5 (increasing by a row). This is called *relative* referencing and is illustrated in Figure 9-1.

Sheet1

	A	B	C	D
1				
2		1234	2345	1234
3		2345	6789	7654
4		4345	4567	7654
5				
6		=SUM(B2:B4)	=SUM(C2:C4)	=SUM(D2:D4)
7		=SUM(B3:B5)		
8				

Figure 9-1
Relative cell addressing

COPY TO ADJACENT CELLS

Copying to adjacent cells in a spreadsheet means that values and text from one cell will be copied to the cells across the same row or down the same column.

1. Sign onto Works and open the spreadsheet **CH8PR2.WKS** created in Chapter 8. You can also retrieve it from the Instructor data disk. It should appear similar to the following example.

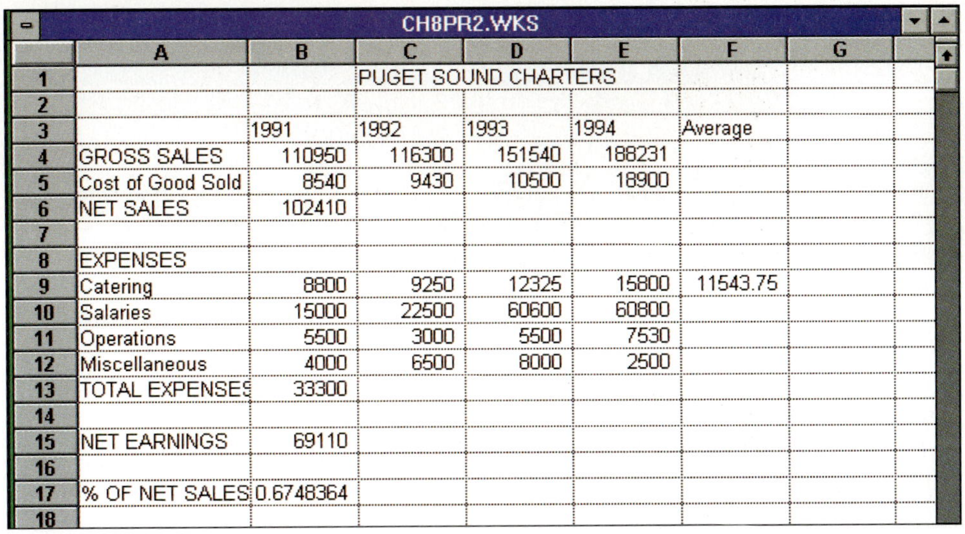

CH8PR2.WKS

	A	B	C	D	E	F	G
1			PUGET SOUND CHARTERS				
2							
3		1991	1992	1993	1994	Average	
4	GROSS SALES	110950	116300	151540	188231		
5	Cost of Good Sold	8540	9430	10500	18900		
6	NET SALES	102410					
7							
8	EXPENSES						
9	Catering	8800	9250	12325	15800	11543.75	
10	Salaries	15000	22500	60600	60800		
11	Operations	5500	3000	5500	7530		
12	Miscellaneous	4000	6500	8000	2500		
13	TOTAL EXPENSES	33300					
14							
15	NET EARNINGS	69110					
16							
17	% OF NET SALES	0.6748364					
18							

Copy a Formula

The following steps will copy a formula in cell B6 to adjacent cells in C6 through E6. To do so, all cells in the range, from the one containing the correct formula through the last cell, are highlighted.

1. Highlight cells **B6, C6, D6,** and **E6** by dragging with the left mouse button over the cells, or pressing the **F8** key and the **Right Arrow** key.

NOTE: The Works spreadsheet tool contains the same **extend** mode (F8) for highlighting large blocks of cells as that used to select large blocks of text in word processing. When the **F8** key is pressed, the EXT mode is turned on and blocks of cells can be highlighted using a few quick keystrokes.

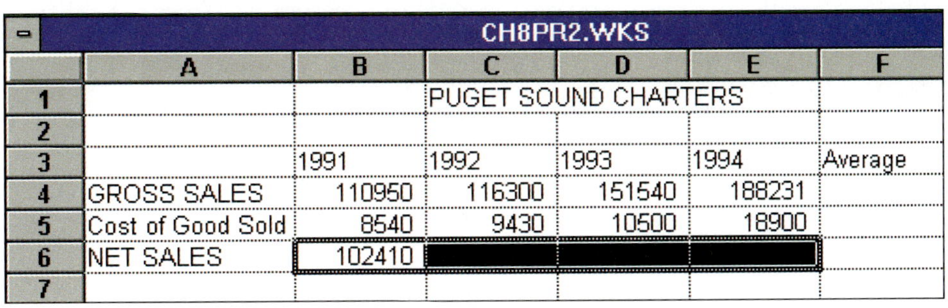

CH8PR2.WKS

	A	B	C	D	E	F
1			PUGET SOUND CHARTERS			
2						
3		1991	1992	1993	1994	Average
4	GROSS SALES	110950	116300	151540	188231	
5	Cost of Good Sold	8540	9430	10500	18900	
6	NET SALES	102410				
7						

Cell B6 contains a value (the NET SALES amount). The formula is shown in the upper left corner of the screen. All cells to which B6 will be copied are also highlighted at this time, and the upper left corner shows the range is B6:E6 as shown in the illustration following step 1.

2. Choose **Edit, Fill Right.**
3. Look at the formula in the cell **B6** shown in the formula bar.
4. Press the **Right Arrow** key once or click in cell C6.

C6 =C4-C5

CH9PR1.WKS

	A	B	C	D	E	F
1			PUGET SOUND CHARTERS			
2						
3		1991	1992	1993	1994	Average
4	GROSS SALES	110950	116300	151540	188231	
5	Cost of Good Sold	8540	9430	10500	18900	
6	NET SALES	102410	106870	141040	169331	
7						

This cell shows the NET SALES for column C and the formula is relative to the column to which it was copied.

5. Press the **Right Arrow** key two more times and look at the formula in each of the cells.

Copy Formula to Additional Cells

The following steps will copy the formula contained in cell F9 to the adjacent cells down through F13.

1. Highlight cells **F9 through F12.**
2. Choose **Edit, Fill Down.**

In step 3, the formula in cell B13 will be copied to the right through cell E13.

3. Highlight cells **B13 through E13** as shown here.

8	EXPENSES					
9	Catering	8800	9250	12325	15800	11543.75
10	Salaries	15000	22500	60600	60800	39725
11	Operations	5500	3000	5500	7530	5382.5
12	Miscellaneous	4000	6500	8000	2500	5250
13	TOTAL EXPENSES	33300				
14						

4. Choose **Edit, Fill Right** to display the results of copying the formula.
5. Highlight the following cells as shown here, and use **Edit, Fill Right** to copy the results of the formulas in cells B15 and B17 to adjacent cells.

14						
15	NET EARNINGS	69110				
16						

Cells **B15 through E15**

16						
17	% OF NET SALES	0.6748364				
18						

Cells **B17 through E17**

When finished, the spreadsheet should appear similar to the following example.

CH8PR2.WKS

	A	B	C	D	E	F	G
1			PUGET SOUND CHARTERS				
2							
3		1991	1992	1993	1994	Average	
4	GROSS SALES	110950	116300	151540	188231		
5	Cost of Good Sold	8540	9430	10500	18900		
6	NET SALES	102410	106870	141040	169331		
7							
8	EXPENSES						
9	Catering	8800	9250	12325	15800	11543.75	
10	Salaries	15000	22500	60600	60800	39725	
11	Operations	5500	3000	5500	7530	5382.5	
12	Miscellaneous	4000	6500	8000	2500	5250	
13	TOTAL EXPENSES	33300	41250	86425	86630		
14							
15	NET EARNINGS	69110	65620	54615	82701		
16							
17	% OF NET SALES	0.6748364	0.614017	0.3872306	0.4883985		
18							

Copy to Non-adjacent Cells

Copying to nonadjacent cells involves copying one or more cells to other areas of the worksheet not directly adjacent to the current cell(s). When this is the case, use the Copy and the Paste buttons in place of the **Fill** command.

1. Highlight cells **A17 through E17** by either dragging with the left mouse button through the cells, or using the **F8** key and the **Right Arrow** key.

16						
17	% OF NET SALES	0.6748364	0.614017	0.3872306	0.4883985	
18						

2. Click on the Copy button, or choose **Edit, Copy** or press **Ctrl/C.**
3. Highlight cell **A16.**
4. Click on the Paste button, or choose **Edit, Paste** or press **Ctrl/V.**

NOTE: Relative referencing is in effect with the cell addresses used in the formulas in this row. Because the new cell addresses in the formulas do not contain the correct values, an ERR message appears or a "0" will be displayed in the cells as shown here This will be corrected later.

15	NET EARNINGS	69110	65620	54615	82701	
16	% OF NET SALES	0	0	0	0	
17	% OF NET SALES	0.6748364	0.614017	0.3872306	0.4883985	
18						

5. Highlight cell **B16** to see the formula *=B14/B5.* This cell is not really doing anything because B14 does not contain a value.

COPYING ABSOLUTE CELL ADDRESSES

Cell addresses that are absolute are "locked" into position so that they will always display the same cell address regardless of where they are copied in the spreadsheet. If a dollar sign ($) is typed in the formula bar with the cell addresses, it locks either the column, the row, or both the column and the row. The following examples show how to lock these addresses.

To lock both columns and rows

To lock both columns and rows in a formula, and thus have a formula that is totally absolute when it is copied, dollar signs ($) are inserted in front of both the column addresses and the row addresses. This formula would read

=$B$15/$B$6

in which case column B is locked and rows 15 and 6 are locked. Wherever this formula is copied, such as to cell F25, it will always divide the contents of cells B15 and B6.

To lock only the columns

To lock only the columns in a formula, insert the dollar sign ($) in front of the columns in the formula as shown in the following example.

=$B15/$B6

Rows 15 and 6 will change relative to the new row location; column B will always read column B.

To lock only rows

To lock only the rows, insert the dollar sign ($) in front of the row numbers in the formula as shown in the following example.

=B$15/B$6

This locks the *row* addresses so that they will not change when copied. Wherever the formula is copied in the worksheet, the rows will remain the same. but the columns can change. You will be locking in row addresses in the following steps.

Copy Absolute Cell Addresses

1. Highlight cell **B17**.
2. Press **F2** to go to the formula bar where you can edit the cell address.
3. Move the cursor in the Formula bar prior to the 15 and prior to the 6 and type the dollar sign. Text will move right automatically. See the following illustration

4. Press **Enter** when the formula is correct.

Copy the New Formula

The following steps will copy the formula in B17 to cells C17 through E17.

1. Highlight cells **B17 through E17.**

15	NET EARNINGS	69110	65620	54615	82701	
16	% OF NET SALES	0	0	0	0	
17	% OF NET SALES	0.6748364	0.614017	0.3872306	0.4883985	
18						

2. Choose **Edit, Fill Right**. This will copy the new formula for the absolute reference to the cells in columns C through E.
3. Highlight each of the cells C17 through E17 to see the change in formulas.

MOVING A RANGE OF CELLS

When the data in row 17 was copied previously, it remained in its original location and was also inserted into row 16. This time, with the formula corrected, this row will be moved rather than copied. It will be deleted from its old location in row 17, and inserted in row 16 where the current contents of that row will be replaced automatically.

Move a Range of Cells

1. Highlight cells **A17 through E17.**

16	% OF NET SALES	0	0	0	0	
17	% OF NET SALES	0.6748364	0.614017	0.3872306	0.4883985	
18						

2. Click on the Cut button, or choose **Edit Cut or press** Ctrl/X.
3. Highlight cell **A16.**
4. Click on the Paste button, or choose **Edit Paste** or press **Ctrl/V.**

14						
15	NET EARNINGS	69110	65620	54615	82701	
16	% OF NET SALES	0.6748364	0.614017	0.3872306	0.4883985	
17						

The data in row 17 is removed and is now inserted into row 16, replacing the data (that had been copied there earlier in this chapter) with the correct percentages.

VIEWING CELL ADDRESSES

To understand further how absolute references change (or do not change) when they are moved or copied to a new location, you can position the highlight in any cell into which an absolute formula is copied.

View Cell Addresses

1. Highlight cell **B16.**

The formula still reads rows 15 and 6. When it was copied the first time, without the dollar signs inserted, the rows were adjusted accordingly to 14 and 5. With the rows locked, 15 and 6 remained stationary.

MOVING CELLS WITH THE MOUSE

You practiced moving a range of cells using Cut, Copy, and Paste. A single cell or a group of cells can also be moved quickly by highlighting them and dragging the block to a new location using the left mouse button which becomes a pointer and shows the word Drag.

Move a Range of Cells

1. Highlight cells **F3 through F12** as shown in the following example.

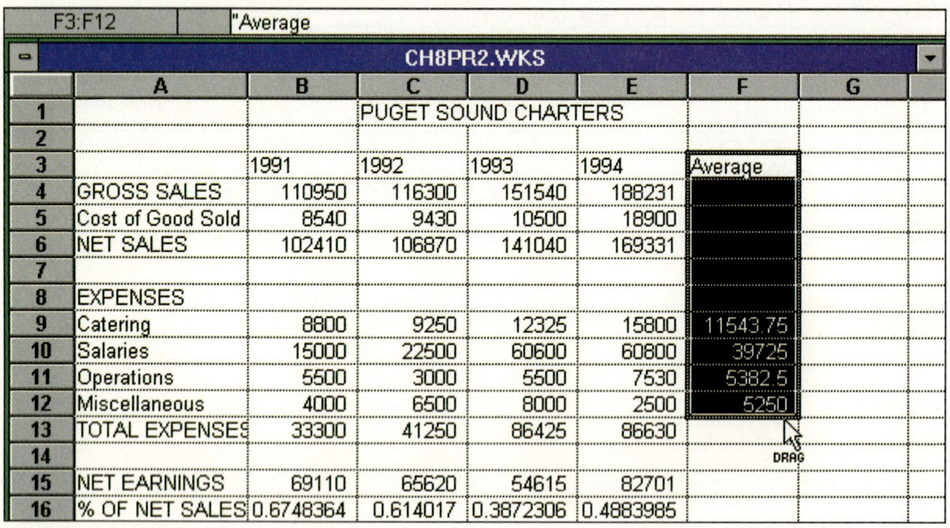

F3:F12 "Average

CH8PR2.WKS

	A	B	C	D	E	F	G
1			PUGET SOUND CHARTERS				
2							
3		1991	1992	1993	1994	Average	
4	GROSS SALES	110950	116300	151540	188231		
5	Cost of Good Sold	8540	9430	10500	18900		
6	NET SALES	102410	106870	141040	169331		
7							
8	EXPENSES						
9	Catering	8800	9250	12325	15800	11543.75	
10	Salaries	15000	22500	60600	60800	39725	
11	Operations	5500	3000	5500	7530	5382.5	
12	Miscellaneous	4000	6500	8000	2500	5250	
13	TOTAL EXPENSES	33300	41250	86425	86630		
14						DRAG	
15	NET EARNINGS	69110	65620	54615	82701		
16	% OF NET SALES	0.6748364	0.614017	0.3872306	0.4883985		

2. Point — to the border of the highlighted cells so that the word "drag" appears with the pointer as shown in the preceding example.

3. Hold — the left mouse button down and drag the entire block of cells to the right one column as shown in the following example.

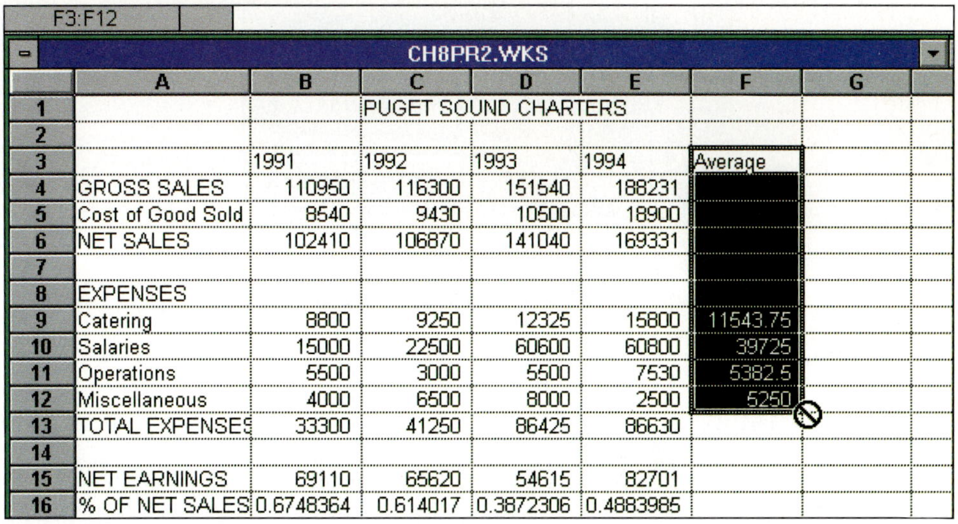
F3:F12

CH8PR2.WKS

	A	B	C	D	E	F	G
1			PUGET SOUND CHARTERS				
2							
3		1991	1992	1993	1994	Average	
4	GROSS SALES	110950	116300	151540	188231		
5	Cost of Good Sold	8540	9430	10500	18900		
6	NET SALES	102410	106870	141040	169331		
7							
8	EXPENSES						
9	Catering	8800	9250	12325	15800	11543.75	
10	Salaries	15000	22500	60600	60800	39725	
11	Operations	5500	3000	5500	7530	5382.5	
12	Miscellaneous	4000	6500	8000	2500	5250	
13	TOTAL EXPENSES	33300	41250	86425	86630		
14							
15	NET EARNINGS	69110	65620	54615	82701		
16	% OF NET SALES	0.6748364	0.614017	0.3872306	0.4883985		

NOTE: You can drag the block to any location in the spreadsheet using this method.

4. Release the left mouse button when in column **G**.

5. Highlight and point to the block again and drag back to column **F**.
6. Save the spreadsheet as **CH9PR1**.

INSERTING AND DELETING ROWS OR COLUMNS

Rows or columns can be inserted and deleted in a spreadsheet. A new row is inserted above a highlighted row. A new column is inserted to the left of a highlighted column. It is also possible to insert or delete *several rows* or columns using the **Insert, Row/Column** or **Insert, Delete Row/Column** commands.

Insert a Single Row or Column

1. Highlight cell **A16**.

NOTE: It is not necessary to highlight the entire row. When the command is given to insert a row, Works knows to insert all the way across the worksheet. The same is true when deleting a row and inserting or deleting columns.

2. Choose **Insert, Row/Column** to display the Insert dialog box as shown on the next page.

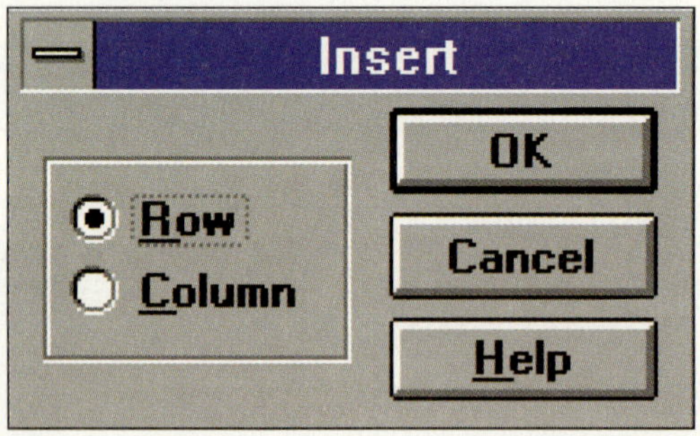

3. Choose **Row** (it should be selected).
4. Choose **OK** or press **Enter**.

Row 16 is now the new blank row and the remaining rows are moved down.

NOTE: When rows or columns are inserted, formulas may change. This spreadsheet is okay. The formulas in cells B17 through E17 refer to the contents of row 15, which has not been moved. However, if these rows had been changed, it may be necessary to change formulas to absolute or partial absolute formulas so that the values remain the same when columns and rows are inserted

SELECTING CELLS IN A SPREADSHEET

You can use extend mode, by pressing the **F8** key and then use the arrow keys to select block of cells, or if you are familiar with using the mouse for highlighting, you may prefer that method.

Select Cells Using a Mouse

1. Highlight cells **A3 through F4** by dragging the left mouse button.

	A	B	C	D	E	F	G
1			PUGET SOUND CHARTERS				
2							
3		1991	1992	1993	1994	Average	
4	GROSS SALES	110950	116300	151540	188231		
5	Cost of Good Sold	8540	9430	10500	18900		
6	NET SALES	102410	106870	141040	169331		
7							

Select Cells Using Extend

1. Move the insertion point to **A6** and press **F8**. EXT is displayed in the status bar. If you press any key now, the selection will be extended.
2. Press the **Right Arrow** enough times to extend the highlighting through **E6**.
3. Press **F8** to turn off extend. The EXT is no longer showing in the status bar, and the selection will not be extended when you press any key.

Make Other Spreadsheet Selections

Table 9-1 shows ways in which other selections can be made in the spreadsheet tool.

1. Read through them and practice each on the current worksheet.

To highlight this	Do this
A single cell	Press the **Arrow** keys or click the left mouse button.
A row	Press **Ctrl/F8**; or choose **Select Row** from the **Edit** menu; or click the left mouse button on any row number.
NOTE: This will select the entire row through column IV.	
A column	Press **Shift/F8**; choose **Select Column** from the **Edit** menu; or click the left mouse button on the column letter.
NOTE: This will select the entire column through row 16,384.	
The entire spreadsheet	Press **Ctrl/Shift/F8**, choose **Select All** from the **Edit** menu, or click the left mouse button in the corner of the window to the left of column A and above row 1. The pointer becomes a cross as shown in the following example.

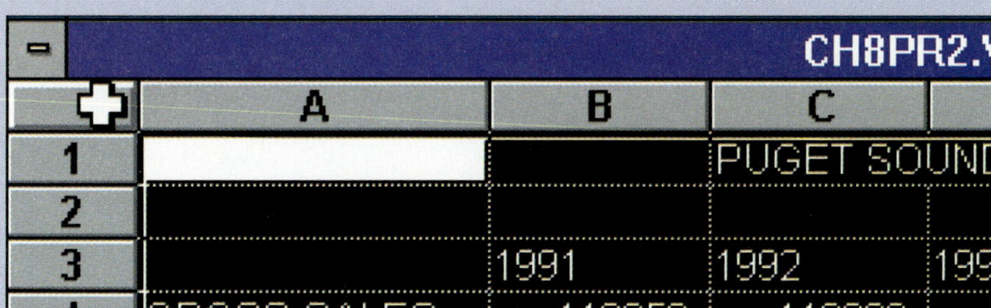

NOTE: This command selects the entire spreadsheet from A1 through IV16,384.

Table 9-1
Making selections on a spreadsheet

INSERTING MULTIPLE ROWS OR COLUMNS

Inserting multiple rows or columns is a matter of highlighting the area into which they will be inserted (as done in selecting cells in a spreadsheet) and then using the **Row/Column** command from the **Insert** menu.

Insert Multiple Rows or Columns

1. Select cells **A3 through F4** again.
2. Choose **Insert, Row/Column** to display the Insert dialog box.
3. Choose **Row** if necessary.
4. Choose **OK** or press **Enter**. All rows are pushed down on the spreadsheet and two new rows are inserted.

Type a Subheading

1. Highlight cell **C2**.
2. Type **Comparison of Earnings**.
3. Press **Enter** or click in the cell. Your screen should resemble the following. example.

	A	B	C	D	E	F
1			PUGET SOUND CHARTERS			
2			Comparison of Earnings			
3						

DELETING ROWS OR COLUMNS

Deleting rows or columns follows the same procedure as inserting rows or columns. The command is located in the **Insert** menu and the row or column is highlighted prior to using the command.

Delete Rows or Columns

1. Highlight cell **A4**.

   NOTE: You could use any cell in row 4 if this is the row to be deleted.

2. Choose **Insert, Delete Row/Column.**
3. Choose **Row** (if necessary).
4. Choose **OK** or press **Enter**. Your screen should look similar to the following example.

	A	B	C	D	E	F
1			PUGET SOUND CHARTERS			
2			Comparison of Earnings			
3						
4		1991	1992	1993	1994	Average
5	GROSS SALES	110950	116300	151540	188231	
6	Cost of Good Sold	8540	9430	10500	18900	
7	NET SALES	102410	106870	141040	169331	
8						

All rows are moved upward and row 3 is the only blank row between the main heading and the column headings.

Insert an Additional Row

1. Highlight cell **A5**.
2. Insert a new row at this position.
3. Click on the Save button  or choose **File, Save** to save the changes.

The final spreadsheet, **CH9PR1**, should appear similar to the following example.

	A	B	C	D	E	F	G	H
1			PUGET SOUND CHARTERS					
2			Comparison of Earnings					
3								
4		1991	1992	1993	1994	Average		
5								
6	GROSS SALES	110950	116300	151540	188231			
7	Cost of Good Sold	8540	9430	10500	18900			
8	NET SALES	102410	106870	141040	169331			
9								
10	EXPENSES							
11	Catering	8800	9250	12325	15800	11543.75		
12	Salaries	15000	22500	60600	60800	39725		
13	Operations	5500	3000	5500	7530	5382.5		
14	Miscellaneous	4000	6500	8000	2500	5250		
15	TOTAL EXPENSES	33300	41250	86425	86630			
16								
17	NET EARNINGS	69110	65620	54615	82701			
18								
19	% OF NET SALES	0.6748364	0.614017	0.3872306	0.4883985			
20								

CLEARING A RANGE OF CELLS

Sometimes it is desirable to clear an entire range of cells. To do so, use one of the highlight methods listed in Table 9-1 or discussed in this chapter to highlight all of the cells to be deleted and choose **Clear** from the **Edit** menu. Since this spreadsheet is complete, it is not necessary to delete any large blocks of cells at this time; however, if you have made errors or if you need to make corrections when doing practice documents, you may decide to use the **Clear** command. It is the fastest way to remove text and values in large ranges of cells.

1. Save the changed spreadsheet as **CH9PR1**.
2. Close the document.

GUIDED TUTORIAL

What You'll Do

- Copy cell contents.
- Create formulas containing cell addresses.
- Insert columns and rows.

How To Do It

1. Open the spreadsheet **CH8TUT2** which you created in Chapter 8.

	A	B	C	D	E	F	G
1			PAYROLL				
2							
3	EMPLOYEE	Hours	Rate	Total	Tax	Net	
4	Eiler	40	12	480	38.4	441.6	
5	Kennedy	40	8				
6	MacRannall	42	12				
7	Walker	41	10				
8							
9	Total	163					
10							

2. Highlight cells **D4 through D7,** the Total range for all employees.
3. Choose **Edit, Fill Down.**
4. Highlight cells **E4 through E7,** the Tax range for all employees.
5. Choose **Edit, Fill Down.**
6. Fill in the **Net** values in column F for all employees using the same techniques as steps 4 and 5.
7. Position the highlight in cell **B9** and select all cells through **F9.**
8. Choose **Edit, Fill Right.**

The spreadsheet should appear similar to the following.

	A	B	C	D	E	F	G
1			PAYROLL				
2							
3	EMPLOYEE	Hours	Rate	Total	Tax	Net	
4	Eiler	40	12	480	38.4	441.6	
5	Kennedy	40	8	320	25.6	294.4	
6	MacRannall	42	12	504	40.32	463.68	
7	Walker	41	10	410	32.8	377.2	
8							
9	Total	163	42	1714	137.12	1576.88	
10							

To add text and a value for the expected percentage rate of payroll increase

9. Position the highlight in cell **A11** and type **Rate of payroll increase.**
10. Move the insertion point to cell **B11** and type 0.07. Press **Enter** when done. This value is the amount of expected pay increase over the next year.

	A	B	C	D	E	F
1				PAYROLL		
2						
3	EMPLOYEE	Hours	Rate	Total	Tax	Net
4	Eiler	40	12	480	38.4	441.6
5	Kennedy	40	8	320	25.6	294.4
6	MacRannall	42	12	504	40.32	463.68
7	Walker	41	10	410	32.8	377.2
8						
9	Total	163	42	1714	137.12	1576.88
10						
11	Rate of payroll increase	0.07				

11. Position the highlight in cell **A12.**
12. Type **Payroll Increase.**
13. Adjust the column width if necessary.
14. Highlight cell **B12.**
15. Type **=D4*$B$11+D4** and press **Enter.**

B12 =D4*$B$11+D4

	A	B	C	D	E	F
1				PAYROLL		
2						
3	EMPLOYEE	Hours	Rate	Total	Tax	Net
4	Eiler	40	12	480	38.4	441.6
5	Kennedy	40	8	320	25.6	294.4
6	MacRannall	42	12	504	40.32	463.68
7	Walker	41	10	410	32.8	377.2
8						
9	Total	163	42	1714	137.12	1576.88
10						
11	Rate of payroll increase	0.07				
12	Payroll Increase	513.6				

This formula will multiply Eiler's Total pay times the percentage rate found in cell B11 and add that increase to the Total pay, showing the increase above the present total. The dollar signs ($) are included to show an absolute cell address, which is one that will not change when copied to other cells in the spreadsheet.

16. Select cells **B12 through B15.**
17. Choose **Edit, Fill Down** to insert the results of copying the formula.

NOTE: Because D4 is used in the formula and does not contain dollar signs, it is a relative cell address. Therefore, it will increase in value as it is copied down. When D4 is copied down one cell address lower, it will change to D5 (Kennedy's Total amount), then to D6 (MacRannall's Total), and so on, as shown in the following example.

	A	B	C	D	E	F
1				PAYROLL		
2						
3	EMPLOYEE	Hours	Rate	Total	Tax	Net
4	Eiler	40	12	480	38.4	441.6
5	Kennedy	40	8	320	25.6	294.4
6	MacRannall	42	12	504	40.32	463.68
7	Walker	41	10	410	32.8	377.2
8						
9	Total	163	42	1714	137.12	1576.88
10						
11	Rate of payroll increase	0.07				
12	Payroll Increase	513.6				
13		342.4				
14		539.28				
15		438.7				

18. Save the spreadsheet as **CH9TUT.**

To insert a row

19. Highlight cell **A4.**

20. Choose **Insert, Row/Column** to display the Insert dialog box.

21. Choose **Row** (it should be selected).

22. Choose **OK** or press **Enter,**

To move data

23. Highlight **B13 through B16.**

24. Position the pointer so that the drag arrow appears.

25. Drag the entire block so that the first cell, B13, is positioned in B14 as shown here.

	A	B	C	D	E	F
1				PAYROLL		
2						
3	EMPLOYEE	Hours	Rate	Total	Tax	Net
4	Eiler	40	12	480	38.4	441.6
5	Kennedy	40	8	320	25.6	294.4
6	MacRannall	42	12	504	40.32	463.68
7	Walker	41	10	410	32.8	377.2
8						
9	Total	163	42	1714	137.12	1576.88
10						
11	Rate of payroll increase	0.07				
12	Payroll Increase	513.6				
13		342.4				
14		539.28				
15		438.7				
16						

MOVE

26. Release the left mouse button.

27. Highlight cells **A5 through A8.**

28. Copy the block of cells to **A14** using the Copy and the Paste buttons.

The spreadsheet should appear similar to the following.

	A	B	C	D	E	F	G
1				PAYROLL			
2							
3	EMPLOYEE	Hours	Rate	Total	Tax	Net	
4							
5	Eiler	40	12	480	38.4	441.6	
6	Kennedy	40	8	320	25.6	294.4	
7	MacRannall	42	12	504	40.32	463.68	
8	Walker	41	10	410	32.8	377.2	
9							
10	Total	163	42	1714	137.12	1576.88	
11							
12	Rate of payroll increase	0.07					
13	Payroll Increase						
14	Eiler	513.6					
15	Kennedy	342.4					
16	MacRannall	539.28					
17	Walker	438.7					
18							

29.	Save	again under the same name, **CH9TUT**.
30.	Print	the spreadsheet and close Works when done.

REVIEW QUESTIONS

Answer the following questions concerning commands from the **Edit** menu.

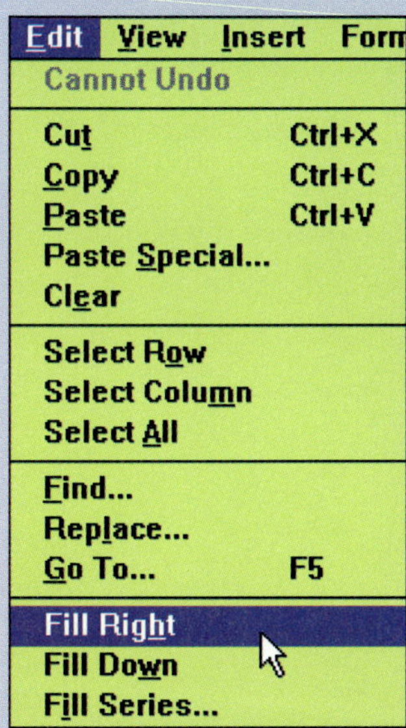

1. What is the function of the **Fill Right** command?

____

____

____

2. Which command is used to move values from one location to another nonadjacent location in the spreadsheet?

____

____

____

3. State two ways to move quickly from one cell to another remote cell.

____

____

____

4. What does the following formula do? What do the dollar signs ($) indicate?

=$A$2*B$1

____

____

____

5. List the steps used to move a range of cells from one location to another.
6. What is the fastest way to move a range of cells from one location to another?
7. Which of the commands from the **Edit** menu is used to remove all contents and formats from cells?

True or False:

8. ______ An absolute cell address changes when copied to other cells in a spreadsheet.
9. ______ Only one cell needs to be highlighted to insert a new row or column in a spreadsheet.
10. ______ All cells in the rows affected must be highlighted to insert multiple rows in a spreadsheet.

Hands-on Exercises

Exercise 1

1. Create the spreadsheet shown below and name it **CH9HO1A** or retrieve it from the Instructor data disk.

   HINT: The formula for the Change column is **=C5-B5**; the formula for the % of Change column is **=D5/B5**. Also, be sure to type double quotes in front of each year used as a heading.

	A	B	C	D	E	F
1			SALES BY BOAT			
2						
3	BOAT NAME	1993	1994	CHANGE	% OF CHANGE	
4						
5	Delano	37890	42520	4630	0.12219583	
6	The Spirit	35550	41236			
7	Sea Wolf	38950	45800			
8	Irish Sea	41250	58695			
9						
10	TOTAL					
11	AVERAGE					
12	MINIMUM					
13						

2. Choose Edit, fill down to copy the **Change** formula for **Delano** to pertinent cells for each of the boats in the spreadsheet.
3. Copy the **% of Change** formula for **Delano** to pertinent cells.
4. Calculate the **Total, Average,** and **Minimum** for 1993.
5. Choose edit, Fill Right to copy the **Total, Average,** and **Minimum** formulas for **1993** sales to the **1994** column using **Fill Right** from the **Edit** menu.
6. Insert a blank row between Total and Average.

The final spreadsheet should appear similar to the following.

	A	B	C	D	E	F
1			SALES BY BOAT			
2						
3	BOAT NAME	1993	1994	CHANGE	% OF CHANGE	
4						
5	Delano	37890	42520	4630	0.12219583	
6	The Spirit	35550	41236	5686	0.159943741	
7	Sea Wolf	38950	45800	6850	0.175866496	
8	Irish Sea	41250	58695	17445	0.422909091	
9						
10	TOTAL	153640	188251			
11						
12	AVERAGE	38410	47062.75			
13	MINIMUM	35550	41236			
14						
15						

7. Save as **CH9HO1B.**
8. Print the spreadsheet and close the window.

Exercise 2

1. Open the spreadsheet **CH8HO5** which you created in Chapter 8 or retrieve it from the Instructor data disk.

	A	B	C	D	E	F	G
1			PUGET SOUND CHARTERS				
2							
3		Current	Next	Five-year	Ten-year	Percentage	
4		Year	Year	Projection	Projection	of Increase	
5							
6	Delano	37890	41679	45846.9	59600.97	0.6357279	
7	The Spirit	35550					
8	Sea Wolf	38950					
9	Irish Sea	41250					
10							

2. Copy the formulas for **Next Year, Five-year Projection, Ten-year Projection,** and **Percentage of Increase** to other pertinent cells in the column for each of the boats.

   HINT: You can copy all formulas in adjacent columns at one time. To do so, highlight all formulas and cells to be copied in the cell range, C6 down and to the right through F9. Then choose **Fill Down** from the **Edit** menu.

3. Position the highlight in **A11**.
4. Type **Total**.
5. Compute the total for the **Current Year** in cell **B11** and copy it to compute totals for each column except **Percentage of Increase.**

   HINT: Use the Autosum button [Σ]. Then to reduce the highlight by one cell, hold the **Shift** key down and press the **Up Arrow** key once. Finally, press **Enter.**

	A	B	C	D	E	F
1			PUGET SOUND CHARTERS			
2						
3		Current	Next	Five-year	Ten-year	Percentage
4		Year	Year	Projection	Projection	of increase
5						
6	Delano	37890	41679	45846.9	59600.97	0.635727908
7	The Spirit	35550	39105	43015.5	55920.15	0.635727908
8	Sea Wolf	38950	42845	47129.5	61268.35	0.635727908
9	Irish Sea	41250	45375	49912.5	64886.25	0.635727908
10						
11	Total	153640	169004	185904.4	241675.72	
12						

6. Save the spreadsheet under the new name **CH9HO2.**
7. Insert two new rows after the one-line main heading.
8. Point and drag the **Total** line to the second blank line below the main heading.
9. Edit the **Total** cell and change it to **Grand Totals.**
10. Adjust the width of all columns to **15.**

HINT: Highlight (by clicking on the row number at the far left) any row across all columns (such as row 3), then choose **Format, Column Width**.

11. Save the spreadsheet again. It should appear similar to the following.

	A	B	C	D	E	F
1			PUGET SOUND CHARTERS			
2						
3	Grand Totals	153640	169004	185904.4	241675.72	
4						
5						
6		Current	Next	Five-year	Ten-year	Percentage
7		Year	Year	Projection	Projection	of increase
8						
9	Delano	37890	41679	45846.9	59600.97	0.635727908
10	The Spirit	35550	39105	43015.5	55920.15	0.635727908
11	Sea Wolf	38950	42845	47129.5	61268.35	0.635727908
12	Irish Sea	41250	45375	49912.5	64886.25	0.635727908
13						

12. Print a copy of the spreadsheet and close the window.

Exercise 3

1. Retrieve **CH8HO1** from your data disk.
2. Calculate the **Total** value in **E4**; then copy the formula down the column through **Vessel Collision Lessons.**
3. Calculate and copy the value for the **TOTAL, AVERAGE,** and **MAXIMUM** for **January** to the **February** and **March** columns.
4. Insert a blank row below the column headings **January** through **Total.**

For practice:

5. Highlight and move all values in the **January** column to cell **E15.**
6. Move the values back to their original location.
7. Save the file as **CH9HO3.**
8. Preview and then print a copy of the spreadsheet.

Exercise 4

1. Retrieve **CH8HO4** from your data disk.
2. Copy the monthly total for **January** to the **Total** cells for **February** and **March** cells C20 and D20.
3. Copy the **Total** in cell E6 (to the right of **March**) down through **Mending Holes.**
4. Copy the values **Total, Average, Minimum** and **Maximum** for **January** to **February** and **March.**
5. Insert one blank row below the column headings, **January** through **Total.**

6. Save it as **CH9HO4.**
7. Preview and print a copy of the worksheet.

Example of Exercises

Exercise 3: CH9HO3

	A	B	C	D	E	F
1			MISCELLANEOUS EXPENDITURES WORKSHEET			
2						
3		January	February	March	Total	
4						
5	Passenger Overboard Fees	200	500	300	1000	
6	Stress Management	1600	1000	2500	5100	
7	Food Replacement	1200	1600	1400	4200	
8	Safety Training	2000	3000	1500	6500	
9	Vessel Collision Lessons	800	350	700	1850	
10						
11	TOTAL	5800	6450	6400		
12	AVERAGE	1160	1290	1280		
13	MAXIMUM	2000	3000	2500		
14						

Exercise 4: CH9HO4

	A	B	C	D	E	F
1			STAFF TRAINING COURSES			
2			ENROLLMENT FIGURES			
3						
4	COURSE TITLE:		Date of Course			
5		January 15	February 10	March 08	Total	
6	Galley Safety Tips	5	4	6	15	
7	Crash Courses					
8	Captaining	82	80	75	237	
9	Deck Hand	2	3	4	9	
10	Life Saving	82	85	87	254	
11	First Aid	4	6	3	13	
12	Jumping Overboard	80	79	88	247	
13	Personal Safety First	2	3	1	6	
14	Emergency Evacuation	67	89	76	232	
15	Avoiding Sharks	6	7	8	21	
16	Narrow Misses	17	24	19	60	
17	Riding the Storm	77	71	76	224	
18	Mending Holes	4	9	6	19	
19						
20	Total	428	460	449		
21	Average	35.6666667				
22	Minimum	2				
23	Maximum	82				

CHAPTER 10

Formatting

OBJECTIVES

Change character formats

Format values

Create patterns and borders

Create headers and footers

Preview the spreadsheet

Insert page breaks

Change margins

Adjust column width and height

Print the spreadsheet

PREVIEW

Formatting a spreadsheet includes using commands from the **Format** menu that will change the appearance of the values and text in the spreadsheet. From this menu, it is possible to add the missing commas and decimal points to the values and to enhance the appearance of headings by using different fonts or character styles such as bold and underline.

CHANGING THE CHARACTER FORMATS

Character formats include anything that affects the appearance of the individual characters in the spreadsheet. Options may include changing the text to bold print, underline, or italics. It also includes changing the type of font and the color.

Change the Font

1. Open the spreadsheet **CH9PR1**, which you created in Chapter 9, or retrieve it from the Instructor data disk. It is shown below.

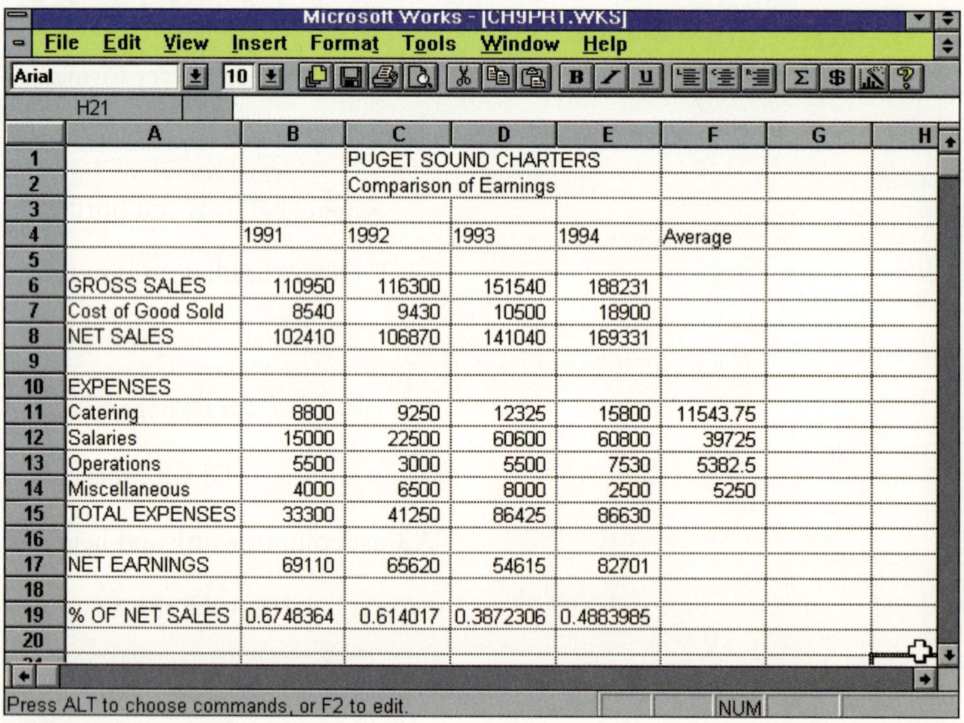

	A	B	C	D	E	F	G	H
1			PUGET SOUND CHARTERS					
2			Comparison of Earnings					
3								
4		1991	1992	1993	1994	Average		
5								
6	GROSS SALES	110950	116300	151540	188231			
7	Cost of Good Sold	8540	9430	10500	18900			
8	NET SALES	102410	106870	141040	169331			
9								
10	EXPENSES							
11	Catering	8800	9250	12325	15800	11543.75		
12	Salaries	15000	22500	60600	60800	39725		
13	Operations	5500	3000	5500	7530	5382.5		
14	Miscellaneous	4000	6500	8000	2500	5250		
15	TOTAL EXPENSES	33300	41250	86425	86630			
16								
17	NET EARNINGS	69110	65620	54615	82701			
18								
19	% OF NET SALES	0.6748364	0.614017	0.3872306	0.4883985			
20								

2. Highlight the two-line main heading in the worksheet (remember, you only need to highlight the cells containing the heading, such as C1 and C2).

3. Choose **Format, Font and Style** to display a dialog box similar to the one shown in Figure 10-1.

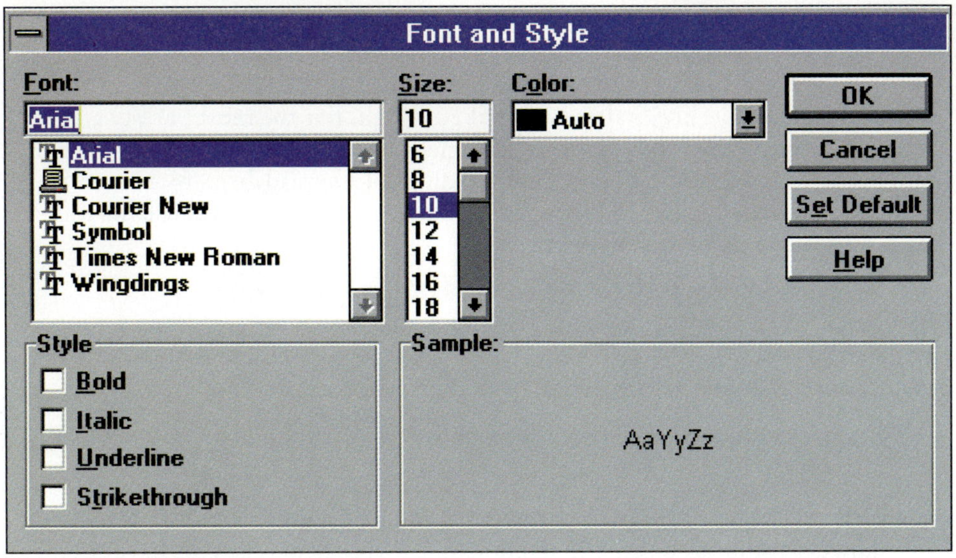

Figure 10-1
Font and style dialog box

This dialog box is similar to the **Font and Style** dialog box in word processing. The selections from this dialog box are shown in Table 10-1.

Use this option	To do this
Font	Change the format of the text or values in highlighted cells in the spreadsheet.
Size	Change the size of the text or values in highlighted cells in the spreadsheet. The larger the number; the larger the font size.
Color	Change the color of the text or values in highlighted cells. The color will appear only if you have a color monitor, and will appear in the printed document only if you have a color printer.
Style	Change the style of text or values in highlighted cells.
Sample	View the changes made to the highlighted cells prior to closing the Font and Style dialog box.

Table 10-1

Options in the Font and Style dialog box

4. Scroll through the list of fonts available. Notice that the point sizes that are available may change depending upon the font that is selected.
5. Choose **Arial** in the **Font** list box if it is not already selected, or choose a different font if you like.
6. Choose **12** in the **Size** box.
7. Choose **Bold** in the **Style** box. View the Sample box.
8. Choose **OK** or press **Enter**.

Change the Style

Changing the style includes altering the appearance of individual characters such as adding bold, underline, italics, and strikethrough. For the most part, changing the appearance of characters involves changing the formatting of text for the column headings, side headings, and main headings of a spreadsheet. Menu commands are discussed in the following steps; however, you may also use the toolbar as a shortcut to formatting text and values.

1. Highlight all column headings from **1991** through **Average.**
2. Choose **Format, Font and Style.**
3. Choose **Bold** and **Underline** from the **Style** box.
4. Choose **Blue** or another color from the **Color** list box.

   NOTE: The color change will appear if you have a color monitor. It will not, however, appear when the document is printed unless you have a color printer, such as a color ink jet printer.

5. Choose **OK** or press **Enter** and click anywhere in the window to deselect text.

The spreadsheet now appears similar to the following (partially shown).

	A	B	C	D	E	F
1			PUGET SOUND CHARTERS			
2			Comparison of Earnings			
3						
4		1991	1992	1993	1994	Average
5						
6	GROSS SALES	110950	116300	151540	188231	
7	Cost of Good Sold	8540	9430	10500	18900	
8	NET SALES	102410	106870	141040	169331	
9						
10	EXPENSES					
11	Catering	8800	9250	12325	15800	11543.75
12	Salaries	15000	22500	60600	60800	39725
13	Operations	5500	3000	5500	7530	5382.5
14	Miscellaneous	4000	6500	8000	2500	5250
15	TOTAL EXPENSES	33300	41250	86425	86630	

6. Highlight all headings in column A.
7. Choose Format, Font and Style.
8. Choose **Helvetica, Bold, 10 point,** and **Blue** from the appropriate boxes or other selections different from those in use if the suggested ones are not available.
9. Choose **OK** or press **Enter**. The column and side headings now appear in blue and in a different font. Depending on your screen, the change in format may appear shaded rather than in color.

Using the toolbar

While it is important to know where to locate format commands in the menus, practice using the toolbar as often as possible. The toolbar options include those shown in the following examples.

> *NOTE:* When you position the pointer on each of the tools on the toolbar, you will see the same messages as shown below.

Format from the toolbar

To use the toolbar, highlight the cells to be formatted and then click on the toolbar button.

1. Highlight all column headings in the spreadsheet from **1991** through **Average.**
2. Click on the **Right Align** button on the **toolbar** and note the change.
3. Click on the **Center Align** button on the **toolbar** and note the change.
4. Choose **Save As** from the **File** menu and save this document as **CH10PR1.** This file will be used throughout this chapter

FORMATTING VALUES

Commands for changing the appearance of values in a spreadsheet are found in the **Number** command in the **Format** menu. Currency values may also be formatted from the **toolbar**. Value formatting is also added when dollar signs are typed with the number (such as $1500). Works assumes that you are formatting the value as currency and turns on the Currency button on the **toolbar**, . Then, when the value is embedded into the cell, the dollar sign and commas appear automatically. In other words a value entered as $1500 will appear as $1,500. However, it is often easier to simply enter the value as a whole number (such as 1500) and apply formatting to large groups of values all at once.

Format Values

1. Highlight cells **B6 through E8** (use the mouse or press **F8** to turn on the EXTand use the arrow keys).

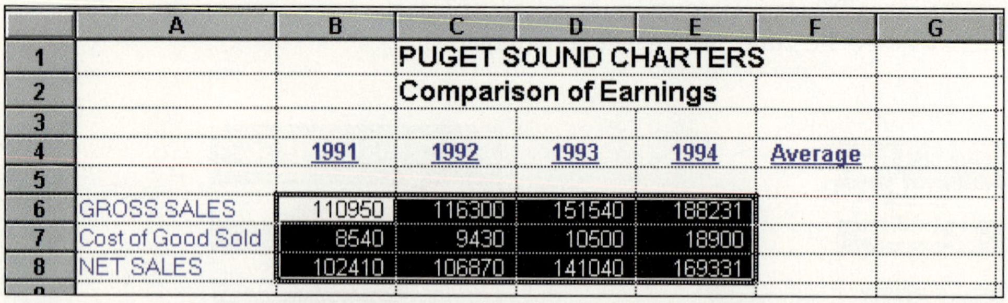

2. Choose **Format, Number.** The Number dialog box is displayed. Options here are explained in Table 10-2.

Table 10-2
Options in the Number dialog box

Use this option	To do this
Format	Change the format of the highlighted values.
Options	Choose variations on the format selected in the Format list.
Sample	View the changed format prior to choosing **OK**.

3. Choose **Currency** in the **Format** list. The Number dialog box changes to that shown in Figure 10-2.

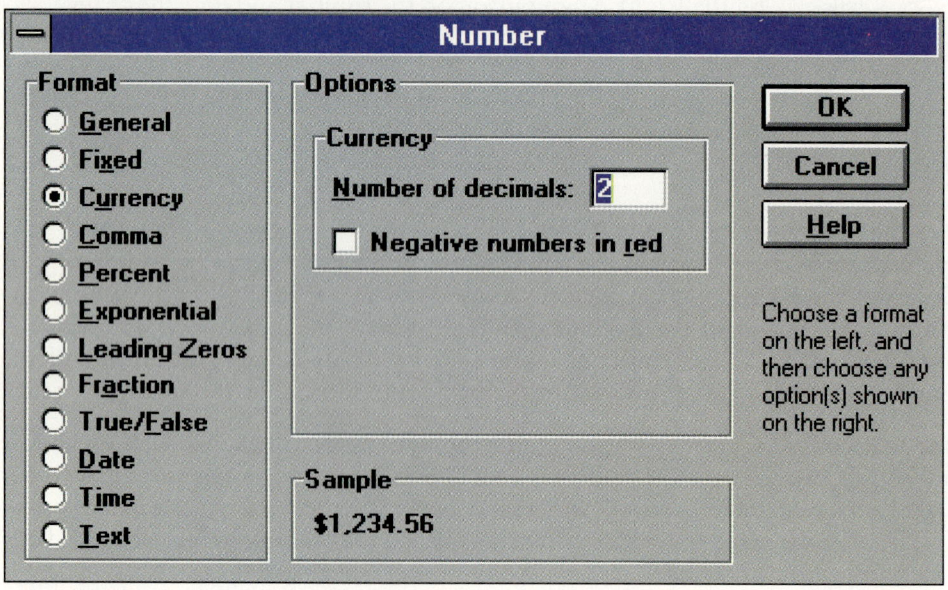

Figure 10-2
The Number dialog box with Currency selected

When the **Currency** format is chosen, the **Options** box displays other selections available with this option. The number of decimals may be changed and an option to show negative values in red is also available. Notice that as changes are made, the **Sample** box shows the affect they will have on the highlighted values. Other options found in the **Format** list include those shown in Table 10-3.

When this option is used	and if this is entered	It will be formatted as
General	876	876
Fixed	876	876.00
Currency	876	$876.00
Comma	1876	1,876.00
Percent	876	87600.00%
Exponential	876	@LX:8.76E+02
Leading Zeros	876	00876
Fraction, Rounded to 1/2	876.25	876 1/2
True/Falso	876	True
Date	9/28/94	9/28/94
Time	12	12:00 AM
Text	876	876

Table 10-3
Options in the Format list

In Table 10-3, the first column lists the options available in the Format list in the Number dialog box, the second column shows the number as it was entered in the spreadsheet, and the third column shows the result of using each option. The formats shown are those that come with the default settings, such as two places to the right of decimals. These can be changed to any number of decimal places the user wants. The **Fraction** option is applied to decimal numbers. The fraction will round the decimal digits to the next highest level. **Dates** should be entered at the keyboard in the date format, such as 9/28/93. You can then format the date to any of the formatted options available, including spelling the date out. **Times** are entered as whole values and then formatted. If you want the time to be shown as PM, then it must be typed as 12 PM otherwise Works will use the default AM setting. The **Text** format is used to identify a number as text rather than a value to be used in a calculation and aligns the entry at the left side of the cell. This is a useful setting for column headings, such as years, that are not to be used in calculations. Values in text format will not be included in totals.

4. Choose **OK** or press **Enter** to accept the settings. Your screen should resemble the following example.

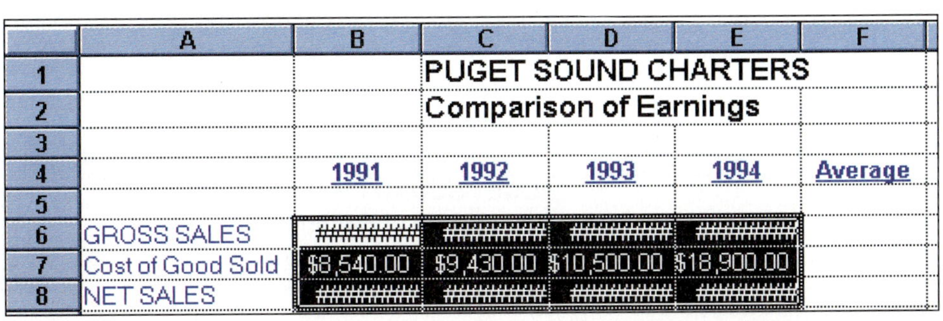

Some values appear showing the dollar sign ($); however, other cells show only number signs (##########). This occurs when the column is not wide enough to hold the values entered into it, such as a very wide, formatted currency value. When the values were changed to currency, commas, dollar signs, decimal places, and zeroes were added to each value. This makes the value much wider than when originally entered.

Change the Column Width

Whenever number signs (###########) appear, change the column width. Once it is changed, the numbers will show in the cells.

With all of the value cells in B6 through E8 still highlighted

1. Choose **Format, Column Width** to display the Column Width dialog box as shown here.

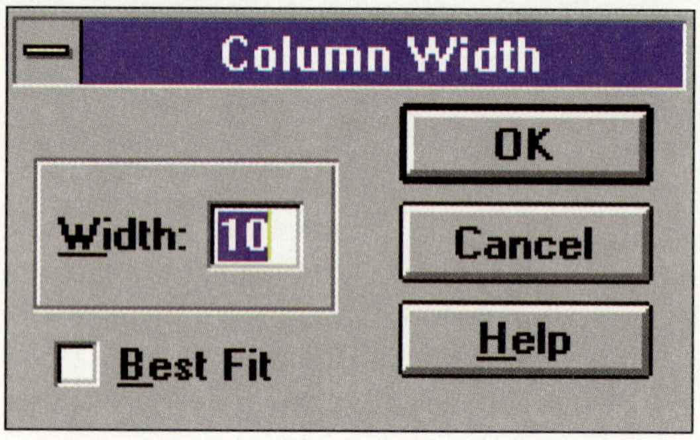

A new width may now be entered in the **Width** box. The number entered will affect the entire width of the column for each of the cells highlighted. You need to highlight only one cell in a column to adjust the width. You can also choose **Best Fit**, which adjusts the column width automatically so the values still appear formatted in the cells.

2. Type **15** in the **Width** box.

   NOTE: It is necessary to guess how wide the columns need to be. Since the default is 10, and 10 was too narrow, adding five spaces should accommodate the larger, formatted figures.

3. Choose **OK** or press **Enter**. The values appear as shown in the following example.

	A	B	C	D	E	F
1			PUGET SOUND CHARTERS			
2			Comparison of Earnings			
3						
4		1991	1992	1993	1994	Avera
5						
6	GROSS SALES	$110,950.00	$116,300.00	$151,540.00	$188,231.00	
7	Cost of Good Sold	$8,540.00	$9,430.00	$10,500.00	$18,900.00	
8	NET SALES	$102,410.00	$106,870.00	$141,040.00	$169,331.00	

Format from the Toolbar

1. Highlight cells **B11 through F17**.
2. Choose the Currency button $ from the toolbar. The values appear in currency format with two zeros to the right of the decimal, which is the default setting when using the toolbar. Click in the window to remove the selection.

Change Column width (Mouse)

Here you will widen Column A by using the mouse. You used this procedure in the previous chapter on editing a spreadsheet.

1. Position the pointer on the column border between columns **A and B**.
2. Hold the left mouse button down and drag the column border to the right until it is approximately under the **F** in the **Format** menu.

Change the Row Height

Row height can be changed quickly by pointing to the row border and using the left mouse button to drag the border to a new height.

1. Position the pointer on the row border between the first and second rows of your spreadsheet as follows.

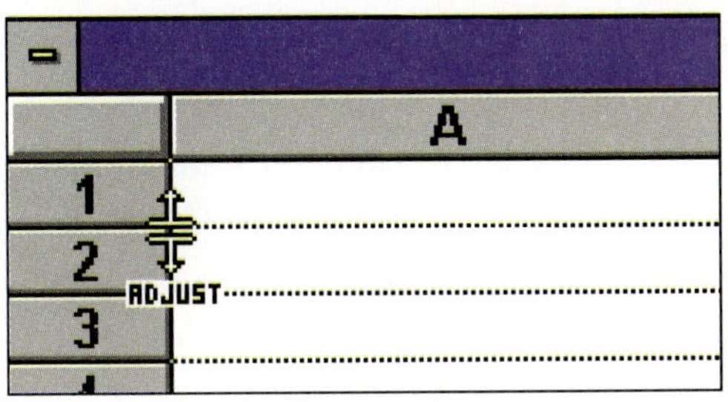

2. Hold the left mouse button down and drag the border downward so that it is approximately the height of two rows and appears similar to the following.

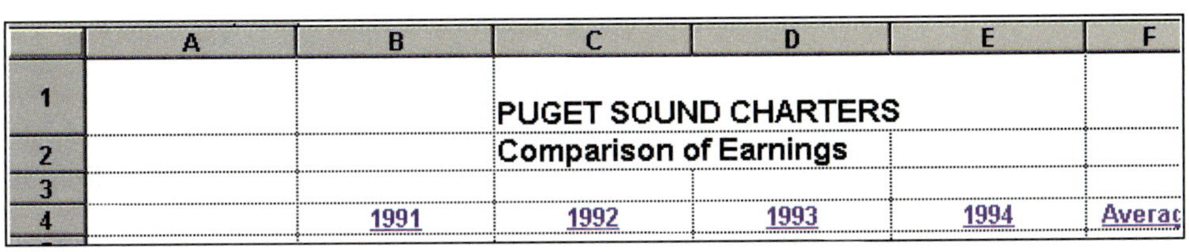

3. Drag the row border between 2 and 3 downward so that it is approximately the same size as row 1.

	A	B	C	D	E	F
1			PUGET SOUND CHARTERS			
2			Comparison of Earnings			
3						
4		1991	1992	1993	1994	Averag

4. Save the spreadsheet again.

Format Percentages

The percentage values on this spreadsheet should be changed and are formatted using the **Number** command from the **Format** menu.

1. Position the pointer on the row number containing the percentage values as shown in the following example.

17	NET EARNINGS	$69,110.00	$65,620.00	$54,615.00	$82,701.00
18					
19	% OF NET SALES	0.674836442	0.61401703	0.387230573	0.488398462

2. Click the left mouse button once. The entire row is highlighted.

   NOTE: Columns can be selected using the same technique as in steps 1 and 2. Point to the column letter and click the left mouse button once.

3. Choose **Format, Number.**
4. Choose **Percent in the Format list.**
5. Type **3** as the number of decimal places.
6. Choose **OK** or press **Enter**. The values are changed as shown here.

18					
19	% OF NET SALES	67.484%	61.402%	38.723%	48.840%
20					

CREATING PATTERNS AND BORDERS

Once the basic spreadsheet is completed, features such as borders, shading, and patterns may be added to the spreadsheet to draw attention to values, text, or headings or to enhance the overall appearance of the spreadsheet.

Change the Patterns

The pattern of highlighted cells or blocks of cells may be changed using the **Patterns** command in the **Format** menu. This command allows you to change the shading, foreground, and background of a cell.

1. Highlight cells **A1 through F2** (both lines of the main heading).
2. Choose **Format, Patterns** to display the dialog box shown in Figure 10-3.

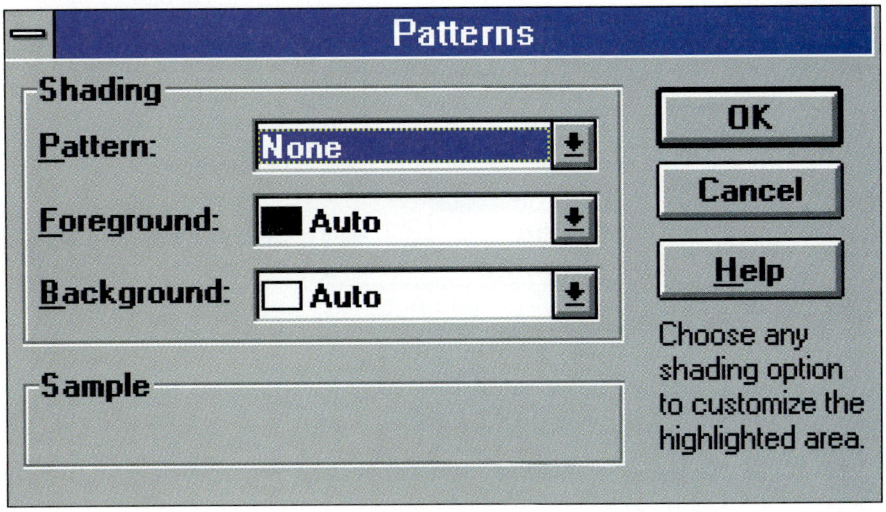

Figure 10-3
The Patterns dialog box

The **Patterns** list box contains options for adding pattern or shading to the highlighted cell(s). After a pattern is selected, the **Foreground** option can be used to change the color or shading of the individual dots or other markings making up the pattern. The **Background** option will change the color again by affecting the area within the cells and behind the pattern markings.

3. Click on the selection arrow to the right of the **Pattern** list box.
4. Select the fifth pattern down. (**None** is the first pattern choice.) That is the pattern showing the widest spacing of small dots.

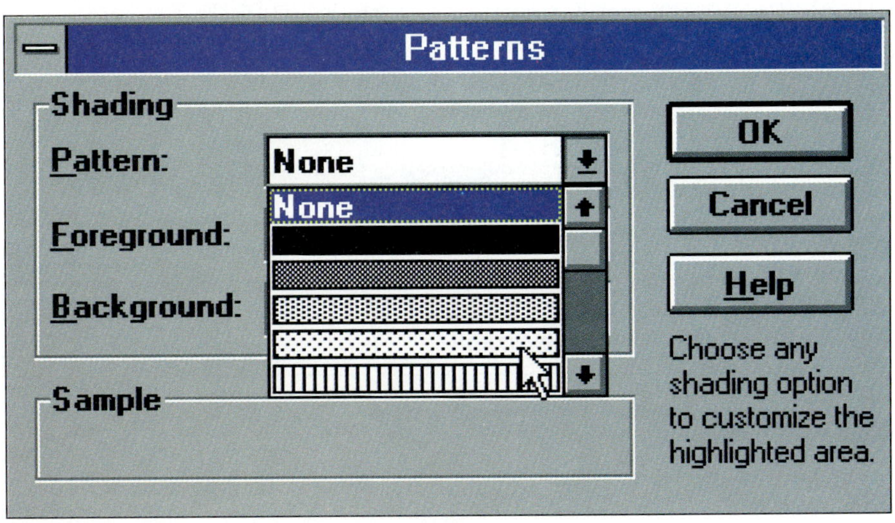

5. Click on the arrow at the right of the **Foreground** list and select **Cyan**.

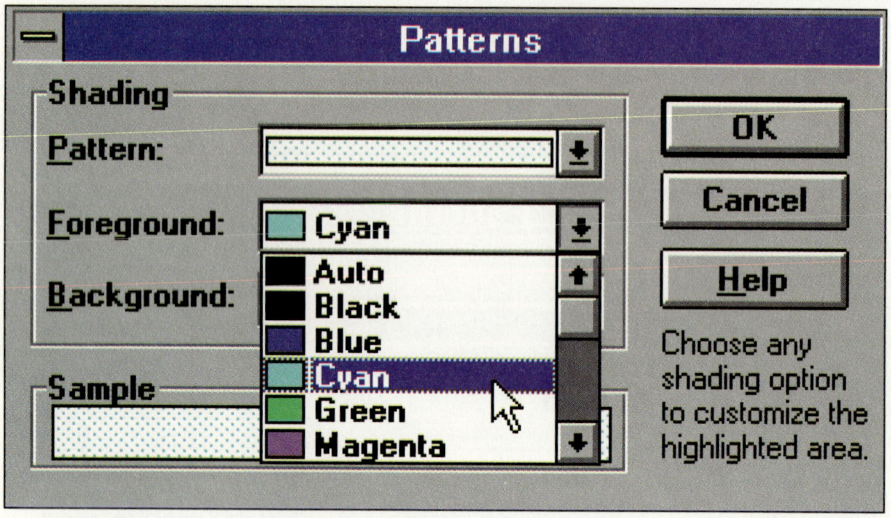

Notice the Sample box as selections are made.

6. Scroll through the **Background** list box as shown below, and choose **Light Gray**.

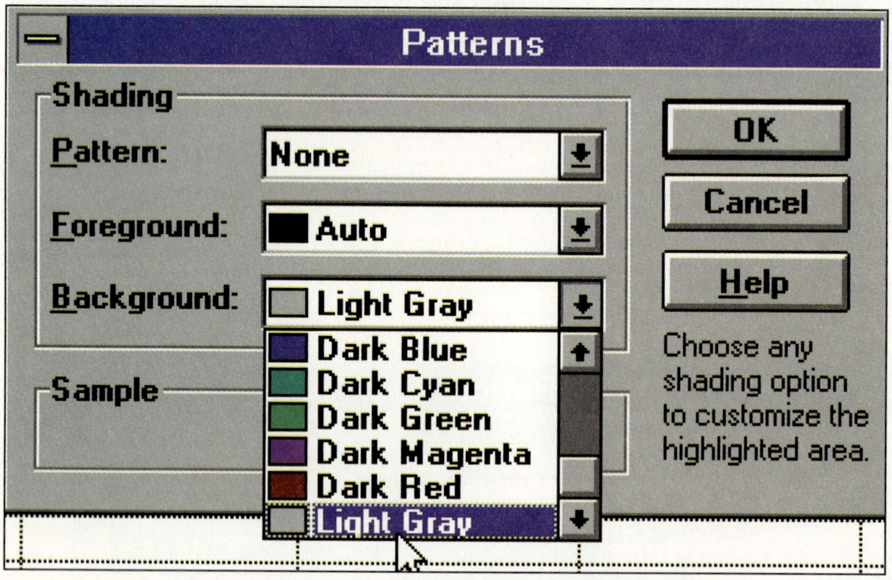

7. Choose **OK** or press **Enter**. Click to deselect the cells. The heading is similar to the following example.

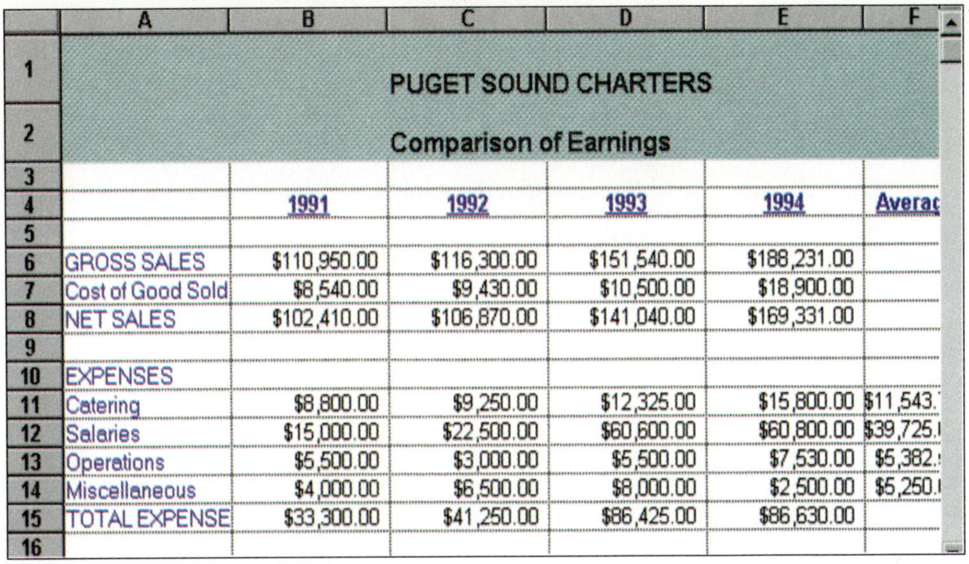

	A	B	C	D	E	F
1	PUGET SOUND CHARTERS					
2	Comparison of Earnings					
3						
4		1991	1992	1993	1994	Averag
5						
6	GROSS SALES	$110,950.00	$116,300.00	$151,540.00	$188,231.00	
7	Cost of Good Sold	$8,540.00	$9,430.00	$10,500.00	$18,900.00	
8	NET SALES	$102,410.00	$106,870.00	$141,040.00	$169,331.00	
9						
10	EXPENSES					
11	Catering	$8,800.00	$9,250.00	$12,325.00	$15,800.00	$11,543.
12	Salaries	$15,000.00	$22,500.00	$60,600.00	$60,800.00	$39,725.
13	Operations	$5,500.00	$3,000.00	$5,500.00	$7,530.00	$5,382.
14	Miscellaneous	$4,000.00	$6,500.00	$8,000.00	$2,500.00	$5,250.
15	TOTAL EXPENSE	$33,300.00	$41,250.00	$86,425.00	$86,630.00	
16						

8. Save the spreadsheet again.

Add Borders

Borders can be added to groups of cells or individual cells. A border is a solid line that appears on all sides of a cell or on selected sides of a cell or group of cells. For example, the column headings in this spreadsheet could have a border along the bottom side of each of the cells. This is different from using the underline feature, which underlines each of the individual characters or values within the cell. The border feature applies to the entire cell border—left, right, bottom, or top, or all sides.

1. Highlight all column headings from **1991** through **Average.**
2. Choose **Format, Border** to display the Border dialog box as shown in Figure 10-4.

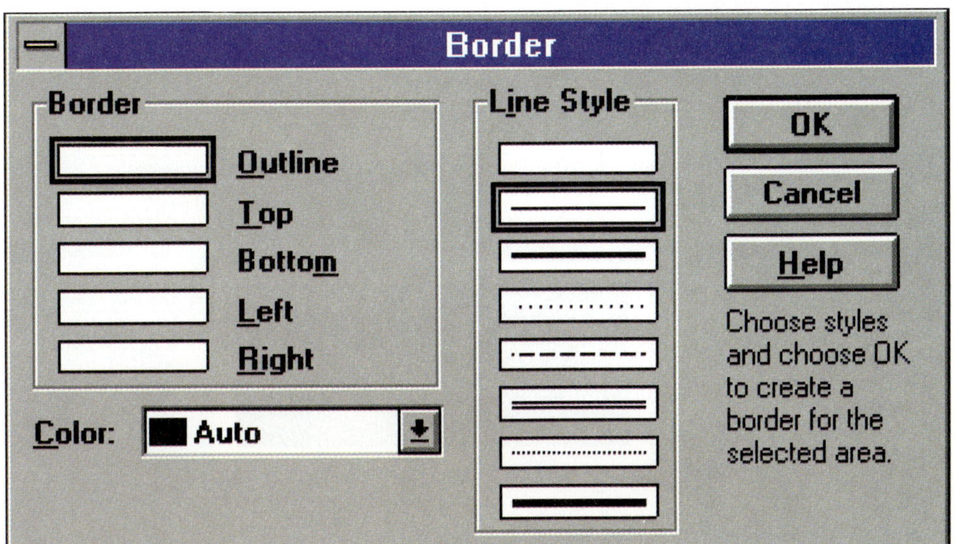

Figure 10-4
The Border dialog box

This dialog box contains options for adding borders to all sides of a cell or group of highlighted cells. The color of the border can also be changed using the **Color** option. The **Line Style** options include formats for changing the width and style of the border.

3. Choose **Bottom** in the **Border** box.
4. Choose the second line down in the **Line Style** box (the heavier solid line).
5. Choose **OK** or press **Enter**.
6. Click on the **Underline** button in the toolbar to remove the underline format. The spreadsheet is now similar to the one shown below.

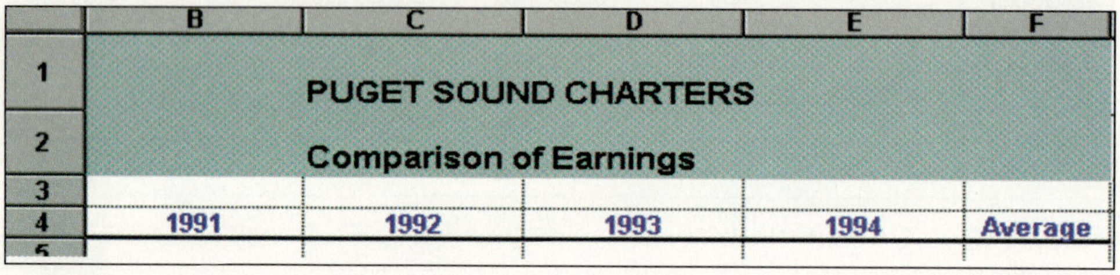

7. Save the spreadsheet again.

USING AUTOFORMAT

Works contains several automatic formats for spreadsheets. These formats can be applied either before or after a spreadsheet is created. The advantage of automatic formats is that extensive formatting such as shading, currency, borders, and so on, does not need to be done one step at a time. You can just highlight certain cells and apply the auto format to them. Or you can choose a format first, and then just fill in the values.

Add AutoFormat

1. Highlight cells **A8 through E8** (Net Sales and the net sales amounts).
2. Choose **Format, AutoFormat**. A dialog box similar to the one shown in Figure 10-5 appears.

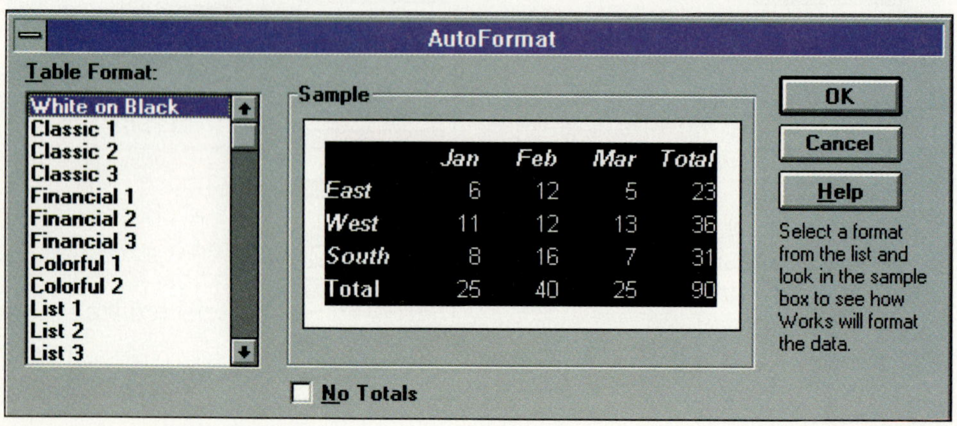

Figure 10-5
The AutoFormat dialog box

Choosing options from the **Table Format** list box changes the display in the Sample box. It will show you the different layouts for each of the options.

3. Choose	**Classic 1** from the **Table Format** list box and note the change to the sample spreadsheet in the Sample box
4. Choose	various options down the **Table Format** list box to view the format.
5. Choose	**List 1** from the list.
6. Choose	**OK** or press **Enter**. NET SALES now appear as follows.

	A	B	C	D	E	F
1			PUGET SOUND CHARTERS			
2			Comparison of Earnings			
3						
4		1991	1992	1993	1994	Average
5						
6	GROSS SALES	$110,950.00	$116,300.00	$151,540.00	$188,231.00	
7	Cost of Good S	$8,540.00	$9,430.00	$10,500.00	$18,900.00	
8	NET SALES	*$102,410.00*	*$106,870.00*	*$141,040.00*	*$169,331.00*	

7. Change	the format for the Total Expenses and the Net Earnings to **List 1**. The formatted spreadsheet is now similar to the following example.

	A	B	C	D	E	F
2			Comparison of Earnings			
3						
4		1991	1992	1993	1994	Average
5						
6	GROSS SALES	$110,950.00	$116,300.00	$151,540.00	$188,231.00	
7	Cost of Good Sold	$8,540.00	$9,430.00	$10,500.00	$18,900.00	
8	NET SALES	*$102,410.00*	*$106,870.00*	*$141,040.00*	*$169,331.00*	
9						
10	EXPENSES					
11	Catering	$8,800.00	$9,250.00	$12,325.00	$15,800.00	$11,543.75
12	Salaries	$15,000.00	$22,500.00	$60,600.00	$60,800.00	$39,725.00
13	Operations	$5,500.00	$3,000.00	$5,500.00	$7,530.00	$5,382.50
14	Miscellaneous	$4,000.00	$6,500.00	$8,000.00	$2,500.00	$5,250.00
15	TOTAL EXPENSES	*$33,300.00*	*$41,250.00*	*$86,425.00*	*$86,630.00*	
16						
17	NET EARNINGS	*$69,110.00*	*$65,620.00*	*$54,615.00*	*$82,701.00*	
18						
19	% of Net Sales	67.484%	61.402%	38.723%	48.840%	
20						

8. Adjust the width of column A if necessary.
9. Highlight the **Average** values and format them in any desired format.

   HINT: Use any of the commands in the **Format** menu discussed here.

10. Save the spreadsheet again.

Change the Alignment

The alignment of text and values can be changed using the **Alignment** command in the **Format** menu. This command is very useful for aligning main headings over spreadsheets or for changing the alignment of column headings or values all in one highlighted block.

1. Highlight cells **A1** through **F2** containing the two-line main heading.

   NOTE: This is the block of text that will be centered over the entire spreadsheet (from the leftmost column to the rightmost column).

2. Choose **Format, Alignment** to display the Alignment dialog box as shown in Figure 10-6.

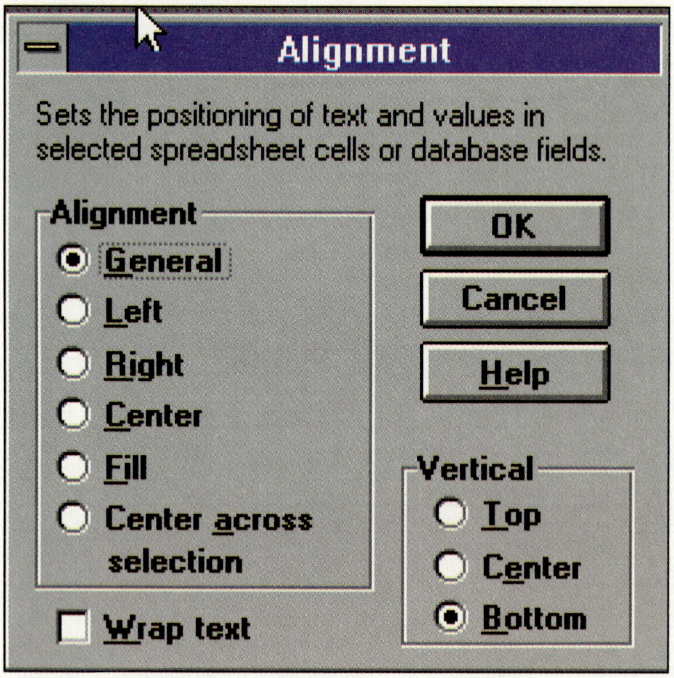

Figure 10-6
The Alignment dialog box

This dialog box allows you to change the alignment of values or text within highlighted blocks of cells. For example, this heading could be centered both vertically and horizontally within the block of cells we have just highlighted (A1 through F2). You also have the option of wrapping text within a cell. For example, when text overlaps into adjacent cells to the right, you could select the cell containing the text and choose the **Wrap text** option in this dialog box. The text would then wrap within the cell borders rather than overlap into adjacent cells.

3. Choose **Center** in the **Alignment** box. This will center the text horizontally in the selected block of cells.
4. Choose **Center** in the **Vertical** box. This will center the text vertically between the top and bottom of the selected block of cells.
5. Choose **OK** or press **Enter**. The spreadsheet is now similar to the following example with the two-line main heading centered evenly between the borders of the spreadsheet.

	A	B	C	D	E	F	G
1	PUGET SOUND CHARTERS						
2	Comparison of Earnings						
3							
4		1991	1992	1993	1994	Average	
5							
6	GROSS SALES	$110,950.00	$116,300.00	$151,540.00	$188,231.00		
7	Cost of Good Sold	$8,540.00	$9,430.00	$10,500.00	$18,900.00		
8	NET SALES	$102,410.00	$106,870.00	$141,040.00	$169,331.00		

CREATING HEADERS AND FOOTERS

Spreadsheets can contain headers and footers like those created in word processing that enhance the overall formatting. A header appears at the top of every page (the first page is optional); a footer appears at the bottom of every page (the first page is optional). The **Headers and Footers** command is found in the **View** menu. The header or footer does not appear on the screen, but it does appear when the spreadsheet is printed or in Print Preview. For more information, see the word processing section of this book.

Create Headers and Footers

1. Choose **View, Headers and Footers** to display the dialog box shown in Figure 10-7.

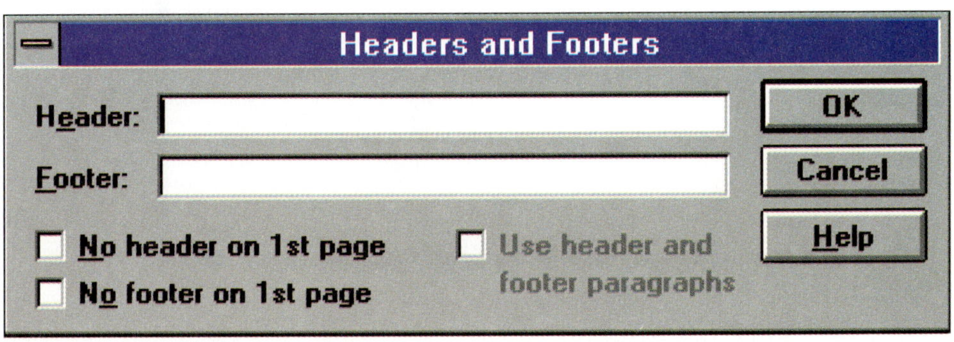

Figure 10-7
The Headers and Footers dialog box

2. Type **Payroll Report, Puget Sound Charters** in the **Header** box.
3. Type **&cPage - &p -** in the **Footer** box.

   NOTE: The code **&c** will center the word Page and its number. The page number is inserted using **&p**. Check Chapter 7 in the word processing section for further information on headers and footers.

4. Choose **OK** or press **Enter.**

PREVIEWING THE SPREADSHEET

A spreadsheet can be viewed in Print Preview, as can any other document created using Works. Since the header does not appear on the spreadsheet and since all columns are not visible on the screen, this option enables you to see the spreadsheet as it will print.

Preview the Spreadsheet

1. Click on the Print Preview button or choose **File, Print Preview**
   A screen similar to the one shown in Figure 10-8 appears.

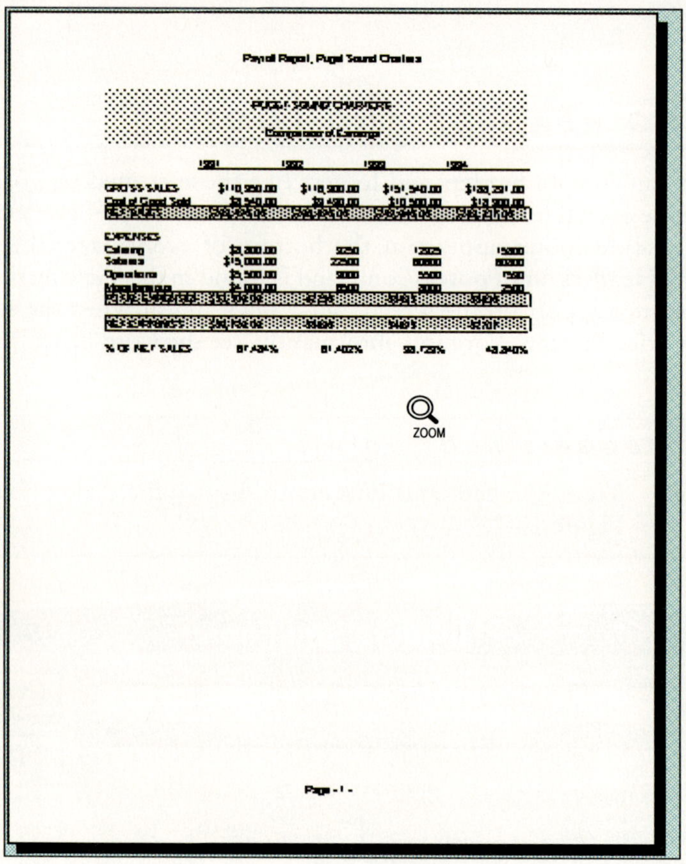

Figure 10-8
Print Preview

The mouse pointer becomes a small magnifying glass. Clicking the left mouse button once will zoom the image first to one increment and a second time to a larger increment. Clicking on the left mouse button a third time will reduce the image so that the entire document is again visible on the screen. If a document contains multiple pages, the **Next** and **Previous** buttons are used to move from page to page.

2.	Click	the left mouse button once or choose **Zoom In**. The image increases in size.
3.	Click	the left mouse button again or choose **Zoom In**. The image zooms to a larger size.
4.	Click	the left mouse button one more time or choose **Zoom Out** twice. The image is reduced to show the full document.

NOTE: When the document is full size, the header and footer are visible. You can use the mouse pointer to zoom in on any area of the document.

5.	Choose	**Next** to view the second page of the spreadsheet.
6.	Choose	**Previous** to move back to the first.
7.	Choose	**Print** to print a copy of the spreadsheet.
8.	Choose	**OK** to the **Print** dialog box that appears.
9.	Save	the document again as **CH10PR1**.

CHANGING PAGE LAYOUT

The text in the last column was pushed to a second page. You have some options available as to how to handle this document. You can do one of the following: leave it as it is and print the spreadsheet on two pages; change the layout of the page so that the spreadsheet prints in landscape (horizontal) mode; or change the position of the page break in the document. Both landscape mode and page breaks will be used here.

Insert a Page Break

A page break is added by positioning the highlight in the column that is to be to the right of the new page break (or the row that is to follow a page break). For example, if you want the page break to appear after column C, position the highlight in any cell in column D.

1.	Position	the highlight in any cell in column **D**.
2.	Choose	**Insert, Page Break** to display the Insert Page break dialog box.
3.	Choose	**Column** in the dialog box that appears as shown in the following example.

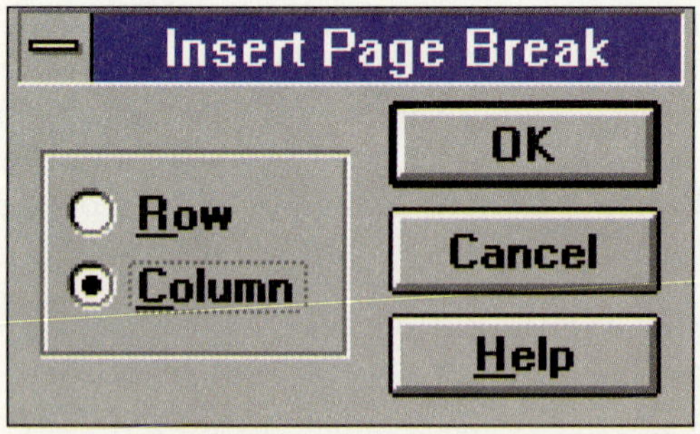

4. Choose **OK** or press **Enter**. A page break is added after column C.

5. Choose **File, Print Preview**. Choose both **Next** and **Previous** to see pages 1 and 2.

Notice that the main heading is now divided between page 1 and page 2. Notice also that the page numbers and the header automatically appear. For the most part, the division of this spreadsheet is okay with the exception of the heading.

6. Choose **Cancel** to leave Print Preview.

7. Highlight cells **C1** and **C2** (or the two cells containing the two-line main headings).

8. Point to the border of the cells and drag the heading to column B as follows.

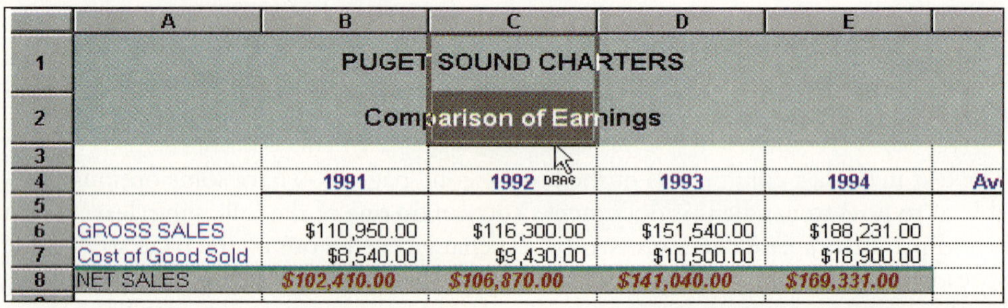

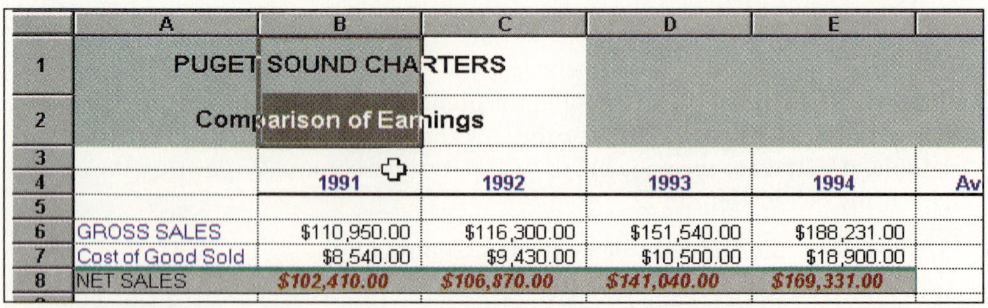

9. Highlight cells **C1** and **C2**.

10. Choose **Format, Patterns.**

11. Choose the fifth pattern in the **Pattern** list box (the light dots).

12. Choose **Cyan** in the **Foreground** box.
13. Choose **Light Gray** in the **Background** box.
14. Choose **OK** or press **Enter**.
15. Click on the Print Preview button  or choose **File, Print Preview** to see the changes in the document.
16. Choose **Cancel** to leave Print Preview.

The document is almost complete. To make it look even better, the margins should be adjusted so that they are approximately even on the left and right sides.

Change the Margins

1. Choose **File, Page Setup** to see the dialog box shown in Figure 10-9.

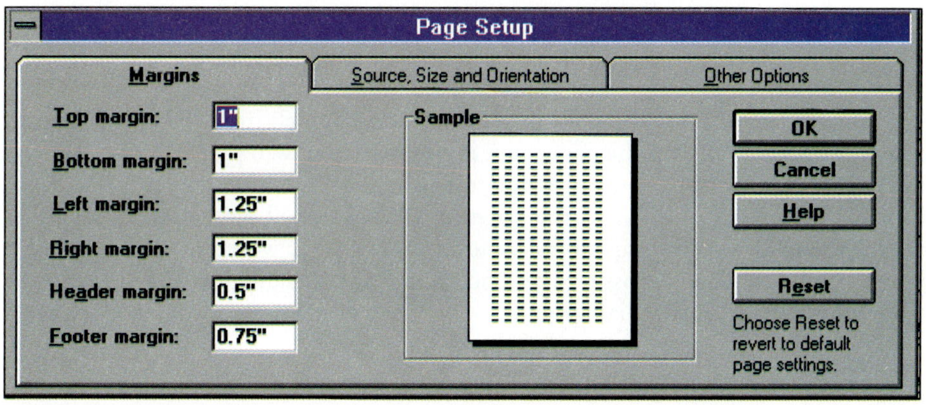

Figure 10-9
The Page Setup dialog box

2. Choose **Margins** if it is not already selected. The default margin settings appear in the boxes under the **Margins** heading. An image of the document with the current settings appears in the Sample box.
3. Type **2.5** in the **Left margin** box by highlighting the box and then typing over the existing margin setting.
4. Choose **OK** or press **Enter**.
5. Click on the Print Preview button  to look at the changes in the document. The margins are now much better. The header, however, would look better if it were left aligned.
6. Choose **Cancel** to return to the document.
7. Choose **View, Headers and Footers.**
8. Type **&L** at the beginning of the header line as follows.

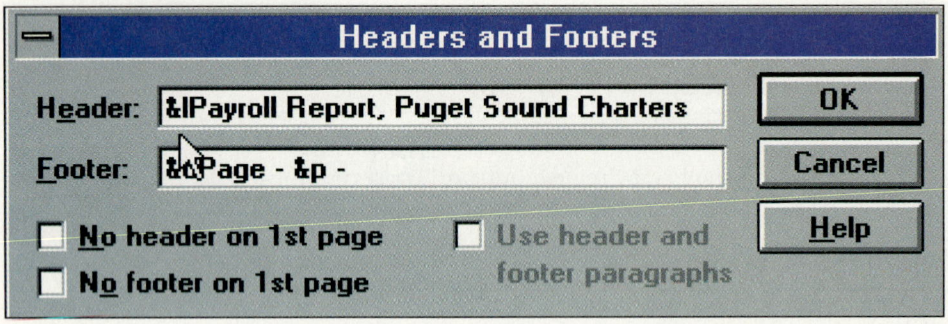

9.	Choose	**OK** or press **Enter**.
10.	Click	on the Print Preview button .
11.	View	both pages of the document.
12.	Choose	**Print**.

CHANGING PAGE ORIENTATION

The page setup for this document is in portrait mode, which means that the spreadsheet will print vertically on the page, and, if it is too wide, will print on two or more pages. This is the default layout for a document in Works. Sometimes it is better if a document prints horizontally on the page in what is called landscape mode. This allows for the length of the page to become the new width, which in turn allows for many more columns to fit across a page. The options for changing the page orientation are found in the **Page Setup** dialog box.

Change Page Orientation

First, remove the page break. Your insertion point must be in the column that follows the page break.

1.	Position	the highlight in any cell in column **D**.
2.	Choose	**Insert, Delete Page Break.**

Now, change the page layout.

3.	Choose	**File, Page Setup.**
4.	Choose	**Source, Size and Orientation** if it is not already selected. The dialog box appears similar to the one shown in Figure 10-10.

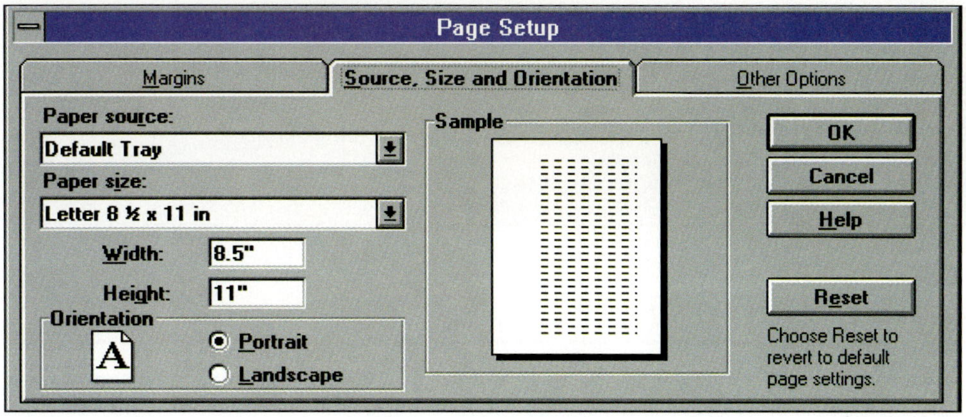

Figure 10-10
Source, Size and Orientation options

The Sample box shows the current page orientation and the layout of the document within the page limitations.

5. Choose **Landscape** in the **Orientation** box.

Note the change in the Sample image.

6. Choose **Margins** again.
7. Change the left margin to **2**.
8. Choose **OK** or press **Enter**.
9. Click on the Print Preview button.

   NOTE: The titles are not centered. If you like, use the procedure given earlier in this chapter for moving the text and for formatting the unshaded cells with patterns.

10. Choose **Print**.
11. Save the spreadsheet again.

PRINTING SELECTED CELLS

A block of selected cells can be printed using the **Set Print Area** command in the **Format** menu. This command allows for specific areas of a spreadsheet to be printed rather than the entire spreadsheet.

Print Selected Cells

1. Highlight cells **A4 through E8**.
2. Choose **Format, Set Print Area**.
3. Choose **OK** to the box that appears.
4. Click on the Print Preview button.
5. Choose **Print**.
6. Highlight the entire spreadsheet (**Choose Edit, Select All**).

7. Choose **Format, Set Print Area.**
8. Choose **OK** to the box that appears.
9. Save the spreadsheet again and close the window.
10. Quit or continue to the tutorial.

GUIDED TUTORIAL

What You'll Do

- Change font and point size.
- Apply character and page formats.
- Print selected blocks of the spreadsheet.
- Print the entire spreadsheet.

How To Do It

1. Open **CH9TUT** which you created in Chapter 9, or retrieve it from the Instructor data disk.

	A	B	C	D	E	F	G
1				PAYROLL			
2							
3	EMPLOYEE	Hours	Rate	Total	Tax	Net	
4							
5	Eiler	40	12	480	38.4	441.6	
6	Kennedy	40	8	320	25.6	294.4	
7	MacRannall	42	12	504	40.32	463.68	
8	Walker	41	10	410	32.8	377.2	
9							
10	Total	163	42	1714	137.12	1576.88	
11							
12	Rate of payroll increase	0.07					
13	Payroll Increase						
14	Eiler	513.6					
15	Kennedy	342.4					
16	MacRannall	539.28					
17	Walker	438.7					
18							
19							
20							

2. Highlight the main heading, **PAYROLL.**
3. Choose **Format, Font and Style.**
4. Choose a font different from the one you are using.
5. Choose **14** from the **Size** box.
6. Choose **Bold** from the **Style** box.
7. Choose a color from the **Color** list box.

8. Choose OK or press **Enter**.
9. Highlight cells **A1 through F1**.
10. Choose **Format, Alignment**.
11. Choose **Center** from the **Alignment** list.
12. Choose **OK** or press **Enter**. The heading appears approximately as follows.

	A	B	C	D	E	F	G
1				PAYROLL			
2							
3	EMPLOYEE	Hours	Rate	Total	Tax	Net	
4							

13. Highlight all currency values (all values except the Hours).
14. Choose the **Currency** button on the toolbar **$**.
15. Highlight columns **A through F** of any row in the spreadsheet.
16. Choose **Format, Column Width**.
17. Change the width to **18** and choose **OK** or press **Enter**.
18. Use **Print Preview** to look at both pages of the document.
19. Choose **Cancel** to return to the document.
20. Choose **File, Page Setup**.
21. Choose **Size, Source and Orientation**.
22. Choose **Landscape** in the **Orientation** box.
23. Choose **OK** or press **Enter**.
24. Choose **Print Preview** to see the changes in the document.
25. Choose **Cancel**.
26. Save the document as **CH10TUT**.
27. Choose **View, Headers and Footers**.
28. Type **&LPAYROLL REPORT, March** in the **Header** box.
29. Type **&C&P** in the **Footer** box.
30. Choose **OK** or press **Enter**.
31. Choose **Print Preview** to see the document with changes. It should appear similar to the following.

PAYROLL REPORT, March

PAYROLL

EMPLOYEE	Hour	Rate	Total	Tax	Net
Eiler	40	$12.00	$480.00	$38.40	$441.60
Kennedy	40	$8.00	$320.00	$25.60	$294.40
MacRannall	42	$12.00	$504.00	$40.32	$463.68
Walker	41	$10.00	$10.00	$32.80	$377.20
Total	163	$42.00	$1,714.00	$137.12	$1,576.88
Rate of payroll increase	0.07				
Payroll Increase					
Eiler	$513.60				
Kennedy	$342.40				
MacRannall	$539.28				
Walker	$438.70				

ZOOM

33. Choose **Cancel.**

34. Add borders and patterns to the spreadsheet in any location you think would improve its overall appearance and readability.

35. Save the spreadsheet again.

36. Choose **Print Preview** to look at the final results. The final spreadsheet might appear similar to the following.

PAYROLL REPORT, March

PAYROLL

EMPLOYEE	Hour	Rate	Total	Tax	Net
Eiler	40	$12.00	$480.00	$38.40	$441.60
Kennedy	40	$8.00	$320.00	$25.60	$294.40
MacRannall	42	$12.00	$504.00	$40.32	$463.68
Walker	41	$10.00	$10.00	$32.80	$377.20
Total	163	$42.00	$1,714.00	$137.12	$1,576.88
Rate of payroll increase	0.07				
Payroll Increase					
Eiler	$513.60				
Kennedy	$342.40				
MacRannall	$539.28				
Walker	$438.70				

ZOOM

37. Choose **Print**. Then save and close the spreadsheet.

38. Quit or continue to the review questions.

Briefly explain some of the options found in each of the following.

1. 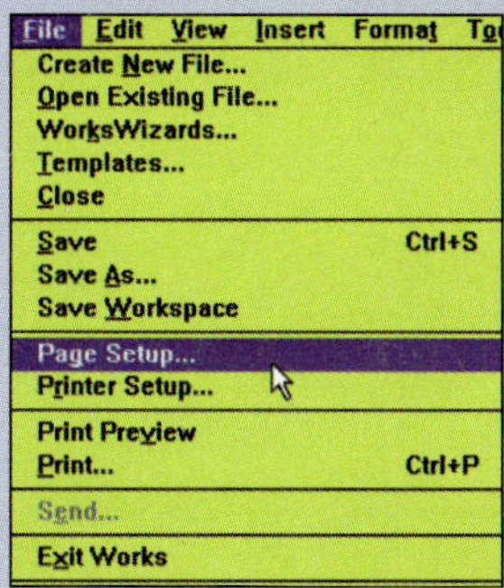

2. 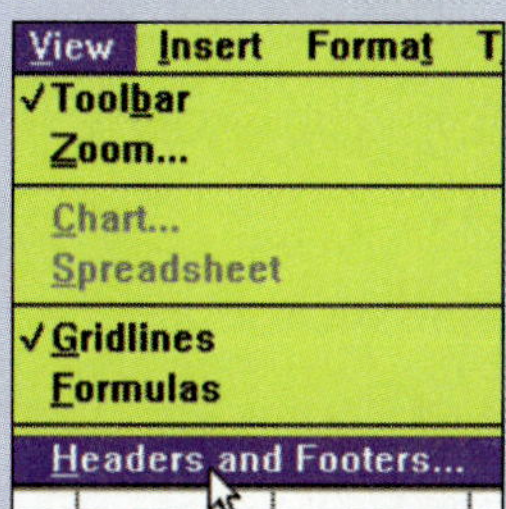

3. 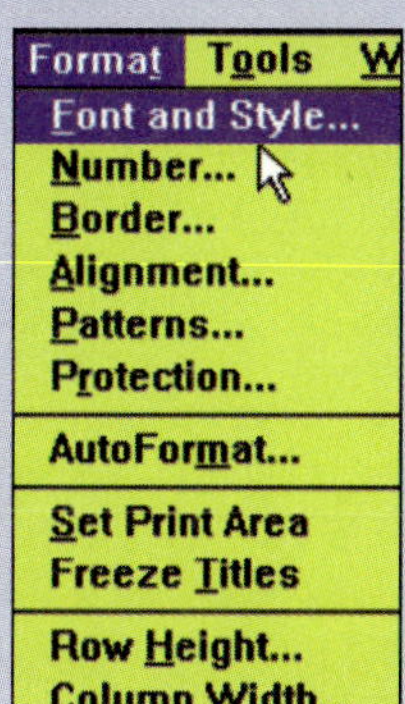

4.

Format
Tools
W
Font and Style...
Number...
Border...
Alignment...
Patterns...
Protection...
AutoFormat...
Set Print Area
Freeze Titles
Row Height...
Column Width...

5.

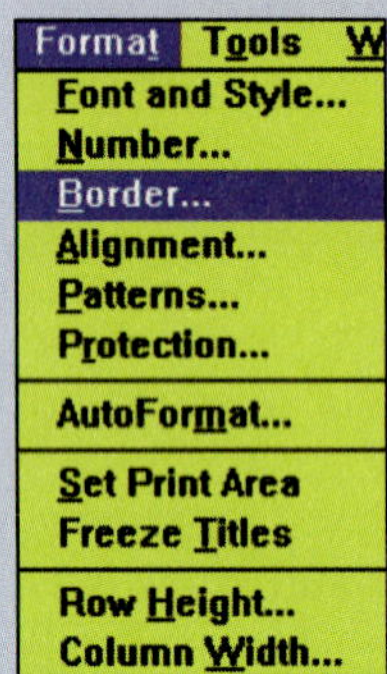
Format
Tools
W
Font and Style...
Number...
Border...
Alignment...
Patterns...
Protection...
AutoFormat...
Set Print Area
Freeze Titles
Row Height...
Column Width...

6.

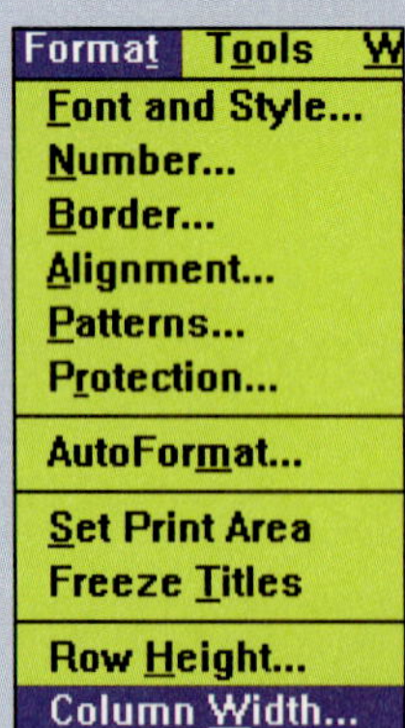
Format
Tools
W
Font and Style...
Number...
Border...
Alignment...
Patterns...
Protection...
AutoFormat...
Set Print Area
Freeze Titles
Row Height...
Column Width...

7. 

8. List two ways to format values as currency.

9. What command is used to print only selected cells of a spreadsheet?

10. What command is used to print in landscape mode?

11. What command is used to insert a page break? What cell is highlighted when the command is chosen?

12. How are percentages formatted?

Hands-on Exercises

Exercise 1

1. Create the following partial spreadsheet as shown. Enter the values and labels in the columns and rows shown. Adjust the column widths as necessary. Do not worry about alignment and formatting at this time.

	A	B	C	D	E	F	G
1		LOAN SCHEDULE					
2							
3	Loan Amount	$25,000					
4	Interest Rate	7%					
5	Term:	12			Payment:		
6							
7			Starting	Ending	Total	Principal	
8		Month	Balance	Balance	Paid	Paid/Monthly	
9							
10							
11							

2. Center the main heading, **LOAN SCHEDULE.**
3. Bold and change the color of the headings in column A.
4. Underline (using a border format) the column headings in B through F in row 8.
5. Bold the label, **Payment,** in cell E5 and the column headings in rows 7 and 8.
6. Shade and change the pattern of the labels in column A. The spreadsheet should appear similar to the following.

	A	B	C	D	E	F	G
1		LOAN SCHEDULE					
2							
3	**Loan Amoun**	$25,000					
4	**Interest Rate**	7%					
5	**Term:**	12			**Payment:**		
6							
7			**Starting**	**Ending**	**Total**	**Principal**	
8		**Month**	**Balance**	**Balance**	**Paid**	**Paid/Monthly**	
9							
10							
11							

Inserting formulas and functions

NOTE: An example of the final spreadsheet is on the next page.

1. For the Payment (in cell F5), use a function called PMT, which computes the amount of payments to be made based on the term, loan amount, and interest rate. The formula is written as follows:

   =PMT(B3,B4/12,B5)

   and is interpreted as:

   =PMT(Loan Amount, Interest rate/12, Term)

2. In cell B9 enter the number **12**. In cell B10 enter the formula **=B9-1.** Copy this formula through cell B20 (**Fill Down**). This spreadsheet will show the accumulation of an investment through the next 12 months.
3. In cell C9 insert the value for Loan Amount by typing **=B3.**

4. In cell C10 insert the value for the Ending Balance, **=D9**. (The values will fill in as the rest of the spreadsheet is completed.)
5. Copy the formula in C10 down the column through cell C20. (The values will fill in later.)
6. In cell D9 enter a formula to compute the Ending Balance. To do this, add the starting balance to the amount that is the result of multiply this amount by the interest rate, and then subtract the amount of the payment. Use the following formula:

   =C9+(C9*$B$4/12)-$F$5
7. Copy the formula in D9 down the column through cell D20.
8. In cell E9, enter the value for payments made, **=F5**.
9. In cell E10, enter a formula to add the absolute cell address value in F5 (**$F$5**) to the value in E9. The dollar signs in this absolute address will lock both the column and row so that it remains the same wherever it is copied. Copy this formula to other cells in the column.
10. In cell F9 insert the formula to compute the principal, **=C9-D9**, and copy down the column.
11. Save the spreadsheet as **CH10HO1**.
12. Format all dollar values as currency with no decimal places and save the spreadsheet again.
13. Proof the spreadsheet. The final spreadsheet should appear similar to the following.

	A	B	C	D	E	F	G	H
1			LOAN SCHEDULE					
2								
3	Loan Amoun	$25,000						
4	Interest Rate	7%						
5	Term:	12			Payment:	$2,163		
6								
7			Starting	Ending	Total	Principal		
8		Month	Balance	Balance	Paid	Paid/Monthly		
9		12	$25,000	$22,983	$2,163	$2,017		
10		11	$22,983	$20,954	$4,326	$2,029		
11		10	$20,954	$18,913	$6,490	$2,041		
12		9	$18,913	$16,860	$8,653	$2,053		
13		8	$16,860	$14,795	$10,816	$2,065		
14		7	$14,795	$12,718	$12,979	$2,077		
15		6	$12,718	$10,629	$15,142	$2,089		
16		5	$10,629	$8,528	$17,305	$2,101		
17		4	$8,528	$6,415	$19,469	$2,113		
18		3	$6,415	$4,289	$21,632	$2,126		
19		2	$4,289	$2,151	$23,795	$2,138		
20		1	$2,151	$0	$25,958	$2,151		

14. Print a copy of the spreadsheet.
15. Change the values of **Loan Amount, Interest Rate,** and **Term** to note the change on the spreadsheet. Print a second copy with the adjustments. Close the spreadsheet without saving these changes.

Exercise 2

1. Open the following documents, **CH9HO1B** and **CH9HO2**, which you created in Chapter 9, or retrieve them from the instructor's data disk.

	A	B	C	D	E	F	G
1			SALES BY BOAT				
2							
3	BOAT NAME	1993	1994	CHANGE	% OF CHANGE		
4							
5	Delano	37890	42520	4630	0.12219583		
6	The Spirit	35550	41236	5686	0.159943741		
7	Sea Wolf	38950	45800	6850	0.175866496		
8	Irish Sea	41250	58695	17445	0.422909091		
9							
10	TOTAL	153640	188251				
11							
12	AVERAGE	38410	47062.75				
13	MINIMUM	35550	41236				
14							
15							

CH9HO1B

	A	B	C	D	E	F
1			PUGET SOUND CHARTERS			
2						
3	Grand Totals	153640	169004	185904.4	241675.72	
4						
5						
6		Current	Next	Five-year	Ten-year	Percentage
7		Year	Year	Projection	Projection	of increase
8						
9	Delano	37890	41679	45846.9	59600.97	0.635727908
10	The Spirit	35550	39105	43015.5	55920.15	0.635727908
11	Sea Wolf	38950	42845	47129.5	61268.35	0.635727908
12	Irish Sea	41250	45375	49912.5	64886.25	0.635727908
13						
14						

CH9HO2

Complete the following steps for each of the documents.

2. Center and bold all main and column headings.
3. Add a border to all sides of the column headings.
4. Bold all headings in column A.
5. Add patterns to all column headings.
6. Format all dollar values as currency using the Currency button in the toolbar. Format all percentages with three places to the right of the decimal.
7. Change the column width for all columns to 20.
8. Change the top margin to **2.0**. Change the left margin to **1** and the right margin

to **1**. Change the layout for both spreadsheets to landscape mode.

9. Add headers to each of the spreadsheets that include your name and class.
10. Add footers on both spreadsheets to include a centered page number.
11. Add a border around each of the spreadsheets. Make the border any thickness and pattern you want.
12. The final documents should appear similar to the following (as partially shown in Print Preview).

Your name, Your class

SALES BY BOAT

BOAT NAME	1993	1994	CHANGE	% OF CHANGE
Delano	37890	42520	4630	12.22%
The Spirit	35550	41236	5686	15.99%
Sea Wolf	38950	45800	6850	17.59%
Irish Sea	41250	58695	17445	42.29%
TOTAL	153640	188251		
AVERAGE	38410	47062.75		
MINIMUM	35550	41236		

CH9HO1B

Your name, Your class

PUGET SOUND CHARTERS

	Current Year	Next Year	Five-year Projection	Ten-year Projection	Percentage of increase
Grand Totals	153640	169004	185904.4	241675.72	
Delano	$37,890.00	$41,679.00	$45,846.90	$59,600.97	63.573%
The Spirit	$35,550.00	$39,105.00	$43,015.50	$55,920.15	63.573%
Sea Wolf	$38,950.00	$42,845.00	$47,129.50	$61,268.35	63.573%
Irish Sea	$41,250.00	$45,375.00	$49,912.50	$64,886.25	63.573%

ZOOM

CH9HO2

13. Save both spreadsheets again under the following new names. **CH9HO1B** as **CH10HO2A** and **CH9HO2** as **CH10HO2B**.
14. Print a copy of each spreadsheet.

Exercise 3

1. Retrieve **CH9HO3** from your data disk.
2. Bold and center the main and column headings.
3. Bold and italicize the words Total, Average, and Maximum in column A.
4. Change all values to currency with two places to the right of the decimal.
5. Adjust the column width if necessary.
6. Change the font of the main heading to a different style and size.
7. Add a double-line border around the main and column headings. Include shading within the border boundaries.
8. Preview the document and print a copy.
9. Save as **CH10HO3**.
10. Change the page layout to landscape mode.
11. Preview the change and make necessary adjustments in margins or the main heading position.
12. Print a copy.
13. Close without saving the changes.

Exercise 4

1. Retrieve **CH9HO4** from your data disk.
2. Bold and center the main headings.
3. Add a border below the row containing the months **January** through **March**.
4. Highlight and add a border around all labels in column A.
5. Shade the area within the border in column A.
6. Insert a page break after **Jumping Overboard**.
7. Preview both pages of the document.
8. Remove the page break.
9. Add a border around the entire document (decide on an appropriate width and color).
10. Increase the row height of the main heading to 1 inch (72 points, which is the amount to enter in the **Format, Row Height** box).
11. Preview the worksheet and make any necessary adjustments in the appearance. You may want to adjust the column widths.
12. Print a copy of the worksheet.

13. Save as **CH10HO4.**
14. Close the spreadsheet and exit Works.

Example of Exercises

Exercise 3: CH10HO3

MISCELLANEOUS EXPENDITURES WORKSHEET

	January	February	March	Total
Passenger Overboard Fees	$200.00	$500.00	$300.00	$1,000.00
Stress Management	$1,600.00	$1,000.00	$2,500.00	$5,100.00
Food Replacement	$1,200.00	$1,600.00	$1,400.00	$4,200.00
Safety Training	$2,000.00	$3,000.00	$1,500.00	$6,500.00
Vessel Collision Lessons	$800.00	$350.00	$700.00	$1,850.00
TOTAL	$5,800.00	$6,450.00	$6,400.00	
AVERAGE	$1,160.00	$1,290.00	$1,280.00	
MAXIMUM	$2,000.00	$3,000.00	$2,500.00	

Exercise 4: CH10HO4

STAFF TRAINING COURSES
ENROLLMENT FIGURES

COURSE TITLE:		Date of Course		
	January 15	February 10	March 08	Total
Galley Safety Tips	5	4	6	15
Crash Courses			0	
Captaining	82	80	75	237
Deck Hand	2	3	4	9
Life Saving	82	85	87	254
First Aid	4	6	3	13
Jumping Overboard	80	79	88	247
Personal Safety First	2	3	1	6
Emergency Evacuation	67	89	76	232
Avoiding Sharks	6	7	8	21
Near Misses	17	24	19	60
Riding the Storm	77	71	76	224
Mending Holes	4	9	6	19
Total	423	456	443	
Average	35.66666667	38.33333333	37.41666667	
Minimum	2	3	1	
Maximum	82	89	88	

CHAPTER 11

Increased Spreadsheet Power

OBJECTIVES

Calculate with dates and times

Enter a series of values

Use range names

Sort contents of cells

Search for conditions

Understand function hierarchy

Insert a spreadsheet into a word processing document

PREVIEW

In this chapter we cover additional features that make working with a spreadsheet easier. These features include inserting the date and time and using them in formulas; freezing titles so that they are visible when scrolling; filling in a series of numbers on a spreadsheet; referencing cell ranges; sorting cell contents; searching for conditions; and integrating a spreadsheet and a word processing document.

INSERTING DATE AND TIME

The date or time may be inserted on a spreadsheet and either of them can then be used as part of the formula. Once dates and times are logged, they can be subtracted or added to each other to count the total hours and minutes or the total number of days. Ways in which dates and times may be entered are shown in Table 11-1.

Table 11-1
Format for typing dates and times

Type this	To display this
Nov 1, 1994	Month, day, year
Nov, 1994	Month, year
Nov 30	Month, day
Nov	Month only
11/1/94	Month, day, year
11/91	Month, year
11/30	Month, day
24-HOUR TIME	
15:30:00	Hour, minute, second
15:30	Hour, minute
12-HOUR TIME	
3:30:00 PM	Hour, minute, second
3:30 PM	Hour, minute
3 PM	Hour only

Type the Date and Time

Works recognizes the formats given in Table 11-1 as those that can be used in calculations. It is necessary when typing the time to include AM or PM if this information is important.

1. Create the following worksheet. Type the dates and times as they are displayed here. The format for the times will be changed later. Underline and center the column headings; and adjust the column width as necessary.

	A	B	C	D	E	F
1			CHARTER TIME SCHEDULE			
2						
3		Dates Scheduled		Total		
4		This Month		Days		
5						
6	Delano	11/1/94	11/26/94			
7	The Spirit	11/2/94	11/29/94			
8	Sea Wolf	11/1/94	11/30/94			
9	Irish Sea	11/5/94	11/25/94			
10						
11	Next scheduled cruise:					
12						
13		Date	Start	End	Total Hours	
14						
15	Delano	12/2/94	12:00 PM	4:00 PM		
16	The Spirit	12/4/94	1:00 PM	5:00 PM		
17	Sea Wolf	12/1/94	4:00 PM	10:30 PM		
18	Irish Sea	12/2/94	4:00 PM	9:00 PM		

FREEZING TITLES

Titles on a spreadsheet can be frozen so that text *above* and *left* of the selected cell always appears on the screen. This is useful when the spreadsheet is longer or wider than the screen. When you scroll down or to the right, for example, the titles are always visible. This allows you to see the column headings as they relate to the data in all parts of the worksheet.

Freeze Titles

1. Highlight cell **B5**.
2. Choose **Format, Freeze Titles.**
3. Scroll to the far right and down in the worksheet. The titles and a vertical and a horizontal line are displayed below and to the right of the titles.

NOTE: You can move into the title area to make changes if you like.

CHANGING THE TIME FORMAT

The 24-hour format, which will show for examples 22:30 for 10:30 PM, is required to calculate the amount of elapsed time. Since it is often easier to enter the more familiar 12-hour format, (10:30 PM or 11 AM) the times were entered in that format. They an then be adjusted quickly to the 24-hour format using the **Time** and **Date** options found in the **Number** command in the **Format** menu.

Change the Time Format

1. Highlight cells **C15 through E18.**

   NOTE: It is necessary to select the Total Hours column and format it for a 24-hour time format as well so that the correct number will show when the hours are calculated.

2. Choose **Format, Number.**
3. Choose **Time** from the **Format** list.
4. Choose the 24-hour format, which will be the current time shown as **11:12** (or whatever the time is when you do this step). The Sample box will show **12:00** or some similar number. PM or AM will not be displayed.
5. Choose **OK** or press **Enter**. The spreadsheet format appears as follows. Because the times were entered using PM, Works knows to change the hours according to the 24-hour format. For example, 12:00 AM becomes 0:00.

10						
11	Next scheduled cruise:					
12						
13		Date	Start	End	Total Hours	
14						
15	Delano	12/2/94	12:00	16:00		
16	The Spirit	12/4/94	13:00	17:00		
17	Sea Wolf	12/1/94	16:00	22:30		
18	Irish Sea	12/2/94	16:00	21:00		
19						

CALCULATING THE DATES OR TIMES

Times can be entered in any format and then changed to the 24-hour format if calculations are to be performed. When calculating dates, any long or short format may be used.

Calculate the Dates or Times

1. Highlight cell **D6.**

   Puget Sound Charters would like to know how many total days each boat was scheduled during the past month. This is done as any other calculation would be done, by subtracting one cell from another. In this case, the beginning date should be subtracted from the ending date to calculate the total days.

2. Type **=C6-B6** and press **Enter.**
3. Copy this formula, using **Edit, Fill Down** through cell **D9**. The total days for each vessel is computed as shown in the following example.

	A	B	C	D	E
1			CHARTER TIME SCHEDULE		
2					
3		Dates Scheduled		Total	
4		This Month		Days	
5					
6	Delano	11/1/94	11/26/94	25	
7	The Spirit	11/2/94	11/29/94	27	
8	Sea Wolf	11/1/94	11/30/94	29	
9	Irish Sea	11/5/94	11/25/94	20	
10					

To compute the total time of each upcoming cruise, subtract the ending time from the starting time, as follows.

4. Highlight **cell E15.**
5. Type **=D15-C15.**
6. Press **Enter.** A 4:00 appears in cell E15. This format is interpreted differently from the time format in columns C and D. In this case, it is read as the total hours and the number of minutes of the cruise.
7. Copy the formula in **E15** down the column through cell **E18.** The final result is shown in the following example.

10						
11	Next scheduled cruise:					
12						
13		Date	Start	End	Total Hours	
14						
15	Delano	12/2/94	12:00	16:00	4:00	
16	The Spirit	12/4/94	13:00	17:00	4:00	
17	Sea Wolf	12/1/94	16:00	22:30	6:30	
18	Irish Sea	12/2/94	16:00	21:00	5:00	
19						

8. Save the spreadsheet as **CH11PR1.**
9. Print a copy of the spreadsheet.

ENTERING A SERIES

In practice exercise 1 at the end of Chapter 10, a spreadsheet was created using a series of numbers indicating the total years for the term of an investment. The spreadsheet used a formula to accumulate the total years by adding one to the value in the previous cell. There is, however, another way to build a series of values or dates on a spreadsheet. It is the **Fill Series** command found in the **Edit** menu.

Enter a Series

Here you will add a schedule for each of the boats going out on specific days in December. You can enter every day of the month down a column using the **Fill Series** command.

1. Choose **Format, Freeze Titles** to turn off the option. Your insertion point can be at any position when you do this.
2. Highlight cell **A20.**
3. Type **Schedules for the month of December** in bold print (let it overlap into the cells to the right).

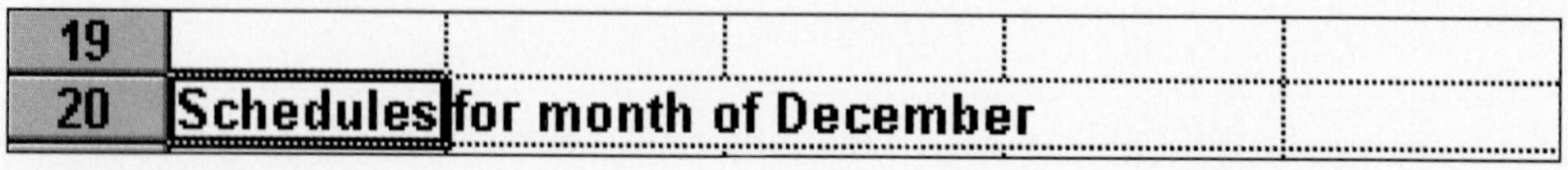

4. Highlight cell **A22.**
5. Type **1.**
6. Press **Enter.**
7. Highlight cells **A22 through A32** (assume that the remainder of the month will be added later).

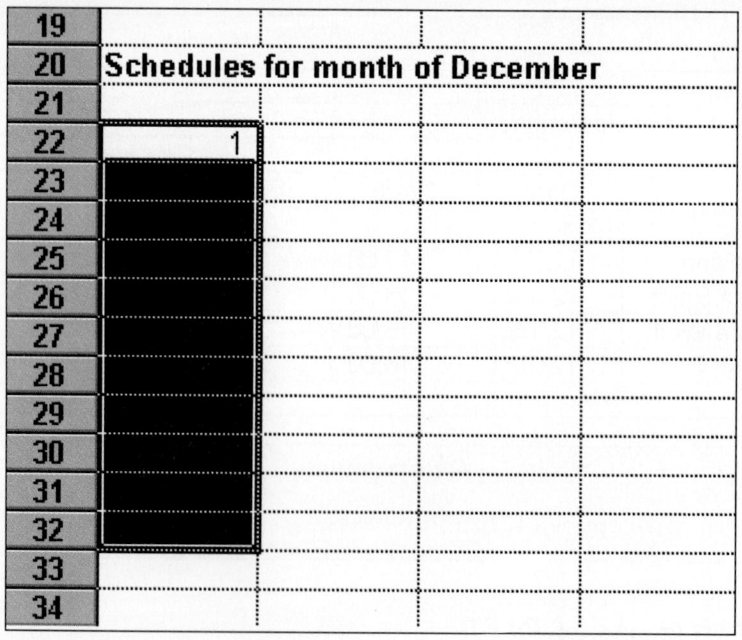

8. Choose **Edit, Fill Series** from the menu. A dialog box similar to the one in Figure 11-1 appears.

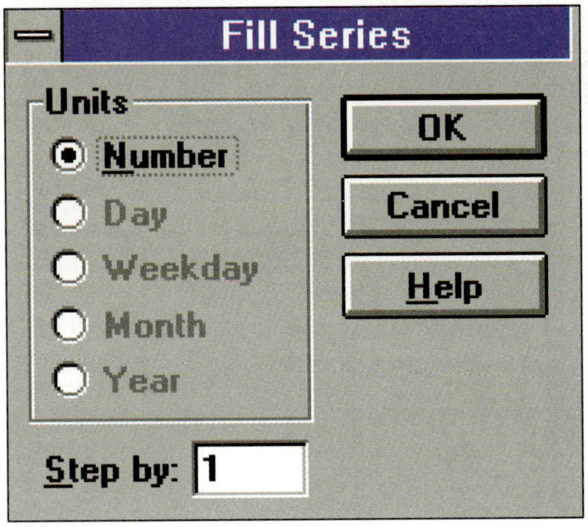

Figure 11-1
The Fill Series dialog box

Depending upon the format entered in the selected cell(s) in the spreadsheet, a selection will be made in the **Units** box. If dates needed were increments, they would be selected in the box. The **Step by** option is used to increment by any number such as 1 (the default), 5, 10, and so on.

9. Leave the settings as shown-increments by one for the days of the month.
10. Choose **OK** or press **Enter**. Numbers 1 through 11 are inserted into the selected cells.
11. Complete the worksheet as shown below and save again as **CH11PR1**.

19						
20	**Schedules for month of December**					
21		Delano	The Spirit	Sea Wolf	Irish Sea	
22	1			4:00 PM		
23	2	12:00 PM			4:00 PM	
24	3					
25	4		1:00 PM			
26	5	12:00 PM		6:30 PM		
27	6		6:00 PM		11:00 AM	
28	7	3:00 PM				
29	8	12:00 PM	6:00 PM		3:00 PM	
30	9	6:00 PM		7:00 PM		
31	10			8:00 PM		
32	11	4:30 PM				
33						

USING RANGE NAMES

Ranges have been used in various formulas throughout this section of the book. A range is any area of a spreadsheet—a single cell, a row or column, a block of cells, or the entire spreadsheet. When a range is more than one cell, it is considered the area from the upper left cell to the lower right cell, such as A1 through G37. You can give names to cell ranges and then use the range name in a formula. This saves time in rewriting formulas or in identifying frequently used ranges in a spreadsheet.

In the current spreadsheet, Puget Sound Charters would like to know how many days each of the vessels is committed at any given time in the month. Right now the spreadsheet shows days 1 through 11 for the month of December, but additional rows can be added later. To complete the calculations on this spreadsheet, an additional row will be added below the last day (11th) shown thus far. It will use a formula to count the total number of days that each vessel is booked. The range used in the individual totals will be named. The formula using the named range will be copied to other areas of the spreadsheet just like any other formula.

Create a Range

1. Highlight cells **B22 through B32** as the range to name.
2. Choose **Insert, Range Name.**

A dialog box appears as shown in Figure 11-2.

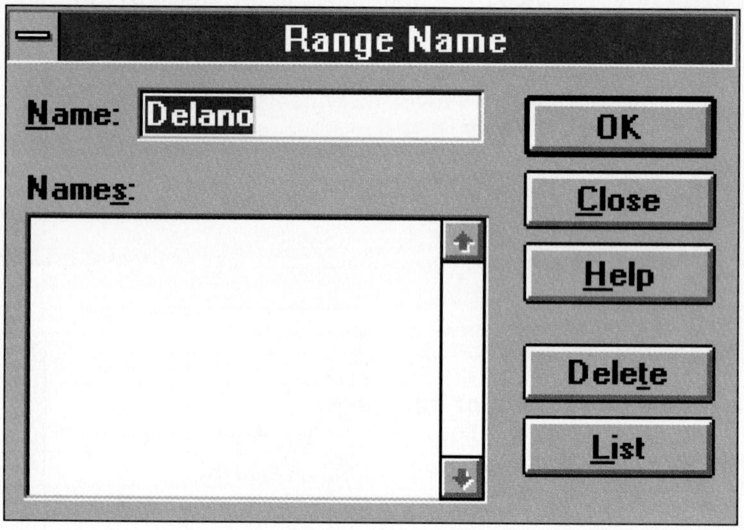

Figure 11-2
The Range Name dialog box

The name, Delano, is suggested because the range is within this column heading. (You will, however, enter a different name here.) As range names are given, the list of names will appear in the **Names** box. You can **List**, **Delete**, access **Help**, or **Cancel** this dialog box. Choosing **OK** will create the new name for the range.

3. Type **total days** in the **Name** box.
4. Choose **OK** or press **Enter**. A new range has been created called **total days.** Open the Range Name dialog box again to see the named range.

USING A RANGE

This range name (total days) can now be applied in a formula in place of the cell addresses.

Use a Range

1. Highlight cell **B34**.
2. Type **=COUNT(total days)**. This formula will count the number of cells containing entries in the designated range (total days in cells B22 through B32).
3. Press **Enter**. The Delano is booked for six days this month as shown here.

	A	B	C	D	E	F
19						
20	**Schedules for month of December**					
21		Delano	The Spirit	Sea Wolf	Irish Sea	
22	1			4:00 PM		
23	2	12:00 PM			4:00 PM	
24	3					
25	4		1:00 PM			
26	5	12:00 PM		6:30 PM		
27	6		6:00 PM		11:00 AM	
28	7	3:00 PM				
29	8	12:00 PM	6:00 PM		3:00 PM	
30	9	6:00 PM		7:00 PM		
31	10			8:00 PM		
32	11	4:30 PM				
33						
34		6				
35						

4. Copy this formula using **Edit, Fill Right** through cell **E34** in the same row. The total days, 6, 3, 4, and 3, appear in row 34. When changes are made, such as deletions or additions in the bookings, the total days will be recalculated automatically, just as with a formula containing the cell addresses.

SORTING CONTENTS OF CELLS

Text, dates, or values can be sorted in a worksheet. Sorting rearranges the cell contents alphabetically or numerically in ascending order (from A to Z or from 1 through the highest number). Works can also sort the contents in descending order. Sorts can be performed on one column, such as on the boat names in this spreadsheet, or a sort can be performed within a sort, such as dates for each vessel. The most useful sort in the current spreadsheet would be on just one column, such as the boat's name or on a date. When the column list to be sorted is selected, all values in the right of the column will also be sorted. For example, all dates to the right of the boat name would be adjusted when the boat name is sorted in ascending or descending order.

Sort on Selected Cells

1. Highlight cells **A6 through A9**.
2. Choose **Tools, Sort Rows** to display the dialog box shown in Figure 11-3.

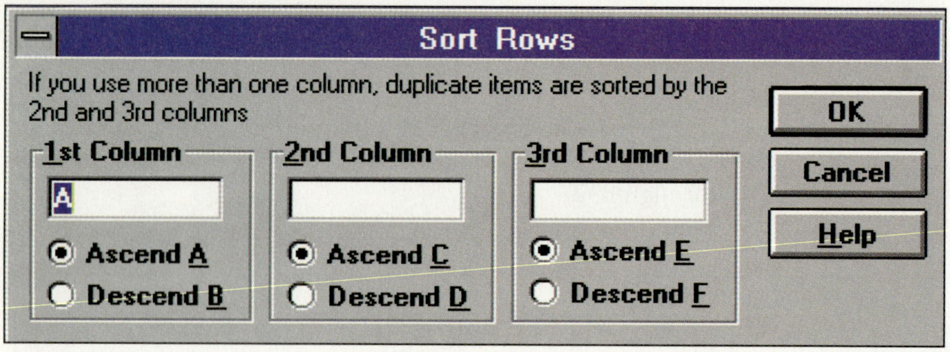

Figure 11-3
The Sort Rows dialog box

This dialog box shows text boxes for the 1st Column, 2nd Column, and 3rd Column sorts. When you want to do a sort within a sort, the additional columns being used in the sort are selected and the ascending or descending order of the sort can be decided for each column. The Ascend option (selected) is the default choice. In this case, only the boat names from column A are selected, so the 1st Column text box shows the letter A.

All options selected in the dialog box at this time are correct for this sort.

3. Choose **OK** or press **Enter** to accept the default settings. The names of the vessels now appear in ascending order as shown here.

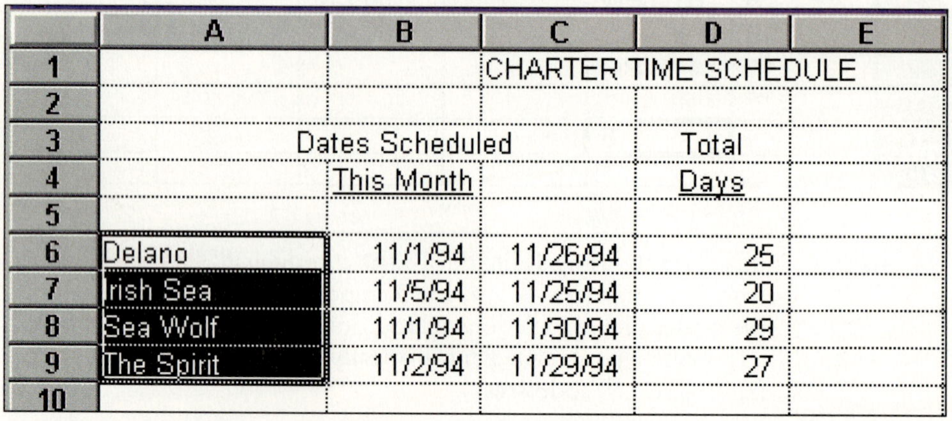

4. Save the spreadsheet again and print a copy.
5. Close the spreadsheet window.

SEARCHING FOR TRUE OR FALSE CONDITIONS

The IF-THEN-ELSE function is used to search for existing conditions. If the function locates a true condition, it will perform one command; if a false condition, it will perform another command. In other words, IF it locates a true condition, THEN it performs one command, ELSE it performs another. The formula used for this type of search uses the built-in Works function, IF.

This type of function can be used to perform calculations if certain values are located. If a certain amount is located in a cell, for example that amount could be multiplied by a given percentage. Suppose that you had a spreadsheet that contained sales amounts and that any amount greater than $10 should be taxed 0.08 percent. The IF function to search for those values and then compute the tax would be written as follows:

= IF(B9>10,B9*.08,B9)

The function looks in cell B9 for a value greater than 10. IF that value is located (a TRUE condition), it multiplies the value by 0.08 percent; ELSE if it is not located (a FALSE condition), it inserts the value of B9 in the current cell. The answer to this function would be either the computed percentage or the value in B9. You could also write the function to add the computed tax to the value in B9 as follows:

=IF(B9>10,B9*.08+B9,B9)

Search for True or False Conditions

1. Open the file **CH10PR1.**

To enter text in cells

2. Highlight cell **A21.**
3. Type **PROFIT** to label the column.
4. Highlight cell **A22** and type **Yes (1).**
5. Highlight cell **A23** and type **No (0).**

To enter the conditions

6. Highlight cell **B21.**
7. Type **=IF(B17<=0,0,1)** and press **Enter** to show the result in cell B21, as displayed in the example below.

This function looks in cell B17. If it locates a value less than or equal to zero (0), which would mean no profit, THEN it inserts a zero for No (also a TRUE condition); ELSE it inserts a 1 for Yes (a FALSE condition), meaning that it located a value greater than zero (0).

B21 =IF(B17<=0,0,1)

	A	B	C	D	E
10	EXPENSES				
11	Catering	$8,800.00	$9,250.00	$12,325.00	$15,800.00
12	Salaries	$15,000.00	$22,500.00	$60,600.00	$60,800.00
13	Operations	$5,500.00	$3,000.00	$5,500.00	$7,530.00
14	Miscellaneous	$4,000.00	$6,500.00	$8,000.00	$2,500.00
15	TOTAL EXPENSES	$33,300.00	$41,250.00	$86,425.00	$86,630.00
16					
17	NET EARNINGS	$69,110.00	$65,620.00	$54,615.00	$82,701.00
18					
19	% of Net Sales	67.484%	61.402%	38.723%	48.840%
20					
21	PROFIT	1			
22	Yes (1)				
23	No (0)				
24					

8. Save as **CH11PR2.**

UNDERSTANDING FUNCTION HIERARCHY

Works evaluates expressions/formulas based on the hierarchy shown in Table 11-2. It follows the standard algebraic rules when evaluating and includes:

- Evaluation of the contents of parentheses ( ) first, with the innermost parenthesis having priority, for example:

  =(F6*3(G6*(H6-H4)))

- Evaluation of operators as shown in the following table.
- Evaluation of two or more operators, that are the same from left to right.

This operator	Is evaluated
^ exponential	first
- negative; + positive	second
* multiplication; / division	third
+ addition; - subtraction	fourth
= equal to; < > not equal to	fifth
< less than; > greater than	
<= less than or equal to	
>= greater than or equal to	
~ NOT	sixth
I OR, & AND	seventh

Table 11-2
Hierarchy of operators in formulas

INTEGRATING DOCUMENTS

Integration (combining files) is Works' most powerful feature. You can easily combine word processing and spreadsheet documents. For example, if you have stored data about a company's earnings in a spreadsheet and want to include these values in a report created in the word processor, you can easily copy them from the spreadsheet to the word processing document.

> *NOTE:* You also can create a spreadsheet directly in a word processing document using the Table button. This procedure is discussed in Exercise 3 at the end of this chapter for those who want to learn how to do this. However, it is usually easier to create the spreadsheet and then bring it in to the word processing document.

Here you will learn how to include a spreadsheet in a word processing document using the **Spreadsheet/Table** command found in the **Insert** menu.

Create a Range

A spreadsheet can be copied to a word processing document or to a database file. The easiest way to insert a spreadsheet into a word processing document is to create a range using the spreadsheet cells you wish to insert.

> *NOTE:* Spreadsheets (or any other document produced with Works) can also be sent to another computer.

1. Open the spreadsheet **CH11PR2**, which you just created, if necessary.
2. Highlight cells **A4 through F23**. Leave out the main heading since the company logo will appear on the word processing document.

NOTE: Do not select the entire spreadsheet (including all other blank rows and columns). Doing so will copy all cells on the entire spreadsheet, not just those containing values or text.

3. Choose **Insert, Range Name.**
4. Type **earnings** in the **Name** box.
5. Choose **OK** or press **Enter**. The range is now stored with **CH11PR2**.

NOTE: Next, you will use the *Insert* menu in a word processing document to quickly position the range from the spreadsheet.

Create a New Document

1. Open a new word processing file.
2. Create the logo shown in the following example. Use a double-line border above and below the heading. Use any font that you want for the text.

PUGET SOUND CHARTERS
East Lake Union Way
Seattle, WA 98108
(206) 555-9200

Insert the Spreadsheet Range

1. Move the insertion point several blank lines below the bottom border.
2. Choose **Insert, Spreadsheet/Table.**
3. Highlight **CH11PR2** in the **Spreadsheets** list to display names in the **Ranges** list box.
4. Highlight **earnings** in the **Ranges** list box as shown below.

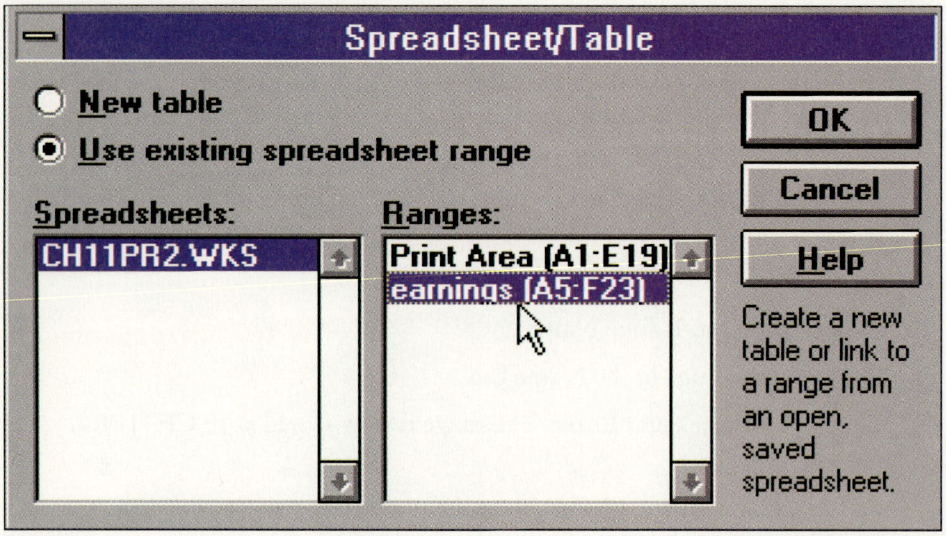

5.	Choose	**OK** or press **Enter**. The spreadsheet is inserted into the word processing document as shown in the following **Print Preview** screen.

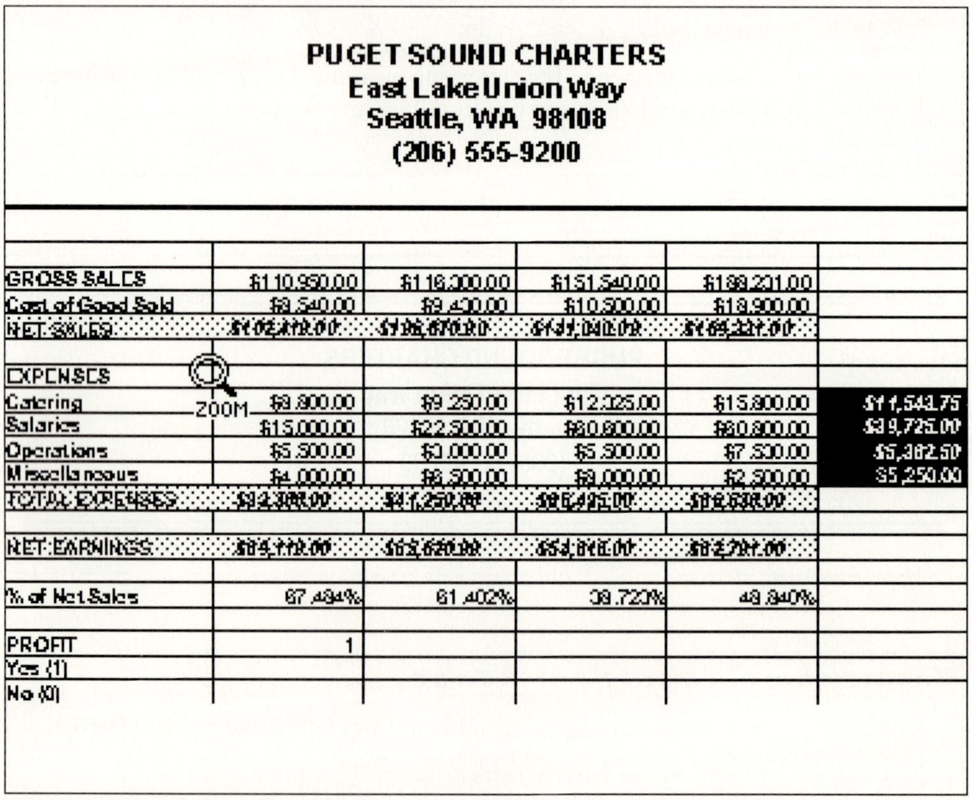

PUGET SOUND CHARTERS
East Lake Union Way
Seattle, WA 98108
(206) 555-9200

GROSS SALES	$110,950.00	$116,300.00	$151,540.00	$188,201.00	
Cost of Good Sold	$8,540.00	$9,430.00	$10,500.00	$18,900.00	
NET SALES	[illegible]	[illegible]	[illegible]	[illegible]	
EXPENSES					
Catering	$8,800.00	$9,250.00	$12,325.00	$15,800.00	$11,543.75
Salaries	$15,000.00	$22,500.00	$60,800.00	$60,800.00	$39,725.00
Operations	$5,500.00	$3,000.00	$5,500.00	$7,500.00	$5,382.50
Miscellaneous	$4,000.00	$6,500.00	$9,000.00	$2,500.00	$5,250.00
TOTAL EXPENSES	[illegible]	[illegible]	[illegible]	[illegible]	
NET EARNINGS	[illegible]	[illegible]	[illegible]	[illegible]	
% of Net Sales	67.484%	61.402%	38.720%	48.840%	
PROFIT	1				
Yes (1)					
No (0)					

6.	Choose	**Print Preview** to look at the document as a full page. **Cancel** to return to the document.
7.	Save	this document as **CH11PR3** and print a copy.
8.	Close	this document, and also save and close **CH11PR2** if necessary.

NOTE: When you open a word processing file containing a spreadsheet, you will be prompted to update links. Choose **Yes** to update. Any changes made in the original spreadsheet file, will be automatically updated in the spreadsheet integrated with the word processing document.

GUIDED TUTORIAL

What You'll Do

- Compute time and date values.
- Format fills for time and date.

How To Do It

1. Create a spreadsheet that shows your class schedule. In it include the title of each of the classes and start/end time similar to that shown below.

	Start time	End time
Class 1	9:00 AM	9:50 AM
Class 2	11:00 AM	11:50 AM
Class 3	1:10 PM	2:00 PM
Class 4	2:10 PM	3:00 PM

2. Create an appropriate main heading for the spreadsheet.
3. Create a column heading called **TOTAL TIME** in a column to the right.
4. Format each of the items, including the blank cells in the TOTAL TIME column, with the 24-hour format using the **Time** option from the **Number** command in the **Format** menu. The following is an example of how you might create this spreadsheet.

	A	B	C	D	E
1			CLASS SCHEDULE		
2					
3		Start time	End time	TOTAL TIME	
4	Class 1	9:00	9:50		
5	Class 2	11:00	11:50		
6	Class 3	13:10	14:00		
7	Class 4	14:10	15:00		
8					

5. Subtract the End time from the Start time and insert the results into the TOTAL TIME column.

	A	B	C	D	E
1			CLASS SCHEDULE		
2					
3		Start time	End time	TOTAL TIME	
4	Class 1	9:00	9:50	0:50	
5	Class 2	11:00	11:50	0:50	
6	Class 3	13:10	14:00	0:50	
7	Class 4	14:10	15:00	0:50	
8					

6. Enter the values in rows 9 through 11 as shown in the example below.

7. Copy the class names in A4 through A7 to A12 through A15 at the bottom of the spreadsheet. To do this, select cells **A4 through A7**, click on the Copy button, move the insertion point to cell A12, and click on the Paste button.

	A	B	C	D	E
1			CLASS SCHEDULE		
2					
3		Start time	End time	TOTAL TIME	
4	Class 1	9:00	9:50	0:50	
5	Class 2	11:00	11:50	0:50	
6	Class 3	13:10	14:00	0:50	
7	Class 4	14:10	15:00	0:50	
8					
9			Last day of		
10		Today's	quarter/	Days	
11		date	semester	remaining	
12	Class 1				
13	Class 2				
14	Class 3				
15	Class 4				

8. Enter the column headings and dates as shown in the following example.

	A	B	C	D	E
1			CLASS SCHEDULE		
2					
3		Start time	End time	TOTAL TIME	
4	Class 1	9:00	9:50	0:50	
5	Class 2	11:00	11:50	0:50	
6	Class 3	13:10	14:00	0:50	
7	Class 4	14:10	15:00	0:50	
8					
9			Last day of		
10		Today's	quarter/	Days	
11		date	semester	remaining	
12	Class 1	9/30/94	12/10/94		
13	Class 2	9/30/94	12/5/94		
14	Class 3	9/30/94	12/7/94		
15	Class 4	9/30/94	12/9/94		

9. Be sure that the date cells are formatted as dates in the short format. To do this, choose **Format**, **Number** and turn on **Date.**

10. Subtract the last day from today's date to compute the total days remaining in the quarter or semester. To do this, type **=C12–B12** in cell D12. Then use **Edit**, **Fill Down** to copy the formula down through D15.

11. Save the spreadsheet as **CH11TUT**.

REVIEW QUESTIONS

1. List two or more formats that are available for time and date in a spreadsheet.

____

____

2. State the function of the following command.

____

3. What are some of the functions of the following command?

4. Explain briefly how you would calculate dates and times.

5. Give an example of when you would use the **Fill Series** command from the **Edit** menu.

6. Give an example of when you would use a range name.

7. Explain briefly the options found in the following dialog box.

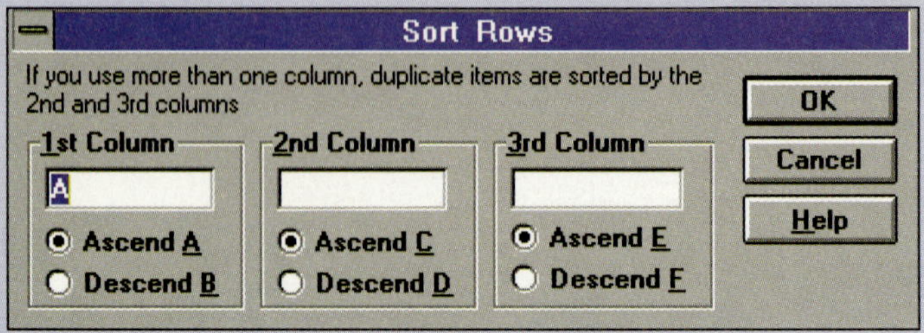

8. Explain the difference between **Ascend** and **Descend** in the box above.

Hands-on Exercises

Exercise 1

In this exercise, you will create a memorandum pertaining to the December charter schedule that you created in **CH11PR1**. The December schedules will be saved with a range name and inserted in the memorandum.

1. Open the word processor window and type the text in the box below.

   Center MEMORANDUM, and insert the special character for printing a long date.

MEMORANDUM

TO:	All staff of Puget Sound Charters
FROM:	P. J. MacRannall
DATE:	*longdate*
SUBJECT:	December charter schedules

The following schedules have been proposed for the month of December. Please let me know if you are aware of any events that could conflict with these schedules.

To insert the December schedules:

2. Open **CH11PR1**.
3. Select all rows in the December schedules, including the title. This will include rows 20 through 32 and columns A through E. (Do not include the totals below the schedules.)
4. Use the **Insert** menu in the spreadsheet to name the range, "schedules."
5. Return to the word processor window.
6. Move the insertion point two lines below the text, and use the **Insert** menu in the word processor document to insert the spreadsheet range "schedules."
7. Center the table. To do this, click with the left mouse button once on the table (handles will be displayed around the table), and then click on the Center button.
8. Save the document as **CH11HO1**.
9. Print a copy of the document and close the window.
10. Save **CH11PR1** again with the new range name "schedules" and close the window.

Exercise 2

This worksheet shows the six-month expenditures of CTech Corporation, a small consulting firm. It would like you to print two copies of the worksheet, first in its original format, and then considering the following possibility: What if expenditures increased in all categories by 10 percent and income remained the same? CTech would like a hard copy (printed copy) of both spreadsheets.

1. The input document is shown below. Enter the values and labels as shown.

	A	B	C	D	E	F	G	H
1				CTech Corporation				
2				Six-month Expenditures				
3								
4		January	February	March	April	May	June	TOTAL
5								
6	EXPENDITURES							
7	Insurance	450	450	450	450	450	450	
8	Supplies	200	500	250	600	400	250	
9	Salary	10000	10000	10000	10000	10000	10000	
10	Equipment	2000	0	0	0	500	1500	
11	Manuals/Productior	4000	4000	5000	3500	4000	5000	
12	Consulting Fees	500	250	550	600	500	500	
13	Copy Machine	500	450	400	550	600	500	
14	Distribution	200	250	200	250	300	250	
15	TOTAL							
16								
17	INCOME							
18	Training	12000	10000	12000	16200	13500	17500	
19	Manuals	3000	4000	6000	7000	8000	9000	
20	Consulting	7000	4000	8000	12000	8000	8500	
21	TOTAL							
22								
23	Profit/Loss:							

2. Adjust the column widths as necessary
3. Create formulas to compute the **TOTAL** in **H7**, **TOTAL** in **B15, TOTAL** in **B21**, and **Profit/Loss** in **B23**. Copy these formulas to appropriate cells. Save the worksheet as **CH11HO2**.
4. Copy all side headings in column **A to A27**. See the following example.

	A	B	C
26			
27	EXPENDITURES		
28	Insurance		
29	Supplies		
30	Salary		
31	Equipment		
32	Manuals/Production		
33	Consulting Fees		
34	Copy Machine		
35	Distribution		
36	TOTAL		
37			
38	INCOME		
39	Training		
40	Manuals		
41	Consulting		
42	TOTAL		
43			
44	Profit/Loss:		
45			

5. Beginning in cell **B28** (**Insurance**), create a formula to increase the original January insurance value by 10 percent (**=B7*1.10**).

B28 =B7*1.10

	A	B	C
26			
27	EXPENDITURES		
28	Insurance	=B7*1.10	
29	Supplies		
30	Salary		
31	Equipment		
32	Manuals/Production		

6. Select cells **B28 through G35**. Use **Edit, Fill Down** and **Edit, Fill Right** to copy. You will have to use both commands to do this. When done your screen should resemble the following.

	A	B	C	D	E	F	G
26							
27	EXPENDITURES						
28	Insurance	$495.00	$495.00	$495.00	$495.00	$495.00	$495.00
29	Supplies	$220.00	$550.00	$275.00	$660.00	$440.00	$275.00
30	Salary	$11,000.00	$11,000.00	$11,000.00	$11,000.00	$11,000.00	$11,000.00
31	Equipment	$2,200.00	$0.00	$0.00	$0.00	$550.00	$1,650.00
32	Manuals/Production	$4,400.00	$4,400.00	$5,500.00	$3,850.00	$4,400.00	$5,500.00
33	Consulting Fees	$550.00	$275.00	$605.00	$660.00	$550.00	$550.00
34	Copy Machine	$550.00	$495.00	$440.00	$605.00	$660.00	$550.00
35	Distribution	$220.00	$275.00	$220.00	$275.00	$330.00	$275.00
36	TOTAL						

7. Compute the total in all expenditure columns for both sections. In cells H15, H21, H36, and H42, compute the totals in column H in each corresponding section above these cells.
8. Copy the **Income** values and totals from the first half of the worksheet to the second. These values should remain the same.
9. Compute the new net profit.
10. Format all values as currency with two places to the right of the decimal. You may select all values in the spreadsheet and then click on the dollar sign ($) in the toolbar to format the values quickly.
11. Adjust the column widths as necessary.
12. Use Print Preview to look at the worksheet prior to printing.
13. Print the entire worksheet to reflect predictions. If necessary, print in landscape mode so that the worksheet fits on one page. Also, you may have to change the top and bottom margins to **.5**.
14. Save the final copy under the same name.

Exercise 3

In the following exercise, you will create a table in the word processing document that contains spreadsheet information. Earlier in this chapter, you imported a spreadsheet into a word processing document using a range name to identify a range of cells making up the spreadsheet. For this exercise, you will use the table feature in Works word processing tool to create columns and rows.

1. Create a new word processing document and type the following text. The centered main heading is in bold, Helvetica, 10 point. Use it or another font different from the text in the body of the document.

SALES PROJECTIONS

Below is a summary of sales projections as submitted recently by the Marketing Department. It shows an increase in the next year of 10 percent, five years of 10 percent over next year's projection, and ten years of 30 percent over the five-year projection. This summary is based on past earnings as stated in the recent profit report and on future predictions and expectations of marketing strategies.

2. Save this document as **CH11HO3**.
3. Open the spreadsheet document called **CH10HO2B** or retrieve it from the Instructor data disk.
4. Print a copy of the spreadsheet for a reference for this exercise and then close the document.
5. Switch to **CH11HO3** using the **Window** menu and move the insertion point several lines below the text.
6. Click once on the **Table** tool in the **toolbar** 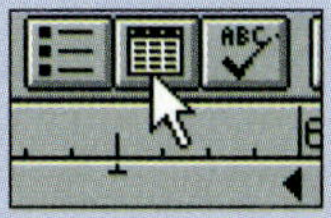.
7. Choose **New Table** in the **Spreadsheet/Table** dialog box and choose **OK.**
8. Point to the lower right corner of the box (the corner handle) and drag the box to the right and downward to increase its size through column F.

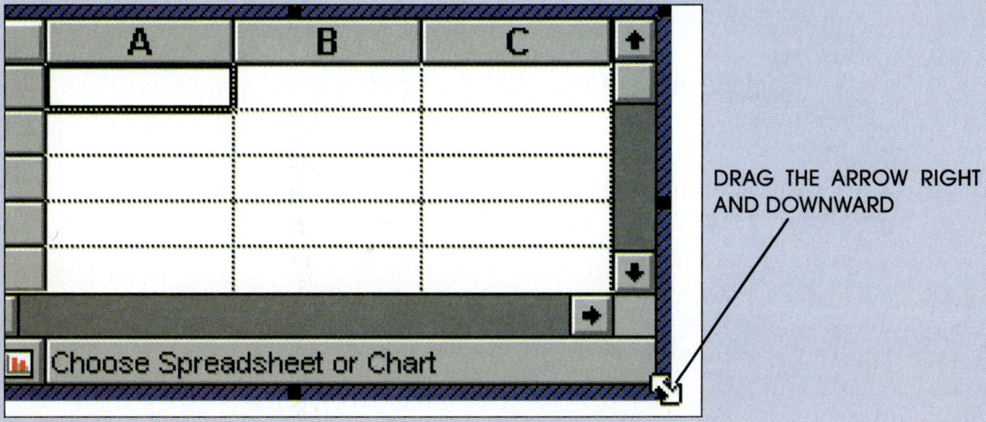

Do not worry exactly how wide or narrow the worksheet appears on the screen. If the number of columns appearing on the screen are not equal to those you need in the spreadsheet, press the arrow keys or the **Tab** key to scroll into additional columns and rows. The new spreadsheet window in the word processing document is exactly like a new spreadsheet document-it is in the word processing document but may be used as though you were starting a new spreadsheet.

The **toolbar** options change when you are working in the spreadsheet window. When the spreadsheet appears as a window, the toolbar applies to the spreadsheet. When it appears as a table inserted into the word processing document, the toolbar applies to word processing functions.

9. Click the left mouse button anywhere outside the spreadsheet. The spreadsheet changes from a spreadsheet window to an embedded table in the word processing document as shown in the following example.

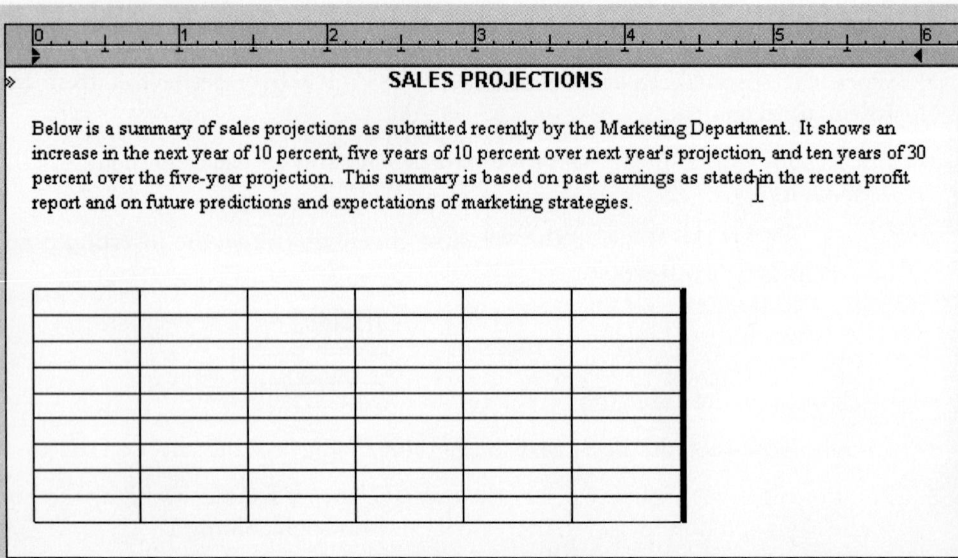

10. Click the left mouse button twice anywhere on the spreadsheet. The table changes back to a spreadsheet window and the toolbar also changes.

    NOTE: You must be in the spreadsheet mode to enter text or values into the spreadsheet cells.

11. Fill in the values as shown in the following example.

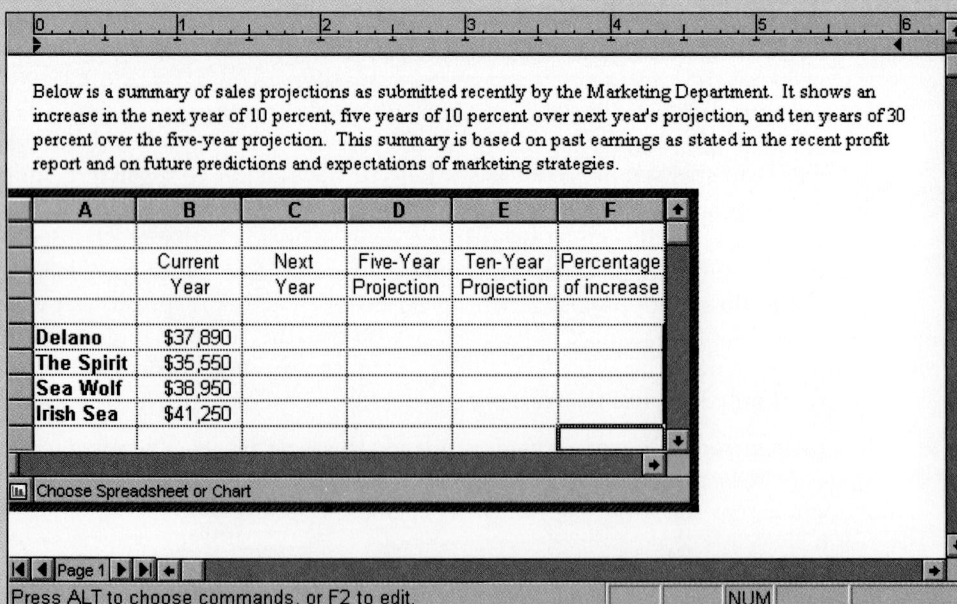

12. Compute the **Next Year, Five-Year Projection, Ten-Year Projection,** and **Percentages** as you did in the original document. Use formulas and functions when appropriate. The increases are given below.

Next Year	10 percent above the Current Year
Five-Year	10 percent above Next Year
Ten-Year	30 percent above the Five-Year
Percentage of Increase	Divide Ten-year into the Current Year

13. Center all column headings. Bold the title Sales Projections and side headings. Format all currency values as whole numbers and all percentages two places to the right of the decimal.
14. Center the spreadsheet by clicking on it to display handles, and then click on the Center Align button.
15. Add the following text two lines below the spreadsheet.

> We expect the projections to be accurate and look forward to continued success and growth in the future. The Puget Sound area is growing rapidly due to increases in high-tech industry as well as in the airline and shipping industries. With this continued optimistic outlook on the future of the geographic area, the chartering business looks bright as well.

16. Run a spell check on the document, and save the document again as **CH11HO3**.

    NOTE: If edits in the table are required, double-click on it with the left mouse button. When done editing, click anywhere outside the table with the left mouse button to return to the word processing document.

17. Preview it in Print Preview and print a copy. The table in the finished document should appear similar to the following.

SALES PROJECTIONS

Below is a summary of sales projections as submitted recently by the Marketing Department. It shows an increase in the next year of 10 percent, five years of 10 percent over next year's projection, and ten years of 30 percent over the five-year projection. This summary is based on past earnings as stated in the recent profit report and on future predictions and expectations of marketing strategies.

	Current Year	Next Year	Five-Year Projection	Ten-Year Projection	Percentage of increase
Delano	$37,890	$41,679	$45,847	$59,601	63.57%
The Spirit	$35,550	$39,105	$43,016	$55,920	63.57%
Sea Wolf	$38,950	$42,845	$47,130	$61,268	63.57%
Irish Sea	$41,250	$45,375	$49,913	$64,886	63.57%

We expect the projections to be accurate and look forward to continued success and growth in the future. The Puget Sound area is growing rapidly due to increases in high-tech industry as well as in the airline and shipping industries. With this continued optimistic outlook on the future of the geographic area, the chartering business looks bright as well.

In this exercise you will create the following agenda for an upcoming Puget Sound Charters meeting. The **Spreadsheet/Table** tool in a word processing document is used.

In a new word processing document

1. Press the **Enter** key twice to insert blank lines at the top of the page.
2. Click on the **Insert Table** button in the **toolbar** 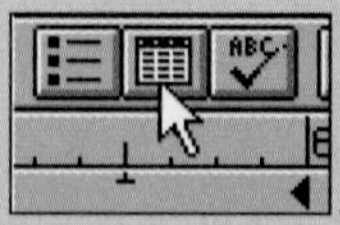.
3. Choose **New Table** and **OK** from the dialog box.
4. Point and drag the lower right handle down and to the right so that it reaches the right margin approximately as shown.

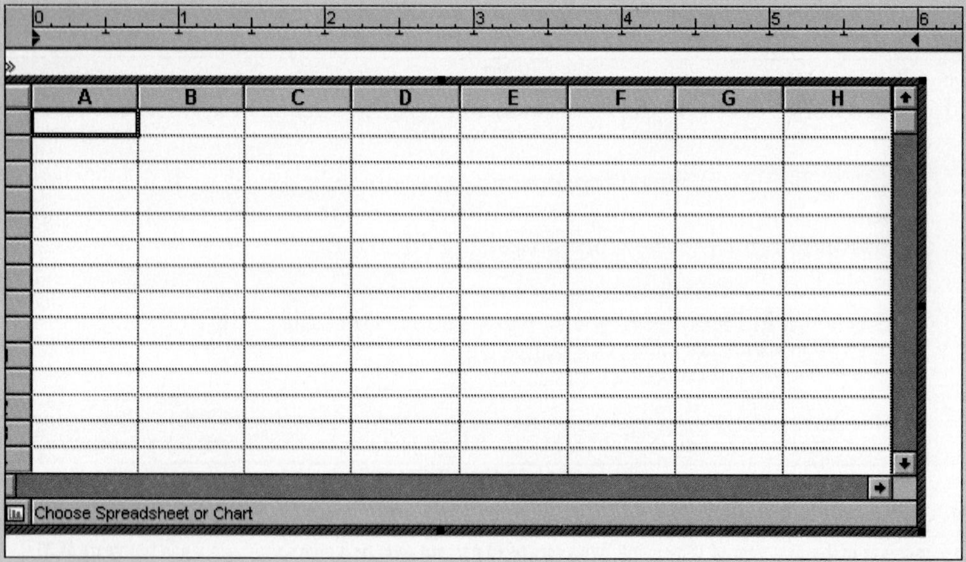

5. Enter the labels and column headings into cells as shown below. As you are doing so, adjust the width of the columns so that they appear similar to those shown here.

	A	B	C	D	E	F
1				**PUGET SOUND CHARTERS**		
2				**Agenda for the February Meeting**		
3						
4		**TIME**		**TOPICS**		**LOCATION**
5						
6		9:00 AM		Opening Keynote Speaker		
7				Past and Present Trends		Elliott Bay Room
8						
9		10:00 AM		Break and Discussion Groups		Main Foyer
10						
11		12 Noon		Lunch		On Your Own
12						
13		2:00 PM		Increasing Sales/Decreasing Costs		Puget Conference
14						Hall
15						
16		4:00 PM		Wrap-Up Discussion Groups		Elliott Bay Room
17						

6. Position the two-line main heading in column D and center both lines.
7. Center and bold the column headings.
8. Complete the agenda as shown. Adjust the width of the columns if necessary.
9. Right align **12 Noon** in column B.
10. Click anywhere outside the spreadsheet window.
11. Center the table and delete column A, if necessary.
12. Use Print Preview to view the document as it will print.
13. If necessary, adjust the size of the table by dragging on the handles.
14. Save the document as **CH11HO4** and print a copy.
15. Close the document and exit Works.

Exercise 3: HO11HO3

SALES PROJECTIONS

Below is a summary of sales projections as submitted recently by the Marketing Department. It shows an increase in the next year of 10 percent, five years of 10 percent over next year's projection, and ten years of 30 percent over the five-year projection. This summary is based on past earnings as stated in the recent profit report and on future predictions and expectations of marketing strategies.

	Current Year	Next Year	Five-Year Projection	Ten-Year Projection	Percentage of Increase
Delano	$37,890	$41,679	$45,847	$59,601	63.57%
The Spirit	$35,550	$39,105	$43,106	$55,920	63.57%
Sea Wolf	$38,950	$42,845	$47,130	$61,268	63.57%
Irish Sea	$41,250	$45,375	$49,913	$64,886	63.57%

We expect the projections to be accurate and look forward to continued success and growth in the future. The Puget Sound area is growing rapidly due to increases in high-tech industry as well as in the airline and shipping industries. With this continued optimistic outlook on the future of the geographic area, the chartering business looks bright as well.

Exercise 4: CH11HO4

PUGET SOUND CHARTERS

Agenda for the February Meeting

TIME	TOPICS	LOCATION
9:00 AM	Opening Keynote Speaker	
	Past and Present Trends	Elliott Bay Room
10:00 AM	Break and Discussion Groups	Main Foyer
12 Noon	Lunch	On Your Own
2:00 PM	Increasing Sales/Decreasing Costs	Puget Conference Hall
4:00 PM	Wrap-Up Discussion Groups	Elliott Bay Room

CHAPTER 12

Charts

OBJECTIVES

Create charts

Make modifications to charts

Name charts

Copy charts

Change chart format

Change display of values

Create a pie chart

Print charts and spreadsheets together

PREVIEW

Charts allow you to represent spreadsheet information in graphic format that interprets data values otherwise shown in rows and columns. It can be easier for those looking at spreadsheet information to better see a representation of the information in chart form. A chart can show values using various size bars in a bar chart, sections in a pie chart, by comparisons in line charts, and other formats.

Works contains eight different chart formats, and you can create and save up to eight charts with each spreadsheet created. Examples are shown on the following pages.

The bar chart

The bar chart explains the differences between categories of selected values on a spreadsheet. Those belonging to different groups are shown in different shades or patterns. Usually, the Y-axis (the left side of the chart) contains values increasing in order up the chart (Figure 12-1). The X-axis (the bottom of the chart) shows the categories. For example, if you created a bar chart on one of the spreadsheets created in previous lessons in this book, the Y-axis might show the total sales values and the X-axis the categories into which the sales are broken down.

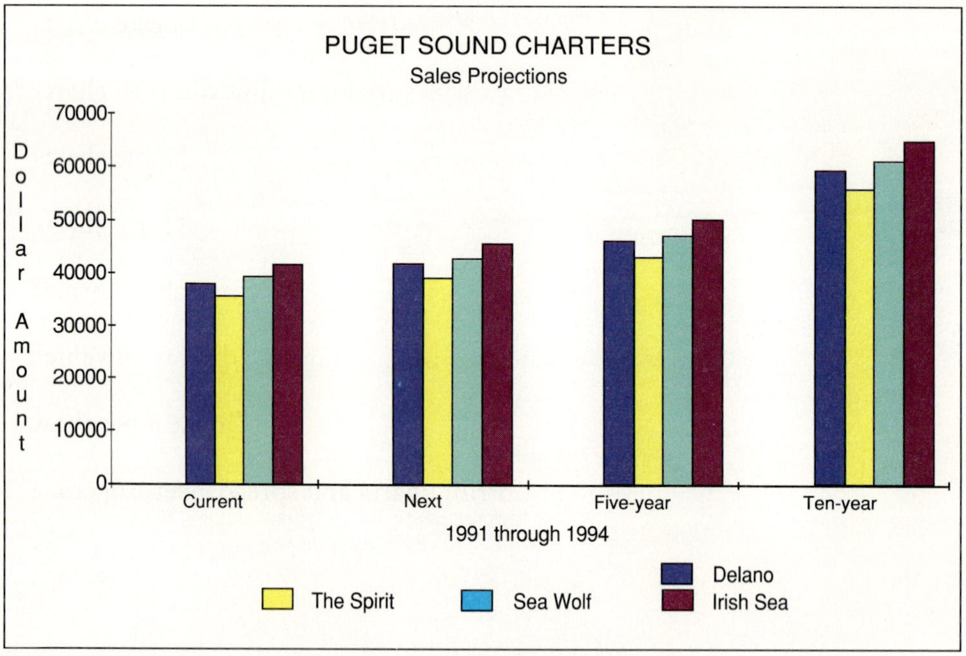

Figure 12-1
Bar chart

The Line chart

A line chart represents data in lines across the chart (Figure 12-2). Three or four groups of data, such as sales over a period of time, may be represented. Line charts are commonly used to show comparisons and trends, such as increases and decreases over a period of time.

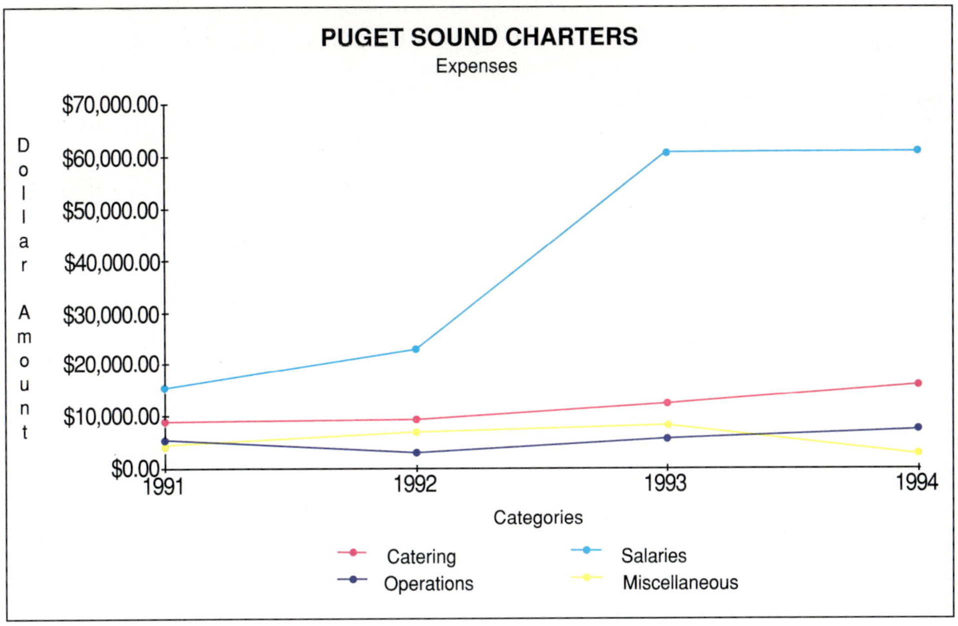

Figure 12-2
Line chart

The Pie chart

A pie chart shows the percentages of a group of selected values as they relate to the whole (Figure 12-3). A pie chart represents one column or row in a spreadsheet.

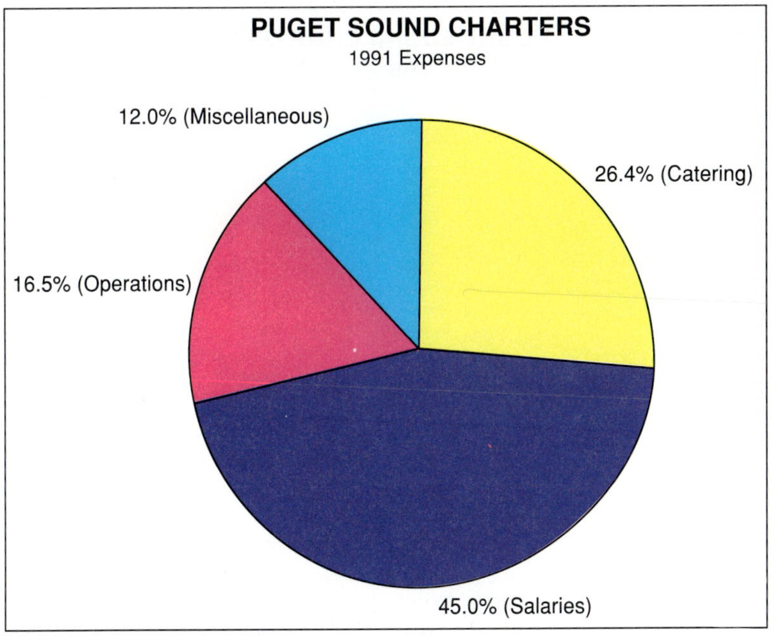

Figure 12-3
Pie chart

The Stacked line chart

An area line chart stacks or combines values to show the total amount in a given category (Figure 12-4). For example, each line's values are added to the previous line's values. If making a comparison of sales over a period of time, sales of the Delano might be added to sales of The Spirit, and so on.

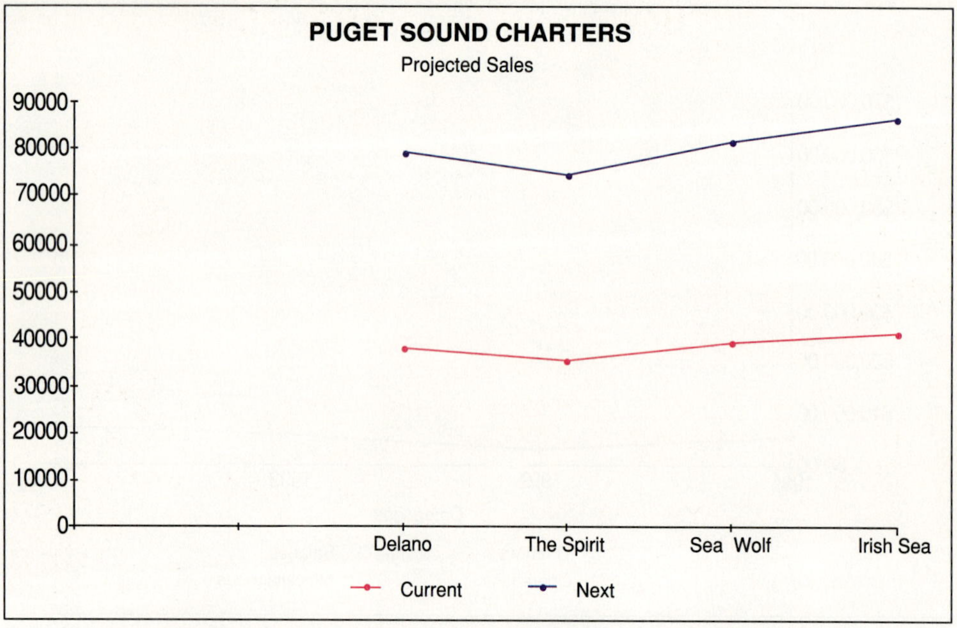

Figure 12-4
Stacked line chart

The X-Y (scatter) chart

This chart shows the relationship between X and Y values in the form of a scatterplot in which no lines or bars are shown, only the points on the graph where a value falls (Figure 12-5).

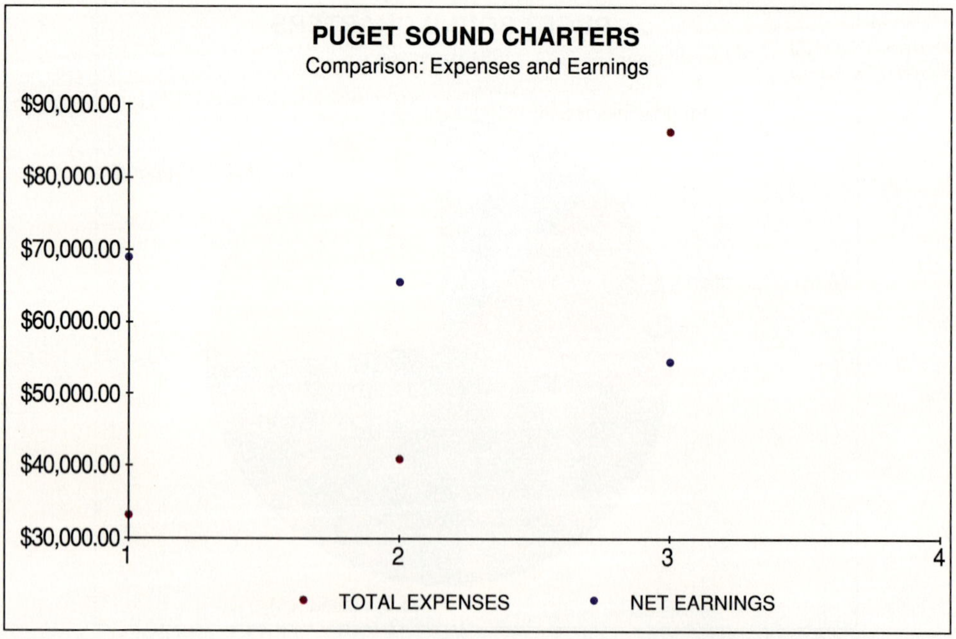

Figure 12-5
X-Y (scatter) chart

The Radar chart

A radar chart shows values as they relate to each other (Figure 12-6). It pivots on a center point. Lines connect all data markers in a series, such as those that affect the catering expenses. These charts are useful for making comparisons between items and showing how items relate to one another.

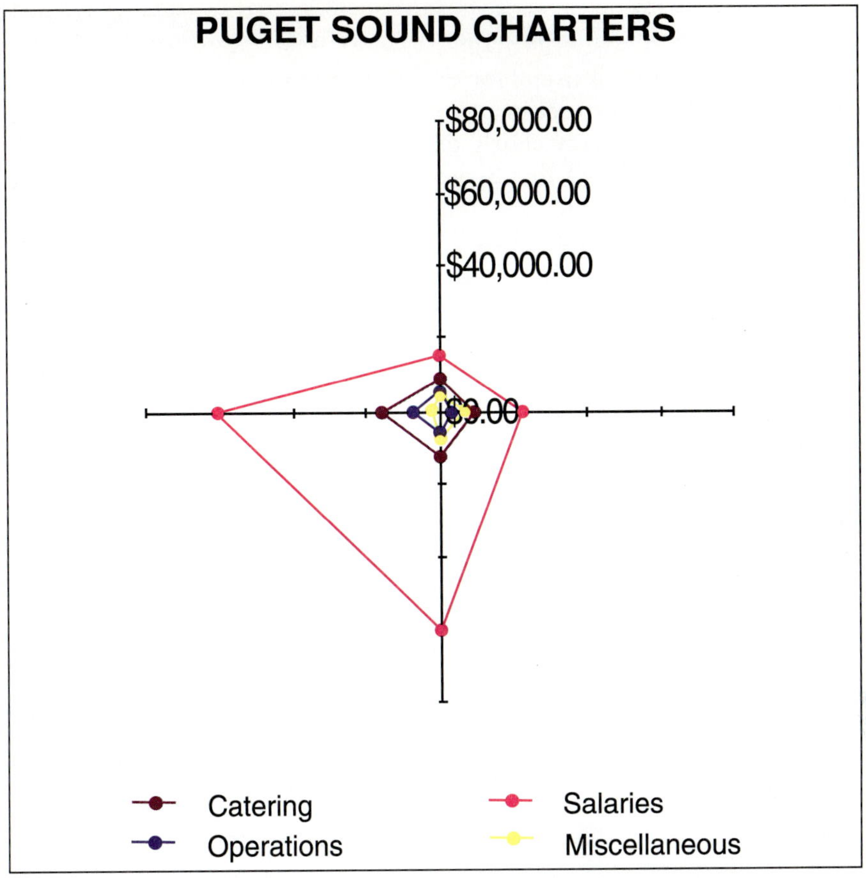

Figure 12-6
Radar chart

The Combination chart

Combination charts show a mix of lines and bars in the same chart (Figure 12-7). This type of chart is useful for making one series of values stand out against another series.

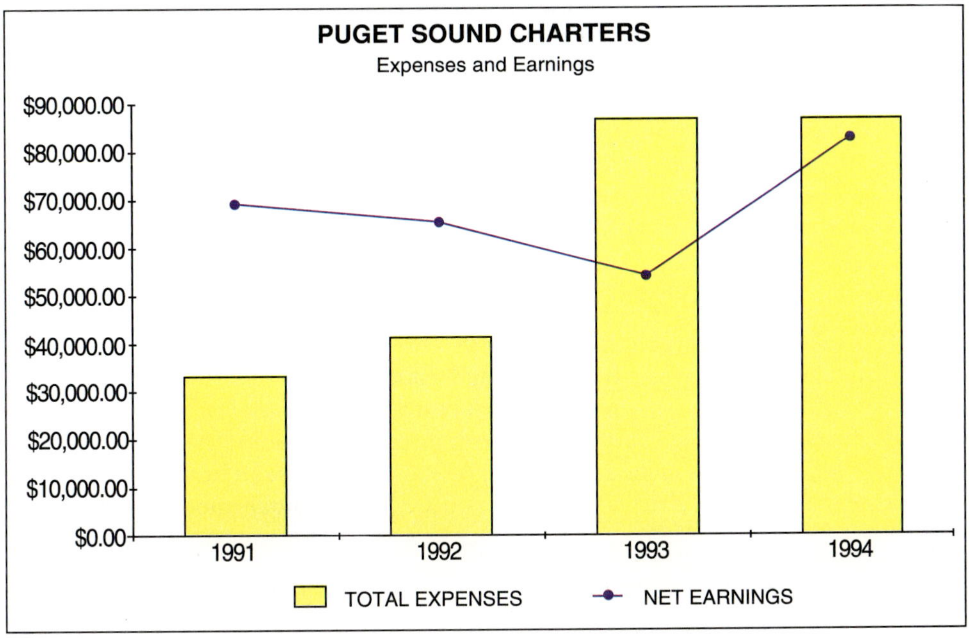

Figure 12-7
Combination chart

3-D area chart

The 3-D area chart option is useful for showing large amounts of data (Figure 12-8). Sometimes data is difficult to see or compare against other sets of values. A 3-D can make values stand out and very clearly display high and low points of data. The following example clearly shows that Series 2 values consume a large chunk of Puget Sound Charters expenses.

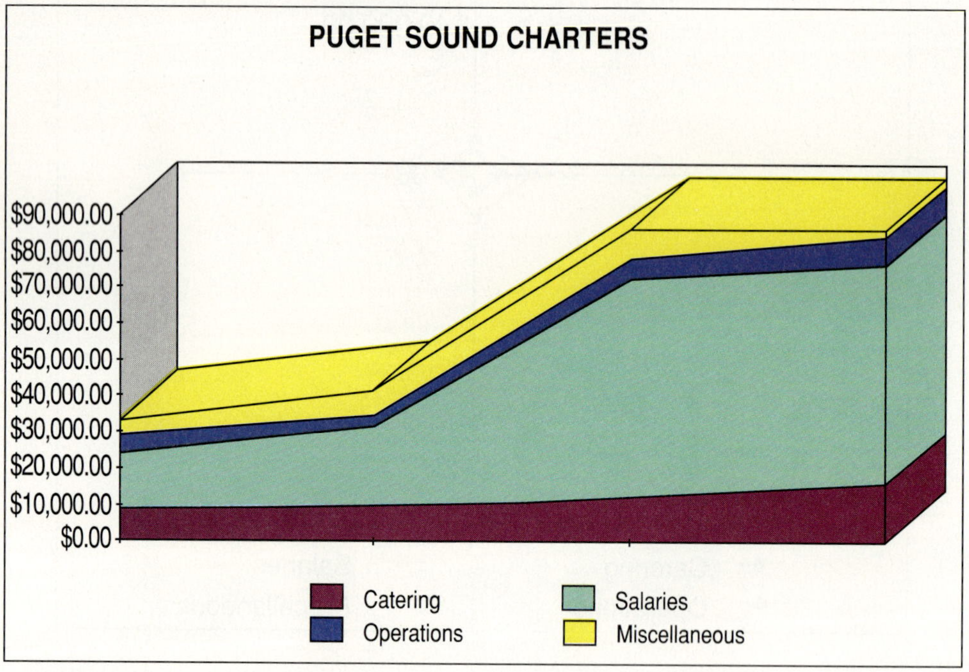

Figure 12-8
A 3-D area chart

CREATING CHARTS

Every chart is based on the text and values found in a spreadsheet and is attached to that spreadsheet. The values are selected to represent bars, lines, scatterplots, or sections of a pie chart. If the values are changed, the chart is updated automatically.

Up to as many as six rows and columns may be used in a single chart. Usually, charts are easier to read and interpret when they represent a limited number of comparisons.

In most spreadsheets, text appears in the first row or the first column of a spreadsheet, and that text automatically becomes the X-axis labels. The selected numbers in a row or column become the Y-series. Once a chart is created, there are many options available to change the appearance of the chart, such as adding legends or X- and Y- titles and main subheadings.

Create a Bar Chart

The first step in creating a chart is to open the spreadsheet file containing the values you want to display graphically. The text and values are then selected (up to six adjacent rows or columns). The New Chart button from the toolbar is then used and the first dialog box appears on the screen. After making some initial settings, the chart appears. These steps are the basic ones used to create an instant chart with Works. After the initial chart appears and you are in chart mode, modifications can be made to it.

1. Sign onto **Works** (if necessary).

2. **Open** the file **CH10HO2A.WKS** which you created in Chapter 10; or retrieve it from the Instructor data disk.

3. **Select** cells **A5 through C8** as shown below.

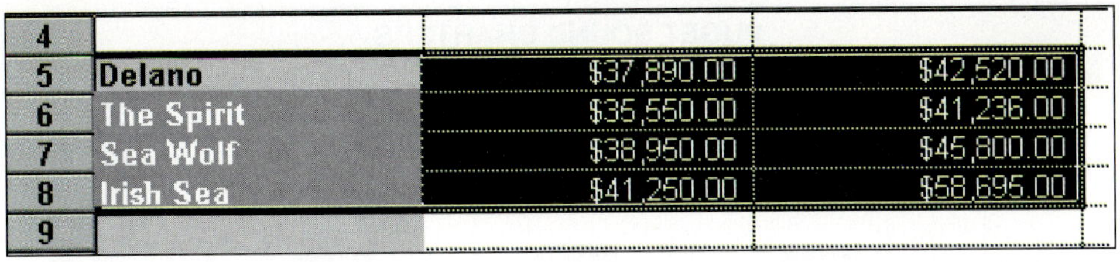

4. **Click** on the **New Chart** button on the **toolbar** or choose **Tools, Create New Chart**. The dialog box shown in Figure 12-9 appears.

NOTE: If **Bar** is not displayed in the **What type of chart . . .** box, click on the down arrow and select it.

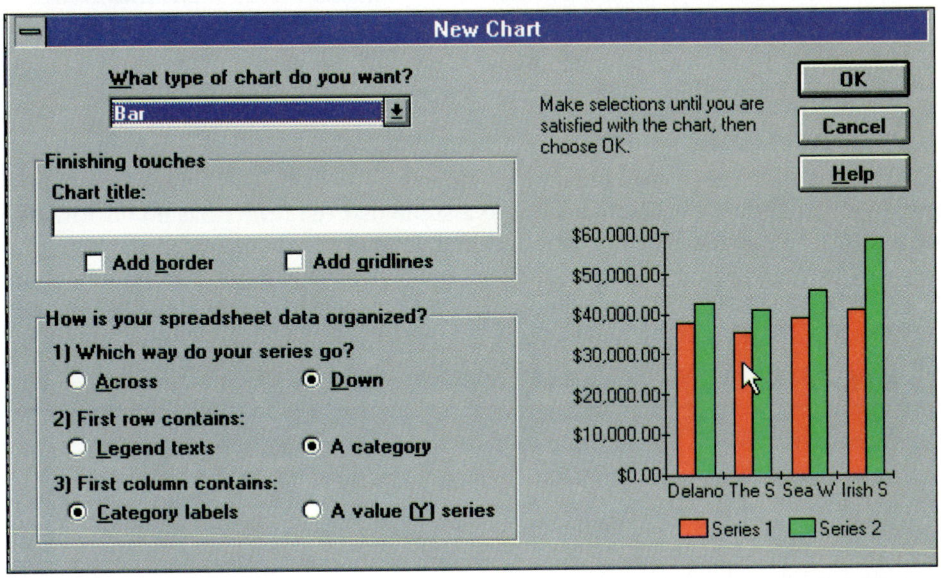

Figure 12-9
The New Chart dialog box

This dialog box shows a partial sample of what the chart looks like using the highlighted cells. The default settings are for a bar chart. The type of chart can be changed using the list box at the upper left corner of this box. In addition, the Finishing touches box allows you to add a chart title, a border around the chart, or gridlines. The data organization box below contains options for changing the way the data values appear, adding legends, and changing how the first column contents are used. Most of the time, the values you select will apply correctly in the layout of the chart. For example, the bar chart X-axis labels are correctly shown as the names of the boats and the Y-axis values are shown as the dollar value of the cruises. When you make changes in this box, the selections are reflected in the Sample.

5. Type PUGET SOUND CHARTERS in the **Chart title** box.
6. Choose **OK** or press **Enter**. The following chart appears and you are switched to chart mode.

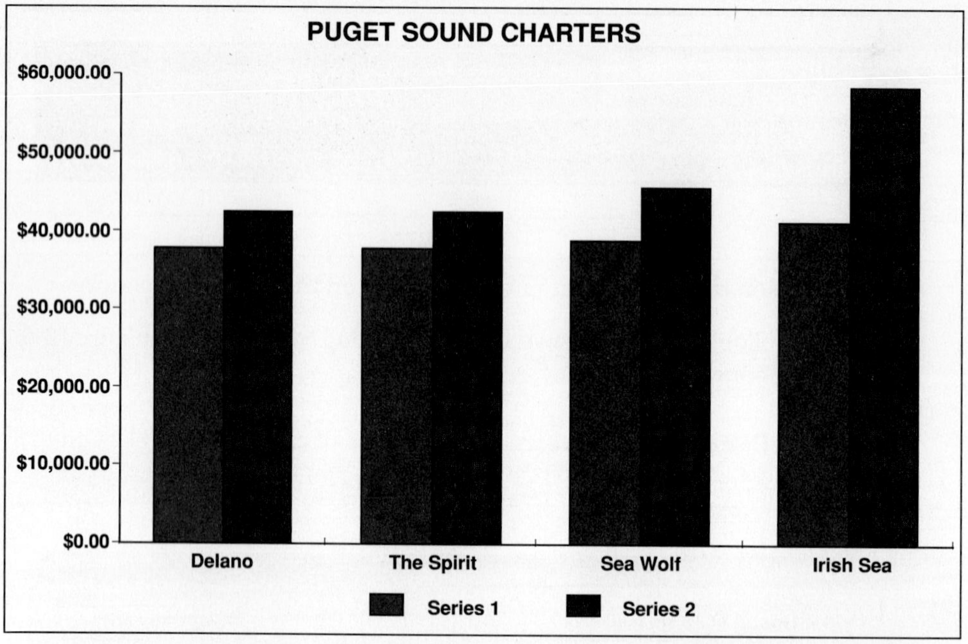

This chart is already nearly complete. However, we could do things to enhance its clarity and readability. You always want to assume that the reader has no information about what is presented on the chart, and therefore the chart must tell all there is to know. For example, Series 1 and Series 2 does not give us very much information about what each bar stands for. You may know that Series 1 is 1993, but the reader may not.

MAKING MODIFICATIONS

The current chart could be modified in a number of ways. Among those that would enhance the readability of the current chart are adding data labels and additional chart titles.

Change Series Labels

Commands used to change legend labels and add other labels or titles are found in the **Edit** menu. The command used to change the legend labels on this worksheet is the **Legend/Series Labels** command.

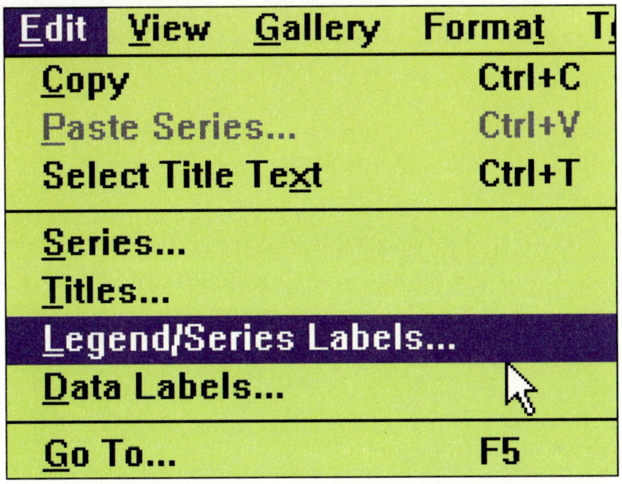

1. Choose **Edit, Legend/Series Labels**. The following dialog box appears (Figure 12-10).

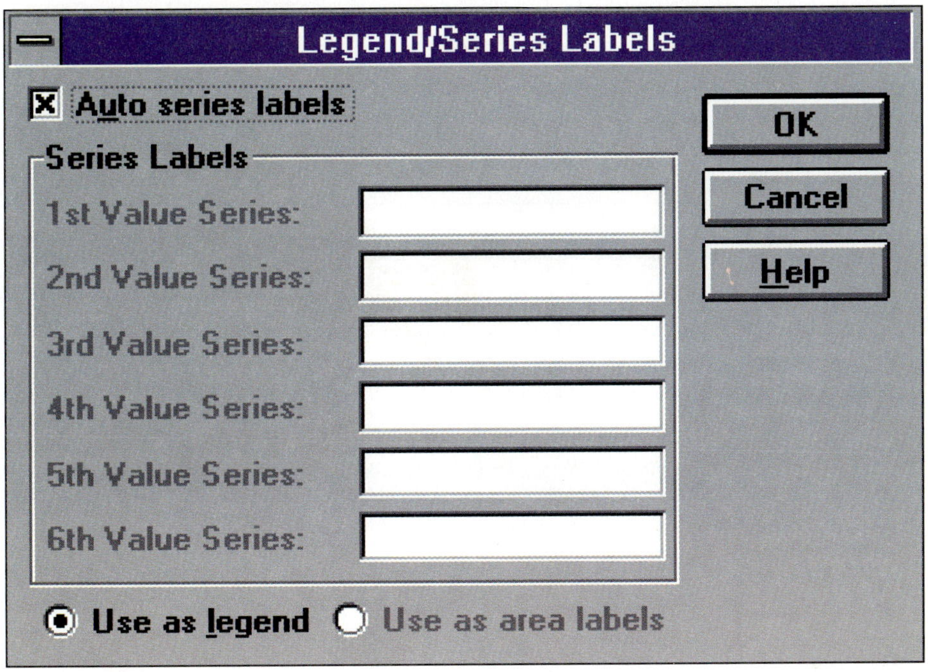

Figure 12-10
The Legend/Series Labels dialog box

2. Click **once** on the **Auto series labels** box to remove the X. The Auto series option uses the labels **Series 1, Series 2,** and so on for each of the sets of data values (1993 and 1994 in this worksheet).
3. Type **1993** in the **1st Value Series** box.
4. Type **1994** in the **2nd Value Series** box.
5. Choose **OK** or press **Enter**. The chart now shows 1993 and 1994 as the legend labels and clearly tells the reader what each bar stands for.

Switch Between Chart and Spreadsheet Mode

The **Window** menu is used to toggle (move) between the chart and the spreadsheet.

1. Choose **CH10HO2A.WKS** from the **Window** menu. The spreadsheet is now active.
2. Choose **CH10HO2A.WKS - Chart 1** from the **Window** menu. The chart and its menu options and toolbar are now active.

NOTE: Remember you can also resize the window the dragging with the left mouse button on the border or on the corners so that both documents are displayed at the same time. The Guided Tutorial in Chapter 2 gives instructions for resizing a window.

Add Data Labels

Data labels are used to give values or add text to each of the individual sets of data values. For example, in the current bar chart, data labels would add the exact values to each of the bars, thus giving the reader more information about the content of the chart. Labels are added by indicating the cell range containing the values.

1. Drag with the left mouse button on the upper left corner of the **Chart** window to reduce it so that it appears as shown below. This enables you to see both the spreadsheet values and the chart.

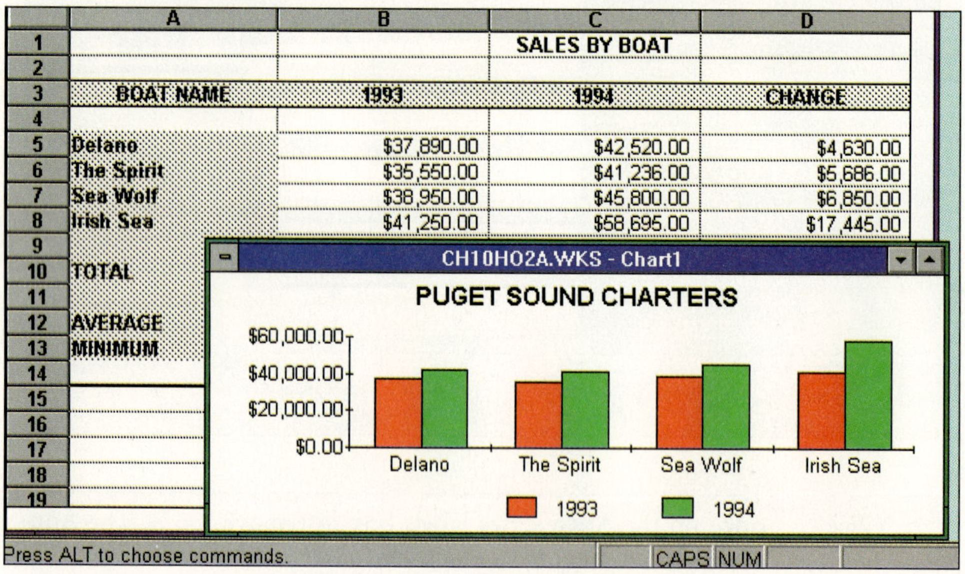

2. Choose **Edit, Data Labels** (with the chart window active).
3. Type **B5:B8** in the **1st** box.
4. Type **C5:C8** in the **2nd** box. Your entries should appear similar to the following as shown in Figure 12-11.

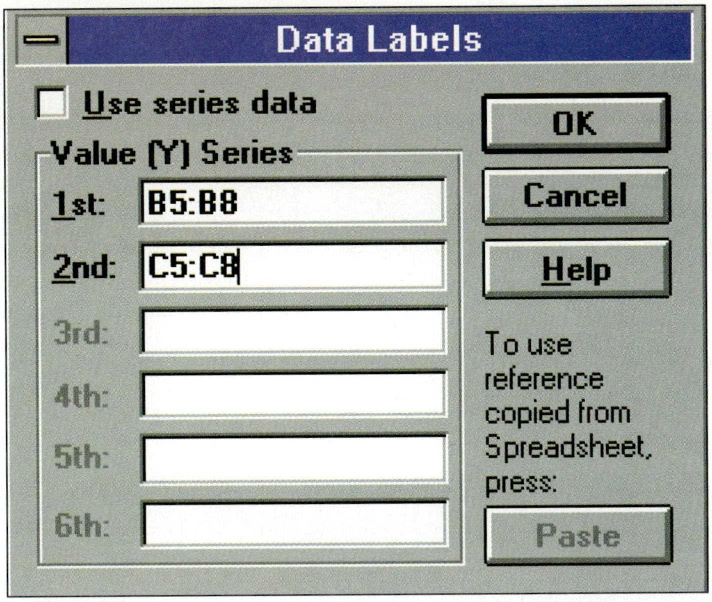

Figure 12-11
The Data Labels dialog box

5. Choose **OK** or press **Enter**. The values are inserted above each bar; however, they are difficult to view in the reduced window size.
6. Click on the **Maximize** button  in the upper right corner of the chart window. The chart now appears similar to the following example.

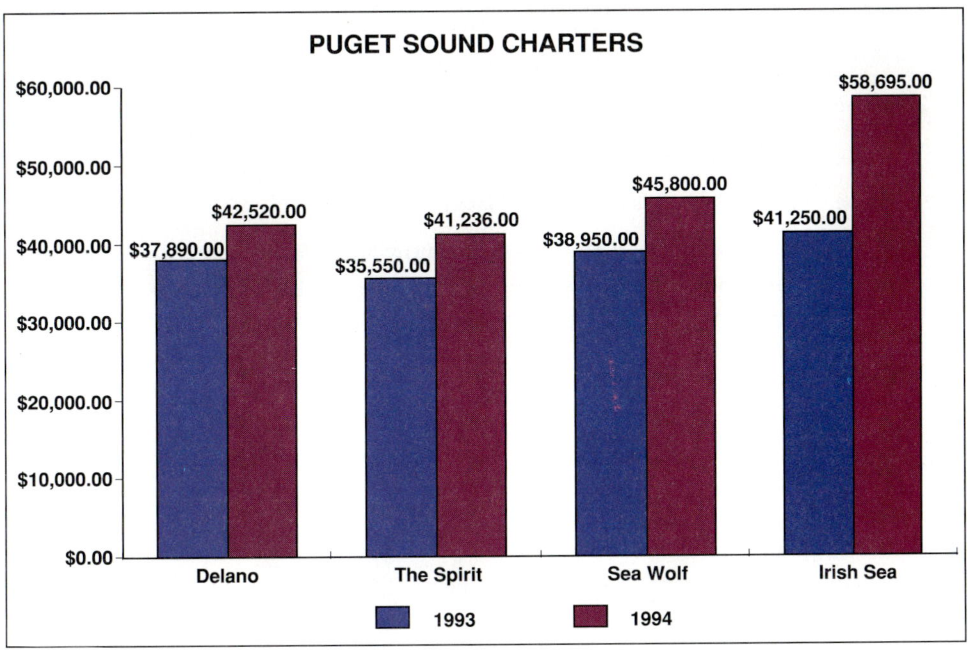

NOTE: To add data labels that are **not** in columns **adjacent** to the value columns, highlight the text in the column for the labels; then go to the chart and choose **Edit, Paste Series,** choose **Category** and **OK**. See exercise 1 in Hands-on Exercises in this chapter for specific instructions for this.

Add Chart Titles

This chart and others can be enhanced further by adding titles. Titles can be added as chart titles, subtitles, X- and Y- axis titles, and Right Y-axis titles. Usually, the more information that can be added to a chart, the easier it is to interpret. A chart title and X- and Y-axis titles will be used on the present chart. Right Y-axis titles are used to identify values appearing on the right side of a chart. This is a format that is used when two values, such as Total and Individual sales, will be shown on the chart. The Total sales amounts would then appear on the left side with individual breakdowns on the right. This is an unusual format with which you can experiment on your own.

With the Chart window active

1. Choose **Edit, Titles**. The following dialog box appears as shown in Figure 12-12.

Figure 12-12
The Titles dialog box

2. Type **1993 and 1994 Sales Figures** in the **Subtitle** box.
3. Type **Active Boats** in the **Horizontal (X) Axis** box.
4. Type **Sales Dollars** in the **Vertical (Y) Axis** box.
5. Choose **OK** or press **Enter**. The chart now appears similar to the following.

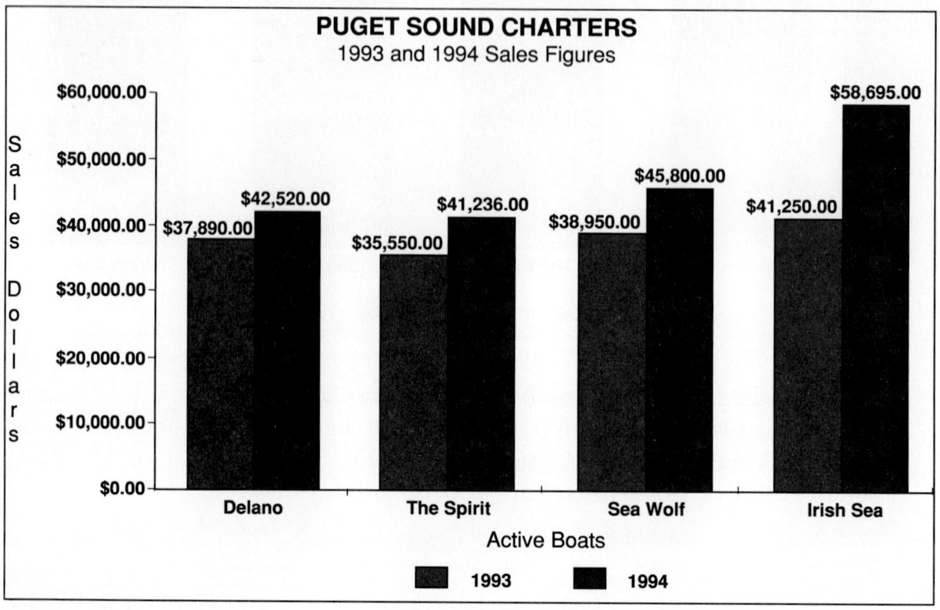

NAMING A CHART

When the chart is complete, it is a good idea to name it. Works has already named this chart, CHART1. If you were experimenting with creating many variations of charts on a single spreadsheet, Works would create each one as CHART2, CHART3, and so on. Each chart is then added to the **Window** menu so that any chart can be quickly retrieved for viewing. It is optional to change the name that Works assigns to a chart. As with any document, a name given by you, the user, often makes it easier to identify.

Name a Chart

With the **Chart** window active

1. Choose **Tools, Name Chart**. Notice that other chart options are found in this menu as well.

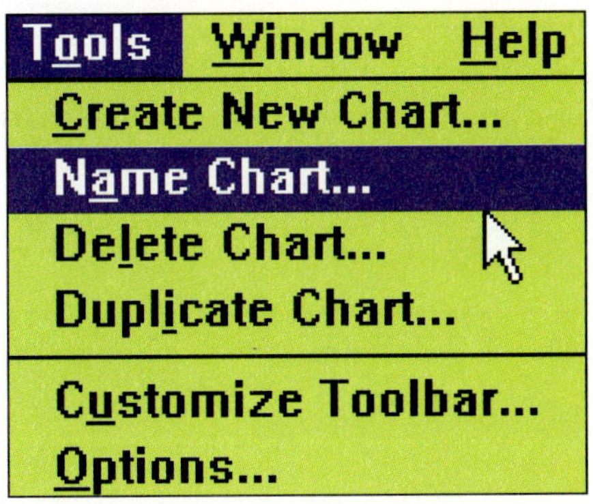

The following dialog box (Figure 12-13) appears.

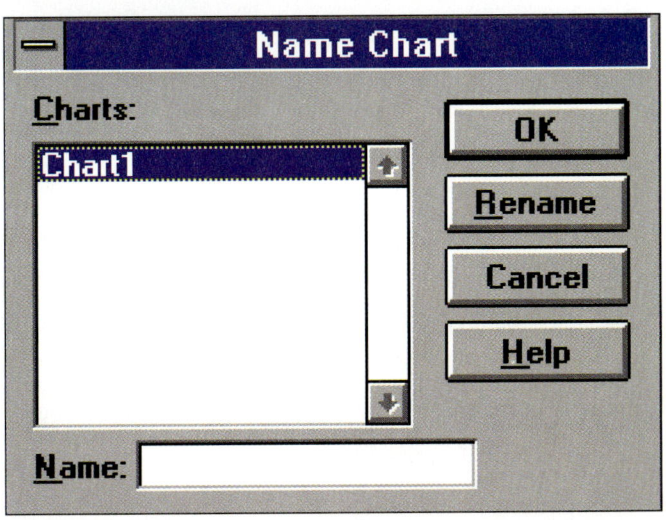

Figure 12-13
The Name Chart dialog box

With **Chart1** highlighted in the **Charts** list box

2. Type **Sales Chart** in the **Name** box.
3. Choose **Rename**. The chart title changes.
4. Choose **OK** or press **Enter**.
5. View the document names in the **Window** menu and note the new chart title attached to the document.

COPYING A CHART

Copying a chart has two primary functions: (1) it creates an automatic backup of a chart, and (2) it allows the user to make changes and experiment with a chart without changing the original.

Copy a Chart

Here, you will make a copy of the current chart, Sales Chart, and experiment with changing the type of chart (such as creating a line chart). The original chart will remain intact.

1. Choose **Tools, Duplicate Chart**. A dialog box similar to the one shown in Figure 12-14 appears.

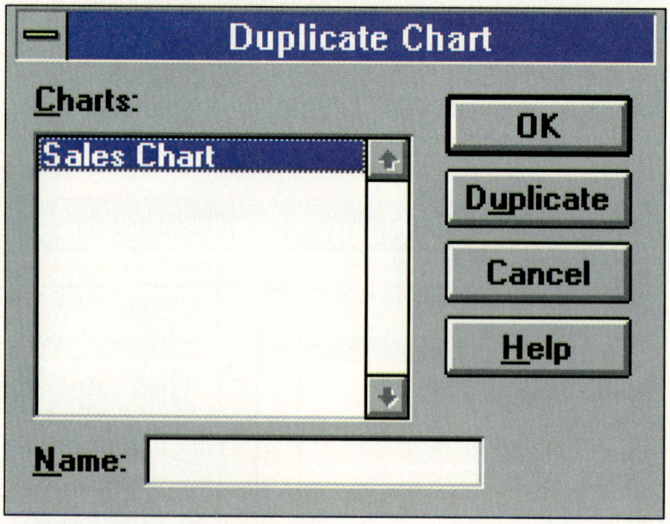

Figure 12-14 The Duplicate Chart dialog box

2. Click **once** on the **Sales Chart** name in the **Charts** list box.
3. Type **Sales Chart 2** in the **Name** box.
4. Choose **Duplicate**.

A new chart is added to the list.

5. Choose **OK** or press **Enter**.

The lowest and highest values on the Y-axis can be set using the Minimum and Maximum boxes. The intervals at which the values will increase is set using the Interval box. Gridlines and a logarithmic scale may also be added. This box can be used to change the general arrangement of the Y-axis values. You can experiment with the changes these settings will make to a chart.

2. Type 30000 in the **Minimum** box.

3. Type 60000 in the **Maximum** box.

These two values encompass the range of all values we are viewing.

4. Type 5000 in the **Interval** box.

This will allow for values to appear more spread out on the chart.

5. Choose **Show Gridlines.**

6. Choose **OK** or press **Enter** to view the changes. The chart should look similar to the following. With these changes, the line chart becomes easier to read, and the highs and lows are more evenly distributed.

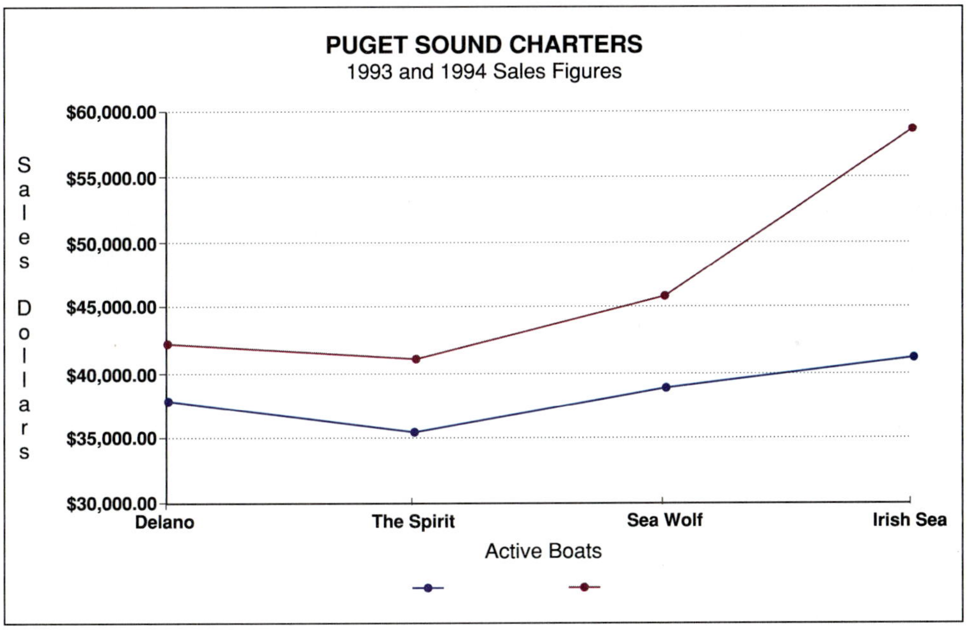

7. Choose **Window** and return to the spreadsheet.

8. Save the spreadsheet as **CH12PR1**. This action also saves the attached charts. You will be using the same spreadsheet in the next section.

CREATING A PIE CHART

A pie chart is used when you want to show comparative values in a *single* category. It shows an individual percentage of a group of values, such as what percentage one boat's sales is of all boats' sales combined. Creating a pie chart will display the values as sections of a pie that clearly show the volume of one when compared to other items in the group. The pie sections may also be labeled and the patterns of the sections formatted so that they stand out. Three-dimensional pie charts are also an option as are 3-D charts of other types. In this exercise, you will explore some of these and other options.

Create a Pie Chart

1. Switch — to the spreadsheet using the **Window** menu (if necessary).
2. Select — the values under the **Change** column of each of the boats as follows.

	BOAT NAME	1993	1994	CHANGE
4				
5	Delano	$37,890.00	$42,520.00	$4,630.00
6	The Spirit	$35,550.00	$41,236.00	$5,686.00
7	Sea Wolf	$38,950.00	$45,800.00	$6,850.00
8	Irish Sea	$41,250.00	$58,695.00	$17,445.00
9				

3. Click — on the **New Chart** button in the toolbar, or choose **Tools, Create New Chart.**
4. Choose — **Pie** from the **What type . . .** box at the top of the New Chart dialog box. The pie image chart appears as shown in Figure 12-17.

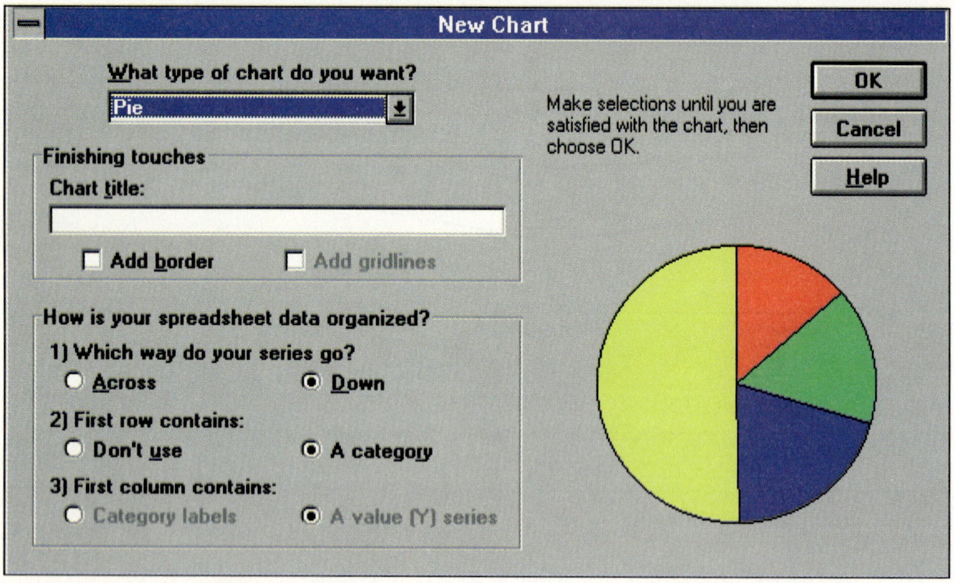

Figure 12-17
The New Chart dialog box

5. Type — **PUGET SOUND CHARTERS** as the **Chart title.**
6. Choose — **Add border.** The Sample box now shows the title and border.
7. Choose — **OK** or press **Enter.**

Add Data Labels

The chart now appears with a main heading and the pie divided into sections. The **Data Labels** option in the **Edit** menu can be used to add percentages and values for the sections.

1. Choose **Edit, Data Labels.** (Note that the options in the Data Label dialog box are different for pie charts than for other charts.)
2. Choose **Percentages** from the **1st Label** box.
3. Choose **Values** from the **(2nd Label)** box.
4. Choose **OK** or press **Enter**. The chart appears similar to the following.

NOTE: The (2nd Label) will appear in parentheses.

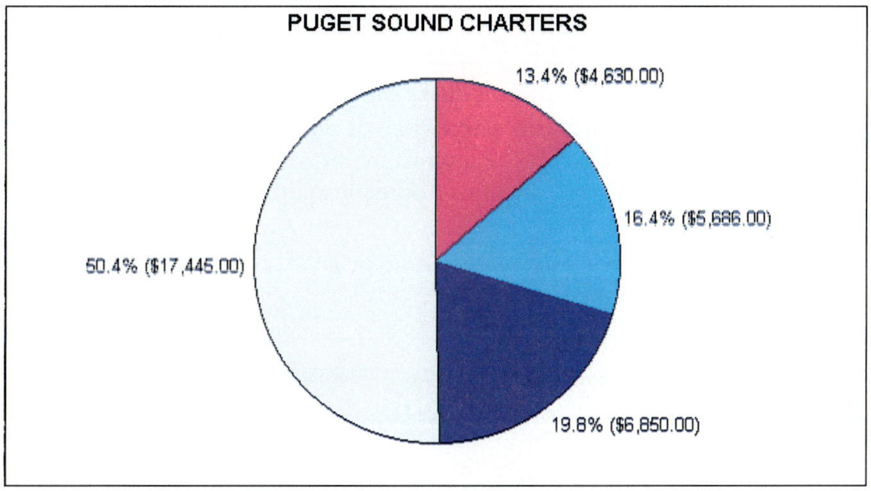

Add Cell Contents

The names of the boats can be added in place of the percentages using the **Add Cell Contents** option in the **Data Labels** dialog box.

Be sure the pie chart is active.

1. Choose **Edit, Data Labels.**
2. Choose **Cell Contents** in the **1st Label** box to turn it on. The Percentages option is turned off automatically. Only one choice can be turned on for each of the labels.
3. Type **A5:A8** in the **Cell Range** box to indicate the range.
4. Choose **OK** or press **Enter**. The chart now shows the boat name and value for each slice.

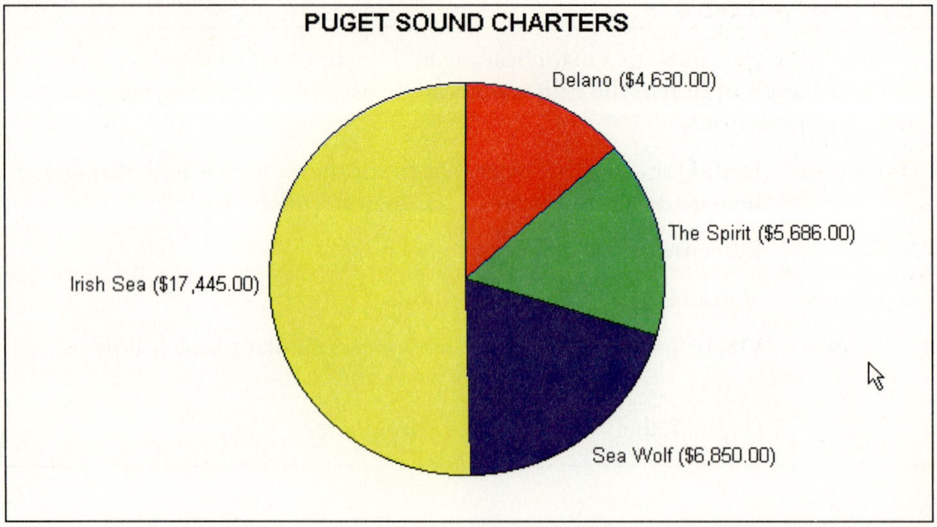

Change Patterns and Shapes

The color and pattern of one or more of the pie sections can be changed to make them more distinctive. In addition, parts or all of the pie can be changed to a 3-D image. This can make the chart more interesting by adding depth to the image. It draws attention to one or more sections of the pie and helps to catch the attention of the reader.

1. Choose **Format, Patterns and Colors** to display the dialog box shown in Figure 12-18.

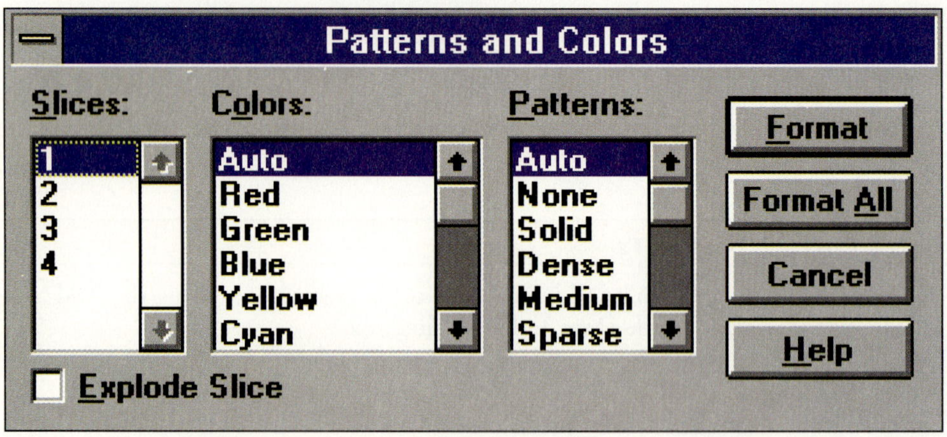

Figure 12-18
The Patterns and Colors dialog box

The number of slices in the current pie chart are given in the Slices list box. A variety of colors and patterns are shown in the boxes to the right. When a pattern is changed, the Format button is chosen to make the change on the pie chart. As each change is made, the new pattern will be displayed on the chart in the background.

2. Choose **1** in the **Slices** box (if necessary).
3. Choose **Blue** in the **Colors** box.
4. Scroll through the list of patterns in the **Patterns** box and choose the **Light //** pattern shown in the following example.

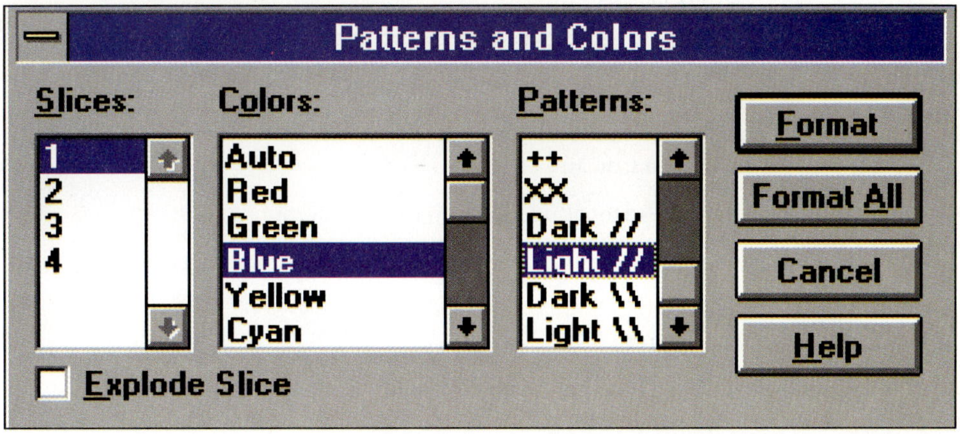

5. Choose **Format** to change the first pie section.

   NOTE: You should be able to view the change on the pie chart in the background. If you cannot, point to the dialog box title bar and drag the box toward the lower right corner of the window so that more of the chart is visible.

Explode a Slice

Remain in the Patterns and Colors dialog box; or if you have exited from it, choose **Format, Patterns and Colors** again.

1. Choose **3** in the **Slices** box to select the third slice.
2. Choose **Explode Slice** to display an **X** in the box.
3. Choose a different color, if you like.
4. Choose a different pattern, if you like.
5. Choose **Format** to apply the formatting to slice number 3.
6. Change the patterns and colors for each of the other pie sections.
7. Choose **Close** when done. When finished, the chart may be similar to the following.

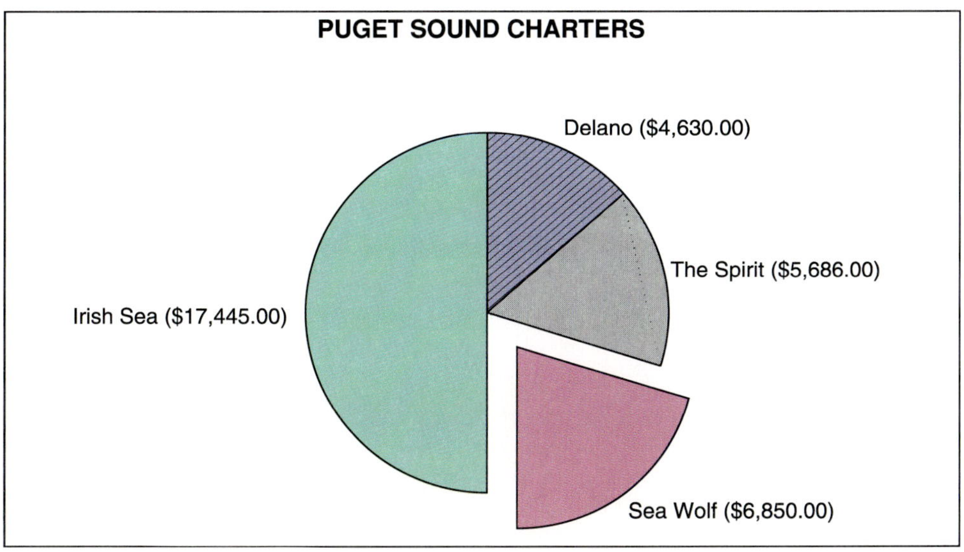

8. Change the name of the chart to **Sales Pie** using the **Tools, Name Chart** command.

   NOTE: Highlight the name of the chart, type the new name in the **Name** box, and choose **Rename** and choose **OK**.

9. Switch to the spreadsheet using the **Window** menu.
10. Save the spreadsheet document as **CH12PR2** (all charts will also be saved).
11. Choose **View, Chart.**
12. Choose **Sales Pie** from the **Chart** list and choose **OK** or press **Enter.**
13. Choose **File, Print Preview.**
14. Choose **Print** to print a copy of the chart.

PRINTING A CHART AND SPREADSHEET TOGETHER

A spreadsheet and chart can be shown together on one page by inserting them both into a word processing document. To do so, a word processing document is opened, the spreadsheet is given a range name and then inserted into the document, and the chart is inserted using its name. The **Range Name** and **Chart** commands from the **Insert** menu are used to insert both documents into the word processing document. The **Print Preview** command can be used to see how the document will appear when printed.

Display Spreadsheet and Chart

1. Switch to the spreadsheet document **CH12PR2** if necessary.
2. Highlight all cells in the spreadsheet including the heading, **A1:E14.**
3. Choose **Insert, Range Name.**
4. Type **Sales** in the **Name** box.
5. Choose **OK** or press **Enter.**
6. Open a new word processing document.

To insert the spreadsheet

7. Choose **Insert, Spreadsheet/Table.**
8. Choose the name of the spreadsheet, **CH12PR2.WKS,** in the Spreadsheets list box.
9. Choose the name of the range, **Sales,** in the Ranges list box as shown in Figure 12-19.

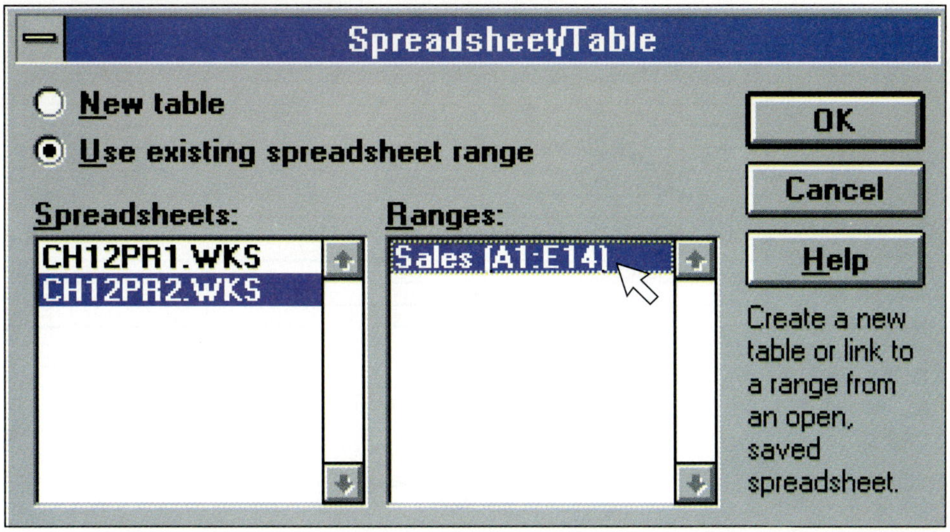

Figure 12-19
The Spreadsheet/Table dialog box

10. Choose **OK** or press **Enter** to insert the spreadsheet.

To insert the chart

11. Press **Enter** twice below the spreadsheet.
12. Choose **Insert, Chart**.
13. Choose the name of the spreadsheet and the name of the chart, **Sales Pie**, as shown in Figure 12-20.

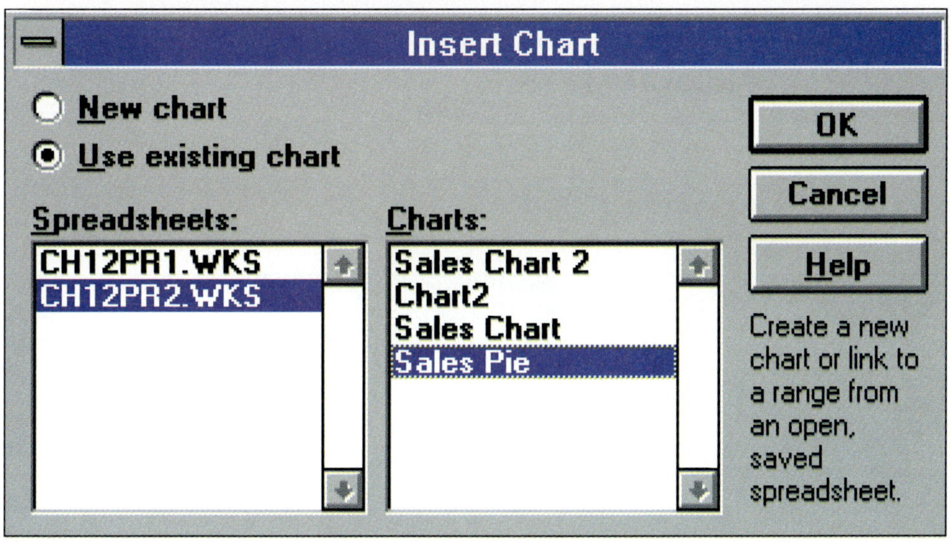

Figure 12-20
The Insert Chart dialog box

14. Choose **OK** or press **Enter**.
15. Choose **Print Preview** to see the merged documents as shown in the following example. You may want to insert a blank line between the chart and the spreadsheet.

		SALES BY BOAT		
BOAT NAME	1993	1994	CHANGE	X OF CHANGE
Delano	$37890.00	$42,450.00	$4,630.00	12.220%
The Spirit	$35,550.00	$41,236.00	$5,686.00	15.994%
Sea Wolf	$38,950.00	$45,800.00	$6,850.00	17.587%
Irish Sea	$41,250.00	$58,695.00	$17,445.00	42.291%
TOTAL	$153,640.00	$188,251.00		
AVERAGE	$38,410.00	$47,062.00		
MINIMUM	$35,550.00	$41,236.00		

PUGET SOUND CHARTERS

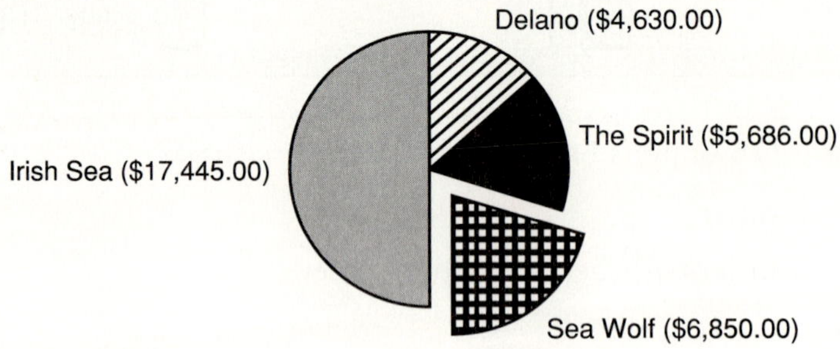

16. Save this word processing document as **CH12PR3.**
17. Choose **Print** to print a copy.
18. Quit or continue to the tutorial.

GUIDED TUTORIAL

What You'll Do

- Create bar charts.
- Modify charts to include legends and titles.
- Preview and print charts.

How To Do It

1. Open the spreadsheet **CH10HO2B.**
2. Change the format of all currency values so that they are whole numbers (no places to the right of the decimal). Keep the dollar signs ($).
3. Select cells **A9 through C12,** the boat names and the Current and Next Year sales figures.

4.	Choose	**Tools, Create New Chart.**
5.	Type	**SALES PROJECTIONS** in the **Chart title** box.
6.	Choose	**Add border** and **Add gridlines.**
7.	Choose	**3-D Bar** from **What type of chart do you want?** box.
8.	Choose	**OK** or press **Enter.**
9.	Choose	**Edit, Legend/Series Labels.**
10.	Turn	off the **Auto series labels** (no X in the box).
11.	Type	**Current Year** in the **1st** and **Next Year** in the **2nd** Value Series boxes and choose **OK** or press **Enter.**
12.	Choose	**Edit, Titles** from the menu.
13.	Type	**Boat Names** in the **Horizontal (X) Axis** box.
14.	Type	**Total Sales** in the **Vertical (Y) Axis** box.
15.	Choose	**OK** or press **Enter.** The chart should be similar to the following.

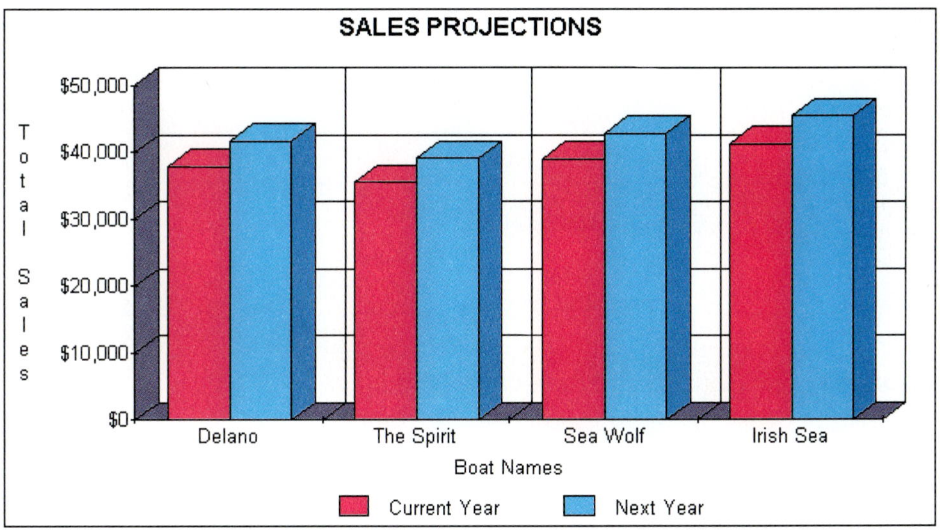

16.	Practice	changing the bar type, using the **Gallery** menu, to each of the following or to others. Stacked line Line 3-D line
17.	Change	the chart back to the original 3-D bar chart.
18.	Choose	**Tools, Name Chart.**

With **Chart1** selected

19.	Type	**Sales Chart 1** in the **Name** box.
20.	Choose	**Rename.**
21.	Choose	**OK** or press **Enter.**
22.	Choose	**File, Save.**
23.	Choose	the spreadsheet, **CH10HO2B.WKS,** from the **Window** menu.
24.	Save	the spreadsheet as **CH12TUT.**
25.	Move	to the chart again using the **Window** menu (**CH12TUT.WKS Sales Chart1**).
26.	Choose	**Print Preview** to see how the chart looks. Then choose **Print** to print the chart.
27.	Close	the document window.
28.	Quit	or continue to the Review Questions.

REVIEW QUESTIONS

1. List at least two ways to view a chart from the spreadsheet document.

   ____

   ____

2. The ____________ command from the ________ menu is used to add headings to a chart.
3. The ____________ command from the ________ menu is used to start a new chart.
4. List one other method of starting a new chart.

   ____

5. What is the first step prior to choosing a new chart option?

   ____

6. Match each of the following to the correct term.

   _____ The values on the vertical axis
   _____ The labels along the horizontal axis
   _____ The component of a chart that identifies each unique bar or line
   _____ The identifying labels in a pie chart
   _____ The text in a chart that shows information about every bar or line

   a. X-series
   b. X-axis
   c. Y-axis
   d. legend
   e. data labels

7. Chart type is changed using which dialog box?

____

8. Adding values to each of the bars in a bar chart is done through which dialog box?

____

9. The __________ command from the ____________ menu is used to rename or delete a chart.

True or False:

10. _______ Charts may be printed using both the Print command from the Print menu and the Print Preview.

Hands-on Exercises

Exercise 1

1. Open the spreadsheet **CH10HO2B.WKS**, which you created in Chapter 10, or retrieve it from the Instructor data disk.
2. Create a bar chart that includes the **Current Year** and **Next Year Sales** amount. Select both the boat names (this will include them as labels in the chart) and the current year and next year values in the spreadsheet before clicking on the Chart button or choosing **Tools, Create New Chart.**
3. Create an appropriate title describing the chart.
4. Change the series labels to show Current Year and Next Year. To do this, choose **Edit, Legend/Series Labels**, turn off **Auto Series Labels**, and enter **Current Year** for the first value series, and **Next Year** for the second value series.
5. Use **Tools, Name Chart** to name the bar chart **CH12BAR**.
6. Print a copy of the bar chart.

To create another similar chart based on different values

7. Select the values (not the headings) and create a similar bar chart on the five- and ten-year projections.
8. Change the series labels to **Five-year projections** and to **Ten-year projections** following the instructions given in step 4 above.
9. Include an appropriate title and subtitle.
10. Add boat names as category labels using the steps given below:

    To add category labels that are not adjacent to the values: (Boat names are separated from the selected columns.)

    a. Return to the spreadsheet.
    b. Highlight the boat names.
    c. Choose **Copy**
    d. Return to the chart.
    e. Choose **Edit, Paste Series**.
    f. Choose **Category**.
    g. Choose **OK**.

11. Adjust the format of the bar by changing the pattern and color of each series. Add gridlines to the background and use the **Gallery** menu to make the bar a 3-D image.
12. Name this chart **CH12SBAR.**
13. Print a copy of this second bar chart.
14. Save the spreadsheet containing these charts as **CH12HO1.**

Exercise 2

Integrating a chart into a word processing document.

1. Open a new word processing document and copy the logo from the document **CH11PR3.WPS** created in Chapter 11. (Hint: Open **CH11PR3.WPS** and select the logo. Then click on the **Copy** button, switch to the new word processing document, and click on the **Paste** button.)
2. Type the following text two blank lines below the logo.

> The following chart shows the five- and ten-year projection for sales above the projected 10 percent increase in sales for the next year. We feel that this projection is a modest one. It shows a 25 percent increase in sales beyond next year's for a total 35 percent increase during the next six years. Another 25 percent increase is projected for the five years following. This averages to an approximate 58 percent increase in the next eleven years.

3. Open **CH12TUT.**
4. Highlight all cells **A1:F13.**
5. Assign a range name to the selection. (Hint: Use a **Range Name** from the **Insert** menu.)
6. Move to the word processing document.
7. Insert the spreadsheet range at the bottom of this document. (Hint: Use the **Insert** menu.)
8. Insert the chart, **Sales Chart1**, below the spreadsheet. (Hint: If you need help here, use the steps given in the instructions under Heading 1, "Printing a Chart and Spreadsheet Together.")

   The finished document should appear similar to the one shown below in Print Preview.

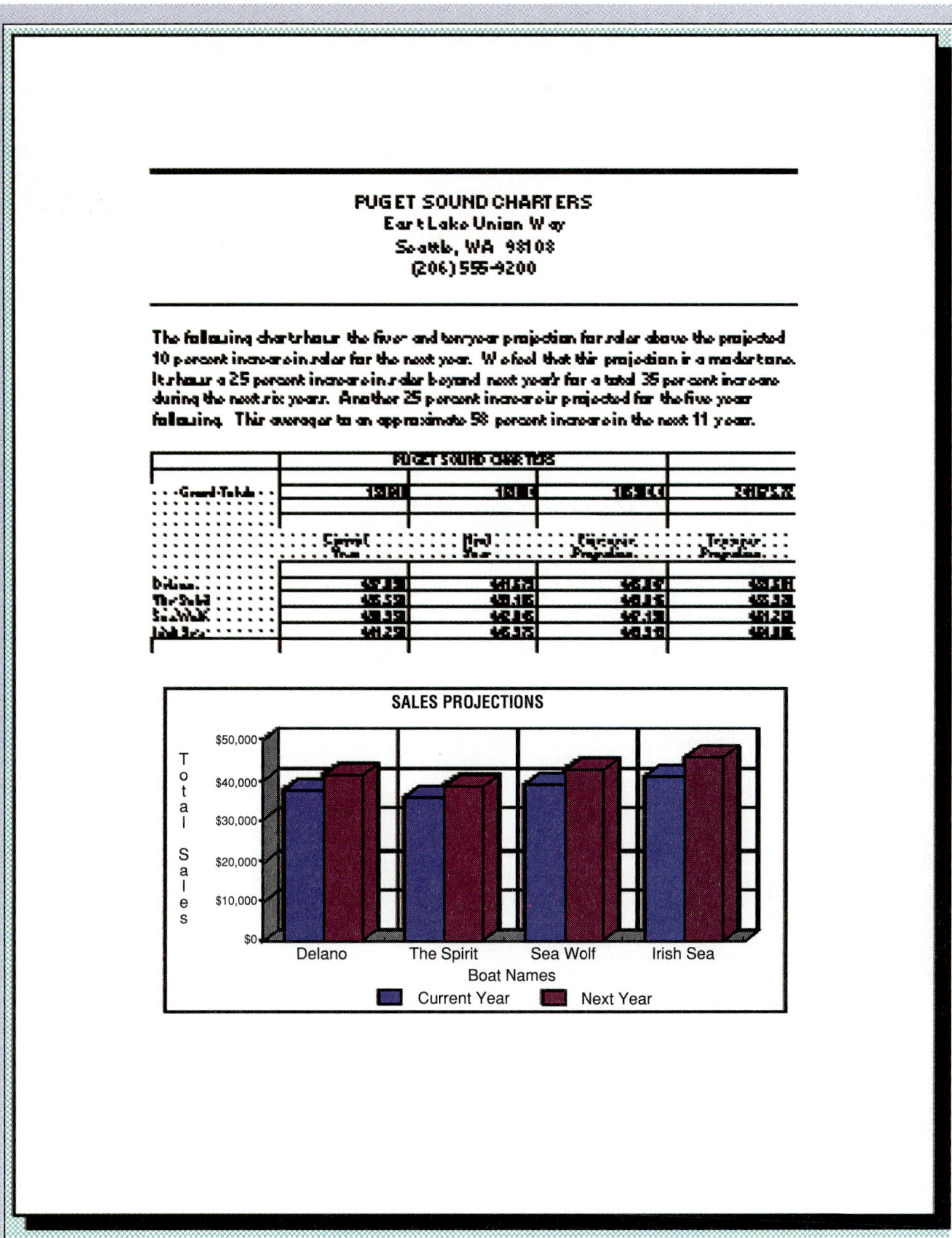

9. Run a spell check and then save this document as **CH12HO2**.
10. Print a copy.

Exercise 3

1. Retrieve **CH10HO3** from your data disk.
2. Delete blank row 4. Now, if you select the items in Column A along with the values, these labels will show in the chart—if the blank line was included in the selection the labels in Column A would not show in the chart. Also, when you

delete the blank line, you will not have a box at the bottom of the chart with no label for it. (If blank lines are selected, they are included in the chart which is why you may see extra boxes.)

2. Create a bar chart showing a comparison of all expenditures for January through March. Include the labels in Column A in the selected cells. (You can abbreviate the items in Column A in the spreadsheet so that the labels in the chart are easier to read.) Add an appropriate title and subtitle.
3. Name the bar chart **CH12BAR.**
4. Print a copy of the chart.
5. Create another chart as a 3-D line chart. Save this chart as **CH12LINE** and print a copy.
6. Create a pie chart on all average values for the three months.
7. Change the settings of the pie chart to 3-D pie and include the following:
   a. an exploded section showing the greatest value.
   b. each section displayed in different patterns and colors.
   c. an appropriate main heading.
   d. the name of the month identifying each section using **Edit, Data Labels.**
   e. values identifying each section of the pie.
8. Rename the pie chart CH12PIE and print a copy.
9. Save the spreadsheet as CH12HO3.

Exercise 4

1. Retrieve **CH10HO4** from your data disk.
2. Create a 3-D area chart with a grid background on the five Crash Course enrollment figures for January through March.
3. Include an appropriate main heading, and change the patterns and colors of each of the area sections.
4. Choose **Edit, Legend/Series Labels** and enter dates for each series as follows:
   a. Turn off **Auto series labels**
   b. Enter dates in the Value Series boxes as follows:
      1st Value Series = January 15
      2nd Value Series = February 10
      3rd Value Series = March 8
5. Rename the chart **CH12AREA** and print a copy.
6. Save the spreadsheet as **CH12HO4.**
7. Close all charts and spreadsheets.

Exercise 3: Bar chart (CH12BAR)

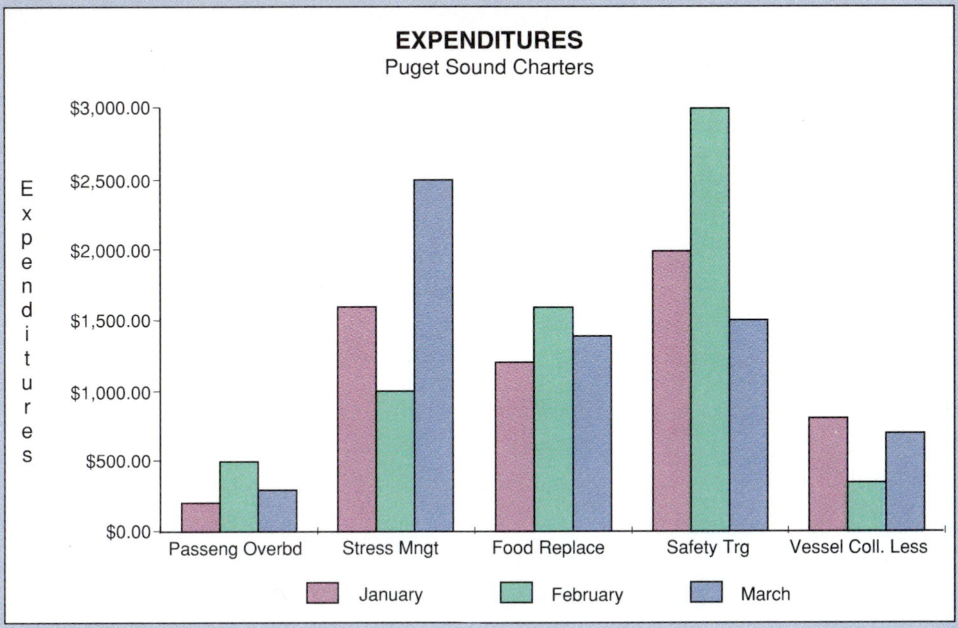

Exercise 3: 3-D line chart (CH12LINE)

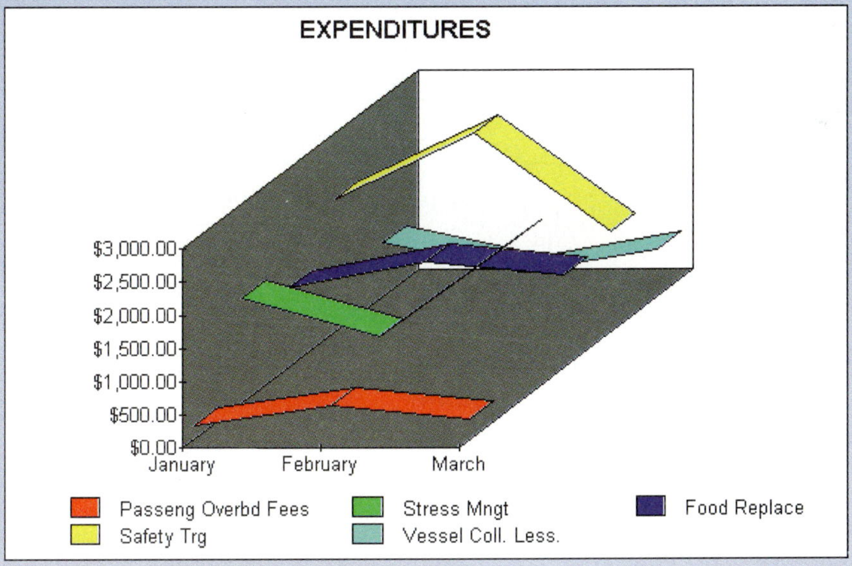

Exercise 3: 3-D pie chart (CH12PIE)

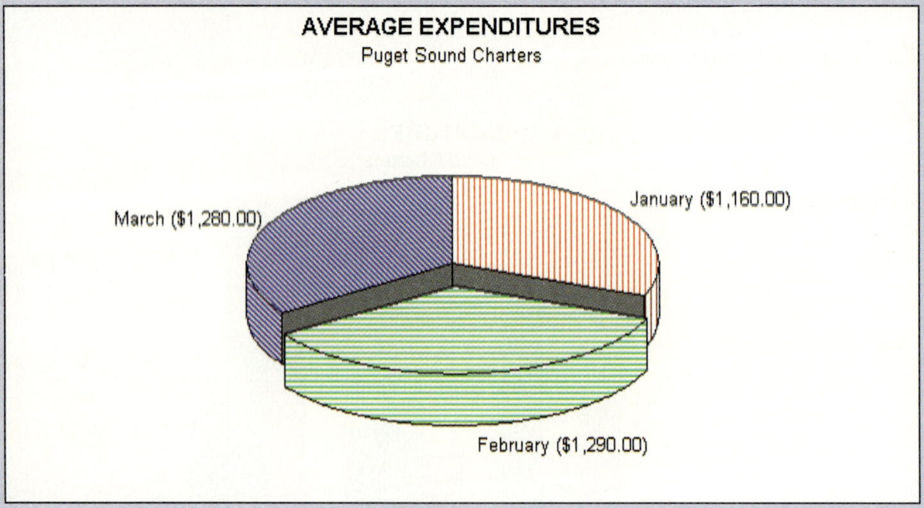

Exercise 4: Area chart (CH12AREA)

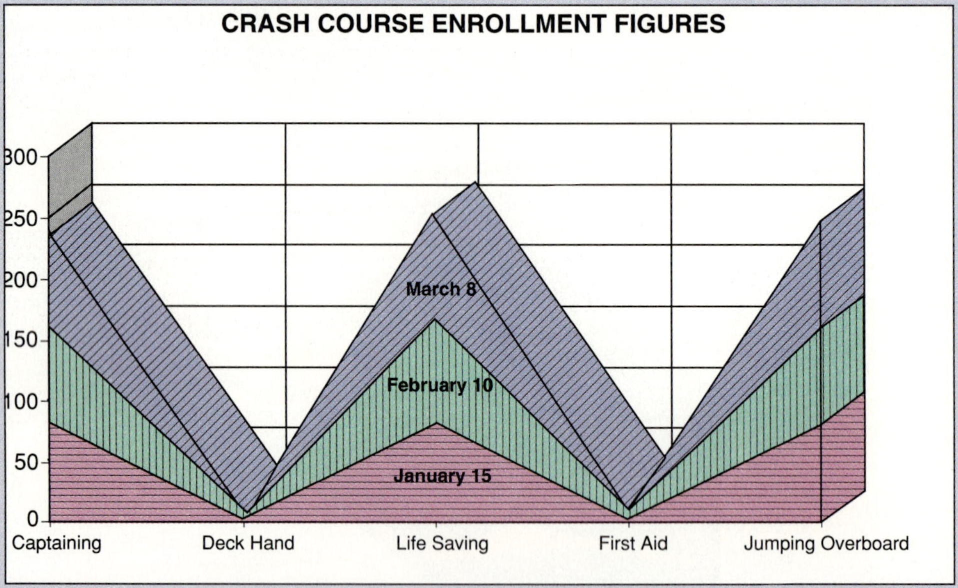

CHAPTER 13

Creating A Database

OBJECTIVES

Understand database design

Create a database

Enter data

Edit a database using list view

Edit a database using form view

Insert a new field in form view

Print data

PREVIEW

A database program is a system for using a computer to store information (data) in an organized fashion. Filing cabinets, address books, Rolodexes, and telephone books are all examples of databases. Information is usually stored in alphabetical order and grouped in various categories. A database management program, such as the Works tool, operates in much the same way. The advantage of using a computer program for keeping data is that you can use the program not only to enter and store the information but also to sort the information, to display it in forms, or to print it as a report.

UNDERSTANDING DATABASE DESIGN

Before creating a database, take some time to plan it. First, ask the question, What kind of output is needed? It is important to know what you want from the database prior to creating and storing the data in it. For example, you might want a report that shows several characteristics of a general population group, and then you might want to see the data sorted by age groups or by zip code area. Or you might want to know where most of your clients live or who are the clients—businesses or individuals—that use your service most often. You need answers to these questions to design the original database. In that way, the data you need can be available and easily retrieved.

Once you know what information you need from a database, you can answer the second question, What data shall I put into the database? Suppose, for instance, that you want to start a database system for Puget Sound Charters. You have decided that you would like some information on the demographics of its clients: who they are, where they work, the company or home address, city, state, and so on. You compile a survey to collect this data into a database file called CLIENTS. From this data you can create reports or do sorts and queries to gather information about the kinds of clients you attract. This is the basis of good database design.

After determining the answers to the questions about the output that you want and the information that needs to be stored to produce that output, you can then determine the *fields* that will be included that will store this information. Each field consists of both a field name and field entries (data) and stores one item of information—such as a name, an address, or a phone number—about the individuals listed in the database. All information pertaining to one individual is a *record.* In the Works tool there are some limitations to field names and to databases. Field names may consist of up to 15 characters. Information stored in each field can contain up to 256 characters, and each record can contain up to 256 fields. A database file can contain up to 32,000 records.

In the example database discussed in the previous paragraphs, the fields would store the following information: name of the individual, name of the organization or company, address, and telephone number. It is also advisable to include a unique identifier for each of the clients. This identifier could be a client ID number. This number improves the accuracy of queries and also avoids replication of data such as storing two or more identical records. The exact field names that store this information could be:

Client id
Lname
Fname
Company
Address
City
State
Zip
Phone

Planning a database is critical. It is a good idea to sketch on paper what you want in a database file before you create it in Works.

CREATING A DATABASE

Creating a database is similar to creating any other Works file. You can choose the Database tool from the Startup dialog box, or if you are already in a Works tool window, choose File, Create New File.

Open a Database Window

In this section create a database that stores the information about Puget Sound Charters' clients and contains the field names just listed above.

1. **Start** up Works and go to the Startup dialog box.
2. **Choose** **Database** 

.

Or if you are in a Works window,

Choose **File, Create New File** to return to the Startup dialog box and then choose **Database**. The Works screen now displays the **Data1** window as shown in Figure 13-1. See Table 13-1 for an explanation of the parts of the database window.

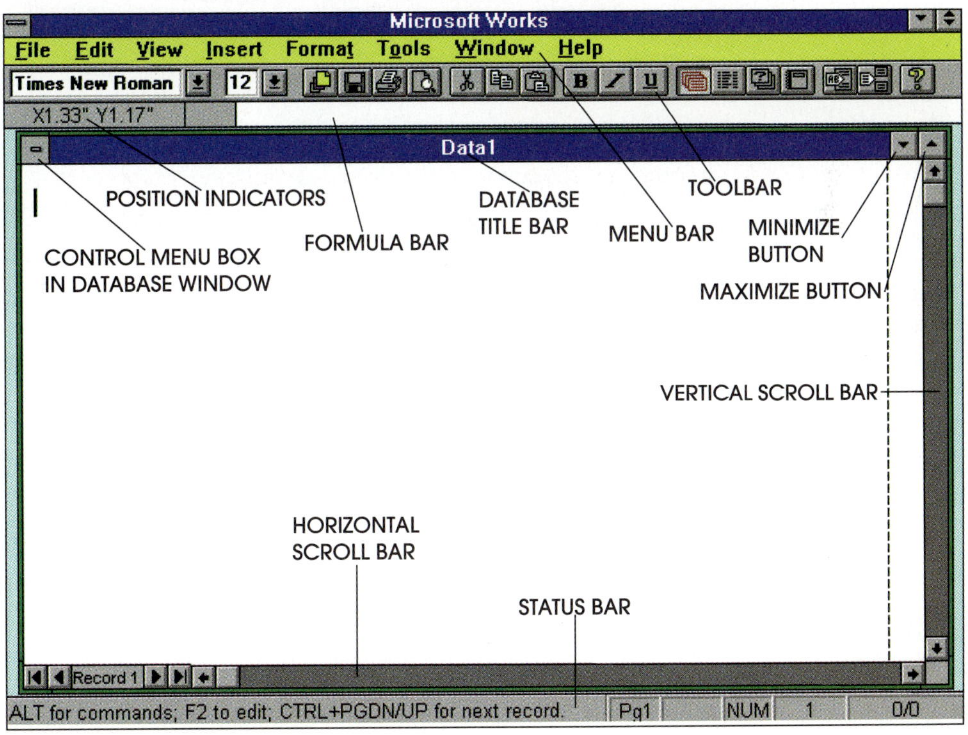

Figure 13-1
The database window

The following table gives a list of the components of the database window and a description of each.

Table 13-1

The components of the database window

Item	Description
Control menu box in database window	Click on this icon to close the current database window, switch to the next window, or restore, move, size, minimize, or maximize the current window.
Position indicators	Display the position of the insertion point as defined by X and Y axes.
Formula bar	The bar where text and formulas are displayed as they are typed in fields. Edits are made to text in the formula bar just as in a spreadsheet.
Toolbar	Displays the buttons that are available for use in the database window. Table 13-2 lists the buttons and describes each.
Menu bar	Similar to the word processor and spreadsheet menus and is used to perform various Works functions in the database window.
Database title bar	Displays the active filename. If the file is not named, a default title, Data#, is displayed.
Minimize button	Reduces the window to an icon.
Maximize button	Enlarges the window to full screen size.
Vertical scroll bar	Drag the shaded box up or down, or click on the up or down arrows to move the data up or down in the window.
Horizontal scroll bar	Drag the shaded box to the left or right, or click on the arrows to move the display from left to right. You can also click on the arrows on either side of the Record# to move to other records as shown in this example. 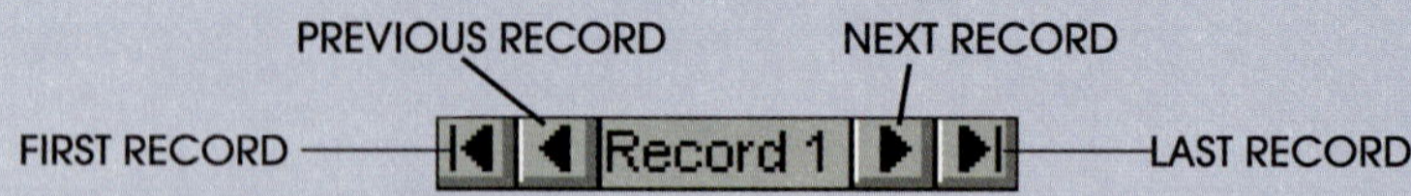
Status bar	Displays instructions to press **Alt** to access the menu bar, press **F2** to edit, press **Ctrl/Page Down** or **Ctrl/Page Up** for next record, as well as shows the page number and the number of records.

The toolbar that is available in the database window is similar to the toolbar in the word processor and in the spreadsheet windows-the buttons from the Font Name through the Underline buttons are the same in all windows; however, there are several different buttons that are used only for the database. Table 13-2 lists these new buttons and describes each.

Button	Description
Form View	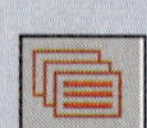 The default view for the database window. It displays all fields in each record. The fields can be arranged to resemble a printed form.

Button		Description
List View		Shows all information in a table format in columns and rows. Each row is a record and each column is a field.
Query View		Use Query View to search for specific records based on conditions that you can enter in the query view screen.
Report View	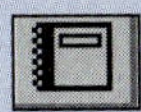	Use this view to rearrange the fields in a format that you want to print. You can also group data in a report and enter formulas that perform calculations on groups of data.
Insert Field	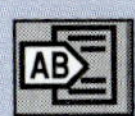	Allows you to name a field and specify its size-width and height.
Insert Record	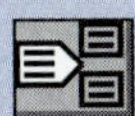	Allows you to insert information at any position in the database based on the fields that have been included in the file.
Learning Works		Goes to the Learning Works dialog box where you can choose from among several options that will help you learn to use Works.

Table 13-2

The toolbar in the database window

Create a Database in Form View

You are now ready to enter the fields for the database. The field names are: Client ID, Lname, Fname, Company, Address, City, State, Zip, and Phone.

1. Move the insertion point to X1.33" Y1.17" (top left corner of the screen) if it is not already there.

NOTE: X is the horizontal position. Y is the vertical position.

2. Click on the Insert Field button  , or choose **Insert, Field** to display the Insert Field dialog box as shown in Figure 13-2.

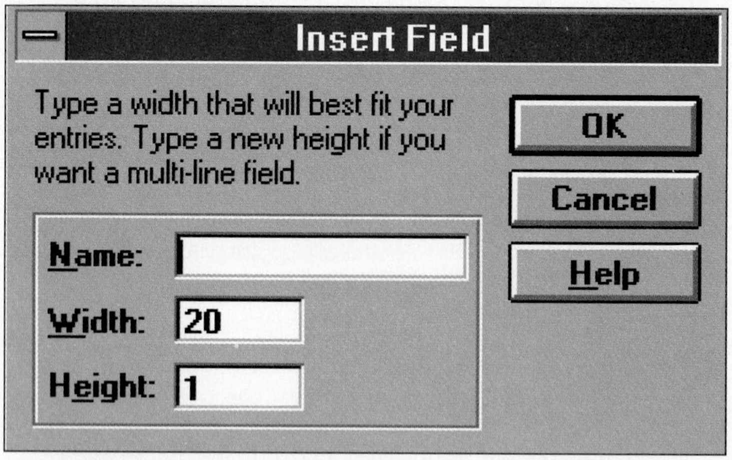

Figure 13-2
The Insert Field dialog box

3. Type **Client ID** in the **Name** text box.

   NOTE: The field name can contain up to 15 characters, and can contain spaces.

4. Choose **Width** and type **5** for the number of characters that you can enter in this field.

5. Leave **Height** at 1 line. The Insert Field dialog box should now look like that shown in Figure 13-3.

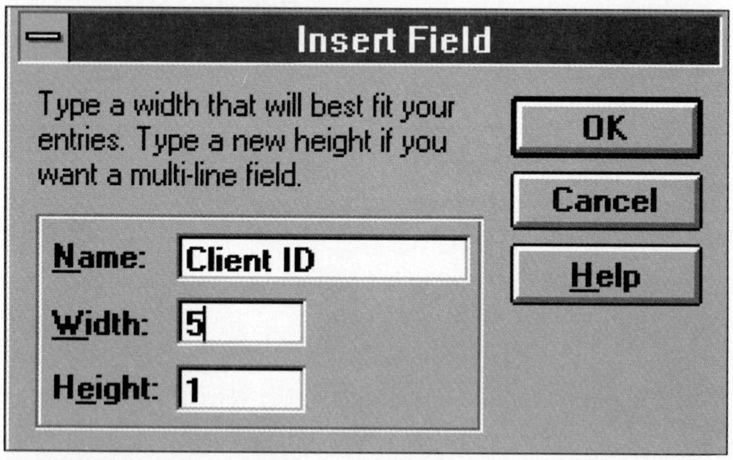

Figure 13-3
The Insert Field dialog box showing information in the text boxes

6. Choose **OK** or press **Enter** to return to the database window. The field is now placed at the insertion point as shown here. Notice the change in the position indicator box.

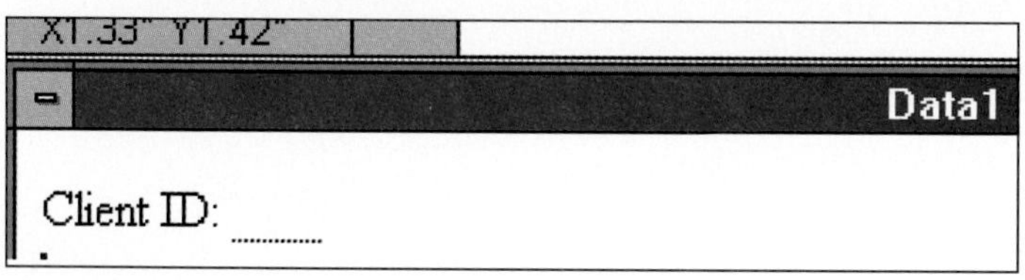

NOTE: All field names are followed by a colon, which is entered automatically when the field name is inserted. You do not need to type the colon in the **Name** text box.

Another way to enter a field name is to move the insertion point to the position where you want the field to be inserted, type the **field name followed by a colon**, and press **Enter**. A Field Size dialog box will then be displayed in which you can enter the number of characters for the field. Choose **OK** or press **Enter** to return to the database window.

To insert the next field:

7. Move — the insertion point to X1.33" Y1.50"—either click on the position or press the appropriate arrow keys to go to the position. This is two lines below the previous field.

8. Click — on the Insert Field button 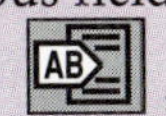, or choose **Insert, Field** to display the Insert Field dialog box again.

9. Type — **Lname** in the **Name** box.

10. Leave — width and height at the default settings.

11. Choose — **OK** or press **Enter** when done to insert the field. Your screen should now resemble the following example.

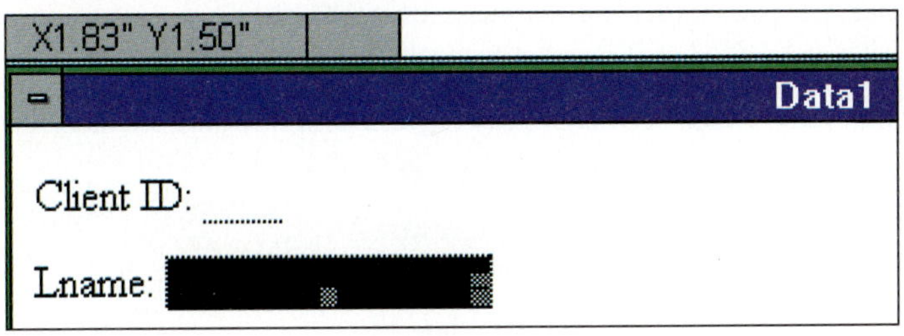

To enter additional fields:

12. Repeat — steps 7 (but move to a different position) through 11 above to insert the following fields. The position and width are given below; however, leave the height (number of lines in the field) set at 1 for each field.

Field name	Position	Width
Fname	X4.25" Y1.50"	20
Company	X1.33" Y1.83"	20
Address	X1.33" Y2.17"	20
City	X1.33" Y2.50	20
State	X4.25" Y2.50"	2
Zip	X5.17" Y2.50"	10
Phone	X1.33" Y2.83	12

When done your screen should resemble the following example.

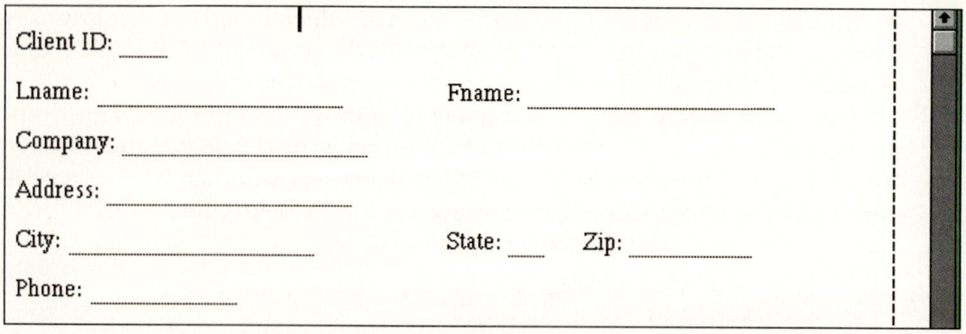

Save the Database

1. Click on the Save button, or choose **File, Save As** to display the Save As dialog box. See Figure 13-4.
2. Select the drive or directory to which you are saving your files if it is different from the default drive or directory.
3. Type **CH13PR1** as the name of the database in the **File Name** text box. See the example in Figure 13-4. The extension **WDB** will be added automatically to this file just as **WPS** is added to a word processing document and **WKS** is added to a spreadsheet file.

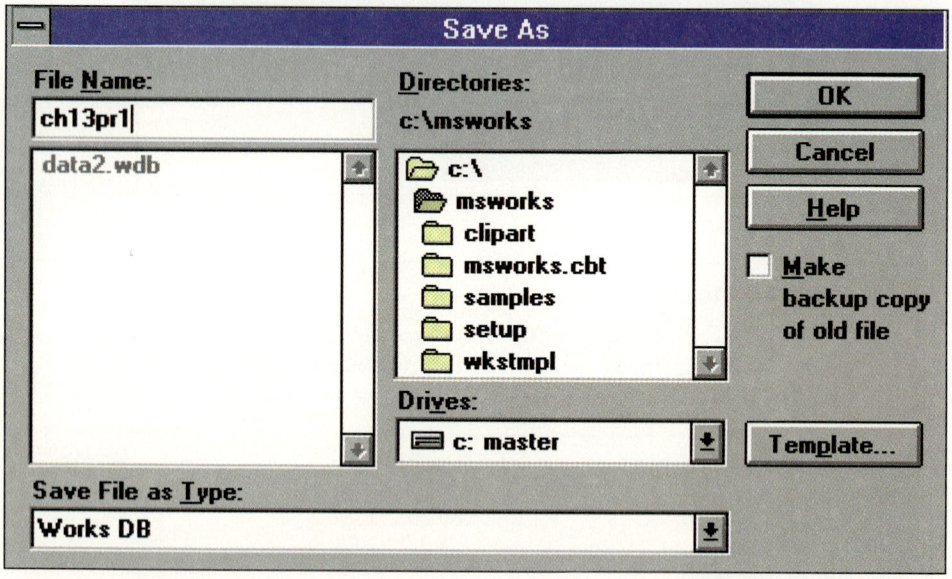

Figure 13-4
The Save As dialog box for saving a database

4. Choose **OK** or press **Enter** to return to the document. The title bar now displays the filename as shown here.

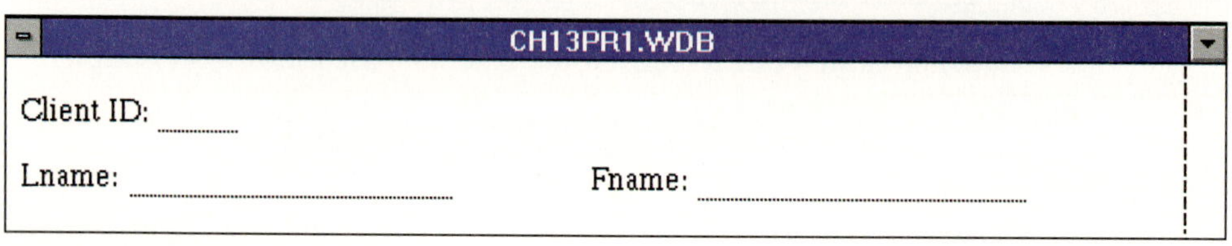

ENTERING DATA

You can enter data in either form view or in list view. In this section, form view will be used because it is generally easier to enter data in this view. In the following section, list view, which displays multiple records in rows and columns, will be used to edit data. In addition to entering data in fields, you can also insert formulas and objects in a database; however, an object can only be inserted in a database in form view.

Enter Data in Form View

1. Open the database **CH13PR1** if it is not already open.
2. Highlight the field to the right of **Client ID:** by clicking to the right of the field name or by pressing the arrow keys to move to the field. Your screen should resemble the following example.

3. Type **101** in the Client ID field. The data is displayed in the field and also in the formula bar as shown here. Notice the insertion point is now at the end of the text displayed in the formula bar.

NOTE: If you make a mistake as you enter data, press **Backspace** to delete the text and type the correction.

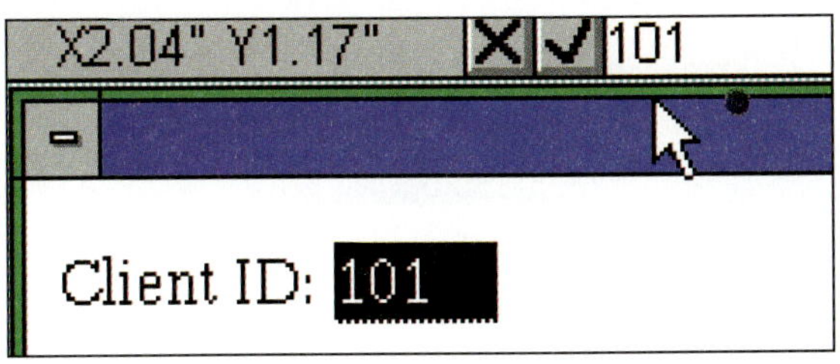

4. Press **Tab** to go to the next field as shown in the example here. The number **101** now appears only in the Clicnt ID field and does not show in the formula bar.

NOTE: You can also press **Enter** to return to the database from the formula bar, or you can press any of the arrow keys, or click on the next field to leave the Client ID field and go on to the next field. To return to the previous field, press **Shift/Tab**.

5. Type **Hammersmith** in the Lname field.
6. Press **Tab** to go to the Fname field.
7. Repeat steps 5 and 6 to enter the following data in the remaining fields.

Field	Text
Fname	Michael
Company	Software Unlimited
Address	1984 Newton Road
City	Seattle
State	WA (see the following note)
Zip	98102
Phone	206 555-1297

NOTE: As you enter data if the Client ID field is not large enough to display the numbers—number signs (#) are displayed rather than the actual numbers—on the screen, point to the right side of the field (the pointer will become a double sided arrow and show the word **Resize**) and drag the side to the right to increase the size. It is necessary to change the field size before printing in form view; otherwise, only the number sign will be printed.

In the next section, you will learn how to change the field size in list view.

When done with the first record,

8. Press **Tab** to go to the next blank record as shown in the following example.

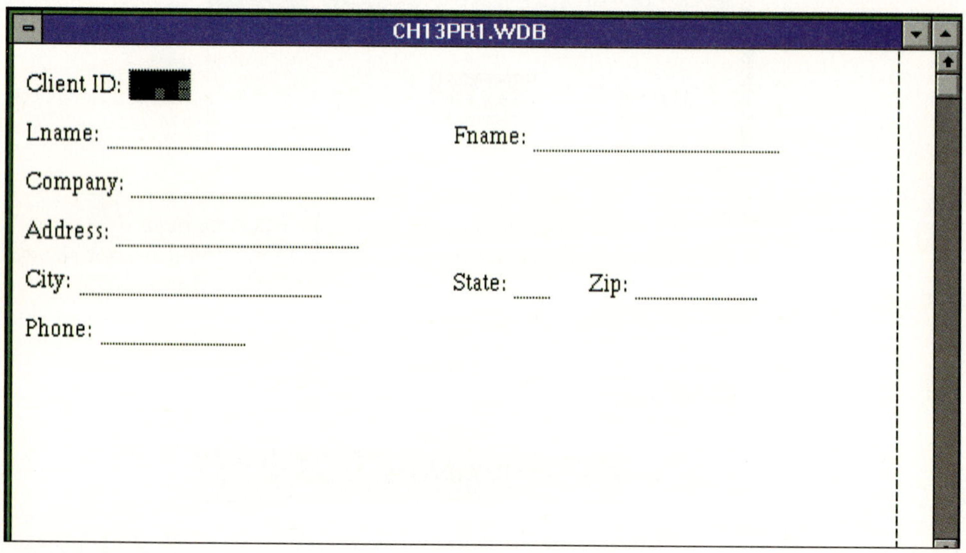

Notice that the status bar now displays Record 2. If you want to return to the first record, click on the left pointing arrow to the left of the record number or press **Ctrl/PageUp**. You can click on the right arrow to the right of the record number or press **Ctrl/Page Down** to return to Record 2.

9. Continue entering the following records. If you need to correct typing errors, highlight the field and press **F2** to move the insertion point to the formula bar where you can make corrections.

102
Ho, Selena
The Northwest Bank
1900 Wilson Plaza
Bellevue WA 98004
206 455-7855

103
Baker, Charles
IMS Consultants
19451 N. E. 45th
Seattle WA 98107
206 296-1278

104
Schuster, Simon
CTech Corporation
2100 Plaza Center
Kirkland WA 98032
206 883-1129

105
Sills, Bonnie
CTech Corporation
East Hills Branch
Tukwila WA 98152
206 925-5500

106
Long, Robert
Long and Tukes
9800 Plaza Suite
Bellevue WA 98007
206 454-9825

107
Krogstad, Sandra
Krogstad and Company
5125 Compton Way
Woodinville WA 98042
206 821-9978

108
Judd, Thomas
Software Express
North Cromlin Blvd.
Issaquah WA 98027
206 391-2857

109
Smith, Trisha
Julien's Computers
1001 South Plaza
Seattle WA 98108
206 284-9711

110
Grover, Douglas
Grover and Associate
123 Fourth Avenue N. E.
Seattle WA 98119
206 887-3455

111
Mills, Nevell
The Baldwin Co.
98 Baldwin Place
Seattle WA 98101
206 821-9942

112
Gonzales, Theodore
The Best Store
Century Plaza #20
Bellevue WA 98005
206 455-2396

10. Press any key to insert the last phone number.

11. Save the file again as **CH13PR1**.

EDITING A DATABASE

In this section, list view will be used to edit field sizes and also to edit information in the database. Because list view displays multiple records on the screen, it is easier to proof data than in form view; however, you can edit fields and data in either view. In list view, a column contains both the field name and the data entries.

Change to List View

1. Click on the list view button, or choose **View, List**, or press **F9**. Your screen should now resemble the following example.

	Client ID	Lname	Fname	Company	Address	City	State	Zip	
1	101	Hammersr	Michael	Software U	1984 Newt	Seattle	WA	98102	20
2	102	Ho	Selena	The Northv	1900 Wilse	Bellevue	WA	98004	20
3	103	Baker	Charles	IMS consu	19451 N. E	Seattle	WA	98107	20
4	104	Schuster	Simon	CTech Cor	2122 Plaza	Kirkland	WA	98032	20
5	105	Sills	Bonnie	CTech Cor	East Hills	Tukwila	WA	98152	20
6	106	Long	Robert	Long and T	9800 Plaza	Bellevue	WA	98007	20
7	107	Krogstad	Sandra	Krogstad a	5125 Com	Woodinville	WA	98042	20
8	108	Judd	Thomas	Software E	North Cron	Issaquah	WA	98027	20
9	109	Smith	Trisha	Julien's Co	1001 Sout	Seattle	WA	98108	20
10	110	Grover	Douglas	Grover and	123 Fourth	Seattle	WA	98119	20
11	111	Mills	Nevell	The Baldw	98 Baldwir	Seattle	WA	98101	20
12	112	Gonzales	Theodore	The Best S	Century Pl	Bellevue	WA	98005	20
13									
14									
15									
16									
17									
18									

Change Field Size

You can use either the mouse or the keyboard to change the field size. In several columns in this database, the entire contents of the field are not displayed. Editing the field size can increase the size of the field width so that all data is displayed. You can easily change the size of the field to display all data using either the mouse or the keyboard to access the **Format** menu.

To use the mouse to change the field size:

1. Double-click on the field name **Lname**. The entire column width changes to fit the existing data. See the following example.

CH13PR1.WDB

	Client ID	Lname	Fname	Company	Address	City	State	Zip
1	101	Hammersmith	Michael	Software Ur	1984 Newt	Seattle	WA	98102
2	102	Ho	Selena	The Northw	1900 Wilse	Bellevue	WA	98004
3	103	Baker	Charles	IMS consult	19451 N. E	Seattle	WA	98107
4	104	Schuster	Simon	CTech Corp	2122 Plaza	Kirkland	WA	98032
5	105	Sills	Bonnie	CTech Corp	East Hills	Tukwila	WA	98152
6	106	Long	Robert	Long and Tu	9800 Plaza	Bellevue	WA	98007
7	107	Krogstad	Sandra	Krogstad ar	5125 Com	Woodinville	WA	98042
8	108	Jackson	Karen	Supermarke	South Perl	Issaquah	WA	98027
9	109	Smith	Trisha	Julien's Cor	1001 Sout	Seattle	WA	98108
10	110	Grover	Douglas	Grover and	123 Fourth	Seattle	WA	98119
11	111	Mills	Nevell	The Baldwir	98 Baldwir	Seattle	WA	98101
12	112	Gonzales	Theodore	The Best St	Century Pl	Bellevue	WA	98005

or

Point — to the right side of the Lname column. The pointer displays the word **adjust** as shown here.

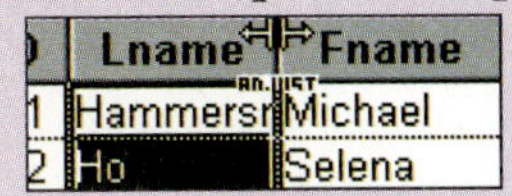

and drag — the right side of the Lname column to the right until the entire word **Hammersmith** is displayed, and then release the left mouse button.

To use the keyboard to change the field size:

1. Move — the insertion point to any row in the **Company** field. (Other columns are also too narrow to display all data.)
2. Choose — **Edit, Select Field** to select the entire column.

   NOTE: When you use a mouse, you can select the entire column by clicking once on the Field name at the top of the column.

3. Choose — **Format, Field Width** to display the Field Width dialog box as shown in Figure 13-5.

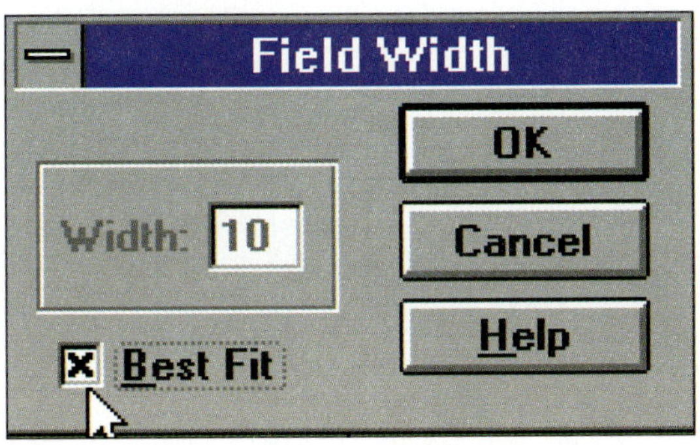

Figure 13-5
The Field Width dialog box

4. Choose — **Best Fit**. This choice will enlarge the field width to display all text in the record based on the most characters in the **Company** field.
5. Choose — **OK** or press **Enter** to return to the document. Your screen should now resemble the following example.

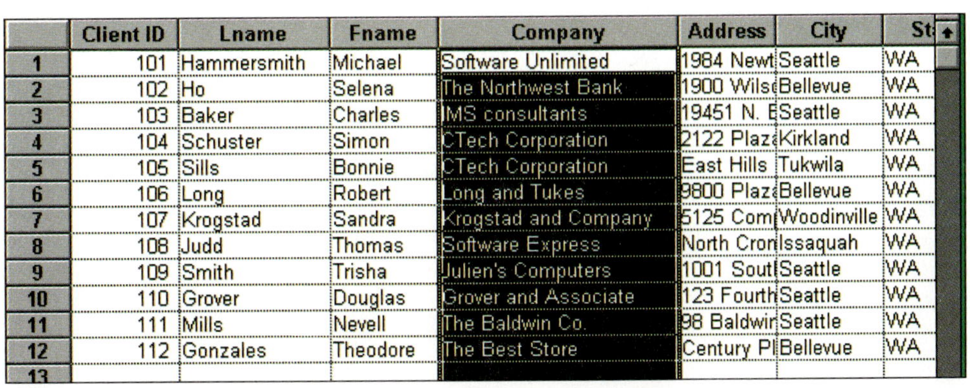

	Client ID	Lname	Fname	Company	Address	City	St
1	101	Hammersmith	Michael	Software Unlimited	1984 Newt	Seattle	WA
2	102	Ho	Selena	The Northwest Bank	1900 Wils	Bellevue	WA
3	103	Baker	Charles	IMS consultants	19451 N. E	Seattle	WA
4	104	Schuster	Simon	CTech Corporation	2122 Plaz	Kirkland	WA
5	105	Sills	Bonnie	CTech Corporation	East Hills	Tukwila	WA
6	106	Long	Robert	Long and Tukes	9800 Plaz	Bellevue	WA
7	107	Krogstad	Sandra	Krogstad and Company	5125 Com	Woodinville	WA
8	108	Judd	Thomas	Software Express	North Cro	Issaquah	WA
9	109	Smith	Trisha	Julien's Computers	1001 Sout	Seattle	WA
10	110	Grover	Douglas	Grover and Associate	123 Fourth	Seattle	WA
11	111	Mills	Nevell	The Baldwin Co.	98 Baldwi	Seattle	WA
12	112	Gonzales	Theodore	The Best Store	Century Pl	Bellevue	WA
13							

6. Repeat any of the steps using either the mouse or the menu to adjust remaining columns so that all data are displayed.
7. Save the edited database using the same name.

Edit Field Contents (Data)

With the entire contents of the fields visible on the screen, you can easily spot errors in the contents and make other editing changes. To change data, select the cell and press **F2** to make changes. Table 13-3 lists actions in the formula bar. Table 13-4 lists actions in both form view and list view.

1. Select any cell.
2. Press **F2** to move to the formula bar and then use any of the following actions to move around in data displayed in the formula bar.

NOTE: A quotation mark is inserted automatically in front of the data displayed in the formula bar. This identifies the text as data rather than as a field name.

Table 13-3

The actions in the formula bar

Press this key	To do this
Home	Go to the beginning of the line.
End	Go to the end of the line.
Left Arrow	Go left one character.
Right Arrow	Go right one character.
Backspace	Delete the character to the left of the insertion point.
Shift/Left or Shift/Right arrow	Select one or more characters to the left or right.
Delete	Remove a selected character(s).

3. Press **Enter** to move the insertion point back to the database window.
4. Use any of the actions listed in Table 13-4 to move around in the database in either list view or in form view.

In list view	In form view	To move to this
Left or Right arrow	Left or Right arrow	Left or right one field or cell
Up or Down arrow	Up or Down arrow	Up or down one record or row
Tab key	Tab key	Next field
Shift/Tab	Shift/Tab	Previous field
Home	Home	Leftmost field or cell
End	End	Rightmost field or cell
Page Down	Page Down	Down one window
Page Up	Page Up	Up one window
Ctrl/Home	Ctrl/Home	First cell in first record
Ctrl/End	Ctrl/End	Last cell in the last record
	Ctrl/Page Down	Next record
	Ctrl/Page Up	Previous record

Ctrl/Page Up	Ctrl/Left arrow	Left one window
Ctrl/Page Down	Ctrl/Right arrow	Right one window
Ctrl/Arrow keys		Up, down, left, or right by one block of data

Table 13-4

The selection movements and scrolling in a database

5. **Proof** the contents of the database and make any corrections.
6. **Save** the database again as **CH13PR1** after making corrections.

Copy Field Contents

Sometimes it is useful to copy field contents rather than retype them. For example, if you know that you have new clients who live in Seattle and have the same zip code, you could copy the contents of the fields for the city, state, and zip code to the corresponding fields of another record.

To copy field contents in list view:

1. Click on the List View button or press **F9** to switch to list view if you are not already there.
2. Select the **City, State,** and **Zip** fields for Record 7 (Woodinville WA 98042). To do this, select Woodinville. Then either drag with the left mouse button to the zip code number, or hold down the **Shift** key and press the **Right Arrow** to select all three fields. The first cell may be outlined and the two following cells will be highlighted.
3. Click on the Copy button, or press **Ctrl/C**, or choose **Edit, Copy.**
4. Select the **City** field in row 13 (the blank row at the end of the file).
5. Click on the Paste button, or press **Ctrl/V**, or choose **Edit, Paste**.
6. Repeat step 5 in row 14 to paste the same information to row 14.
7. Add the following data in rows 13 and 14. Press **Tab** to go from one column to the next. After entering all data for client 113, press the **Down Arrow** and press **Home** to go to the beginning of row 14.

113	114
Kimball, Elizabeth	Bell, Pat
Downtown Pets	The Furniture Emporium
23rd and Forest	2525 16th Ave. N. E.
206 832-8877	206 833-9000

To copy to adjacent fields using Fill Down or Fill Right:

These commands are in the **Edit** menu.

1. Select — the **City** and the **State** fields from row 14 through row 17 as shown in the following example.

13	Elizabeth	Downtown Pets	23rd and Forest	Woodinville	WA	9804
14	Pat	The Furniture Emporium	2525 16th Ave. N. E.	Woodinville	WA	9804
15						
16						
17						
18						

2. Choose — **Edit, Fill Down** to copy the information from row 14 to the fields in rows 15 through 17 as shown here.

14	Pat	The Furniture Emporium	2525 16th Ave. N. E.	Woodinville	WA	9804
15				Woodinville	WA	
16				Woodinville	WA	
17				Woodinville	WA	
18						

Move a Record in List View

You can move a record from one position to another in list view, if you like.

1. Select — the entire row (click on the row 2 label at the far left) in Record 2, or just select the first cell and then choose **Edit, Select Record**.
2. Click — on the Cut button, or press **Ctrl/X**, or choose **Edit, Cut**.
3. Move — the insertion point to the first field in row 13.
4. Click — on the Paste button, or press **Ctrl/V**, or choose **Edit, Paste**. The record is moved to row 13 and the records above row 13 have been moved up one row as shown in the following example.

12	112	Gonzales	Theodore	The Best Store	Century Plaza #20	Bellevue
13	102	Ho	Selena	The Northwest Bank	1900 Wilson Plaza	Bellevue
14	114	Bell	Pat	The Furniture Emporium	2525 16th Ave. N. E.	Woodinv

5. Repeat — steps 1 through 4 to move Record 2 (Client ID 102) back to row 2.

Delete Field Contents in a Row or Column

1. Select — the cells in the **City** and **State** fields in rows 15 through 17.
2. Press — **Delete** to remove the data.

Undo an Edit

You can easily reverse the last edit by choosing **Edit, Undo**. Be sure, however, the Undo command is invoked before you go on to perform other editing tasks; otherwise, you will not be able to reverse the edit.

1. Leave   the **City** and **State** fields selected in rows 15 through 17 as shown here.

2. Choose   **Edit, Undo Clear** or press **Ctrl/Z** to reinsert the deleted text.

Redo an Edit

The Redo command reverses the Undo command.

1. Leave   the **City** and **State** fields selected.
2. Choose   **Edit, Redo Clear** or press **Ctrl/Z** to remove the data again.
3. Save   the document again as **CH13PR1**.

EDITING IN FORM VIEW

Moving quickly from field to field using list view mode is usually the fastest way to scan records and make editing changes. However, using form view allows you to concentrate on one record at a time.

Edit Field Contents in Form View

Refer to Table 13-4 for keystrokes used to move around in a database in form view.

To change data in an address:

1. Switch   to form view by clicking on the Form View button  or by pressing **F9**.
2. Click   on the far left arrow in front of the Record # 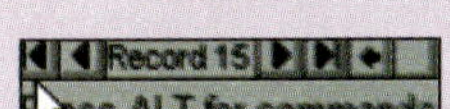, or press **Ctrl/Home** to go to the first record.

3. Click   on the right arrow to the right of the Record # 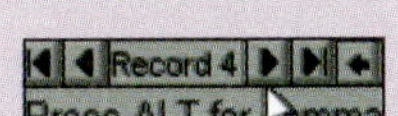, or press **Ctrl/Page Down** until you reach Client 104.

4. Select   the **Address** field.
5. Press   **F2** to edit the field. The insertion point is now flashing in the formula bar.

6. **Use** the arrow keys and the **Delete** or **Backspace** keys to change the number in the address to **2122**.

7. **Press** **Enter** to leave the formula bar.

Insert a New Record

As you entered data originally, you went automatically from one record to the next by pressing the **Tab** key. After entering data, it is sometimes desirable to insert a new record in the middle of a file. This can be done by clicking on the Insert Record button or by choosing **Insert, Record.**

To insert a new record at Record 8:

1. **Go** to Record 8. Confirm that this is Client 108. If you see number signs (#) in the Client ID space, it means the field is not large enough to show the number. Look at the formula bar to see the ID number.

   NOTE: You can drag the right side of the field-the pointer becomes a double-sided arrow and shows the word **Resize**—so that numbers are displayed in it.

2. **Click** on the Insert Record button  , or choose **Insert, Record.** Your screen should now resemble the following example.

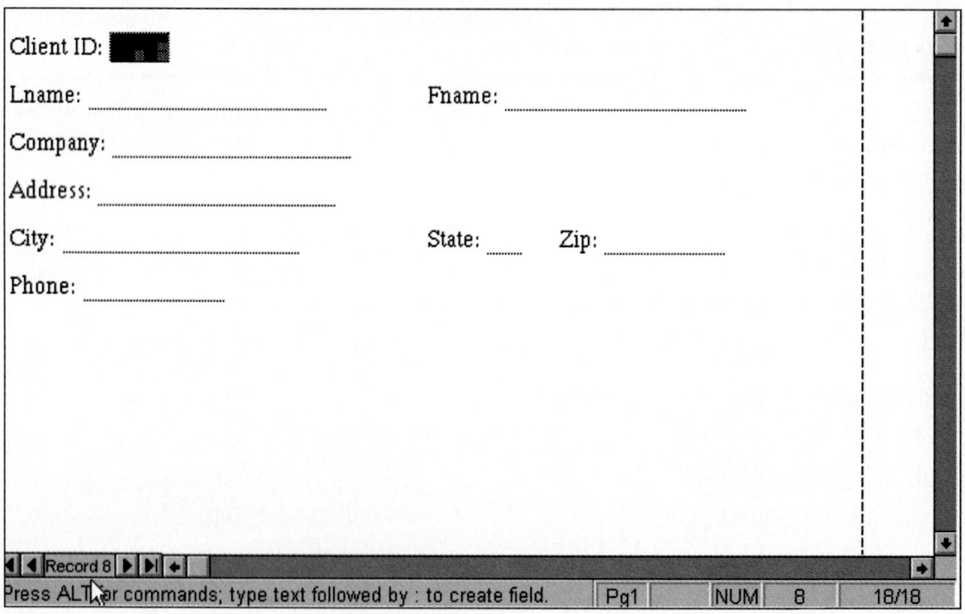

3. **Type** the following data for the new Client 108.

108
Jackson, Karen
Supermarkets, Inc.
South Perkins Blvd.
Issaquah WA 98027
206 392-5634

Delete a Record

As a result of inserting a record in the previous section, you now have two records for Client 108. The original record needs to be deleted.

1. Click on the right arrow at the right side of the Record # or press **Ctrl/Page Down** to go to the original record. (Thomas Judd is the client.)
2. Choose **Insert, Delete Record** to remove the original record.

INSERTING A FIELD

You can insert additional fields in a database at any time. Here, a new field called **Note** is added in form view. The **Note** field can be used to add information about the clients.

Insert a Field in Form View

Be sure you are in form view, if you are not already there.

1. Move the insertion point to X1.33" Y3.17" in any record.

2. Click on the Insert Field button, or choose **Insert, Field** to display the Insert Field dialog box as shown in Figure 13-6.
3. Type **Note** in the **Name** text box.
4. Choose **Height**.
5. Type **5** to format the field with 5 lines. See Figure 13-6.

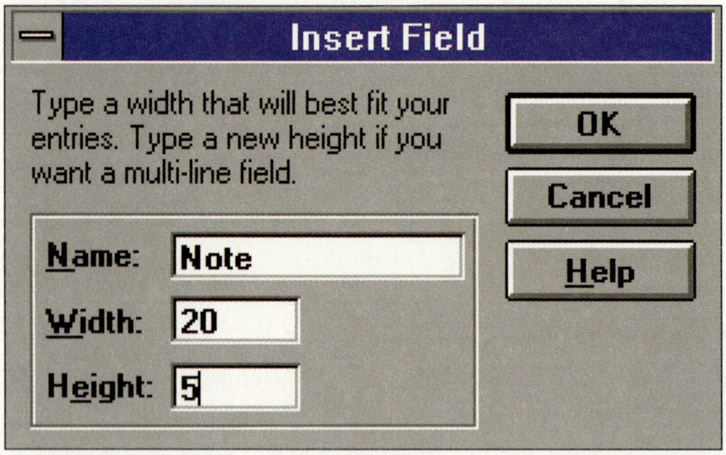

Figure 13-6
The Insert Field dialog box

6. Choose OK or press **Enter** to return to the database. The **Note** field is now in each record as shown here.

Enter Information in the New Field

1. Move the insertion point to the **Note** field in Record 9 (Client 109). All five lines will be highlighted.
2. Type **Requested additional information about charters.** Let text wrap to the next line within the **Note** field.

At the space following **charters,**

3. Press **Shift/Enter** to insert a paragraph mark to go to the next line.
4. Type **11/94** for the date and press **Enter** to leave the formula bar.
5. Move from one record to another to see the **Note** field in other records, if you like.
6. Save the document again as **CH13PR1**.

PRINTING DATA

You can preview the data and print it in much the way same as you print word processing documents or spreadsheets. You can do this from either form view or from list view. Form view will print each record on a separate page, and the field names will be printed. List view will print the records one after the other on the same page as they are displayed on the screen. In list view the default setting does not print field names and record numbers; however, this can be changed so that they, as well as the gridlines, will be printed. Additional pages can be printed in list view, if needed.

Use Print Preview

1. Be sure the database **CH13PR1** is open. Display it in either form or list view.
2. Click on the Print Preview button, or choose **File, Print Preview**.

If you are in form view,

3. Choose **Next** and **Previous** to move from one record to another. Each record is on a separate page.

If you are in list view,

Choose **Next** and **Previous** to go from one page to another if there is more than one page for the database. Next and Previous will be darkened, if there are additional pages.

4. Choose **Zoom In** and **Zoom Out** in either view to change the size of the display.
5. Choose **Cancel** when done.

Print Data

The following shows what happens when you are in form view

1. Click on the Print button to send all data directly to the printer.

   or

   Press **Ctrl/P** or choose **File, Print** to display the Print dialog box as shown in Figure 13-7.

NOTE: This Print dialog box shown in Figure 13-7 is displayed when you are in form view. The Print dialog box is somewhat different when you are in list view.

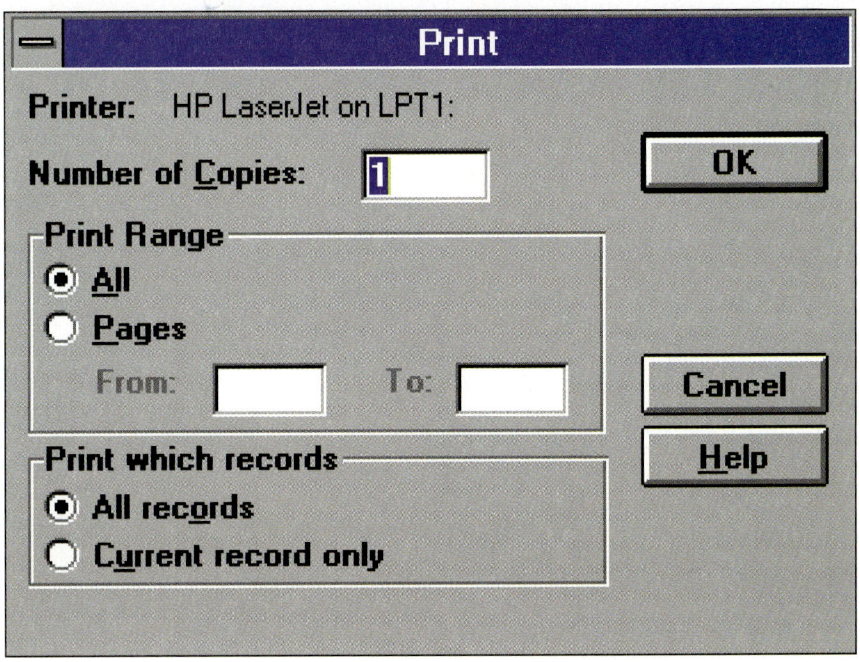

Figure 13-7
The Print dialog box

The options available in the Print dialog box for a database are described in Table 13-5.

Option	Usage
Number of Copies	Enter the number of copies that you want. If you choose only a specific page, this will print any amount of that page.
Print Range	The default is All. Choose **Pages** and then enter the beginning page number and the ending page number that you want printed. If you want to print only page 5, enter **5** in both the **From** and the **To** boxes.
All records	This is the default and will print all records in the active database.
Current record only	Turn this on to print the record in which the insertion point is located.

Table 13-5
The options in the Print Dialog box

If you are in form view

2. Choose **Current record only** and choose **OK** or press **Enter** to print only that record. If you leave **All records** turned on, you will print 14 separate records.

Or

If you are in list view

Leave the settings as is and choose **OK** or press **Enter** to print the database. Depending upon the font size that you are using, your database may be printed on three separate pages.

Print Field Names and Gridlines in List View

The **File, Page Setup** dialog box is used to turn on the command to print field names, record numbers, and gridlines.

1. Be sure the file **CH13PR1** is open and displayed in list view.
2. Choose **File, Page Setup** to display the Page Setup dialog box as shown in Figure 13-8. This dialog box contains three tabs.

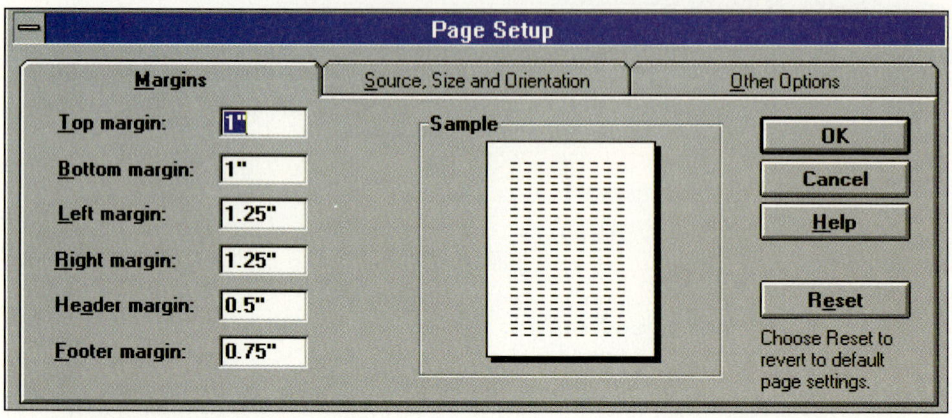

Figure 13-8
The Page Setup dialog box

3. Choose **Other Options** to display the Other Options tab as shown in Figure 13-9.

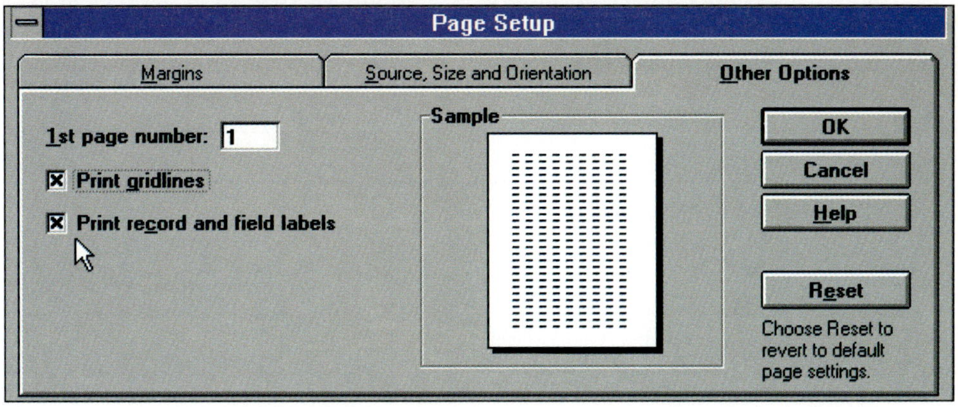

Figure 13-9
The Other Options tab in the Page Setup dialog box

4. Choose **Print gridlines** to turn it on. (See Figure 13-9.)
5. Choose **Print record and field labels** to turn it on as shown in Figure 13-9.
6. Choose **OK** or press **Enter** to return to the database window.
7. Click on the Print Preview button , or choose **File, Print Preview** to see how the database will look when it is printed.

NOTE: If necessary, return to list view and adjust column widths.

When the information is displayed as you want it,

8. Click on the Print button ; or choose **File, Print, OK** to print the database showing record numbers, field names, and gridlines.

NOTE: If you want to print only the field names and record numbers (not the gridlines), do not turn on **Print gridlines** in the **Other Options** tab in the **Page Setup** dialog box.

9. Save the file again as **CH13PR1**. When you save the database, the print settings are also saved, so the next time you print this file, the gridlines and field names will be printed automatically.

GUIDED TUTORIAL

What You'll Do

- Create a database file.
- Adjust column widths.
- Edit records.
- Print a database.

How To Do It

1. **Open** a new database window.
2. **Insert** the following fields using the widths given here. Use your own judgment in placing the fields in the form, but make the form similar to the example shown below. Leave the height for each field at 1.

ID Number	9
Last Name	12
First Name	12
Membership Date	6
Dues Owing	4

ID Number: ....

Last Name: .... First Name: ....

Membership Date: ....

Dues Owing: ....

3. **Save** the file as **CH13TUT**.

While still in form view,

4. **Enter** the following records.

ID Number	Last/First Name	Membership Date	Dues Owing
359345678	Randle, Colleen	1/2/94	3.25
329542198	Jones, Randall	1/3/94	2.95
295754444	Wilson, Richard	1/4/94	3.80
329951897	Costner, Jeremy	1/5/94	2.00
297882917	Mitchell, Sandra	1/4/94	4.00
278374758	Madsen, Olivia	1/3/94	3.00
378577611	Petrella, Harold	1/5/94	3.95
278574199	Ferrier, Karen	1/4/94	3.50
327899511	Jackson, Martha	1/3/94	3.60
547178594	McReynolds, Sally	1/2/94	3.70

5. Change to list view—either click on the List View button , or press **F9** and move to the beginning of the file.

6. Adjust the width of all the fields so that all data and field names are visible. Either drag the right side of a field or double-click on the field name to enlarge it. The following example shows how your file should look.

	ID Number	Last Name	First Name	Membership Date	Dues Owing
1	359345678	Randle	Colleen	1/2/94	3.25
2	329542198	Jones	Randall	1/3/94	2.95
3	295754444	Wilson	Richard	1/4/94	3.8
4	329951897	Costner	Jeremy	1/5/94	2
5	297882917	Mitchell	Sandra	1/4/94	4
6	278374758	Madsen	Olivia	11/3/94	3
7	378577611	Petrella	Harold	1/5/94	3.95
8	278574199	Ferrier	Karen	1/4/94	3.5
9	327899511	Jackson	Martha	1/3/94	3.6
10	547178594	McReynolds	Sally	1/2/94	3.7
11					

To use* Fill Down*:

7. Select the data in the Membership Date and the Dues Owing fields of the last record, McReynold's, and also select the row below it as shown here.

10	547178594	McReynolds	Sally	1/2/94	3.7
11					
12					
13					

8. Choose **Edit, Fill Down**. Your screen should now look like the following.

9	327899511	Jackson	Martha	1/3/94	3.6
10	547178594	McReynolds	Sally	1/2/94	3.7
11				1/2/94	3.7
12					

9. Enter the following information in the first three fields in row 11.

457882298 Newman Julie

To move the last record so that it is in row 12:

10. Select the entire row 11.

11. Click on the Cut button , or choose **Edit, Cut**, or press **Ctrl/X.**

12. Move the insertion point to the first cell at the left in row 12.

13. Click — on the Paste button, or choose **Edit, Paste**, or press **Ctrl/V**. Your screen should now resemble the following example.

8	278574199	Ferrier	Karen		1/4/94	3.5
9	327899511	Jackson	Martha		1/3/94	3.6
10	547178594	McReynolds	Sally		1/2/94	3.7
11						
12	457882298	Newman	Julie		1/2/94	3.7
13						

14. Repeat — steps 10 through 13 to move the last record back to row 11.

To insert a new record in row 6:

15. Switch — to form view by clicking on the Form View button, or press **F9**.

16. Move — the insertion point to Record 6. Confirm your position in the status bar, which should display the following when you are at the correct position. The Membership Date field displays only number signs (#) indicating it is not large enough to display all characters.

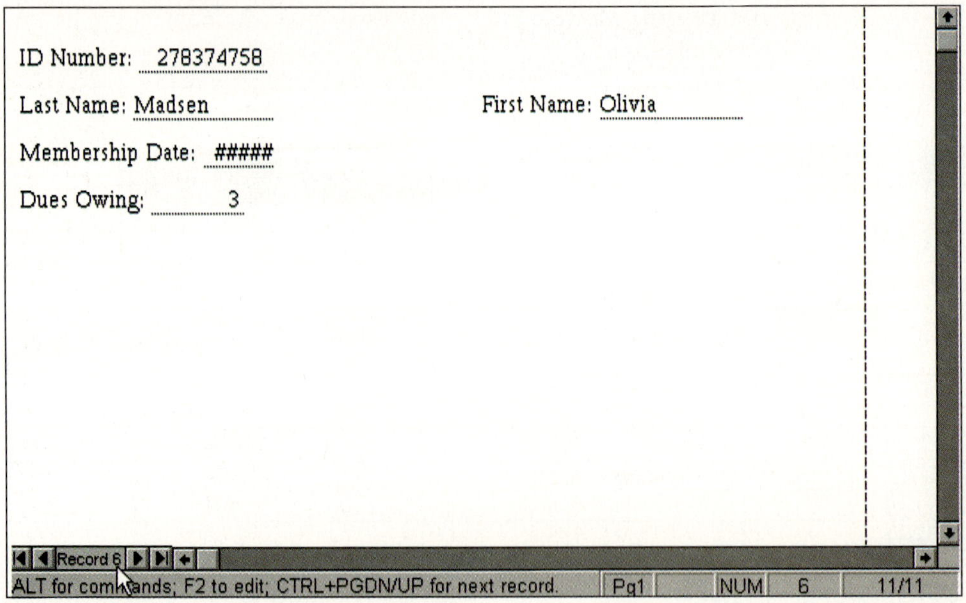

17. Drag — the right side of the Membership Date field to enlarge it enough so that all numbers in it are displayed.

18. Choose — **Insert, Record**.

19. Enter — the following information in Record 6.

238844768	Thiry	Jacques	1/5/94	4.50

20.	Save	the database again as **CH13TUT**.
21.	Print	a copy from list view and close the window.

REVIEW QUESTIONS

1. Define each of the following.

   Database

   ____

   ____

   ____

   Record

   ____

   ____

   ____

   Field

   ____

   ____

   ____

2. Identify each of the parts of the status bar shown here.

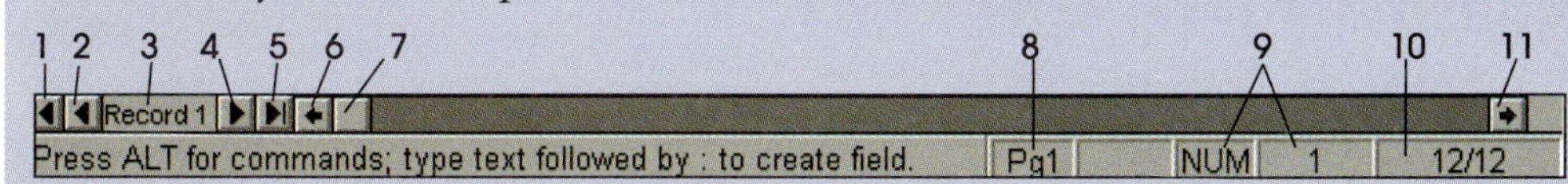

1 ______________________________

2 ______________________________

3 ______________________________

4 ______________________________

5 ______________________________

6 ______________________________

7 ______________________________

8 ______________________________

9 ______________________________

10 ______________________________

11 ______________________________

3. Identify and describe the use of each of the following buttons.

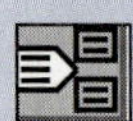

4. Use the ______________________________ command from the ______________________________ menu to insert and increment numbers or dates when filling in fields.

5. List the keystrokes used to move to the previous and to the following records in form view.

Hands-on Exercises

Exercise 1

1. Use form view to create a database file for the following survey responses, or retrieve **CH13HO1** from the Instructor data disk.
   a. The field names are: **Survey Number**, **Response**, **Date**.
   b. Use your own judgment in placing the fields and determining the width.
   c. Use either the Insert Field button, or choose **Insert**, **Field**, or type the field name followed by a colon (the colon is required to designate the text as a field name) in Field view, press **Enter**, enter the numbers of characters for the width, and choose **OK** or press **Enter** to insert the field.

2. Use either form view or list view to enter the following data in response to: Customers heard about Puget Sound Charters through one of the following media:
   NP = Newspaper* **M** = Magazine **C** = Current or previous client
   P = Phone book **O** = Other publication **W** = Word of Mouth **T** = Other

   * Enter NP rather than N because the character N is a reserved character used in database functions to indicate a Range Reference. Reserved characters are those used by Works in various functions. For example, MAX, MIN, IF, OR, NOT are all characters designating Works functions.

Survey Number	Response	Date
101	M	8/8/94
105	O	8/8/94
109	P	8/10/94
116	NP	8/10/94
107	C	8/11/94
122	W	8/11/94
126	T	8/12/94
138	P	8/15/94
104	W	8/15/94
126	P	8/16/94
148	W	8/16/94
129	O	8/16/94
149	C	8/17/94
152	T	8/18/94
106	NP	8/18/94

3. Save the file as **CH13HO1**.
4. Adjust the fields in list view as necessary.
5. Proof the records and save the file again as **CH13HO1**. Print a copy from list view. and close the window

Exercise 2

1. Create a database file to store the following payroll data. The field names are displayed in the first row. Be sure to type **Hours** with an "s." If you use **Hour** for the field name, you will not be able to use it later in a formula, because **Hour** is the name of a Works function.

Name	Salary	Hours	Total	Tax	Net
Kendall	15.50	45			
Snelling	15.00	42			
Randle	18.75	51			
Jensen	112.35	40			
Thiry	15.50	44			

2. Enter the data and adjust the column widths as appropriate.
3. Save the file as **CH13HO2**. This file will be used in Chapter 14 to enter formulas that will fill in the blank fields.
4. Print the file and close the window.

Exercise 3

1. Create the database file shown here. Use the following widths:

Description	15
In stock	6
Month	10
Rented	8
Cost	8

2. Fill in the data as shown here.

	Description	In stock	Month	Rented	Cost
1	crazy hats	100	March	2500	1
2	water balloons	1030	March	1250	0.5
3	roller skates	1500	March	500	2.5
4	roller blades	500	March	650	3.5
5	knee pads	2000	March	1300	1
6	life jackets	1000	March	100	5
7	skate boards	850	March	450	2.5
8					

3. Change the following values.
   In stock:
   250 crazy hats
   820 water balloons
   1500 knee pads
4. Edit each of the descriptions so that they begin with an uppercase letter as in the following example.
   Crazy hats
   Water balloons
5. Save the file as **CH13HO3**.
6. Change the width of the following fields using list view.

Description	20
In stock	8
Rented	10
Cost	10

7. Save the file again and print a copy from List View with gridlines and record and field labels.
8. Close the window.

1. Create the following database file. Decide appropriate field widths and fill in the data as shown. Use **Edit, Fill Series** to enter the **Event** numbers.

	Event	Description	Date	Destination	Departure	Return
1	1	Lake Union Roundup	7/1/95	Lake Union & Ship Canal	4:00 PM	8:30 PM
2	2	Loop the Locks	7/5/95	Elliott Bay	1:00 PM	8:00 PM
3	3	Islands A-Go-Go	8/12/95	San Juan Islands	7:00 AM	7:00 PM
4	4	Do The Lake	8/15/95	Kirkland	5:00 PM	10:00 PM
5	5	Ride the Waves	7/20/95	Snohomish River	10:00 AM	4:00 PM
6						

2. Adjust the column widths if necessary.
3. Save the file as **CH13HO4**.
4. Add a new field called **Hours** following the **Return** field, which will be used in Chapter 14 to store the computed total time of each trip.
5. Save the file again and print a copy in List View.
6. Close the window and Exit Works.

Example of Exercises

Exercise 3: CH13HO3

	Description	In stock	Month	Rented	Cost
1	Crazy hats	250	March	2500	1
2	Water balloons	820	March	1250	0.5
3	Roller skates	1500	March	500	2.5
4	Roller blades	500	March	650	3.5
5	Knee pads	1500	March	1300	1
6	Life jackets	1000	March	100	5
7	Skate boards	850	March	450	2.5
8					

Exercise 4: CH13HO4

	Event	Description	Date	Destination	Departure	Return	Hours
1	1	Lake Union Roundup	7/1/95	Lake Union & Ship Canal	4:00 PM	8:30 PM	
2	2	Loop the Locks	7/5/95	Elliott Bay	1:00 PM	8:00 PM	
3	3	Islands A-Go-Go	8/12/95	San Juan Islands	7:00 AM	7:00 PM	
4	4	Do The Lake	8/15/95	Kirkland	5:00 PM	10:00 PM	
5	5	Ride the Waves	7/20/95	Snohomish River	10:00 AM	4:00 PM	
6							

CHAPTER 14

Formatting a Database

OBJECTIVES

Hide field names and data

Add labels (text)

Format field names, labels, and data

Insert a new field in list view

Use formulas to display computed values

Protect data and form design

PREVIEW

In this chapter you will learn how to change the appearance of your database. These changes include hiding data in fields so that only specified information is displayed; adding labels such as titles to the database to help identify the purpose of the database; adding formatting such as bold, italic, and underlining to text; applying various types of number formatting to data; and locking data so that it cannot be changed by others who may have access to the database.

HIDING FIELD NAMES AND DATA

In some databases, you may want to hide field names and enter new text that better explains the contents of the field. Also, you can hide columns so that information in columns that are not adjacent can be viewed in one window. Or records that contain information that others should not see, can be hidden. You can hide information in either form view or in list view.

Hide a Field Name in Form View

In form view, hide the field names **City**, **State**, and **Zip** so that the information in these fields appears as it might be typed in an address.

1. Start — Works, if necessary.
2. Open — the file **CH13PR1**.
3. Change — to form view if you are not already there. Click on the Form View button or press **F9**.
4. Move — to Record 13 (Client ID 113, the first record with Woodinville as the city).
5. Select — the **City** field as shown here.

City: Woodinville

6. Choose — **Format, Show Field Name**. The option had a check mark in front of it. It is now removed and the field name is hidden as shown here.

Address: 23rd and Forest
Woodinville

7. Repeat — steps 5 and 6 to hide the fields **State** and **Zip**.

To drag the data so that the city, state, and zip are closer together on the same line:

8. Click — on **Woodinville** to select it and drag it so that it is under the beginning of the address information above it. See the following example.

Address: 23rd and Forest
Woodinville WA 98042

9. Repeat step 8 to move **WA** and the zip code as shown in the following illustration.

Address: 23rd and Forest
Woodinville WA 98042

10. Press **Ctrl/Page Up** or **Ctrl/Page Down** to move from record to record to see the change in the display of these fields.

To show the field names again:

1. Select any city.
2. Choose **Format, Show Field Name.**
3. Drag the **City** field to the left to its original position.
4. Repeat steps 1 through 3 for the **State** and **Zip** fields. Show the field name for the Zip field and move it to the right before showing the field name for the State field. This avoids overlapping fields and makes it easier to see what you are doing.

Hide Data in List View

In list view you may want to show data in nonadjacent columns in the same window. For example, here you will hide the company names and addresses so that the cities in which clients live will be displayed adjacent to the clients' names.

1. Click on the List View button or press **F9**.
2. Point to the right side of the **Company** field name as shown here

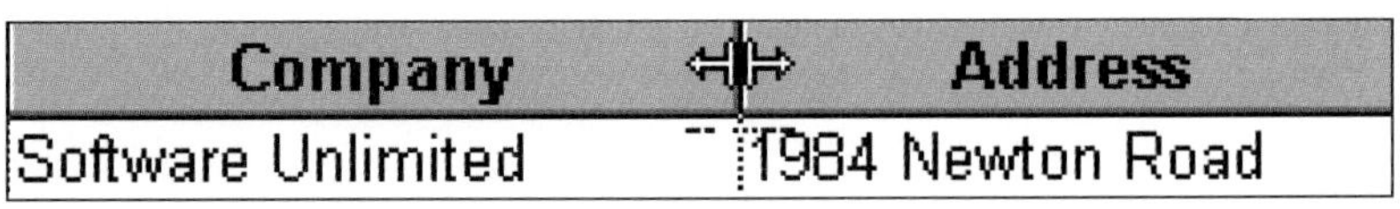

3. Drag the right side of the column all the way to the left side

   or

   Choose **Format, Field Width**, type 0 in the Width text box, and choose **OK.** (You do not have to select the column for this-just move the insertion point to any cell in the column.) The entire column is now hidden.

4. Repeat step 3 for the **Address** field. Your screen should now resemble the following example.

	Client ID	Lname	Fname	City	State	Zip	Phone
1	101	Hammersmith	Michael	Seattle	WA	98102	206 555-1297
2	102	Ho	Selena	Bellevue	WA	98004	206 455-7855
3	103	Baker	Charles	Seattle	WA	98107	206 296-1278
4	104	Schuster	Simon	Kirkland	WA	98032	206 883-1129
5	105	Sills	Bonnie	Tukwila	WA	98152	206 925-5500
6	106	Long	Robert	Bellevue	WA	98007	206 454-9825
7	107	Krogstad	Sandra	Woodinville	WA	98042	206 821-9978
8	108	Jackson	Karen	Issaquah	WA	98027	206 392-5634
9	109	Smith	Trisha	Seattle	WA	98108	206 284-9711
10	110	Grover	Douglas	Seattle	WA	98119	206 887-3455
11	111	Mills	Nevell	Seattle	WA	98101	206 821-9942
12	112	Gonzales	Theodore	Bellevue	WA	98005	206 455-2396
13	113	Kimball	Elizabeth	Woodinville	WA	98042	206 832-8877
14	114	Bell	Pat	Woodinville	WA	98042	206 833-9000

To go to a field:

Since you cannot see the field, use the Go To command to locate a hidden field to show it again.

1. Press **Ctrl/Home** to go to the beginning of the database.
2. Choose **Edit, Go to** or press **F5** to display the Go To dialog box as shown in Figure 14-1.

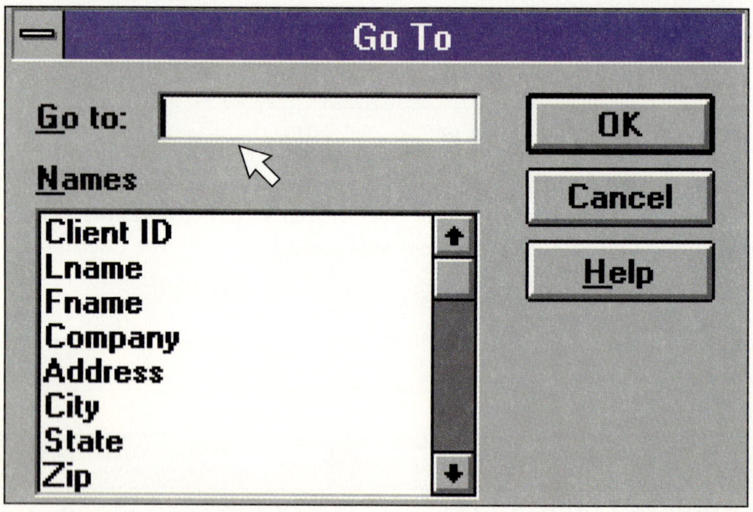

Figure 14-1
The Go To dialog box

3. Choose **Company** as the field.
4. Choose **OK** to go to that field. The data in the first record is displayed in the formula bar as shown here  , but the column is not displayed in the window. Notice that the insertion point is located between the Fname and the City fields.

To show the field in list view:

1. Choose **Format, Field Width** to display the Field Width dialog box.
2. Choose **Best Fit** as shown in Figure 14-2.

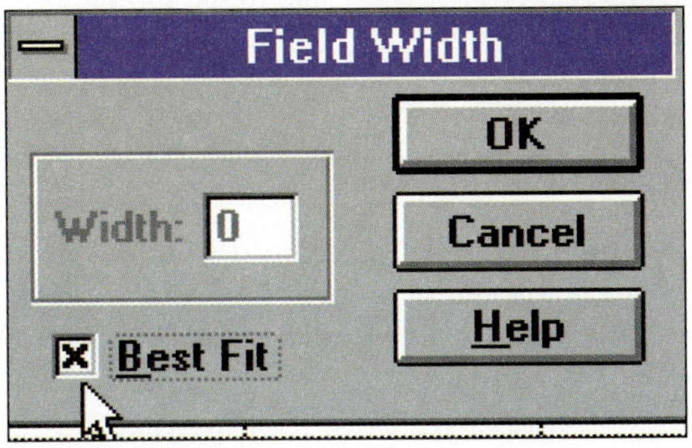

Figure 14-2
The Field Width dialog box

3. Choose **OK** to return to the database window. The data in the **Company** field is now displayed.
4. Choose **Edit, Go To** to go to the **Address** field, and then repeat steps 1 through 3 here to show all data.

ADDING A LABEL

You can add text, such as a title, that is not contained in a field in order to add information or explanations to your database.

Add a Title

Add a title at the top of the database that will show in **form view**.

1. Switch to form view-click on the Form View button or press **F9**.
2. Move the insertion point to X3.25" Y1.00" in any of the records in this database.
3. Choose **Insert, Label** to display the Label Entry dialog box as shown in Figure 14-3.

Figure 14-3
The Label Entry dialog box

4. Type **Clients for Puget Sound Charters, Inc.** in the text box.
5. Choose **OK** or press **Enter** to return to the database window. The title is now displayed at the top of each record.
6. Save the file as **CH14PR1**.
7. Close the database window.

FORMATTING A DATABASE

A database file can be formatted similar to a spreadsheet or a word processing file. The margins can be adjusted, fields and forms can be protected, and page breaks can be added to any database file. You can also format numbers and create formulas in database fields.

Format a Database

A new database will be created in this section.

1. Open a new database file—either choose **Database** from the Startup dialog box, or choose **File, Create New File,** to return to the Startup dialog box and select **Database.**

To insert a label at the top of the database:

2. Move the insertion point to X3.17" Y1.00" and choose **Insert, Label** to display the Label Entry dialog box.
3. Type **PUGET SOUND CHARTERS** in the text box.
4. Choose **OK** or press **Enter** to return to the document window.

To insert fields:

5. Insert the following fields at the locations shown (or as close to these locations depending upon the font you are using). Click on the Insert Field button 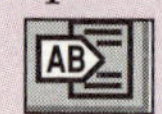, or choose **Insert, Field** and enter the field name, width, and height as listed below for each.

Field	Position	Width	Height
Invoice No.	X1.67 Y1.33	5	1
Invoice Date	X1.67 Y1.58	8	1
Client ID	X1.67 Y1.83	5	1
Boat Name	X1.67 Y2.17	20	1
Date Booked	X5.25 Y2.17	8	1
Hours	X5.25 Y2.42	2	1
Deposit	X1.67 Y2.75	6	1
Tax	X1.67 Y3.00	6	1
Balance	X1.67 Y3.25	6	1
Notes	X1.67 Y3.58	20	4

NOTE: In form view, if you need to change the width of any field, select it and drag on the handles, or choose **Format, Field Size** to display the Field Size dialog box and enter different measurements for the width and height.

Your final format should be similar to the following example.

PUGET SOUND CHARTERS

Invoice No.: ....
Invoice Date: ....
Client ID: ....

Boat Name: .... Date Booked:
Hours: ....

Deposit: ....
Tax: ....
Balance: ....
Notes: ....
....
....
....

6. Save the file as **CH14PR2**.
7. Click on the List View button or press **F9** to switch.
8. Adjust the column widths so that the complete field names are visible. Make the **Boat Name** field at least 12 characters wide.

Enter a Series of Values

If it is known that a series of consecutive values will be entered into cells, such as 1 through 10 for invoice numbers or dates from 1 through 20, then the **Edit, Fill Series** command can be used, which eliminates the necessity of typing each value individually. This command is similar to the **Edit, Fill Series** command used in spreadsheets that was discussed in Chapter 11, "Increased Spreadsheet Power",

Here the invoice numbers and dates can be entered using this command.

1. Select the first cell in the Invoice No. field, Record 1.
2. Type **501** as the invoice number and press **Enter**.
3. Select rows 1 through 10. To do this, point to row 1 in the Invoice field, hold down the left mouse button and drag to row 10. If you are using the keyboard, move the insertion point to row 1, hold down the **Shift** key and press the **Down Arrow** to row 10 as shown here.

	Invoice No.	Invoice Date	Client ID	Boat Name	Date Booke	Hours
1	501					
2						
3						
4						
5						
6						
7						
8						
9						
10						
11						
12						

4. Choose **Edit, Fill Series** to display the dialog box shown in Figure 14-4.

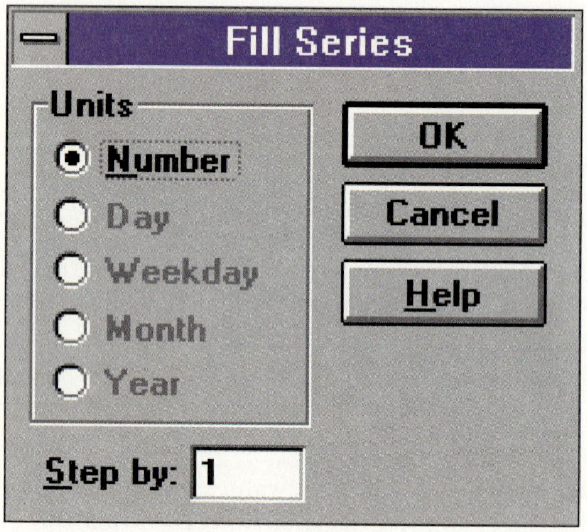

Figure 14-4
The Fill Series dialog box

The default Unit is **Number**, which will be used here since you want to enter invoice numbers automatically. And **Step by** will be left at **1** because the numbers are to be incremented by 1 unit in each cell.

5. Choose **OK** or press **Enter** to return to the document. Your screen should now resemble the following example.

	Invoice No.	Invoice Date	Client ID	Boat Name
1	501			
2	502			
3	503			
4	504			
5	505			
6	506			
7	507			
8	508			
9	509			
10	510			
11				
12				
13				

Fill a Series of Dates

As you can see, the Fill Series command can save a lot of time, and it can also be used to enter a series of dates.

1. Select Record 1 in the Invoice Date field.
2. Type **1/1/94** as the invoice date for Record 1.
3. Select the cells in the Invoice Date column from Records 1 through 10 as shown here.

	Invoice No.	Invoice Date	Client ID	Boat
1	501	1/1/94		
2	502			
3	503			
4	504			
5	505			
6	506			
7	507			
8	508			
9	509			
10	510			
11				
12				

4. Choose **Edit, Fill Series** to display the Fills Series dialog box. Because you entered a date, Day is automatically turned on. Leave **Step by** set at **1**.

5. Choose **OK** or press **Enter** to return to the document. The Invoice Date field should now look like the following.

	Invoice No.	Invoice Date	Client ID	Boat
1	501	1/1/94		
2	502	1/2/94		
3	503	1/3/94		
4	504	1/4/94		
5	505	1/5/94		
6	506	1/6/94		
7	507	1/7/94		
8	508	1/8/94		
9	509	1/9/94		
10	510	1/10/94		
11				
12				
13				

To complete the file:

6. Enter the following data in the appropriate fields.

Client ID	Boat Name	Date Booked	Hours	Deposit
105	Delano	1/20/94	3	100
113	The Spirit	1/25/94	4	200
102	Sea Wolf	1/15/94	4	500
109	Irish Sea	1/19/94	3	100
104	The Spirit	1/7/94	3	200
106	Delano	1/10/94	4	100
110	Irish Sea	1/27/94	3	200
111	Delano	1/28/94	3	100
114	Irish Sea	1/17/94	4	150
105	The Spirit	1/29/94	4	150

2. Save the file again as **CH14PR2**.

Change the Font and Size

As with other tools in Works, you can change the character font and the point size. The changes can be made for each field, or you can change the entire file if you select it and then format it with a new font and size.

To change the font type and size for the entire file in list view:

1. Choose **Edit, Select All.**
2. Click on the arrow at the right end of the Font Name button .

3. Choose **Times New Roman,** if that is available, or some similar font.
4. Click on the arrow at the right end of the Font Size button .

5. Choose 12 for the point size.
6. Click anywhere in the file or press an arrow key to remove the highlighting.

NOTE: You can change the font and style for an entire column by moving the insertion point to any row in the column (you do not need to select the entire column) and then use steps 2 through 5 to format it.

You can also choose **Format, Font and Style** and select the fonts and sizes from the Font and Style dialog box to format the entire document, an entire column, or selected cells.

Add Bold

Add bold to the title and to the field names in form view.

1. Click on the Form View button or press **F9.**
2. Select the title.
3. Click on the Bold button.
4. Repeat steps 2 and 3 for all field names. See the following example.

PUGET SOUND CHARTERS

Invoice No.: 501
Invoice Date: 1/1/94
Client ID: 105

Boat Name: Delano

Date Booked: 1/20/94
Hours: 3

Deposit: 100
Tax:
Balance:
Notes:

5. Save the file again as **CH14PR2.**

INSERTING A NEW FIELD IN LIST VIEW

In Chapter 13, "Creating a Database" you inserted a new field in form view. Here, you will learn how to insert a field in list view.

Insert a Field in List View

To insert a new field, Total, ***between the*** Deposit ***and the*** Tax ***columns, do the following.***

1. Change to list view-click on the List View button.

2. Move the insertion point to any position in the **Tax** column.

3. Click on the **Insert Field** button.

To enter a field name for the new column, be sure the insertion point is in the new column.

4. Choose **Edit, Field Name** to display the Field Name dialog box as shown here.

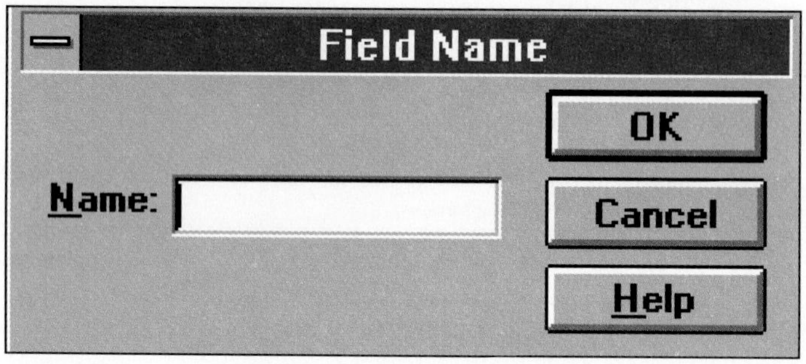

5. Type **Total** in the **Name** text box, and choose **OK** or press **Enter.** Your screen should now be similar to the following example.

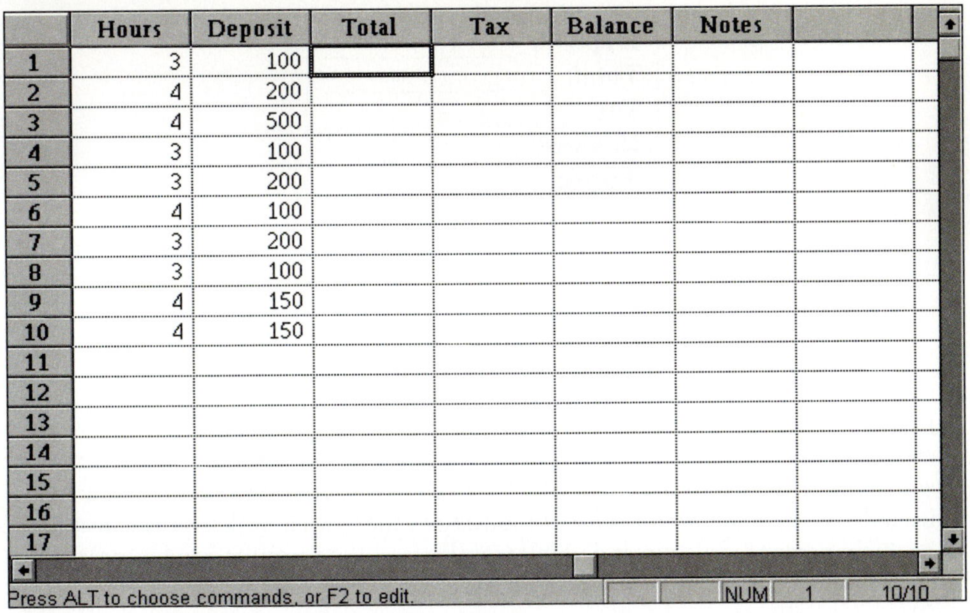

Move the Field in Form View

The new field will not be at an approrpiate position in form view,

1. Click on the Form View button. Your screen may resemble the following illustration with the new **Total** field in the upper left corner

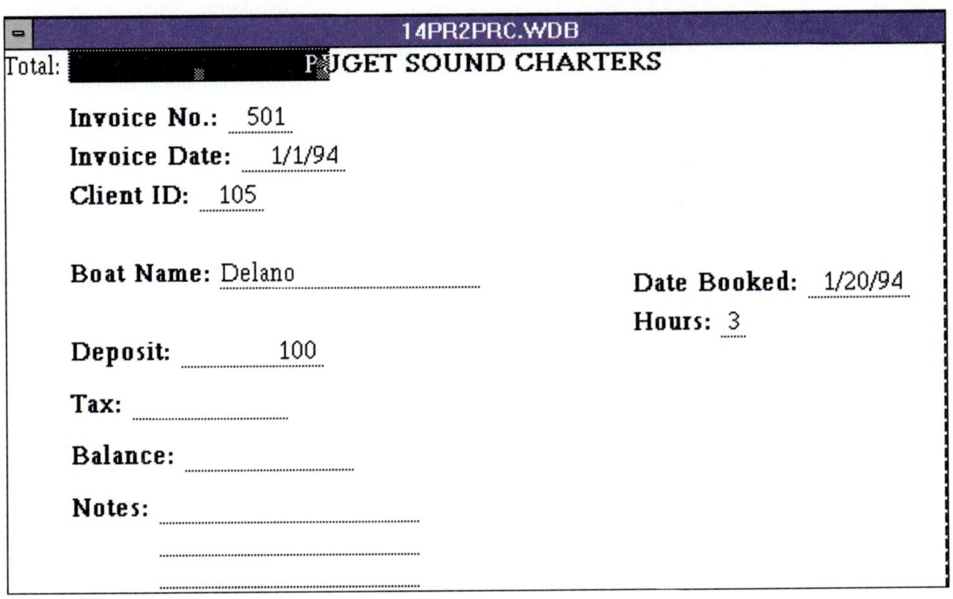

2. Point to the new field, **Total**, and drag it down to an appropriate position between the **Deposit** field and the **Tax** field. Make other adjustments to the form until your screen resembles the example that follows step 3.
3. Select the word **Total** and click on the Bold button to format it in bold.

Deposit: ....
Total: ....
Tax: ....
Balance: ....
Notes: ....
....
....
....

INCLUDING FORMULAS IN A DATABASE

Formulas are written into the cells which will show the computed value. They are written using the same symbols for computing as those used in the spreadsheet functions. Field names are also included in formulas, and the formulas can be entered in either form view or in list view. Both will be covered here.

NOTE: If you get an error message when you enter the formula, check the name of the field being used. If it is a name that is the same as a Works function, such as Hour, Date, or Rate, you will not be able to perform the calculation. Check the Works Help menu for a list of all Works functions.

As with spreadsheet formulas, all begin with the equal sign and can include the operands for division, addition, subtraction, and so on. Three formulas will be written in this exercise: (1) one that multiplies the number of hours by $500, which is the cost per hour for chartering a vessel; (2) one that multiplies the total amount by .08, which is the tax rate; and (3) one that calculates the balance by adding the total amount and the tax rate and subtracting the amount of the deposit.

Write a formula in form view

Be sure you are still in form view.

1. Select the field to the right of **Total**. You can be in any record.
2. Type **=Hours*500** and press **Enter**. The screen immediately shows the results of the formula as displayed here. The amount shown depends upon the location of your insertion point.

Boat Name: Delano **Date Booked:** 1/20/94
Hours: 3

Deposit: 100
Total: 1500
Tax: ....
Balance: ....
Notes: ....

Write a Formula in List View

1. **Click** on the List View button. The new **Total** values in all records are now showing.
2. **Move** the insertion point to any cell in the **Tax** field.
3. **Type** **=Total*.08** in the formula bar as shown here This will multiply the total by the amount of the tax.

=Total*.08

Deposit	Total	Tax
100	1500	=Total*.08
200	2000	
500	2000	
100	1500	
200	1500	
100	2000	
200	1500	
100	1500	
150	2000	
150	2000	

4. **Press** **Enter** to display the new values.
5. **Move** the insertion point to any cell in the **Balance** column.
6. **Type** **=Total+Tax-Deposit** in the formula bar, and press **Enter**. Your screen should now resemble the following illustration.

	Date Booke	Hours	Deposit	Total	Tax	Balance	Notes
1	1/20/94	3	100	1500	120	1520	
2	1/25/94	4	200	2000	160	1960	
3	1/15/94	4	500	2000	160	1660	
4	1/19/94	3	100	1500	120	1520	
5	1/7/94	3	200	1500	120	1420	
6	1/10/94	4	100	2000	160	2060	
7	1/27/94	3	200	1500	120	1420	
8	1/28/94	3	100	1500	120	1520	
9	1/17/94	4	150	2000	160	2010	
10	1/29/94	4	150	2000	160	2010	
11							
12							
13							
14							
15							

Format Data Values

You can change the format for values to the currency format, which displays numbers with two decimals. The default format for numbers is **General**, which displays numbers without decimals or commas.

1. Select any cell in the **Deposit** field.
2. Choose **Format, Number** to display the Number dialog box. See Figure 14-5.
3. Choose **Currency**. The Options box now displays 2 for the **Number of decimals** as shown in Figure 14-5. Also, the Sample box at the bottom of the dialog box now shows the currency format for numbers.

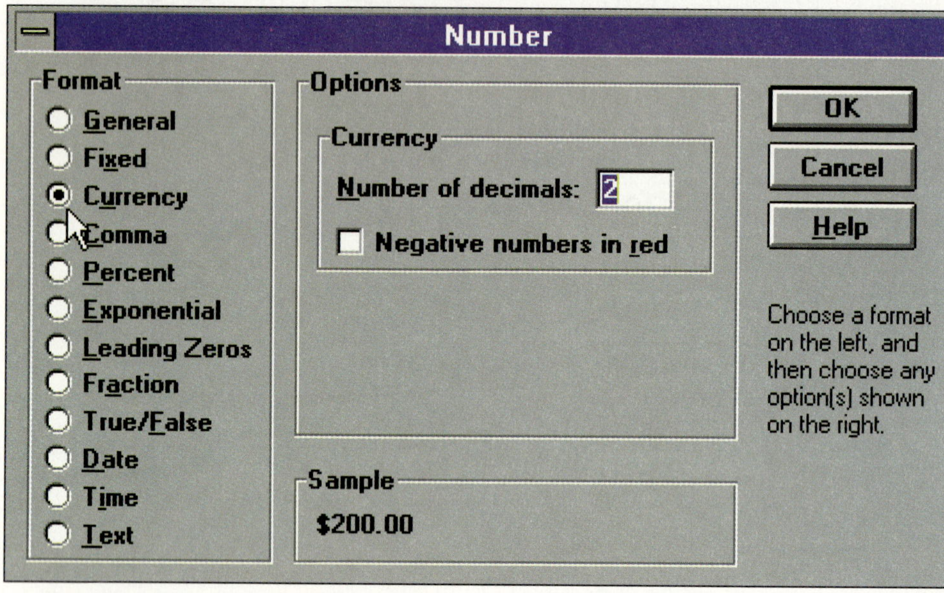

Figure 14-5
The Number dialog box

4. Choose **OK** or press **Enter** to return to the database window.
5. Repeat steps 1 through 4 to change the data value to Currency for the **Total, Tax,** and **Balance** fields.
6. Switch to form view by clicking on the Form View button.

NOTE: Some fields in form view may show a series of number signs (####) in place of the values. This indicates that the field is not large enough to display the values. To adjust the field width, select the field contents and either drag the handles to the right, or choose **Format, Field Size** and enter a large enough width to display the currency values.

If any of the columns in list view had also shown only number signs (#), you could adjust the size there by dragging the right border of the field name to the right; or by choosing **Format, Field Width** and entering a measurement for the **Width**, or by turning on **Best Fit**.

7. Save the file again as **CH14PR2**.

PROTECTING DATA

You can protect data from being changed by turning on Protection. This prevents others from making changes to all existing data in a file. You can also protect only specified fields, if you like. In addition, you can protect the form design from being changed.

Choose **Format, Protection** to display the Protection dialog box. **Locked** is on by default for all Work's databases; however this does not prevent you, or others, from making changes. **Protect Data** must also be turned on in order to prevent changes to all entries in the database as well as any formatting changes

Protect Data in all Fields

Open **CH14PR2** if it is not already open.

1. Switch to list view.
2. Choose **Format, Protection** to display the Protection dialog box.
3. Choose **Protect Data** to turn it on. An X is displayed in the check box as shown in Figure 14-6.

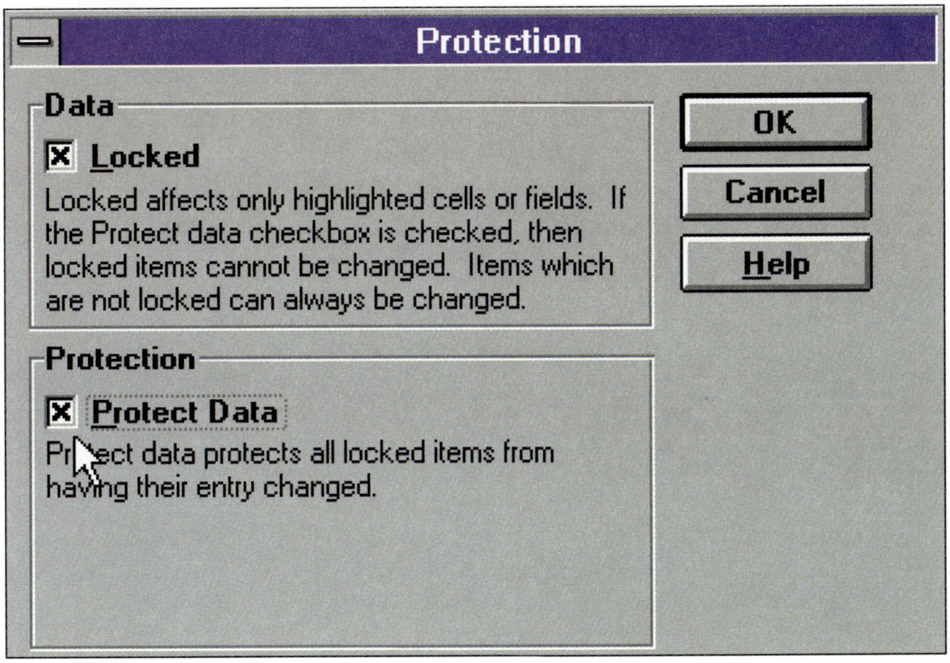

Figure 14-6
The Protection dialog box

4. Choose **OK** or press **Enter** to return to the database window.

To test the protection:

5. Move the insertion point to any field and change the data.
6. Press **Enter** or move the insertion point to another position. When you do this, a prompt is displayed as shown in the following example telling you that the data is locked and cannot be changed.

7. Choose **OK** to return to the database.

Turn Off Protection for Specified Fields

If you want to allow others access to some fields in your database but not all fields, you must first turn on both **Lock** and **Protect Data** for all fields, then turn off Lock for only those fields that you want to allow others to access. In this section, turn off protection to the Invoice Date field.

1. Choose **Format, Protection** and be sure that both **Lock** and **Protect Data** are turned on for all fields.
2. Move the insertion point to the Invoice Date field.
3. Choose **Format, Protection** and choose **Locked** to turn it off. See Figure 14-7.

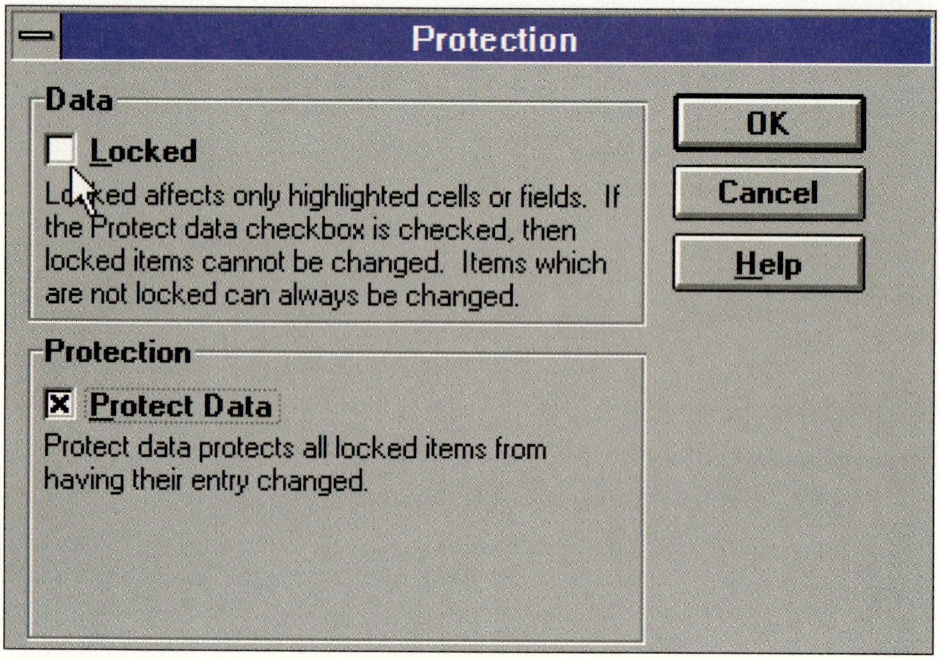

Figure 14-7
The Protection dialog box with Locked turned off

4. Choose **OK** or press **Enter** to return to the document.

To test the change:

5. Move the insertion point to row 10.
6. Type **1/15/94** and then press **Enter**. No prompt is displayed indicating the data is protected. The data is now changed.

NOTE: You can remove protection from all fields by choosing **Format, Protection** and turning off **Protect Data**. Your insertion point can be in any field. If the insertion point is in a field that you have unlocked, you should turn on **Locked** and then turn off **Protect Data.**

Protect Form Design

You can prevent your form design from being changed in much the same way you protect data.

1. Switch to form view-either click on the Form View button  or press **F9.**
2. Choose **Format, Protection.**
3. Choose **Protect Form** to turn it on as shown in Figure 14-8.

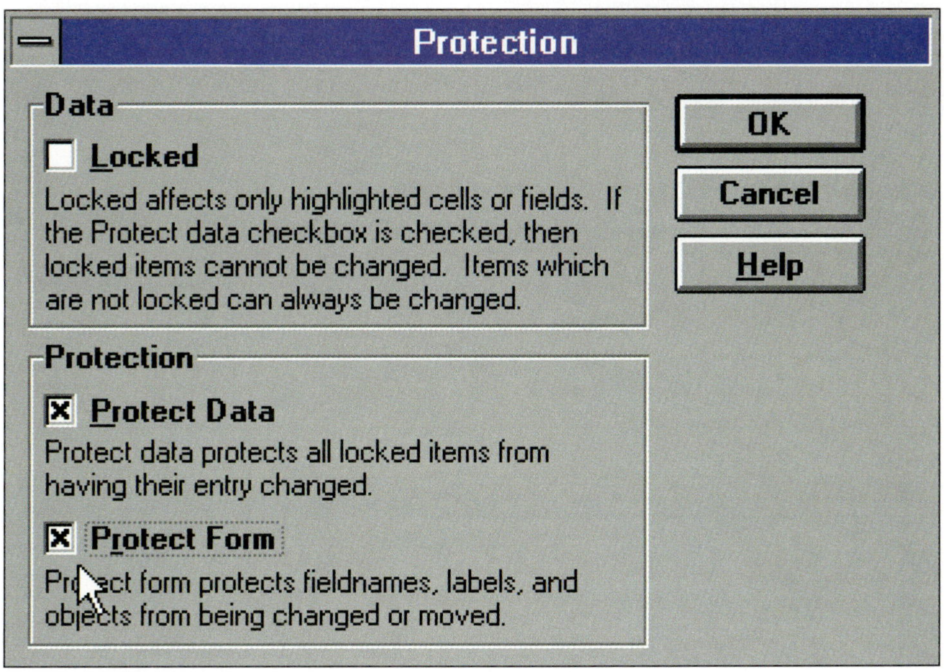

Figure 14-8
The Protection dialog box showing Protect Form turned on

4. Choose **OK** or press **Enter** to return to the database window.

To test the protection:

5. Click on any field name. It cannot be selected when Protection is turned on.

To turn off form protection:

6. Repeat steps 2 through 4, except at step 3 choose **Protect Form** to turn it off. Now when you select a field name, it will be highlighted and you can make changes, if you like.
7. Save the file again as **CH14PR2**.
8. Print the database from either form or list view and close the window.

GUIDED TUTORIAL

What You'll Do

- Format numbers.
- Insert a field in list view and edit the field name.
- Use the Fill Series command.

How To Do It

1. Open **CH13TUT**.
2. Switch to list view.

To format the* Dues Owing *field as currency:

3. Move the insertion point to any cell in the Dues Owing column.
4. Choose **Format, Number** to go to the Number dialog box and choose **Currency**.
5. Choose **OK** or press **Enter** to return to the database window. Your screen should resemble the following example.

	ID Number	Last Name	First Name	Membership Date	Dues Owing	
1	359345678	Randle	Colleen	1/2/94	$3.25	
2	329542198	Jones	Randall	1/3/94	$2.95	
3	295754444	Wilson	Richard	1/4/94	$3.80	
4	329951897	Costner	Jeremy	1/5/94	$2.00	
5	297882917	Mitchell	Sandra	1/4/94	$4.00	
6	238844768	Thiry	Jacques	1/5/94	$4.50	
7	278374758	Madsen	Olivia	1/3/94	$3.00	
8	378577611	Petrella	Harold	1/5/94	$3.95	
9	278574199	Ferrier	Karen	1/4/94	$3.50	
10	327899511	Jackson	Martha	1/3/94	$3.60	
11	547178594	McReynolds	Sally	1/2/94	$3.70	
12	457882298	Newman	Julie	1/2/94	$3.70	
13						

To insert a new field in list view:

6. Press **Ctrl/Home** or click on the first cell in row 1.
7. Click on the **Insert Field** button or choose **Insert, Record/Field,** choose **Field** and choose **OK** or press **Enter**. A new field is inserted and the following fields are moved to the right as shown here. (A field name will be inserted later.)

		ID Number	Last Name	First Name	Membership Date	Dues Owing
1		359345678	Randle	Colleen	1/2/94	$3.25
2		329542198	Jones	Randall	1/3/94	$2.95
3		295754444	Wilson	Richard	1/4/94	$3.80
4		329951897	Costner	Jeremy	1/5/94	$2.00
5		297882917	Mitchell	Sandra	1/4/94	$4.00
6		238844768	Thiry	Jacques	1/5/94	$4.50
7		278374758	Madsen	Olivia	1/3/94	$3.00
8		378577611	Petrella	Harold	1/5/94	$3.95
9		278574199	Ferrier	Karen	1/4/94	$3.50
10		327899511	Jackson	Martha	1/3/94	$3.60
11		547178594	McReynolds	Sally	1/2/94	$3.70
12		457882298	Newman	Julie	1/2/94	$3.70
13						
14						

To enter text and use Fill Series to enter additional data in a series:

8. Type **1** in the first row.
9. Select row 1 through row 12 in the new field.
10. Choose **Edit, Fill Series** to display the Fill Series dialog box as shown here.

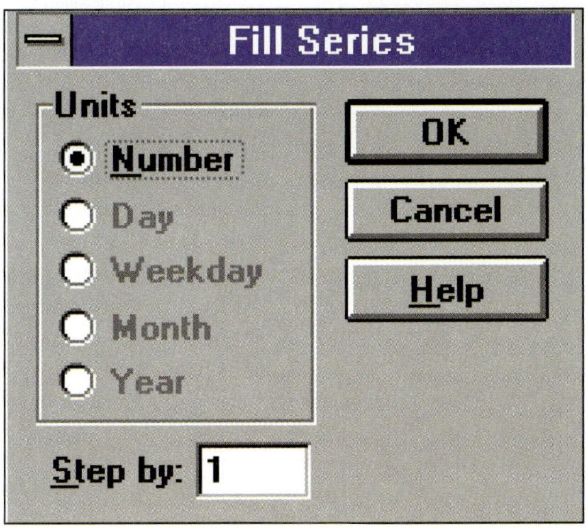

11. Leave **Number** turned on and also leave **Step by** set at **1**.
12. Choose **OK** or press **Enter** to return to the database window. Your screen should now resemble the following.

	Field1	ID Number	Last Name	First Name	Membership Date	Dues Owing
1	1	359345678	Randle	Colleen	1/2/94	$3.25
2	2	329542198	Jones	Randall	1/3/94	$2.95
3	3	295754444	Wilson	Richard	1/4/94	$3.80
4	4	329951897	Costner	Jeremy	1/5/94	$2.00
5	5	297882917	Mitchell	Sandra	1/4/94	$4.00
6	6	238844768	Thiry	Jacques	1/5/94	$4.50
7	7	278374758	Madsen	Olivia	1/3/94	$3.00
8	8	378577611	Petrella	Harold	1/5/94	$3.95
9	9	278574199	Ferrier	Karen	1/4/94	$3.50
10	10	327899511	Jackson	Martha	1/3/94	$3.60
11	11	547178594	McReynolds	Sally	1/2/94	$3.70
12	12	457882298	Newman	Julie	1/2/94	$3.70
13						
14						

Notice that the field name **Field1** is inserted automatically.

To edit (change) this name:

13. Select any cell in the **Field1** column.

14. Choose **Edit, Field Name** to display the Field Name dialog box.

15. Type **Member** in the **Name** text box as shown in the following example.

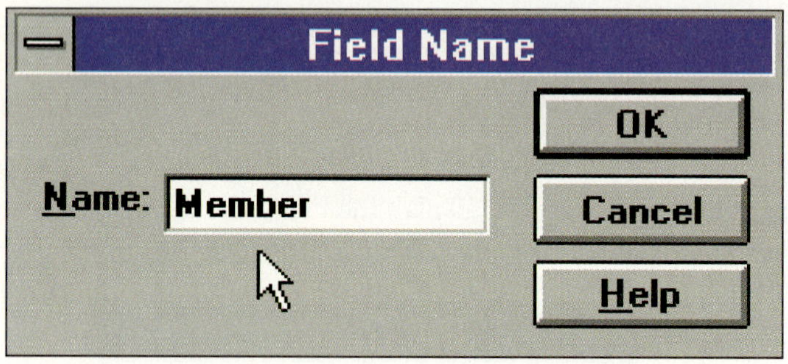

16. Choose **OK** or press **Enter** to return to the list view. The new name is now displayed as shown here.

	Member	ID Number	Last Name	First Name	Membership Date	Dues Owing
1	1	359345678	Randle	Colleen	1/2/94	$3.25
2	2	329542198	Jones	Randall	1/3/94	$2.95
3	3	295754444	Wilson	Richard	1/4/94	$3.80
4	4	329951897	Costner	Jeremy	1/5/94	$2.00
5	5	297882917	Mitchell	Sandra	1/4/94	$4.00
6	6	238844768	Thiry	Jacques	1/5/94	$4.50
7	7	278374758	Madsen	Olivia	1/3/94	$3.00
8	8	378577611	Petrella	Harold	1/5/94	$3.95
9	9	278574199	Ferrier	Karen	1/4/94	$3.50
10	10	327899511	Jackson	Martha	1/3/94	$3.60
11	11	547178594	McReynolds	Sally	1/2/94	$3.70
12	12	457882298	Newman	Julie	1/2/94	$3.70
13						

17.	Save	the document as **CH14TUT**.
18.	Print	a copy of the database and close the window.

REVIEW QUESTIONS

1. Choose the ______________________________ command from the ____________________ menu to hide a field name in form view.
2. After hiding data in a field in list view, use the ____________________ command to locate it.
3. The following dialog box is displayed by choosing ____________________, ____________________,

and it is used to ____.

4. The following dialog box is displayed by choosing ____________________, ____________________,

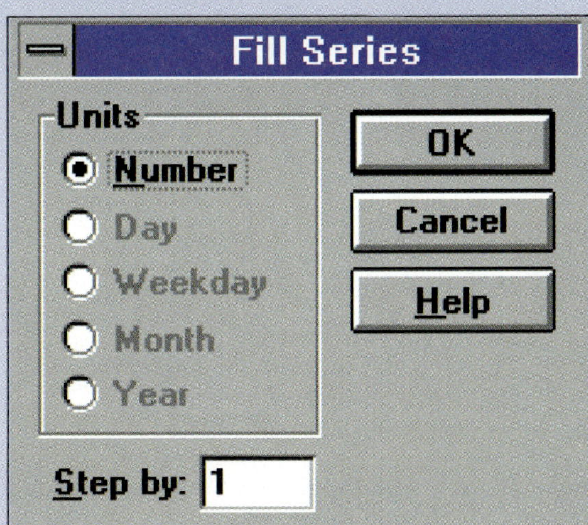

and it is used to ____.

5. To select the entire database, choose the ________________________ command from the ____________________ menu.
6. Write a formula that will compute the tax of 8% on total pay and subtract that amount from the total pay to show a net amount.

    ____

    ____

    ____

7. List three items in a database that can be protected by preventing others from making changes.

    ____

    ____

    ____

Hands-on Exercises

Exercise 1

1. Open **CH13HO1**.
2. In list view, insert a new field, **Response No.**, to the left of **Survey Number** and use **Edit, Fill Series** to enter consecutive numbers beginning with 1 and going through 15.
3. Format the Date field so that it is in long format showing the month, date, and year. (Select any cell and choose **Format, Number,** turn on **Date** and choose the format that will display the date as August 01, 1994.) You may have to adjust the width of the field to display all text.
4. Locate survey number 122 and change the response to T.
5. Select the entire file and format it in Times New Roman, 12 point.
6. Switch to form view and add a title, **1994 CLIENT SURVEY**. (*HINT:* Drag all fields down so there is room to add a title at the top of the form.)
7. Format the title in bold.
8. Save as **CH14HO1** and print a copy in list view.
9. Print one record in form view and close the window.

Exercise 2

1. Open **CH13HO2**.
2. Compute the Total by multiplying the Salary times the Hours.
3. Compute the Tax by multiplying the Total times 20.2 percent.
4. Compute the Net by subtracting the Tax from the Total.
5. Format all dollar values as currency with 2 decimals.
6. Adjust the column widths as appropriate.

7. Proof the file and save it as **CH14HO2.**
8. Print a copy from list view with gridlines and record and field labels.
9. Close the window.

Exercise 3

1. Retrieve **CH13HO3** from your data disk.
2. Bold all field names and all data in the Description field. (*HINT:* You need to be in form view to add bold to field names.)
3. Save the file as **CH14HO3** and print a copy in list view with gridlines and record and field labels.
4. Change the field width and move fields so that only the following fields appear in the table and in the order shown:

   Description   In Stock   Cost
5. Add a title called **ITEMS IN STOCK** in form view.
6. Bold the title.
7. Preview the database in list view, make any adjustments, and save the changes. Dollar amounts will be formatted as currency in Chapter 15.
8. Print a copy in list view showing gridlines and record and field labels.

Exercise 4

1. Retrieve **CH13HO4** from your data disk.
2. Enter the formula **=Return–Departure** and press **Enter** in rows 1 through 8 in the Hours field.
3. Reformat the layout of the fields in form view so that they are similar to the following.

Date: 7/1/95   **Event No.:** 1
Departure: 4:00 PM
Return: 8:30 PM
Hours: 4:30

Destination: Lake Union & Ship Canal

Description: Lake Union Roundup

3. Add the following new records in form view.

Event No.	Description	Date	Destination	Departure	Return
6	Party-Till-U-Drop	8/20/95	Seward Park	5:00 PM	11:00 PM
7	Up All Night	7/30/95	The Lakes	8:00 PM	8:00 AM (*HINT:* You will have to edit the data in the Hours field by typing 12 in place of the 0 in front of the colon in 0:00.)

4. Adjust the column widths, if necessary.
5. Add the title: **TOURS O' MYSTERY AND INTRIGUE**.
6. Format the title in bold, italic.
7. Bold and underline all field names in form view. Adjust positions of any fields in the form, if you like.

HINT:

8. Print one copy each of trips 1 and 4. (*HINT:* Switch to form view, and move the insertion point to any position in record 1. Then in the print dialog box, turn on **Current record only**. Repeat this procedure for the trip listed in record 4.)
9. Save the file as **CH14HO4** and switch to list view.
10. Adjust the field widths as necessary, and print a copy.
11. Close the window and exit Works.

Examples of Exercises

Exercise 3: CH14HO3

	Description	In stock	Cost	
1	Crazy hats	250	1	
2	Water balloons	820	0.5	
3	Roller skates	1500	2.5	
4	Roller blades	500	3.5	
5	Knee pads	1500	1	
6	Life jackets	1000	5	
7	Skate boards	850	2.5	
8				
9				

TOURS O'MYSTERY AND INTRIGUE

Date: 8/20/95 **Event No.:** 6
Departure: 5:00 PM
Return: 11:00 PM
Hours: 6:00

Destination: Seward Park

Description: Party-Till-U-Drop

CHAPTER 15

Sorting, Searching, Querying, and Reporting

OBJECTIVES

Sort records by one field and by multiple fields

Find and replace text and values

Query a database

Manage the queries

Create a report

Customize a report

PREVIEW

This chapter will show you how to sort records, how to use search and replace, how to extract information from a database by querying it, and how to create a report that presents the data in an effective way. Sorted records can be rearranged on the basis of either one field or multiple fields, and they can also be sorted in ascending or descending order. Querying a database means to search the file for and display records that contain specific characteristics. For example, a query can be performed that will show all clients living in a specific zip code area. A report allows you to add titles and print data from all fields or from selected fields in an attractive format.

SORTING RECORDS

In this section information will be sorted on the basis of one field, and also on the basis of multiple fields. When sorting information on multiple fields, a sort is done within a sort. For example, you can sort on state, then city, then by name, by first sorting all states, then cities within each state, and finally names within each city.

Sort on One Field

When sorting on a field, it is not necessary to select the field first. The name of the field is typed in the **Sort Records** dialog box, and the choice of ascending or descending order is made for each field to be sorted. The instructions below are to sort the database file **CH14PR2** on the **Date Booked** field.

1. Open **Works** if necessary and open the database file **CH14PR2** or retrieve it from the Instructor data disk.

2. Switch to list view.

NOTE: You can sort in either view, however, it is easier to view the results in list view.

3. Choose **Tools, Sort Records** to display the Sort Records dialog box as shown in Figure 15-1.

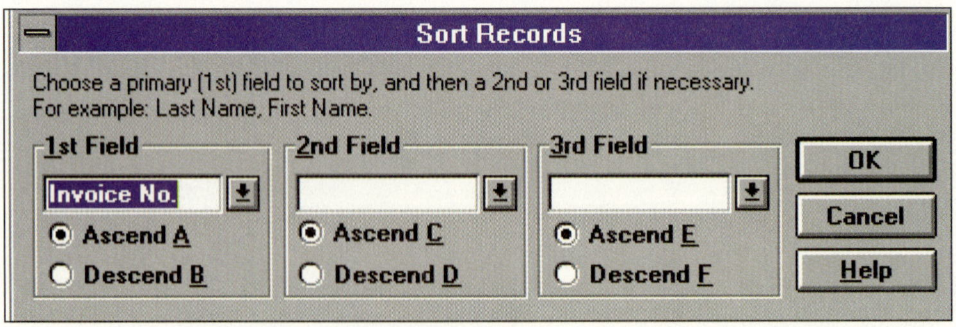

Figure 15-1
The Sort Records dialog box

4. Click on the down arrow at the right end of the list in the **1st Field** list box and drag down until **Date Booked** is selected as shown in the following example.

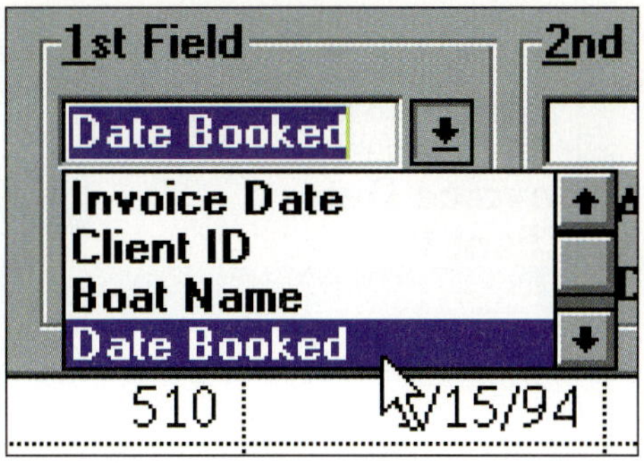

5. Release the left mouse button. The new field name is now displayed in the text box as shown here.

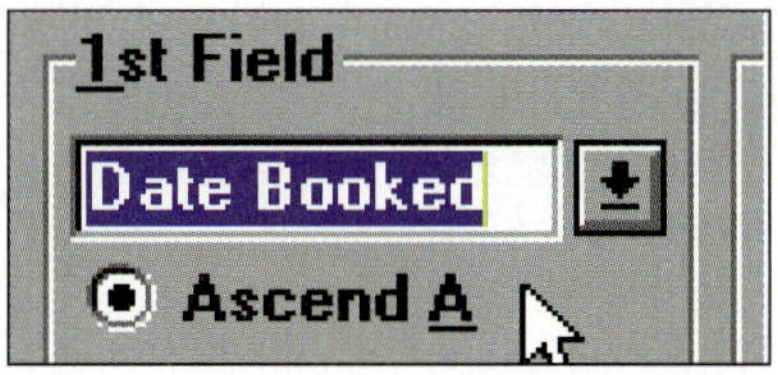

6. Leave the sort order set at **Ascend A**.

7. Choose **OK** or press **Enter** to return to the file. The records are now rearranged, and the dates in the **Date Booked** field are in ascending numerical order as shown in Figure 15-2.

	Invoice No.	Invoice Date	Client ID	Boat Name	Date Booke	Hours
1	505	1/5/94	104	The Spirit	1/7/94	3
2	506	1/6/94	106	Delano	1/10/94	4
3	503	1/3/94	102	Sea Wolf	1/15/94	4
4	509	1/9/94	114	Irish Sea	1/17/94	4
5	504	1/4/94	109	Irish Sea	1/19/94	3
6	501	1/1/94	105	Delano	1/20/94	3
7	502	1/2/94	113	The Spirit	1/25/94	4
8	507	1/7/94	110	Irish Sea	1/27/94	3
9	508	1/8/94	111	Delano	1/28/94	3
10	510	1/15/94	105	The Spirit	1/29/94	4
11						

Figure 15-2
Completed sort on one field

Sort on Multiple Fields

More useful information about the bookings of boats might be to sort on the boat name first and then on the date the boat is booked.

1. Choose **Tools, Sort Records** to display the Sort Records dialog box.

2. Click on the down arrow at the right end of the **1st Field** list box and select **Boat Name** as shown in the following example.

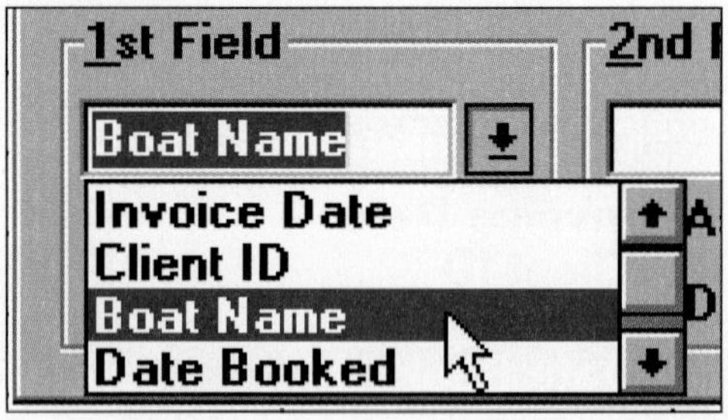

3.	Click	on the down arrow at the right end of the blank **2nd Field** list box and select **Date Booked** as shown in the following example. Leave **Ascend A** and **Ascend C** as is.

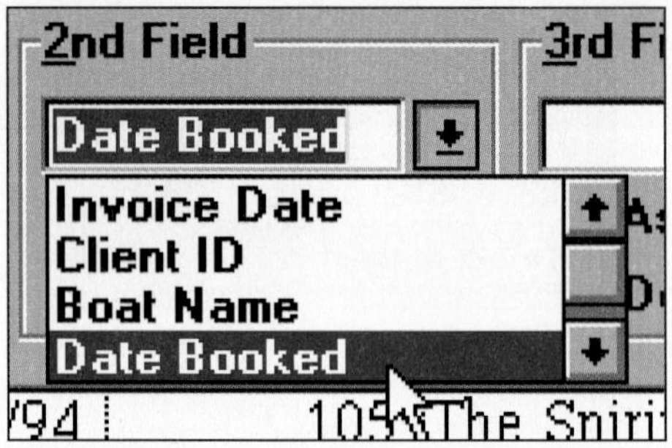

4.	Choose	**OK** or press **Enter** to sort on two fields. The results are shown in Figure 15-3. Notice that the boat names are listed in alphabetical order and that the dates are listed in ascending order for each boat name in the **Date Booked** field.

	Invoice No.	Invoice Date	Client ID	Boat Name	Date Booke	Hours
1	506	1/6/94	106	Delano	1/10/94	4
2	501	1/1/94	105	Delano	1/20/94	3
3	508	1/8/94	111	Delano	1/28/94	3
4	509	1/9/94	114	Irish Sea	1/17/94	4
5	504	1/4/94	109	Irish Sea	1/19/94	3
6	507	1/7/94	110	Irish Sea	1/27/94	3
7	503	1/3/94	102	Sea Wolf	1/15/94	4
8	505	1/5/94	104	The Spirit	1/7/94	3
9	502	1/2/94	113	The Spirit	1/25/94	4
10	510	1/15/94	105	The Spirit	1/29/94	4
11						

Figure 15-3
Completed sort on multiple fields

5.	Save	the file as **CH15R1**. The data protection features, **Locked** and **Protect Data**, are turned on because they were on in **CH14PR2**.

The **Edit** menu contains the **Find** option that allows you to move the insertion point to specific text and values in the database. The **Replace** option in the **Edit** menu is used to go to specific information and replace it with other information. You can either replace each occurrence individually, or you can replace all occurrences in one procedure.

Find Specific Text

The instructions given in this section will use the **Find** command in the **CH14PR1** file to locate the client whose last name is **Bell.** If you had a large database, and this name was not displayed on the screen when you open the database, it would save time to use the **Find** command to locate the name.

1. Open — the database file **CH14PR1** or retrieve it from the Instructor data disk.
2. Choose — **Edit, Find** to display the Find dialog box. See Figure 15-4. You can be in either list for form view, and your insertion point can be at any record.
3. Type — **Bell** in the **Find What** text box as shown in the figure below.

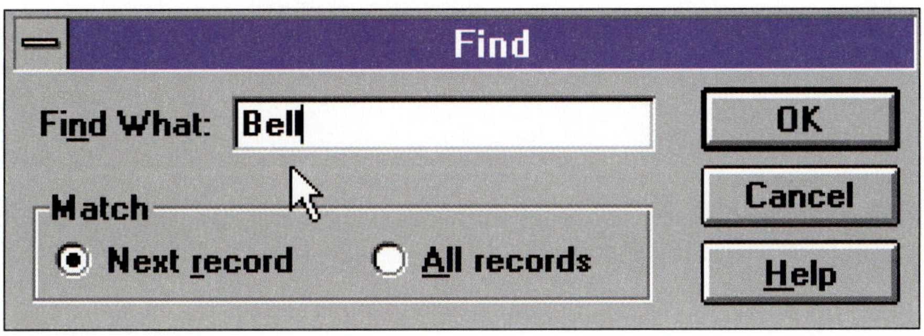

Figure 15-4
The Find dialog box

4. Leave — **Next record** turned on. This will specify that the next occurrence of **Bell** will be located.

   NOTE: If you turn on **All records**, all records containing **Bell** will be displayed and other records will be hidden. When you do this, you can then choose **View, Switch Hidden Records** to display all other records that do not contain **Bell,** or you can choose **View, Show All Records** to show all records in the database. It is not necessary to show all records before performing another Find or Replace. These functions search through all records in the file even when they are not showing in the database window. Practice this, if you have time.

5. Choose — **OK** or press **Enter** to locate the first occurrence of **Bell,** which, in this case, is in **Bellevue.**

Repeat Find

1. Press F7 to go to the next occurrence of **Bell**. Again, **Bellevue** is located.
2. Repeat pressing **F7** until the client named **Bell** is located.

NOTE: If you want to search only in a specific field, be sure you are in **list view**. Select the entire column for the field in which you want to perform the search, then choose **Edit, Find**, enter the characters to be located, and choose **OK**. In the instructions just given, if the **Lname** field had been selected, the Find function would not have located **Bellevue**, but would only have located the name **Bell**. Practice this if you have time.

Replace Text and Values

In this section, change the zip code **98042** to **98043**.

1. Switch to list view, if you are not already there.

NOTE: The **Replace** option is not available in the **Edit** menu in **form view**.

2. Press **Ctrl/Home** to go to the beginning of the file if you are not already there. (This is not required; however, it is the procedure used here.)
3. Choose **Edit, Replace** to display the Replace dialog box as shown in Figure 15-5.

Figure 15-5
The Replace dialog box

4. Type **98042** in the **Find What** text box. The word **Bell** will be deleted as soon as you start typing. See Figure 15-6.
5. Choose **Replace With** and type **98043** in the text box.
6. Choose **Find Next** 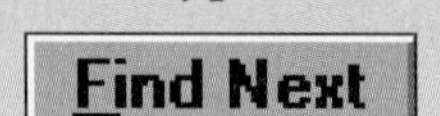
. The insertion point moves to the first occurrence of 98042; the Replace dialog box is still displayed. Your screen should now resemble the following.

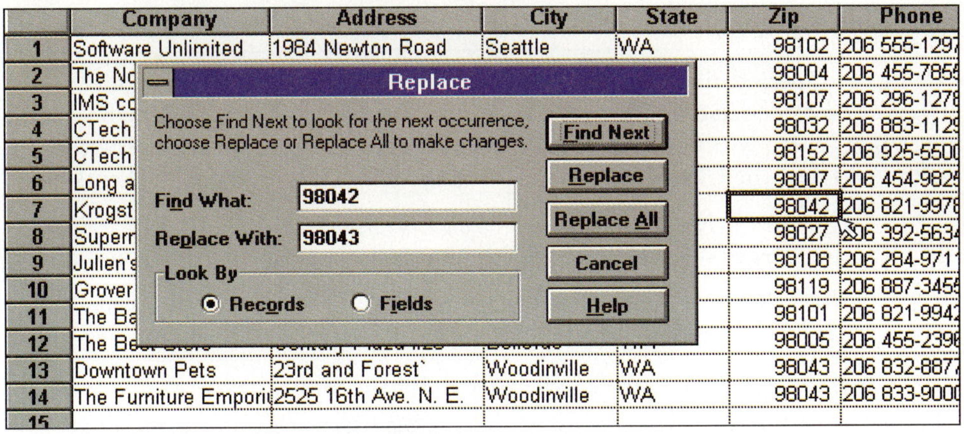

Figure 15-6
Select the first occurrence of text to be replaced

7. Choose **Replace** Replace. The value **98042** is replaced with **98043** and the next occurrence of 98042 is selected.

NOTE: In the Replace dialog box, the Records option is turned on by default. This means that Works will search across each row, and then go to the next row and search. If Fields is turned on, Works will search down through the first column, then down through the next column, and so on. Choose whichever method of searching seems most efficient.

8. Choose **Replace All** Replace All. All remaining occurrences of **98042** are replaced with **98043**.

NOTE: You can use wildcard characters such as the question mark (?) to search for one character, or the asterisk (*) to search for multiple characters.

For example, in the database shown here, if you type **?ills** in the **Find What** text box (either in the Find dialog box or in the Replace dialog box), you will locate **Sills, Hills,** and **Mills** (you are searching for one character followed by **ills**).

If you type **The *** (type the word **The,** space once, and type an asterisk), you will locate all entries beginning with the word "The" because you are searching for the word **The** followed by any number of characters. The asterisk is often used to locate words where you are not sure of the spelling. For example, type **K*D** to locate **Krogstad** if you are not sure how to spell it.

9. Save the database as **CH15PR2**.

QUERYING A DATABASE

To query a database means to locate specific records for display. Locating the records is done through the use of the **Query** commands in the **Tools** menu. In a query you can specify certain conditions that will display only information that you want to view. Other information will not be displayed in the query result.

Create a Query

Using the Query dialog box, you can enter up to three conditions for your query. You can be in either form view or in list view to perform a query; however, it is generally easier to view the final output of the query when you are in list view. Here, the **CH15PR2** file will be used, and you will locate all clients living in Seattle.

1. Open — the file **CH15PR2** if it is not already open and switch to list view.
2. Choose — **Tools, Create New Query** to display the **New Query** dialog box shown in Figure 15-7.

   Or, if this is the *first* query to be created for this file (which it is in this case),

   Click — on the Query View button  to display the dialog box.

   NOTE: The Query View button displays the New Query dialog box *only* if the file does not have other queries saved with it. If other queries exist, the Query View button displays the last query that has been used.

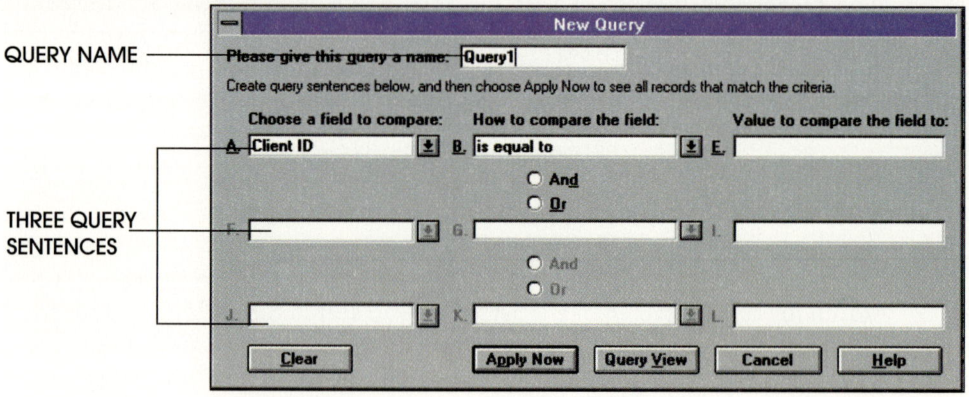

Figure 15-7
The New Query dialog box

Works provides a query name; however, you can enter a new name if you like. Here, you will use the supplied name, **Query1**.

3. Click — on the down arrow at the right end of the **A** list box and select **City** as shown here.

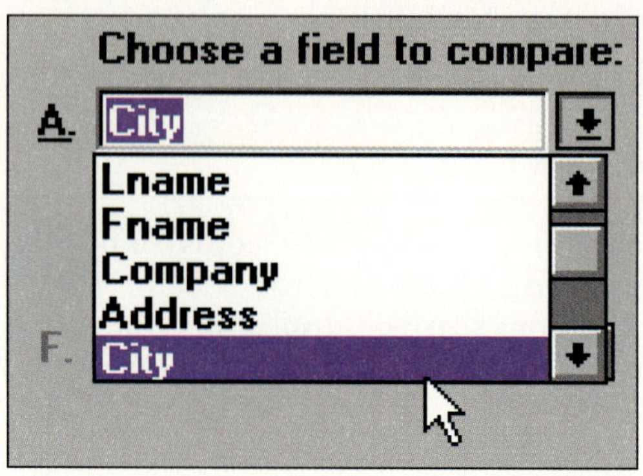

4. Click	on the down arrow at the right end of the **B** list box, or press **Alt/B** to choose **B** which will move the selection to the **How to compare the field** box to display the list of options as shown here. The condition will remain set at **is equal to**. See Table 15-1 for examples of results from using these comparisons.

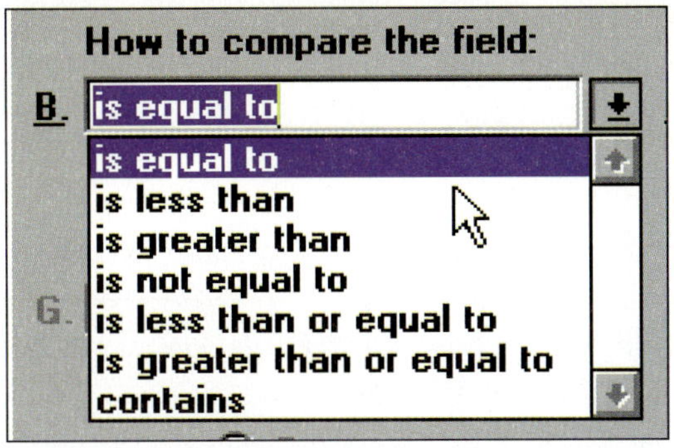

Use this comparison	Enter text in the *Value to compare field to* box	To locate these records
is equal to	enter a value *Example*: Seattle	only records of those living in Seattle
is less than	enter a value *Example*: 98100	only records of those in zip code areas with numbers less than 98100
is greater than	enter a value *Example*: 98100	only records of those in zip code areas with numbers greater than 98100
is not equal to	enter a value *Example*: Seattle	all records of those who do not live in Seattle
is less than or equal to	enter a value *Example*: 98104	all records of those who live in the zip code area 98104 or zip code areas with numbers less than 98104
is greater than or equal to	enter a value *Example*: 98104	all records of those living in the zip code area 98104 or zip code areas with numbers larger than 98104
contains	enter a value *Example*: Northwest	records where a company name includes the word "Northwest"

Table 15-1
The options in the *How to compare the field* list box

5. Choose	**E** to move to the **Value to compare the field to** text box.
6. Type	**Seattle** in the text box as shown in the following example.

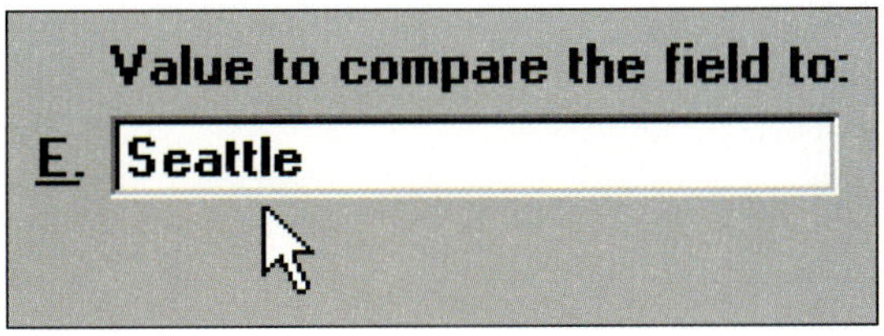

7. Choose **Apply Now** Apply Now to perform the query. Your screen should resemble the following example.

	Client ID	Lname	Fname	Company	Address	City
1	101	Hammersmith	Michael	Software Unlimited	1984 Newton Road	Seattle
3	103	Baker	Charles	IMS consultants	19451 N. E. 45th	Seattle
9	109	Smith	Trisha	Julien's Computers	1001 South Plaza	Seattle
10	110	Grover	Douglas	Grover and Associate	123 Fourth Ave. N. E.	Seattle
11	111	Mills	Nevell	The Baldwin Co.	98 Baldwin Place	Seattle
15						

Display all Records

In this section, use the **View, Show All Records** command to see all the original records that were stored in the database.

1. Choose **View, Show All Records**. The original records are now showing in the database window.

   NOTE: Showing all records is not required before performing another query. When the next query is used, it will automatically query all records.

Apply an Existing Query

The query you just created is named **Query1** and can be used again if you like. For example, if additional records were entered including those of clients from Seattle, you can use this same query to display those additional records.

1. Choose **View, Apply Query** or press **F3** to display the **Apply Query** dialog box as shown in Figure 15-8.

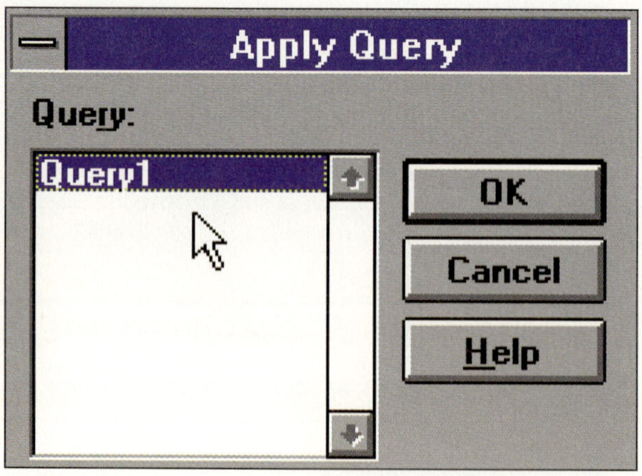

Figure 15-8
The Apply Query dialog box

Only one query is displayed; however, as other queries are created they will all be listed here. Remember, you can give them a different name if you like.

2. Choose **Query1** as shown in Figure 15-8.
3. Choose **OK** or press **Enter** to perform the query again. No changes will be made because additional records have not been added here; however, if new records of clients from Seattle had been added, they would be shown in the query.
4. Choose **View, Show All Records** to display all records again.

Query for Two Conditions

You can locate records that meet one condition or a different condition; or you can locate records that must meet two or three conditions. The **OR** condition is used to display all records that meet one condition, such as a specific date, or a different condition, such as a different date. All records containing one or the other of these conditions will be displayed as the result of the query. Here you will display records of boats that were chartered on either January 7 *or* January 17.

In this section, use the database **CH15PR1.**

1. Be sure the file **CH15PR1** is open and active.

To use the OR condition:

1. Choose **Tools, Create New Query.**
2. Choose **Date Booked** in the **Choose a field to compare** list box.
3. Choose **E** to go to the **Value to compare the field to** text box. (Skip over the **How to compare the field** text box and leave it set at **is equal to.**)
4. Type **1/7/94.**
5. Choose **Or** to turn it on.
6. Choose **F** to go to the second **Choose a field to compare** list box and select **Date Booked** again.
7. Choose **G** to go to the second **How to compare the field** list box and select **is equal to.**
8. Choose **I** to go to the **Value to compare the field to** text box.
9. Type **1/17/94.** Your dialog box should look like the following illustration.

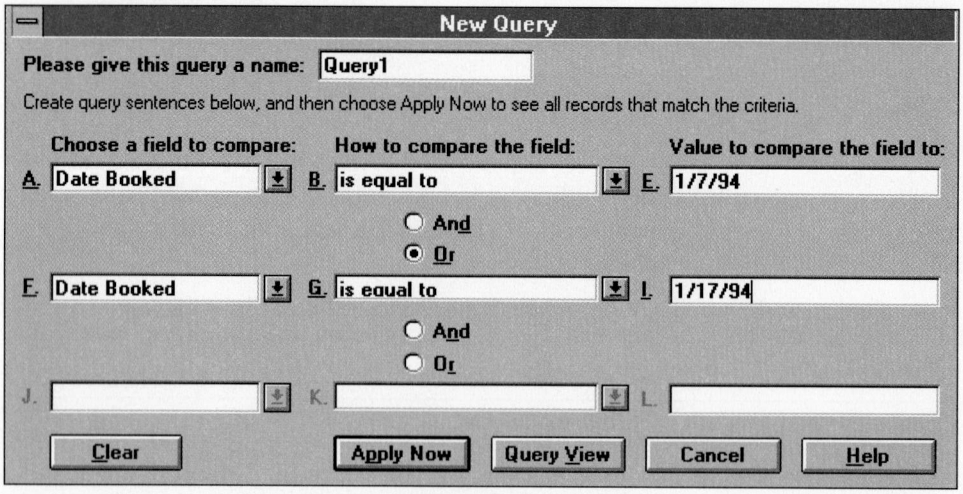

10. Choose **Apply Now** **Apply Now** to perform the query. Your screen should resemble the following example.

	Invoice No.	Invoice Date	Client ID	Boat Name	Date Booke	Hours	D
4	509	1/9/94	114	Irish Sea	1/17/94	4	
8	505	1/5/94	104	The Spirit	1/7/94	3	

11. Display all records again by choosing **View, Show All Records.**

To use the AND condition:

The **AND** condition means that the query displays records that meet two or three conditions, such as a specific state *and* a specific city. You can also use the AND condition to locate records that are greater than *and* less than specific values. Here, the records of boats with balances greater than $1500 and less than $2000 will be displayed.

1. Choose **Tools, Create New Query** to display the New Query dialog box.
2. Choose **Balance** for the field in the first **Choose a field to compare** list box.
3. Choose **B** to go to the **How to compare the field** text box and select **is greater than.**
4. Choose **E** to go to the **Value to compare the field to** text box.
5. Type 1500.
6. Choose **And.**
7. Choose **F** and select **Balance** for the field in the second **Choose a field to compare** list box.
8. Choose **G** to go to the **How to compare the field** text box and select **is less than.**
9. Choose **I** to go to the **Value to compare the field to** text box.
10. Type 2000. The dialog box should resemble the following illustration.

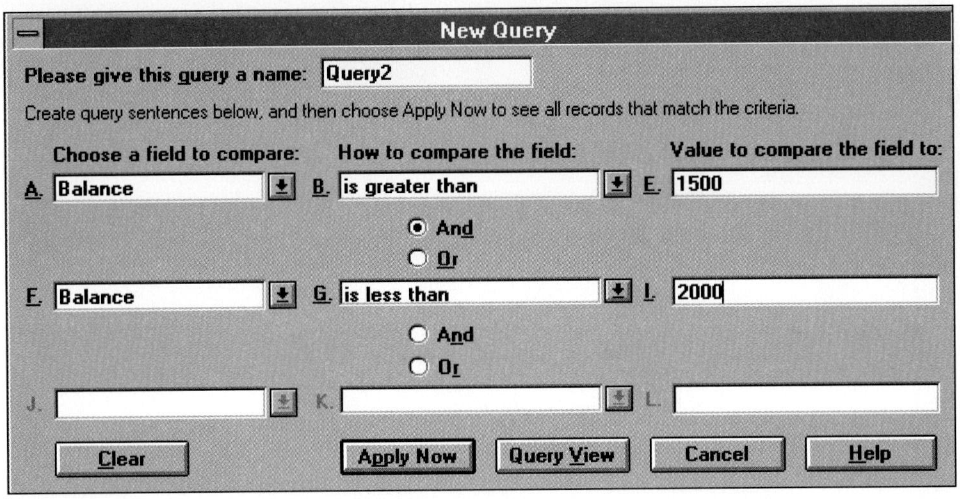

11. Choose **Apply Now** to display the results of the query. Your screen should look like the following example.

	Invo	Invoice	Clien	Boat Na	Date Boo	Hou	Deposit	Total	Tax	Balance
2	501	1/1/94	105	Delano	1/20/94	3	$100.00	$1,500.00	$120.00	$1,520.00
3	508	1/8/94	111	Delano	1/28/94	3	$100.00	$1,500.00	$120.00	$1,520.00
5	504	1/4/94	109	Irish Sea	1/19/94	3	$10[illegible]00	$1,500.00	$120.00	$1,520.00
7	503	1/3/94	102	Sea Wolf	1/15/94	4	$500.00	$2,000.00	$160.00	$1,660.00
9	502	1/2/94	113	The Spirit	1/25/94	4	$200.00	$2,000.00	$160.00	$1,960.00
11										

Use More Than Three Conditions in a Query

To enter more than three conditions, you must be in form view. See Table 15-2 for a list of operators that can be used in comparison conditions. In the following steps, conditions will be entered in the Query form. See Figure 15-10.

NOTE: By using the Query form rather than the Query dialog box, you can enter conditions in each field in the database; or you can enter a string (list) of conditions in one field.

1. Make the file **CH15PR1** active or open it if it is not already open, or retrieve it from the Instructor data disk. Choose **View, Show All Records.**
2. Choose **Tools, Create New Query** to display the New Query dialog box.
3. Choose **Clear** 

to remove all the previous information that is showing in the text boxes. Your screen should now resemble Figure 15-9.

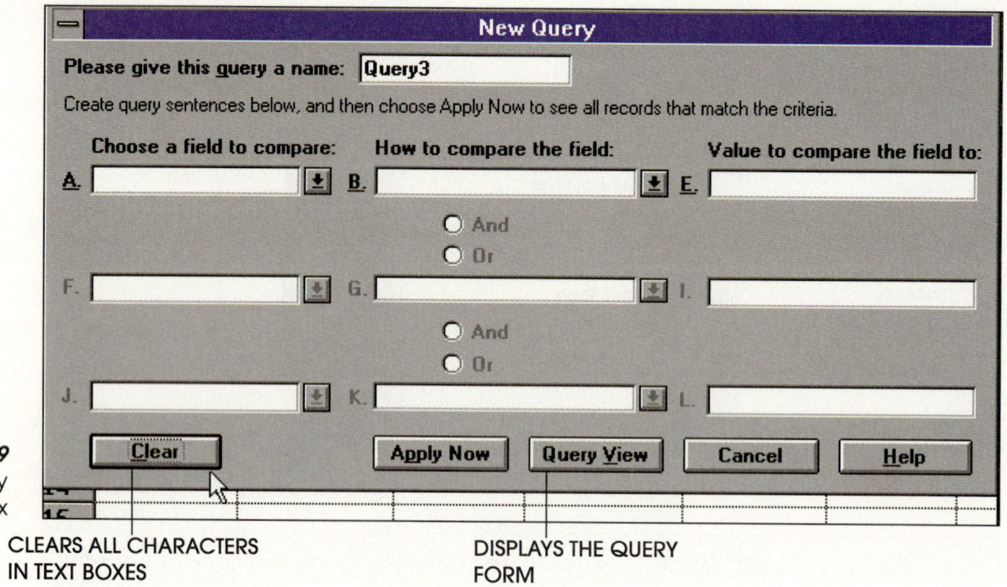

Figure 15-9
The New Query dialog box

4. Choose Query View **Query View** to display the Query form. See the example in Figure 15-10.

Figure 15-10
The Query form

NOTE: The Query form looks just like the form view for this database file, and you can enter conditions in each field to select specific records; or you can enter a string of conditions in one field. The following instructions will show you how to do both.

Operator	Example	Results
> (greater than)	Amount field: >150	Displays records in which all values in the **Amount** field are larger than 150.
	City field: >"M"	Displays records in the **City** field that begin with letters above "M." The text must be enclosed in double quotes.
< (less than)	Amount field: < 150	Displays records in which all values in the **Amount** field are less than 150.
	City field: <"M"	Displays records in the **City** field that begin with letters lower than "M." The text must be enclosed in double quotes.
>= (greater than or equal to)	Amount field: >=150	Displays records in which all values in the **Amount** field are 150 or more.
<= (less than or equal to)	Amount field: <=150	Displays records in which all values in the **Amount** field are 150 or less.
< > (not equal)	City field: < >"Seattle"	Displays all records in which the **City** field contains cities other than Seattle.
#AND#	Amount field: >150#AND#<350	Displays all records in which the value in the **Amount** field is over 150 and is less than 350.
	City field: = "Seattle"#AND#Amount =150	Displays all records in which the **City** field contains Seattle and the **Amount** field contains 150.

NOTE: Text must be enclosed in double quotes and the field names must be included in the condition statement when you are querying on more than one field. Although you can only enter this statement in one field, you can include as many conditions as you need. You can also combine the #AND# operator with the #OR# operator using these same procedures.

Operator	Example	Results
#OR#	City field: = "Seattle"#OR#"Bellevue"	Displays all records in which the **City** field contains either Seattle or Bellevue.
+ (addition)	Total field: = (Total+Tax)>2000	Displays all records in which the **Total** amount plus the amount of **Tax** is greater than 2000.
- (subtract)	Total field: = (Total-Deposit)<=1500	Displays all records in which the **Total** amount minus the amount of the **Deposit** is equal to or less than 1500.
* (multiply)	Hours field: = (hours*rate)>1000	Displays all records in which the **Hours** times the **Rate** produces an amount greater than 1000.
/ (divide)	Hours field: = (Total/hours)=500	Displays all records in which the **Total** divided by the **Hours** will produce an amount equal to 500.

Table 15-2

The operators used in the Query form

Enter conditions in four fields

When you finish the following instructions, the Query form will resemble that shown in Figure 15-11. These conditions will locate all records showing charters booked for *Irish Sea,* between January 1 and January 31, 1994, for 3 hours, with a deposit of $200; You just type the condition that you want to match in each field. You can also enter operators in each field, such as greater than (>) and less than (<) or the logical operators #AND# or #OR#. See Table 15-2 for a list of operators that can be used in conditions.

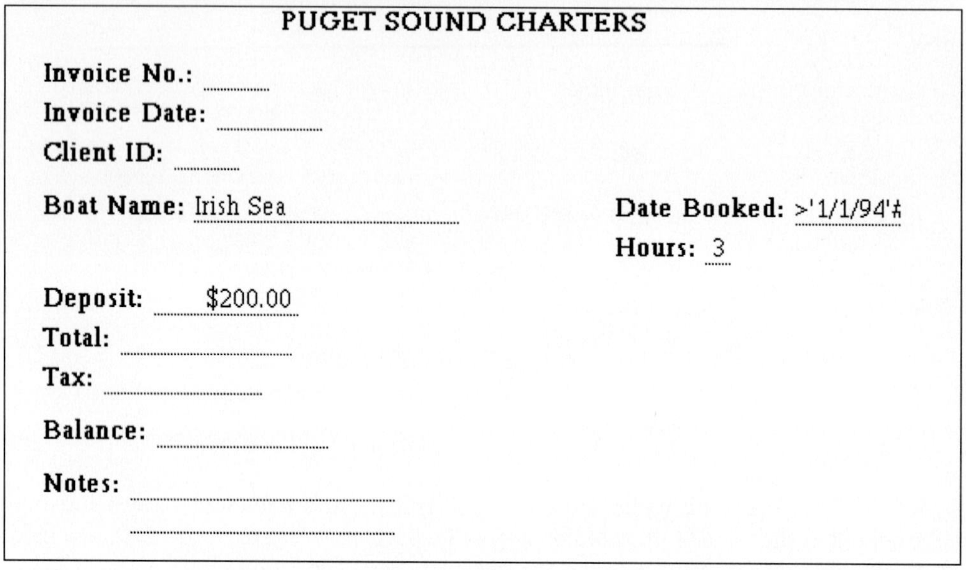
PUGET SOUND CHARTERS

Invoice No.:
Invoice Date:
Client ID:
Boat Name: Irish Sea
Date Booked: >'1/1/94'#
Hours: 3
Deposit: $200.00
Total:
Tax:
Balance:
Notes:

Figure 15-11
The filled-in Query form

5. Move the insertion point to the **Boat Name** field to select it.

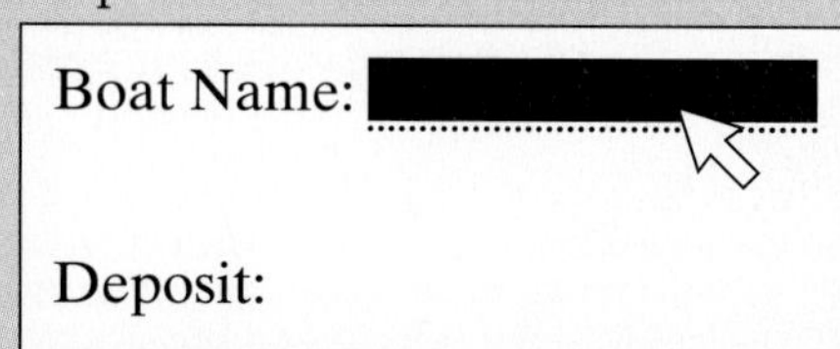

6. Type *Irish Sea* to enter the boat name you want to locate in the query.
7. Move the insertion point to the **Date Booked** field to select it. The field on your screen may not be as large as that shown in Figure 15-11, but you can still enter as much text as required for the condition.
8. Type **>'1/1/94'#AND#<'1/31/94'**. The full text will be displayed in the formula bar as shown in the following example.

This condition will locate all records for boat charters for *Irish Sea* that occurred after January 1, 1994, and before January 31, 1994.

NOTE: When entering dates in conditions, enclose the dates in single quotation marks. Also, the logical operators AND, OR, and NOT are enclosed in number signs (#).

9. Move the insertion point to the **Hours** field.
10. Type **3** to locate only the charters that were booked for 3 hours.
11. Move the insertion point to the **Deposit** field and type **200**.
12. Compare your screen with Figure 15-11 to confirm the accuracy of your entries.
13. Move the insertion point away from any field.

NOTE: If a field is selected, the query cannot be performed.

14. Click on the List view button , or choose **View, List** to display the results of the query as shown in the following example.

	Invoice No.	Invoice Da	Client II	Boat Na	Date Booke	Hour	Deposit	Total
6	507	1/7/94	110	Irish Sea	1/27/94	3	$200.00	$1,500.00
11								

NOTE: You can also click on the Form View button or choose **View, Form** if you like; however, it is easier to view the results of the query in list view.

15. Choose **View, Show All Records.**

To enter several conditions in one field:

You do not necessarily have to move to different fields to enter several conditions in one field. All conditions can be entered in one field when you want to specify two or more conditions to be met in that field. Figure 15-12 shows an example of four conditions entered in one field that will display the boats *Delano* and *The Spirit* when they are chartered for 4 hours and have had deposits of less than $150. See Table 15-2 for a list of operators and examples of how they are used in a Query form.

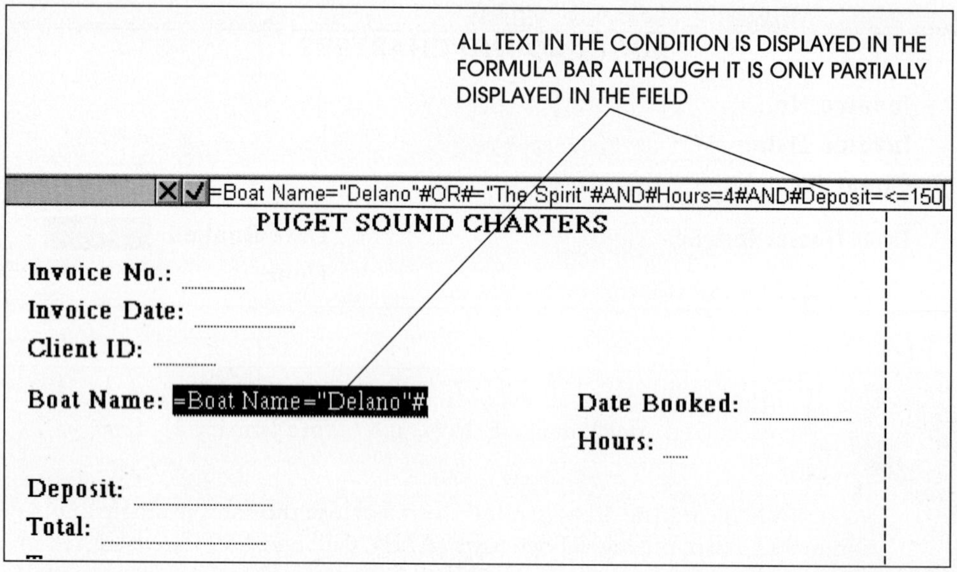

Figure 15-12
The Query form showing several conditions in one field

1. Be sure the file **CH15PR1** is open and is active.
2. Choose **Tools, Create New Query** to display the New Query dialog box.
3. Choose **Clear** [Clear] to remove all the previous information that is showing in the text boxes.
4. Choose **Query View** [Query View] to display the form.
5. Move the insertion point to the **Boat Name** field to select it.

6. Type **=Boat Name="Delano"#OR#="The Spirit"#AND#Hours= 4#AND#Deposit<=150**. (See Figure 15-12.) The condition statement is showing in the formula bar. Then move the insertion point away from the field.

NOTE: When entering text, such as the boat names, in conditions asking for multiple comparison, enclose the text in double quotation marks. Also, field names entered for each comparison are followed by equal signs (=). All statements begin with an equal sign (=).

7. Click on the List View button or choose **View, List** to display the results of the query as shown in the following example.

	Invoice No.	Invoice Da	Client II	Boat Na	Date Booke	Hour	Deposit	Total
1	506	1/6/94	106	Delano	1/10/94	4	$100.00	$2,000.00
10	510	1/15/94	105	The Spirit	1/29/94	4	$150.00	$2,000.00

8. **Save** the file again as **CH15PR1**.

NOTE: Queries are saved with the database and can be used later even if you exit and start up again.

MANAGING QUERIES

The queries are automatically named (Query1, Query2, Query3, etc.) and saved with each database file. You can, however, use the **Tools** menu to rename these queries, to duplicate them, or to delete them.

Name a Query

For **CH15PR1**, it would be helpful to give the queries names that would more easily identify them. Query 4 will therefore be named **4 Hour charters**.

1. Be sure the **CH15PR1** file is open and active. You can be in any view.
2. Choose **Tools, Name Query** to display the Name Query dialog box.
3. Select **Query4**. See Figure 15-13.
4. Choose **Name** to go to the Name text box at the bottom of the dialog box.
5. Type **4 hour charters** in the text box as shown.

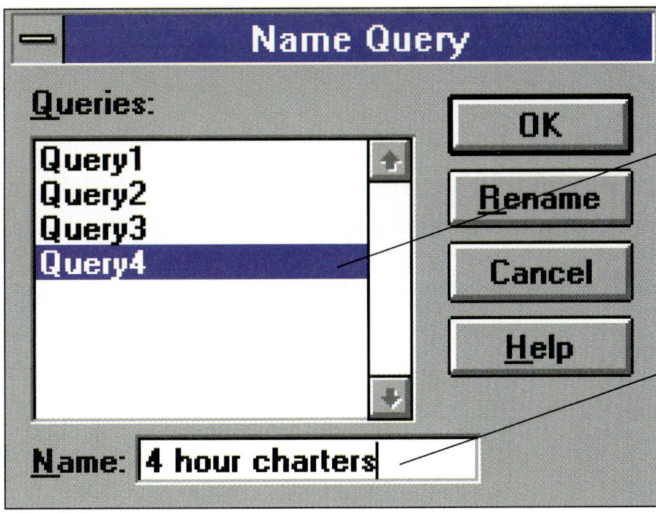

SELECT THE QUERY

TYPE A NEW NAME

Figure 15-13
The Name Query dialog box

6. Choose **Rename** Rename. The new name is now displayed in the Queries list box as shown in the following example.

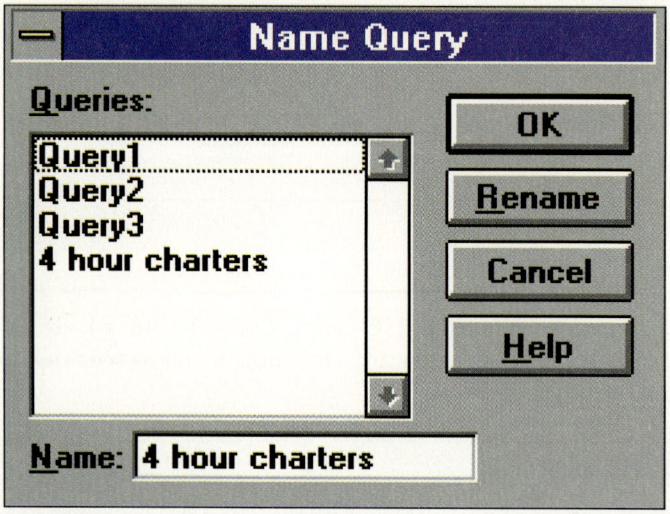

7. Choose **OK** or press **Enter** to return to the database window.

Duplicate a Query

You may find that you want to use a query containing some conditions, but you would like to make one to two changes to the query. You can use the Duplication command to do this. The following instructions will duplicate Query3 for the **CH15PR1** database. Then in the following section, "Select a Query" the condition looking for *Irish Sea* will be changed to locate *The Spirit* with the remaining conditions left as is.

1. Be sure the **CH15PR1** database is open and active.
2. Choose **Tools, Duplicate Query** to display the Duplicate Query dialog box.
3. Select **Query3**. See Figure 15-14.

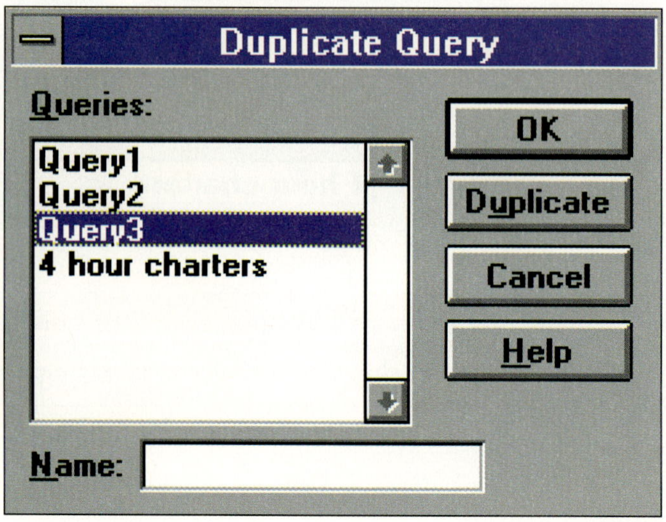

Figure 15-14
The Duplicate Query dialog box

4. Choose **Duplicate** Duplicate. The duplicate of Query3 is now named Query4 and is in the **Queries** list box as shown here.

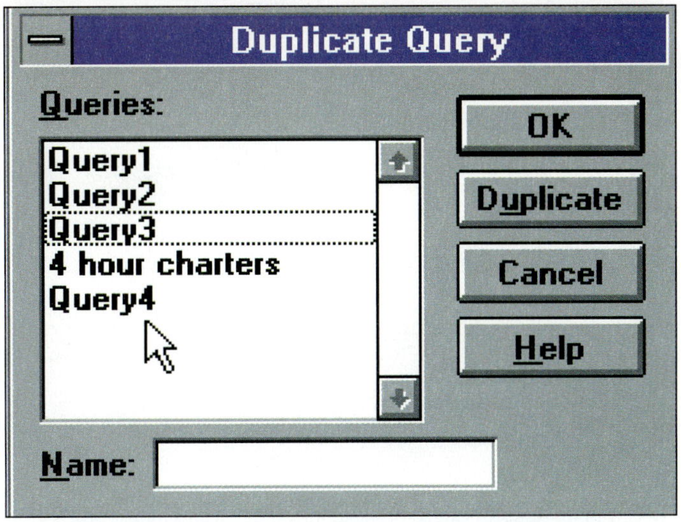

5. Choose **OK** or press **Enter** to return to the database window.

Select a Query

To display a query, use **View, Query**. Here, select the new **Query4** and change it.

1. Choose **View, Query**.
2. Select **Query4** and choose **OK** to display it in Query form.
3. Move the insertion point to the **Boat Name** field.
4. Delete ***Irish Sea*** and type ***The Spirit*** in the field.
5. Click on the List View button to see the results of the new query.

Delete a Query

You can remove a query from the list if you find that you are no longer using it. In this section, delete Query4 that you just created as a result of duplicating Query3.

1. Be sure the **CH15PR1** database is open and active.
2. Choose **Tools, Delete Query** to display the Delete Query dialog box.
3. Select **Query4** as shown in Figure 15-15. (It may already be selected.)

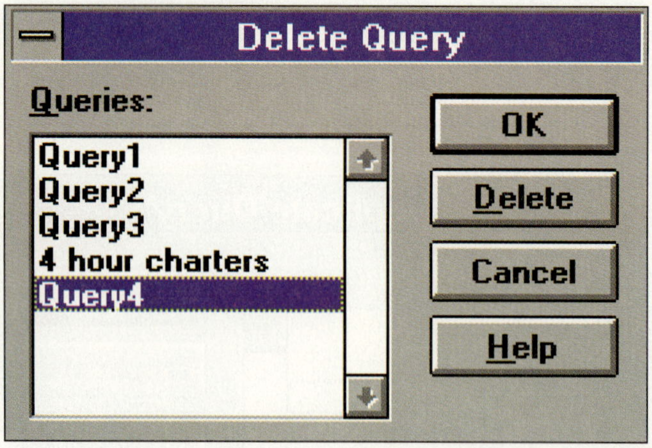

Figure 15-15
The Delete Query dialog box

4. Choose **Delete** 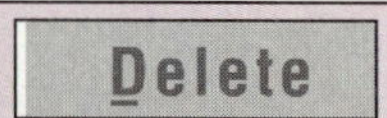 to remove the query name from the list as shown in the following example.

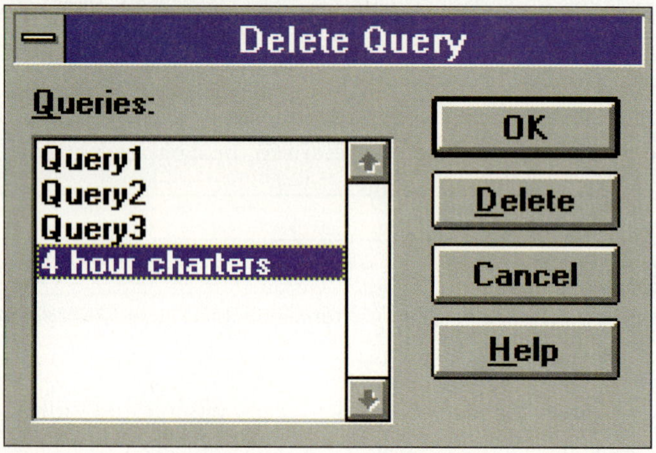

5. Choose **OK** or press **Enter** to return to the database window.
6. Save the file again as **CH15PR1**. The queries are saved with the file.

CREATING A REPORT

Reports are used to organize and present data in ways that are different from printing the database information from list view or from form view. You can create a report that shows all fields or only selected fields, and you can then customize the report by adding subtitles, formatting, blank rows, and other text that explain the report.

Create a Basic Report

The basic report displays data from selected fields in columns, and a title can be added to the report. Here you will create a report which is a telephone list of clients, based on the database **CH15PR2**, and includes the fields for the first and last name, company names, and phone numbers. (An additional field will be inserted later when you customize this report.)

1. Open **CH15PR2** You can be in either form or list view.
2. Choose **Tools, Create New Report** to display the New Report dialog box.

   NOTE: If this is the first time that a report is being created for the active database, you can also click on the Report View button in the toolbar to display the New Report dialog box. If, however, other reports have been created for the file, the last report form that has been used will be displayed when you click on the Report View button.

3. Type **Client Telephone List** in the **Report Title** text box as shown here.

***To add fields* Lname, Fname, Company, *and* Phone:**

4. Select **Lname** and choose Add>> **Add >>**. The field name is now also displayed in the **Fields in Report** list box. The next field name, **Fname**, is selected.
5. Choose Add>> **Add >>** again to add **Fname** to the list box at the right.
6. Repeat steps 4 and 5 for **Company** and for **Phone**. Your **Fields in Report** list box in the New Report dialog box should now resemble the following.

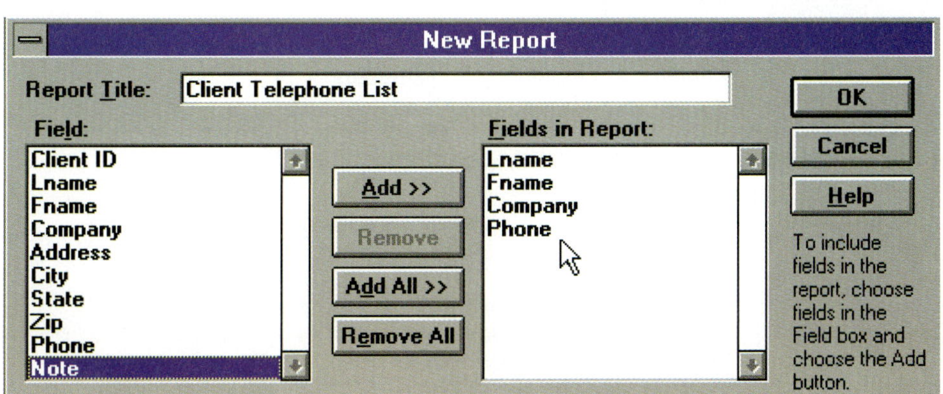

NOTE: If you inadvertently added a field that you do not want to include in the report, select it in the **Fields in Report** box and choose **Remove**

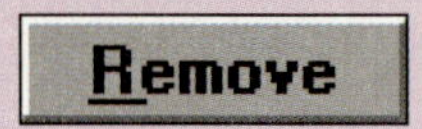

.

If you choose **Add All >>**

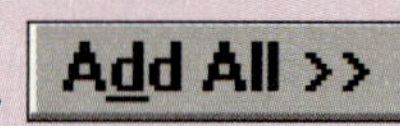

, all field names will be displayed in the Fields in Report list box.

7. Choose **OK** to display the Report Statistics dialog box The Report Statistics dialog box makes it easy to perform calculations on designated fields and to display the results in the report.

8. Select **Lname** and choose **Count** to display a count of the total names in the list. Your screen should resemble Figure 15-16.

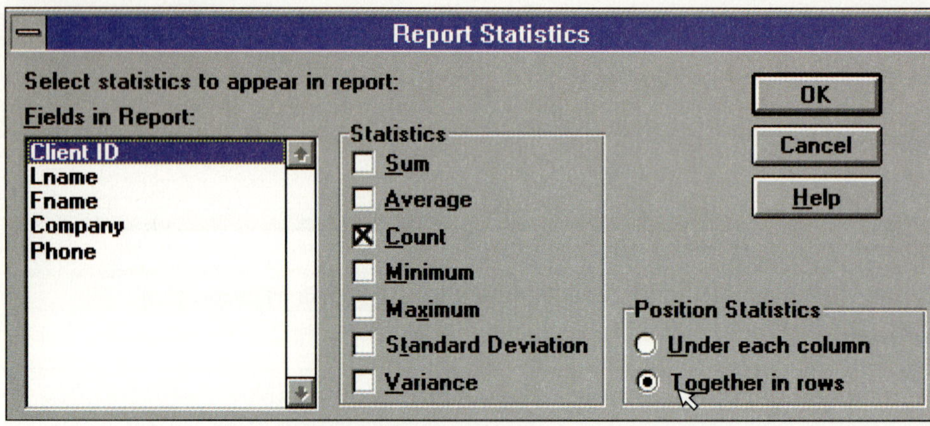

Figure 15-16
The Report Statistics dialog box

9. Choose **OK** or press **Enter**. The prompt telling you the report definition has been created will be displayed.

10. Choose **OK** or press **Enter** to go to the report definition view. Your screen should resemble the following. See Table 15-3 for an explanation of the labels in the leftmost column.

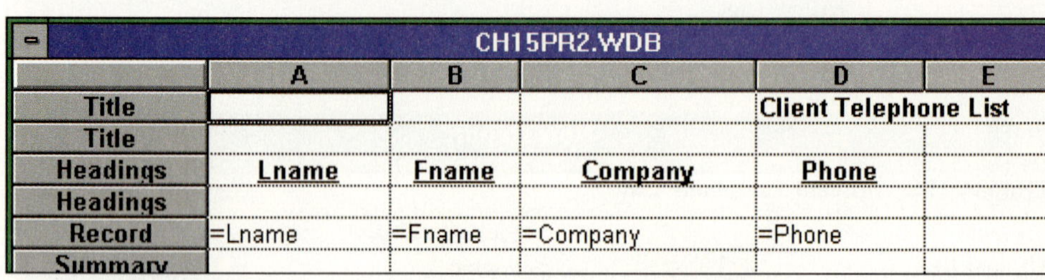

Row label	Is used to
Title	Enter a title and subtitle for the report. Prints only on the first page. The text that is displayed here is the text that was entered in the New Report dialog box; however, this text can be edited.

Headings	Enter headings for each column or page headings for other text which are printed at the top of each page. The default is to use the field names; however, these can be edited to better define the information in each column.
Record	Specify the fields that will be printed in the report.
Summary	Display the results of calculations or statistical summaries. Prints information at the end of the report.

Table 15-3

The labels in the report definition view

11. Click on the Print Preview button  to see how the report will look when printed. Click the left mouse button to enlarge. Your screen should resemble the following. If not all text in a column is displayed, choose **Cancel** to return to the report definition view and drag on the right borders of columns A, B, and C to enlarge the fields. Then return to print preview to confirm the adjustments.

NOTE: In the following section on customizing the report, a subtitle will be added, formatting will be applied, a new column for the **City** field will be inserted, and the title and subtitle will be moved to another column so that they are more centered on the page.

Client Telephone List

Lname	**Fname**	**Company**	**Phone**
Hammersmith	Michael	Software Unlimited	206 555-1297
Ho	Selena	The Northwest Bank	206 455-7855
Baker	Charles	IMS consultants	206 296-1278
Schuster	Simon	CTech Corporation	206 883-1129
Sills	Bonnie	CTech Corporation	206 925-5500
Long	Robert	Long and Tukes	206 454-9825
Krogstad	Sandra	Krogstad and Compa	206 821-9978
Jackson	Karen	Supermarkets, Inc.	206 392-5634
Smith	Trisha	Julien's Computers	206 284-9711
Grover	Douglas	Grover and Associate	206 887-3455
Mills	Nevell	The Baldwin Co.	206 821-9942
Gonzales	Theodore	The Best Store	206 455-2396
Kimball	Elizabeth	Downtown Pets	206 832-8877
Bell	Pat	The Furniture Emporium	206 833-9000
COUNT OF Lname		**14**	

11. Choose **Cancel** to return to the report definition view.

To leave report definition view

12. Click on either the Form View button 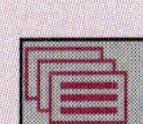 or the List View button  to leave report definition view.

Save the Report with the File

When you save the database file, any reports that have been created for it are automatically saved with the file.

To save the file with a new name:

1. Choose **File, Save As** to display the Save As dialog box.
2. Type **CH15PR3** in the **File Name** text box and choose **OK** or press **Enter**.

Select a Report

Use **View, Report** to see a list of reports and choose the one you want to use.

In either list view or in form view:

1. Choose **View, Report** to display the Reports dialog box. See Figure 15-17.

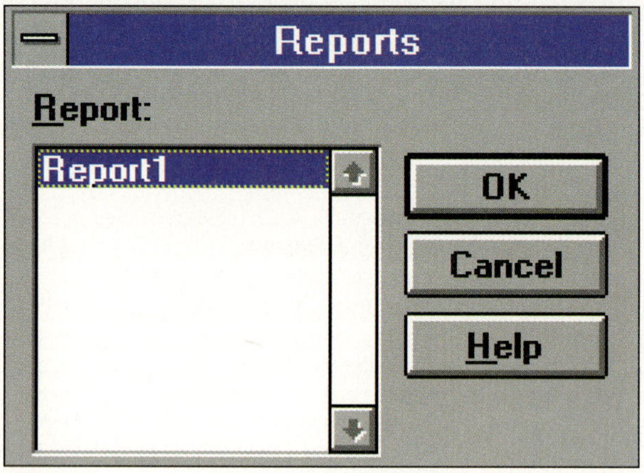

Figure 15-17
The Reports dialog box

2. Select **Report1** and choose **OK**. As other reports are created, they will be listed here.

CUSTOMIZING THE REPORT

The basic report format may not show all of the information you would like to have in the final output. For example, a subtitle can be added, or you can replace the field names with more detailed column headings that would better define the contents of each column. Blank separator rows can be inserted that would make the report easier to read.

Add a Subtitle

Here you will add a subtitle, **Puget Sound Charters**, in the second title row. Text in **Title** rows is printed only at the top of the first page.

1. Select the cell in the second **Title** row in column D.
2. Type **Puget Sound Charters** as shown in the following example.

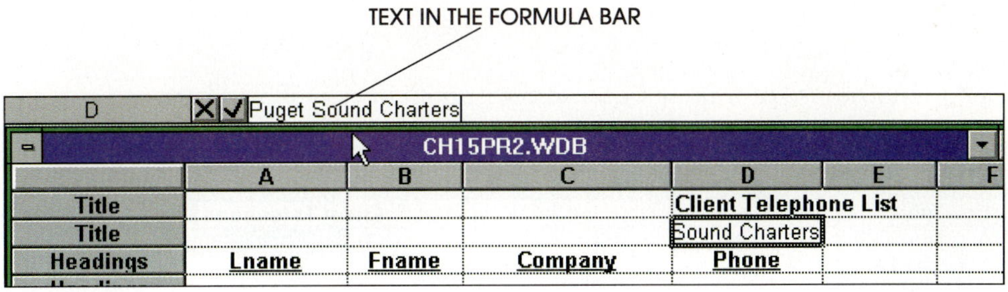

3.	Press	**Enter** to leave the formula bar. These titles will be moved to column C later.

Center Text

To center both headings:

1.	Select	the text in both rows of the title as shown here. To do this, point to **Client** and drag down to **Puget**.

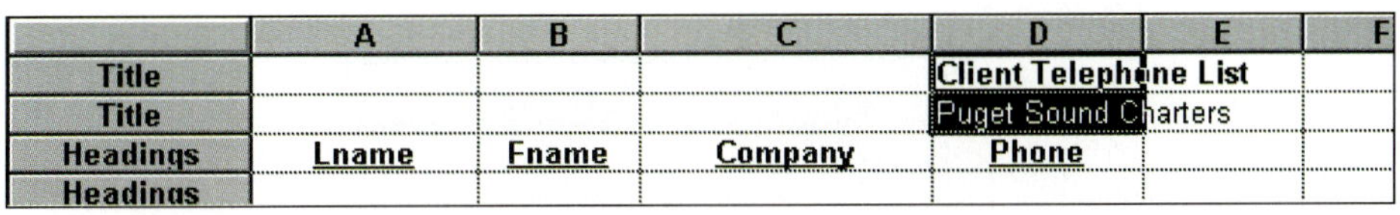

2.	Choose	**Format, Alignment** to go to the Alignment dialog box. See Figure 15-18.

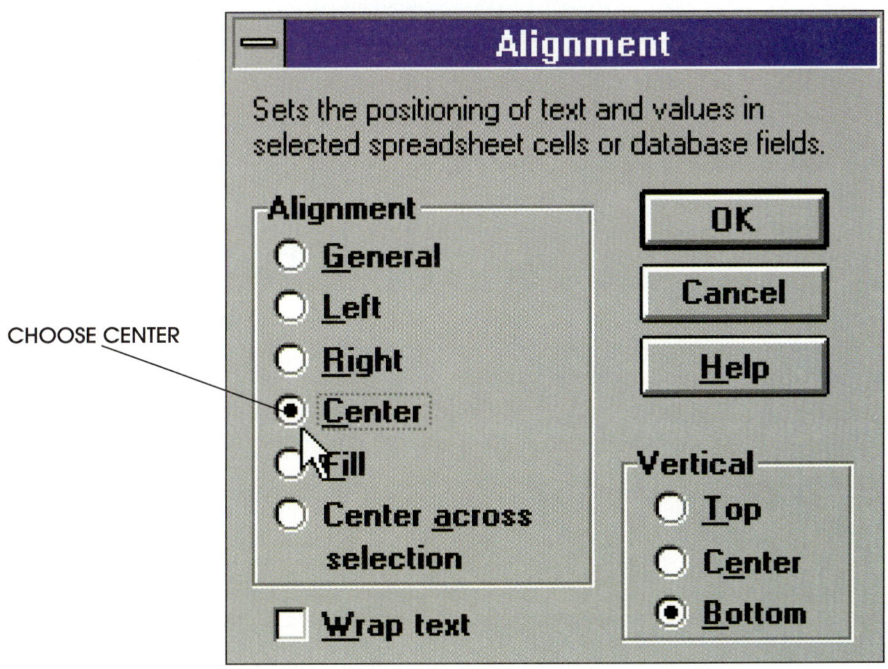

Figure 15-18
The Alignment dialog box

3. Choose **Center** to turn it on.

4. Choose **OK** or press **Enter** to center both titles as shown here.

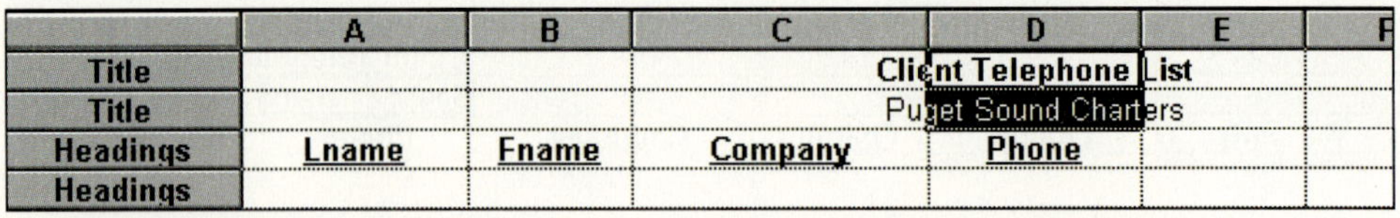

Insert a New Row

You now have text directly above the first **Headings** row. It would improve the layout to insert a blank line between the second **Title** row and the first **Headings** row.

1. Select **Lname** as shown here. You do not necessarily have to select the first cell—any cell can be selected to insert a blank row above it.

2. Choose **Insert, Row/Column** to display the Insert dialog box as shown in Figure 15-19.

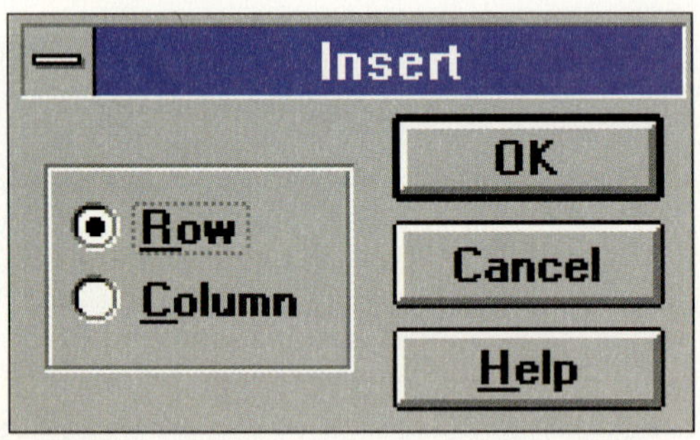

Figure 15-19
The Insert dialog box

3. Leave **Row** turned on.

4. Choose **OK** or press **Enter** to display the Insert Row dialog box as shown in Figure 15-20.

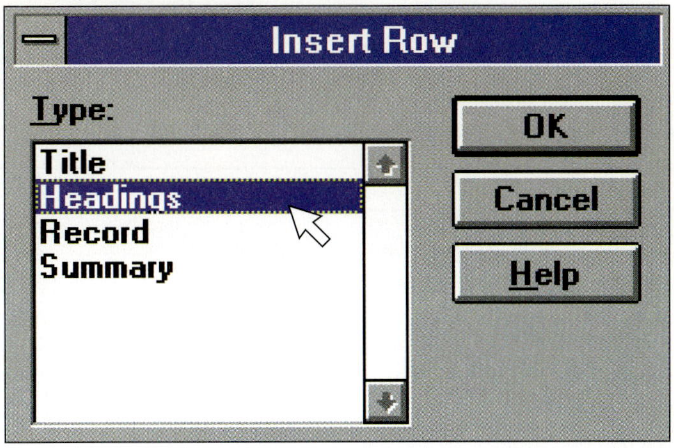

Figure 15-20
The Insert Row dialog box

Headings is automatically selected because that is the row in which you have selected the cell containing **Lname**; however, you can choose any type of row to insert.

5. Leave the selection as is.

6. Choose **OK** or press **Enter** to insert the additional row as shown here.

	A	B	C	D	E	F
Title				Client Telephone List		
Title				Puget Sound Charters		
Headings						
Headings	Lname	Fname	Company	Phone		
Headings						

NOTE: To remove a row, select the *entire* row and choose **Insert, Delete Row/Column.**

Edit Headings

The field names are entered automatically as column headings, but they do not always clearly identify the contents of the field, because they may be abbreviated as in this report. For example, **Lname** is used instead of **Last name**. Here changes will be made and the final **Headings** row will look like the following example.

Title				Client Telephone List	
Title				Puget Sound Charters	
Headings					
Headings	Last name	First name	Company	Phone	
Headings					
Record	=Lname	=Fname	=Company	=Phone	
Summary					

1. Select **Lname** in the Headings row and press **Delete** to remove the text.
2. Type **Last name** and press **Enter** to leave the formula bar.
3. Repeat steps 1 and 2 to replace **Fname** with **First name.**

Format Text in Bold

Add bold formatting to the subtitle. The Bold button on the toolbar is used here; however, you can also choose **Format**, **Font and Style** and turn on **Bold**.

1. Select **Puget Sound Charters** in column D in the second **Title** row as shown here. Not all text is shown in the cell; however, all of it is displayed in the formula bar so you know that it is all selected.

Title				**Client Telephone List**	
Title				Puget Sound Charters	
Headings					

2. Click on the Bold button **B**.

Insert a Column and Field

Insert a new column and data from the **City** field between **Company** and **Phone**.

To insert a column

1. Move the insertion point to any cell in column D (the **Phone** column).
2. Choose **Insert, Row/Column** to display the Insert dialog box.
3. Choose **Column** to turn it on and then choose **OK** or press **Enter**. A new column is inserted as shown in the following example.

Title				**Client Telephone**	
Title				**Puget Sound Char**	
Headings					
Headings	**Last name**	**First name**	**Company**		**Phone**
Headings					
Record	=Lname	=Fname	=Company		=Phone
Summ Lname					
Summary					

To insert a field name

You can use the Insert menu to insert both a field name and a field entry.

1. Move the insertion point to column D (the new column) in the second **Headings** row as shown in the following example.

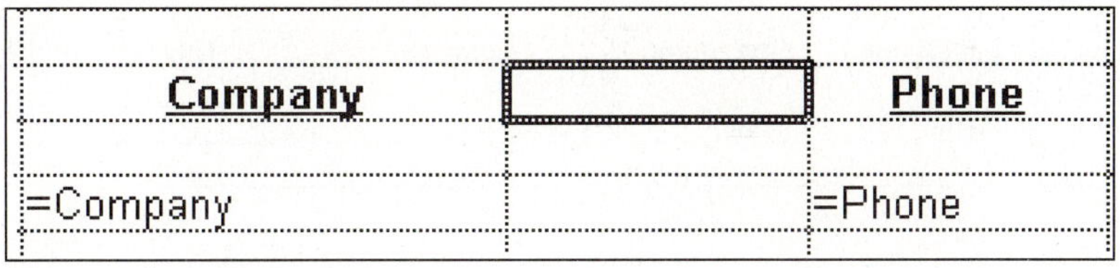

2. Choose **Insert, Field Name** to display the Insert Field Name dialog box.

3. Select **City** as shown in Figure 15-21.

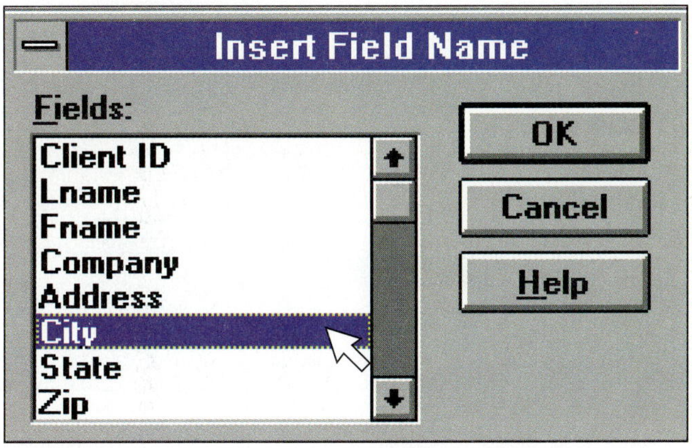

Figure 15-21
The Insert Field Name dialog box

4. Choose **OK** or press **Enter** to insert the field name in the cell

5. Click on the Bold and Underline buttons, if necessary to add formatting to the new text. Also, if necessary, choose **Format, Alignment, Center** and **OK** Your report should resemble the following.

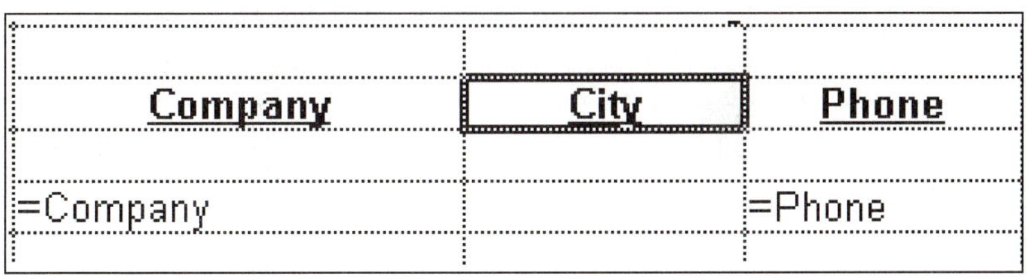

To insert a field entry

You now need to insert the data from the City field into the report. Use the *Insert, field entry* command to display the data from the selected field in the report.

1. Move the insertion point to the cell in column D that is in the **Record** row as shown in the following example.

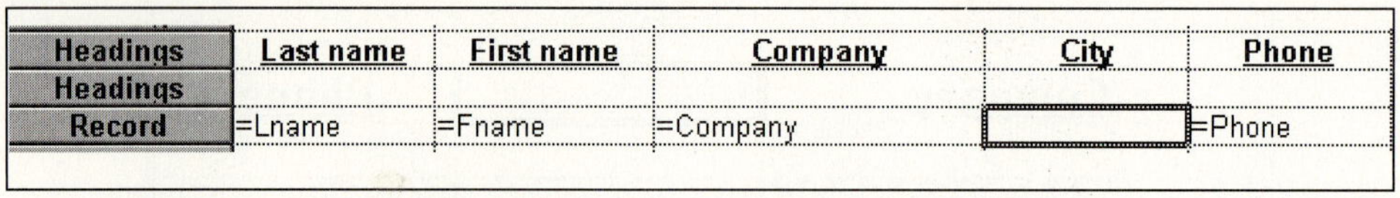

2. Choose **Insert, Field Entry** to display the Insert Field Entry dialog box.
3. Select **City** as shown in Figure 15-22.

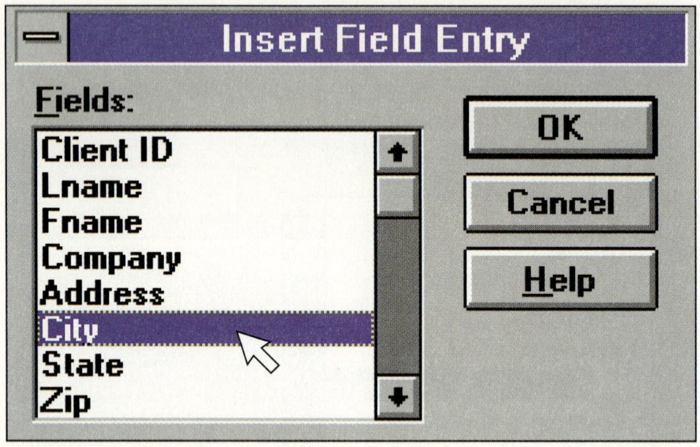

Figure 15-22
The Insert Field Entry dialog box

4. Choose **OK** or press **Enter** to insert the field as shown here.

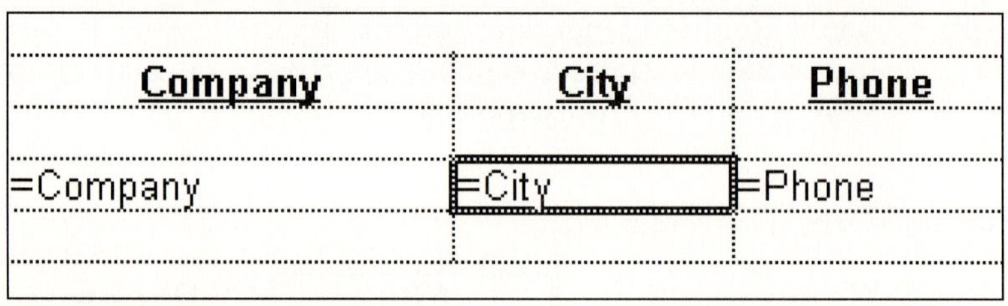

Move Text from One Column to Another

Instructions are given here for moving the title and subtitle to column C so that it is more centered on the page.

1. Select both cells in column E in the **Title** rows. You may not have all of the text displayed as shown here.

2. **Click** on the Cut button 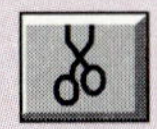 or choose **Edit, Cut,** or press **Ctrl/X.**
3. **Move** the insertion point to the first **Title** row in column C.
4. **Click** on the Paste button , or choose **Edit, Paste,** or press **Ctrl/V** to insert the text in a different cell as shown here.

Group Data

Here you will group the data on the basis of the first letter in the Lname field. This will group all names beginning with the same first letter—all A's in one groups, B's in another, and so on. The insertion point can be at any location in the report definition view.

1. **Choose** **Tools, Sort Records** to display the Sort Records dialog box.
2. **Click** on the down arrow at the end of the **1st Field** box to display the list of field names and select **Lname.**
3. **Choose** **Break G** to turn on the break (grouping).
4. **Choose** **1st Letter I** to group on the basis of the first letter of the names in the **Lname** field. The dialog box should look like Figure 15-23.

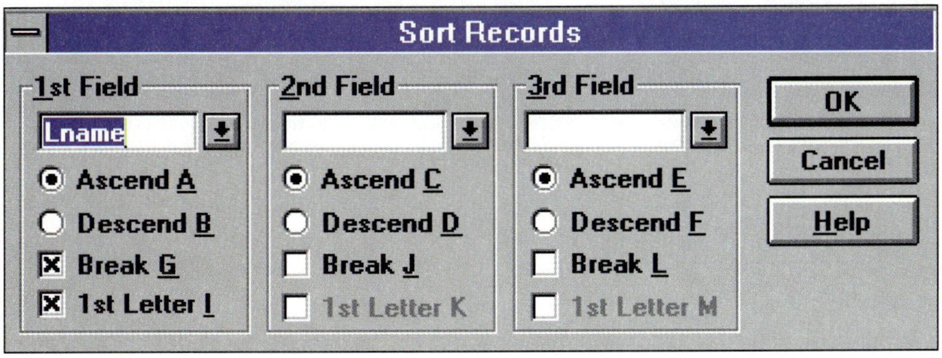

Figure 15-23
The Sort Records dialog box

5. **Choose** **OK** or press **Enter** to return to the report as shown here.

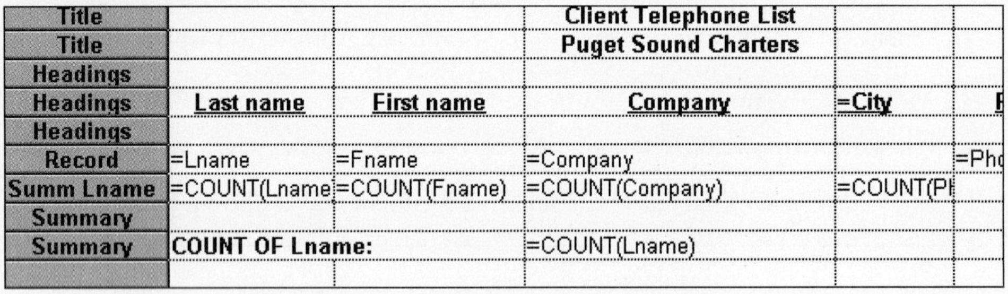

Title			Client Telephone List		
Title			Puget Sound Charters		
Headings					
Headings	Last name	First name	Company	=City	P
Headings					
Record	=Lname	=Fname	=Company		=Pho
Summ Lname	=COUNT(Lname	=COUNT(Fname)	=COUNT(Company)	=COUNT(Pl	
Summary					
Summary	COUNT OF Lname:		=COUNT(Lname)		

To delete the COUNT formulas in the new Summ Lname row (they show counts of names in each group which are not necessary in this report)

6. Select all COUNT formulas in the Summ Lname row and press **Delete**.

7. Choose **Print Preview** to see how the report now looks. Zoom the display, return to the report definition view to make any adjustments, if necessary. Your final output should resemble the following example.

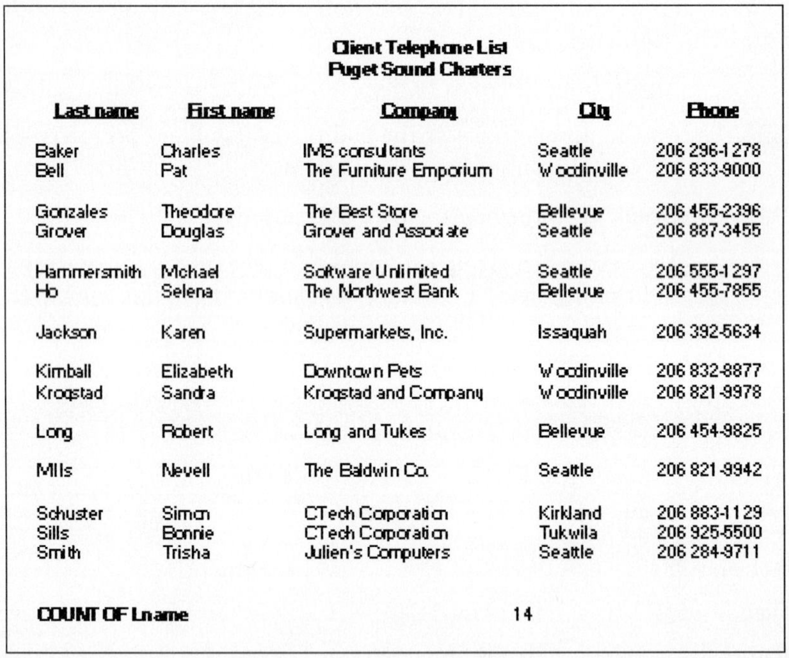

Client Telephone List
Puget Sound Charters

Last name	First name	Company	City	Phone
Baker	Charles	IMS consultants	Seattle	206 296-1278
Bell	Pat	The Furniture Emporium	Woodinville	206 833-9000
Gonzales	Theodore	The Best Store	Bellevue	206 455-2396
Grover	Douglas	Grover and Associate	Seattle	206 887-3455
Hammersmith	Michael	Software Unlimited	Seattle	206 555-1297
Ho	Selena	The Northwest Bank	Bellevue	206 455-7855
Jackson	Karen	Supermarkets, Inc.	Issaquah	206 392-5634
Kimball	Elizabeth	Downtown Pets	Woodinville	206 832-8877
Krogstad	Sandra	Krogstad and Company	Woodinville	206 821-9978
Long	Robert	Long and Tukes	Bellevue	206 454-9825
Mills	Nevell	The Baldwin Co.	Seattle	206 821-9942
Schuster	Simon	CTech Corporation	Kirkland	206 883-1129
Sills	Bonnie	CTech Corporation	Tukwila	206 925-5500
Smith	Trisha	Julien's Computers	Seattle	206 284-9711

COUNT OF Lname 14

8. Choose **Cancel** 

to return to the report definition view.

9. Save the file again as **CH15PR3**.

Print the Report

Be sure you remain in the report definition view.

1. **Click** on the Print button [print button icon] to send the report to the printer

or

Choose **File, Print** or press **Ctrl/P** to go to the Print dialog box and choose **OK** or press **Enter** to print.

GUIDED TUTORIAL

What You'll Do

- Sort records.
- Practice query commands.
- Perform wildcard searches.
- Create a report.

How To Do It

1. **Open** the **CH14TUT** file that you created in Chapter 14 or retrieve it from the Instructor data disk.
2. **Switch** to list view as shown here.

	Member	ID Number	Last Name	First Name	Membership Date	Dues Owing
1	1	359345678	Randle	Colleen	1/2/94	$3.25
2	2	329542198	Jones	Randall	1/3/94	$2.95
3	3	295754444	Wilson	Richard	1/4/94	$3.80
4	4	329951897	Costner	Jeremy	1/5/94	$2.00
5	5	297882917	Mitchell	Sandra	1/4/94	$4.00
6	6	238844768	Thiry	Jacques	1/5/94	$4.50
7	7	278374758	Madsen	Olivia	1/3/94	$3.00
8	8	378577611	Petrella	Harold	1/5/94	$3.95
9	9	278574199	Ferrier	Karen	1/4/94	$3.50
10	10	327899511	Jackson	Martha	1/3/94	$3.60
11	11	547178594	McReynolds	Sally	1/2/94	$3.70
12	12	457882298	Newman	Julie	1/2/94	$3.70
13						

3. **Choose** **Tools, Sort Records** to display the Sort Records dialog box.
4. **Click** on the down arrow at the right end of the **1st Field** list box and select **Membership Date** as shown in the following example.

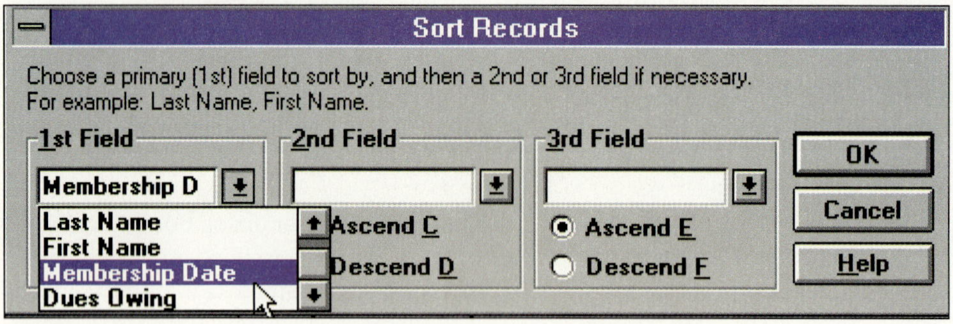

5. Leave **Ascend A** turned on.

6. Choose **OK** or press **Enter** to sort the records. See the following example.

	Member	ID Number	Last Name	First Name	Membership Date	Dues Owing
1	1	359345678	Randle	Colleen	1/2/94	$3.25
2	11	547178594	McReynolds	Sally	1/2/94	$3.70
3	12	457882298	Newman	Julie	1/2/94	$3.70
4	2	329542198	Jones	Randall	1/3/94	$2.95
5	7	278374758	Madsen	Olivia	1/3/94	$3.00
6	10	327899511	Jackson	Martha	1/3/94	$3.60
7	3	295754444	Wilson	Richard	1/4/94	$3.80
8	5	297882917	Mitchell	Sandra	1/4/94	$4.00
9	9	278574199	Ferrier	Karen	1/4/94	$3.50
10	4	329951897	Costner	Jeremy	1/5/94	$2.00
11	6	238844768	Thiry	Jacques	1/5/94	$4.50
12	8	378577611	Petrella	Harold	1/5/94	$3.95
13						

To print a copy of the sorted records:

7. Click on the Print button, or choose **File, Print**, or press **Ctrl/P** to display the Print dialog box, and choose **OK** or press **Enter**.

Next, sort records by **Membership Date** in ascending order and by **Dues Owing** in descending order, using the following instructions.

8. Choose **Tools, Sort Records** to go to the Sort Records dialog box.

9. Leave **1st Field** as is.

10. Click on the down arrow at the right end of the **2nd Field** list box and select **Dues Owing** as shown here.

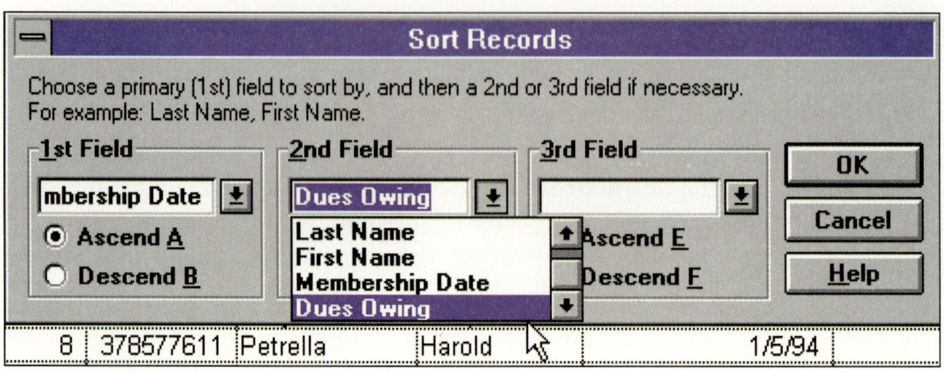

11. Choose **Descend D** to turn it on.

12. Choose **OK** or press **Enter** to sort the records. See the following example.

	Member	ID Number	Last Name	First Name	Membership Date	Dues Owing
1	11	547178594	McReynolds	Sally	1/2/94	$3.70
2	12	457882298	Newman	Julie	1/2/94	$3.70
3	1	359345678	Randle	Colleen	1/2/94	$3.25
4	10	327899511	Jackson	Martha	1/3/94	$3.60
5	7	278374758	Madsen	Olivia	1/3/94	$3.00
6	2	329542198	Jones	Randall	1/3/94	$2.95
7	5	297882917	Mitchell	Sandra	1/4/94	$4.00
8	3	295754444	Wilson	Richard	1/4/94	$3.80
9	9	278574199	Ferrier	Karen	1/4/94	$3.50
10	6	238844768	Thiry	Jacques	1/5/94	$4.50
11	8	378577611	Petrella	Harold	1/5/94	$3.95
12	4	329951897	Costner	Jeremy	1/5/94	$2.00
13						

To query the database for all records between January 2, 1994, and January 4, 1994:

13. Choose **Tools, Create New Query** to display the New Query dialog box.

14. Select **Membership Date** from the list in the **A** list box as shown here.

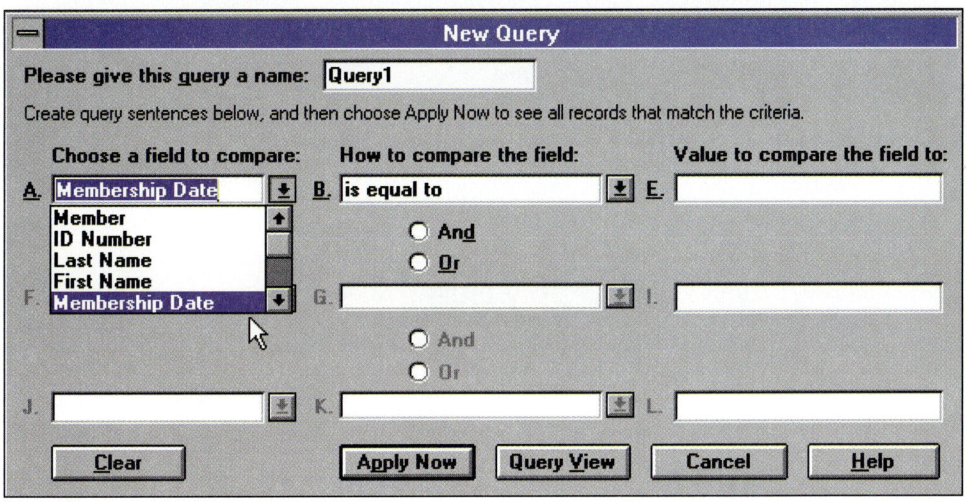

15. Select **is greater than or equal to** in the **How to compare the field** text box.

16. Move the insertion point to **E** and type **1/2/94** as shown here.

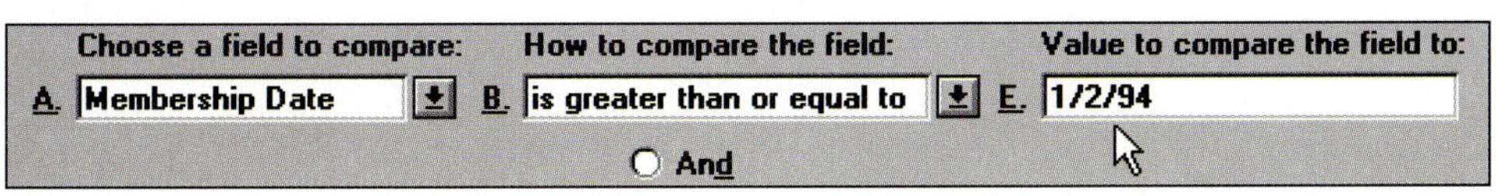

17. Choose **And** to turn it on and to make the next line of boxes active.

18. Move the insertion point to the **F** list box and select **Membership Date** again.

19. Move the insertion point to the **G** list box and select **is less than or equal to** as shown here.

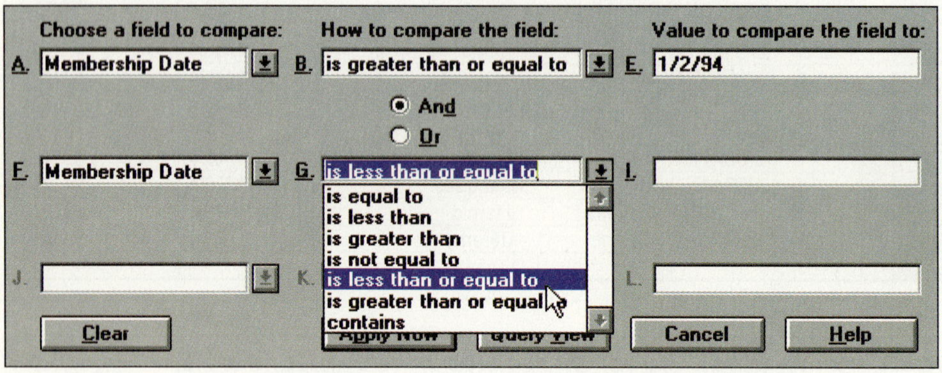

20. Move the insertion point to **I** and type **1/4/94** as shown here.

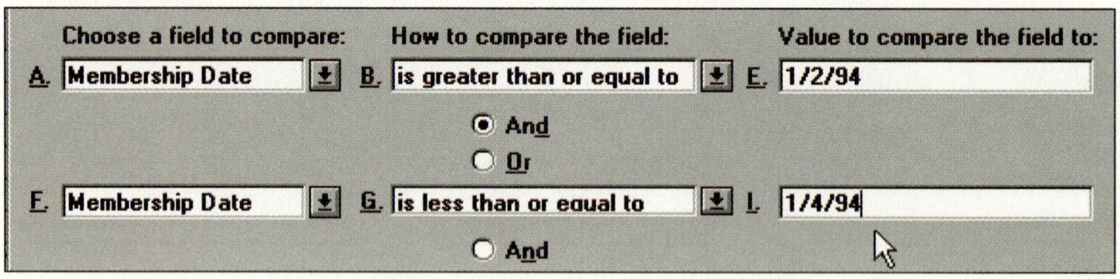

21. Choose **Apply Now** Apply Now to query on two conditions. The results should be similar to the example shown here.

	Member	ID Number	Last Name	First Name	Membership Date	Dues Owing
1	11	547178594	McReynolds	Sally	1/2/94	$3.70
2	12	457882298	Newman	Julie	1/2/94	$3.70
3	1	359345678	Randle	Colleen	1/2/94	$3.25
4	10	327899511	Jackson	Martha	1/3/94	$3.60
5	7	278374758	Madsen	Olivia	1/3/94	$3.00
6	2	329542198	Jones	Randall	1/3/94	$2.95
7	5	297882917	Mitchell	Sandra	1/4/94	$4.00
8	3	295754444	Wilson	Richard	1/4/94	$3.80
9	9	278574199	Ferrier	Karen	1/4/94	$3.50
13						

22. Choose **View, Show All Records** to see the original records in the database.

To query for records where the Dues Owing field contains a value greater than 3.50:

23. Choose **Tools, Create New Query** to display the New Query dialog box.
24. Select **Dues Owing** in the **A** list box.
25. Choose **B** (the **How to compare the field** box).
26. Select **is greater than**.
27. Choose **E** (the **Value to compare the field to** box).
28. Type **3.50**. Your dialog box should resemble the following example.

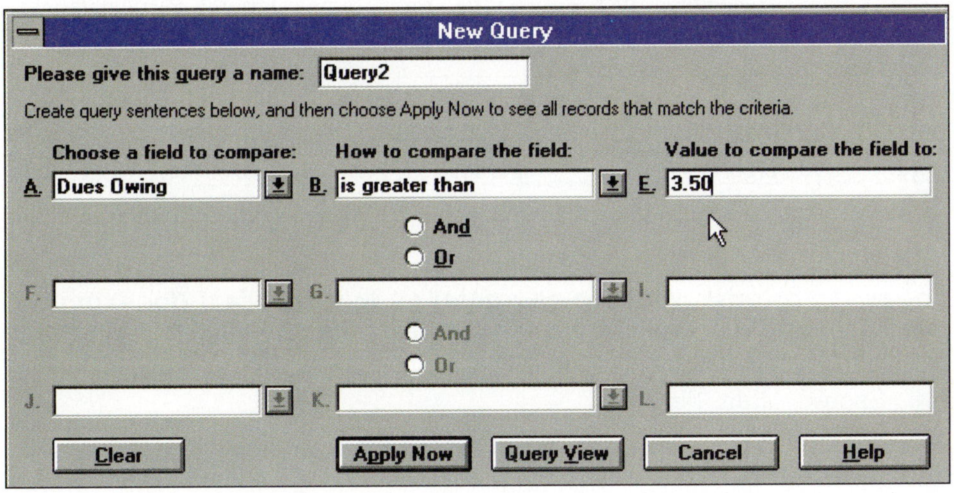

29. Choose **Apply Now** Apply Now. The result should be like that shown in the following example. Then show all records again (choose **View, Show All Records**) if you like.

	Member	ID Number	Last Name	First Name	Membership Date	Dues Owing
1	11	547178594	McReynolds	Sally	1/2/94	$3.70
2	12	457882298	Newman	Julie	1/2/94	$3.70
4	10	327899511	Jackson	Martha	1/3/94	$3.60
7	5	297882917	Mitchell	Sandra	1/4/94	$4.00
8	3	295754444	Wilson	Richard	1/4/94	$3.80
10	6	238844768	Thiry	Jacques	1/5/94	$4.50
11	8	378577611	Petrella	Harold	1/5/94	$3.95
13						

To search for the record(s) containing the last name Ferrier:

30. Choose **Edit, Find** to display the Find dialog box.
31. Type **Ferrier** in the text box as shown in the following example.

32. Choose **All records** to turn it on (see the preceding example).

33. Choose **OK** or press **Enter** to show the results as displayed in the following example. Choose **View, Show All Records** if you like; however, this is not required. The Find function searches through all records in the file even when they are not showing in the database window.

	Member	ID Number	Last Name	First Name	Membership Date	Dues Owing
9	9	278574199	Ferrier	Karen	1/4/94	$3.50
13						

To use the asterisk wildcard character (*) to locate text (for example, McReynolds) when you are not sure of the spelling (Is it* Mac *or* Mc, *and how is* Reynolds *spelled?):

34. Choose **Edit, Find.**

35. Type **M*R*nolds** in the **Find What** text box as shown here.

NOTE: You do not necessarily have to match case when you type the text in the text box. If you type **m+r_nolds,** Works will still locate the data.

36. Choose **All records** to turn it on as shown in the preceding example.

37. Choose **OK** or press **Enter** to locate **McReynolds**, then choose **View, Show All Records.**

To sort records by last name and create a report of the members with dues owing:

38. Choose **Tools, Sort Records** and select **Last Name** in the **1st Field** list. Be sure **Ascend A** is turned on. Leave **Dues Owing** in the **Find Field** and **Descend D** turned on.

39. Choose **OK** or press **Enter** to sort.

To create the report

40. Click on the Report View button to go to the New Report dialog box.

41. Type **Members with dues owing** in the Report Title text box.

42. Select and choose **Add >** for each of the following: **Last Name, First Name,** and **Dues Owing.**

43. Choose **OK** to display the Report Statistics dialog box, choose **OK** to display the prompt telling you the report is created, and choose **OK** to go to report definition view.

44. Click on the Print Preview button to see the report. Choose **Cancel** to return to the report definition view.

45. Select the title in Column D, click on the Cut button, move the insertion point to Column B and click on the Paste button to move the title.

46. Drag on the column border of columns A and B to the right to move the data so that it is more centered on the page. Your final report should resemble the following when viewed in Print Preview.

Members with dues owing

Last Name	First Name	Dues Owing
Costner	Jeremy	$2.00
Ferrier	Karen	$3.50
Jackson	Martha	$3.60
Jones	Randall	$2.95
Madsen	Olivia	$3.00
McReynolds	Sally	$3.70
Mitchell	Sandra	$4.00
Newman	Julie	$3.70
Petrella	Harold	$3.95
Randle	Colleen	$3.25
Thiry	Jacques	$4.50
Wilson	Richard	$3.80

47. Save the database as **CH15TUT.**

In report definition view

48. Click on the Print button to print the report.

REVIEW QUESTIONS

1. What commands do you use to display the following dialog boxes?

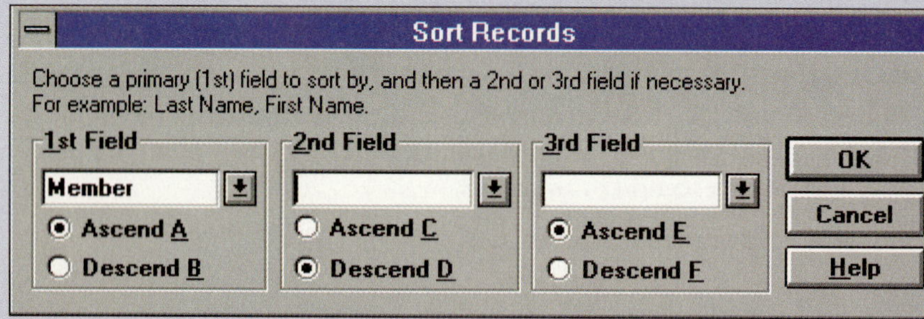

Choose ______________________________

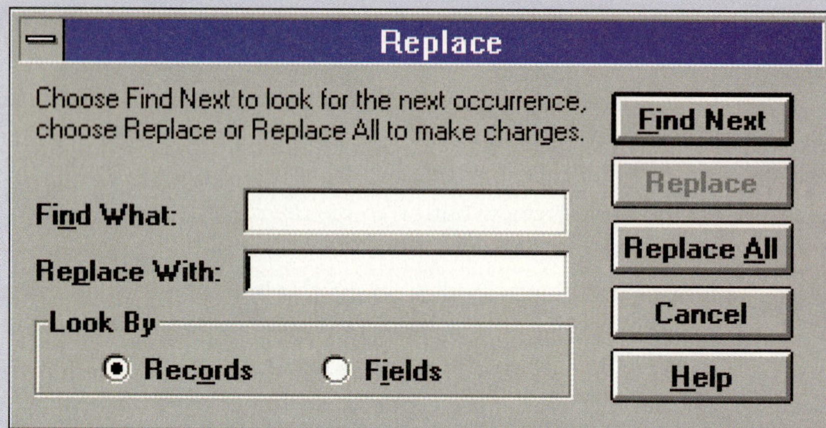

Choose ______________________________

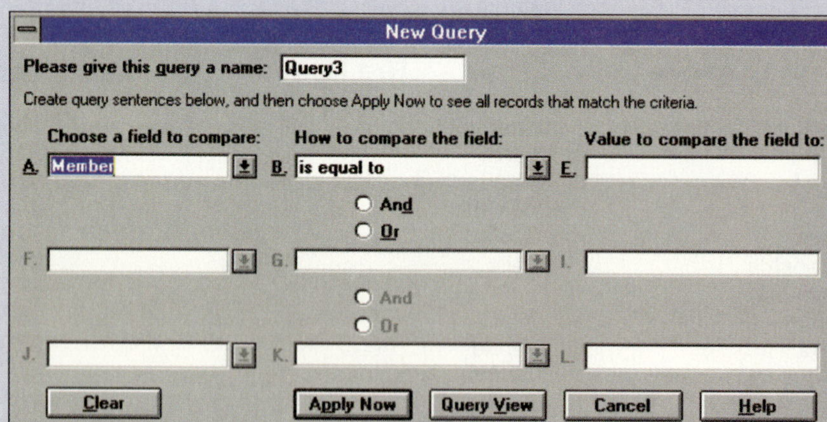

Choose ______________________________

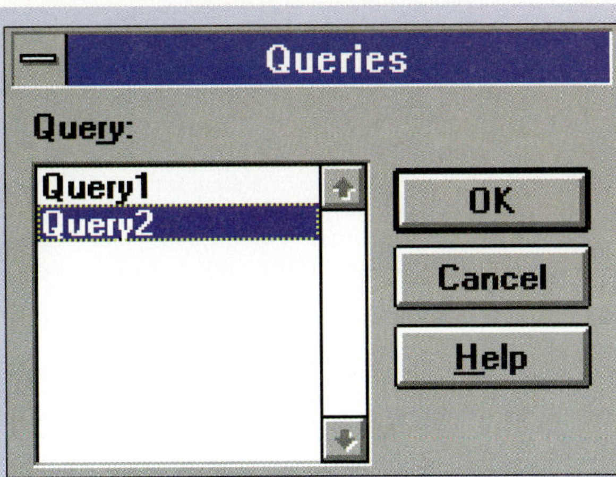

Choose ____

2. Describe the results of choosing each of the following in the Find dialog box.

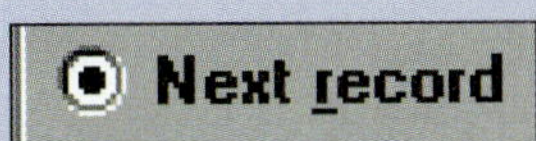

____

____

____

____

____

____

3. Describe the results of choosing each of the following in the Look By box in the Replace dialog box.

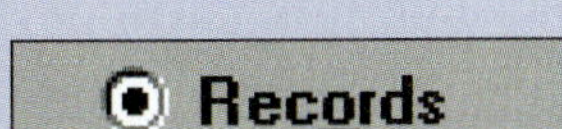

____

____

____

4. Dates in a query instruction must be enclosed in ____________________.
5. Text in an instruction entered in a Query form that includes operators must be enclosed in ____________________.
6. Logical operators are always surrounded by ____________________.
7. Describe the results of the following queries.

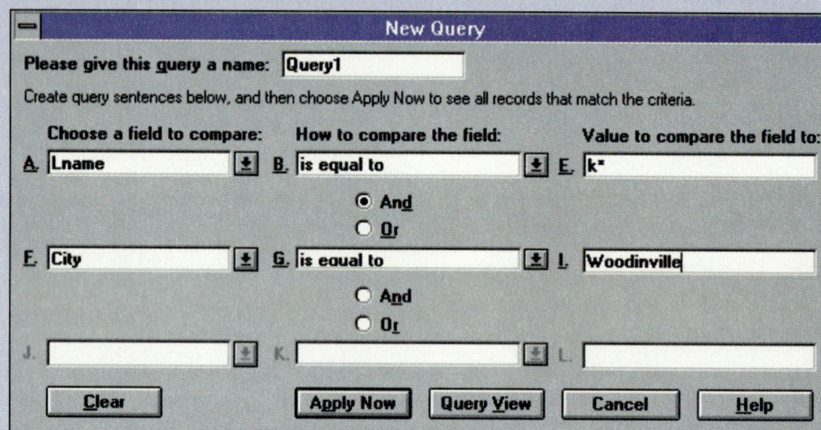

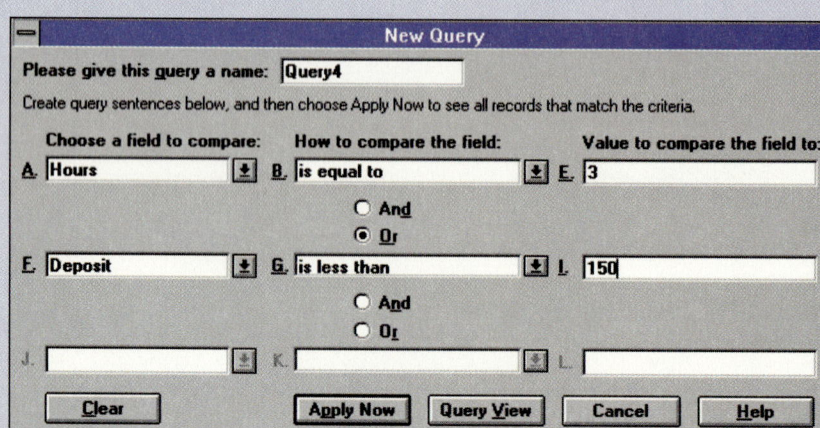

8. When do you use the Query form rather than the Query dialog box?

9. Choose the ______________________ command from the ______________________ to create a new report.

10. List the menu and command that is selected to display each of the dialog boxes and briefly describe the box's use.

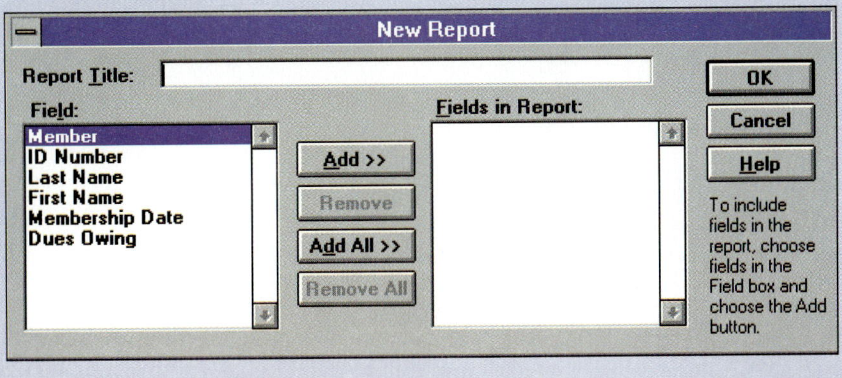

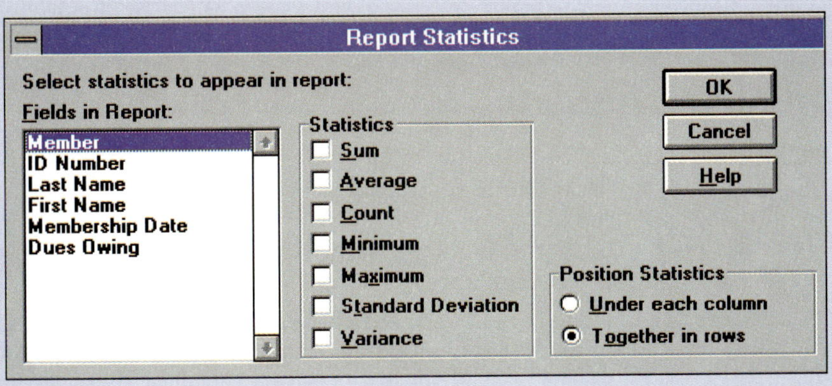

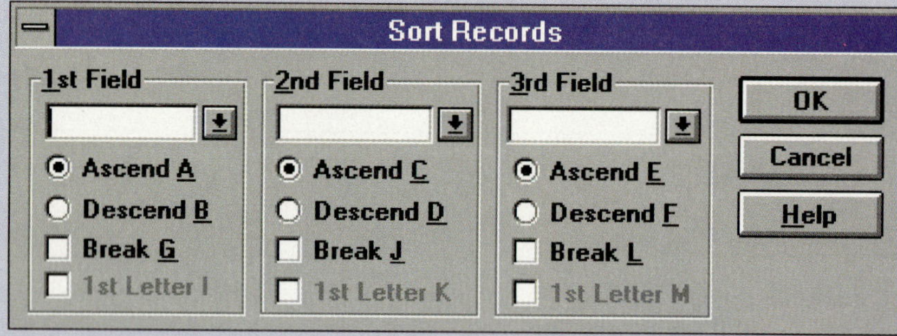

___

___

___

Hands-on Exercises

Exercise 1

1. Open the database file **CH14HO1** that you created in Chapter 14.
2. Sort the file on the **Response** field in ascending order and print a copy of the output.
3. Perform a query for each of the following. Print a copy of each result.
   a. All M responses
   b. All responses received on August 15 or August 16
   c. All T or W responses
   d. All W responses received on August 15
   e. All C or NP responses
4. Sort the file by **Date** in ascending order and print a copy of the output.
5. Sort the file by **Survey Number** in ascending order and print a copy.
6. Save the file as **CH15HO1** and close the window.

Exercise 2

1. Create the following database file showing registration and licensing information on each of the vessels in Puget Sound Charters' ownership.

Boat Name	Reg. No.	Captain	Persons	License	Length	Tonnage	Beam	Speed
Delano	WN6655L	Randle	200	ICL	74	28	22	7
The Spirit	WN6291L	Kennedy	225	OCL	130	74	34	14
Sea Wolf	WN3251J	Eiler	49	IC	62	29	24	11.5
Irish Sea	WN7210S	Brodie	150	ICL	90	60	28	12

2. Save the file as **CH15HO2**.

3. Include the following list in Form View. It explains the information in the **License** field for each of the vessels. This information is defined as follows and should be added in form view at the bottom of the form using **Insert, Label.**
   - I Inland waters
   - O Oceangoing
   - C Catering facilities
   - L Liquor license
4. Sort the records by boat name and print a copy in list view.
5. Query for all boats licensed for inland waters (perform a wildcard search). (*HINT:* Type ***I*** in the **Value to Compare . . .** text box.)
6. Print a copy of the results.
7. Query for all boats that can carry 200 or more passengers. Print a copy of the results.
8. Query for all boats that can carry 200 or more passengers and that are licensed for ocean waters. (*HINT:* Type **O*** in the **Value to Compare . . .** text box.)
9. Print a copy of the results.
10. Query for all boats that can carry 200 or more passengers or have a length greater than 90 feet. Print a copy of the results.
11. Save the file again and close the window.

Exercise 3

1. Retrieve **CH14HO3** from your data disk.
2. Use **Edit, Go To** to locate any fields that may not be showing in list view, and then choose **Format, Field Width, Best Fit** to display the contents of the column.
3. Sort the records on **Description** in ascending order and print a copy.
4. Sort the file on **In Stock** in descending order and print a copy.
5. Sort the file on **Description** in ascending order and then sort **Rented** in descending order. Print a copy.
6. Perform a search to locate Roller skates and change the name to Ice skates.
7. Perform a search and change the **In stock** amount for roller blades to 650. (Hint: Search for "500" and then change it to "650." It may be necessary to drag on the Replace dialog box title bar to move it to a different position in the window.)
8. Add a new field called **Total** and compute the total by multiplying **Rented** times **Cost**.
9. Format all dollar amounts as currency with two decimals.
10. Save this file as **CH15HO3**.
11. Preview the file and print a copy. Close the window when done.

Exercise 4

1. Retrieve **CH14HO4**.

2. Sort the file on **Date**.
3. Query for the following and print a copy of each result.
   a. All trips scheduled for July.
   (*HINT:* The New Query dialog box should show the following:)

In **Choose a field . . .**	In **How to Compare . . .**	In **Value . . .**
Show **Date**	Show **Is greater then or equal to** turn on **And**	Type **7/1/95**
Show **Date**	Show **Is less than or equal to**	Type **7/31/95**

   b. All trips including the word **Lake** in their description. Use the wildcard character * (asterisk) on either side of **Lake** here.
   c. All trips scheduled for August and going to the San Juan Islands. (*HINT:* Three conditions will be entered here—the first two conditions are needed to query for the August dates similar to the query in Step 3a.) There will be only one record.
4. Name the last query, **San Juan**.
5. Add the following record to the file.
   8 Island Hop 8/25/95 Orcas and San Juan Islands 8:00 AM 7:00 PM
6. Use the San Juan query again to search for all trips that include a San Juan destination. Only one record will be displayed. To correct this, choose **View, Query** and edit the Query conditions in the formula bar by adding an asterisk (*) in front of San Juan Islands. Then perform the query again.

   NOTE: This will locate all records with San Juan preceded by any other text. If you typed ***San Juan***, it would locate records with San Juan and any additional text on either side of the name.

7. Print a copy of the query results.
8. Save this file as **CH15HO4**.
9. Close the window and exit Works.

Examples of Exercises

Exercise 3: CH15HO3

	Description	In stock	Month	Rented	Cost	Total
1	Crazy hats	250	March	$2,500.00	$1.00	$2,500.00
2	Ice skates	1500	March	$500.00	$2.50	$1,250.00
3	Knee pads	1500	March	$1,300.00	$1.00	$1,300.00
4	Life jackets	1000	March	$100.00	$5.00	$500.00
5	Roller blades	650	March	$650.00	$3.50	$2,275.00
6	Skate boards	850	March	$450.00	$2.50	$1,125.00
7	Water balloons	820	March	$1,250.00	$0.50	$625.00
8						

	Even	Description	Date	Destination	Departure	Return	Hours
1	1	Lake Union Roundup	7/1/95	Lake Union & Ship Canal	4:00 PM	8:30 PM	4:30
2	2	Loop the Locks	7/5/95	Elliott Bay	1:00 PM	8:00 PM	7:00
3	5	Ride the Waves	7/20/95	Snohomish River	10:00 AM	4:00 PM	6:00
4	7	Up All Night	7/30/95	The Lakes	8:00 PM	8:00 AM	12:00
9							

Step 3a.

	Even	Description	Date	Destination	Departure	Return	Hours
1	1	Lake Union Roundup	7/1/95	Lake Union & Ship Canal	4:00 PM	8:30 PM	4:30
6	4	Do The Lake	8/15/95	Kirkland	5:00 PM	10:00 PM	5:00
9							

Step 3b.

	Even	Description	Date	Destination	Departure	Return	Hours
5	3	Islands A-Go-Go	8/12/95	San Juan Islands	7:00 AM	7:00 PM	12:00
8							

Step 3c.

	Even	Description	Date	Destination	Departure	Return	Hours
5	3	Islands A-Go-Go	8/12/95	San Juan Islands	7:00 AM	7:00 PM	12:00
8	8	Island Hop	8/25/95	Orcas and San Juan Islar	8:00 AM	7:00 PM	11:00
9							
10							
11							
12							
13							
14							
15							
16							
17							
18							
19							
20							

Queries

Query:

Query1
Query2
San Juan

OK
Cancel
Help

Step 4 Query dialog box showing all queries for this file

CHAPTER 16

Integrating Files

OBJECTIVES

Create a form document

Preview and print the merged output

Create mailing labels

Preview and print labels

Copy database information to a word processing document

PREVIEW

A form letter, or other form document, is one that can be sent to many different individuals when merged with records from a database file. Using the word processing tool and the database tool, many different names and addresses (or other fields) can be merged with a single form document to produce standard letters, mailing labels, or other types of forms.

In this chapter you will produce a letter that will be sent to the clients in the **CH15PR2** database file. You will then create mailing labels using the same database information to accompany the letters. Creating a form document is similar to any other document. Just type the text that you want in the document and insert field names from the database file at the positions in the document where you want to merge the information from the database file. For example, in a form letter, insert the field names for first and last names, company names, and addresses at the appropriate position for an inside address in a business letter. Other fields can be inserted at other positions as needed, and you can also insert the same field at more than one position.

In addition, this chapter will give instructions for selecting a block of data and copying it to a word processing document.

CREATING A FORM DOCUMENT

The form document for this exercise will be a business letter. Keep in mind, however, that you could create any type of document with the word processing tool. All you need to merge it with a database file is the inclusion of the field names within the body of the document. The field names enclosed in chevrons (<< >>) are called *placeholders*.

Since the database document that will be used with this exercise has already been created **(CH15PR2)**, you will not need to create a new one. You will, however, create the form letter that is shown here.

longdate

<<Fname>> <<Lname>>
<<Company>>
<<Address>>
<<City>>, <<State>> <<Zip>>

SUMMER PROMOTION

This summer season begins early for the boat charter business. May begins a busy time that usually continues through mid-October.

This year we are offering 25 percent off all tickets purchased by corporations prior to May 1, 1994. This includes tickets for any of our cruises: lunch, weekend brunches, or evening dinners.

If you are interested in receiving this once-a-year offer, please call our office for further details. Hope to see you on board!

PUGET SOUND CHARTERS

Create a Form Document

1. Start — Works if necessary.
2. Open — the **Word Processor** tool to display a new document window.
3. Press — **Enter** about five times to insert five blank lines at the top of the document.

To insert a code that prints the current date whenever the document is printed:

4. Choose — **Insert, Special Character, Print long date.**
5. Choose — **OK** or press **Enter** to insert the *longdate* code.
6. Press — **Enter** four more times to insert four blank lines following the date.

Inserting database fields

Inserting database fields is a procedure that inserts placeholders such as <<Fname>>, <<Lname>>, for the database fields. In this exercise, these placeholders are where the names and addresses of the clients to whom you are sending this letter will be printed when the form document is merged with the database information. The database does not necessarily have to be open before inserting the fields.

1. Choose — **Insert, Database Field** to display the Insert Field dialog box as shown in Figure 16-1.

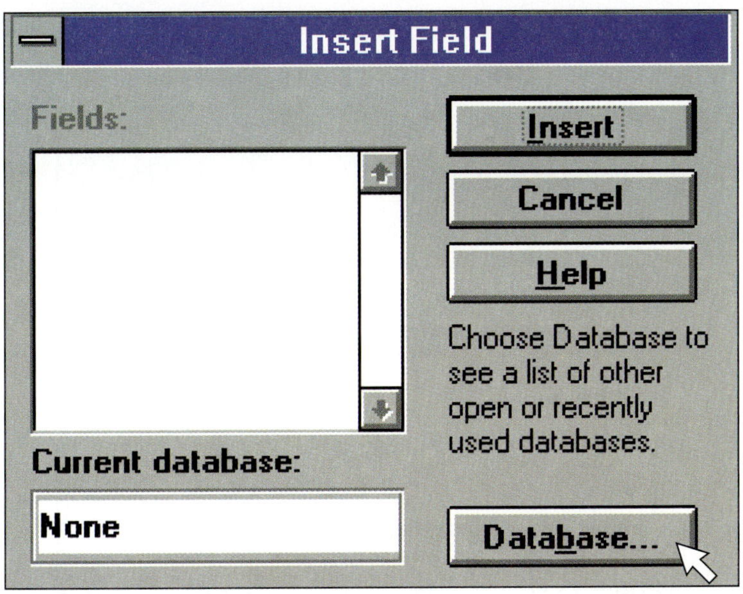

Figure 16-1
The Insert Field dialog box

2. Choose — **Database**  to display a list of current databases that are saved in the Works directory.
3. Select — **CH15PR2.WDB** as shown in Figure 16-2.

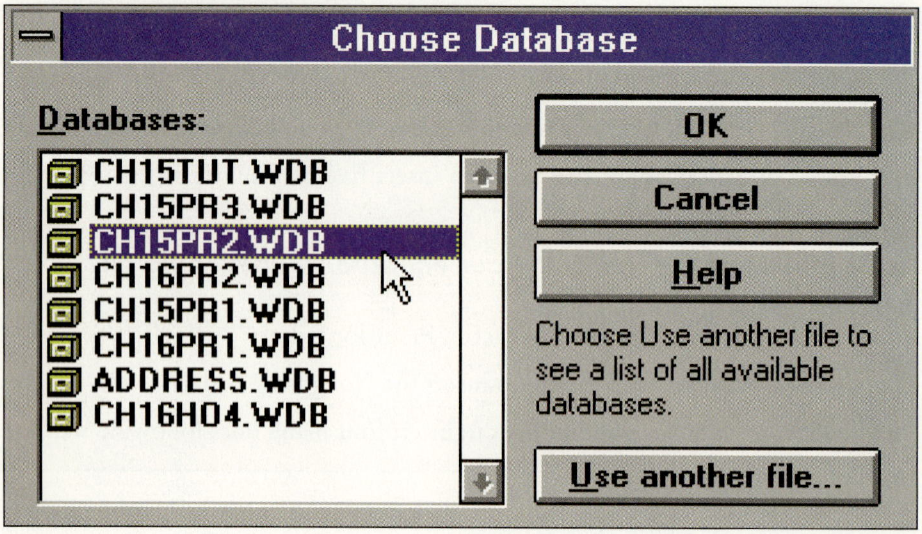

Figure 16-2 The Choose Database dialog box

NOTE: If the database that you want is not displayed in the list box, choose **Use another file**. Another dialog box will be displayed in which you can search through all of the files in the directory or you can select another directory for the search.

4. Choose **OK** or press **Enter**. The Insert Field dialog box is displayed again; however, this time it contains a list of the fields in the selected database file.

5. Select **Fname** for the first field to be inserted. Your screen should now resemble Figure 16-3.

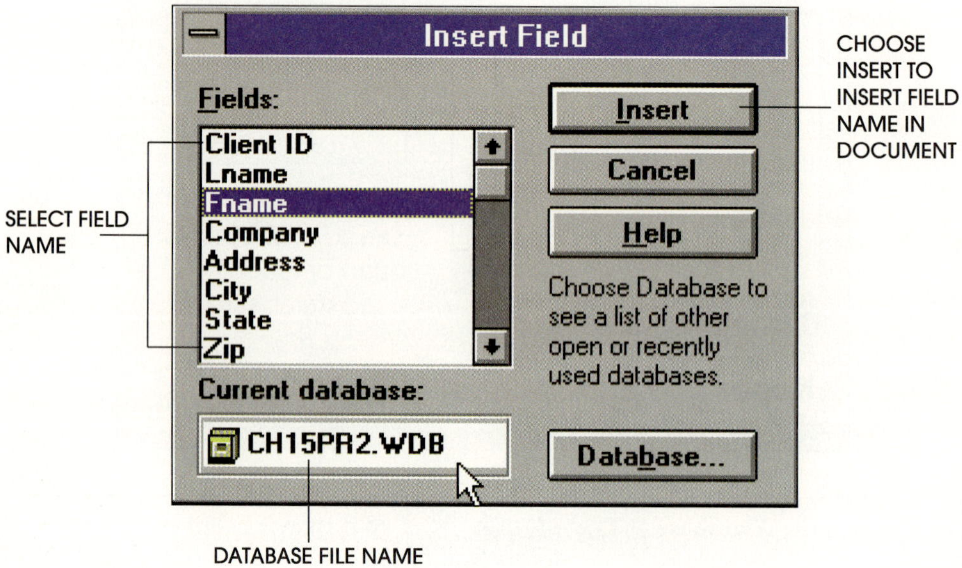

Figure 16-3 The Insert Field dialog box containing field names from a database file

6. Choose **Insert** 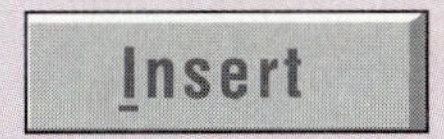

. The field is now inserted in the document at the insertion point as shown here. The Insert Field dialog box remains displayed until you choose **Close**.

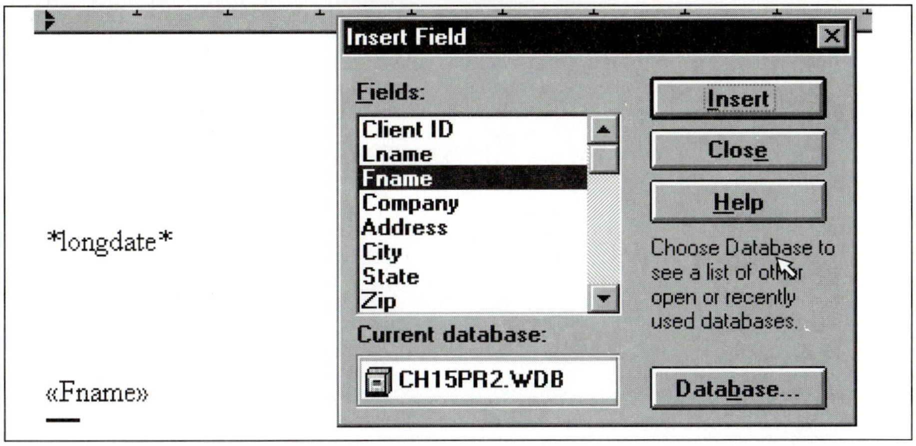

7. Leave the Insert Field box displayed and select **Lname**.

8. Choose **Insert** 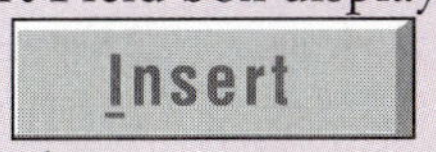

to insert the <<Lname>> placeholder as shown here.

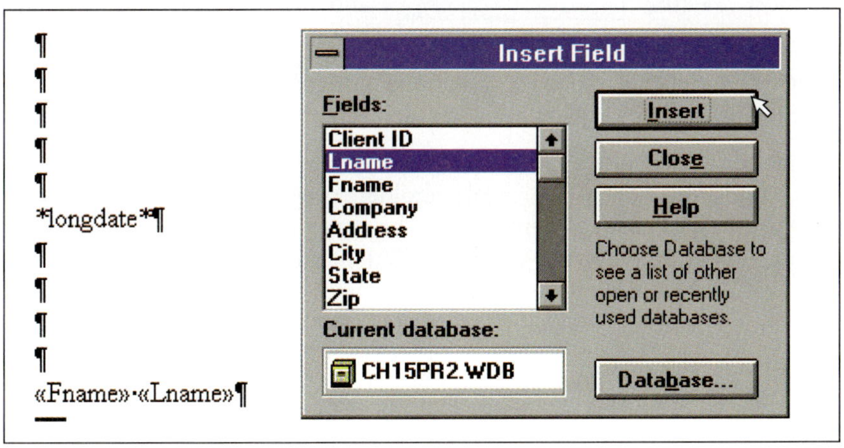

9. Choose **Close** 

to return to the document window.

The insertion point is following the <<Lname>> placeholder. Notice that a space is automatically inserted between the <<Fname>> and the <<Lname>> placeholders.

10. Press **Enter** to go to the next line.

To insert the placeholder for the* Company *field name:

11. Choose **Insert, Database Field** to again display the Insert Field dialog box, which contains the field names.

12. Select **Company** and choose **Insert** 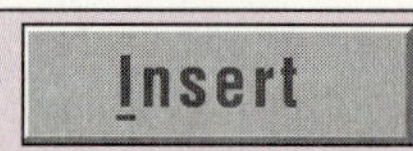

. Your document now shows the <<Company>> placeholder as shown here.

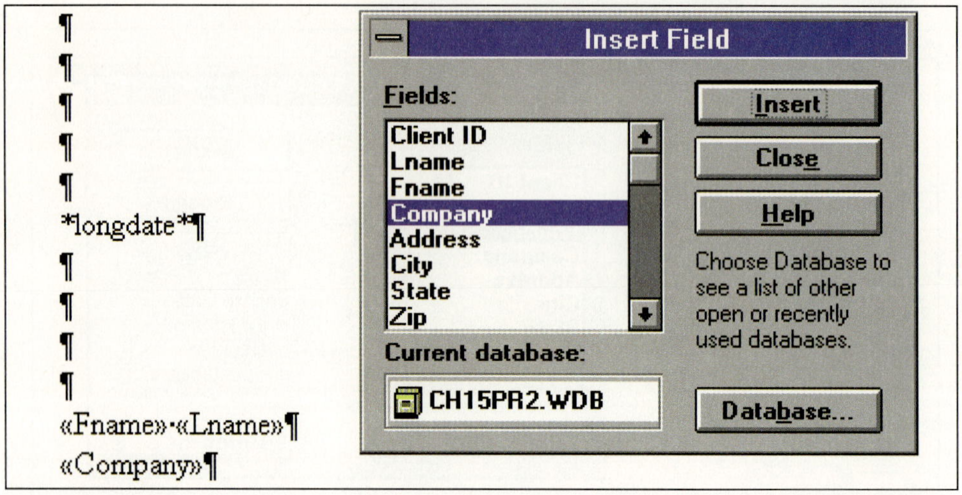

NOTE: If you inadvertently inserted the placeholder on the same line with other placeholders, you can move the insertion point in front of the first chevron and press **Enter** to move the placeholder down one line after you finish working in the Insert Field dialog box.

13. Choose **Close** 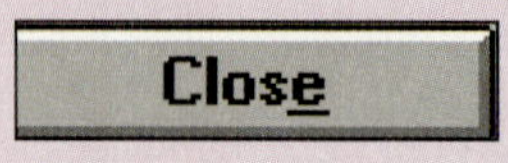

and press **Enter** to go to the next line.

14. Repeat steps 11 through 13 to insert the placeholders for <<Address>> and <<City>>.

15. Move the insertion point to the space directly following the last chevron for the <<City>> placeholder, type a comma (,), and press the **spacebar**. Then insert the two remaining placeholders for <<State>> and <<Zip>>. When done, your form should resemble the following.

```
»  ¶
   ¶
   ¶
   ¶
   ¶
   *longdate*¶
   ¶
   ¶
   ¶
   ‹‹Fname››·‹‹Lname››¶
   ‹‹Company››¶
   ‹‹Address››¶
   ‹‹City››,·‹‹State››·‹‹Zip››¶
```

NOTE: If you like, you can select each field name and choose **Insert** before closing the dialog box. All field names will be placed on one line. After inserting the last field name, choose **Close**, and then in the document window, move the insertion point in front of the field placeholders that are to be moved to the following line, and press **Enter**. You can also insert spaces, commas, blank lines, or move the placeholders to other positions.

16. Type the text shown in the box below for the body of the form letter. When done your document should resemble that shown here.

longdate

<<Fname>> <<Lname>>
<<Company>>
<<Address>>
<<City>>, <<State>> <<Zip>>

SUMMER PROMOTION

This summer season begins early for the boat charter business. May begins a busy time that usually continues through mid-October.

This year we are offering 25 percent off all tickets purchased by corporations prior to May 1, 1994. This includes tickets for any of our cruises: lunch, weekend brunches, or evening dinners.

If you are interested in receiving this once-a-year offer, please call our office for further details. Hope to see you on board!

PUGET SOUND CHARTERS

17.	Run	a spell check.
18.	Save	the form letter as **CH16PR1**.

MERGING AND PRINTING THE FORM LETTER

The **Print** command from the **File** menu is used to print the form letter in much the same way other files are printed. The form document must be active and the **Print merge** box in the Print dialog box checked to print the merged output.

> *NOTE:* If the **Print merge** box is not checked, the form document will be printed showing the placeholders rather than merging with the database file.

Preview the Form Letter

You can see how the merged output will look before printing, if you like.

1.	Make	the form letter **CH16PR1** active if it is not already active.
2.	Choose	**File, Print** or press **Ctrl/P** to display the Print dialog box as shown in Figure 16-4.

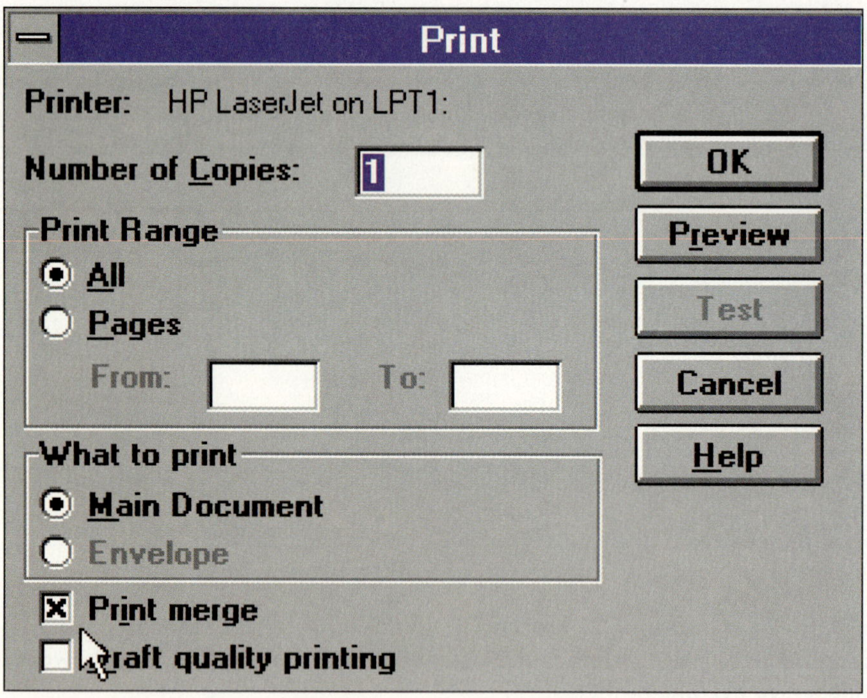

Figure 16-4
The Print dialog box

3.	Be sure	the Print merge check box has an X in it as shown in Figure 16-4. This is automatic because the file contains placeholders that indicate it is a form document used to merge with information in a database file.
4.	Choose	**Preview** Preview . The Choose Database dialog box will be displayed as shown here in Figure 16-5.

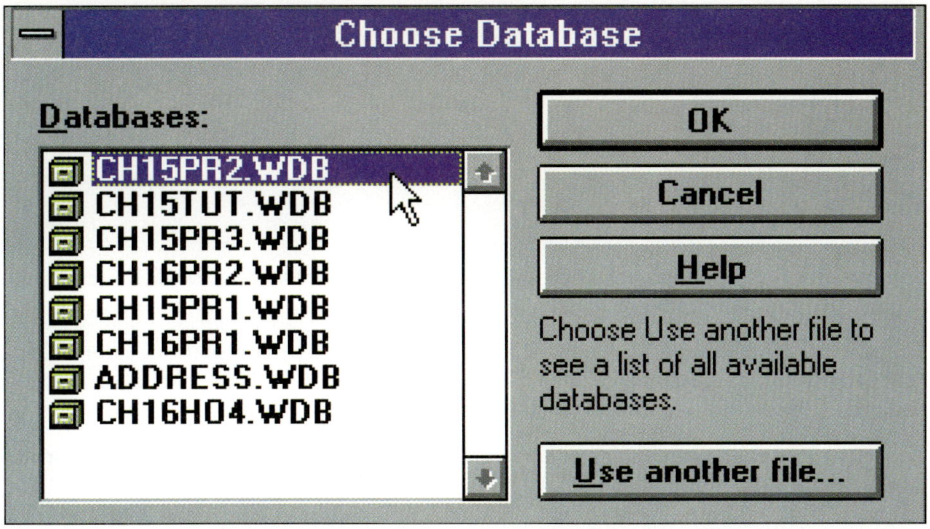

Figure 16-5
The Choose Database dialog box

5.	Select	the **CH15PR2.WDB** database file as shown in Figure 16-5.
6.	Choose	**OK** or press **Enter**. Because the database file is not already open, a prompt asking if you want to merge all records will be displayed as shown here in Figure 16-6. The box also tells you that you can perform a query to select only specified files to be merged if you like.

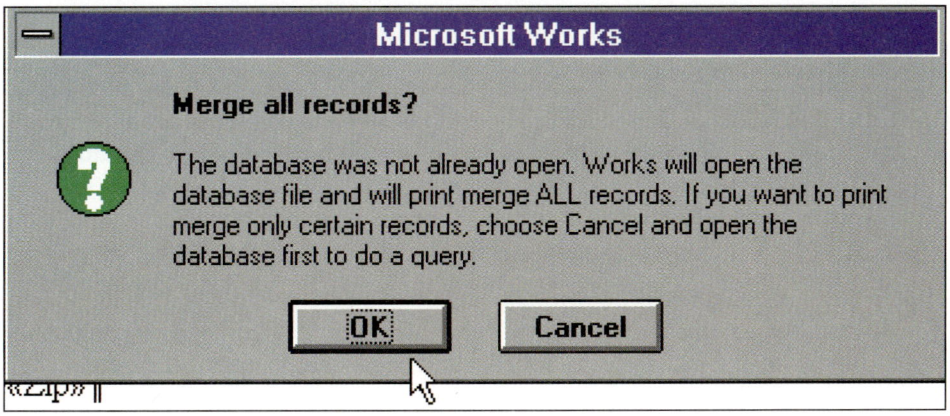

Figure 16-6
The prompt to open the database file

7.	Choose	**OK** to display the Print Preview screen showing the merged output. Your screen should resemble the following example.

Septermbter 05, 1994

Michael Hammersmith
Software Unlimited
1984 Newton Road
Seattle, WA 98102

SUMMER PROMOTION

The summer season begins early for the boat charter business. May begins a busy time that usually continues through mid-October.

This year we are offering 2.5 percent off all tickets purchased by corporations prior to May 1, 1994. This includes tickets for any of our curises: lunch, weekend brunches, or evening dinners.

If you are interested in receiving this once-a-year offer, please call our office for further details. Hope to see you on board!

PUGET SOUND CHARTERS

8. Choose **Next** 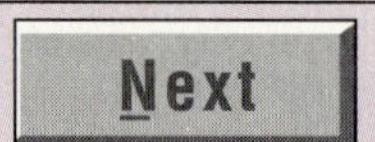

to see the next form.

9. Choose **Print** 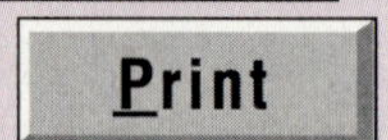

to return to the Print dialog box as shown previously in Figure 16-4.

Print the Form Letter

Now that you have confirmed that the output is correct, you can send it to the printer, if you like. This will print 14 pages. If you do not want to do this now, read the instructions and go on to the next section, "Creating Mailing Labels." (Check with your instructor on this.)

> *NOTE:* All pages will be printed, even if you give instructions in the Print dialog box to print only specified pages. When printing merged documents, you can only use a query (as indicated in the prompt to open the database file (see Figure 16-6) to limit the number of forms that will be printed. Exercise 4 at the end of this chapter covers how to use a query to produce a merged document.

1. Be sure the Print dialog box is displayed. If it is not, choose **File, Print**. The Print merge box should have an X in it. See Figure 16-4.
2. Choose **OK** or press **Enter**. The Choose Database dialog box, as shown in Figure 16-5, will be displayed again.
3. Select **CH15PR2.WDB** and choose **OK**. The prompt asking if you want to merge all records is displayed as shown in Figure 16-6.
4. Choose **OK** or press **Enter** to send the output to the printer.
5. Close the document.

NOTE: You can also use WorksWizard to create a form letter. Choose **WorksWizard** from the Startup dialog box to display a list of the WorksWizards and choose **Form Letter**.

CREATING MAILING LABELS

Creating mailing labels has been made easy in Works 3.0. The **Envelopes and Labels** option in the **Tools** menu is used to select the label size. Then the procedure is similar to creating a form document in that you insert the placeholders you want to use at the appropriate position in the label box.

Create the Form for the Labels

1. Open a new word processor document window. Choose **File, Create New File** and choose the **Word Processor** tool.

NOTE: You do not necessarily have to open a new document window. You could create the label form and include it in the file with the form letter. By creating a separate file for the label form, however, it is available with other forms that use the same database file for addresses and such.

2. Choose **Tools, Envelopes and Labels** to display the Envelopes and Labels dialog box as shown in Figure 16-7. The Envelopes section is active.

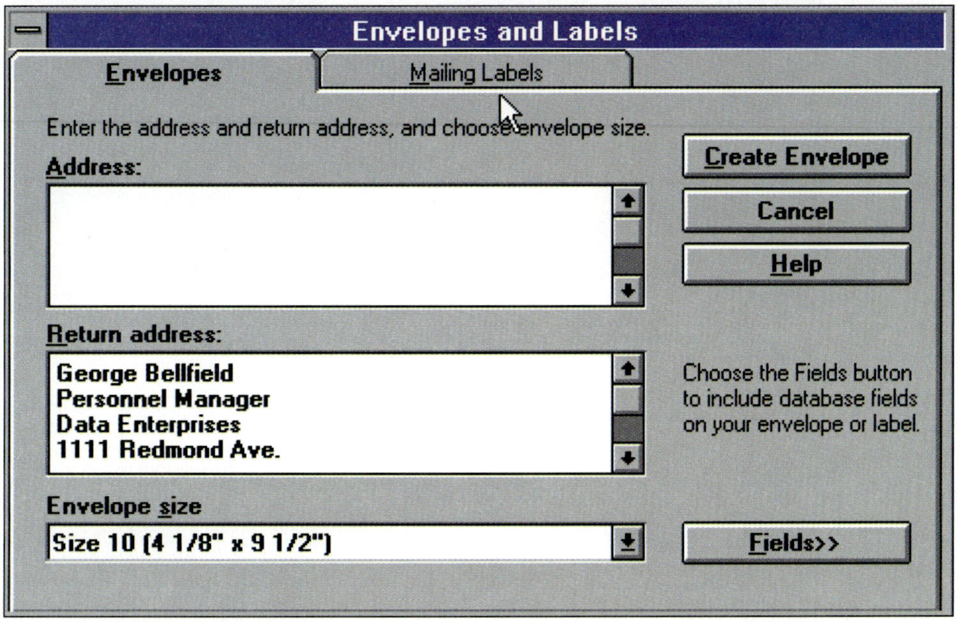

Figure 16-7
The Envelopes and Labels dialog box

This dialog box has two tabs (sections)-one for Envelopes and one for Mailing Labels.

3. Choose **Mailing Labels** tab to make it active as shown in Figure 16-8.

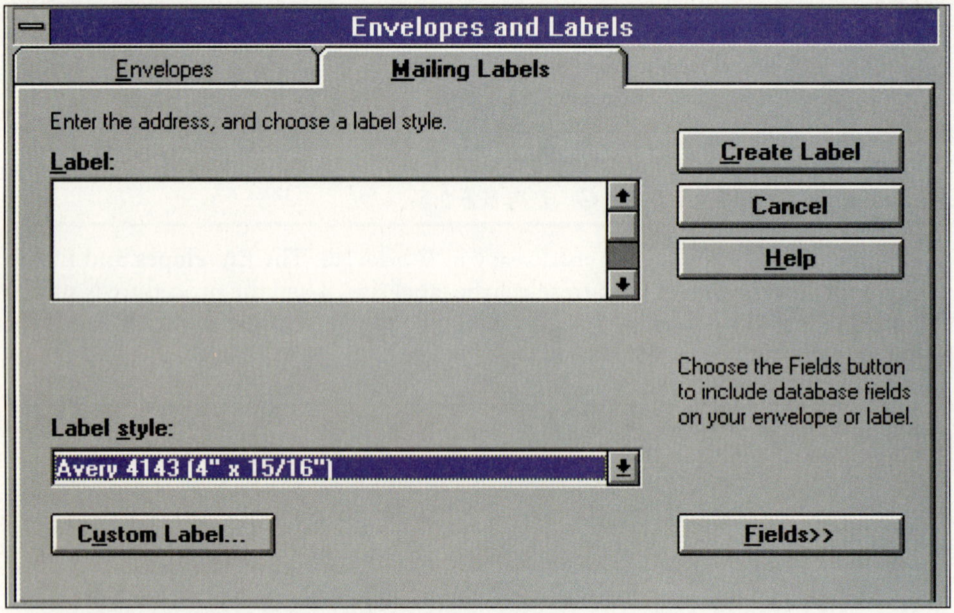

Figure 16-8
The Mailing Labels tab in the Envelopes and Labels dialog box

To insert placeholders for the field names:

4. Choose fields>> 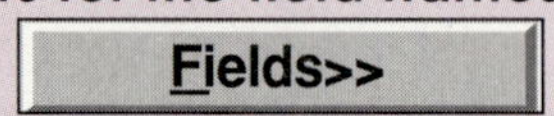

. A new section is now added at the bottom of the Mailing Labels tab as shown in Figure 16-9.

ADDED SECTION TO SELECT FIELD NAMES

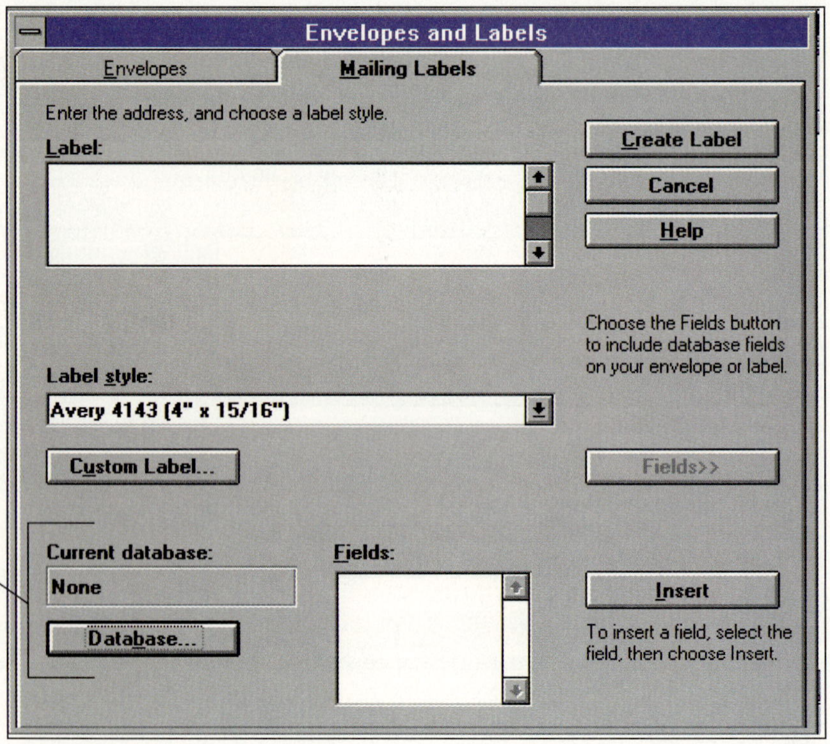

Figure 16-9
The additional section in the Mailing Labels tab section

The **Current database** box displays **None**.

To select the database you want to use for the labels:

5. Choose **Database** 

to display the Choose Database dialog box as shown in Figure 16-10.

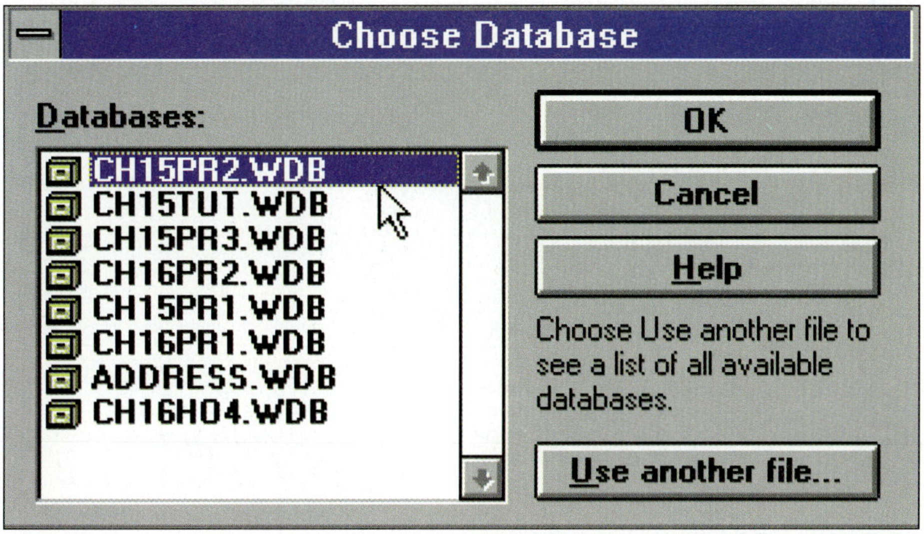

Figure 16-10
The Choose Database dialog box

6. Select **CH15PR2.WDB** and choose **OK** or press **Enter** to return to the Mailing Labels tab. The fields in the database are now showing in the **Fields** list box, and the insertion point is flashing in the **Label** box in which you can start inserting field placeholders the same way you did in the form letter in the previous section. Your screen should resemble Figure 16-11.

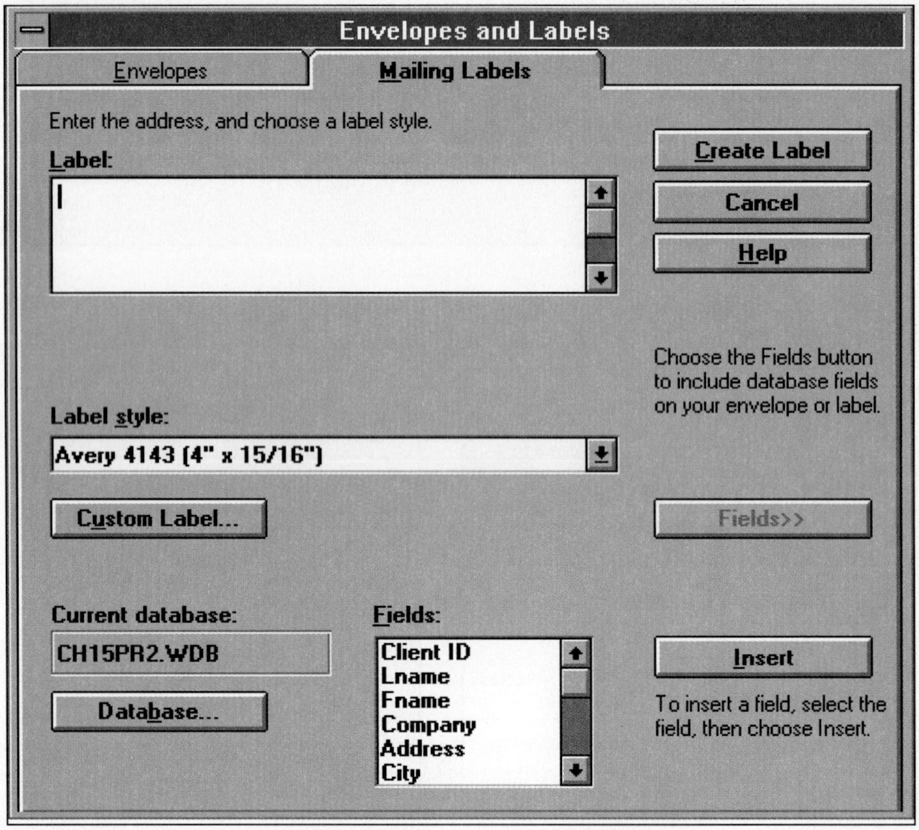

Figure 16-11
The field names displayed in the Mailing Labels tab section

7. Select **Fname** and choose **Insert** 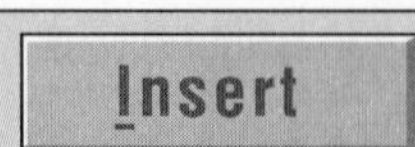

.
8. Repeat step 7 for **Lname** and press **Enter** to go to the next line in the **Labels** box.
9. Select **Company** and choose **Insert** 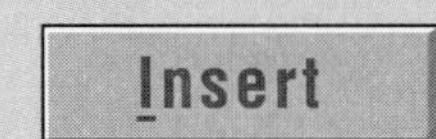

.
10. Press **Enter** to go to the next line.
11. Repeat steps 9 and 10 for the following fields. Press **Enter** to end each line when necessary.
    Address
    City
    State
    Zip

When done, your **Label** box should resemble the following example. Be sure to insert a comma (,) and an extra space following <<City>>.

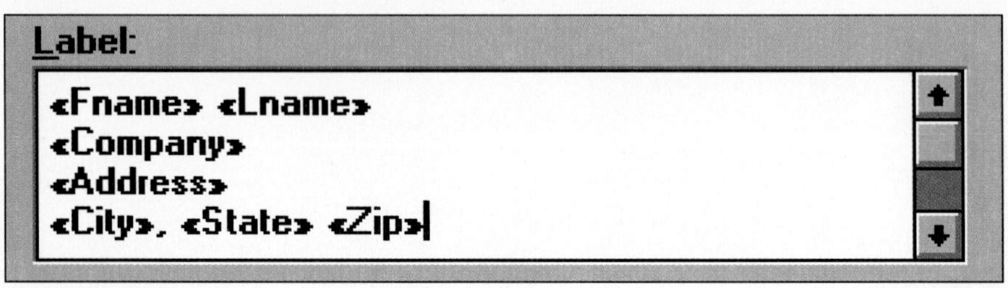

12. Choose **Label style** and click on the up and down arrows at the right end of the box to display the available label sizes as shown in Figure 16-12.

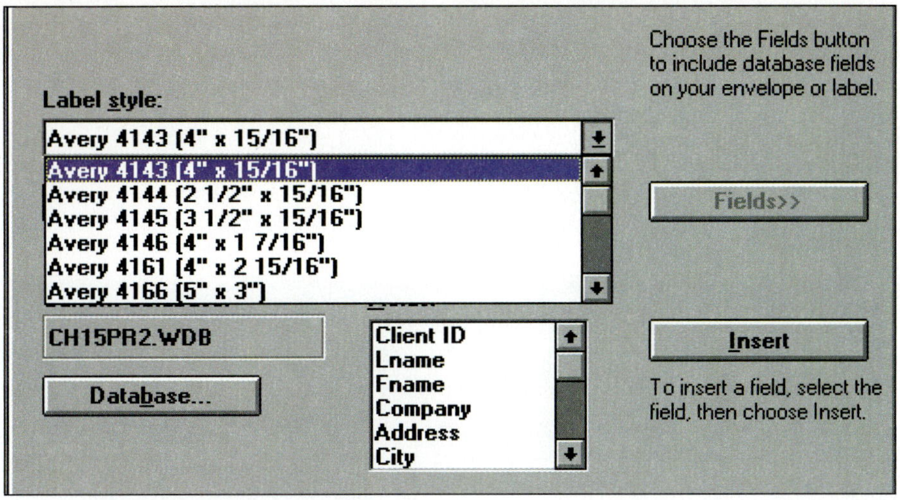

Figure 16-12
The list of available label styles

13. Select the label style that you want.

NOTE: If there is no label style that you want, choose **Custom Label** 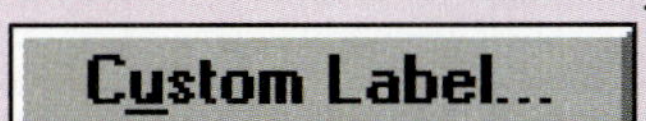 to display a dialog box in which you can enter the measurements for the labels that you want. Instructions for this are in the next section in this chapter, "Creating Custom Labels."

14. Choose **Create Label** 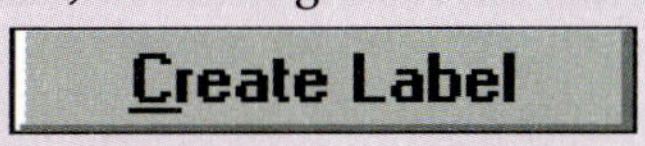. The placeholders for the field names are now inserted in the new document window. Notice in the following example that the Ruler displays a new right margin depending upon the label style you chose. Also, a page break line is showing below the placeholders.

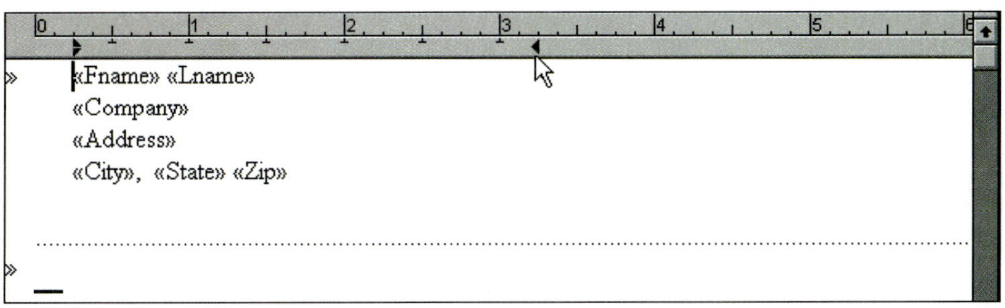

15. Save the form for the mailing labels as **CH16PR2**. Saving the file is not required to print the labels; however, if you save it, it can be used later to produce other labels without having to create the form again.

PREVIEWING AND PRINTING THE MAILING LABELS

Preview the Mailing Labels

You can see how the mailing labels will look before printing the same way you viewed the merged output for the form letter. The procedure given below will be somewhat different-the Print Preview button will be used rather than the **File, Print** command, however, the results will be the same.

1. Click on the Print Preview button. The Choose Database dialog box is displayed as shown here.

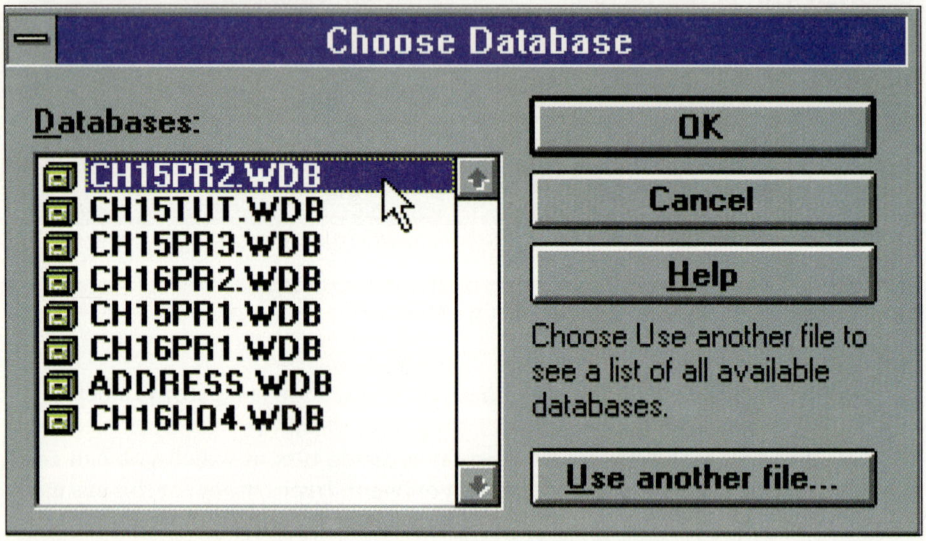

2. Select **CH15PR2.WDB** and choose **OK** or press **Enter**. The prompt asking if you want to merge all records is displayed as shown here.

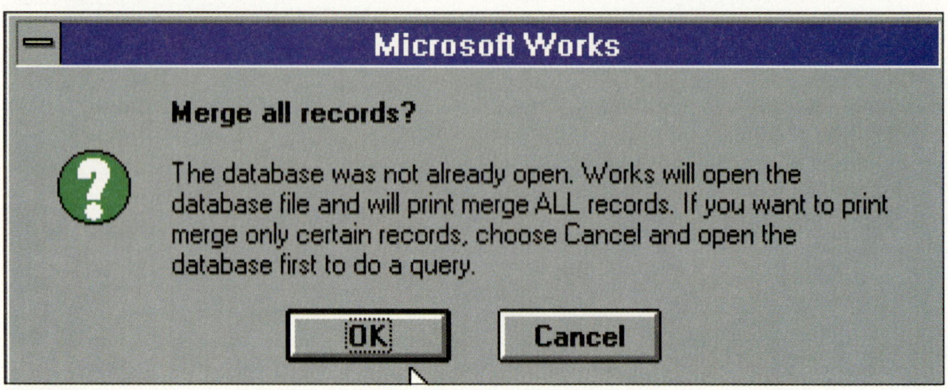

3. **Choose** **OK** or press **Enter**. The names and addresses stored in the database file are now displayed as they will be printed on labels. Depending upon the label style that you chose, your Print Preview screen may be similar to the following example.

Michael Hammersmith
Software Unlimited
1984 Newton Road
Seattle, WA 98102

Charles Baker
IMS consultants
19451 N. E. 45th
Seattle, WA 98107

Bonnie Sills
CTech Corporation
East Hills Branch
Tukwila, WA 98152

Sandra Krogstad
Krogstad and Company
5125 Compton Way
Woodinville, WA 98043

Trisha Smith
Julien's Computers
1001 South Plaza
Seattle, WA 98108

Nevell Mills
The Baldwin Co.
98 Baldwin Place
Seattle, WA 98101

Elizabeth Kimball
Downtown Pets
23rd and Forest
Woodinville, WA 98043

Selena Ho
The Northwest Bank
1900 Wilson Plaza
Bellevue, WA 98004

Simon Schuster
CTech Corporation
2122 Plaza Center
Kirkland, WA 98032

Robert Long
Long and Tukes
9800 Plaza Suite
Bellevue, WA 98007

Karen Jackson
Supermarkets, Inc.
South Perkins Blvd.
Issaquah, WA 98027

Douglas Grover
Grover and Associate
123 Fourth Ave. N. E.
Seattle, WA 98119

Theodore Gonzales
The Best Store
Century Plaza #20
Bellevue, WA 98005

Pat Bell
The Furniture Emporium
2525 16th Ave. N. E.
Woodinville, WA 98043

Print the Labels

You can choose **Print** from the Print Preview screen, or you can choose **Cancel** and then choose **File, Print** if you want to print the labels later.

1. Choose **Print** 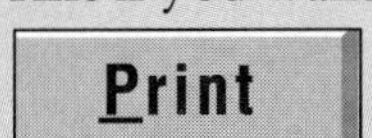

from the Print Preview screen to display the Choose Database dialog box again.
2. Select **CH15PR2.WDB** and choose **OK** or press **Enter**. The prompt asking if you want to merge all records is displayed again.
3. Choose **OK** or press **Enter** to print.
4. Close the document when done.

Create Custom Labels

1. **Open** a new word processing document window.
2. **Choose** **Tools, Envelopes and Labels, Mailing Labels** to display the Mailing Labels tab section in the Envelopes and Labels dialog box as shown here.

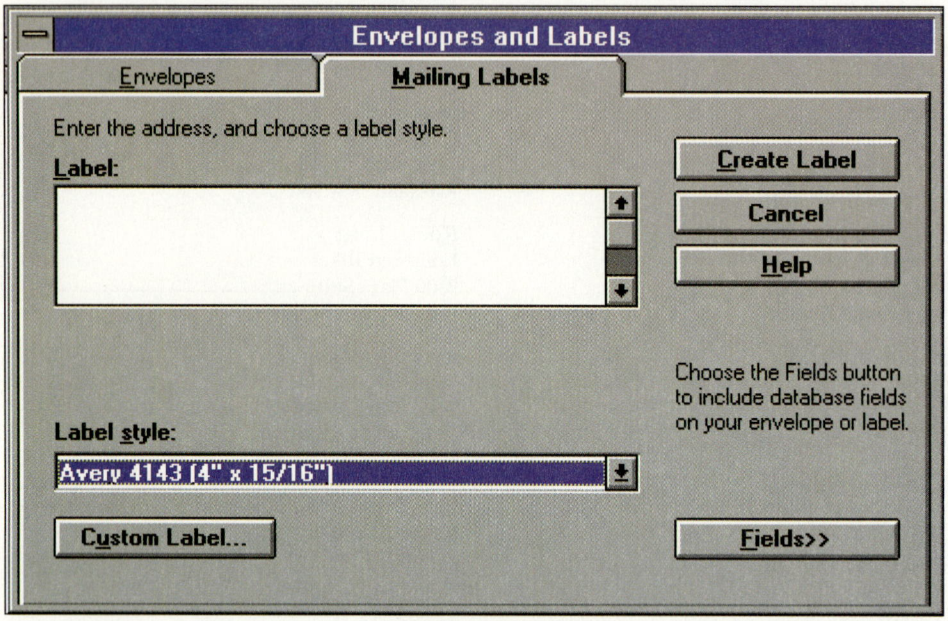

3. **Choose** **Custom Label** 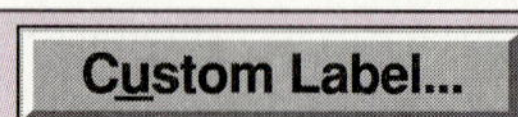

to display the Custom Labels dialog box as shown in Figure 16-13

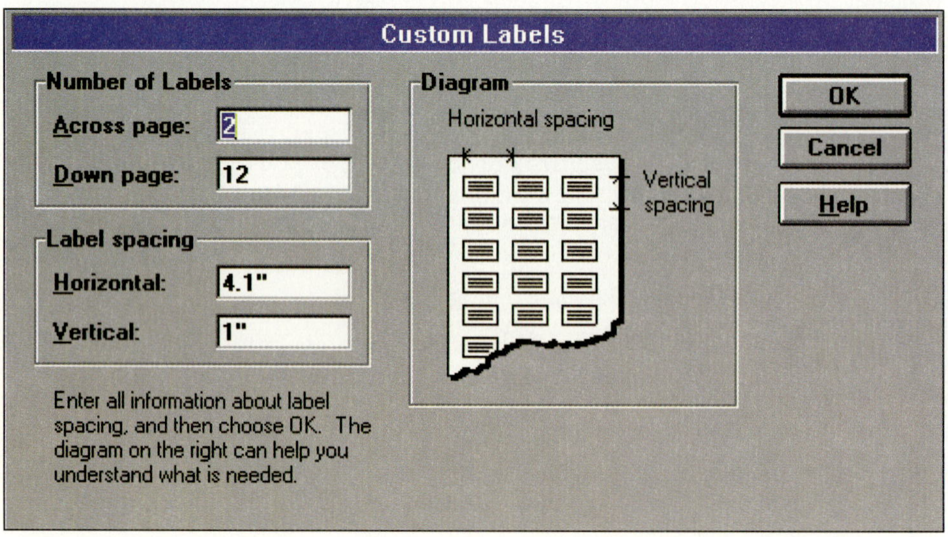

Figure 16-13
The Custom Labels dialog box

4. Type 3 for the number of labels across the page. (The number that is displayed there depends upon the type of label you chose in the previous instructions.)

5. Choose **Down page** and type **9** in the text box.

6. Choose **Horizontal** and type **2.5** for the horizontal width plus distance between labels.

7. Leave **Vertical** set at **1"**.

NOTE: In steps 4 through 7, the settings are arbitrary. When you create your own labels, you can enter whatever measurements are appropriate for your work.

8. Choose **OK** or press **Enter** to display the next Custom Labels dialog box as shown in Figure 16-14.

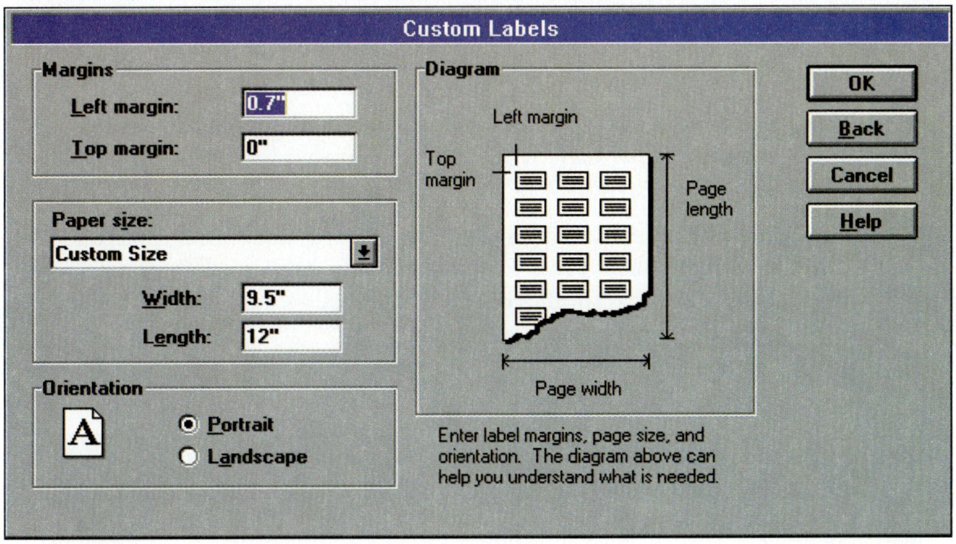

Figure 16-14
The next Custom Labels dialog box

9. Leave Margins set as is. The margin settings are the result of your choice of label style in the previous instructions.

10. Choose **Paper size** to display a list of choices as shown in Figure 16-15.

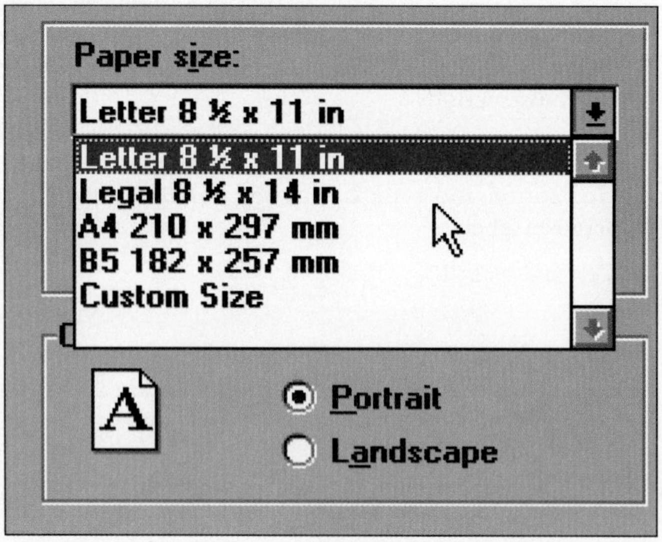

Figure 16-15
The list of paper sizes

11. Choose **Letter 8 1/2 x 11 in**. See Figure 16-15 above.

12. Choose **OK** to return to the Mailing Labels tab.

13. Choose **Fields>>**  . If the current database box does not show **CH15PR2**, choose **Database** and select it from the list.

14. Select the field names shown in the following illustration and choose **Insert** for each. Press **Enter** to move to the next line in the Label box. The box should resemble the following example when all placeholders are inserted.

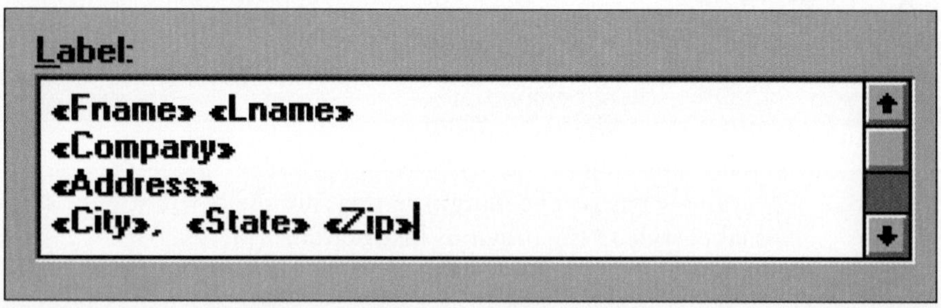

15. Choose **Create Label**  to display the form for the label in the document window as shown here. Notice the right margin marker position is at 2.25.

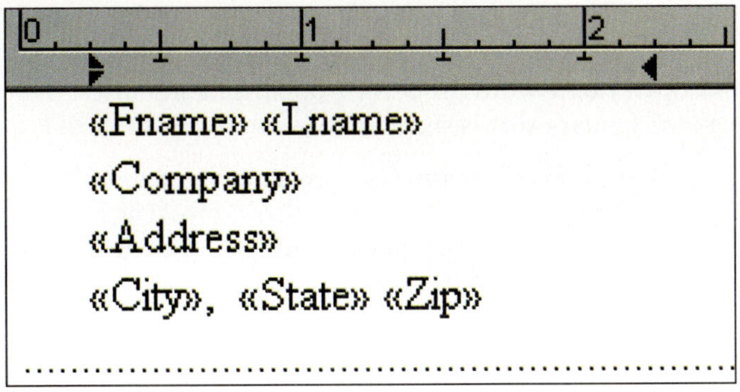

16. Choose	**Print Preview** and then select **CH15PR2** for the database to be used for the merge Your screen may resemble the following example.

Michael Hammersmith Software Unlimited 1984 Newton Road Seattle, WA 98102	Selena Ho The Northwest Bank 1900 Wilson Plaza Bellevue, WA 98004	Charles Baker IMS consultants 19451 N. E. 45th Seattle, WA 98107
Simon Schuster CTech Corporation 2122 Plaza Center Kirkland, WA 98032	Bonnie Sills CTech Corporation East Hills Branch Tukwila, WA 98152	Robert Long Long and Tukes 9800 Plaza Suite Bellevue, WA 98007
Sandra Krogstad Krogstad and Company 5125 Compton Way Woodinville, WA 98043	Karen Jackson Supermarkets, Inc. South Perkins Blvd. Issaquah, WA 98027	Trisha Smith Julien's Computers 1001 South Plaza Seattle, WA 98108
Douglas Grover Grover and Associate 123 Fourth Ave. N. E. Seattle, WA 98119	Nevell Mills The Baldwin Co. 98 Baldwin Place Seattle, WA 98101	Theodore Gonzales The Best Store Century Plaza #20 Bellevue, WA 98005
Elizabeth Kimball Downtown Pets 23rd and Forest Woodinville, WA 98043	Pat Bell the Furniture Emporium 2525 16th Ave. N. E. Woodinville, WA 98043	ZOOM

17. Choose	**Cancel** to leave the Print Preview window. Do not print these labels.
18. Save	the label form as **CH16PR3** and close the document.

INSERTING DATABASE INFORMATION IN A WORD PROCESSING DOCUMENT

You can insert information stored in a database into a word processing document by selecting the information in the database and choosing **Cut**, then moving to the word processing document and choosing **Paste**.

Insert Data

Here you will open a new word processing document and insert the information about charters for January that is stored in the database **CH15PR1.**

1. Open — a new word processing document and enter the logo shown in the following example. You can either create it again; or you can open the **CH12HO2** document, select the logo, click on the Copy button, switch to the new open word processing document, and click on the Paste button.

››

PUGET SOUND CHARTERS
East Lake Union Way
Seattle, WA 98108
(206) 555-9200

February 1, 1994

TO: All employees

FROM: Accounting Department

The following information shows the total amount from charters for the month of January 1994.

2. Type — the text below the logo as it is shown in the example above. Press **Enter** twice following **January, 1994.**
3. Save — the document as **CH16PR4.**

To insert information from the database

4. Open — the database **CH15PR1.**
5. Select — the information in all columns from **Boat Name** through **Balance** as shown here

	Client I	Boat Name	Date Booked	Hours	Deposit	Tax	Balance	Note:
1	106	Delano	1/10/94	4	$100.00	$160.00	$2,060.00	
2	105	Delano	1/20/94	3	$100.00	$120.00	$1,520.00	
3	111	Delano	1/28/94	3	$100.00	$120.00	$1,520.00	
4	114	Irish Sea	1/17/94	4	$150.00	$160.00	$2,010.00	
5	109	Irish Sea	1/19/94	3	$100.00	$120.00	$1,520.00	
6	110	Irish Sea	1/27/94	3	$200.00	$120.00	$1,420.00	
7	102	Sea Wolf	1/15/94	4	$500.00	$160.00	$1,660.00	
8	113	The Spirit	1/25/94	4	$200.00	$160.00	$1,960.00	
9	105	The Spirit	1/29/94	4	$150.00	$160.00	$2,010.00	
10	104	The Spirit	1/7/94	3	$200.00	$120.00	$1,420.00	
11								

6. **Click** on the Copy button or choose **<u>E</u>dit, <u>C</u>opy**.

To switch to the word processing document:

7. **Choose** **<u>W</u>indow, CH16PR4.**
8. **Move** the insertion point to two lines below the text.
9. **Click** on the **Paste** button or choose **<u>E</u>dit, <u>P</u>aste**. Your document will resemble the following.

TO: All employees

FROM: Accounting Department

The following information shows the total amount from charters for the month of January 1994.

Delano	1/10/94	4	$100.00	$160.00	$2,060.00
Delano	1/20/94	3	$100.00	$120.00	$1,520.00
Delano	1/28/94	3	$100.00	$120.00	$1,520.00
Irish Sea	1/17/94	4	$150.00	$160.00	$2,010.00
Irish Sea	1/19/94	3	$100.00	$120.00	$1,520.00
Irish Sea	1/27/94	3	$200.00	$120.00	$1,420.00
Sea Wolf	1/15/94	4	$500.00	$160.00	$1,660.00
The Spirit	1/25/94	4	$200.00	$160.00	$1,960.00
The Spirit	1/29/94	4	$150.00	$160.00	$2,010.00
The Spirit	1/7/94	3	$200.00	$120.00	$1,420.00

10. **Save** the document again as **CH16PR4**.

NOTE: You can select all data or only specified rows and columns in the database, as you did here. You may have to adjust the columns in the word processing document, by selecting all rows of the data and moving the tab stops to new positions. You can do this by either dragging the tab stops in the **Ruler** or choosing **Format, Tabs** and typing new positions.

GUIDED TUTORIAL

What You'll Do

- Create a form letter that includes placeholders for field names within the body of the letter.
- Create a label form.
- Print the output of the merge for both the form letter and the mailing labels.

How To Do It

1. Open a new word processor document window.
2. Create the following form letter using steps 3 through 11.

longdate

<<Fname>> <<Lname>>
<<Company>>
<<Address>>
<<City>>, <<State>> <<Zip>>

To the attention of: <<Fname>>

This letter is to thank you for your continued support of Puget Sound Charters. You have been an outstanding client for the past few years, and your company, <<Company>>, has served us as an excellent public relations representative.

We at Puget Sound Charters like to reward good customers. We would like to offer you and six top employees from <<Company>> complimentary dinner tickets any night during the next month.

Please contact us within the next week to set up a time and confirm reservations.

Again thank you for your continued support. We look forward to serving your company in the years to come.

Sincerely,

P. J. MacRannall
President

To insert the *longdate* code:

3. Move the insertion point down to about the fifth line from the top of the window and choose **Insert, Special Character, Print long date** and choose **OK** or press **Enter**.
4. Press **Enter** four times to insert four blank lines.

To insert the placeholders:

5. Choose **Insert, Database Field** to display the Insert Field dialog box shown here.

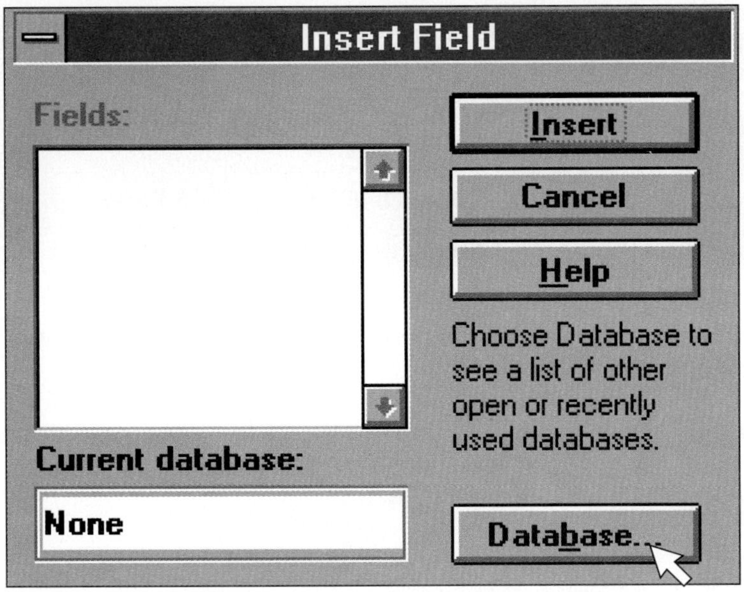

6. Choose **Database** 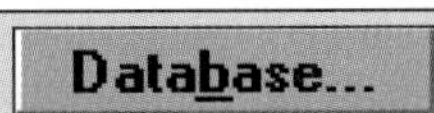

to display the Choose Database dialog box.

7. Select **CH15PR2.WDB** and choose **OK** or press **Enter** to display the Insert Field dialog box again that now displays the field names.

8. Select **Fname** and choose **Insert** 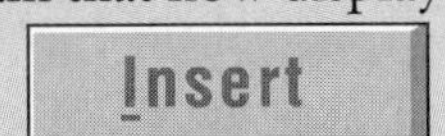

.

9. Repeat selecting and inserting the field names at the positions indicated in the sample letter shown on the first page of the Guided Tutorial.

NOTE: If you like, select and insert all placeholders on one line. Then choose **Close**, and in the document window press **Enter** in front of each placeholder to move it to the next line. Also insert needed spaces and the comma following the <<City>> placeholder.

10. Type the text, and at the positions where you want to insert the placeholders <<Fname>> and <<Company>>, choose **Insert, Database Field** to display the Insert Field dialog box showing the field names. Then select the field name and choose **Insert** and then choose **Close**.

When done with the form letter:

11. Save as **CH16TUT1**.

To preview and print the form letter:

12. Choose **File, Print** or press **Ctrl/P** to display the Print dialog box.

13. Choose **Preview** to display the Choose Database dialog box.

14. Select **CH15PR2.WDB** and choose **OK** or press **Enter.**

15. Choose **OK** or press **Enter** at the prompt asking if you want to merge all records.

To print all 14 letters from the Print Preview screen, or skip this if you do not want to print all letters:

16. Choose **Print** , choose **OK** or press **Enter,** and repeat steps 14 and 15 to print the merged output.

To create labels:

17. Open a new word processor document window.

18. Choose **Tools, Envelopes and Labels** to display the Envelopes and Labels dialog box.

19. Choose **Mailing Labels** tab to make it active.

20. Choose an appropriate **Label style.**

21. Choose **Fields>>** to display the new section at the bottom of the Mailing Labels tab.

22. Choose **Database** to display the Choose Database dialog box.

23. Select **CH15PR2.WDB** and choose **OK** or press **Enter** to return to the Mailing Labels tab.

24. Select the field names shown in the following example and choose **Insert** for each. The **Label** box should resemble the following when done.

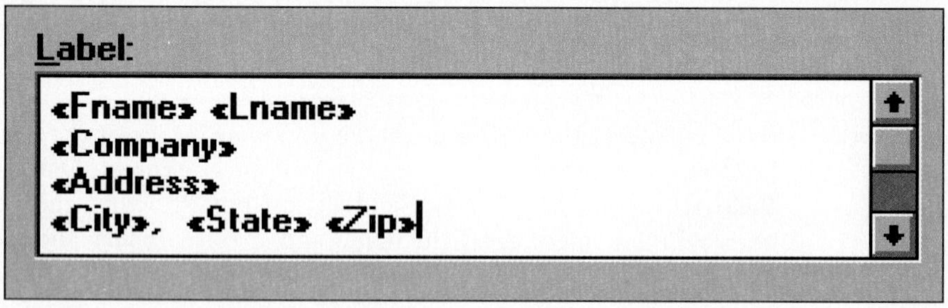

24. Choose **Create Label.** Your window should resemble the following depending upon the label style this is used.

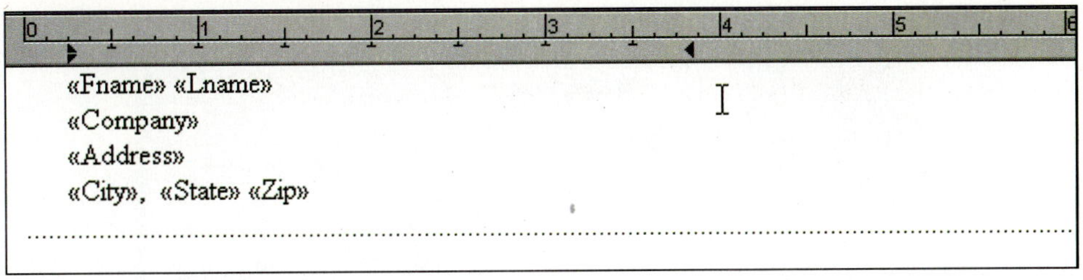

25.	Save	the labels as **CH16TUT2**.
26.	Choose	**Print Preview** and select **CH15PR2** as the database. Respond to the prompts to go to the Print Preview window. Your screen display depends upon the label style that is used.
27.	Choose	**Print** and respond to the screen prompt to print the labels.
28.	Close	the document.

REVIEW QUESTIONS

1. Name the two files that are used to merge information.

    ____

    ____

2. The ______________________ document is active when performing the merge.

3. Describe the purpose of each of the following dialog boxes.

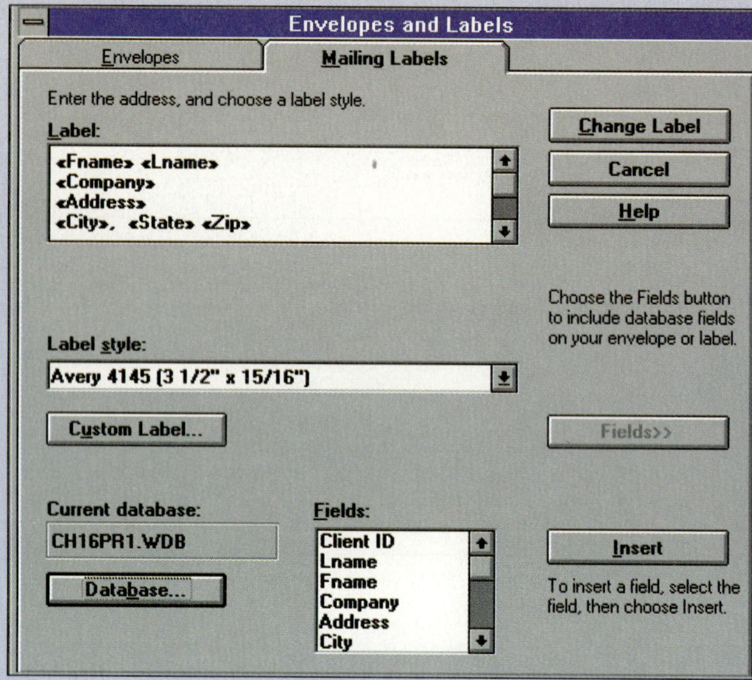
Envelopes and Labels
Envelopes
Mailing Labels
Enter the address, and choose a label style.
Label:
«Fname» «Lname»
«Company»
«Address»
«City», «State» «Zip»
Change Label
Cancel
Help
Choose the Fields button to include database fields on your envelope or label.
Label style:
Avery 4145 (3 1/2" x 15/16")
Custom Label...
Fields>>
Current database:
CH16PR1.WDB
Database...
Fields:
Client ID
Lname
Fname
Company
Address
City
Insert
To insert a field, select the field, then choose Insert.

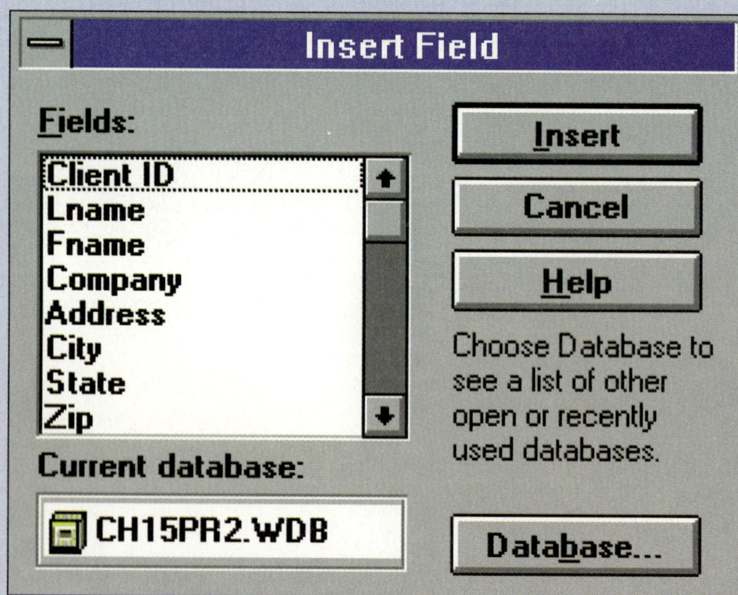
Insert Field
Fields:
Client ID
Lname
Fname
Company
Address
City
State
Zip
Insert
Cancel
Help
Choose Database to see a list of other open or recently used databases.
Current database:
CH15PR2.WDB
Database...

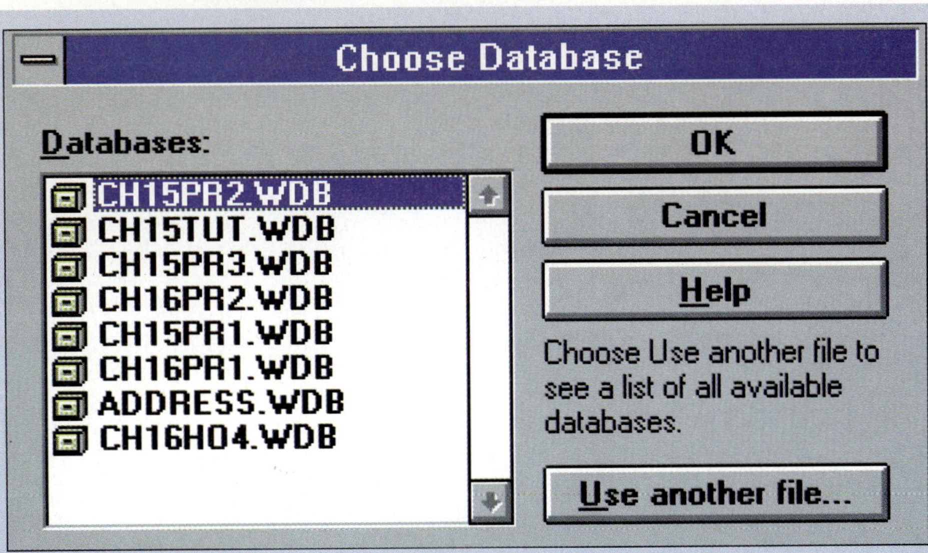

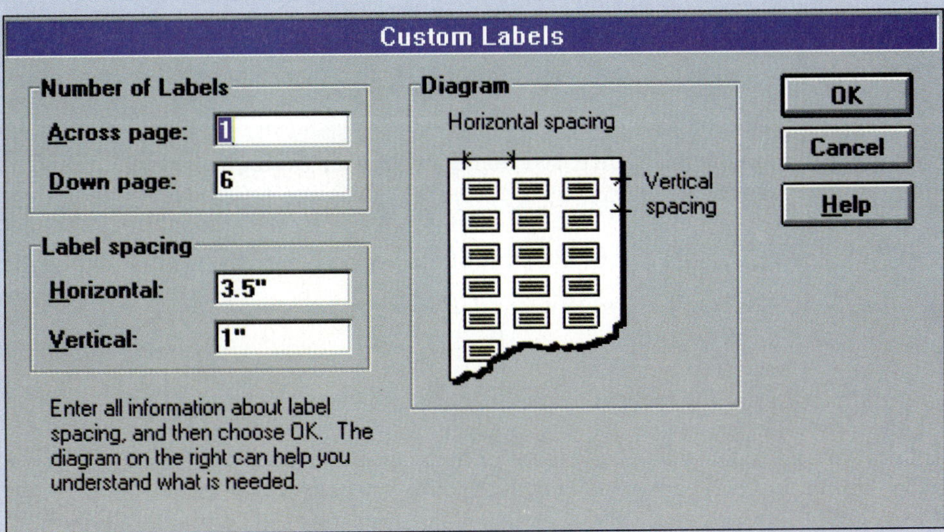

4. List the menu and commands used to print the form document showing the placeholders.

Exercise 1

1. Create the following form document and use the **CH15HO2** database file to insert the placeholders for the field names. (*HINT:* Open a word processing document, and at the place in the third paragraph where the placeholders are inserted, choose **Insert, Database Field**. Then choose **CH15HO2** as the database to be used.)

longdate

Dear Prospective Client,

This letter is in response to your request for information on our boat, <<Boat Name>>, now in service with Puget Sound Charters. We are happy to provide you with the following specifics about the boat and its services, and we look forward to seeing you aboard in the future.

If you have any questions in addition to the information provided below, please do not hesitate to call. We believe that we offer the finest and most experienced private charter service in the region.

The boat, <<Boat Name>>, is captained by Captain <<Captain>>. It is licensed for <<License>> and can carry a maximum of <<Persons>> persons. Its length is <<Length>> feet.

This vessel is captained by a licensed Merchant Marine captain who has a minimum of five years experience.

The boat licenses are defined as follows:

I	Inland Waters
O	Oceangoing
C	Catering Available
L	Liquor License on board

Inland waters are considered the lakes in the greater Seattle area, and include Lake Union, Lake Washington, and special trips to Lake Sammamish. Oceangoing waters are all waters in the greater Puget Sound region, including the South Sound and the San Juan Islands. Overnight accommodations are available on some of our vessels.

2. Run a spell check.
3. Save the document as **CH16HO1**.
4. Merge the form document with the database file and print.
5. Close the document.

1. Type the memorandum shown in the box below. This is not a form document, but refers to an enclosed document that is a form document. A mailing label section will be added above this memorandum containing the placeholders shown in step 4 below. Refer to "Examples of Exercises" at the end of this chapter to see how the final of this exercise will look.

   NOTE: The advantage of this is that you use the function of merging information from a database in a word processing document, and the mailing label feature, enables you to enter all merged data on one page rather than on separate pages as you have done with form letters.

> *longdate*
>
> MEMORANDUM
>
> TO: Management
>
> FROM: Captain Eiler
>
> SUBJECT: Vessel Statistics
>
> Enclosed is a summary of the activity for each of our boats during the last few months. This is a summary of bookings for the three- and four-hour cruises only.
>
> Let me know if you have any questions after looking over the list.

2. Run a spell check.
3. Save the document as **CH16HO2**.
4. Be sure the memorandum document is active. You will be creating a custom mailing label form (shown below) because it enables you to print all information on one page, rather than to print each record in the database on a separate page. In this exercise a page showing the boat name, hours, and balance is going to be created. Space the placeholders approximately as shown below. The making label section will be placed automatically at the top of the document. See step 5 below for details to enter for the custom label.

   HINT: If the last placeholder is inserted too far to the right, the merge will be unsuccessful, so use Print Preview to check the output before printing and adjust the spacing if necessary.

> <<Boat Name>> <<Hours>> <<Balance>>

5. Choose **Tools, Envelopes and Labels, Mailing Labels.**
6. In the Mailing Labels tab section, choose **Custom Label** and make the following changes:
   a. Set **1** for the number of labels across the page.
   b. Set **10** for the number of labels down the page.

c. Set horizontal spacing at 6".
d. Set vertical spacing at .5".
e. Set left margin at 1".
f. Set top margin at 1".

7. In the Mailing Labels tab section, choose **Fields>>** and then choose **Database, CH15PR1**. Select and insert each of the field names, **Boat Name, Hours**, and **Balance** as shown in the example in step 4. Press the **spacebar** to insert the spaces between the placeholders. Choose **Create Labels**.
8. Save the document again as **CH16HO2**.
9. Use Print Preview to merge and display the merged output. Be sure your insertion point is positioned in the labels section showing the placeholders when you do this.
10. Print the merged output and close the document.

Exercise 3

1. Create the following form document which is a memo to be distributed to members who owe dues. Use **CH15TUT** to insert the field names in the form.

> *longdate*
>
> MEMORANDUM
>
> TO: <<First Name>> <<Last Name>>
> <<ID Number>>
>
> FROM: Jason Paul, Treasurer
>
> According to our records, your membership fee in the amount of <<Dues Owing>> is past due. We would appreciate your attention to this matter as soon as possible.
>
> Thank you.

2. Run a spell check and save the form as **CH16HO3**.
3. Use Print Preview to look at the merged output. Select **CH15TUT** when asked to choose the database.
4. Print the output, or skip this step if you do not want to print all 12 memos.

Exercise 4

In this exercise, use the query created for **CH15PR2** to send the following form letter to only those clients with Seattle addresses. To do this:

1. Open **CH15PR2** and choose **View, Query** and select **Query1**. Click on list view to display the query results. Only records with Seattle addresses are displayed. Leave this query result open.

2. Open a new word processor file and create the following form letter. Use **CH15PR2** as the database for the field names.

> *longdate*
>
> <<Fname>> <<Lname>>
> <<Company>>
> <<Address>>
> <<City>>, <<State>> <<Zip>>
>
> Dear <<Fname>>,
>
> As a valued client, we are pleased to offer a new cruise to employees of your company, <<Company>>. Puget Sound Charters is planning a new weekend tour of the entire Puget Sound area. We are anticipating adding this to our current schedule in the spring of 1995; however, as an introductory offer, we are making this cruise available at this time to our clients working in the Seattle area.
>
> We hope that you can take advantage of this offer and look forward to serving you.
>
> Sincerely,
>
> Puget Sound Charters

3. Run a spell check and save the form as **CH16HO4**.
4. Use Print Preview to view the merged output. Select **CH15PR2**. In the Print Preview screen, choose **Next** to confirm that only records with Seattle addresses are merged.
5. Print a copy of the output.
6. Close the document and exit Works.

Exercise 2: CH16HO2

» «Boat Name» «Hours» «Balance»

»

longdate

MEMORANDUM

TO: Management

FROM: Captain Eiler

SUBJECT: Vessel Statistics

Enclosed is a summary of the activity for each of our boats during the last few months. This is a summary of bookings for the three- and four-hour cruises only.

Let me know if you have any questions after looking over the list.

Custom mailing label form

Delano	4	$2,060.00
Delano	3	$1,520.00
Delano	3	$1,520.00
Irish Sea	4	$2,010.00
Irish Sea	3	$1,520.00
Irish Sea	3	$1,420.00
Sea Wolf	4	$1,660.00
The Spirit	4	$1,960.00
The Spirit	4	$2,010.00
The Spirit	3	$1,420.00

Merged output

Exercise 4: CH16HO4

	Client ID	Lname	Fname	Company	Address	City	Stat
1	101	Hammersmith	Michael	Software Unlimited	1984 Newton Road	Seattle	WA
3	103	Baker	Charles	IMS consultants	19451 N. E. 45th	Seattle	WA
9	109	Smith	Trisha	Julien's Computers	1001 South Plaza	Seattle	WA
10	110	Grover	Douglas	Grover and Associate	123 Fourth Ave. N. E.	Seattle	WA
11	111	Mills	Nevell	The Baldwin Co.	98 Baldwin Place	Seattle	WA
15							

Query results that are to be used in the merge

September 01, 1994

Trisha Smith
Julien's Computers
1001 South Plaza
Seattle, WA 98108

Dear Trisha:

As a valued client, we are pleased to offer a new cruise to employees of your company, Julien's Computers. Puget Sound Charters is planning a new weekend tour of the entire Puget Sound area. We are anticipating adding this to our current schedule in the spring of 1995; however, as an introductory offer, we are making this cruise available at this time to our clients working in the Seattle area.

We hope that you can take advantage of this offer and look forward to serving you,

Sincerely,

Puget Sound Charters.

Merged output of one of the records

APPENDIX I

Works Accessories

Appendix I will cover using features that apply to all Works tools-word processing, spreadsheet, database, and communications. Included here will be information for changing the toolbar and options. Instructions will also be given for inserting drawings, using clip art and word art, and creating equations that are automatically formatted. In addition, the template functions and WorksWizard will be discussed.

CUSTOMIZING THE TOOLBAR

If you find that there is a button in the toolbar for a function that you rarely use, you can remove the button and replace it with a different one for a function that you frequently use. The **Customize Toolbar** option in the **Tools** menu, which is available in all Works windows, is used for this.

Remove a Button

1. Open any Works window.
2. Choose **Tools, Customize Toolbar** to display the **Customize Works Toolbar** dialog box as shown in Figure I-1.

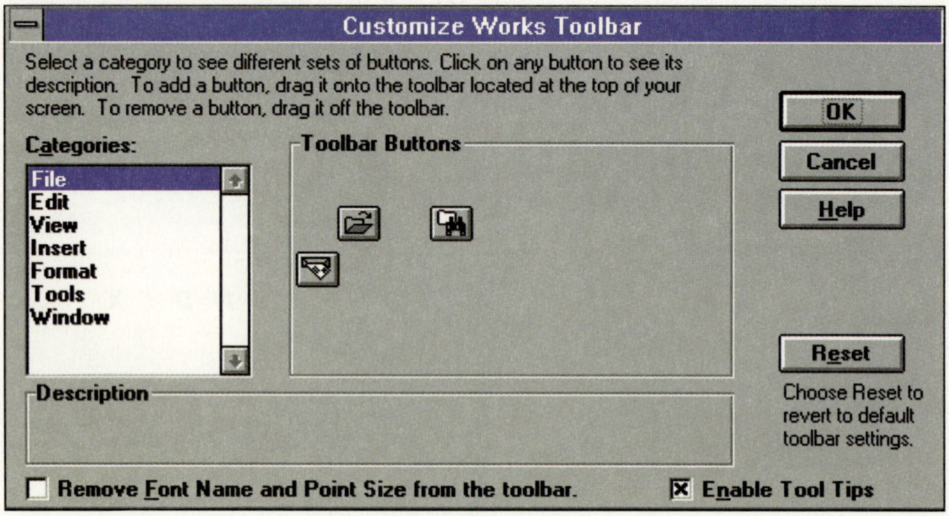

Figure I-1
The Customize Works Toolbar dialog box

3. Point to any button on the toolbar that you want to remove. Hold down the left mouse button, and drag the button away from the toolbar. The remaining buttons adjust to fill in the empty space.

Restore a Default Button

The default buttons are those that are displayed in each of the windows when you first install Works. They can easily be restored after you delete them by using the following steps.

> *NOTE:* You can use this procedure to restore a removed default button at any time, even if you had exited from the dialog box or if you had exited from Works and shut down. Anytime you start up again, the default buttons can be restored.

1. Choose **Tools, Customize Toolbar.**
2. Choose **Reset** 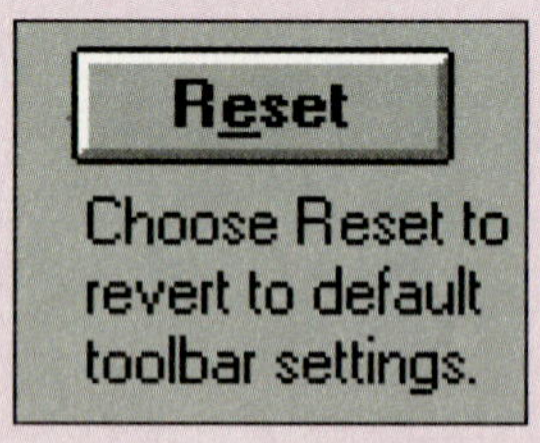 .

3. Choose **OK** or press **Enter** to return to the document window.

Add a Button to the Toolbar

1. Choose **Tools, Customize Toolbar** to display the **Customize Works Toolbar** dialog box. (See Figure I-1.) The **File** category is highlighted and the toolbar buttons for that category are displayed in the **Toolbar Buttons** box.

2. **Click** on any other category to see the buttons for that category that can be added to the toolbar. See an example in Figure I-2.

3. **Click** on the button that you want to add to the toolbar. When you click on the button, its function is displayed in the **Description** box.

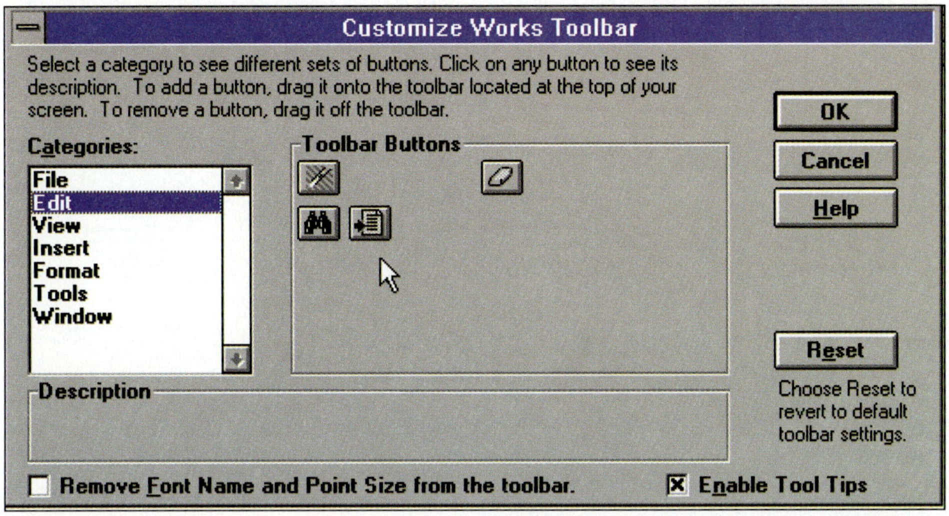

Figure I-2
The Toolbar Buttons box, showing buttons for a specific category and the description of each

4. **Drag** any button you want out of the **Toolbar Buttons** box to the position that seems appropriate in the toolbar.

5. **Repeat** step 4 for any other buttons that you want to add to the toolbar.

NOTE: Leave **Enable Tool Tips** 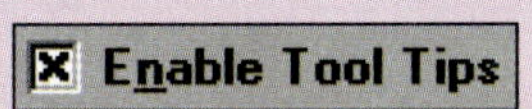

turned on if you want to see the name of the new button when you point to it in the toolbar.

6. **Choose** **OK** or press **Enter** to return to the document. You can now use the button the way you use other buttons in the toolbar. Point to the new button and notice that a label for the new button is now showing.

7. **Use** the steps given earlier in the Restore a Default Button section to remove the added button(s).

NOTE: You can remove the font name and point size from the toolbar in the **Customize Works Toolbar** dialog box by clicking on the **Remove Font Name and Point Size from the toolbar** option. These boxes will be immediately removed. If you click on this option again, they will be restored. When done, choose **OK** or press **Enter** to return to the document.

SETTING OPTIONS

The Options dialog box allows you to specify various settings for using Works. Some of the options available are (1) selecting the way measurements are displayed-(e.g. in inches, centimeters, points, etc); (2) selecting the type of dictionary used for the speller;

and (3) specifying whether or not to save the changes to the workspace when you exit from Works. A complete list and description of the options available are shown in Table I-1. The Options dialog box can be accessed from any Works window-word processor, spreadsheet, database, or communications.

Select Works Options

1. Choose **Tools, Options** to display the Options dialog box as shown in Figure I-3.

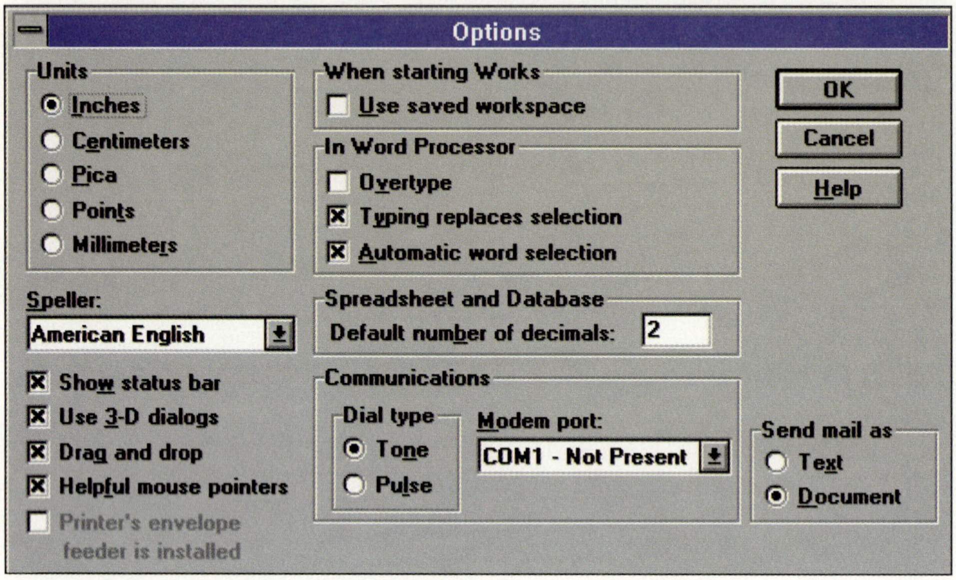

Figure I-3
The Options dialog box

2. Click on any option or press **Alt** and the underlined character to turn it on. An **X** will be displayed in the check box or the **Dot** will be displayed in the radio button when it is turned on. See Table I-1 for a description of each option.

NOTE: As you can see, some of the options are turned on. If you do not choose to use these, use step 2 to turn off any of the options.

3. Choose **OK** or press **Enter** when done.

Option	Description
Units	Select the type of measurement you want displayed in the Ruler as well as page size, margins, tab stops, and paragraph indents.
Speller	Selects the type of dictionary that will be used in the spelling checker.
Show status bar	Displays (it is already turned on) or hides the status bar.
Use 3-D dialogs	Displays the dialog boxes in three-dimensional boxes. This is turned on by default.

Drag and drop	Allows you to drag selected blocks of text to a new location. This is also turned on by default.
Helpful mouse pointers	Displays available mouse actions. Turned on by default.
Printer's envelope feeder is installed	This will be dimmed if you do not have an envelope feeder. Choose this before printing envelopes if you do have an envelope feeder.
Use saved workspace	Turn this option on to display specific documents every time you start Works. It is on by default. To always display certain documents each time you start up, open the documents, arrange them in the Works window, and choose **File, Save Workspace** before exiting Works.
Overtype	This is turned on by default, which means that when **Insert** is pressed, text to the right of the insertion point will be deleted when you type new text.
Typing replaces selection	If a block of text is selected, it will be deleted automatically when you type new text.
Automatic word selection	Whole words will be automatically highlighted.
Spreadsheet and Database Default number of decimals	Enter the number of decimals that you want displayed. The default is two.
Dial type	This will only be available if you have a modem. You can choose the type of dial, either Tone or Pulse, depending upon the telephone you are using.
Modem port	Specify the port for your modem.
Send mail as	Choose to send mail either as text or as a Works document.

Table I-1

The choices in the Options dialog box

SPLITTING A WINDOW

You can split any Works tool window and work on two different sections of the same file simultaneously. You are, however, limited to splitting a word processor window in Normal or Draft view; you cannot split a window in Page Layout view. In the database window, you can only split a window in Form view.

Use the Mouse to Split a Document Window

1. **Open** any Works window or file.
2. **Point** to the split bar icon as shown in the following illustration. (A word processor window is shown here.) When you point to it, the pointer becomes a double-headed arrow and displays the word **Adjust** below it.

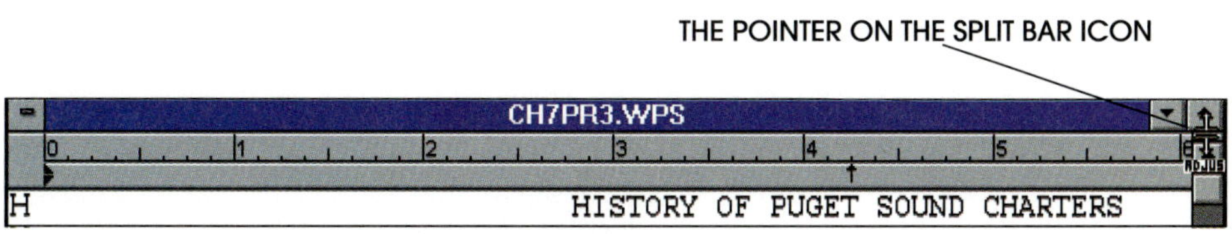

3. **Drag** the icon down. Notice a split bar is displayed across the entire document as shown in Figure I-4.

4. **Release** the left mouse button when the split bar is at the position you want. See the example shown in Figure I-4.

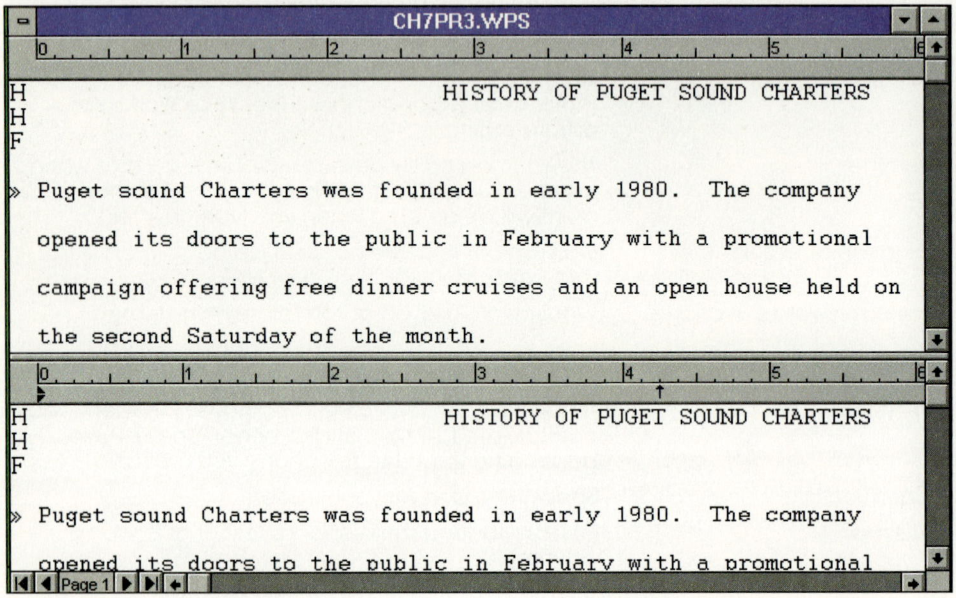

Figure I-4
A split document window

5. **Click** on either the upper or the lower window to move the insertion point.

NOTE: This enables you to look at two different areas of the same document simultaneously. One advantage is that you can easily select data and cut or copy it from its original position. Then move it immediately to a different position that is displayed in the other window.

Use the Mouse to Remove the Split Window

1. Double-click on the split bar. Or drag it up to its original position as shown in Figure I-5. Here it is dragged almost to the top of the window. Continue to drag it up so the window no longer shows the split bar.

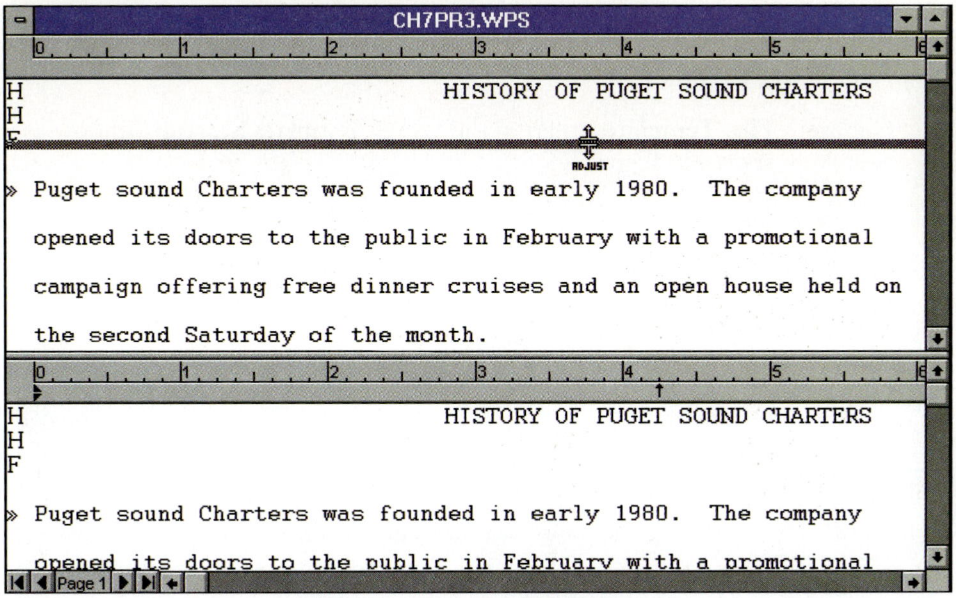

Figure I-5
Dragging the split bar up the window

Use the Keyboard to Open and Close a Window

You can use the keyboard instead of the mouse to split a window, if you like.

To split a window:

1. Choose **Window, Split**. The split bar is displayed and the pointer becomes a double-headed arrow with the word **Adjust** below it.
2. Press the **Down Arrow** or the **Up Arrow** to move the split bar to the position you want and press **Enter** to set it.
3. Press **F6** to move from one window to another.

To remove the split window:

1. Choose **Window, Split**. The pointer moves immediately to the split bar and displays a double-headed arrow.
2. Press the **Up Arrow** to move the split bar to the top of the window.
3. Press **Enter** to restore the full-sized window.

USING TEMPLATES

Works provides you with some documents that are already formatted and contain basic layouts which makes it easy to immediately create professional-looking, consistent documents. A variety of templates for both business and personal use are included; however, you can also create your own template, if you like. Templates can be created for any type of file in Works—word processing, spreadsheet, or database.

You can access a Works template either from a Works tool window or from the Works Startup window

Use a Works Template

From any Works window:

1. Choose **File, Templates** to go to the **Use A Template Startup** window as shown in Figure I-6.

NOTE: If the Works New and Recent Documents Startup window is displayed, click on the **Use a Template** button to display the dialog box shown in Figure I-6.

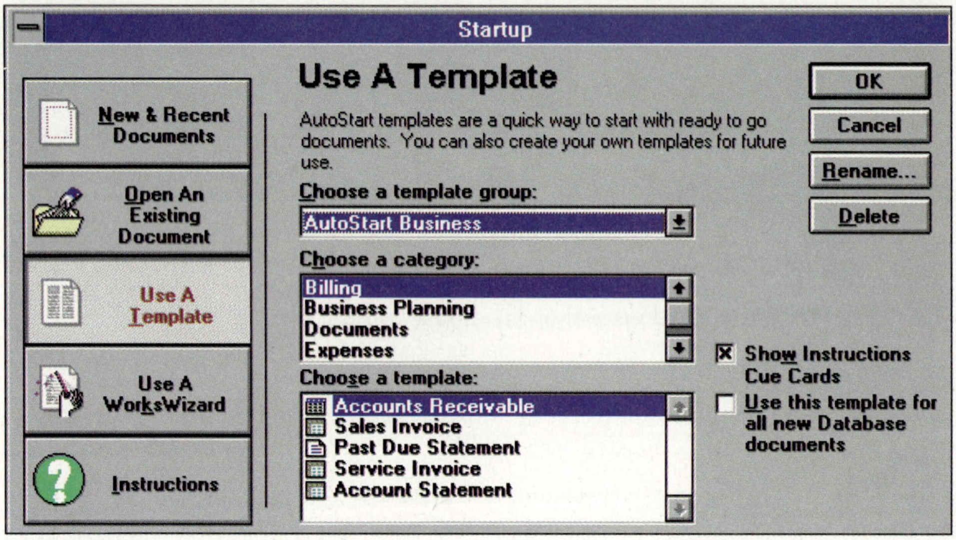

Figure I-6
The Use A Template Startup dialog box

If your screen shows other choices in the list boxes, it means that the template window has been used previously and perhaps other choices have been made. The last selections made are highlighted when you start up the next time.

In Figure I-6, the **AutoStart Business** group is displayed. The **Choose a category** list shows the various types of templates available if you choose the AutoStart Business template. In the **Choose a category** list, **Billing** is selected, and in the **Choose a template** list are displayed the five types of templates that are available if you choose the Billing category.

2. Click on the various choices in the **Choose a template group** to see the different categories that are displayed for each group. Also, click on different categories to see the available templates for each category.

To use a template:

3. Click on the down arrow at the right end of the **Choose a template group** list box.
4. Choose the group you want.
5. Choose the category you want in the **Choose a category** list box. A new list of templates is now displayed in the **Choose a template** list box.
6. Choose the template you want in the **Choose a template** list box.

6. **Choose** the template you want in the **Choose a template** list box.
7. **Choose** **OK** or press **Enter** to display the template. An example of the template used for a résumé is shown in Figure I-7.

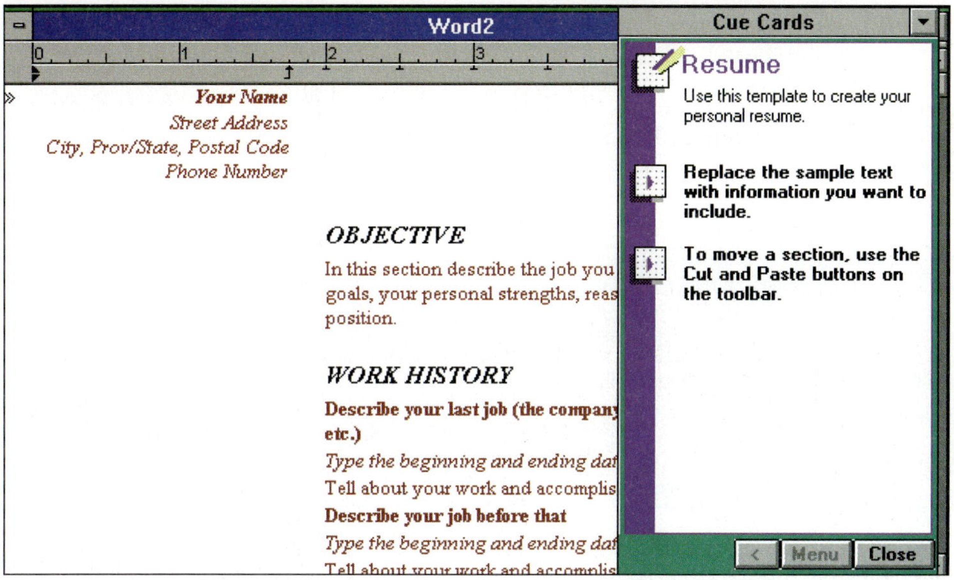

Figure I-7
The Résumé template

A Cue Cards window is displayed at the right and can remain there to guide you in your work with the template if you like, or you can remove it to enlarge the working area of the window.

8. **Respond** to either the Cue Cards window or remove it by choosing **Close**.
9. **Fill in** the information asked for in the template depending on the type of template being used.

When done:

10. **Save** the file as you would save any other file.

Create a Template

To create a template, a file is created in any Works tool window-word processor, spreadsheet, or database-and then it is saved as a template rather than as a regular document. The following are some ideas for creating templates:

- a word processing template that uses your company's logo as a letterhead, format the template with the font style and size that you want, also set margins, line spacing, or other formatting that you want for that particular document.
- a word processing template that contains titles, headings, headers and footers, margins used in reports that are produced on a regular basis.
- create a database that contains the fields for an enrollment or registration form, and objects and pictures can be added to the form view for the database.
- create a spreadsheet template that can be used for an invoice form, monthly statement, or other financial reports.

1. Create the document.

To save the document as a template:

2. Choose **File, Save As** or click on the Save Button to display the Save As dialog box.
3. Choose **Template** Template... to display the Save As Template dialog box.
4. Type a filename in the **Template Name** text box. See the following example. **Report** is the template name shown here.

5. Choose **OK** or press **Enter** to save and return to the document. The title bar in the document window remains unchanged; however, the new template name is now added to the list of custom templates.

Use a Custom Template

1. Choose **File, Templates** to go to the **Use A Template Startup** dialog box.
2. Choose **Custom** from the **Choose a template group** list.
3. Choose the name of the template you want.
4. Choose **OK** or press **Enter**.

You can now enter data or text and save it as you would save any other file.

Edit a Template

You can change a template is much the same way you edit other files. You cannot save changes in one of the templates supplied by Works using the original template name, however, you can use one of these templates as a basis for a new template, make desired changes, and then save it with a different name.

1. Choose **File, Templates** to go to the **Use A Template Startup** dialog box.
2. Choose the template you want.
3. Choose **OK** or press **Enter** to open the template.
4. Make the changes to the template that you want.

To save the edited template:

5. Choose **File, Save As** or click on the **Save** button.

6. Choose **Template** to display the Save As Template dialog box as shown here. The current template name is shown in the text box.

7. Choose **OK** or press **Enter**. A prompt asking if you want to replace the template will be displayed. See the following example.

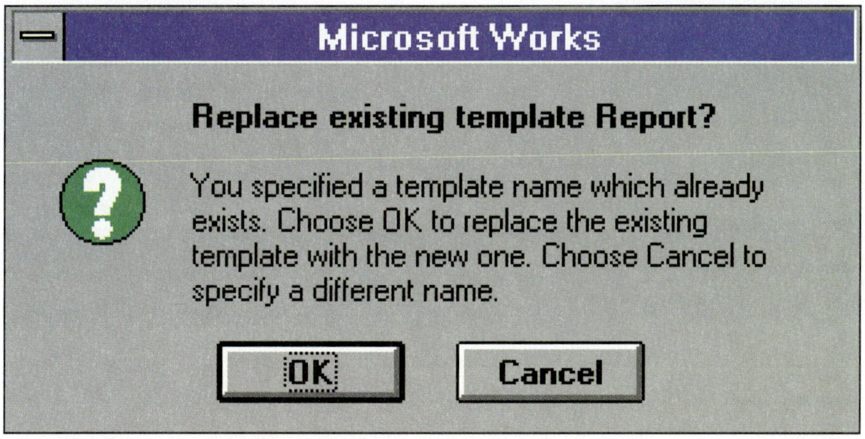

8. Choose **OK** to replace and save the edited template.

NOTE: You can delete a template, rename it, or specify that a certain template always be used for all new word processing documents. To delete or rename a template, choose **File, Templates** and in the **Use A Template Startup** dialog box, select the template, and then choose **Rename** or **Delete**. Depending on your choice here, another dialog box will be displayed. Respond to the prompts to either delete the selected template or enter a new name.

If you want to always use a specific template for all your word processing documents, select the template and turn on **Use this template for all new Word Processor documents** in the Use A Template Startup dialog box. Then choose **OK** or press **Enter** to leave the dialog box. You can use this same procedure for spreadsheet and database templates.

USING WORKSWIZARD

There are a number of WorksWizards that can help you organize files, create letterheads and form letters, and design databases to store various types of information. The advantage of using a WorksWizard, is that it speeds up the process of performing these tasks by responding automatically to the information entered depending on the type of WorksWizard you are using.

Use a WorksWizard

1. Choose **File, WorksWizards** to go to the **Use A WorksWizard Startup** dialog box as shown in Figure I-8.

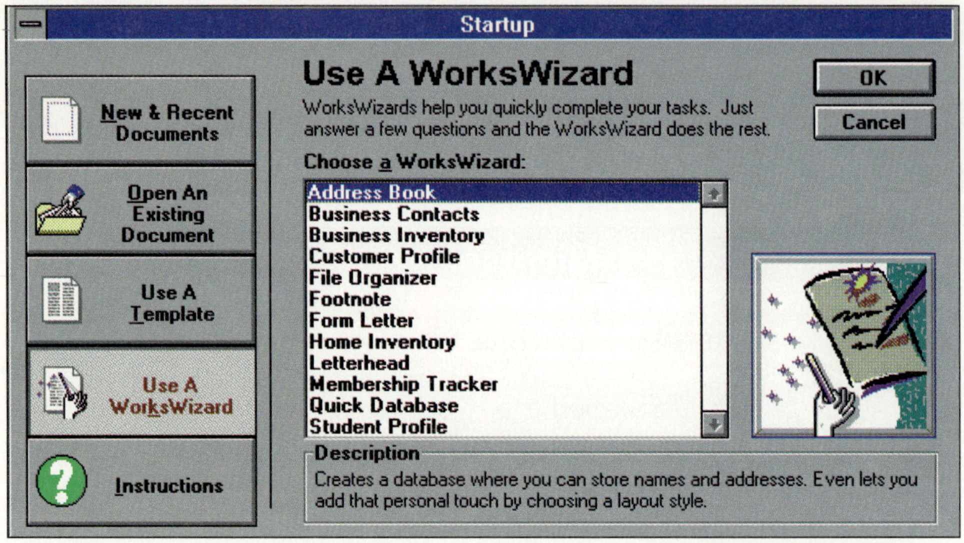

Figure I-8
The Use A WorksWizard Startup dialog box

A list of the available WorksWizards is displayed in the list box. As you select each name, the **Description** box below the list shows the description for that WorksWizard.

2. Choose the WorksWizard you want, and choose **OK** or press **Enter**. The WorksWizard window for your selection will be displayed. Figure I-9 shows the File Organizer WorksWizard.

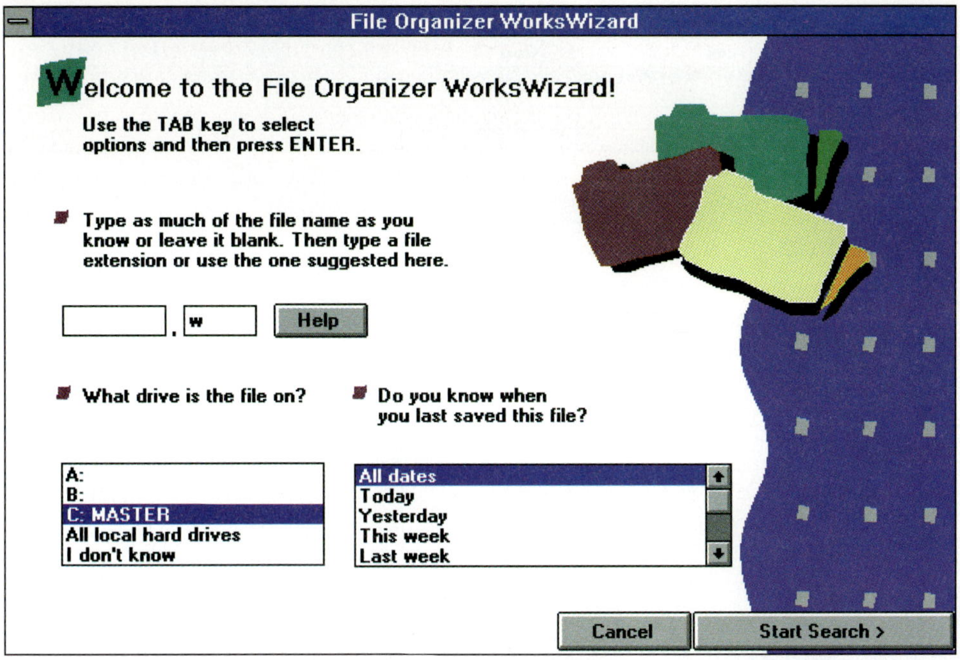

Figure I-9
The File Organizer WorksWizard window

3. Read the instructions on the screen and respond to them to use the WorksWizard you have selected.

When done:

4. Choose **Done** or **Cancel** (depending upon the information displayed) to leave the WorksWizard window.

EMBEDDING OBJECTS

Works provides a variety of objects that can be inserted in either a word processing document or in a database form to enhance the appearance of either of these types of files. Objects include charts, word art, clip art, drawings, equations, and note-its, to name a few. After objects have been inserted in a document, they can be moved, edited, and resized.

Insert WordArt

WordArt allows you to enter letters that are in various creative shapes and sizes that resemble custom-created lettering. These are shapes not available in ordinary fonts, and are frequently used for logos, stationery, and personal initials.

1. Move the insertion point to the position where you want to place the word art.

2. Choose **Insert, WordArt** to display the WordArt menu, button bar, and text dialog box similar to that shown in Figure I-10.

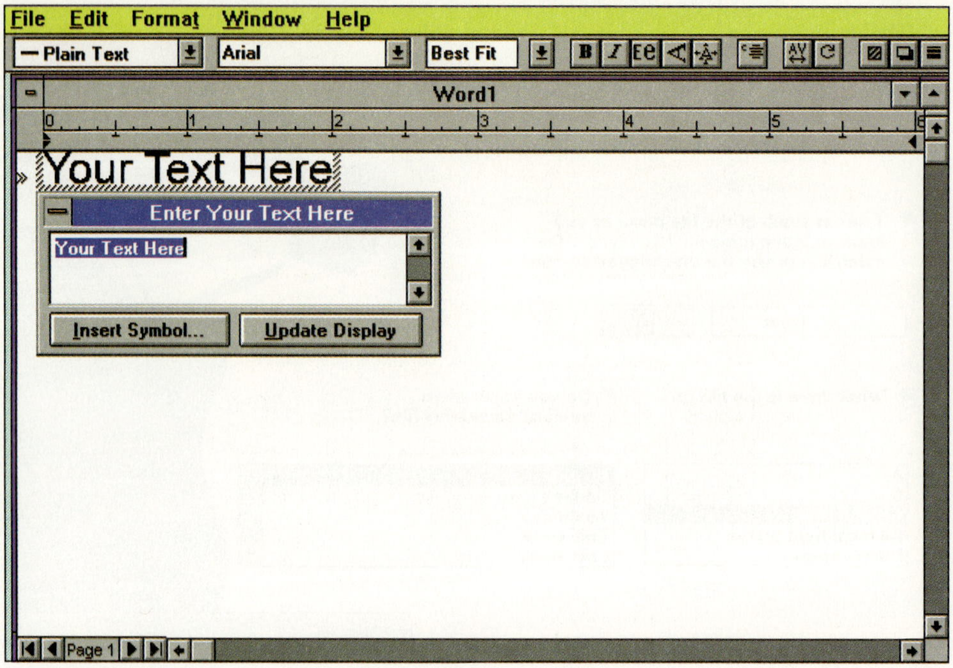

Figure I-10
The WordArt menu, button bar, and text dialog box

The menu items are now changed-a new button bar is displayed and the text dialog box is showing with an example box above it that displays the text as it is formatted with a new shape. The text in the dialog box is highlighted and will be deleted when you type new text.

3. Type the text you want in place of **Your text here.**
4. Choose **Update Display** Update Display to see how the text will look. The following illustration shows an example of word art.

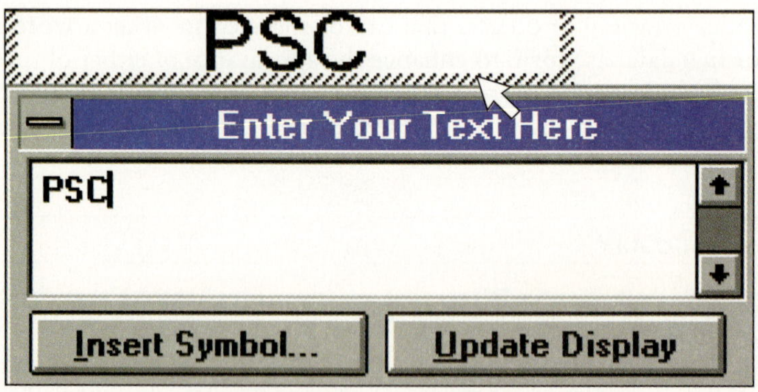

To change the shape of the letters:

5. Click on the down arrow at the right end of the list box in the toolbar showing — **Plain Text** — Plain Text. All of the available shapes for formatting the letters are displayed as shown below.

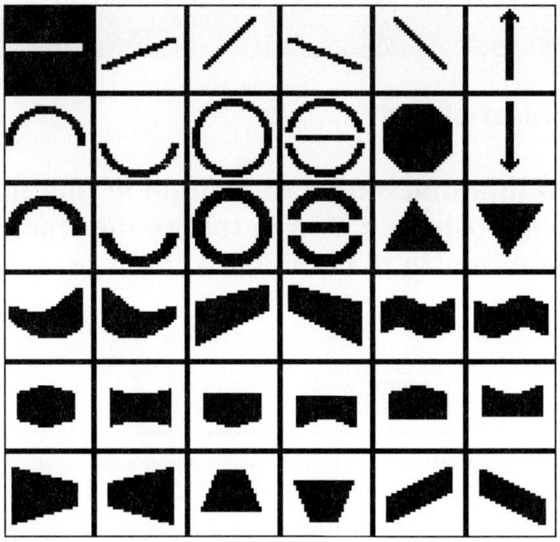

6. Select the shape you want. As soon as you select it, the text box shows the name of the shape and the display in the example box change to the new shape. See an example in the illustration below.

NOTE: You may have to move the **Enter Your Text Here** dialog box.

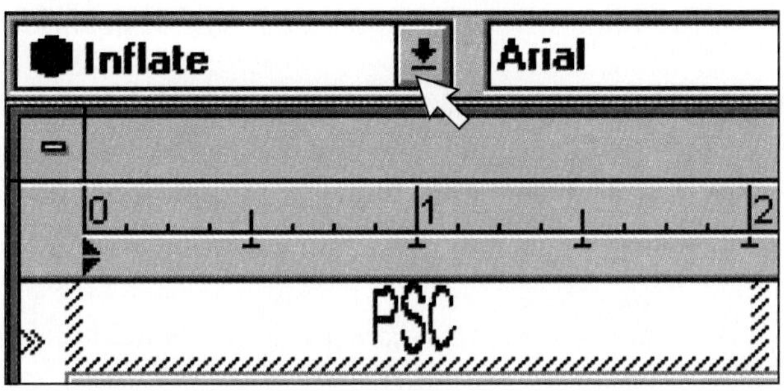

To change the size of the display:

7. Click on the down arrow at the right end of the font size box

A list of font sizes is displayed. The font name and font size correspond automatically to the font name and size used at the location of the insertion point.

8. Choose the font size you want. A prompt may be displayed as shown below, telling you the size is too large for the frame and suggesting you either choose Yes to resize it, or No to leave the frame as is.

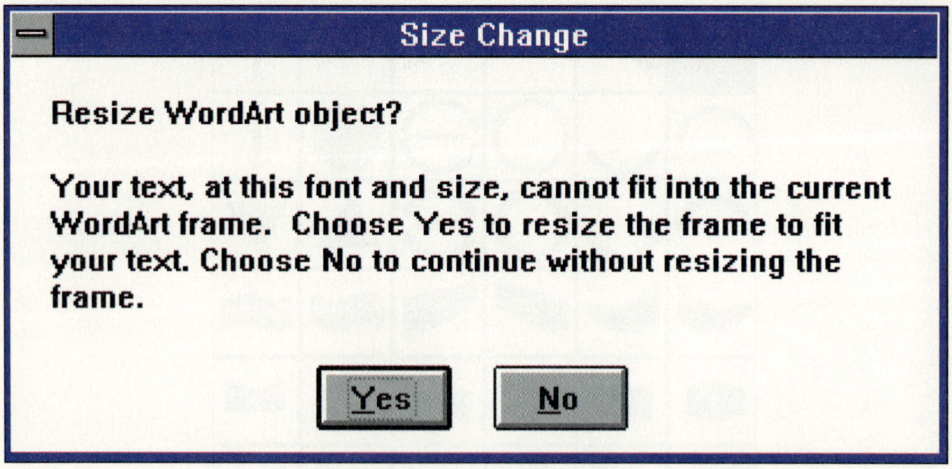

9. **Respond** to the prompt.
10. **Click** anywhere outside the WordArt text box to remove it from the window and return to the document. The letters are now at the insertion point in the document window.

Insert Clip Art

Clip art consists of a collection of pictures and symbols that Works provides for you to insert either in your word processing document or in a database form.

1. **Move** the insertion point to the position where you want to insert clip art.
2. **Choose** **Insert, ClipArt** to go to the ClipArt Gallery as shown in Figure I-11.

NOTE: If the clip art pictures have not been loaded previously, a prompt asking if you want to do that is displayed before the ClipArt Gallery is shown. Choose **Yes** to load the pictures.

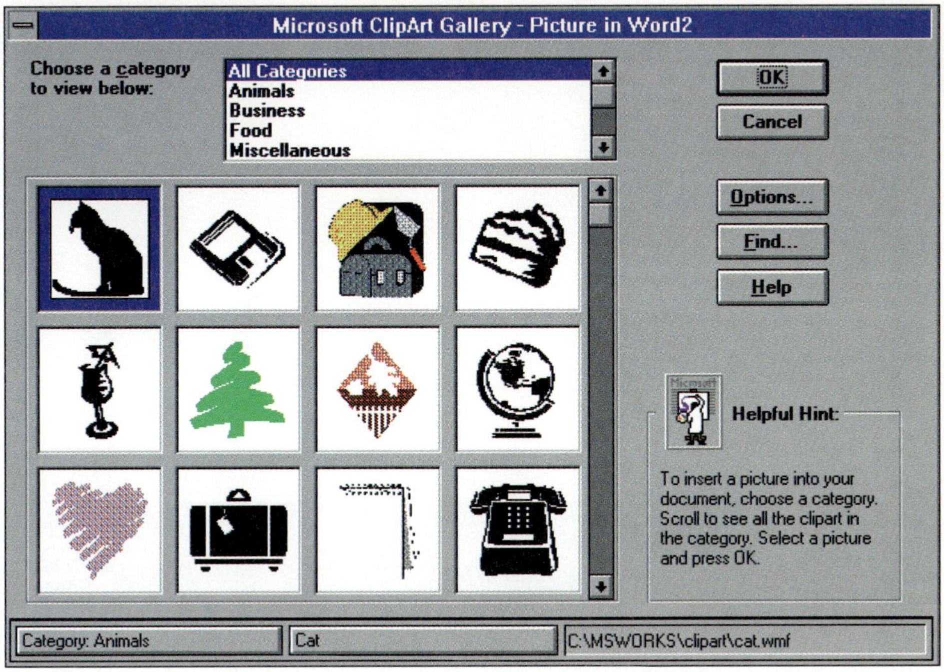

Figure I-11
The ClipArt Gallery window

A list of categories is displayed in the upper left part of the window. The default is for all pictures to be displayed; however, you can select any of the categories to see the pictures available in each.

If you like:

3. Select the categories, one by one, in the **Choose a category to view below** list box, to see the pictures that are available in each.

After looking at all the pictures:

4. Select the picture you want to insert in the document window.

5. Choose **OK** or press **Enter** to return to the document and embed the object.

Insert a Drawing

You can embed a drawing that you create in the Microsoft Draw window in a word processing or database window.

1. Move the insertion point to the position where you want to insert a drawing.

2. Choose **Insert, Drawing** to go to the Microsoft Draw window similar to that shown in Figure I-12.

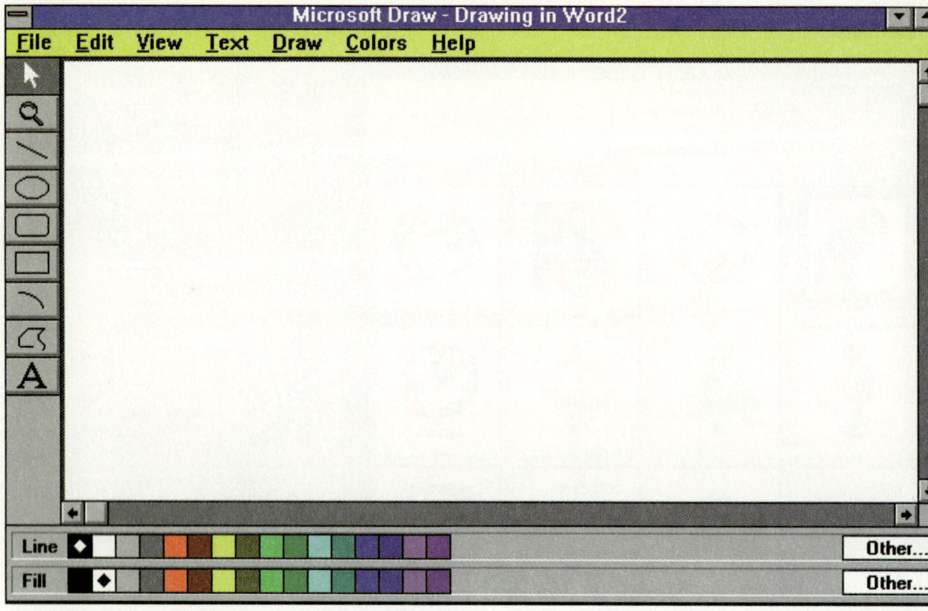

Figure I-12
The Microsoft Draw window

The tools at the left side of the window can be selected and used to draw various types of lines and shapes. See a list of the tools and a description of each in Table I-2. When you select one of these tools, the button is shaded and the pointer changes to that tool. When you select the arrow tool, the pointer is restored to its original use—that of moving around in the window. The bars at the bottom of the screen can be selected to choose colors for lines and for fills, and the items in the menu bar display lists of options that can be used to change the drawings in the window.

Arrow	 The pointer used to move around in the Draw window and ends using any other selection.
Zoom In/Zoom Out	 Enlarges the display in the Draw window.
Line	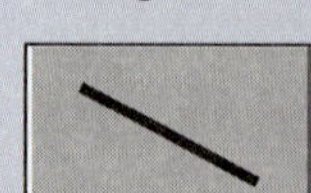 Draws a straight line. Hold down the left mouse button and drag. Release the mouse button to end the line.
Ellipse/Circle	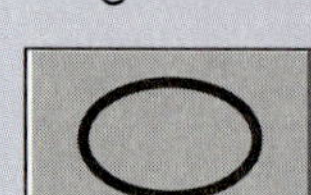 Draws ovals or circles. Point to the position where you want to begin drawing, hold down the left mouse button and drag to a different position to draw an ellipse. To draw a circle, hold down the **Shift** key and drag to a different position.

Tool	Description
Rounded Rectangle/Square	 Draw rectangles or squares with rounded corners. Point to the position where you want to begin drawing, hold down the left mouse button and drag to a different position to draw a rectangle. Hold down the **Shift** key and drag to draw a square.
Rectangle/Square	 Draw rectangles or squares with square corners. Point to the position where you want to begin drawing, hold down the left mouse button and drag to a different position to draw a rectangle. Hold down the **Shift** key and drag to draw a square.
Arcs	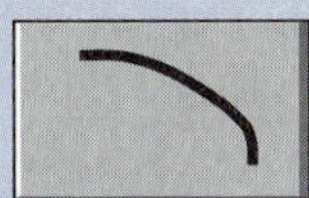 Draw arcs that are 90-degree segments of ovals. Point to the position where you want to begin drawing, hold down the left mouse button and drag to a different position to draw an arc. Hold down the **Shift** key and drag to draw an arc that is part of a circle.
Freeform	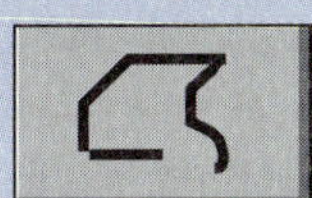 Draws freeform lines. Point to the position where you want to begin and drag to create a design. Click to add a straight line.
Text	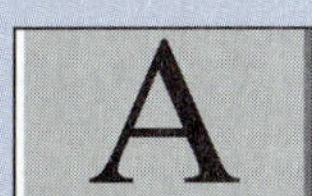 Used to type text in the Draw window. Point and click on the position where you want to insert text and type the characters you want to insert. Use the **Text** menu to format the text the way you want it.

Table I-2

The Draw tools

3. Choose the tool you want and draw the figure you want or insert text in the Draw window.

When done:

4. Double-click on the Close button at the left end of the title bar . or choose **File, Exit and Return to . . .** You will be prompted to update the file as shown here.

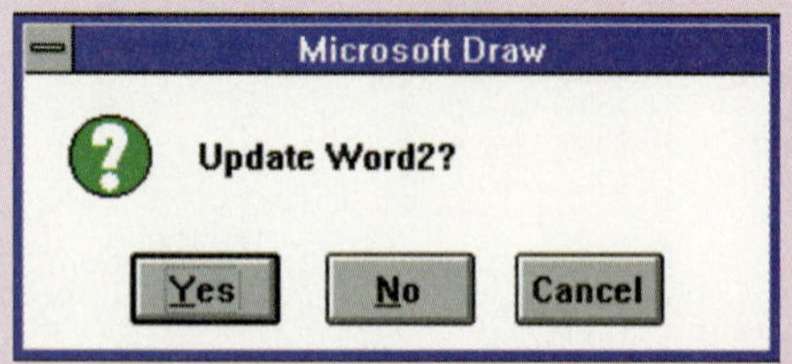

5. Choose **Yes** to return to the document. The drawing is placed at the insertion point.

Insert an Equation

You can use the Equation window to format an equation and insert it in either the Works word processor window or the database form window. Inserting an equation does not include calculation. Rather it is used to format equations accurately.

1. Move the insertion point to the place where you want to insert the equation.

2. Choose **Insert, Object** to go to the Insert Object dialog box as shown in Figure I-13.

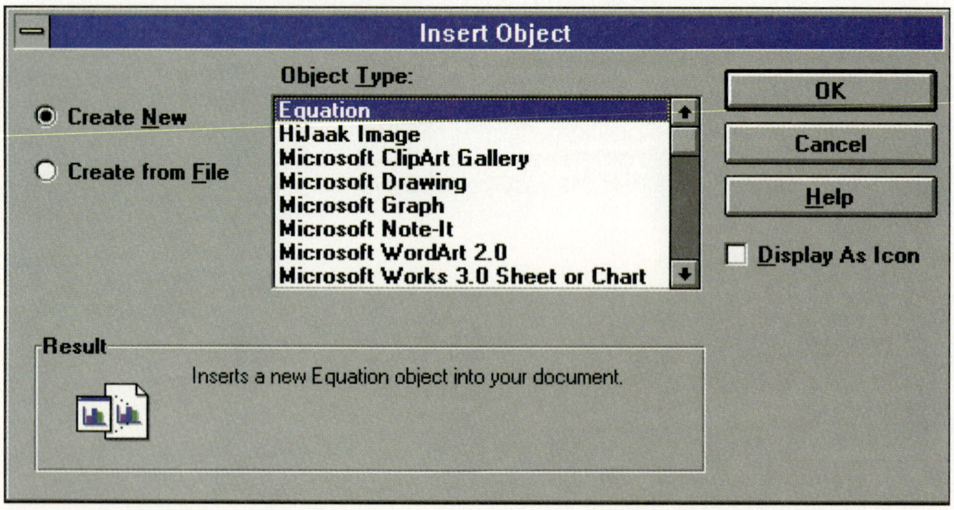

Figure I-13
The Insert Object dialog box

The Object Type list box displays a list of objects that can be selected and embedded in your document. As you can see, clip art, word art, and drawings could be inserted from this dialog box; however, it is quicker to select them directly from the **Insert** menu.

Be sure **Create New** is turned on.

3. Select **Equation** in the **Object Type** list box, if it is not already selected.

4. Choose **OK** or press **Enter** to go to the Equation Editor. The Equation Editor is displayed as shown in Figure I-14.

NOTE: If a prompt warning you that some fonts are not available because of your printer, choose **OK** to go on. Several prompts may be displayed. Choose **OK** to all prompts. You can choose a different printer later if necessary and if it is available. Some printers will not support all equation characters.

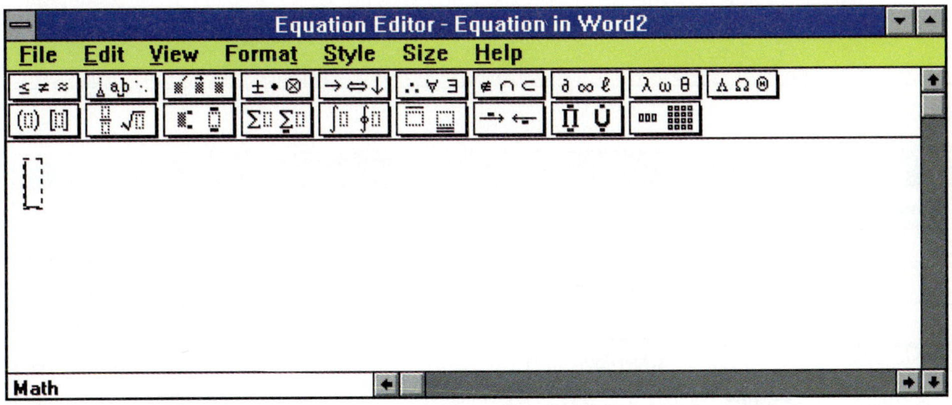

Figure I-14
The Equation Editor

The menu bar displays items that allow you to edit, view, and change the format of the equations. In addition, a group of buttons is displayed below the menu bar. When you point to any of the buttons and hold down the left mouse button, a variety of equation items appropriate for that button will be displayed. You can then drag to the item you want and release the left mouse button to insert the item in the equation window.

The rectangle displayed in the window showing the flashing insertion point is where you can type

5. Select the group button to display equation items. Then select the equation item you want to insert in the equation window.

6. Type any text that is necessary in the outline box. The box will expand as you enter text.

NOTE: In some equations you may type text in the outline box before selecting an equation item.

When done:

7. Double-click on the Close button at the left end of the title bar, or choose **File, Close** A prompt will be displayed asking if you want to save changes to the document.

NOTE: If you edited the equation, the File menu will display the option **Exit and Return to . . .** rather than **Close**.

8. Choose **Yes** to return to the document and insert the equation.

Insert a Note-It

Works has provided some icons called "note-its" that can be inserted in a word processing document or in a database form that are used to call attention to specific portions of the text, for annotations, or for any other task that is appropriate. Also, captions and text can be associated with these icons.

1. Move the insertion point to the position where you want to place the note-it.

2. Choose **Insert, Note-It** to display the Note-It window as shown in Figure I-15.

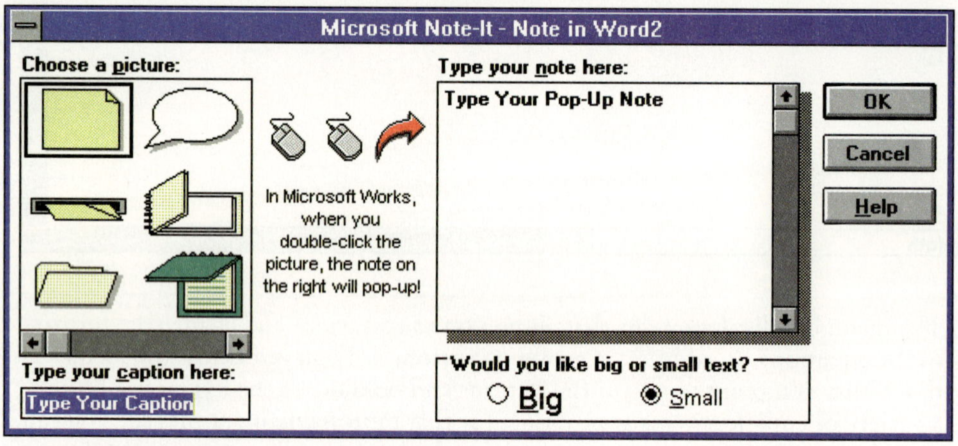

Figure I-15
The Note-It window

You can select items and enter text in any order. The **Choose a picture** box at the left shows the available pictures that can be used for the note-it. Below that box, you can type a caption that will be displayed along with the picture if you like. At the right in the **Type your note here** box is where you enter the text that will be displayed in a pop-up note when you double-click on the picture.

3. Click on the horizontal scroll bar in the **Choose a picture** box to scroll to the right to see the variety of pictures that are available.

4. Click on the picture you want. A box is displayed around the selected picture as shown in the following example.

5. Press **Alt/C** to choose **Type your caption here**. The existing text is automatically highlighted as shown here.

6. Type the text for the caption. The previous text is deleted automatically.
7. Press **Alt/N** to choose **Type your note here**. The text in the **Type your note here** text box is highlighted.
8. Type the text for the pop-up note. This is similar to entering text in the regular document. You can select it and delete it or add text just as you do in the document window. After entering the text, check it for errors. Figure I-16 shows an example of pop-up text.
9. Choose either **Big** or **Small**.

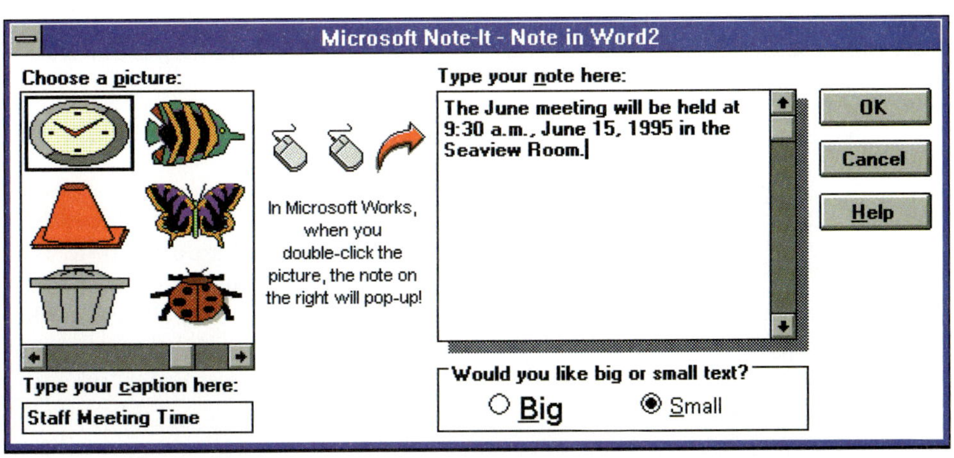

Figure I-16
The Note-It window showing the information that will be embedded in the document

10. Choose **OK** or press **Enter** when done to return to the document. Figure I-17 shows an example of a clock note-it inserted in a document.

Figure I-17
The document containing the embedded note-it object

To see the note attached to the picture:

11. Double click on the object. The pop-up note will be displayed at the top of the window. See the following example.

NOTE: You can also display the pop-up text for the note by selecting the note-it object and choosing **Edit, Microsoft Note-It Object,** and **Read.**

12. Click anywhere in the document window to remove the pop-up text.

NOTE: If you frequently create documents that include embedded objects, you can add a button to the toolbar that will go directly to the appropriate object window. There is a button for each of the following: charts, drawings, note-its, clip art, and word art. To do this, choose **Tools, Customize Toolbar,** select the **Insert** category, and drag the button or buttons that you want to the toolbar. Then choose **OK** or press **Enter** to return to the document.

EDITING AN OBJECT

All Works objects (with the exception of a note-it) can be easily edited by double-clicking on the picture or object, or by using the **Edit, Object** (text that is displayed here depends upon the type of object to be edited)**, Edit** command from the menu bar. Either returns you to the window that was used to create the object. Then you can make changes the same way you created the object originally.

Edit a Word Art, Clip Art, or Draw Object

1. Double-click on the object

   or

   Select the object by clicking on it once. Handles will be displayed as shown here.

   and

   Choose **Edit** and the appropriate option. The choice displayed above corresponds to the object that has been selected. If you had selected the clip art picture, this option would be **Edit Microsoft ClipArt Gallery Object**, for example. If your computer is slow, you may have to wait several seconds. The pointer becomes an hourglass. Soon the menu, toolbar, and the text box for the object will be displayed.

2. Make any changes the same way you created the object originally.
3. Double-click on the Control menu box at the left end of the title bar in whatever object window you are in to return to the document.

NOTE: To edit a note-it, select the note-it object, then choose **Edit, Microsoft Note-It Object, Edit**. Make changes in the edit window the same way you entered information originally for the note-it object.

RESIZING AN OBJECT

Resizing clip art, drawings, note-its, or equations will change the size of the picture. It will not, however, change the size of text in a word art object; it will only change the size of the box around the text.

Resize Embedded Objects

1. Click on the object to display the handles and outline. The following illustration shows an example of a word art object that is selected, showing the handles .

2. Drag any of the handles to a different position to change the size of the box.

   NOTE: Be sure you are resizing, not dragging. When you are resizing, the pointer becomes a double-headed arrow and the word **Resize** is displayed on it. When you are dragging the object, the word **Drag** will appear on the pointer.

3. Click anywhere in the document away from the object to deselect it (that is, to remove the handles and outline).

   NOTE: You can also resize an object by selecting it, then choosing **Format, Picture/Object** and entering a specific measurement for the picture in the Picture/Object dialog box.

MOVING AN OBJECT

You can move an object by selecting it and then dragging it to a new position, or, after selecting it, you can click on the **Cut** button to copy the object to Clipboard, move to the new position and click on the **Paste** button. The procedure for moving an object is the same as for moving a block of text.

Move an Embedded Object

1. Click on the object to select it. When you point to it, the pointer shows the word **Drag** below it as displayed in the following example.

2.	Hold	down the left mouse button and drag the object to a new position.
3.	Release	the mouse button when the object is placed where you want it.

NOTE: You can copy objects the same way you copy blocks of text. Select the object, click on the **Copy** button, move the insertion point to the place where you want to copy the object, and click on the **Paste** button.

SETTING TEXT WRAP

Text wrap applies only to text in a word processing window. The default setting for an object is *in line* with accompanying text. That means that the object will move up and down as text is entered above it or deleted, or it will move from side to side as text is added or deleted in front of it. If you want the object to be at a fixed position on the page, you can specify that in the Picture/Object dialog box from the **Format** menu. Then, regardless of text that is added or deleted, it will always remain in the same place on the page.

1.	Select	the object.
2.	Choose	**Format, Picture/Object** to display the Picture/Object dialog box as shown in Figure I-18.

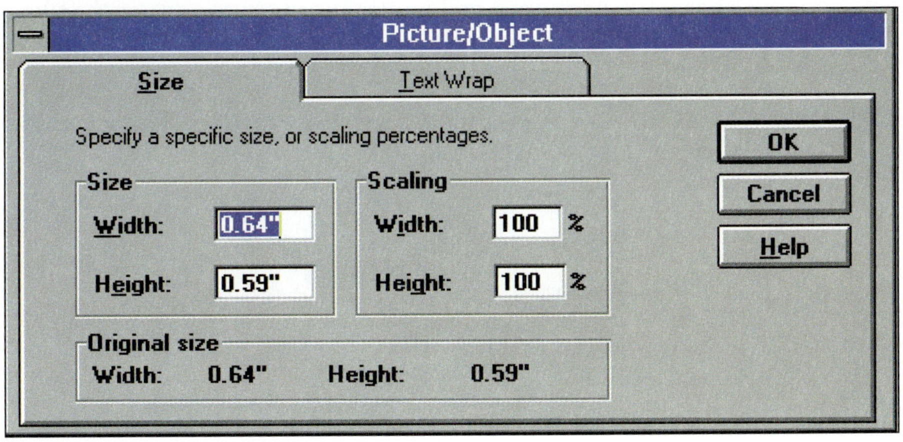

Figure I-18
The Picture/Object dialog box

NOTE: The Picture/Object dialog box contains two sections—**Size** and **Text Wrap**. The Size tab displays the current size of the selected object. If this object had been resized, the new measurements would be showing in the **Width** and **Height** boxes. The original width and height of the object are displayed in the Original size box at the bottom of the dialog box. If you want to restore any of the objects that you resized, you can select the object, choose **Format, Picture/Object**, and enter the original measurements in the Width and Height text boxes.

3. Choose **Text Wrap** tab. Your screen now resembles the example shown in Figure I-19. The Text Wrap tab allows you to specify whether the object will be formatted as an in-line object or if it will be at a fixed position on the page.

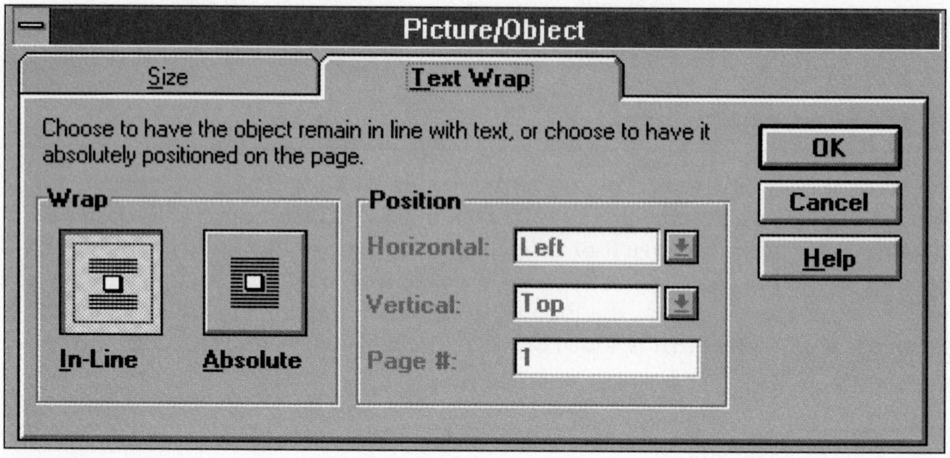

Figure I-19
The Text Wrap tab section of the Picture/Object dialog box

In-Line is turned on as the default choice in the Wrap box, and a description of In-Line is displayed above the In-Line picture.

4. Choose **Absolute**. The **Position** box at the right of the **Wrap** box now shows the horizontal and vertical position choices of the object. (The information displayed here may vary depending upon the exact placement of your object.)

5. Click on the down arrow at the right of **Horizontal** to display a list of choices as shown here.

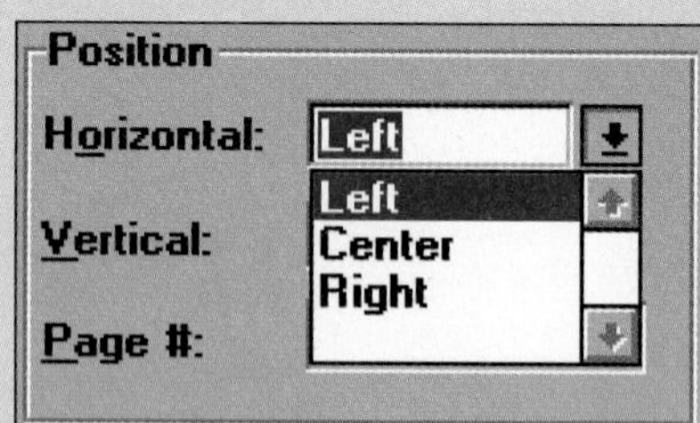

6. Choose the alignment you want.

7. Click on the down arrow at the right of **Vertical** as shown here.

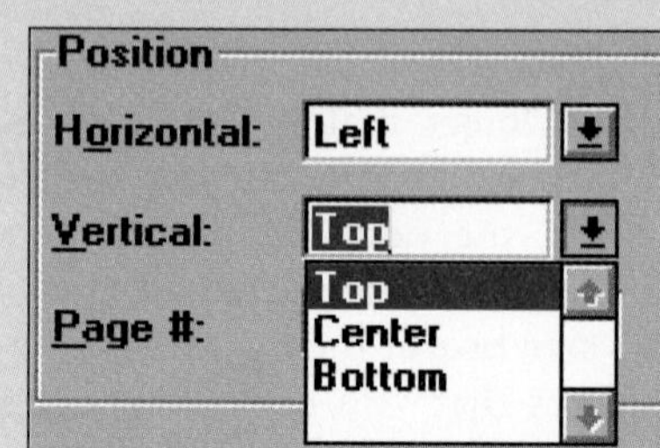

8. Choose the alignment you want.

NOTE: You can also enter measurements for the Horizontal and the Vertical positions if you know exactly where you want to place the object. Once the object is set at a fixed position, it will not move as text is entered around it. You can, however, move it to another absolute position by dragging it the same way you drag other objects.

9. Choose **OK**. A prompt, as shown here, asking if you want to change to Page Layout will be displayed if you are working in some other view.

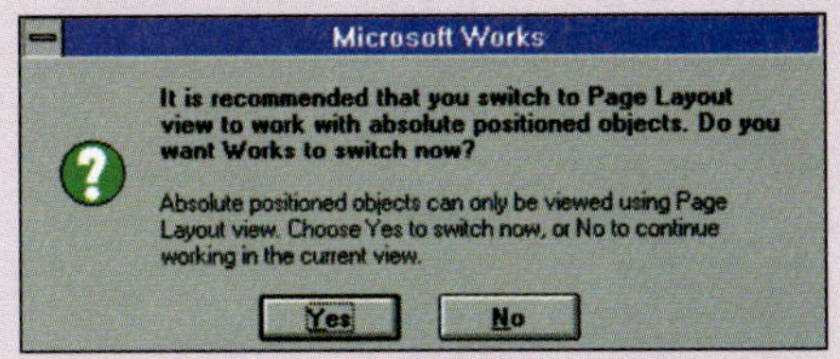

10. Choose **Yes** to return to the document. The object is now moved to the specific position set in the Text Wrap section of the Picture/Object dialog box.

NOTE: You can drag an object to a different fixed (absolute) position if you like. The only requirement is that the object must be formatted with text wrap set at **Absolute**.

APPENDIX II

The Communications Tool

Appendix II covers features of the Works communications tool. If you have communications capabilities-a modem is required for using the Works communications tool-you can use this appendix as a general guideline. It is to be used as a reference tool rather than an instructional practice tool, because communication capabilities vary with individual systems.

The communications tool allows you to access information services or bulletin boards or to communicate with others through their computers. You can collect data from another computer or send information to one or more computers. The procedures for communicating with other computers will be discussed here as well as how to send files, such as word processing documents.

BEGINNING A COMMUNICATIONS SESSION

The communications tool is used to sign on to a bulletin board or information service, where you can receive information or communicate with the service, or to communicate directly with another computer. When making connections with a service or with another computer, be sure the settings for your computer match those of the other computer or service. (Changing settings is covered later in this appendix.)

Start a Communications Session

Before connecting to another computer or to a service, be sure your modem is properly connected and that it is turned on.

1. Open — Works, or if you are already using a Works tool, choose **File, Create New File.**
2. Choose — the **Communications** tool  from the Startup window.

If this is the first time you are starting a communications session, the Modem Setup dialog box may be displayed as shown in Figure II-1. (If the Modem Setup dialog box is not displayed, skip to step 6.)

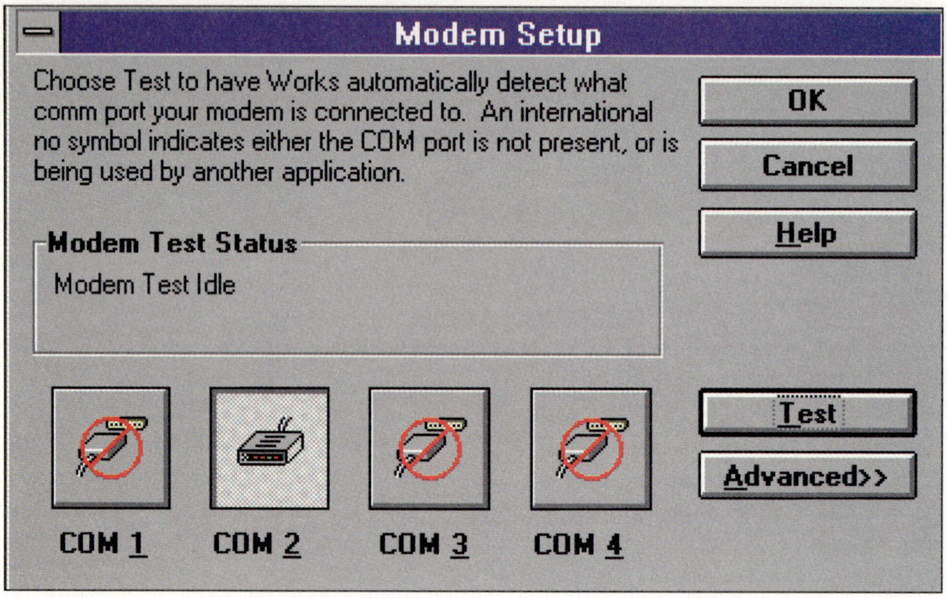

Figure II-1
The Modem Setup dialog box

3. Be sure — a **Com** number is selected.
4. Choose — **Test** to confirm that the modem is properly connected. If the test shows it is not connected properly, or if it is not turned on, make the necessary corrections, then run the test again.

When done:

5. Choose — **OK** to close the dialog box. The Easy Connect dialog box is then displayed as shown in Figure II-2.

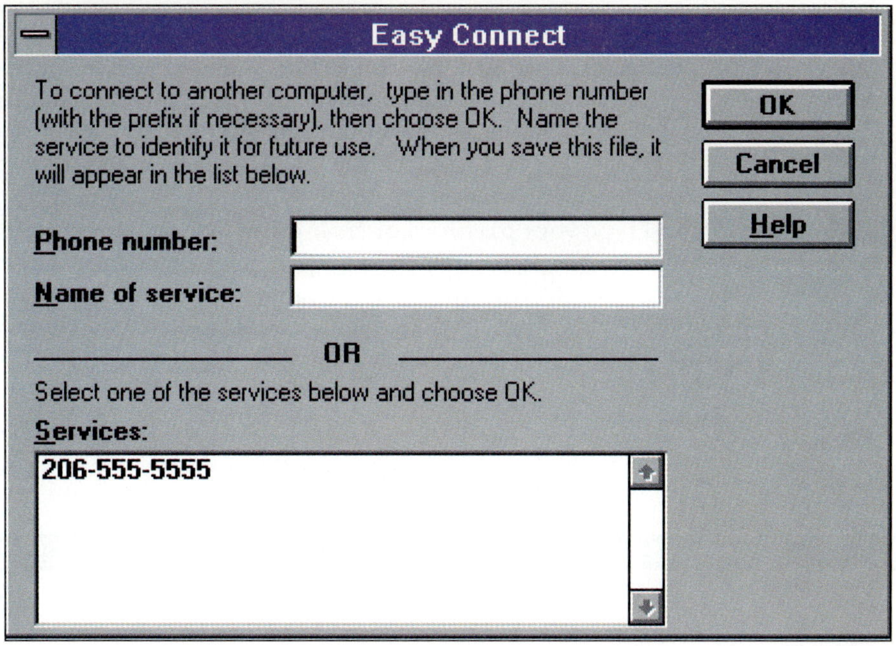

Figure II-2
The Easy Connect dialog box

If this is the first time you are calling a service or individual:

6. Type — the phone number you want to connect with in the **Phone number** text box. (Hyphens are optional when typing the number.)

7. Type — the name of the service or person with whom you wish to communicate in the **Name of service** text box.

or — if this is not the first time you are calling, a list of services that you have communicated with previously will be displayed in the **Services** list box.

Select — the service or individual with whom you want to communicate listed in the **Services** box. The eight most recent connections are here.

8. Choose — **OK** or press **Enter**. A prompt is displayed as shown in Figure II-3, asking if you want to connect to another computer or if you want to choose **Cancel** to work off-line.

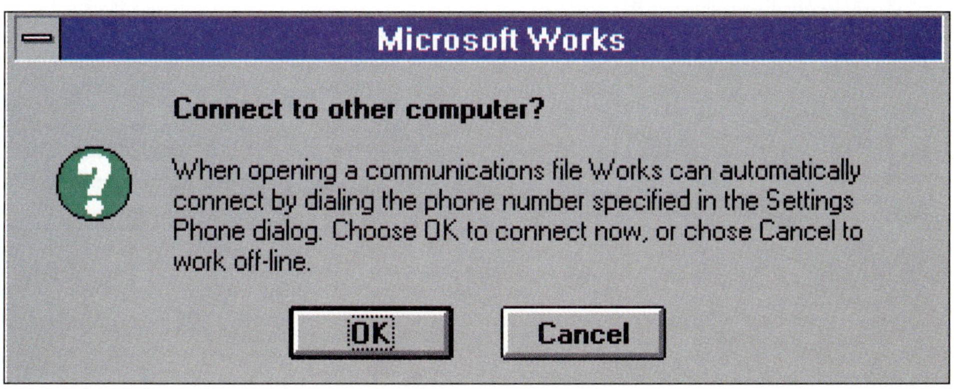

Figure II-3
The prompt asking if you want to make the connection

NOTE: Working off-line allows you to change settings or use the Tools menu in the Communications window. You cannot, however, enter any text in the window when you are off-line. You can display the Easy Connect dialog box again by clicking on the Phone button  or by choosing **Phone, Easy Connect**.

9. Choose **OK** and type your password or enter other required information. Respond to the screen depending upon the connection you are making. Most services or bulletin boards give instructions when you connect with them. A communications document window similar to that shown in Figure II-4 is displayed that shows this information.

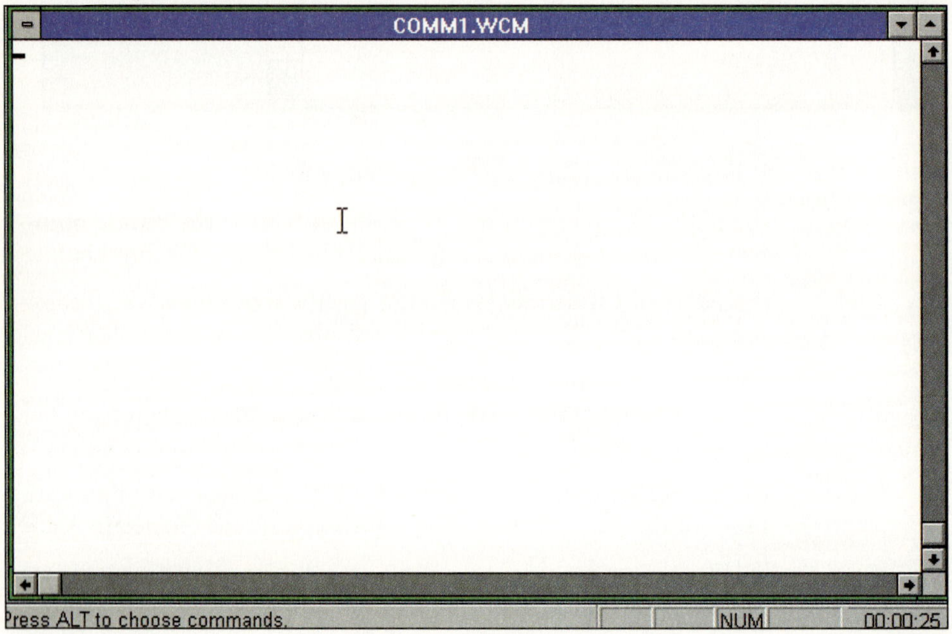

Figure II-4
The Communications window

Notice the status bar displays information about the current communications action. (No connection was made here.) A message will be displayed in the lower right corner of the status bar showing the elapsed time of the connection.

When done:

10. Click on the Dial/Hangup button  or choose **Phone, Hang Up** to display the "OK to diconnect?" prompt shown in Figure II-5.

Figure II-5
The prompt to disconnect

11.	Choose	**OK** to disconnect. The status bar now displays OFFLINE.

SAVING THE COMMUNICATIONS DOCUMENT

You can save the information that is displayed in the Communications window which is the information that is required to make the connection. Saving this information as a document allows you to open it later to call the same service or computer.

1.	Choose	**File, Save As** to display the Save As dialog box shown in Figure II-6.

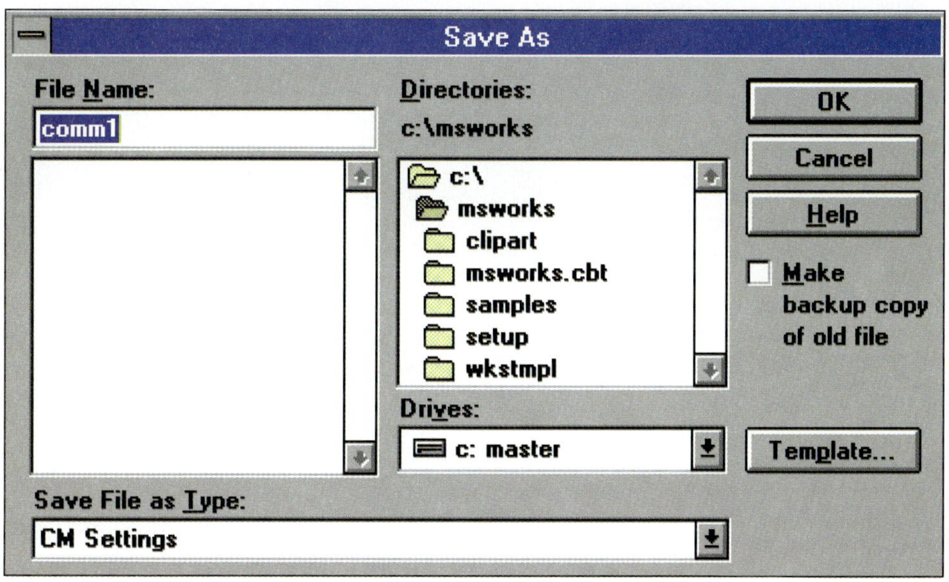

Figure II-6
The Save As dialog box in the communications tool

2.	Type	a filename in the **File Name** text box or leave the default name, **comm1**, as is. This procedure is similar to saving other Works files.
3.	Choose	**OK** or press **Enter** to save.

USING THE COMMUNICATIONS MENU

The menu options available in the Communications tool are described in Table II-1.

Table II-1
Menus in the communications tool window

Menu	Options in the menu
File	Similar to other Works tools.
Edit	Copy, Paste, and Select All.
View	Turns the toolbar on or off.
Setting	Changes the settings for Phone, Communication, Terminal, or Transfer, or selects the Modem to be used.
Phone	Easy Connect, Dial, Dial Again, Pause, or Break.
Tools	Customize Toolbar, Options (similar to other Works tools options), Receive File, Send File, Capture Text, Send Text, Record Script, Cancel Recording, and Edit Script.
Window	Same as other Works Window options.
Help	Provides information about using the various Works tools and features.

USING THE TOOLBAR

The toolbar contains buttons that can be used to perform the various communications functions. The buttons that are different from those in other Works windows are listed in Table II-2 with a description of each.

Button	Function
Communication Settings	 Displays the Communication tab section in the Settings dialog box.
Terminal Settings	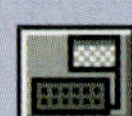 Displays the Terminal tab section in the Settings dialog box.
Phone Settings	 Displays the Phone tab section in the Settings dialog box.
Transfer Settings	 Displays the Transfer tab section in the Settings dialog box.
8-N-1 settings	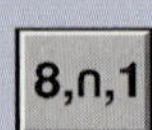 Changes the communication settings to 8 data bits, no parity, and 1 stop bit if these settings have been set differently.
7-E-1	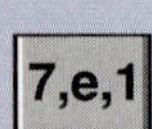 Changes the communication settings to 7 bits, even parity, and 1 stop bit if these settings have been set differently.

<table>
<tr><td>Easy Connect</td><td>
Displays the Easy Connect dialog box in which you can enter the number you want to call.</td></tr>
<tr><td>Dial/Hangup</td><td>
Either disconnects a connection or dials the current phone number.</td></tr>
<tr><td>Pause</td><td>
Delays incoming text if it is coming in faster than you can copy or review it.</td></tr>
<tr><td>Capture Text</td><td>
Displays the Capture dialog box in which you can name and save the incoming text to a file.</td></tr>
<tr><td>Send Text</td><td>
Displays the Send Text dialog box in which you can enter the name of a file that you want to send. This sends text as an ASCII file (one that does not contain formatting).</td></tr>
<tr><td>Send Binary File</td><td>
Displays the Send File dialog box in which you can enter the name of the file that you want to send. This sends text as a binary file, which can contain formatting.</td></tr>
<tr><td>Receive Binary File</td><td>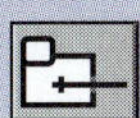
Receives a binary file that contains formatting.</td></tr>
</table>

Table II-2
Buttons in the communication toolbar

CHANGING SETTINGS

Various communications settings can be changed that will allow you to communicate with other computers or information services. These settings include Phone, Communications, Terminal, and Transfer settings.

Change Phone Settings

1. Click on the Phone Settings button  or choose **Settings, Phone** to display the Phone section in the Settings dialog box as shown in Figure II-7.

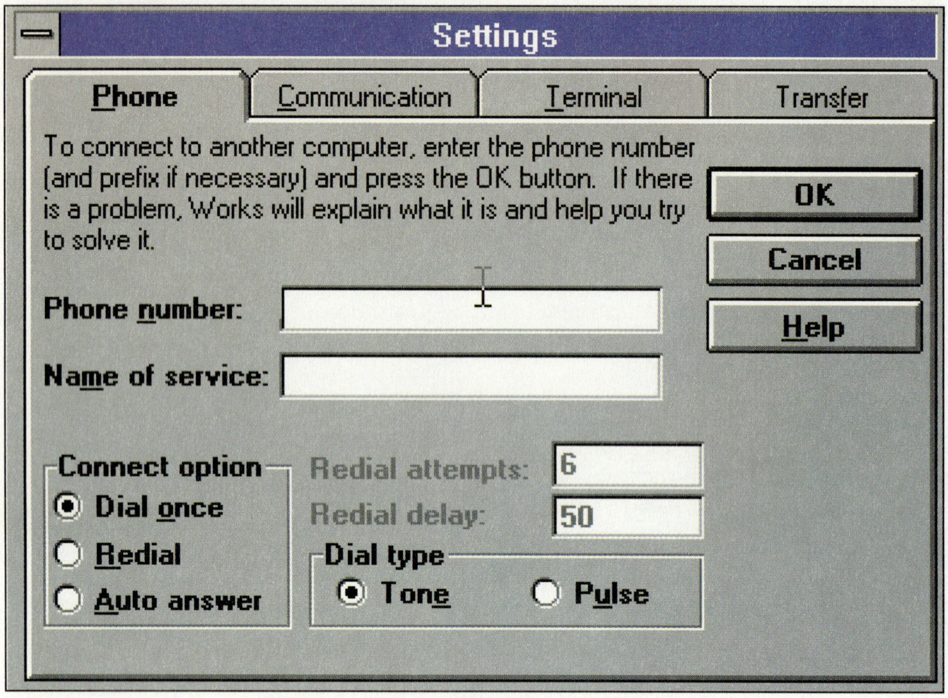

Figure II-7
The Phone tab in the Settings dialog box

Changes that can be made are listed in Table II-3.

Table II-3
Phone setting options

Option	Results or response
Dial once	Default setting. Dials the phone number once.
Redial	Dials the number again if the line is busy. If Redial is turned on, you can enter the number of times to redial in the Redial attempts text box. You can also enter the length of the delay between redial attempts in the Redial delay text box.
Auto answer	Allows an incoming communication from another computer.
Dial Type	Choose Tone for a touch-tone phone, or Pulse for a rotary dial.

2. Make any changes that you want.
3. Choose **OK** or press **Enter**.

Change Communication Settings

1. Click on the Communication Settings button 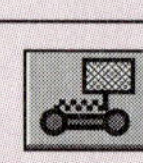 , or choose **Settings, Communication** to display the Communication tab in the Settings dialog box. See an example in Figure II-8.

Table II-4 contains a list of the options and description of each.

2. Make any changes to the communication settings and choose **OK** or press **Enter** when done.

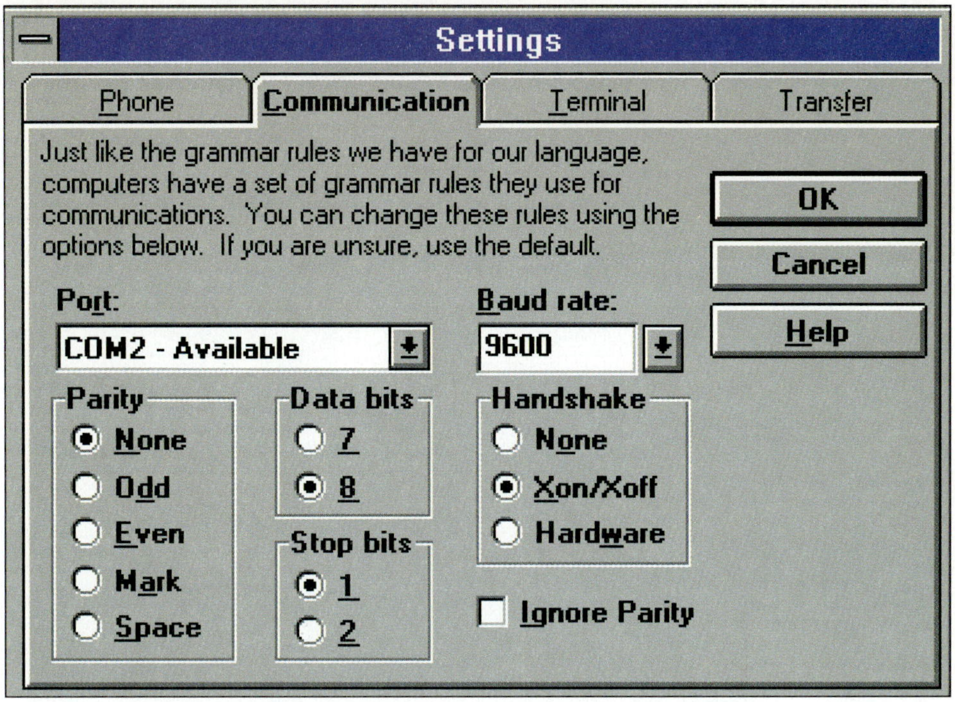

Figure II-8
The Communication tab in the Settings dialog box

Table II-4
Communication settings options

Options	Response
Port	Displays the port you are currently connected to. Click on the down arrow to display a list of available ports.
Parity	Leave the option set at None if you are not sure of the other computer's settings, or choose one of the parity options that matches the other computer's settings. (Parity refers to a parity bit that is added to a byte to ensure there is either an odd or an even number of bits, depending on the system's logic.) Parity, here in the Communication Settings, checks for errors if a bit is lost in transmission.
Data bits	Choices here should match the other computer's settings. The default is 8. If you need to change this to 7, you can either make that change here, or click on the 7-E-1 button 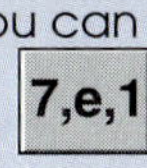 in the toolbar.
Stop bits	Choices here should match the other computer's settings. The number of stop bits is used to represent the end of each character.
Baud rate	This number is the rate of data transfer. Choose the highest rate for your modem and for the other computer's modem. You may have to refer to the User's Guide for your modem to determine the correct rate.
Handshakes	X on/X off controls how data transfers from one computer to another. If you are using a cable connection, turn on Hardware.
Ignore Parity	Clear the check box here, if necessary, to use a different parity setting.

Change Terminal Settings.

1. Click on the Terminal Settings button, or choose **Settings, Terminal. See** Figure II-9.

See a list of the options and their description in Table II-5.

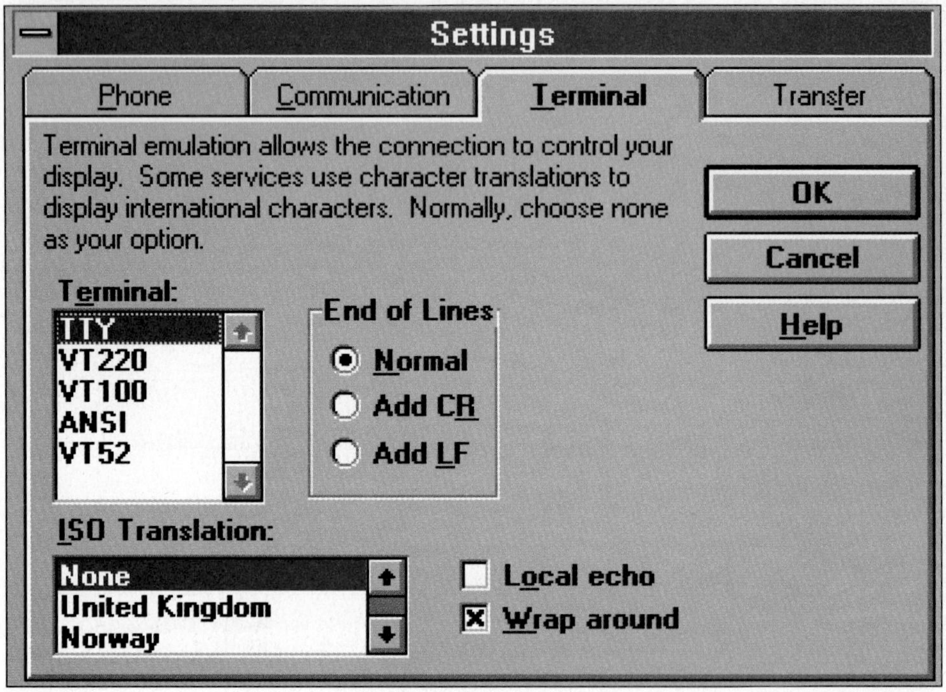

Figure II-9
The Terminal tab in the Settings dialog box

Table II-5
The Terminal options

Options	Response
Terminal	Choose a type of terminal that matches the computer you are communicating with.
End of Lines	The default setting is Normal; however, if incoming text is displayed on one line, choose Add CR (a carriage return) or Add LF (a line feed).
ISO Translation	The default is None; however, if the incoming data needs to be translated, choose an appropriate language by clicking on the down arrow to display the choices.
Local echo	If your typing doesn't appear on the screen, turn this option on. If you see duplicate characters, turn it off.
Wrap around	Turn this option off so that text does not wrap to the next line in the window.

2. Make any changes that you want.
3. Choose **OK** or press **Enter** to return to the Communications window.

Change Transfer Settings

Change the transfer settings, if necessary, when sending or receiving text or binary files. The transfer settings allow you to choose the protocol used for sending and receiving files.

1. Click on the Transfer Settings button , or choose **Settings, Transfer** to display the Transfer tab section of the Settings dialog box. See an example in Figure II-10.

See a list of options and a description of each in Table II-6.

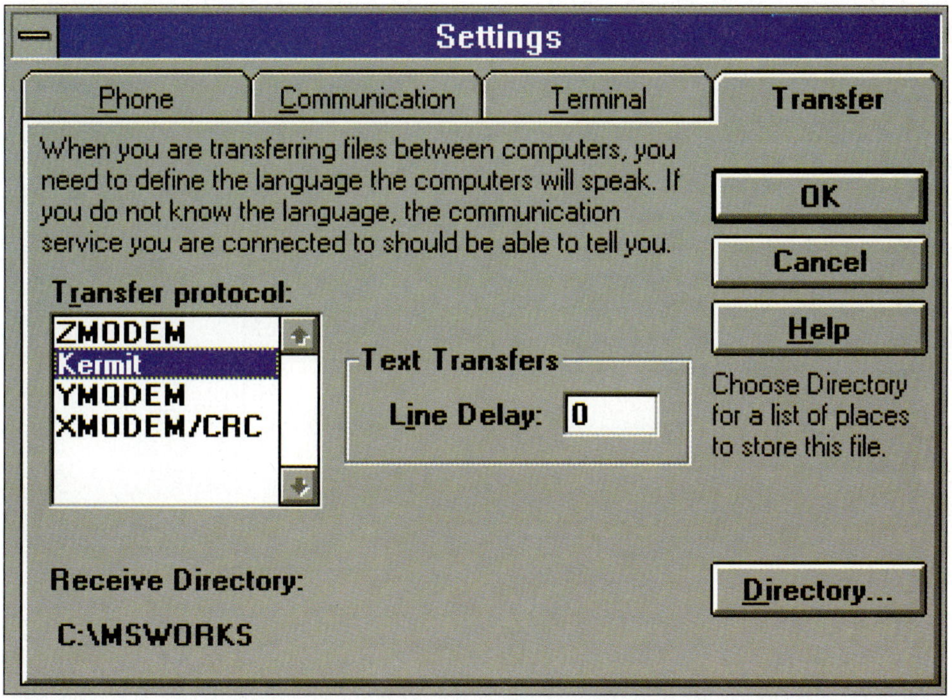

Figure II-10
The Transfer tab in the Settings dialog box

Option	Response
Transfer protocol	Select the protocol that you want to use to control sending and receiving. The choice must match the computer with which you are communicating. ▪ ZMODEM is the fastest choice. ▪ Kermit is the slowest choice, but is very reliable. You can transfer several files during one download, and it can recover from a transfer failure. ▪ YMODEM is faster than an XMODEM, but slower than ZMODEM It is generally reliable and can transfer several files. ▪ XMODEM is slow but reliable. You can transfer only one file at a time.
Text Transfers Line Delay	Sets the amount of time to delay sending your next line in an ASCII text file. The number will be in tenths of a second that Works delays sending the next line.

Table II-6
Transfer options

2. Make any changes you want and choose **OK** or press **Enter** when done.

RECEIVING INCOMING COMMUNICATIONS

Make sure the communication settings are the same for both computers, and that you are in the Communications window.

1. Click on the Phone Settings button  or choose **Settings, Phone** to display the Phone tab as shown in Figure II-11.

TURN ON AUTO ANSWER

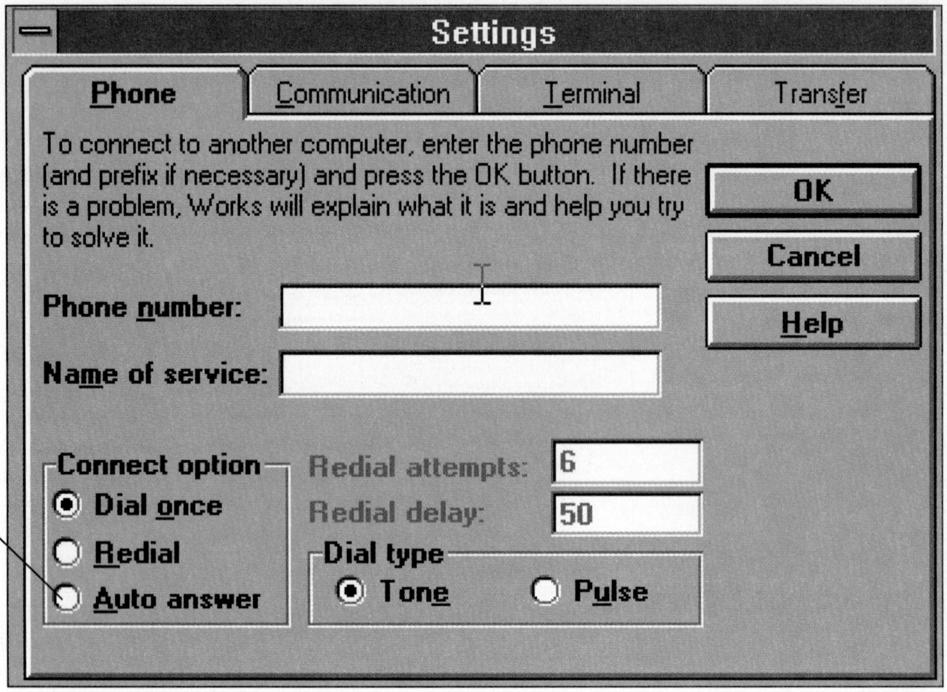

Figure II-11
The Phone settings tab

3. Choose **Auto answer** and choose **OK** or press **Enter**. You can now receive incoming calls.

SENDING TEXT

You can send text that you type in the Communications window, or you can copy text from the word processor, the spreadsheet, or the database windows to the Communications window and send it. You can also send text files or files created in other applications such as the draw program which is discussed in Appendix I, page 17 and 18, or the chart program which is discussed in Chapter 12.

Send Text That Is Typed in the Communications Window

1. Open the **Communications** tool 

. The Easy Connect window is displayed.
2. Type the phone number and enter the name of the service if that is appropriate.
3. Choose **OK** or press **Enter** to display the Communications window. A prompt is displayed asking if you want to connect to another computer.
4. Choose **OK** to connect.

NOTE: Or you can choose **Cancel** to go off-line, make settings changes or use the Tools option. Then click on the Easy Connect button  or choose **Phone, Easy Connect** and proceed with steps 2 through 4 above. You can also click on the Dial/Hangup button  to redial the same number or service entered in step 2.

5. Type the text that you want to send. *It will be sent without formatting as you type.*

When done:

6. Click on the Dial/Hangup button  , or choose **Phone, Hang Up** to display the prompt asking if you want to disconnect.
7. Choose **OK** or press **Enter** to disconnect.

Send Text That Is Copied from a Works File

1. Open the Communications window if it is not already open.
2. Type the phone number and name of service in the Easy Connect dialog box.

   or if the Communications window is already open:

   Choose **Phone, Easy Connect** and type the phone number and name of the service in the dialog box.
3. Choose **OK** or press **Enter**.

In the Communications window:

4. Choose **File, Open Existing File** to go to the Open dialog box.
5. Select the file that you want to copy from and choose **OK** or press **Enter** to open the file.
6. Select the block of text that you want to send. See example in Figure II-12.

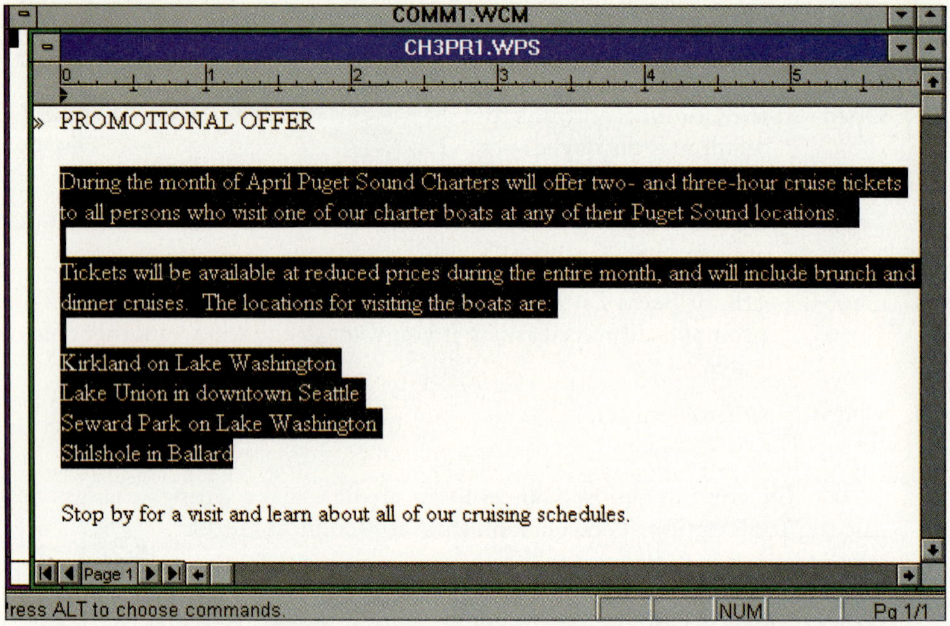

Figure II-12
Selected text in word processing window

7. Click on the Copy button, or choose **Edit, Copy**, or press **Ctrl/C.**

8. Switch to the Communications window. To do this, either click on the title bar in the Communications window; or choose **Window** to select the Communications window. An example is shown in Figure II-13.

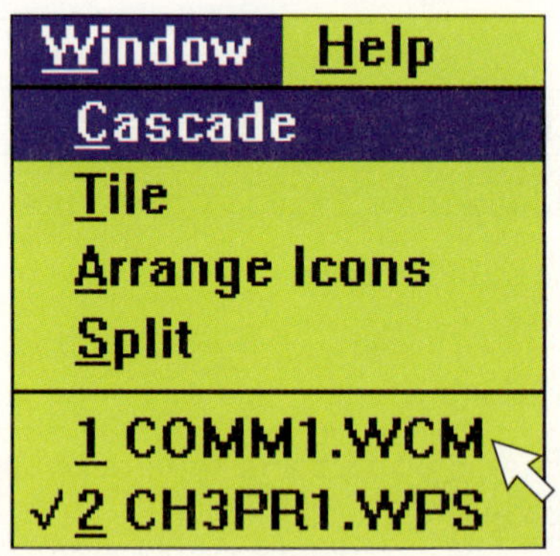

Figure II-13
The Window menu

In the Communications window:

9. Click on the Paste button, or choose **Edit, Paste**, or press **Ctrl/V.** The first line of the selected text will be displayed and the Send Text dialog box as shown in Figure II-14 will be open in the Communications window.

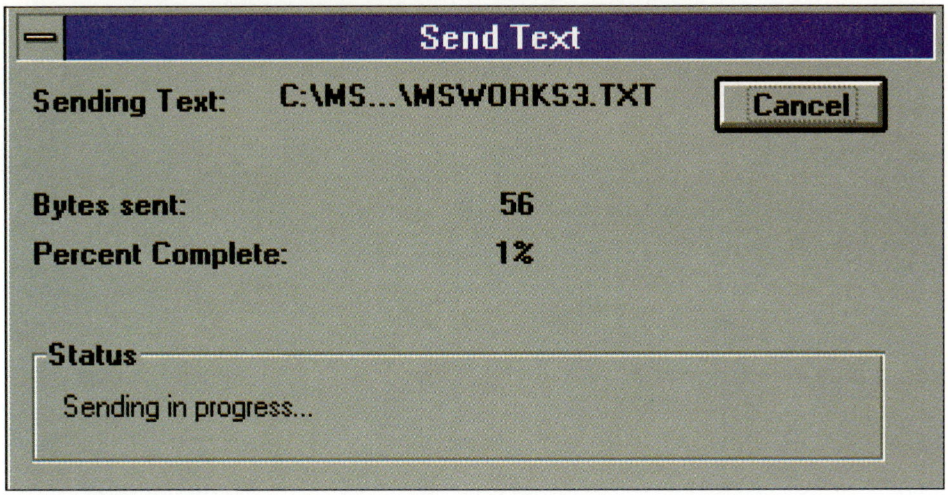

Figure II-14
The Send Text dialog box

When the transfer is complete:

10. Click on the Dial/Hangup button  or choose **Phone, Hang Up**. The OK to disconnect dialog box is displayed.

11. Choose **OK** to disconnect.

NOTE: Text is sent without formatting. If text is sent too fast for the receiving computer, click on the Pause button , or choose **Phone, Pause**, or click anywhere in the Communications window. To begin transmitting again, click on the Pause button or choose **Phone, Pause**.

SENDING A FILE

You can send any of the files that have been created in a Works tool—a word processing file, a spreadsheet file, or a database file. You can also send files from other programs such as draw or chart if you like.

Send a File

1. Open the Communications window if it is not already open and type the phone number and name of service in the Easy Connect dialog box.

or if the Communications window is already open:

Choose **Phone, Easy Connect** to display the Easy Connect dialog box, and type the phone number and name of service. Choose **OK** or press **Enter** to dial and go to the Communications window.

2. Choose **Tools, Send File** to display the list of files. All the Works files-word processing, spreadsheets, and database files-are listed here. If you like, you can choose a different drive or directory and select a filename from the new list.

NOTE: If you choose **Tools, Send Text**, only a list of text files with the .txt extension will be displayed. You can use this option when you know you do not want to see a list of other files.

3. Select the file you want to send.
4. Choose **OK** or press **Enter** to begin sending the file. A Send File dialog box is displayed that shows the progress of the transmission. See an example in Figure II-15.

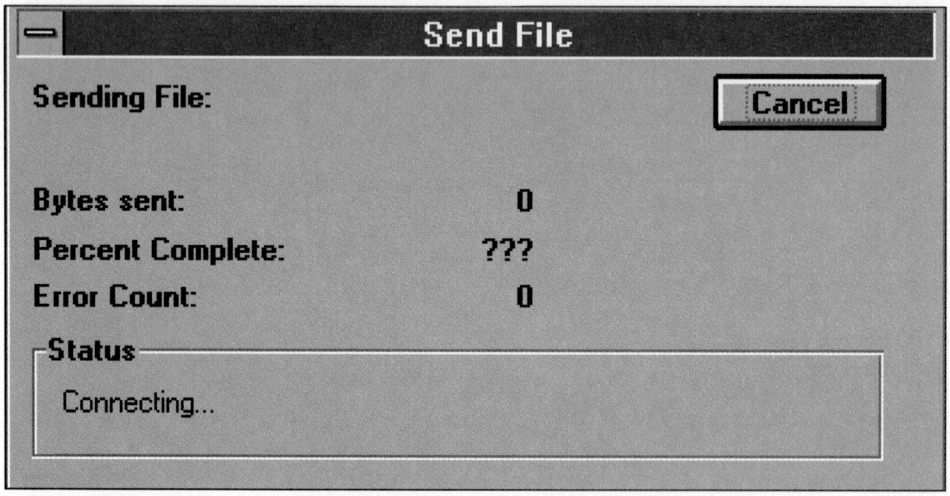

Figure II-15
The Send File dialog box

When the transmission is complete:

5. Click on the Dial/Hangup button  or choose **Phone, Hang Up**. The OK to Disconnect dialog box is displayed.
6. Choose **OK** to disconnect.

NOTE: If you are having a problem in sending the text or file, such as the other computer is not recognizing your signals or you cannot quit the function, enter a Break signal by choosing **Phone, Break**.

RECEIVING TEXT

Text that is received from another computer is displayed in the Communications window and stored temporarily in a buffer. This text can then be selected and saved as a Works file, if you like. *Files* that are received are saved automatically.

Receive Text

1. Open the Communications window if it is not already open. If the Easy Connect dialog box is then displayed, choose **Cancel** to remove it from the window. Be sure your settings are the same as the settings for the computer from which you are receiving information.
2. Choose **Settings, Phone,** to display the Phone tab section in the Settings dialog box. See Figure II-16.
3. Choose **Auto answer** as shown in Figure II-16 and choose **OK** or press **Enter**

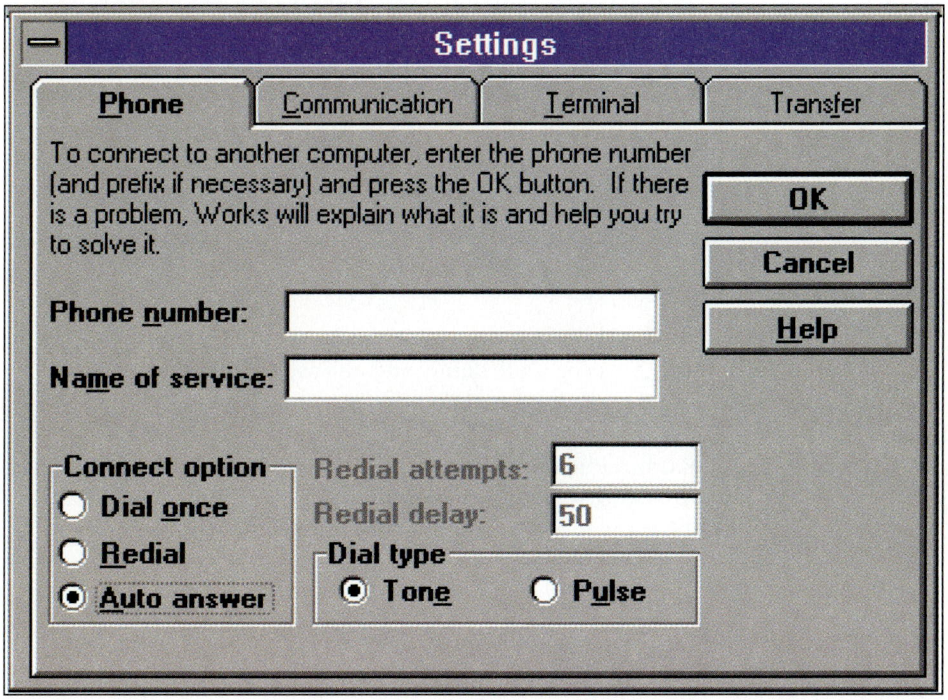

Figure II-16
The Phone tab in the Settings dialog box

Your computer is now ready to receive the text that will be displayed in the Communications window as it comes in. If it is coming in faster than you can read it, you can choose **Pause**—either click on the Pause button or choose **Phone, Pause.**

View Text In Buffer

1. Scroll up through the text that is in the Communications window. If more text has been received than can be displayed in the window, the first lines will be out of view.

SAVING TEXT

The buffer is only a temporary storage area. If you save the Communications window, the text in the buffer will not be saved—only the settings for receiving will be saved. To save the text, you can either copy it from the buffer to a Works tool window (word processor, spreadsheet, or database) and name and save it, or as text comes in, you can save it to a file using **Tools, Capture Text**.

Copy and Save Text

Text stored temporarily in the buffer can be saved by copying it to another Works tool and saving it there, as you save other Works files.

1. Select all of the text in the buffer that you want to save.
2. Click on the Copy button , or choose **Edit, Copy**, or press **Ctrl/C**.
3. Open the Works tool window where you want to save the incoming text (the word processing, the spreadsheet, or the database window).
4. Click on the Paste button , or choose **Edit, Paste**, or press **Ctrl/V**.

To save the text:

5. Choose **File, Save As**, type a file name, and choose **OK** or press **Enter**.

When done:

6. Return to the Communications window, and end the session and save the Communications settings if you like. If you had entered a **Pause**, begin the transmission again to allow more text to come in.

Capture Incoming Text as a File

1. Open the communications tool and make sure your settings are the same as the settings for the computer that is sending you the file.
2. Choose **Settings, Phone** and turn on **Auto Answer**, then choose **OK** or press **Enter**. Let the other user know you are ready to receive the file.
3. Choose **Tools, Capture Text** to go to the Capture Text dialog box. See Figure II-17. A default filename is displayed; however, you can enter any name you want.
4. Type a filename in the File Name text box. See example in Figure II-17.

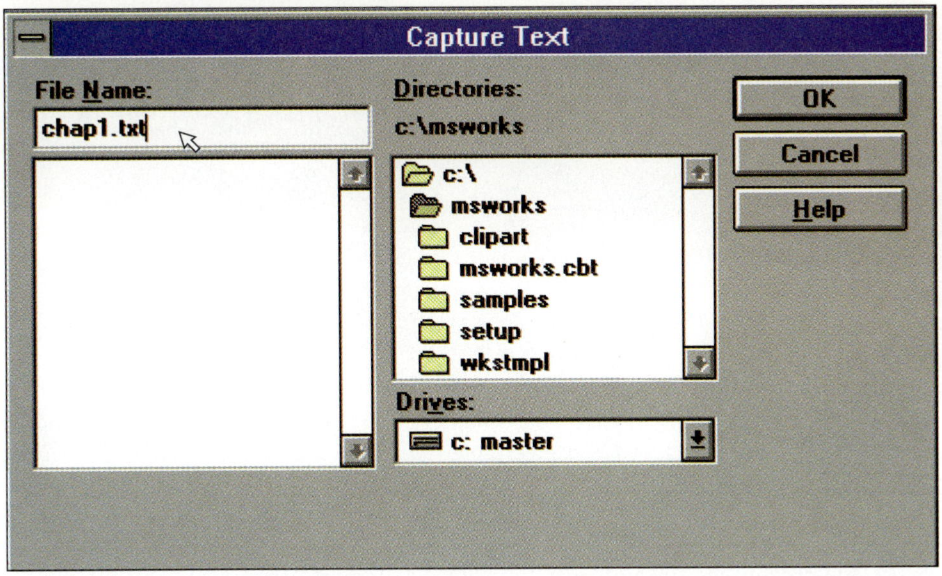

Figure II-17
The Capture Text dialog box

5. Choose **OK** or press **Enter** return to the Communications window. All incoming text will be saved to the file during the communications session.

To end the capture:

6. Choose **Tools, End Capture Text.**

RECEIVING A FILE

1. Open the communications tool and make sure your settings are the same as those of the computer sending you the file. If the Easy Connect dialog box is displayed, choose **Cancel** to remove it from the window.
2. Choose **Settings, Phone** and turn on **Auto Answer** if it is not already on.
3. Let the other computer user know you are ready to receive the file.
4. Choose **Tools, Receive File** to display the Receive File dialog box. See Figure II-18.

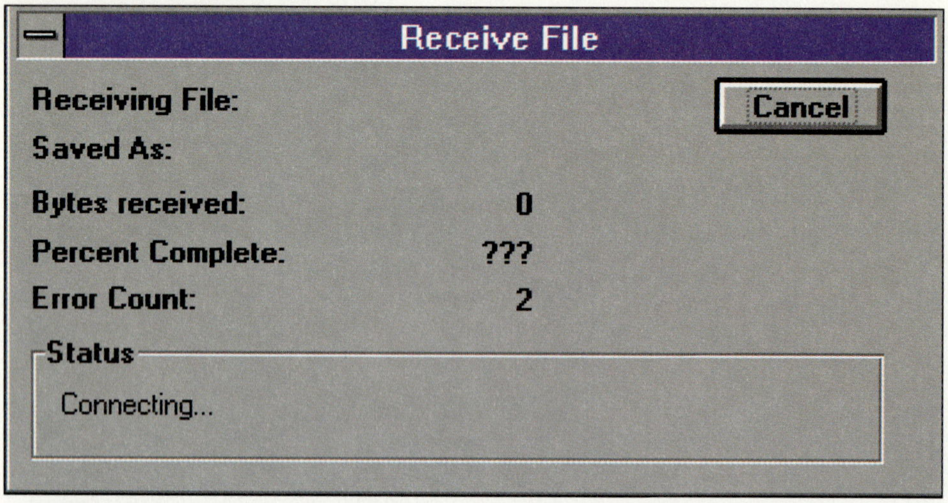

Figure II-18
The Receive File dialog box

Works will receive the file and save it automatically as it is received. The progress of the transmission and the filename will be displayed in the Receive File box. When done, leave the Communications window, or remain in the window and send or receive another communication.

QUITTING A COMMUNICATIONS SESSION

Save any communications document if necessary.

If you are leaving an information service:

1. Follow the steps that the service requires for signing off. Most services will provide instructions for this.

If you are disconnecting from another computer:

1. Click on the Dial/Hangup button  ; or choose **Phone, Hang Up**.

   The prompt asking you if you want to disconnect is displayed.
2. Choose **OK** or press **Enter** to disconnect.
3. Choose **File, Close** to leave the Communications window.

Index

A

B

C

D

E

F

G

H

N

O

P

Q

R

T

U

V

W

X

Y

Z